An Spechte

Kurt Eshlem

M000314013

MANAGING CYBER ATTACKS IN INTERNATIONAL LAW, BUSINESS, AND RELATIONS

This book presents a novel framework to reconceptualize Internet governance and better manage cyber attacks. It makes an original contribution by examining the potential of polycentric governance to enhance cybersecurity. It also synthesizes aspects of contemporary cybersecurity research, bringing features of the cloak-and-dagger world of cyber attacks to light and comparing and contrasting the cyber threat to key stakeholders. Throughout the book, cybersecurity is treated holistically, covering outstanding issues in the law, science, economics, and politics. This interdisciplinary approach is an exemplar of how strategies from different disciplines, as well as the private and public sectors, may cross-pollinate to enhance cybersecurity. Case studies and examples illustrate what is at stake and help to identify best practices. The book is written in an informal, straightforward manner and is designed to inform readers about the interplay between Internet governance and cybersecurity and the potential for polycentric governance to help foster cyber peace.

Professor Scott J. Shackelford serves on the faculty of Indiana University, where he teaches cybersecurity law and policy, sustainability, and international business law among other courses, and is a senior Fellow at the Center for Applied Cybersecurity Research. A graduate of Stanford Law School and the University of Cambridge, he has written more than forty articles, essays, and book chapters that have been published in outlets such as the *American Business Law Journal, Stanford Journal of International Law, Stanford Environmental Law Journal,* and the *Berkeley Journal of International Law.* Professor Shackelford has also written op-eds on the topic of cybersecurity that have been published in the *Huffington Post, Washington Times,* and the *San Francisco Chronicle,* and his research has been covered by National Public Radio, *The Atlantic Wire,* and *USA Today.* Professor Shackelford's academic work and teaching both have been recognized with awards, including a Fulbright Award in law, Notre Dame Institute for Advanced Study Distinguished Fellowship, Academy of Legal Studies in Business Outstanding Paper Award, Stanford Law School Steven Block Civil Liberties Award for Writing on Civil Rights, Indiana University Trustees' Teaching Award for Excellence, Kelley School of Business Innovative Teaching Award, and the Campus Sustainability Award for Teaching Excellence. He was also the recipient of the 2014 Indiana University Outstanding Junior Faculty Award. A frequent speaker to a variety of audiences, Professor Shackelford has presented his research on cybersecurity at diverse forums, including Notre Dame, Stanford, Australian National University, the Prime Minister and Cabinet Office of the Government of Australia, the Croatian Chamber of Commerce, NATO, the Swedish National Defense College, the International Telecommunication Union World Summit on the Information Society, the Indiana Counter Proliferation Task Force, and the *Harvard Business Review.*

Managing Cyber Attacks in International Law, Business, and Relations

IN SEARCH OF CYBER PEACE

SCOTT J. SHACKELFORD, JD, PHD

Kelley School of Business, Indiana University

CAMBRIDGE
UNIVERSITY PRESS

32 Avenue of the Americas, New York, NY 10013-2473, USA

Cambridge University Press is part of the University of Cambridge.

It furthers the University's mission by disseminating knowledge in the pursuit of education, learning, and research at the highest international levels of excellence.

www.cambridge.org
Information on this title: www.cambridge.org/9781107004375

© Scott J. Shackelford 2014

First published 2014

A catalog record for this publication is available from the British Library.

Library of Congress Cataloging in Publication Data
Shackelford, Scott J.
Managing cyber attacks in international law, business, and relations : in search of cyber peace / Scott J. Shackelford.
   p.   cm.
Includes index.
ISBN 978-1-107-00437-5
1. Information warfare (International law)   2. Cyberspace – Security measures.
3. Cyberterrorism.   4. Computer crimes.   5. Computer networks – Security measures.   I. Title.
KZ6718.S53   2013
343.09'99–dc23   2012035324

ISBN 978-1-107-00437-5 Hardback

For the women in my life, who are my world – my lovely wife, Emily, and our beautiful daughters, Avery and Samantha.

We have a faith-based approach [to cybersecurity], in that we pray every night nothing bad will happen.
— James Lewis, Center for Strategic and International Studies[1]

[1] Ken Dilanian, *Privacy Group Sues to Get Records About NSA-Google Relationship*, L.A. TIMES (Sept. 14, 2010), http://www.latimes.com/business/la-fi-nsa-google-20100914,0,5669294.story.

Contents

Tables and Figures

Foreword

Dr. Hamadoun I. Touré
Secretary-General, International Telecommunication Union

Cybersecurity is a matter of global importance as is evidenced by the spate of attacks at individual, corporate, national, and international levels. Professor Scott J. Shackelford's book is a timely intervention to press for cyber peace at a time when many nations, global institutions, and enterprises are threatened by cyber attacks.

I urge all readers of this excellent treatise to take its lessons to heart and seek greater multistakeholder cooperation to combat the growing array of cyber threats around the world. Safeguarding cyberspace and preventing cyber war depends entirely on the willingness of countries and businesses to cooperate and share expertise. As part of this process, we need to strengthen national legislation, push for the adoption of international norms, and adopt the technical measures required to plug the loopholes to stem the annual loss of more than $100 billion as a result of cybercrime. Overall, we need to bolster confidence in our networks, which are today the bulwarks of international commerce depended on by nations and citizens around the world.

The exponential growth of the Internet and the convergence of communication devices and applications in an increasingly networked world have brought about a transformation in the way we conduct our lives, manage our relationships, and do business.

Professor Shackelford ably explores the dynamics of cyber threats and the security implications of fractured Internet governance, the weapons that are continuously evolving to strike at the vulnerabilities in cyberspace, and the urgent need to secure critical national infrastructure in the digital age and embrace cybersecurity best practices in order to prevent cyber war and secure cyber peace.

Our common vision of the information society envisages safe, secure, and affordable access to global networks. It is a key component in ensuring social and economic progress and sustainable development for people in every corner of the world. Enhancing cybersecurity and achieving cyber peace are fundamental challenges that we must address urgently.

Preface

In June 1982, there was a massive explosion deep in Siberia. It was not a missile test or nuclear accident.[2] Rather, a gas pipeline had exploded, and it was not an accident.[3] Soviet spies allegedly stole a Canadian company's software that had been implanted with a CIA-sponsored logic bomb, resulting in "the most monumental non-nuclear explosion and fire ever seen from space."[4] That was more than thirty years ago.

Flash forward to June 2010 and the discovery of the Stuxnet worm – a sophisticated cyber weapon designed to target Iranian nuclear facilities. It exploited flaws in Microsoft Windows, disrupting plant processes that were controlled by Siemens-manufactured systems.[5] Thousands more computers around the world were also affected because components of the equipment in question are used in everything from traffic lights to nuclear power plants.[6] The worm's unusual complexity along with other revelations led many to argue that one or more national governments,

---

[2] *See Cyberwar: War in the Fifth Domain*, ECONOMIST, July 1, 2010, at 25 [hereinafter *Cyberwar*].

[3] *See* Clay Wilson, *Computer Attack and Cyberterrorism: Vulnerabilities and Policy Issues for Congress*, CONG. RES. SERV., RL 32114 at 29 (2005), http://www.history.navy.mil/library/online/computerattack .htm. *But see* Anatoly Medetsky, *KGB Veteran Denies CIA Caused '82 Blast*, MOSCOW TIMES (Mar. 18, 2004), http://www.themoscowtimes.com/news/article/kgb-veteran-denies-cia-caused-82-blast/232261 .html (reporting on a retired KGB official who denies this accounting of events, arguing that the explosion was caused by poor construction). Questions surrounding this episode help to highlight the difficulties of investigating cyber attacks and enhancing cybersecurity.

[4] THOMAS REED, AT THE ABYSS: AN INSIDER'S HISTORY OF THE COLD WAR 269 (2005); *see also Cyberwar, supra* note 2, at 25 (expanding on this episode and discussing the use of other logic bombs).

[5] *See, e.g.*, Aleksandr Matrosov et al., *Stuxnet Under the Microscope*, ESET at 17 (Rev. 1.31, 2011). Logic bombs and worms are discussed, along with other methods of cyber attack, in Chapter 3.

[6] *See* Steven Cherry, *How Stuxnet Is Rewriting the Cyberterrorism Playbook*, IEEE SPEC-TRUM (Oct. 13, 2010), http://spectrum.ieee.org/podcast/telecom/security/how-stuxnet-is-rewriting-the-cyberterrorism-playbook; Grant Gross, *Experts: Stuxnet Changed the Cybersecurity Landscape*, PC WORLD (Nov. 17, 2010), http://www.pcworld.com/article/210971/article.html; *Stuxnet: Computer Worm Opens New Era of Warfare*, CBS NEWS 60 MINUTES (Mar. 4, 2012), http://www.cbsnews.com/video/ watch/?id=7400904n&tag=contentBody;storyMediaBox.

such as Israel and the United States, backed the attacks rather than cybercriminals or terrorists.[7] Analysts viewed it either as a limited if groundbreaking covert action, or as the first act of cyber warfare in history.[8]

Finally, consider what happened in late 2011 when a man opened an email with the innocuous subject line, "2011 Recruitment Plan."[9] He proceeded to download a spreadsheet, unintentionally "allowing hackers to raid the computer networks of his employer, RSA[,]" whose cybersecurity products help protect the networks of the U.S. government and many Fortune 500 companies.[10] According to U.S. General Keith Alexander, former National Security Agency director and commander of U.S. Cyber Command (CYBERCOM), the blame for the attack lies with an organized campaign orchestrated by elements within China.[11] Among the companies targeted in the aftermath of the successful breach was Lockheed Martin, which reportedly lost "data on the F-35 Lightning II [jet] fighter[,]" the Defense Department's most expensive weapons program.[12] Since then, reports have surfaced revealing that dozens of U.S. weapons systems have been similarly compromised.[13]

What do these events have in common? Each reveals some of the many facets of "cyber attacks," which make up a vast, evolving, and controversial class of incidents. Now that everything from refrigerators to stock exchanges can be connected to a ubiquitous Internet, how can we better enhance cybersecurity across networks and borders? As we will see, a great deal of uncertainty and debate surrounds this question, and the stakes are high – everything from U.S. national and international

---

[7] *See, e.g.*, DAVID E. SANGER, CONFRONT AND CONCEAL: OBAMA'S SECRET WARS AND SURPRISING USE OF AMERICAN POWER 206–07 (2012); William J. Broad, John Markoff, & David E. Sanger, *Israeli Test on Worm Called Crucial in Iran Nuclear Delay*, N.Y. TIMES, Jan. 15, 2011, at A1; Transcript of Debate, Deterrence in Cyberspace: Debating the Right Strategy with Ralph Langner and Dmitri Alperovitch (Brookings Inst., Sept. 27, 2011), http://www.brookings.edu/events/2011/09/20-cyberspace-deterrence [hereinafter Deterrence in Cyberspace].

[8] *See, e.g.*, *Are 'Stuxnet' Worm Attacks Cyberwarfare?*, NPR (Oct. 1, 2010), http://www.npr.org/templates/story/story.php?storyId=130268518; *Cyberwar: The Meaning of Stuxnet*, ECONOMIST, Sept. 30, 2010, at 14; David P. Fidler, *Was Stuxnet an Act of War? Decoding a Cyberattack*, IEEE SEC. & PRIVACY, July–August 2011, at 56, 56–59; Ellen Messmer, *Stuxnet Cyberattack by US a 'Destabilizing and Dangerous' Course of Action, Security Expert Bruce Schneier Says*, NETWORK WORLD (June 18, 2012), http://www.networkworld.com/news/2012/061812-schneier-260303.html.

[9] Michael Joseph Gross, *Enter the Cyber-Dragon*, VANITY FAIR (Sept. 2011), http://www.vanityfair.com/culture/features/2011/09/chinese-hacking-201109.

[10] *Id.*

[11] *See* J. Nicholas Hoover, *NSA Chief: China Behind RSA Attacks*, INFO. WK. (Mar. 27, 2012), http://www.informationweek.com/government/security/nsa-chief-china-behind-rsa-attacks/232700341.

[12] *See, e.g.*, Siobhan Gorman, August Cole, & Yochi Dreazen, *Computer Spies Breach Fighter-Jet Project*, WALL ST. J. (Apr. 21, 2009), http://online.wsj.com/article/SB124027491029837401.html; William Jackson, *RSA Confirms its Tokens Used in Lockheed Hack*, GCN (June 7, 2011), http://gcn.com/articles/2011/06/07/rsa-confirms-tokens-used-to-hack-lockheed.aspx. For more on this attack, see Chapter 3.

[13] *See* Ellen Nakashima, *Confidential Report Lists U.S. Weapons System Designs Compromised by Chinese Cyberspies*, WASH. POST (May 27, 2013), http://www.washingtonpost.com/world/national-security/confidential-report-lists-us-weapons-system-designs-compromised-by-chinese-cyberspies/2013/05/27/a42c3e1c-c2dd-11e2-8c3b-0b5e9247e8ca_story.html.

security to the competitiveness of firms and the future of the Internet itself may be affected by how the cyber threat is managed.[14]

Difficulties stem in part from the rate of technological advancement,[15] along with geopolitical divides and legal ambiguities. Throughout the long and tumultuous history of conflict, new technologies have revolutionized both battlefields and businesses, either gradually as with gunpowder and the industrial revolution, or abruptly as with nuclear fission. Information technology (IT) is no exception. Networked computers have given tremendous advantages to and exposed vulnerabilities of the cyber powers, including China, Israel, Russia, the United States, and the United Kingdom.[16] These nations can now launch sophisticated cyber attacks, but their own militaries, economies, and critical national infrastructures (CNI) are also vulnerable. Elements within the U.S. government, for example, have admitted that they are unprepared for a cyber conflict.[17] The rise of new cyber powers underscores the shift in international relations after the Cold War from a bipolar world order dominated by the United States and the former Soviet Union to a multipolar one featuring more emerging power centers.[18] This shift complicates international efforts to reach

[14] Part of the cyber threat is the so-called cybersecurity dilemma. The security dilemma suggests that national security strengths can be provocative to other nations in the sense that "efforts by states to enhance their security can decrease the security of others." Nicholas C. Rueter, The Cybersecurity Dilemma, at iv (2011) (unpublished Masters thesis, Duke University) (on file with Duke Library). Establishing cooperation to enhance cybersecurity may be made more difficult by this security dilemma. *Id.*

[15] An example of this rapid technological advancement is Moore's Law, the prediction by Intel co-founder Gordon Moore that "the number of transistors on a chip will double approximately every two years[,]" speeding up processing times and overall computer performance. *Moore's Law Inspires Intel Innovation*, Intel, http://www.intel.com/content/www/us/en/silicon-innovations/moores-law-technology .html (last visited Jan. 5, 2014). *But see* Brooke Crothers, *End of Moore's Law: It's Not Just About Physics*, CNET (Aug. 28, 2013), http://news.cnet.com/8301-1001_3-57600373-92/end-of-moores-law-its-not-just-about-physics/ (discussing the potential end of Moore's Law, and highlighting the economic factors that may bring it about).

[16] There are also "'up-and-coming' cyber powers" to consider, including Iran. Tom Gjelten, *Is All the Talk about Cyberwarfare Just Hype?*, NPR (Mar. 15, 2013), http://www.npr.org/2013/03/15/174352914/ is-all-the-talk-about-cyberwarfare-just-hype?sc=17&f=1001; *see also* Valéry Marchive, *Cyberdefence to Become Cyber-Attack as France Gets Ready to Go on the Offensive*, ZDNet (May 3, 2013), http:// www.zdnet.com/cyberdefence-to-become-cyber-attack-as-france-gets-ready-to-go-on-the-offensive- 7000014878/ (reporting on France's cyber warfare capabilities). The cyber powers are discussed in Chapter 4.

[17] *See* Dennis Fisher & Paul Roberts, *U.S. House Committee Questions Ability to Secure Wall Street Data*, ThreatPost (July 14, 2011), http://threatpost.com/en_us/blogs/us-house-committee-questions-ability-secure-wall-street-data-071411; Sarah N. Lynch, *Senator Shelby Seeks Hearing on SEC's Cybersecurity Lapse*, Reuters, Nov. 30, 2012, http://www.reuters.com/article/2012/11/30/ net-us-sec-cyber-congress-idUSBRE8AT17P20121130; Claudette Roulo, *Cybercom Chief: U.S. Unprepared for Serious Cyber Attacks*, Am. Forces Press Serv. (July 27, 2012), http://www.af.mil/news/story .asp?id=123311659.

[18] *See, e.g.,* Fareed Zakaria, *Excerpt: Zakaria's 'The Post-American World'*, Newsweek (May 3, 2008), http://www.thedailybeast.com/newsweek/2008/05/03/the-rise-of-the-rest.html (conveying the perceived sentiment that the United States no longer dominates in many areas seen to denote global power). *But see* Richard N. Haass, *The Age of Nonpolarity: What Will Follow U.S. Dominance,*

consensus on improving cybersecurity through multilateral organizations such as the United Nations (UN),[19] hampering policy making as the political and economic costs of the cyber threat mount.[20]

87(3) FOREIGN AFF., May/June 2008, at 44 (arguing for the emergence of "a nonpolar international system . . . characterized by numerous centers with meaningful power.").

[19] *See* COMMISSION ON GLOBAL GOVERNANCE, OUR GLOBAL NEIGHBOURHOOD 10 (1995) (observing that the emerging global power structure has altered the way the international community can and does react to international problems); Danielle Kelh & Tim Maurer, *Did the U.N. Internet Governance Summit Actually Accomplish Anything?*, SLATE (Dec. 14, 2012), http://www.slate.com/blogs/future_tense/2012/12/14/wcit_2012_has_ended_did_the_u_n_internet_governance_summit_accomplish_anything.html (reporting on difficulties during a December 2012 Internet governance conference reviewed in Chapter 7).

[20] *See* REIN MULLERSON, INTERNATIONAL LAW, RIGHTS AND POLITICS: DEVELOPMENTS IN EASTERN EUROPE AND THE CIS 38, 40 (1994) (discussing the shifting character of international relations after the end of the Cold War); Mark MacCarthy, *What Payment Intermediaries Are Doing About Online Liability and Why It Matters*, 25 BERKELEY TECH. L.J. 1037, 1114 (2010) (analyzing the potential for a tragedy of the cyber commons); Elisabeth Bumiller & Thom Shanker, *Panetta Warns of Dire Threat of Cyberattack on U.S.*, N.Y. TIMES, Oct. 11, 2012, at A1. Excerpts of this manuscript have been published previously in various outlets. The following chronological list includes these articles along with the most relevant chapters in which the excerpted material appears: ERIC L. RICHARDS & SCOTT J. SHACKELFORD, LEGAL AND ETHICAL ASPECTS OF INTERNATIONAL BUSINESS (2014) (Chapters 1 and 5); *Governing the Final Frontier: A Polycentric Approach to Managing Space Weaponization and Debris*, 51 AM. BUS. L.J. 429 (2014) (Chapters 2 and 7); *Toward Cyber Peace: Managing Cyber Attacks through Polycentric Governance*, 62 AM. UNIV. L. REV. 1273 (2013) (Preface and Chapters 1, 2, 4, 6, and 7); *The Meaning of Cyber Peace*, NOTRE DAME INST. ADVANCED STUDY Q. (Oct. 2013) (Preface, Chapters 2 and 7); *Neither Magic Bullet Nor Lost Cause: Land Titling and the Wealth of Nations*, 21 N.Y.U. ENVTL. L.J. __ (2014) (Chapter 2); *In Search of Cyber Peace: A Response to the Cybersecurity Act of 2012*, 64 STAN. L. REV. ONLINE 106 (Mar. 8, 2012), http://www.stanfordlawreview.org/online/cyber-peace (Preface, Chapters 4, 5, 7, and Conclusion); *Should Your Firm Invest in Cyber Risk Insurance?*, BUS. HORIZONS (2012), http://www.sciencedirect.com/science/article/pii/S0007681312000377 (Chapters 5 and 7); Scott J. Shackelford & Richard Andres, *State Responsibility for Cyber Attacks: Competing Standards for a Growing Problem*, 42 GEO. J. INT'L L. 971 (2011) (Preface, Chapters 1, 2, 3, 5, 6, and Conclusion); *Was Selden Right?: The Expansion of Closed Seas and Its Consequences*, 47 STAN. J. INT'L L. 1 (2011) (Chapters 1, 2, 6, and 7); *Defining Privacy in the Information Age*, ARIZ. ST. L.J. (Apr. 8, 2011), http://asulawjournal.lawnews-asu.org/?p=191 (Chapter 4); *Cybersecurity: How to Crash the Internet*, YouGov (May 9, 2011), http://www.yougov.polis.cam.ac.uk/?p=493 (Chapter 7); *Estonia Three Years Later: A Progress Report on Combating Cyber Attacks*, 13(8) J. INTERNET L. 22 (Feb. 2010) (Preface and Chapter 4); *The Tragedy of the Common Heritage of Mankind*, 28 STAN. ENVTL. L.J. 109 (2009) (Chapters 2 and 6); *From Net War to Nuclear War: Analogizing Cyber Attacks in International Law*, 27 BERKELEY J. INT'L L. 192 (2009) (Chapter 6 is substantially similar to this article, which is also excerpted in the Preface along with Chapters 2 and 4); *Holding States Accountable for the Ultimate Human Rights Abuse: A Review of the ICJ Bosnian Genocide Decision*, 14 HUMAN RIGHTS BRIEF 21 (2007) (Chapter 6). Excerpts of this manuscript have also been published as op-eds under the following titles: *The Coming Age of Internet Sovereignty?*, HUFF. POST (Jan. 10, 2013), http://www.huffingtonpost.com/scott-j-shackelford/internet-sovereignty-b_2420719.html (Chapters 2 and 7); *How to Enhance Cybersecurity and Create American Jobs*, HUFF. POST (July 16, 2012), http://www.huffingtonpost.com/scott-j-shackelford/how-to-enhance-cybersecurity-b_1673860.html (Chapters 3, 5, and 7); *Getting Burma Back Online*, HUFF. POST (Nov. 5, 2010), http://www.huffingtonpost.com/scott-shackelford/getting-burma-back-online-b_779758.html (Chapter 7); *Google Needs Help Against Online Attackers*, SF GATE (Jan. 24, 2010), http://www.sfgate.com/opinion/article/Google-needs-help-against-online-attackers-3202252.php (Chapter 5). The author wishes to thank all of the editors and staff of these publications for their tremendous help. Further, as of this

Managing cyber attacks is made more difficult by the multifaceted nature of these attacks.[21] A serious cyber attack may disrupt critical networks, damage "military command or information systems," and interrupt "electrical power . . . or . . . financial services."[22] Or, in a worst-case scenario, cyber attacks could trigger satellites to spin out of control, power grids to crash, economies to collapse, and societies – deprived of basic services – to begin to self-destruct.[23] Luckily, this has not happened yet. And there is good reason to hope that it will not in the future. Nevertheless, it does not take a doomsday attack to raise flags. Consider the power grid. In 2007, a logic bomb was reportedly identified that could have disrupted U.S. electrical systems.[24] Many power plants tend not to keep expensive replacement parts on hand, meaning that it could take weeks to fix a widespread outage.[25] U.S. power systems may become more vulnerable to the planting of logic bombs because of the rise of Internet-connected smart grids called Supervisory Control and Data Acquisition (SCADA) networks.[26]

writing there are several forthcoming and working papers building from this material, including: Scott J. Shackelford & Amanda N. Craig, *Beyond the New 'Digital Divide': Analyzing the Evolving Role of Governments in Internet Governance and Enhancing Cybersecurity*, STAN. J. INT'L L. (forthcoming) (Chapters 1, 2, 4, and 7); Amanda N. Craig & Scott J. Shackelford, *Hacking the Planet, the Dalai Lama, and You: Managing Technical Vulnerabilities in the Internet through Polycentric Governance*, FORDHAM INTELL. PROP. MEDIA & ENT. L.J. (forthcoming) (Chapters 2 and 3); Jamie D. Prenkert & Scott J. Shackelford, *Business, Human Rights, and the Promise of Polycentricity*, VAND. J. TRANSNAT'L L. (forthcoming) (Chapter 2); Scott J. Shackelford & Anjanette Raymond, *Building the Virtual Courthouse: Ethical Considerations for Design, Implementation, and Regulation in the World of ODR*, WIS. L. REV. (forthcoming) (Chapter 2); Scott J. Shackelford et al., *Using BITs To Protect Bytes: Promoting Cyber Peace and Safeguarding Trade Secrets through Bilateral Investment Treaties*, 52 AM. BUS. L.J. (forthcoming) (Chapters 1, 2, and 6); Scott J. Shackelford, Timothy L. Fort, & Jamie D. Prenkert, *How Businesses Can Promote Cyber Peace*, 36 UNIV. PENN. J. INT'L L. __ (forthcoming) (Chapters 1 and 5).

[21] *See Cyberwar, supra* note 2, at 25–26.

[22] James A. Lewis, *The "Korean" Cyber Attacks and Their Implications for Cyber Conflict*, CTR. STRATEGIC & INT'L STUD. (CSIS) (Oct. 2009), at 1, http://csis.org/publication/korean-cyber-attacks-and-their-implications-cyber-conflict.

[23] *See* RICHARD A. CLARKE & ROBERT K. KNAKE, CYBER WAR: THE NEXT THREAT TO NATIONAL SECURITY AND WHAT TO DO ABOUT IT 70, 234 (2010); Christopher Helman, *Corporate Attacks Hint of a Coming 'Cyber Pearl Harbor'*, FORBES (Oct. 12, 2012), http://www.forbes.com/sites/christopherhelman/2012/10/12/america-cyber-pearl-harbor/. The 2007 blockbuster *Die Hard 4.0* dramatized the prospect of a large-scale cyber assault: in it, a frustrated former Pentagon insider and a team of hackers interrupted U.S. air traffic control, power, telecommunications, and financial services. According to Richard Clarke, such a scenario is feasible under certain circumstances. *See* Michiko Takutani, *The Attack Coming from Bytes, Not Bombs*, N.Y. TIMES, Apr. 26, 2010, at C1.

[24] *See, e.g.*, Siobhan Gorman, *Electricity Grid in U.S. Penetrated by Spies*, WALL ST. J. (Apr. 8, 2009), http://online.wsj.com/article/SB123914805204099085.html; Robert Mullins, *Bracing for a Cybersecurity Pearl Harbor*, NETWORK WORLD (Mar. 5, 2010), http://www.networkworld.com/community/node/58224.

[25] *See* Brian Wingfield, *Power-Grid Cyber Attack Seen Leaving Millions in Dark for Months*, BLOOMBERG (Feb. 1, 2012), http://www.bloomberg.com/news/2012-02-01/cyber-attack-on-u-s-power-grid-seen-leaving-millions-in-dark-for-months.html.

[26] *See, e.g.*, Dana A. Shea, *Critical Infrastructure: Control Systems and the Terrorist Threat*, CONG. RES. SERV., RL31534 at 1–2 (2003); Elinor Mills, *Just How Vulnerable Is the Electrical Grid?*, CNET (Apr. 10, 2009), http://news.cnet.com/8301-1009_3-10216702-83.html.

Useful for enhancing efficiency and promoting distributed renewable power, such industrial control systems can increase the cyber threat to critical infrastructure.[27] One senior U.S. military source has said, "[I]f any country were found to be planting logic bombs on the grid, it would provoke the equivalent of the Cuban missile crisis."[28] But no one knows for sure how many logic bombs exist, who planted them, and what the legal, economic, or political ramifications might be if they were ever used.[29]

Cyber attacks are often broken down into four main categories: cyber terrorism, warfare, crime, and espionage.[30] Although virtually every terrorist group has an online presence,[31] true cyber terrorism remains rare, potentially because of a lack of technological sophistication and the difficulty of using cyber attacks alone to terrorize a populace.[32] Definitions vary, but cyber warfare generally refers to an attack by one hostile nation against the computers or networks of another to cause disruption or damage, as compared to a criminal act or terrorist attack, which likely involves a private actor.[33] According to General James E. Cartwright, former commander of the U.S. Strategic Command, "[C]yberspace has emerged as a warfighting domain

---

[27] See Kim Zetter, *Report: Critical Infrastructures Under Constant Cyberattack Globally*, WIRED (Jan. 28, 2010), http://www.wired.com/threatlevel/2010/01/csis-report-on-cybersecurity/.

[28] COMMITTEE ON DETERRING CYBERATTACKS: INFORMING STRATEGIES AND DEVELOPING OPTIONS, U.S. NATIONAL RESEARCH COUNCIL COMMITTEE ON DETERRING CYBERATTACKS: INFORMING STRATEGIES AND DEVELOPING OPTIONS FOR U.S. POLICY 140 n.15 (2010) [hereinafter COMMITTEE ON DETERRING CYBERATTACKS] (quoting *Cyberwar*, *supra* note 2, at 25).

[29] Part of the reason for this state of affairs is that the United States has more than 3,200 independent power utilities, unlike Germany, for example, which has four major providers. See U.S. DEP'T ENERGY, A PRIMER ON ELECTRIC UTILITIES, DEREGULATION, AND RESTRUCTURING OF U.S. ELECTRICITY MARKETS V. 2.0, at 2.1 (May 2002); CHRISTIAN SCHÜLKE, THE EU'S MAJOR ELECTRICITY AND GAS UTILITIES SINCE MARKET LIBERALIZATION 130 (2010). Some U.S. firms are taking appropriate steps to secure their systems, but differences in resources and expertise make the uptake of best practices haphazard. See Letter from Michael Assante, NERC Vice President and Chief Security Officer, to Industry Stakeholders (Apr. 7, 2009), http://online.wsj.com/public/resources/documents/CIP-002-Identification-Letter-040609.pdf (discussing the designation of critical cyber assets).

[30] See, e.g., SCOTT CHARNEY, MICROSOFT CORP., RETHINKING THE CYBER THREAT: A FRAMEWORK AND PATH FORWARD 5 (2009), http://www.microsoft.com/downloads/en/details.aspx?displaylang=en&FamilyID=062754cc-be0e-4bab-a181-077447f66877.

[31] See, e.g., PHILIP SEIB, MEDIA AND CONFLICT IN THE TWENTY-FIRST CENTURY 186–87 (2005); Dorothy E. Denning, *Activism, Hacktivism and Cyberterrorism: The Internet as a Tool for Influencing Foreign Policy*, in NETWORKS AND NETWARS: THE FUTURE OF TERROR, CRIME AND MILITANCY 239, 252 (John Arquilla & David Ronfeldt eds., 2001); James J. F. Forest, *Perception Challenges Faced by Al-Qaeda on the Battlefield of Influence Warfare*, 6(1) PERSP. ON TERRORISM 8, 8 (2012).

[32] See Irving Lachow, *Cyber Terrorism: Menace or Myth?*, in CYBERPOWER AND NATIONAL SECURITY 437, 449 (Franklin D. Kramer et al. eds., 2009); cf. DAN VERTON, BLACK ICE: THE INVISIBLE THREAT OF CYBERTERRORISM 1–2 (2003) (quoting the 2002 National Strategy for Homeland Security discussing the growing technological sophistication of terrorist groups).

[33] See CLARKE & KNAKE, *supra* note 23, at 6 (limiting cyber war to actions between nation-states, and defining it as "actions by a nation-state to penetrate another nation's computers or networks for the purpose of causing damage or disruption").

not unlike land, sea, and air, and we are engaged in a less visible but nonetheless critical battle against sophisticated cyberspace attacks."[34] Cyber weapons are being developed around the world without a transparent discussion about the circumstances in which they may be used.[35] As *The Economist* summarizes, "Even as computerized weapons systems and wired infantry have blown away some of the fog of war from the battlefield, they have covered cyberspace in a thick, menacing blanket of uncertainty."[36]

The specter of cyber warfare is not the only problem; crime and espionage are on the rise and pose significant challenges to companies and countries alike.[37] The true extent of cybercrime is unknown, but contested estimates have placed losses at $1 trillion for 2010, prompting U.S. Senator Sheldon Whitehouse, a Democrat from Rhode Island, to suggest, "[W]e are suffering what is probably the biggest transfer of wealth through theft and piracy in the history of mankind."[38] In addition, many nations, including the United States, are engaging in cyber espionage as shown by leaked documents from former NSA contractor Edward Snowden.[39] One recent example is the so-called Red October network unearthed in late 2012, which has been described as "one of the most advanced online espionage operations that's ever been discovered" and appears to have targeted governmental data and scientific research.[40] James Lewis of the Center for Strategic and International Studies (CSIS) has called cyber espionage "the biggest intelligence disaster since the loss of the nuclear secrets [in the late 1940s]," and few think it will slow down anytime soon.[41]

---

[34] NAT'L RES. COUNCIL OF THE NAT'L ACADS., TECHNOLOGY, POLICY, LAW, AND ETHICS REGARDING U.S. ACQUISITION AND USE OF CYBERATTACK CAPABILITIES 162 (William A. Owens, Kenneth W. Dam, & Herbert S. Lin eds., 2009) [hereinafter NATIONAL ACADEMIES].

[35] *See* Paolo Passeri, *What Is a Cyber Weapon?* (Apr. 22, 2012), http://hackmageddon.com/2012/04/22/what-is-a-cyber-weapon/ (discussing some of the difficulties involved with classifying "cyber weapons").

[36] *Cyberwar, supra* note 2, at 25–26.

[37] *See, e.g.,* Jonathan B. Wolf, *War Games Meets the Internet: Chasing 21st Century Cybercriminals with Old Laws and Little Money*, 28 AM. J. CRIM. L. 95, 95 (2000); Debra Wong Yang et al., *Countering the Cyber-Crime Threat*, 43 AM. CRIM. L. REV. 201, 201–02 (2006); *Cybercrime Threat on the Rise, Says PwC Report*, BBC (Mar. 26, 2012), http://www.bbc.co.uk/news/business-17511322.

[38] *Sheldon Speaks in Senate on Cyber Threats*, SHELDON WHITEHOUSE: SPEECHES (July 27, 2010), http://www.whitehouse.senate.gov/news/speeches/sheldon-speaks-in-senate-on-cyber-threats; *see also* Peter Maass & Megha Rajagopalan, *Ask NSA Director Keith Alexander: Does Cybercrime Really Cost $1 Trillion?*, PROPUBLICA (Aug. 1, 2012,), http://www.propublica.org/article/does-cybercrime-really-cost-1-trillion (critiquing McAfee and other estimates on which the $1 trillion figure was based).

[39] *See* FRANKLIN D. KRAMER, STUART H. STARR, & LARRY K. WENTZ, CYBERPOWER AND NATIONAL SECURITY 424–26 (2009); Ian Black, *NSA Spying Scandal: What We Have Learned*, GUARDIAN (June 10, 2013), http://www.theguardian.com/world/2013/jun/10/nsa-spying-scandal-what-we-have-learned (reporting on an NSA wiretapping program code-named PRISM).

[40] Mathew J. Schwartz, *Operation Red October Attackers Wielded Spear Phishing*, INFO. WK. (Jan. 18, 2013), http://www.informationweek.com/security/attacks/operation-red-october-attackers-wielded/240146621.

[41] *Cyberwar, supra* note 2, at 26; Jack Goldsmith, *The Prospects for Cybersecurity Cooperation After Snowden*, FREEMAN SPOGLI INST. (Oct. 24, 2013), http://fsi.stanford.edu/events/the_prospects_for_

It is no simple matter to categorize cyber attacks in this manner, as is discussed more fully in Chapter 1. Motivations can overlap and targets abound in cyberspace. For example, there has been a spate of high-profile cases of cybercrime and espionage, as well as alleged state-sponsored cyber attacks involving criminal organizations targeting both the public and private sectors.[42] Cyber attacks against states in particular are increasingly common and serious, as seen in Estonia in 2007, Georgia in 2008, Iran in 2010, and South Korea in 2013.[43] U.S. government networks are also being targeted: 22,144 attacks on Department of Defense (DOD) networks were reportedly detected in the year 2000, up from 5,844 in 1998.[44] By 2010, Senator Susan Collins stated that U.S. government websites were being attacked more than 1.8 billion times per month.[45] Thus, it could be said that the United States is "under cyber-attack virtually all the time, every day[,]" as did former U.S. Defense Secretary Robert Gates.[46] Emblematic of this new threat, the U.S. Air Force adopted a new mission statement in 2005: "to fly, fight, and win . . . in air, space, and cyberspace."[47]

States are not the only victims, though; far less attention is paid to the many firms and individuals around the world who are regularly suffering cyber attacks. Whereas headlines are devoted to major breaches that result in the theft of millions of dollars or valuable intellectual property, many cyber attacks go largely unreported.

cybersecurity_cooperation_after_snowden/ (arguing that Snowden's revelations make international cybersecurity cooperation more likely).

[42] *See, e.g.*, Lech J. Janczewski & Andrew M. Colarik, *Introductory Chapter, in* CYBER WARFARE AND CYBER TERRORISM xiii, xxvii (Lech J. Janczewski & Andrew M. Colarik eds., 2008) (speaking generally of the increase in cyber attacks particularly focused on the private sector); David E. Sanger & Thom Shanker, *Broad Powers Seen for Obama in Cyberstrikes*, N.Y. TIMES (Feb. 3, 2013), http://www.nytimes.com/2013/02/04/us/broad-powers-seen-for-obama-in-cyberstrikes.html (noting that the U.S. government has increased its readiness for cyber attacks given the growing threat to the public sector); Ian Steadman, *Reports Find China Still Largest Source of Hacking and Cyber Attacks*, WIRED (Apr. 24, 2013), http://www.wired.co.uk/news/archive/2013-04/24/akamai-state-of-the-internet (discussing reports alleging that China is the source of more than 30 percent of global cyber attacks).

[43] *See, e.g.*, Joshua Davis, *Hackers Take Down the Most Wired Country in Europe*, WIRED (Aug. 21, 2007), http://www.wired.com/politics/security/magazine/15-09/ff_estonia (discussing the cyber attacks on Estonia); John Markoff, *Before the Gunfire, Cyberattacks*, N.Y. TIMES, Aug. 13, 2008, at A1 (reporting on the cyber attacks on Georgia); Gross, *supra* note 6 (arguing that a cybersecurity threat in Iran "illustrates the need for governments and businesses to adopt new approaches to cyberthreats"); Mihoko Matsubara, *Lessons from the Cyber-Attacks on South Korea*, JAPAN TIMES (Mar. 26, 2013), http://www.japantimes.co.jp/opinion/2013/03/26/commentary/lessons-from-the-cyber-attacks-on-south-korea/#.UW9fdII8xPk.

[44] Jim Wolf, *Hacking of Pentagon Computers Persists*, WASH. POST, Aug. 9, 2000, at A23.

[45] Press Release, U.S. Senate Comm. on Homeland Sec. & Governmental Affairs, Senator Collins' Statement on Cyber Attack (Mar. 18, 2011), http://www.hsgac.senate.gov/media/minority-media/senator-collins-statement-on-cyber-attack.

[46] *Gates: Cyber Attacks a Constant Threat*, CBS NEWS (Apr. 22, 2009), http://www.cbsnews.com/news/gates-cyber-attacks-a-constant-threat/.

[47] *Our Mission*, U.S. Air Force, http://www.airforce.com/learn-about/our-mission/ (last visited Jan. 5, 2014).

Myriad technology firms including Google were hit in early 2010, for instance,[48] but so were school districts in Illinois, Colorado, Oklahoma, and Pennsylvania, which lost tens of thousands of dollars to cybercriminals.[49] One 2010 Symantec study found "that 75 percent of [surveyed companies have] . . . experienced cyber attacks" costing "an average of $2 million annually[,]"[50] although these figures (like so many cybersecurity statistics) are disputed. This subject is explored in Chapter 5.

Current methods are proving ineffective at managing cyber attacks. What is needed is the comprehensive, proactive, and vigorous use of cybersecurity best practices at the local, national, and global levels to manage cyber attacks more effectively and hold accountable those who launch them. Neither offense nor defense alone is sufficient to achieve this goal; addressing meta challenges, including technical vulnerabilities, legal ambiguities, and governance gaps, is also critical.[51] In other words, new tools demand new rules, as well as a push to clarify the application of existing regimes.

This is not the first time that technology has raced ahead of both military doctrine and international law. Nuclear weapons were developed in 1945, but it was not until the early 1960s that Bernard Brodie, Albert Wohlstetter, Herman Kahn, and the other "Wizards of Armageddon" created the theory of Mutually Assured Destruction,[52] while the International Court of Justice did not rule on the legality of nuclear weapons until 1996.[53] The same evolution is now occurring in cyberspace, and the nuclear analogy has not been lost on victim states.[54] Fears of a doomsday "Electronic Pearl Harbor" may well be overblown, but the general need for enhanced cybersecurity is not.[55] Still, the debate over how to defend against cyber

---

[48] *See, e.g.,* Julian Ryall, *A History of Major Cyber Attacks,* TELEGRAPH (Sept. 20, 2011), http://www.telegraph.co.uk/news/worldnews/asia/japan/8775632/A-history-of-major-cyber-attacks.html.

[49] *E.g., Attention School Districts: You Are Being Targeted by Cyber-Criminals,* HACKER J. (Jan. 13, 2010), http://www.hackerjournals.com/?p=5649.

[50] *See Symantec 2010 State of Enterprise Security Study Shows Frequent, Effective Attacks on Worldwide Business,* SYMANTEC (2010), http://www.symantec.com/about/news/release/article.jsp?prid=20100221_01.

[51] *See* Daniel H. Cole, *From Global to Polycentric Climate Governance,* 2 CLIMATE L. 395, 412 (2011) (clarifying that "governance is 'a continuum between state-based solutions and solutions which do not involve the state, with hybrid forms in between'") (quoting Jouni Paavola, *Climate Change: The Ultimate 'Tragedy of the Commons'?, in* PROPERTY IN LAND AND OTHER RESOURCES 417 (Daniel H. Cole & Elinor Ostrom eds., 2012).

[52] FRED M. KAPLAN, THE WIZARDS OF ARMAGEDDON 248 (1983).

[53] *See* Legality of the Threat or Use of Nuclear Weapons, Advisory Opinion, 1996 I.C.J. 226, ¶ 105 (July 8).

[54] Kevin Poulsen, *'Cyberwar' and Estonia's Panic Attack,* WIRED (Aug. 22, 2007), http://www.wired.com/threatlevel/2007/08/cyber-war-and-e/ (reporting that Ene Ergma, a scientist and member of the Estonian Parliament, has made the comparison, "When I look at a nuclear explosion and the explosion that happened in our country in May [2007], I see the same thing.").

[55] *Doomsday Fears of Terror Cyber-Attacks,* BBC NEWS (Oct. 11, 2001), http://news.bbc.co.uk//hi/science/nature/1593018.stm.

war and promote cyber peace is one that many nations wish to avoid, having "found mutual benefit in a _status quo_ of strategic ambiguity."[56]

CYBER WAR AND PEACE

Assessments of the severity of cyber attacks and the likelihood of cyber war range widely. Some, such as Mike McConnell, a former director of national intelligence for the George W. Bush administration, envision the potential for a catastrophic breakdown.[57] Others, like Howard Schmidt, the former cybersecurity coordinator of the Obama administration, argue that there is currently no cyber war under way, and that an apocalyptic cyber attack against the United States is implausible.[58] Still others point to the rise in "blended" or "combination" attacks involving both kinetic and cyber components as being a key area of common concern.[59] However, framing cyber attacks within the context of a loaded category like war can be an oversimplification that creates confusion and shifts focus away from enhancing cybersecurity against the full range of threats now facing individuals, companies, countries, and the international community. As retired General Michael Hayden, former director of both the National Security Agency (NSA) and the CIA, has said, "I'm reluctant to use the word war. . . . We have created this new domain, this new space called cyber, and, frankly, it's lawless."[60] Lawless is a stretch, as we will see, but General Hayden is correct in that the use of the word "war" suggests preconceived legal notions that may or may not be useful in dealing with the multifaceted problem of cyber attacks. The hype may be based on real vulnerabilities such as zero-day exploits in popular operating systems like Windows, but it can distract us from more pressing concerns.[61]

The truth about the risk posed by cyber attacks is somewhere in between "weapons of mass disruption – as [President] Barack Obama dubbed cyberattacks in

---

[56] Rex B. Hughes, _NATO and Cyber Defence: Mission Accomplished?_, ATLANTISCH PERSPECTIEF 3 (Apr. 2009), http://www.carlisle.army.mil/DIME/documents/NATO%20and%20Cyber%20Defence.pdf.

[57] _See_ Mike McConnell, _Mike McConnell on How to Win the Cyber-War We're Losing_, WASH. POST (Feb. 28, 2010), http://www.washingtonpost.com/wp-dyn/content/article/2010/02/25/AR2010022502493 .html.

[58] _Cyberwar, supra_ note 2, at 25; _see also_ PETER SOMMER & IAN BROWN, ORG. FOR ECON. COOPERATION & DEV. PROJECT ON "FUTURE GLOBAL SHOCKS," REDUCING SYSTEMIC CYBERSECURITY RISK 7 (2011), http://www.oecd.org/dataoecd/3/42/46894657.pdf (arguing that "true cyberwar" involving almost no kinetic element is unlikely).

[59] _See_ Jeffrey Carr, _OECD's Cyber Report Misses Key Facts_, FORBES (Jan. 19, 2011), http://blogs.forbes .com/jeffreycarr/2011/01/19/oecds-cyber-report-misses-key-facts/ (explaining why a true cyber war is relatively unlikely).

[60] Transcript of _Hayden: Hackers Force Internet Users to Learn Self-Defense_, PBS NEWS HOUR (Aug. 11, 2010), http://www.pbs.org/newshour/bb/science/july-dec10/cyber_08-11.html [hereinafter PBS NEWS HOUR].

[61] _See_ Evgeny Morozov, _Battling the Cyber Warmongers_, WALL ST. J. (May 10, 2010), http://online.wsj .com/article/SB10001424052748704370704575228653351323986.html. For more on zero-day exploits, which are attacks targeting previously unknown software vulnerabilities, see Chapter 3.

2009 . . . [and] weapons of mass distraction . . . . "[62] Letting ourselves get carried away by fear of one aspect of this evolving threat matrix can lead to misdirected investments and ill-suited cybersecurity policies at the local, national, and global levels.[63] Instead of worrying about "dystopian futures and limitless vulnerabilities,"[64] we should be focused on proactively addressing concrete vulnerabilities, understanding better how the cyber threat is developing, and strengthening public- and private-sector defenses to more effectively manage cyber attacks and secure some measure of cyber peace. Harvard Professor Joseph Nye, Jr., among others, has called for this type of more constructive dialogue.[65] For example, considering the topic of cybersecurity in light of cyber peace, not war, can help reframe the debate toward creating "a global culture of cybersecurity."[66]

There have been relatively few efforts to date aimed at defining "cyber peace." The International Telecommunication Union (ITU), a UN agency specializing in information and communication technologies, pioneered some of the early work in the field by defining "cyber peace" in part as "a universal order of cyberspace" built on a "wholesome state of tranquility, the absence of disorder or disturbance and violence . . . . "[67] Although certainly desirable, such an outcome is politically and technically unlikely, at least in the near term.[68] Cyber peace is defined here not as the absence of conflict, what may be called negative cyber peace.[69] Rather, it is the construction of a network of multilevel regimes that promote global, just, and sustainable cybersecurity by clarifying the rules of the road for companies and countries alike to help reduce the threats of cyber conflict, crime, and espionage to levels comparable to other business and national security risks. To achieve this goal, a new approach to cybersecurity is needed that seeks out best practices from the public

---

[62] *Id.*

[63] In this context, "threat matrix" refers to a framework constituting the myriad evolving cyber threats facing stakeholders ranging from sophisticated zero-day exploits launched by nation-states to denial of service attacks originating from hactivist groups.

[64] Kristin M. Lord & Travis Sharp, *Executive Summary, in* AMERICA'S CYBER FUTURE: SECURITY AND PROSPERITY IN THE INFORMATION AGE 7, 8 (Kristin M. Lord & Travis Sharp eds., CNAS, 2011) [hereinafter AMERICA'S CYBER FUTURE].

[65] *See* Joseph S. Nye, *Cyber War and Peace*, PROJECT SYNDICATE (Apr. 10, 2012), http://www.project-syndicate.org/commentary/cyber-war-and-peace.

[66] Henning Wegener, *Cyber Peace, in* THE QUEST FOR CYBER PEACE 77, 77 (Int'l Telecomm. Union & Permanent Monitoring Panel on Info. Sec. eds., 2011), http://www.itu.int/dms_pub/itu-s/opb/gen/S-GEN-WFS.01-1-2011-PDF-E.pdf.

[67] *Id.* at 78, 82 (arguing that "unprovoked offensive cyber action, indeed any cyber attack, is incompatible with the tenets of cyber peace").

[68] To its credit, though, the ITU and World Federation of Scientists report recognizes this fact and that the concept of cyber peace should be broad and malleable given an ever-changing political climate and cyber threat landscape. *Id.* at 78 ("The definition [of cyber peace] cannot be watertight, but must be rather intuitive, and incremental in its list of ingredients.").

[69] The notion of negative peace has been applied in diverse contexts, including civil rights. *See, e.g.,* Martin Luther King, *Non-Violence and Racial Justice*, CHRISTIAN CENTURY 118, 119 (1957) (arguing "[t]rue peace is not merely the absence of some negative force – tension, confusion or war; it is the presence of some positive force – justice, good will and brotherhood").

and private sectors to build robust, secure systems, and couches cybersecurity within the larger debate on Internet governance. Working together through polycentric partnerships, we can mitigate the risk of cyber war by laying the groundwork for a positive cyber peace that respects human rights, spreads Internet access along with best practices, and strengthens governance mechanisms by fostering multi-stakeholder collaboration.[70]

Much of the existing literature often offers a false choice between viewing cyberspace as a traditional commons or an extension of national territory,[71] between the need for a grand cyberspace treaty or a state-centric approach,[72] between governments being regulators or resources for at-risk companies,[73] between corporate liability and immunity for data breaches,[74] between Internet sovereignty and Internet freedom,[75] and ultimately, between cyber war and cyber

---

[70] *See* Johan Galtung, *Peace, Positive and Negative, in* THE ENCYCLOPEDIA OF PEACE PSYCHOLOGY 1, 1 (Daniel J. Christie ed., 2011) (comparing the concepts of negative and positive peace). Definitions of positive peace vary depending on context, but the overarching issue in the cybersecurity space is the need to address structural problems in all forms, including the root causes of cyber insecurity such as economic and political inequities, legal ambiguities, and working to build "a culture of peace . . . . " *Id.* ("The goal is to build a structure based on reciprocity, equal rights, benefits, and dignity . . . and a culture of peace, confirming and stimulating an equitable economy and an equal polity."); *see also A Declaration on A Culture of Peace*, UNESCO, A/Res/53/243, www.unesco.org/cpp/ uk/declarations/2000.htm (offering a discussion of the prerequisites for creating a culture of peace including education, multistakeholder collaboration, and the "promotion of the rights of everyone to freedom of expression, opinion and information").

[71] *See, e.g.*, Dan Hunter, *Cyberspace as Place and the Tragedy of the Digital Anticommons*, 91 CALIF. L. REV. 439, 519 (2003) (depicting cyberspace as a traditional commons and warning that inaction will lead to an intractable digital anti-commons); David R. Johnson & David Post, *Law and Borders – The Rise of Law in Cyberspace*, 48 STAN. L. REV. 1367, 1367 (1996) (arguing that "[g]lobal computer-based communications cut across territorial borders, creating a new realm of human activity and undermining the feasibility – and legitimacy – of laws based on geographic boundaries").

[72] *See, e.g.*, Patrick W. Franzese, *Sovereignty in Cyberspace: Can It Exist?*, 64 A.F. L. REV. 1, 41 (2009) (discussing the tension between nations wanting global involvement in cyberspace but concerned that such action would decrease national sovereignty); Rex Hughes, *A Treaty for Cyberspace*, 86 INT'L AFF. 523, 541 (2010) (expressing the advantages of using international treaties to protect cyberspace).

[73] *See, e.g.*, Derek E. Bambauer, *Conundrum*, 96 MINN. L. REV. 584, 662 (2011) (warning that governments should be prepared to shoulder some of the private-sector costs of cyber warfare); Llewellyn Joseph Gibbons, *No Regulation, Government Regulation, or Self-Regulation: Social Enforcement or Social Contracting for Governance in Cyberspace*, 6 CORNELL J.L. & PUB. POL'Y 475, 503 (1997) (expressing the divide between private-sector "Cyberian elites" and government outsiders who impose regulations); Grant Gross, *Lawmaker: New Cybersecurity Regulations Needed*, IDG NEWS SERV. (Mar. 10, 2009), http://www.pcworld.com/article/161023/article.html (conveying the opinions of lawmakers that the U.S. government needs to impose regulations on private firms to enhance national cybersecurity).

[74] *See, e.g.*, Monica Vir, *The Blame Game: Can Internet Service Providers Escape Liability for Semantic Attacks*, 29 RUTGERS COMPUTER & TECH. L.J. 193, 194–95 (2003) (exploring the liability exposure for ISPs of semantic attacks, i.e., posting false or misleading information online).

[75] *See* Press Release, Ind. Univ., London Conference Reveals 'Fault Lines' in Global Cyberspace and Cybersecurity Governance (Nov. 7, 2011), http://newsinfo.iu.edu/news/page/normal/20236.html (highlighting the tension between civil liberties and regulations online); *see also* Johnson & Post, *supra* note 71, at 1367 (arguing that cyberspace would foster regulatory arbitrage and undermine traditional hierarchically structured systems of control); Lawrence Lessig, *The Law of the Horse: What Cyberlaw*

peace.[76] This book attempts to navigate a middle ground between these competing camps and seeks out new models to help build consensus. For example, instead of a traditional area of the "global commons" existing beyond national jurisdiction, this book argues – in the same vein as James Lewis, among others – that cyberspace is at best a "pseudo commons" given the realities of private and governmental control.[77] Whereas certain principles of commons analysis such as collective action problems and the tragedy of the commons scenario arguably apply to cyberspace, they manifest in distinct ways.[78] However, drawing from this interdisciplinary literature provides insights on how we might better govern this unique space to promote cybersecurity.

A novel analytical framework is needed to reconceptualize Internet governance in order to better manage cyber attacks and ultimately secure cyber peace. This search should include an examination of polycentric governance.[79] According to Professor Michael McGinnis, "[t]he basic idea [of polycentric governance] is that any group . . . facing some collective action problem should be able to address that problem in whatever way they best see fit."[80] This could include using existing governance structures or crafting new systems.[81] In other words, "[a] system of governance is *fully polycentric* if it facilitates creative problem-solving at all levels . . . . "[82] This multilevel, multipurpose, multifunctional, and multisectoral model,[83] championed by scholars including Nobel Laureate Elinor Ostrom and Professor Vincent Ostrom,

Might Teach, 113 HARV. L. REV. 501, 507–08 (1999) (introducing the concept of regulatory modalities and their effects both within and outside of cyberspace); Timothy S. Wu, Note, *Cyberspace Sovereignty? – The Internet and the International System*, 10 HARV. J.L. & TECH. 647, 650–51 (1997) (assessing how states can regulate the content of the Internet through regulations affecting access and hardware).

[76] *Cf.* CLARKE & KNAKE, *supra* note 23, at 31 (noting the blurring of peace and war in cyberspace). Moreover, a 2008 collection of essays on cyber warfare largely ignores the topic of sovereignty, which is critical to managing cyber attacks. *See* Janczewski & Colarik, *supra* note 42.

[77] Lewis, *supra* note 22, at 3 n.4 (defining the idea of the pseudo commons, as first outlined by U.S. State Department coordinator for issues Christopher Painter, "as a space where owners have granted the right of way to any and all traffic as long as it does not impose costs or damages upon them"); Eben Moglen, *Freeing the Mind: Free Software and the Death of Proprietary Culture*, 56 ME. L. REV. 1, 1–2, 6 (2004).

[78] Collective action problems are a classic "social dilemma," which are discussed in Chapter 2. Elinor Ostrom, *A Polycentric Approach for Coping with Climate Change* 6 (World Bank, Policy Research Working Paper No. 5095, 2009), http://www.iadb.org/intal/intalcdi/pe/2009/04268.pdf.

[79] This argument is built on the work of numerous scholars, including Professor Andrew Murray's analysis of polycentric cyber regulation. *See* ANDREW W. MURRAY, THE REGULATION OF CYBERSPACE: CONTROL IN THE ONLINE ENVIRONMENT 47–52 (2006).

[80] Michael D. McGinnis, *Costs and Challenges of Polycentric Governance: An Equilibrium Concept and Examples from U.S. Health Care*, Workshop on Self-Governance, Polycentricity, and Development, at 1 (Conference on Self-Governance, Polycentricity, and Development, Renmin University, in Beijing, China) (2011), http://php.indiana.edu/~mcginnis/Beijing_core.pdf.

[81] *Id.* at 1–2.

[82] *Id.* at 3.

[83] Michael D. McGinnis, *An Introduction to IAD and the Language of the Ostrom Workshop: A Simple Guide to a Complex Framework*, 39(1) POL'Y STUD. J. 163, 171–72 (Feb. 2011), *available at* http://php .indiana.edu/~mcginnis/iad_guide.pdf (defining polycentricity as "a system of governance in which authorities from overlapping jurisdictions (or centers of authority) interact to determine the conditions

challenges orthodoxy by demonstrating the benefits of self-organization, networking regulations "at multiple scales,"[84] and examining the extent to which national and private control can in some cases coexist with communal management. It also posits that, due to the existence of free riders in a multipolar world, "a single governmental unit" is often incapable of managing "global collective action problems"[85] such as cyber attacks. Instead, a polycentric approach recognizes that diverse organizations working at multiple levels can create different types of policies that can increase levels of cooperation and compliance, enhancing "flexibility across issues and adaptability over time."[86] This approach has the promise of moving us beyond common classifications of cybersecurity challenges, recognizing that cyberspace is uniquely dynamic and malleable, and that its "stratified . . . structure [underscores] . . . a particularly complex regulatory environment, meaning that mapping or forecasting" the effects of regulations is problematic.[87] Polycentric regulation is not a "keep it simple, stupid" response,[88] but a multifaceted one in keeping with the complexity of the crises in cyberspace.

Not all aspects of polycentric governance easily apply to cyberspace. Given that the online community includes more than two billion users, the concept of self-organization, for example, is strained.[89] Additionally, there are important drawbacks of polycentric regulation to be addressed, such as the fact that a highly fragmented system can also "yield gridlock rather than innovation" due, in part, to an insufficient hierarchy.[90] Since such systems "must meet standards of coherence, accountability, [and] . . . sustainability," an unclear hierarchy may lead to inconsistency and systemic failures.[91] However, viewing cybersecurity through this lens potentially takes the debate about how to address cybersecurity challenges in a more productive direction by helping to eschew false choices, divisive top-down regimes, and all-or-nothing

---

under which these authorities, as well as the citizens subject to these jurisdictional units, are authorized to act as well as the constraints put upon their activities for public purposes").

[84] Elinor Ostrom, *Polycentric Systems as One Approach for Solving Collective-Action Problems* 1 (Ind. Univ. Vincent & Elinor Ostrom Workshop in Pol. Theory & Pol'y Analysis Working Paper No. W08–6, 2008) http://dlc.dlib.indiana.edu/dlc/bitstream/handle/10535/4417/W08-6_Ostrom_DLC .pdf?sequence=1.

[85] Ostrom, *supra* note 78, at 35.

[86] Robert O. Keohane & David G. Victor, *The Regime Complex for Climate Change* 9 PERSP. ON POL. 7, 9 (2011); *cf.* Julia Black, *Constructing and Contesting Legitimacy and Accountability in Polycentric Regulatory Regimes*, 2 REG. & GOVERNANCE 137, 157 (2008) (discussing the legitimacy of polycentric regimes, and arguing that "[a]ll regulatory regimes are polycentric to varying degrees").

[87] MURRAY, *supra* note 79, at 52–53.

[88] Jeffrey Weiss, *Elinor Ostrom and the Triumph of the Commons*, POLITICS DAILY (2009), http://www .politicsdaily.com/2009/10/14/elinor-ostrom-and-the-triumph-of-the-commons/. The author is especially grateful to Professors Fred Cate, David Fidler, Elinor Ostrom, and Anjanette Raymond among others for their comments, suggestions, and insights on developing portions of this argumentation.

[89] *See* Roger Hurwitz, *The Prospects for Regulating Cyberspace: A Schematic Analysis on the Basis of Elinor Ostrom, "General Framework for Analyzing Sustainability of Social Ecological Systems,"* 325 SCI. 419, 419–22 (2009). See Chapter 7 for the important role played by smaller-scale online communities in managing the cyber pseudo commons.

[90] Keohane & Victor, *supra* note 86, at 15.

[91] *Id.* at 8.

choices, as well as challenging all relevant stakeholders to take action through a more inclusive conceptual framework. Given that polycentric regulation has already been applied to both cyberspace generally and global collective action problems such as climate change particularly,[92] the time is ripe to begin investigating what lessons this approach offers toward enhancing cybersecurity.

This book provides more than a synthesis of the current state of interdisciplinary cybersecurity research. It draws from the voluminous literature on this topic to make an original contribution by comparing and contrasting the cyber threat to key stake-holders, including users, companies, countries, and the international community. The book analyzes how and why a subset of existing regimes are failing to adequately manage cyber attacks, and applies lessons from polycentric governance to suggest ways to enhance cybersecurity and promote cyber peace. New data on regime effectiveness and cybersecurity best practices are presented, drawing from interviews, surveys, and a statistical analysis of cyber attacks affecting one large organization. The arguments presented here build upon the work of Professors Ostrom, Lawrence Lessig, Andrew Murray, Robert Keohane, and David Victor, among others, as well as an array of cybersecurity specialists.[93] This book offers a novel perspective on cybersecurity, applying cutting-edge management techniques to a range of cybersecurity challenges that must be overcome to achieve cyber peace, from governance gaps and legal ambiguities to technical vulnerabilities and political impasses. Importantly, this analysis neither attempts to reinvent cybersecurity law and policy nor to solve the problem of cyber attacks. Rather, an effort is made to make some sense out of the extensive, diverse, and sometimes-conflicting information about cybersecurity in order to glean some insights that may prove useful in better managing the multifaceted cyber threat.

Throughout the book, the topic of cybersecurity is treated holistically, including outstanding issues not only in the law, but also the science, economics, and politics of cybersecurity. This interdisciplinary approach is crucial because insufficient attention has been paid to how strategies from different disciplines as well as the private and public sectors may cross-pollinate to enhance cybersecurity.[94] Because this analysis is context specific, case studies and examples are used both to illustrate what is at stake and to help identify best practices. However, this is not a book intended

---

[92] *See* MURRAY, *supra* note 79, at 53; Ostrom, *supra* note 78; Keohane & Victor, *supra* note 86, at 3. Harvard Professor John Ruggie has similarly lauded the benefits of polycentric governance in developing the Guiding Principles for Business and Human Rights. *See* JOHN G. RUGGIE, JUST BUSINESS: MULTINATIONAL CORPORATIONS AND HUMAN RIGHTS 78 (2013) (stating, "The overriding lesson I drew ... was that a new regulatory dynamic was required under which public and private governance systems ... each come to add distinct value, compensate for one another's weaknesses, and play mutually reinforcing roles – out of which a more comprehensive and effective global regime might evolve, including specific legal measures. International relations scholars call this 'polycentric governance.'").

[93] *See, e.g.*, Ostrom, *supra* note 78; MURRAY, *supra* note 79; Keohane & Victor, *supra* note 86, at 2; Lessig, *supra* note 75, at 502; CLARKE & KNAKE, *supra* note 23.

[94] *Cf.* Bambauer, *supra* note 73, at 587 ("[d]rawing upon scholarship in economics, behavioral biology, and mathematics" to address cybersecurity challenges).

solely for specialists – legalese and technical jargon are kept to a minimum. And although technical issues of Internet architecture and cybersecurity are addressed, this book is not a primer on computer science or information systems management. Nor is it a book focusing only on military doctrine or policy making in the Information Age. Rather, the material is presented in an informal manner that is designed to inform (and perhaps even occasionally entertain) the reader about the interplay of Internet governance and cybersecurity and the potential of polycentric regulation to help foster cyber peace.

The book is broken down into three parts. Part I lays the foundations of polycentric regulation in cyberspace. Specifically, Chapter 1 summarizes the cyber threat and uses Internet governance as a lens to analyze some of the reasons why contemporary models are failing to enhance overall cybersecurity. Chapter 2 investigates cyberspace as a pseudo commons juxtaposed against the global commons and introduces the conceptual framework of polycentric governance.

Part II applies polycentric principles to some of the cybersecurity vulnerabilities facing key stakeholders, including technical communities, countries, and companies, in Chapters 3, 4, and 5. Chapter 3 takes a functional approach in analyzing the primary technical vulnerabilities in cyberspace and how they may be conceptualized within a polycentric framework. Chapter 4 investigates the potential for polycentric governance to promote cyber peace by securing critical infrastructure, along with discussing the evolution of cyber conflict and the cybersecurity strategies of the cyber powers. Chapter 5 then critiques survey data about cyber attacks on the private sector and analyzes corporate cybersecurity strategies to identify and implement private-sector best practices in keeping with polycentric theory.

Part III completes the investigation by analyzing how polycentric governance may help reconceptualize legal ambiguities and bridge political divides to help foster cyber peace. Within Part III, Chapter 6 examines the applicable international law to cyber attacks and its utility in enhancing cybersecurity. Chapter 7 then describes the fluid domestic and global politics of Internet governance reform, studies the regime effectiveness of a subset of cyber laws, and summarizes cybersecurity best practices revealed throughout the study. The book concludes with a discussion of the potential for cyber peace and whether it may be attained through a polycentric governance approach.

When China's first Premier, Zhou Enlai, was asked in the early 1970s "for his opinion on the historical significance of the 1789 French Revolution,"[95] he reportedly replied: "It's too soon to tell."[96] As with the French Revolution, so it is with

---

[95] Poul Kjaer, *Law and Order Within and Beyond National Configurations*, at 37 (Normative Orders Working Paper, Feb. 2010).

[96] RICHARD WOLIN, THE WIND FROM THE EAST: FRENCH INTELLECTUALS, THE CULTURAL REVOLUTION, AND THE LEGACY OF THE 1960S (2010). *But see* Richard McGregor, *Zhou's Cryptic Caution Lost in Translation*, FT CHINA (June 10, 2011), http://www.ft.com/intl/cms/s/0/

cyberspace. It is simply too early to write a history of Internet governance or find a panacea for all cybersecurity challenges. Nevertheless, the advent of cyberspace is already changing the course of history. From the ways we make money to how we govern ourselves, start relationships, and even fight wars, cyberspace is in many ways the driving force of the twenty-first century. These changes are occurring so fast that most of us, including business leaders, lawyers, military planners, academics, and policy makers, are struggling to keep up with this rapid pace. What follows, then, is a modest effort to assess the debate over conceptualizing this dynamic space, and to offer some new perspectives on how we may be able to promote cyber peace without sacrificing the openness that drives innovation and has given birth to the Information Age.

KEY TERMS

Cyberspace has become a mainstay of the twenty-first century, but the terminology to describe it is still developing. Science fiction writer William Gibson first coined the term "cyberspace" in 1984.[97] Since then, the term has taken on a much more robust but still somewhat ambiguous meaning. Even the use of the prefix "cyber" is debatable.[98] It has evolved to describe a world of IT despite the fact that many computer and software engineers, and some governments, find it to be nondescript. Some engineers, for example, prefer "information technology" when referring directly to networks, hardware, and software.[99] Likewise, some governments prefer "information security" to "cybersecurity," and focus more on content and censorship than on mitigating vulnerabilities.[100] However, in line with many scholars and policy makers as well as popular references in U.S. and international media, this book uses "cyber" terminology.[101] As such, cybersecurity refers here to the policy field concerned with managing cyber threats, including unauthorized access, disruption, and modification of electronically stored information, software, hardware, services,

---

74916db6-938d-11e0-922e-00144feab49a.html#axzz2J6b2nUqC (reporting that, in fact, Zhou's comment referred to the 1968 riots in Paris, not the 1789 French Revolution).

[97] WILLIAM GIBSON, NEUROMANCER 4 (1984) ("A year here and he still dreamed of cyberspace, hope fading nightly.").

[98] For a tongue-in-cheek exploration of this issue, see http:// willusingtheprefixcybermakemelooklikeanidiot.com/.

[99] *See, e.g.,* MICHAEL E. WHITMAN & HERBERT J. MATTFORD, PRINCIPLES OF INFORMATION SECURITY 9–15 (2011); D. Stepanova, S. E. Parkin, & A. van Moorsel, *Computing Science: A Knowledge Base for Justified Information Security Decision-Making* (Newcastle Univ., Working Paper No. CS-TR-1137, 2009).

[100] *See* Gerry Smith, *State Department Official Accuses Russia and China of Seeking Greater Internet Control,* HUFF. POST (Sept. 28, 2011), http://www.huffingtonpost.com/2011/09/27/russia-china-internet-control_n_984223.html.

[101] *See* COMMITTEE ON DETERRING CYBERATTACKS, *supra* note 28; NATIONAL ACADEMIES, *supra* note 34, at vii–viii. However, this book does use terminology such as "IT security" in Chapters 3 and 5 in reference to technical and corporate cybersecurity best practices.

and networks.[102] Such threats may come from state or non-state actors but are carried out through the use of information technologies, although not necessarily via the Internet. Stuxnet, for example, was reportedly delivered via a flash drive.[103] A similar strategy was employed by a disgruntled contractor to steal the names, credit card information, and social security numbers for nearly half the population of South Korea in January 2014.[104]

"Cyber attack" is another term that is often debated because of the ambiguity in the meaning of both "cyber" and "attack."[105] For example, even though U.S. defense networks are being continuously probed, not all of these probes are "attacks."[106] According to the U.S. National Academy of Sciences, cyber attacks refer to "deliberate actions to alter, disrupt, deceive, degrade, or destroy computer systems or networks or the information and/or programs resident in or transiting these systems or networks."[107] That definition may seem relatively straightforward, but the key words to take notice of are "alter," "disrupt," and "deceive" – what do these verbs mean in the contexts of computers, networks, or software? What exactly has to be altered? Disruptive to what degree? And deceptive to what end?

The term "cyber attack" has tended to refer to a wide range of intrusive and exploitative behaviors, making the use of the word "attack" misleading. According to General Hayden, for cyber activity to constitute an attack it must "degrade his [an opponent's] information, deny him access to information, corrupt his information, delay his information, or destroy his information, or destroy his network."[108] Professor Dan Ryan of the National Defense University prefers to use the phrase "cyber incident" for an intrusion that does not have kinetic effects "because the term

---

[102] *See* 44 U.S.C. § 3542(b)(1) (defining "information security" as "protecting information and information systems from unauthorized access, use, disclosure, disruption, modification, or destruction . . . ").

[103] *See* Daniel Terdiman, *Stuxnet Delivered to Iranian Nuclear Plant on Thumb Drive*, CNET (Apr. 12, 2012 http://news.cnet.com/8301-13772_3-57413329-52/stuxnet-delivered-to-iranian-nuclear-plant-on-thumb-drive/. Stuxnet is discussed further in Chapter 4.

[104] *See Credit Card Details on 20 Million South Koreans Stolen*, BBC (Jan. 20, 2014), http://www.bbc.co.uk/news/technology-25808189.

[105] *See, e.g.*, Alex Stark, Book Review, E-INT'L REL. (Jan. 6, 2014), http://www.e-ir.info/2014/01/06/review-cybersecurity-and-cyberwar/ (reviewing PETER W. SINGER & ALLAN FRIEDMAN, CYBERSECURITY AND CYBERWAR: WHAT EVERYONE NEEDS TO KNOW 68 (2014)) (analogizing the grouping together of cyber attacks to "treating the actions of a prankster with fireworks, a bank robber with a revolver, an insurgent with a roadside bomb, and a state military with a cruise missile as if they were all the same phenomenon simply because their tools all involved the same chemistry of gunpowder").

[106] Sean Lawson, *Just How Big Is the Cyber Threat to the Department of Defense*, FORBES (June 4, 2010), http://www.forbes.com/sites/firewall/2010/06/04/just-how-big-is-the-cyber-threat-to-dod/ (reporting on General Alexander's comments at a Center for Strategic and International Studies event, stating, "DOD systems are probed by unauthorized users approximately 250,000 times an hour, over 6 million times a day").

[107] NATIONAL ACADEMIES, *supra* note 34, at 1. *Cf.* Oona A. Hathaway et al., *The Law of Cyber-Attack*, 100 (817) CAL. L. REV. 817, 822–32 (2012) (defining cyber attacks as consisting "of any action taken to undermine the function of a computer network for a political or national security purpose").

[108] PBS NEWS HOUR, *supra* note 60.

'attack' carries a lot of legal baggage."[109] Others prefer "cyber events"[110] or "Web skirmishes."[111] This debate is representative of a parallel legal struggle, which is discussed in Chapter 6, to define thresholds that describe the severity of different kinds of attacks and the applicable international law. The confusion over terminology is a consequence of cyber attacks being difficult to interpret and categorize. They often impact multiple systems and stakeholders, and the degree of control and intent involved are hard to measure. For example, as was previously mentioned, cyber attacks can be characterized as war; terrorism; political, military, or corporate espionage; or crime.[112]

For purposes of this book, cyber attacks are defined in keeping with the National Academy of Sciences approach, recognizing that not all cyber attacks so labeled are attacks in a legal sense and understanding that this term includes a wide and largely undefined continuum of more or less invasive and disruptive actions.[113] Cyber attacks by any name will continue to evolve, challenging laws, norms, and policies to keep up. Likewise, as systems become more interconnected, the effects of network vulnerabilities may be multiplied.[114] That is precisely why now is the time to organize our efforts and resources to promote cyber peace through polycentric action.

---

[109] Interview with Dan Ryan, professor, National Defense University, in Wash., DC (Jan. 5, 2011).

[110] SOMMER & BROWN, *supra* note 58, at 6.

[111] Patrick Thibodeau, *Black Hat Puts 'Offense' on Its Cyber Agenda*, COMPUTERWORLD (Jan. 18, 2011), http://www.computerworld.com/s/article/9205441/Black_Hat_puts_offense_on_its_cyber_agenda?taxonomyId=17.

[112] Interview with James A. Lewis, director and senior Fellow, Center for Strategic and International Studies, in Wash., DC (Jan. 5, 2011).

[113] *See* NATIONAL ACADEMIES, *supra* note 34, at 15.

[114] *See Age of Cyberwarfare Is 'Dawning'*, BBC NEWS (Nov. 17, 2009), http://news.bbc.co.uk/1/hi/technology/8363175.stm (reporting on the evolving cyber war capabilities of the cyber powers).

Acknowledgments

As with most writing projects, what starts off as a simple idea in the mind of the author evolves into a far better final product through the comments and insights of many far more talented individuals. First and foremost, this book would not have been possible without the invaluable research support of Amanda Craig. Her unfailing energy, vision, and passion have made this study infinitely better than it could ever have been otherwise, and she deserves credit for refining (and in some cases originating) many of the best ideas presented herein, especially in Chapters 1, 3, and 5.

Professors Fred Cate, Daniel Cole, David Fidler, Janine Hiller, Michael Mc-Ginnis, Elinor Ostrom, and Anjanette Raymond all offered invaluable comments on draft sections of this book, and some of the ideas presented in this manuscript are based on conversations with them and others. I am also indebted to the numerous individuals who took the time to explain their perspectives on cybersecurity. In particular, I am thankful to Stewart Baker, Richard Clarke, Jim Dempsey, Michael DuBose, Paul Hoffman, Rex Hughes, Jim Hutchins, Mikko Hypponen, Assaf Keren, Jim Lewis, Steve Lipner, Nemanja Malisevic, Haroon Meer, Charlie Miller, Paul Nicholas, Michael Oppenheimer, Elinor Ostrom, Chris Palmer, Greg Rattray, Dan Ryan, Steve Schneider, Yaron Sheffer, Von Welch, and Charles Williamson.

I am also grateful to Stephanie Dickinson and Hao Guo of the Statistical Consulting Center at Indiana University (IU), the staff and Fellows at the IU Center for Applied Cybersecurity Research, particularly Deputy Director Von Welch, as well as the people at YouGov, especially Sean Kirwan. My thanks also to the Kelley School of Business administration and staff, and my colleagues in the Department of Business Law and Ethics for their much appreciated support and enthusiasm for this project, as well as Frank Alexander, Jason Allen, Brenton Martell, Lief Mattila, Selvanayagam Rangasamy, and Evan Sarosi for their dedicated citation checking and assistance.

In addition, I would like to thank John Berger and the staff at Cambridge University Press for taking a chance on this project, and for their incredible professionalism, patience, and dedication throughout every stage of the production process.

Finally, my thanks go to my family, including my parents – Susan Jean, Jim Shackelford, and Sharon Conner – for their unfailing love and encouragement. Above all, I am indebted in countless ways to my wonderful wife, Emily, who has made all this possible.

Abbreviations

APT	Advanced Persistent Threat
ATS	Antarctic Treaty System
BGP	Border Gateway Protocol
CCDCOE	NATO Cooperative Cyber Defense Committee of Excellence
CDMA	Cyber Defense Management Authority
CERT	Cyber Emergency Response Team
CFAA	Computer Fraud and Abuse Act
CHM	Common Heritage of Mankind
CNI	Critical National Infrastructure
Coll.	Colloquium
Comp.	Comparative
CSI	Computer Security Institute
CSIS	Center for Strategic and International Studies
CYBERCOM	U.S. Cyber Command
DDoS	Distributed Denial of Service
DHS	U.S. Department of Homeland Security
DNS	Domain Name System
DNSSEC	DNS Security Extensions
DOD	U.S. Department of Defense
DOJ	U.S. Department of Justice
EFF	Electronic Frontier Foundation
FBI	Federal Bureau of Investigation
FCRA	Fair Credit Reporting Act
FERC	Federal Energy Regulatory Commission
GCHQ	UK Government Communications Headquarters
IAB	Internet Architecture Board
IANA	Internet Assigned Numbers Authority
ICANN	Internet Corporation for Assigned Names and Numbers

ICC	International Criminal Court
ICJ	International Court of Justice
IDF	Israeli Defense Forces
IETF	Internet Engineering Task Force
IGF	Internet Governance Forum
IHRL	International Human Rights Law
ILA	International Law Association
ILC	International Law Commission
Int'l	International
IP	Internet Protocol
IPsec	Internet Protocol Security
IPv4	Internet Protocol Version 4
IPv6	Internet Protocol Version 6
IRTF	Internet Research Task Force
ISOC	Internet Society
ISP	Internet Service Provider
IT	Information Technology
ITU	International Telecommunication Union
J.	Journal
LOAC	Law of Armed Conflict
LOS	Law of the Sea
MAD	Mutually Assured Destruction
MLAT	Mutual Legal Assistance Treaty
MOD	UK Ministry of Defence
MPLS	Multiprotocol Label Switching
n.	Footnote
NASA	National Aeronautics and Space Administration
NATO	North Atlantic Treaty Organization
NCSS	National Computer Security Survey
NGO	Non-Governmental Organization
OECD	Organisation for Economic Cooperation and Development
OSCE	Organization for Security and Co-operation in Europe
OSI	Open Systems Interconnection
OST	Outer Space Treaty
Proc.	Proceedings
Rev.	Revised
SCADA	Supervisory Control and Data Acquisition
SDL	Security Development Lifecycle
Soc.	Society
SOFA	Status of Forces Agreement
SSH	Secure Shell
SSL	Secure Sockets Layer

TCP/IP	Transmission Control Protocol and the Internet Protocol
TLD	Top-Level Domain
TLS	Transport Layer Security
UN	United Nations
UNCLOS	United Nations Convention on the Law of the Sea
UNGA	UN General Assembly
UNSC	United Nations Security Council
VPN	Virtual Private Network
W3C	World Wide Web Consortium
WLAN	Wireless Local Area Network
WWW	World Wide Web

PART I

Foundations of Polycentric Governance in Cyberspace

The Internet is the first thing that humanity has built that humanity doesn't understand, the largest experiment in anarchy that we have ever had.

— Google Chairman Eric Schmidt[1]

---

[1] *Reproduced in* ANDREW W. MURRAY, THE REGULATION OF CYBERSPACE: CONTROL IN THE ONLINE ENVIRONMENT 233 (2006).

1

Defining the Cyber Threat in Internet Governance

For any complex sociotechnical system, especially one that touches as many people as the Internet, control takes the form of *institutions*, not commands.

– Syracuse Professor Milton Mueller[2]

Architecture is politics.

– Electronic Frontier Foundation (EFF) co-founder Mitchell Kapor[3]

Cyber attacks seem to be proliferating in numbers, sophistication, and severity just as our means of managing them more effectively is fracturing. This is partially because ideological divides over Internet governance are generating political, economic, and governance challenges as well as opportunities for experimenting with novel regulatory frameworks.[4] Finding solutions to cybersecurity challenges requires collaboration between technical communities, the private sector, governments, and

---

[2] MILTON L. MUELLER, RULING THE ROOT: INTERNET GOVERNANCE AND THE TAMING OF CYBERSPACE 11 (2002). Portions of this chapter are scheduled to appear in the *Stanford Journal of International Law* at 50 STAN. J. INT'L L. __ (forthcoming) (2014). When possible and appropriate, please cite to that version.

[3] Mitch Kapor's Blog (Apr. 23, 2006), http://blog.kapor.com/index9cd7.html?p=29.

[4] The term "Internet governance" has been defined in many ways depending on politics, ideology, and economic considerations. In the U.S. context, the term has come to mean the customary management practices developed predominantly by private actors that control much of the Internet's functionality. A leading Chinese information security law scholar, though, has described the U.S. approach as nonsensical. Indeed, some nations, including China, prefer a 2005 UN definition of Internet governance as "the development and application by Governments, the private sector and civil society, in their respective roles, of shared principles, norms, rules, decision-making procedures, and programmes that shape the evolution and use of the Internet." World Summit on the Information Society, Geneva 2003-Tunis 2005, Rep. from the Working Group on Internet Governance, at 10, WSIS-II/PC-3/DOC/5-E (Aug. 3, 2005), http://www.itu.int/wsis/documents/doc_multi.asp?lang=en&id=1695|0. Other formulations, such as Professor Yochai Benkler's approach discussed in Chapter 3, consider Internet governance as being comprised of distinct layers. *See* Yochai Benkler, *From Consumers to Users: Shifting the Deeper Structure of Regulation Toward Sustainable Commons and User Access*, 52 FED. COMM. L.J. 561, 562 (2000). The term is used here consistent with the UN approach but paying special note to the tenants

intergovernmental organizations, but fostering cooperation between these stake-holders can be difficult. Public-private partnerships, for example, try but often fail to bridge sectoral divides,[5] as is discussed in Chapter 5. Worst-case scenario cyber attacks could force these diverse groups over the elusive tipping point into a coordinated response, but that could come too late, if at all.

Although the Internet was originally managed by only a handful of researchers, today, thousands of entities – including companies, organizations, and governments – have a stake in regulating cyberspace, together forming a "regime complex," which is defined by Professors Kal Raustaila and David Victor as "a collective of partially overlapping and nonhierarchical regimes."[6] This complexity can make addressing questions of governance, such as whether a new cybercrime treaty is necessary, more difficult.[7] It also provides an opportunity to take, in the words of Robert Knake, director at Good Harbor Consulting, "a networked and distributed approach to a networked and distributed problem."[8] The issue of cybersecurity is increasingly driving debates about Internet governance. Being among the most important and difficult issues in this field, promoting cybersecurity is a crucial test for the emerging cyber regime complex.[9]

This chapter begins by analyzing the multifaceted cyber threat and examining why current paradigms are not working to effectively manage vulnerabilities. As we will see, technical decisions that have catalyzed the Internet's explosive growth have also made it susceptible to attack. However, some aspects of Internet governance that work relatively well may provide insights into better managing cyber attacks. Making this case requires analyzing the emergence of the Internet and its evolving governance structures, focusing on the Internet address and communications systems and the two distinct organizations that manage them. The chapter concludes with a discussion of how the cyber threat may be better conceptualized within a polycentric framework.

---

of polycentric governance especially the importance of bottom-up multi-stakeholder governance in promoting cybersecurity.

[5] *See, e.g.,* Jim Garrettson, *Melissa Hathaway: America Has Too Many Ineffective Private-Public Partnerships*, NEW INTERNET (Oct. 12, 2010), http://www.thenewnewinternet.com/2010/10/12/melissa-hathaway-america-has-too-many-ineffective-private-public-partnerships/; *cf.* Tom Brewster, *UK Signs up to Cyber Resilience Initiative in Davos*, TECH WK. EUR. (Jan. 25, 2013), http://www.techweekeurope .co.uk/news/uk-cyber-resilience-davos-government-william-hague-105467?id_prob=3095_273195 (reporting that the UK has signed an initiative sponsored by the World Economic Forum's Partnering for Cyber Resilience to help nations and the private sector better manage the cyber threat).

[6] Kal Raustiala & David G. Victor, *The Regime Complex for Plant Genetic Resources*, 58(2) INT'L. ORG. 277, 277 (2004).

[7] *See* ROBERT K. KNAKE, COUNCIL ON FOREIGN RELATIONS, INTERNET GOVERNANCE IN AN AGE OF CYBER INSECURITY 3 (2010), http://i.cfr.org/content/publications/attachments/Cybersecurity_CSR56.pdf (discussing the interplay between Internet governance and addressing cybersecurity challenges).

[8] *Id.*

[9] *See* Daniel H. Cole, *From Global to Polycentric Climate Governance*, 2 CLIMATE L. 395, 412 (2011) (arguing that certain "regime complex[es]" are analogous to polycentric governance).

UNDERSTANDING THE CYBER THREAT

On February 2, 2012, former FBI Director Robert Mueller told a U.S. House Committee, "[T]he cyber threat will equal or surpass the threat from counter terrorism in the foreseeable future."[10] The elements comprising the cyber threat are complex. In brief, they include the following facts: (1) governance gaps hamper efforts to collaboratively manage cyber attacks, (2) integrated cyberspace in an age of advancing national sovereignty online makes crafting tailored responses to specific threats difficult, (3) multiple attack vectors and technical vulnerabilities complicate policymaking, (4) vying national approaches to enhancing cybersecurity can impede multilateral cooperation to secure critical infrastructure,[11] (5) the evolving cyber threat to the private sector coupled with a lagging regulatory environment has made the uptake of best practices haphazard, (6) latent legal ambiguities make it more difficult to enhance accountability and prosecute attackers, and (7) multipolar politics and the prevailing "*status quo* of strategic ambiguity" hinder international cyber regulation.[12] These topics, among others, are analyzed in each respective chapter of this book. It is because cyber attacks take advantage of a range of vulnerabilities at multiple scales that managing them effectively has proven to be so challenging.

Cyber attackers are taking advantage of the fact that no system is secure in the absolute sense. It is possible to covertly raid and damage even the most protected computer networks for those with the will, resources, and patience to commit such acts. Cybersecurity is a continuum in which risk can be better managed, but not eliminated. This is a fact that engineers have long recognized. For example, back in 1991, when computer scientist Phil Zimmermann wrote a program that encrypts email, he called it PGP, or "Pretty Good Privacy."[13] Chris Palmer, a software security engineer at Google and former technology director at the Electronic Frontier Foundation, has said that this acronym is a bit of engineering humor, but it also says something about what kind of privacy or security is possible online.[14]

Technical vulnerabilities, however, are only part of the story of the cyber threat. Other confounding variables include the fact that the applicable international law is

---

[10] Alicia Budich, *FBI: Cyber Threat Might Surpass Terror Threat*, CBS NEWS (Feb. 2, 2012), http://www .cbsnews.com/8301-3460_162-57370682/fbi-cyber-threat-might-surpass-terror-threat/. *See also Poll: Cyber Attacks Biggest Threat to National Security*, DEF. ONE (Jan. 6, 2014), http://www.defenseone .com/threats/2014/01/poll-cyber-attacks-biggest-threat-national-security/76253/?oref=d-interstitial-continue (reporting on a 2014 poll of defense officials, which found cyber attacks to be "the greatest threat to U.S. national security. . . . ").

[11] *See, e.g.*, Arie J. Schaap, *Cyber Warfare Operations: Development and Use Under International Law*, 64 A.F. L. REV. 121, 141 (2009).

[12] Rex B. Hughes, *NATO and Cyber Defence: Mission Accomplished?*, ATLANTISCH PERSPECTIEF 3 (Apr. 2009), http://www.carlisle.army.mil/DIME/documents/NATO%20and%20Cyber%20Defence.pdf.

[13] Philip Zimmerman's Home Page, http://www.philzimmermann.com/EN/background/index.html (last visited Mar. 22, 2013).

[14] Interview with Chris Palmer, Google engineer and former technology director, Electronic Frontier Foundation, in San Francisco, Cal. (Feb. 25, 2011).

often ambiguous or nonbinding, and that businesses and regulators must keep pace with advancing technology that is continually changing the cyber threat matrix.[15] Developments in cybersecurity and data monitoring are also allowing for increased national regulation and censorship of the Internet.[16] This trend toward Internet sovereignty is complicating efforts at enhancing cybersecurity and clarifying governance, as is explored in Chapter 2.[17] To meet the diverse elements of the cyber threat, many commentators have moved from a one-size-fits-all approach to a tiered model, parsing out cyber attacks based on motive and means into the categories of cyber war, crime, espionage, and terrorism introduced in the Preface.[18] These categories help define policy responses to cyber incidents, but as we will see, problems of overlap and attribution – among other challenges – curtail their utility.[19]

Cyber War

The term "cyber war" takes on different meanings dependent on context. It is known as "informationalized warfare" in China.[20] From a U.S. military perspective,

---

[15] *See, e.g.*, SYMANTEC, INTERNET SECURITY THREAT REPORT: 2011 TRENDS 29 (2011), http://www .symantec.com/content/en/us/enterprise/other_resources/b-istr_main_report_2011_21239364.en-us.pdf (reporting, among other statistics, that there "were more than 403 million unique variants of malware" in 2011, compared to 286 million in 2010); Mark MacCarthy, *What Payment Intermediaries Are Doing About Online Liability and Why It Matters*, 25 BERKELEY TECH. L.J. 1037, 1114 (2010) (discussing the tragedy of the cyber commons introduced in Chapter 2 and explaining how the concept of a bordered Internet, in which each country applies its jurisdiction and laws to cyberspace transactions, cannot "scale up" to handle increased international Internet commerce).

[16] *See* Ronald J. Deibert & Nart Villeneuve, *Firewalls and Power: An Overview of Global State Censorship of the Internet, in* HUMAN RIGHTS IN THE DIGITAL AGE 111, 111 (Mathias Klang & Andrew Murray eds., 2005).

[17] *See* KNAKE, *supra* note 7, at 5 (explaining that the Internet was deliberately designed to be run without a centralized operator). The term "Internet sovereignty" as used here refers to the growing state-centric approach to both Internet governance and cybersecurity. For one iteration of the Chinese perspective on this topic, see *White Paper Explains 'Internet Sovereignty,'* PEOPLE'S DAILY (June 9, 2010), http://english.peopledaily.com.cn/90001/90776/90785/7018630.html (defining Internet sovereignty in terms of requiring "foreign IT companies operating in China . . . [to] abide by China's laws and [be] subject to Beijing's oversight.").

[18] *See, e.g.*, SCOTT CHARNEY, MICROSOFT CORP., RETHINKING THE CYBER THREAT: A FRAMEWORK AND PATH FORWARD 5 (2009), http://www.microsoft.com/downloads/en/details.aspx?displaylang= en&FamilyID=062754cc-be0e-4bab-a181-077447f66877; James Lewis, *Assessing the Risks of Cyber Terrorism, Cyber War and Other Cyber Threats*, CSIS 1–2 (2002), http://csis.org/publication/ assessing-risks-cyber-terrorism-cyber-war-and-other-cyber-threats (distinguishing between cyber warfare and cyber terrorism).

[19] For an analysis of the applicable legal challenges, see David P. Fidler, *Inter Arma Silent Leges Redux? The Law of Armed Conflict and Cyber-Conflict, in* CYBERSPACE AND NATIONAL SECURITY: THREATS, OPPORTUNITIES, AND POWER IN A VIRTUAL WORLD 71, 72 (Derek S. Reveron ed., 2011) (arguing that issues of attribution, application, accountability, and assessment contribute to the challenge of applying the law of armed conflict to cyberspace).

[20] JOEL BRENNER, AMERICA THE VULNERABLE: INSIDE THE NEW THREAT MATRIX OF DIGITAL ESPIONAGE, CRIME, AND WARFARE 135 (2011); Johnny Ryan, *"iWar": A New Threat, its Convenience – and Our Increasing Vulnerability*, NATO REV. (2007), http://www.nato.int/docu/review/2007/issue4/english/ analysis2.html.

cyber war falls under "information operations,"[21] which includes computer network defense and exploitation involving the offensive and defensive use of IT to protect critical national infrastructure and eliminate cyber threats to DOD systems.[22] The specific doctrine of cyber war is a classified and evolving topic in U.S. defense circles, but the "[p]revailing military doctrine calls for . . . U.S. dominance" across all "domains of warfare," including cyberspace.[23] This entails the U.S. military having "freedom of access to and use of" cyberspace while denying that freedom to adversaries.[24]

There has not yet been a genuine cyber war as this would likely require that a cyber attack be the equivalent of an armed attack,[25] as is discussed in Chapter 6. "Cyber warfare," then, is often used as a catchall term that does not explain cyber attacks in general, just as the term "cyber attack" has come into common usage, but should not be confused with an "armed attack" activating the law of armed conflict.[26] Indeed, a war framework is inappropriate for managing the vast majority of cyber incidents, including cyber espionage and cybercrime, although we may well be entering a new era of cyber conflict, as is explored in Chapter 4. In this new era, the list of cyber powers continues to lengthen even as non-state actors – including commercial entities, terrorist groups, and organized crime – become more active. Some of these entities are being sponsored by states, further complicating the regulatory picture. This makes drawing the line between cyber war, espionage, crime, and terrorism all the more imperative, and difficult.

Cyber Espionage

Cyber espionage, what some term "computer network exploitation,"[27] comes in many forms but may be understood here as "operations conducted through the use of computer networks to gather data from target or adversary automated information

---

[21] EDWIN L. ARMISTEAD, INFORMATION OPERATIONS: WARFARE AND THE HARD REALITY OF SOFT POWER 11–16 (2004).

[22] *See* Clay Wilson, *Information Operations, Electronic Warfare, and Cyberwar: Capabilities and Related Policy Issues*, CONG. RES. SERV., RL31787 at 4–6 (2007), http://www.history.navy.mil/library/online/infoops_cyberwar.htm.

[23] NAT'L RES. COUNCIL OF THE NAT'L ACADS., TECHNOLOGY, POLICY, LAW, AND ETHICS REGARDING U.S. ACQUISITION AND USE OF CYBERATTACK CAPABILITIES 162 (William A. Owens, Kenneth W. Dam, & Herbert S. Lin eds., 2009) [hereinafter NATIONAL ACADEMIES].

[24] *See id.*; *see also* Larry Greenemeier, *The Fog of Cyberwar: What Are the Rules of Engagement?*, SCI. AM. (June 13, 2011), http://www.scientificamerican.com/article.cfm?id=fog-of-cyber-warfare (discussing evolving U.S. rules of engagement in cyberspace).

[25] *See* THOMAS RID, CYBER WAR WILL NOT TAKE PLACE 10 (2013).

[26] *See* INT'L GRP. OF EXPERTS, TALLINN MANUAL ON THE INTERNATIONAL LAW APPLICABLE TO CYBER WARFARE 7, 15 (Michael N. Schmitt ed., 2013) (explaining the obstacles faced in developing an appropriate lexicon for cyber warfare because many terms are derived from the traditional warfare context); Eneken Tikk et al., *Cyber Attacks Against Georgia: Legal Lessons Identified*, NATO 3 n.2 (Ver. 1, 2008), http://www.carlisle.army.mil/DIME/documents/Georgia%201%200.pdf (distinguishing the term cyber attack from the term "armed attack" used in international humanitarian law).

[27] NATIONAL ACADEMIES, *supra* note 23, at 161.

systems or networks. . . ."[28] General Michael Hayden has argued that many cyber attacks that governments regularly experience are not cyber war: "That's exploitation. That's espionage. States do that all the time."[29] The relative ease of using cyber attacks as a tool for espionage, however, does change the equation somewhat. As one senior U.S. military official has explained: "A spy might once have been able to take out a few books' worth of material . . . [but] [n]ow they take the whole library. And if you restock the shelves, they will steal it again."[30]

To understand the power of cyber espionage, consider the case of FBI double agent Robert Philip Hanssen. Over a period of twenty-two years from 1979 to 2001, Hanssen stole thousands of classified documents on everything from cryptology to U.S. strategies for surviving a nuclear attack and passed it along to the Soviet Union for payment.[31] For his treason, Hanssen was sentenced to life in prison without possibility of parole at a federal super-maximum security prison.[32] At the time, the FBI called Hanssen's actions "possibly the worst intelligence disaster in U.S. history. . . ."[33]

Now consider "that between August 2007 and August 2009, 71 government agencies, contractors, universities, and think tanks with connections to the U.S. military [were reportedly] penetrated by foreign hackers, in some cases multiple times."[34] The DOD has *admitted* to losing some 24,000 files to cyber espionage.[35] It is impossible to calculate the quantity or value of information that has been compromised drawing from publicly available sources, but it is safe to assume that together these attacks likely dwarf the damage that Hanssen did for more than two decades.[36] Nevertheless, the spies responsible for these incidents are usually not being punished by life in prison. To highlight some of the difficulties facing prosecutors, consider the case of Hanjuan Jin, a former Motorola employee who was found at Chicago

---

[28] *Id.; see also* Irving Lachow, *Cyber Terrorism: Menace or Myth?, in* CYBERPOWER AND NATIONAL SECURITY 437, 440 (F. D. Kramer, S. H. Starr & Larry Wentz eds., 2009) (analyzing the terrorist use of cyberspace).

[29] Tom Gjelten, *Extending the Law of War to Cyberspace*, NPR (Sept. 22, 2010), http://www.npr.org/templates/story/story.php?storyId=130023318.

[30] *Cyberwar: War in the Fifth Domain*, ECONOMIST (July 1, 2010), http://www.economist.com/node/16478792 [hereinafter *Cyberwar*].

[31] *See* DAVID A. Wise, THE BUREAU AND THE MOLE: THE UNMASKING OF ROBERT PHILIP HANSSEN, THE MOST DANGEROUS DOUBLE AGENT IN FBI HISTORY 136, 241–44 (2002).

[32] *See* Laura Sullivan, *Timeline: Solitary Confinement in U.S. Prisons*, NPR (July 26, 2006), http://www.npr.org/templates/story/story.php?storyId=5579901.

[33] U.S. DEP'T. JUST., A REVIEW OF FBI SECURITY PROGRAMS 1 (Mar. 2002), http://www.fas.org/irp/agency/doj/fbi/websterreport.pdf.

[34] Andy Greenberg, *For Pentagon Contractors, Cyberspying Escalates*, FORBES (Feb. 17, 2010), http://www.forbes.com/2010/02/17/pentagon-northrop-raytheon-technology-security-cyberspying.html.

[35] *See* Sarah Jacobsson Purewal, *24,000 Pentagon Files Stolen in Major Cyberattack*, PC WORLD (July 15, 2011), https://www.pcworld.com/article/235816/24000_pentagon_files_stolen_in_major_cyberattack.html.

[36] *See, e.g., US Report Warns on China IP Theft*, BBC (May 23, 2013), http://www.bbc.co.uk/news/world-asia-china-22634685 (discussing a report suggesting that IP theft is costing the U.S. economy approximately $300 billion annually).

O'Hare International Airport with more than 1,000 proprietary documents from her employer and a one-way ticket to China.[37] Eventually, Jin was found guilty of trade secrets theft and sentenced to four years in federal prison, but she was found not guilty of economic espionage due to the high evidentiary burden of proof required.[38]

The U.S. government, though, has begun to assert fault with greater certainty in several cyber espionage cases, highlighting in particular the activities of Chinese and Russian spying campaigns.[39] In early 2013, the Obama administration implemented new policies and countermeasures in response to the ongoing theft of trade secrets that includes heightened diplomatic engagement.[40] It is currently unclear what will result from these actions, but the fact that they are happening indicates an altered U.S. perspective on the seriousness of cyber espionage and its impact on geopolitics. Reports by cybersecurity firms such as Mandiant have also further solidified perceptions of the Chinese state-sponsored espionage campaign, such as the activities of People's Liberation Army (PLA) Unit 61398.[41] Eric Schmidt of Google has similarly called China, "'the most sophisticated and prolific' hacker of foreign companies[,]" even as attribution difficulties cloud such conclusions.[42] Indeed, China is often used as a scapegoat for cyber espionage given the extent to which cyber attacks are routed through porous Chinese systems.[43]

Chinese officials have likewise accused the United States of cyber espionage – accusations that have been given added weight by former NSA contractor Edward

---

[37] *See* John Ribeiro, *Former Motorola Employee Sentenced to Four Years Imprisonment for Trade Secrets Theft*, CIO (Aug. 30, 2012), http://www.cio.com/article/715140/Former_Motorola_Employee_Sentenced_to_Four_Years_Imprisonment_for_Trade_Secrets_Theft.

[38] *Id.* (reporting that the judge "found by a preponderance of the evidence" that "Jin 'was willing to betray her naturalized country'...").

[39] *See* OFF. NAT'L COUNTERINTELLIGENCE EXECUTIVE, FOREIGN SPIES STEALING U.S. ECONOMIC SECRETS IN CYBERSPACE: REPORT TO CONGRESS ON FOREIGN ECONOMIC COLLECTION AND INDUSTRIAL ESPIONAGE, 2009–2011 i (Oct. 2011), http://www.ncix.gov/publications/reports/fecie_all/Foreign_Economic_Collection_2011.pdf [hereinafter FOREIGN SPIES].

[40] *See* Victoria Espinel, *Launch of the Administration's Strategy to Mitigate the Theft of U.S. Trade Secrets*, WHITE HOUSE (Feb. 20, 2013), http://www.whitehouse.gov/blog/2013/02/20/launch-administration-s-strategy-mitigate-theft-us-trade-secrets (laying out a five-point plan to manage the theft of trade secrets, including: (1) "diplomatic engagement," (2) the uptake of voluntary industry "best practices," (3) enhancing domestic law enforcement, (4) improving legislation, and (5) increasing "public awareness"); Derek Klobucher, *Obama's Five-Point Plan to Fight Cyber-Crime*, FORBES (Feb. 25, 2013), http://www.forbes.com/sites/sap/2013/02/25/obamas-five-point-plan-to-fight-cyber-crime/.

[41] *See APT1: Exposing One of China's Cyber Espionage Units*, MANDIANT 7 (2013).

[42] *Cybercrime: Smoking Gun*, ECONOMIST, Feb. 23, 2013, at 43 (reporting on the extent of state-sponsored cyber espionage, noting deficiencies in the attribution methodology of the 2013 Mandiant report, and noting that the likes of Iran, Russia, Bulgaria, and Romania "deserve to join China on cybercrime's most-wanted list.").

[43] *See* Oliver Rochford, *A Convenient Scapegoat – Why All Cyber Attacks Originate in China*, SEC. WK. (Sept. 27, 2012), http://www.securityweek.com/convenient-scapegoat-why-all-cyber-attacks-originate-china ("The evidence for China's involvement is often flimsy: an IP traced back to Chinese cyberspace, or a few Chinese characters or references on the digital corpse left on a victim's computing device.").

Snowden's revelations.[44] U.S. ambitions of stewarding global efforts to enhance cybersecurity and stay the course on Internet governance suffered a serious setback after the extent of NSA hacking became better known.[45] Brazilian President Dilma Rousseff canceled a state visit to the United States in response to reports that the NSA had spied on both her and Brazil's national oil company, Petrobras.[46] This has lead to an "unusual alliance" between President Rousseff and the president of the Internet Corporation for Assigned Names and Numbers, discussed later in this chapter, to "spearhead a push for new initiatives in Internet governance[,]" showcasing the extent to which cybersecurity and Internet governance are linked.[47] In addition, President Rousseff's implied concern that the U.S. intelligence program "might have been used to steal trade secrets"[48] has also been voiced by corporate managers in Germany after learning that the NSA had eavesdropped on German Chancellor Angela Merkel.[49] A 2013 Ernst & Young survey of German companies concluded that "the US now poses almost as big a risk as China when it comes to industrial espionage and data theft. . . . "[50] Even though none of the leaked reports provide definitive evidence to confirm the claim that the U.S. government has forwarded stolen trade secrets to U.S. businesses,[51] the damage to U.S. credibility is clear.[52] At least in the short term, the furor over the NSA revelations has forced

---

[44] See, e.g., Jacob Davidson, *China Accuses U.S. of Hypocrisy on Cyberattacks*, TIME (July 1, 2013), http://world.time.com/2013/07/01/china-accuses-u-s-of-hypocrisy-on-cyberattacks/; Marv Dumon, *China Accuses U.S. of Cyber Espionage*, TECHNORATI (June 6, 2013), http://technorati.com/technology/article/china-accuses-us-of-cyber-espionage/.

[45] Geoff Dyer & Richard Waters, *US Admits Surveillance on Foreign Governments 'Reached Too Far,'* FIN. TIMES (Nov. 1, 2013), http://www.ft.com/intl/cms/s/0/e028f49c-4257-11e3-9d3c-00144feabdco .html#axzz2qqrsFKwy ("'US credibility as a neutral steward of the internet has been severely damaged by the NSA revelations,' said Milton Mueller, professor at Syracuse University school of information studies.").

[46] See *Brazilian President Dilma Rousseff Calls Off US Trip*, BBC (Sept. 17, 2013), http://www.bbc.co .uk/news/world-latin-america-24133161.

[47] Milton Mueller & Ben Wagner, *Finding a Formula for Brazil: Representation and Legitimacy in Internet Governance*, INTERNET GOVERNANCE FORUM 1 (2014), http://www.internetgovernance.org/ wordpress/wp-content/uploads/MiltonBenWPdraft_Final.pdf.

[48] Gerald Jeffris, *Brazil's President Pokes at U.S. Spying*, WALL ST. J. (Sept. 25, 2013), http://online.wsj .com/news/articles/SB20001424052702304213904579095210325139486.

[49] Chris Bryant, *NSA Revelations Boost Corporate Paranoia About State Surveillance*, WALL ST. J. (Oct. 31, 2013), http://www.ft.com/intl/cms/s/0/ec02a8ca-422b-11e3-bb85-00144feabdco.html#axzz2qqrsFKwy.

[50] Id.

[51] Id. ("In all the documentation leaked by Mr Snowden, there has, however, been no evidence to date that the US has passed on foreign companies' trade secrets to its own companies."). Cf. James Glanz & Andrew W. Lehren, *N.S.A. Dragnet Included Allies, Aid Groups and Business Elite*, N.Y. TIMES (Dec. 20, 2013), http://www.nytimes.com/2013/12/21/world/nsa-dragnet-included-allies-aid-groups-and-business-elite.html (reporting that a spokesperson for the NSA, while denying that the agency relayed trade secrets to U.S. companies, stressed that the United States had national security reasons for gathering economic intelligence).

[52] See Harry Farrell & Martha Finnemore, *The End of Hypocrisy*, FOREIGN AFF. (Nov.-Dec. 2013), at 22–23 ("When these deeds turn out to clash with the government's public rhetoric, . . . it becomes harder for the U.S. allies to overlook Washington's covert behavior and easier for U.S. adversaries to justify their own.").

the United States "to abandon its naming-and-shaming campaign against Chinese hacking."[53]

What can be done about cyber espionage? Stopping these types of attacks is difficult because "given enough time, motivation, and funding, a determined adversary will always – always – be able to penetrate a targeted system."[54] Moreover, espionage is not illegal under international law,[55] although it can be under domestic law,[56] and many states are content with this state of affairs complicating potential legal remedies, as discussed further in Chapter 6.[57] Over time, though, as firms in emerging markets such as China generate more valuable domestic intellectual property, they may push for enhanced domestic and international legal protections.[58] In June 2013, for example, the United States and China agreed for the first time to hold regular talks on addressing cyber espionage.[59] Yet cyber espionage remains a serious form of cyber exploitation requiring robust defensive strategies – as is cybercrime, with which cyber espionage can overlap.

Cybercrime

The Internet is an open system, and as such, it does not provide significant inherent security for users. This openness has fostered innovation as well as cybercrime, which is among the most significant problems comprising the cyber threat; as some commentators have argued, "cyber war appears to be dominating the conversation

---

[53] *Id.* at 25 ("Protected from major criticism, U.S. officials were planning a major public relations campaign to pressure China into tamping down its illicit activities in cyberspace, starting with threats and perhaps culminating in legal indictments of Chinese hackers.").

[54] *Cyberwar, supra* note 30 (quoting "Steven Chabinsky, a senior FBI official responsible for cybersecurity"); *see* James A. Lewis, *The "Korean" Cyber Attacks and Their Implications for Cyber Conflict,* CTR. STRATEGIC & INT'L STUD. 2 (Oct. 23, 2009), http://csis.org/publication/korean-cyber-attacks-and-their-implications-cyber-conflict.

[55] *See* AN ASSESSMENT OF INTERNATIONAL LEGAL ISSUES IN INFORMATION OPERATIONS 45 (May 2009), http://www.au.af.mil/au/awc/awcgate/dod-io-legal/dod-io-legal.pdf; *Editor's Preface, in* INTERNATIONAL LAW AND ESPIONAGE vii, viii (J. Kish & David Turns eds., 1995).

[56] *See, e.g.,* Economic Espionage Act of 1996, 18 U.S.C. § 1831 et seq. (1996); Espionage Act of 1917, 18 U.S.C. § 792 (2012). For example, according to the U.S. Chamber of Commerce, "Canada, Australia, Malaysia and Singapore are among the . . . countries that have no explicit laws criminalizing the theft of trade secrets whatsoever. . . . "). Jon Cavicchi, *Chamber Seeks Sanctions For Trade Secret Theft In TPP,* UNH Law BLAWGS (Aug. 2013), http://blogs.law.unh.edu/tradesecretsblog/2013/08/.

[57] *See* NATIONAL ACADEMIES, *supra* note 23, at 280 (discussing aspects of the current international legal regime of cyber attacks, and noting that the Council of Europe's Convention on Cybercrime "does not establish espionage as an act that violates international law."). *See also* Gary Brown & Keira Pollet, *The Customary International Law of Cyberspace,* 6 STRATEGIC STUD. Q. 126, 134 (2012), http://www.au.af.mil/au/ssq/2012/fall/fall12.pdf ("Years of state practice accepting violations of territorial sovereignty for the purpose of espionage have apparently led to the establishment of an exception to traditional rules of sovereignty – a new norm seems to have been created.").

[58] *See Cybercrime: Smoking Gun, supra* note 42, at 44.

[59] *See* David E. Sanger & Mark Landler, *U.S. and China Agree to Hold Regular Talks on Hacking,* N.Y. TIMES (June 1, 2003), at A1.

among policymakers even though cyber crime is a much larger and more pervasive problem."[60] Reported cybercrime statistics have risen from $265 million in 2008, to $560 million in 2009, reaching more than $1 trillion in 2010, which is a figure larger than estimates for the global illegal drugs market, although these figures are in dispute.[61] Piracy of software alone is estimated to have yielded a loss of some $23 billion back in 2003, according to FBI figures, while some $250 billion was lost that year to intellectual property theft in the United States, costing as many as 50,000 jobs annually.[62] The U.S. Federal Trade Commission (FTC) has confirmed that cases involving identity theft and fraud are also on the rise around the world.[63] Despite its widespread prevalence, however, relatively few firms report cybercrime losses to law enforcement, as is explored in Chapter 5. Part of the reason for this apathy may come from the fact that the global dimension of cybercrime makes prosecution difficult.[64] As Michael DuBose, head of Cyber Investigations at Kroll Advisory Solutions and former chief of computer crime at the U.S. Department of Justice (DOJ) said, "I think it's fair to say that information sharing and coordination among law enforcement and national security components is key to an effective response to multipronged system attacks, and there continues to be room for improvement in that regard."[65]

Cybercrime itself is not new. An early version of "computer crime," as it used to be called, was used "in the earlier 1970s to misdirect railroad cars worth millions of dollars."[66] As far back as 1974, then Assistant Attorney General Richard Thornburg broke down computer crimes into three categories: "(1) the computer as a victim;

---

[60] Gary McGraw & Nathaniel Fick, *Separating Threat from the Hype: What Washington Needs to Know About Cyber Security*, *in* AMERICA'S CYBER FUTURE: SECURITY AND PROSPERITY IN THE INFORMATION AGE 41, 44 (Kristin M. Lord & Travis Sharp eds., 2011) [hereinafter AMERICA'S CYBER FUTURE].

[61] *See, e.g.*, *U.S. Cybercrime Losses Double*, HOMELAND SEC. NEWS WIRE (Mar. 16, 2010), http:// homelandsecuritynewswire.com/us-cybercrime-losses-double; UN OFF. DRUGS & CRIME, WORLD DRUG REPORT 127 (2005), http://www.unodc.org/unodc/secured/wdr/wdr2013/World_Drug_Report_2013.pdf (estimating the "[s]ize of the global illicit drug market in 2003" at more than $320 billion); Robert Vamosi, *The Myth Of That $1 Trillion Cybercrime Figure*, SEC. WK. (Aug. 3, 2012), http://www.securityweek.com/myth-1-trillion-cybercrime-figure.

[62] *See A Warning with Teeth: N.Y. Rolls up Movie Piracy Rings*, FBI (June 30, 2006), http://www.fbi.gov/news/stories/2006/june/iprny063006.

[63] *See* GEORGE E. HIGGINS, CYBERCRIME: AN INTRODUCTION TO AN EMERGING PHENOMENON 3 (2010).

[64] *Cf.* Mark Clayton, *Hacker's Extradition for Cyber Heist: Sign US is Gaining in Cyber Crime Fight*, CHRISTIAN SCI. MONITOR (Aug. 11, 2010), http://www.csmonitor.com/USA/Justice/2010/0811/Hacker-s-extradition-for-cyber-heist-sign-US-is-gaining-in-cyber-crime-fight (reporting on the increase in successful extraditions of international cyber criminals).

[65] Electronic Interview with Michael DuBose, head of Cyber Investigations at Kroll Advisory Solutions and former chief of the Computer Crime & Intellectual Property Section, Criminal Division, Department of Justice (Apr. 18, 2011).

[66] Samuel Liles, *Cyber Warfare: As a Form of Low-Intensity Conflict and Insurgency*, NATO CCDCOE PROC. 2010, at 47, 49, http://www.ccdcoe.org/publications/2010proceedings/Liles%20-%20Cyber%20warfare%20%20As%20a%20form%20of%20low-intensity%20conflict%20and%20insurgency.pdf (citing THOMAS T. WHITESIDE, COMPUTER CAPERS: TALES OF ELECTRONIC THIEVERY, EMBEZZLEMENT, AND FRAUD 26 (1978)).

(2) the computer as an environment; and (3) the computer as an accomplice. . . . "[67] These categories have not substantially been revised in the following decades.[68] The difference today, however, is the ubiquity of the Internet, and the growing sophistication of criminals in compromising computers and networks. This job is made easier when the targets lack vital protections. For example, according to an AOL and National Cyber Safety Alliance study, "four out of five home PCs lacked at least one of three critical protections: updated anti-virus software, spyware protection, or a working firewall that blocks certain communications."[69] Without these basic defenses, PCs are vulnerable: "[If] you put an unprotected computer on the Internet, I would say with virtual certainty within 30 minutes your computer is going to be compromised," according to an FBI official interviewed on *National Public Radio*.[70] That is one reason why cybercriminals often target personal computers instead of harder targets – not because they cannot get into these other systems, but simply because there is so much low hanging fruit. Unsecured PCs and networks comprise the soft underbelly of cyberspace, a route to more significant targets. They are both the victims and unwitting accomplices of attackers.

Cybercrime, like cyber warfare, is a catchall category. It may be broken down into an array of topics, including cyber harassment and bullying, cyber stalking, cyber fraud and identity theft, and intellectual property theft.[71] Each of these issues requires its own legal and policy responses that are beyond the scope of this book, but serve to highlight the intricate web of regulations at work in cyberspace. For example, the 1986 Computer Fraud and Abuse Act (CFAA), as amended in 2008, criminalizes "unauthorized access" to or "unauthorized transmission" of things like malware (malicious software) into a computer, as well as damage to a protected computer or network, obtaining and trafficking private information, affecting the use of a computer (such as by using a computer to form a botnet), and extortion.[72] However, harmonizing criminal laws across borders, resource constraints, and

---

[67] *Id.* at 50 (citing WHITESIDE, *supra* note 66, at 79).

[68] *See id.*; Clay Wilson, *Cyber Crime, in* CYBERPOWER AND NATIONAL SECURITY 415, 417 (Franklin D. Kramer, Stuart H. Starr, & Larry Wentz eds., 2009).

[69] *Criminals Find New Ways to Attack on the Internet*, NPR (Oct. 9, 2006), https://www.npr.org/templates/story/story.php?storyId=6223908. Note that personal computer (PC) is used here in the generic sense to include Apple computers. For more recent statistics, see Gloria Sin, *Microsoft: Almost 25 Percent of Computers are Still Unprotected from Viruses and Malware*, DIGITAL TRENDS (Apr. 18, 2013), http://www.digitaltrends.com/computing/microsoft-almost-25-of-computers-are-vulnerable-to-viruses-and-malware/.

[70] *Cyber Sleuths Zero In as Web Fraud Takes Toll*, NPR WEEKEND ED. (Jan. 20, 2008), http://www.npr.org/templates/story/story.php?storyId=18117120.

[71] *See ID Theft, Fraud & Victims of Cybercrime*, STAYSAFEONLINE.ORG, http://www.staysafeonline.org/stay-safe-online/protect-your-personal-information/id-theft-and-fraud (last visited Jan. 24, 2013).

[72] *See* 18 U.S.C. § 1030 (3)(10); Jennifer Granick, *Amendments to Computer Crime Law Are a Dark Cloud with a Ray of Light*, EFF (June 15, 2009), http://www.eff.org/deeplinks/2009/06/amendments-computer. A botnet is a network of computers working together to perform some task, such as, in the best case, a citizen science project. Botnets are discussed further in Chapter 3. The CFAA is explored in Chapter 5.

problems of attribution among other challenges underscore the difficulties of managing cybercrime.[73]

Cybercrime is likely the most widely reported kind of cyber attack and the one with which people are most familiar. Many Internet users, for example, have received an email at some point saying that if you send some money now you will receive a larger payoff. An example of such a scheme is the Nigerian 419 scam.[74] Another potential vehicle for cybercrime, eBay, is used for what is known as "quickswapping."[75] To understand quickswapping, Mikko Hypponen, a cybersecurity officer at F-Secure, provides the following example. Consider a hypothetical situation in which there are three people: Chuck (the criminal), Alice (the first victim), and Bob (the second victim). Alice's computer has been infected with a virus, allowing Chuck to steal her credit card information. Chuck could just use her card, but he does not want to get caught, so he posts "Sony PlayStation 4, new in box" for sale on eBay, although he possesses no such item. Bob sees the PlayStation and is the winning bidder. In an email, Chuck congratulates Bob and tells him that he will ship it right away. He suggests that Bob pay him after checking out the device, and Bob agrees. Now Chuck goes to Amazon.com and uses Alice's stolen credit card to purchase a brand new PlayStation, which he then ships to Bob's address. A day later, the PlayStation arrives, and Chuck asks for payment via Western Union or any other anonymous one-way online money transfer mechanism. Bob complies, and everyone is happy. But we have a loser – Alice. On her next credit card bill, she notices an extra PlayStation purchase, calls her bank, and refuses to pay it. The bank then calls Amazon and reverses the charges, and Amazon calls the cops. The cops, however, will not go to Chuck. Nobody knows who Chuck is or where he is. Instead, the cops will go to Bob. They will take away the PlayStation and possibly even charge Bob for possessing stolen property.[76] According to Hypponen, "The bottom line is that when everyday users go to online auctions and look for good value, scenarios like this never occur

---

[73] *But see* Matt Liebowitz, *Interpol Site Attacked After Arrest of Anonymous Hackers*, SEC. NEWS DAILY (Feb. 28, 2012), http://www.securitynewsdaily.com/1575-interpol-attacked-anonymous-arrests .html (illustrating several high-profile successes of law enforcement actions against cybercriminals). For a survey of cybercrime events including successful prosecutions, see *Cyber Crime Stories*, FBI, http://www.fbi.gov/news/stories/story-index/cyber-crimes (last visited Jan. 24, 2014).

[74] Nigerian 419 scams, which began in the 1980s and often involve stealing private information like credit card or bank account numbers, are also known as the "Nigerian Letter" or "419 scam" because "the scammer often claims to be from Nigeria and 419 is the Nigerian criminal code that this scam violates." *Scams that Promise Money, Gifts, or Prizes*, MICROSOFT (Mar. 9, 2010), http://www .microsoft.com/canada/protect/protect-yourself/spam-and-phishing-scams/article.aspx?article=scams-that-promise-money-gifts-or-prizes (last visited June 3, 2013); *see also Email and Web Scams: How to Help Protect Yourself*, MICROSOFT SAFETY & SEC. CTR., http://www.microsoft.com/security/online-privacy/phishing-scams.aspx (last visited Jan. 24, 2014) (reviewing how to recognize, report, and mitigate the risk of falling victim to scams online). For insights into the human cost of these scams, see Geeta Pandey, *Man Travels 1,000 Miles to Claim Bogus Prize*, BBC (Feb. 6, 2014), http://www.bbc.co.uk/news/world-asia-india-26012779.

[75] Electronic Interview, Mikko H. Hypponen, Chief Research Office, F-Secure Corporation (Oct. 1, 2010).

[76] *Id.*

to them. They'd never imagine that the item they are bidding on might not exist at all and instead they are laundering money for online criminals."[77]

There is another bottom line to the story: this can happen to anyone, from anywhere. Cybercrime is global. Although infected systems tend to be concentrated in certain areas, including the United States and China, everywhere the Internet has penetrated, cyber attackers have followed.[78] Zeus – one of the most prolific Trojan horses to date – has infiltrated computers in nearly every nation.[79] This underscores the extent to which multilateral collaboration is critical to enhancing cybersecurity, as is discussed in Chapter 7. To catch cybercriminals, investigators often follow the money trail because digital footprints are so hard to find. However, this is easier said than done, according to DuBose: "For instance, we've investigated fraudsters using eight credit cards to back 20 or more PayPal accounts, most of the accounts opened using stolen IDs, while at the same time conducting their illegal Internet business via a Wi-Fi connection stolen from a neighbor."[80] Problems are exacerbated by jurisdictional difficulties. Even though "police are constrained by national borders, criminals roam freely."[81] As a result, cybercriminals can take advantage of neutral states that tolerate their criminal behavior and do not participate in extradition treaties. Failed or weak states, in particular, are often havens for cybercriminals with Ivory Coast being a case in point,[82] and there is a thriving black market in software attack tools that may be purchased or rented to help avoid detection.[83]

Given this multitude of challenges, what can be done about cybercrime? Nations share a common interest in catching cybercriminals, but so far, efforts have proven insufficient to stem the flood, though some progress is being made. In the United States, the FBI's Cyber Division was created in 2002 to address all cyber attacks that "have international facets and national economic implications."[84] It investigates

[77] *Id.*

[78] *See The Center to Fight CyberCrime*, EUROPOL, http://europol.easyred.com/ (last visited Jan. 24, 2014) (reporting that 23 percent of the global cybercrime surveyed purportedly originated in the United States, with the next highest concentration being China accounting for 9 percent).

[79] *See* Nicolas Falliere & Eric Chien, *Zeus: King of the Bots*, SYMANTEC: SEC. RESPONSE, at 2, http://www.symantec.com/content/en/us/enterprise/media/security_response/whitepapers/zeus_king_of_bots.pdf; Gregory J. Rattray & Jason Healey, *Non-State Actors and Cyber Conflict, in* AMERICA'S CYBER FUTURE, *supra* note 60, at 67, 73 ("Zeus yielded criminal gains of 70 million dollars to just one of the many groups using it."). Trojan horses are programs designed to steal information or harm systems and are discussed further in Chapter 3.

[80] DuBose, *supra* note 65.

[81] *Cyberwar, supra* note 30.

[82] Lewis, *supra* note 54, at 8; *see* Tamisin Ford, *Ivory Coast Cracks Down on Cyber Crime*, BBC (Jan. 16, 2014), http://www.bbc.co.uk/news/business-25735305.

[83] Lewis, *supra* note 54, at 9; Rattray & Healey, *supra* note 79, at 72 (noting that Zeus may be purchased for $700). The sheer number of attacks can also stymie prosecutorial efforts. *See* Carrie Johnson, *U.S. Hunts 'Hacktivists'; Some Ask: Is it Worth It?*, NPR (Dec. 13, 2010), http://www.npr.org/2010/12/13/132015315/as-u-s-hunts-hacktivists-some-ask-is-it-worth-it.

[84] *Cyber Division*, FBI, https://www.fbijobs.gov/311132.asp (last visited Jan. 24, 2014); *see also* JOSEPH F. GUSTIN, CYBER TERRORISM: A GUIDE FOR FACILITY MANAGERS 140 (2004) (discussing the FBI cyber division).

cases that are referred by the Internet Fraud Crime Center, an online reporting service, or by local, state, or federal agencies.[85] After a referral, the FBI's Office of Infrastructure Protection and Computer Intrusion Squad becomes involved. The Squad typically investigates cyber attacks against private companies, educational facilities, and U.S. government agencies.[86] In addition to the FBI, the National Infrastructure Protection Center, part of the Department of Homeland Security (DHS) since 2002,[87] is another player in helping to investigate cybercrime along with the DOJ, which prosecutes cyber attackers under the more than twenty U.S. cybercrime statutes.[88] The DOJ has begun focusing more on cybercrime. From 2005 to 2009, prosecutors at the Computer Crime and Intellectual Property Section (CCIPS) of the DOJ quadrupled the number of investigative matters opened.[89]

Globally, Interpol began efforts to harmonize national cybercrime laws in 1979, an effort that has continued through the G8 but so far with no binding legal effect.[90] The Council of Europe's Convention on Cybercrime, in force since July 1, 2004, and commonly called the "Budapest Convention," provides an operative but limited framework through which to harmonize divergent national cybercrime laws and encourage law enforcement collaboration.[91] The Convention, for example, is stymied by the fact that it allows signatory nations to back out of investigations on fairly broad grounds, including "prejudice[ing] its sovereignty, security, *public order* or other essential interests."[92] A new UK-based body, the International Cyber Security Protection Alliance, was launched in 2011 with the goal of uniting governments, the private sector, and law enforcement agencies to fight cybercrime.[93] This organization joins a growing array of cybersecurity partnerships,[94] such as the

---

[85] Gustin, *supra* note 84, at 140; Internet Fraud Crime Center, http://www.ic3.gov/default.aspx (last visited Jan. 24, 2014).

[86] Gustin, *supra* note 84, at 140–41.

[87] *Id.* at 144. In 2011, the Secret Service – another component of the DHS – arrested some 1,239 suspects for cybercrime and helped prevent more than $1.6 billion in losses. *See* Mark Sullivan, *America's Law Enforcement Officers: Keeping Us Safe Online*, Homeland Sec. (Oct. 11, 2012), http://www.dhs .gov/blog/2012/10/11/america%E2%80%99s-law-enforcement-officers-keeping-us-safe-online.

[88] Gustin, *supra* note 84, at 157–62; U.S. Dep't of Justice, Cybercrime laws of the United States 1 (2006), http://www.oas.org/juridico/spanish/us_cyb_laws.pdf.

[89] DuBose, *supra* note 65.

[90] *See* Stein Schjolberg, *The History of Global Harmonization on Cybercrime – The Road to Geneva*, at 3, 13 (Dec. 2008), http://www.cybercrimelaw.net/documents/cybercrime_history.pdf (discussing the history of G8 efforts to mitigate cybercrime).

[91] *Id.* at 11–13; Council of Europe, Convention on Cybercrime, Mar. 2002, 41 I.L.M. 282 (2002), http://conventions.coe.int/Treaty/EN/Treaties/Html/185.htm [hereinafter Cybercrime Convention].

[92] Cybercrime Convention, art. 27(4).

[93] *See About: ICSPA*, ICSPA, www.icspa.org/about-us/ (last visited Jan. 24, 2014). *See also* Brewster, *supra* note 5 (reporting on the UK's decision to sign up to the World Economic Forum's Partnering for Cyber Resilience initiative, and noting that Foreign Secretary William Hague stated, "We must strive for a model for Internet governance in which governments, business, and users of the Internet work together in a collective endeavour, establishing a balance of responsibility for the benefit of us all.").

[94] *See, e.g.*, Gordon Corera, *Anti-Cyber Threat Centre Launched*, BBC News (Mar. 26, 2013), http:// www.bbc.co.uk/news/uk-21945702 (reporting on an initiative to improve public-private information sharing featuring a "secure Facebook" portal to allow users to share "information in real time. . . . ").

International Multilateral Partnership Against Cyber Threats (IMPACT), a global public-private partnership based in Malaysia and organized by the International Telecommunication Union that has been billed as the "world's first comprehensive alliance against cyber threats."[95] Together, these initiatives and accords have made some progress in the fight to prosecute cybercriminals and enhance global cyber-security, although there is a long way to go given the continued proliferation of cybercrime.[96]

Cyber Terrorism

As with cyber warfare and cybercrime, cyber terrorism too is a complex category of cyber attacks with little in the way of agreed upon terminology even between U.S. government agencies.[97] The "general term, terrorist, is used to denote revolutionaries who seek to use terror systematically to further their views or to govern a particular area."[98] Cyber terrorists, on the other hand, use cyberspace to "disrupt computer or telecommunications service[s]" to illicit widespread disruptions and loss of public confidence in the ability of government to function effectively such as by disrupting critical infrastructure.[99] The means used to accomplish these goals can be similar to the cyber weapons employed by states or cybercriminals, but the ends differ.

Cyber terrorists have used the Internet for a variety of purposes including recruiting, financing, and public relations.[100] For example, Azzam Publications, a fundraising site for Al Qaeda, has posted material in a wide variety of languages (from Somali to Swedish) to avoid investigations into its dealings.[101] So-called "patriotic hackers" are active around the world, notably in Russia and China, but the extent

---

[95] *Strategy*, ITU, http://www.itu.int/en/ITU-D/Cybersecurity/Pages/Strategy.aspx (last visited Jan. 24, 2014); *see* IMPACT, http://www.impact-alliance.org/aboutus/mission-&-vision.html (last visited Jan. 24, 2014).

[96] *See, e.g.*, Nikolaj Nielsen, *EU Cyber-Crime Chief Fears Massive Proliferation*, EU OBSERVER (Sept. 18, 2012), http://euobserver.com/justice/117569 (reporting on the growing cybercrime problem in Europe).

[97] *See* Sam Powers, *The Threat of Cyberterrorism to Critical Infrastructure*, E-INT'L REL. (Sept. 2, 2013), http://www.e-ir.info/2013/09/02/the-threat-of-cyberterrorism-to-critical-infrastructure/.

[98] M. J. Warren, *Terrorism and the Internet*, *in* CYBER WARFARE AND CYBER TERRORISM 42, 42 (Leah Janczewski ed., 2008) (citing PAUL WILKINSON, POLITICAL TERRORISM (1976)).

[99] *Id.* at 49; *see also* COMPUTER SCI. & TELECOMM. BD., NAT'L RES. COUNCIL, INFORMATION TECHNOL-OGY FOR COUNTERTERRORISM: IMMEDIATE ACTIONS AND FUTURE POSSIBILITIES 1–2 (John L. Hennessy et al. eds., 2003) [hereinafter INFORMATION TECHNOLOGY FOR COUNTERTERRORISM] (defining cyber terrorism); Lewis, *supra* note 18, at 1 (defining cyber terrorism as "the use of computer network tools to shut down critical national infrastructures (such as energy, transportation, government operations) or to coerce or intimidate a government or civilian population.").

[100] *See, e.g.*, UN OFF. DRUGS & CRIME, THE USE OF THE INTERNET FOR TERRORIST PUR-POSES 1 (2012), http://www.unodc.org/documents/frontpage/Use_of_Internet_for_Terrorist_Purposes .pdf ("Technology is one of the strategic factors driving the increasing use of the Internet by terrorist organizations and their supporters for a wide range of purposes, including recruitment, financing, propaganda, training, incitement to commit acts of terrorism, and the gathering and dissemination of information for terrorist purposes.").

[101] *See* Warren, *supra* note 98, at 43–44.

to which these groups are independent often remains unclear.[102] Even though virtually every terrorist group is on the web, true cyber terrorism remains rare.[103] At least three reasons may be offered for this state of affairs. First, cyber attacks may not illicit sufficient fear in targeted populations. Second, this could be the result of tacit cooperation between cyber terrorists and host nations.[104] Third, these groups could lack technological sophistication.[105] According to Admiral McConnell, however, "Sooner or later, terror groups will achieve cyber sophistication. It's like nuclear proliferation, only far easier."[106] Indeed, al-Qaeda released a video in 2012 "calling for an 'electronic Jihad[]'" on U.S. critical infrastructure.[107]

Responding to cyber terrorism is difficult given the problem of attribution as well as the issue of terrorist groups operating in failed or failing states. Retaliation may be ineffective given the fact that non-state groups will likely have few IT assets worth targeting, along with the risk of escalating a conflict and galvanizing support for the group's campaign.[108] Maintaining close collaboration with foreign law enforcement and intelligence services, incentivizing information sharing, and infiltrating dangerous non-state networks will be critical to better manage cyber terrorism and ensure that it remains a nascent threat.[109]

Summary

Current methods of conceptualizing cybersecurity challenges are not working. Cybercrime and espionage are on the rise,[110] targeting both state and non-state actors, while the prospects of cyber war and terrorism threaten international peace and security. Parsing out attacks by motive is helpful but neglects the extent to

---

[102] *See* Dorothy E. Denning, *Cyber Conflict as an Emergent Social Phenomenon, in* CORPORATE HACKING AND TECHNOLOGY-DRIVEN CRIME: SOCIAL DYNAMICS AND IMPLICATIONS 170, 180 (Thomas J. Holt & Bernadette H. Schell eds., 2010); William Marmon, *Main Cyber Threats Now Coming from Governments as "State Actors,"* EUR. INST. (2011), http://www.europeaninstitute.org/EA-November-2011/main-cyber-threats-now-coming-from-governments-as-state-actors.html.

[103] *See* James J. F. Forest, *Perception Challenges Faced by Al-Qaeda on the Battlefield of Influence Warfare,* PERSP. ON TERRORISM, Mar. 2012, at 8–9; William L. Tafoya, *Cyber Terror,* FBI L. ENFORCEMENT BULL. (Nov. 2011), http://www.fbi.gov/stats-services/publications/law-enforcement-bulletin/november-2011/cyber-terror.

[104] *See* Lewis, *supra* note 54, at 8 (arguing that cybercriminals often live in a state of sanctuary where they have agreed to target their activity outside the host nation or to strike government-designated targets).

[105] *Id.* at 9; Joseph S. Nye, Jr., *Power and National Security in Cyberspace, in* AMERICA'S CYBER FUTURE, *supra* note 60, at 7, 16.

[106] JOSEPH S. NYE, THE FUTURE OF POWER 145 (2011); Nathan Gardels, *Cyberwar: Former Intelligence Chief Says China Aims at America's Soft Underbelly,* NEW PERSPECTIVES Q., Spring 2010, at 15, 16.

[107] Powers, *supra* note 97.

[108] *See* Lewis, *supra* note 54, at 4–5; NATIONAL ACADEMIES, *supra* note 23, at 313.

[109] *See* NATIONAL ACADEMIES, *supra* note 23, at 313–15; *see also* Powers, *supra* note 97 (noting the need for an overarching U.S. strategy to manage cyber terrorism while engaging with civil society and establishing international norms).

[110] *See, e.g.,* WILL GRAGIDO & JOHN PIRC, CYBER CRIME AND ESPIONAGE: AN ANALYSIS OF SUBVERSIVE MULTI-VECTOR THREATS 8–12 (2011) (offering an analysis of cybercrime and espionage statistics).

which both actors and paradigms overlap, as may be seen in cases of state-sponsored cyber attacks involving criminal organizations for political or economic espionage.[111] Managing the cyber threat effectively is made more problematic by the fragmentation of Internet governance.[112] A new approach to modeling cybersecurity that takes into account current trends such as the growing role of states in Internet governance is needed.[113] Considering cyberspace as a unique arena through the lens of polycentrism can help reshape the way we view governance frameworks, and how cybersecurity should be approached to promote cyber peace. First, though, before these core concepts may be examined, the current framework for Internet governance and the lessons it holds for enhancing cybersecurity must be analyzed.

FRACTURED INTERNET GOVERNANCE AND ITS SECURITY IMPLICATIONS

Internet governance is in the midst of fracturing, which makes addressing cybersecurity challenges all the more difficult.[114] Early theorists viewed cyberspace as either an "environment without borders and free from state control,"[115] or a space where regulation is possible.[116] More recent scholarship has recognized the complexity inherent in cyber regulation and that a dynamic model of Internet governance is required.[117]

---

[111] The "legal vacuum[]" surrounding cyber espionage can be especially problematic for investigators. Jeremy Kirk, *GhostNet Cyber Espionage Probe Still has Loose Ends*, PC WORLD (June 18, 2009), https://www.pcworld.com/article/166901/article.html.

[112] *See, e.g.*, JONAH FORCE HILL, HARV. UNIV., INTERNET FRAGMENTATION: HIGHLIGHTING THE MAJOR TECHNICAL, GOVERNANCE AND DIPLOMATIC CHALLENGES FOR U.S. POLICY MAKERS 17–20 (2012), http://belfercenter.hks.harvard.edu/files/internet_fragmentation_jonah_hill.pdf (explaining the origin of the Domain Name System and the fragility of its future if security and fairness issues are not resolved); Norman Schneidewind, *USA's View on World Cyber Security Issues*, in CYBER WARFARE AND CYBER TERRORISM, *supra* note 98, at 446, 448–49 (discussing Internet service providers' control over a significant portion of Internet infrastructure). *See also* Alex Stark, Book Review, E-INT'L REL. (Jan. 6, 2014), http://www.e-ir.info/2014/01/06/review-cybersecurity-and-cyberwar/ (reviewing PETER W. SINGER & ALLAN FRIEDMAN, CYBERSECURITY AND CYBERWAR: WHAT EVERYONE NEEDS TO KNOW 17, 25 (2014)) (noting "that the Internet is built around 'a dynamic architecture that creates both flexibility and resilience . . . without top-down coordination." However, this model highlights "the importance of the Internet's users and gatekeepers behaving properly, and how certain built-in choke points can create vulnerabilities if they don't.").

[113] *See, e.g.*, Amar Toor, *Will the Global NSA Backlash Break the Internet?*, VERGE (Nov. 8, 2013), http://www.theverge.com/2013/11/8/5080554/nsa-backlash-brazil-germany-raises-fears-of-internet-balkanization.

[114] *See* HILL, *supra* note 112, at 31.

[115] ANDREW W. MURRAY, THE REGULATION OF CYBERSPACE: CONTROL IN THE ONLINE ENVIRONMENT 250 (2006); *see* David R. Johnson & David G. Post, *Law and Borders – The Rise of Law in Cyberspace*, 48 STAN. L. REV. 1367, 1370–72 (1996) (noting that cyberspace, unlike physical space, does not lend itself to "territorially defined rules").

[116] *See* Lawrence Lessig, *The Law of the Horse: What Cyberlaw Might Teach*, 113 HARV. L. REV. 501, 502, 533 (1999) ("I have argued that cyberspace is not inherently unregulable; that its Regulability is a function of its design.").

[117] *See* MURRAY, *supra* note 115, at xii, 250.

As a prerequisite to analyzing whether polycentric governance can enhance cyber-security, the remainder of this Part uses the case studies of the Internet Corporation for Assigned Names and Numbers (ICANN) and the Internet Engineering Task Force (IETF) to begin constructing such a model. To that end, the following section analyzes the evolution of Internet governance, focusing on the Internet address and communications systems and the extent to which security concerns have been pushed aside in favor of other priorities, such as efficiency, flexibility, and anonymity.

The Unplanned, Well-Planned Internet

The story of Internet governance may be broken down into three phases. Phase One encompassed influential network engineers and the ad hoc organizations that they developed, such as the IETF, extending from roughly 1969 to the birth of ICANN in 1998. Phase Two coincided with the commercial success of the Internet and the rise of ICANN and other organizations seeking to address the first global "digital divide" represented by the economic divergence of information and communication technology resources between developed and developing nations, culminating with the Internet Governance Forum (IGF) in 2006. Finally, Phase Three has been defined to date by the extent to which nations have begun to assert a greater role in Internet governance underscoring the potential for a "new 'digital divide'" to emerge not between the "haves and have-nots," but between "the open and the closed[]" crystallizing at the 2012 World Conference on International Telecommunications as is discussed in Chapter 7.[118] This section explores these phases, especially how the evolution of Internet governance contextualizes and offers insights into contemporary debates about promoting cyber peace, while Chapter 2 picks up on the debate between Internet sovereignty and Internet freedom.

The technological heart of the Internet is packet switching, which laid the groundwork for networking. Packet switching consists of transmitting information between linked computers. Early in the predawn of the Information Age, routes between computers were getting jammed with computers trying to transport too many whole messages simultaneously on one network, like a highway being choked with too many semi trucks. So engineers allowed messages to be divided into many smaller "packets" and sent along multiple paths to a destination – as if the semis became smart cars that could use back roads as well as interstate highways. This method resulted in our capacity to move information millions of times faster than we could before.[119]

Many networks were created throughout the 1970s and 1980s by adapting this packet-switching technology. It was first utilized by a U.S. DOD project called

---

[118] Larry Downes, *Requiem for Failed UN Telecom Treaty: No One Mourns the WCIT*, FORBES (Dec. 17, 2012), http://www.forbes.com/sites/larrydownes/2012/12/17/no-one-mourns-the-wcit/.

[119] *Id.* at 70; *Internet History*, COMPUTER HIST. MUSEUM, http://www.computerhistory.org/internet_history/ (last visited Dec. 3, 2012). For a detailed discussion of early Internet history, see KATIE HAFNER & MATTHEW LYON, WHERE WIZARDS STAY UP LATE: THE ORIGINS OF THE INTERNET (1996); *Brief History of the Internet*, INTERNET SOC'Y, http://www.isoc.org/internet/history/brief.shtml.

ARPANET, which was created in 1958 in response to the Sputnik I launch (an early indication of the extent to which international relations, along with technological change, has shaped the Internet).[120] ARPANET first existed as a closed four-node network, connecting computers at the University of California, Los Angeles; Stanford University; the University of California, Santa Barbara; and the University of Utah.[121] Eventually, it linked with other networks, adopted a common set of design protocols called Transmission Control Protocol and the Internet Protocol (TCP/IP) that allowed diverse networks to talk to one another – giving rise to many security implications – and became *the* Internet.[122] An intermediate stage of the Internet's evolution is shown in Figure 1.1.

Initially, there was no guarantee that diverse networks would morph into a single Internet. From the 1970s through the early 1990s, many small networks existed as locally, regionally, or privately funded projects used by particular communities, such as government employees or academic researchers. The ITU was helping to create national networks, which ran on a different set of protocols called Open Systems Interconnection (OSI).[123] With the exception of OSI networks and several others, however, most networks were not designed to be widely compatible.[124] As a result, many networks used different technologies, algorithms, and protocols to move information.

However, Robert Kahn, an Internet pioneer who was working for the U.S. government, had an idea: why not connect these different networks together for both defense and communication purposes?[125] The main problem was that they were technically incompatible, like railways using different gauges – all the networks used packet switching, but they transmitted information through different communications systems.[126] In the spring of 1973, Kahn recruited his former colleague, Vinton Cerf, and together they began creating a new protocol system making the incompatible compatible called TCP/IP.[127] Instead of devising a means for translating

---

[120] *See* MURRAY, *supra* note 115, at 61 (arguing that the Advanced Research Projects Agency was created by President Eisenhower to maintain U.S. technological superiority over the Soviet Union).

[121] *See id.* at 63.

[122] The Transport Control Protocol (TCP) and the Internet Protocol (IP) are the set of protocols that are responsible for the interconnections underpinning the Internet. *See, e.g.,* Howard Gilbert, *Introduction to TCP/IP*, YALE (Feb. 2, 1995), http://www.yale.edu/pclt/COMM/TCPIP.HTM; Joseph Licklider & Wesley Clark, *On-Line Man-Computer Communication*, 1962 PROC. SPRING JOINT COMPUTER CONF. (describing the notion of a 'Galactic Network' allowing scientists to share scarce computer mainframes – an idea that was to become the Internet); MURRAY, *supra* note 115, at 61, 64.

[123] *See* DAVID G. POST, IN SEARCH OF JEFFERSON'S MOOSE: NOTES ON THE STATE OF CYBERSPACE 140 (2009) (noting that as late as the early 1990s, OSI networks practically were "the Internet"; in fact, until 1994, much of the U.S. government used OSI); MURRAY, *supra* note 115, at 68–69; John R. Aschenbrenner, *Open Systems Interconnection*, 25(3) IBM SYSTEMS J. 369, 369 (1986).

[124] *See* MURRAY, *supra* note 115, at 68 (noting that the ARPANET community felt that OSI was too complex, whereas TCP/IP was more straightforward and had been proven to work).

[125] *See id.* at 65–67.

[126] *See* JANET ABBATE, INVENTING THE INTERNET 122 (2000).

[127] *See* MURRAY, *supra* note 115, at 67–68. Cerf and Kahn's goal was to create a new, simple, and widely connective protocol suite for ARPANET, a project of the U.S. Department of Defense's Advanced

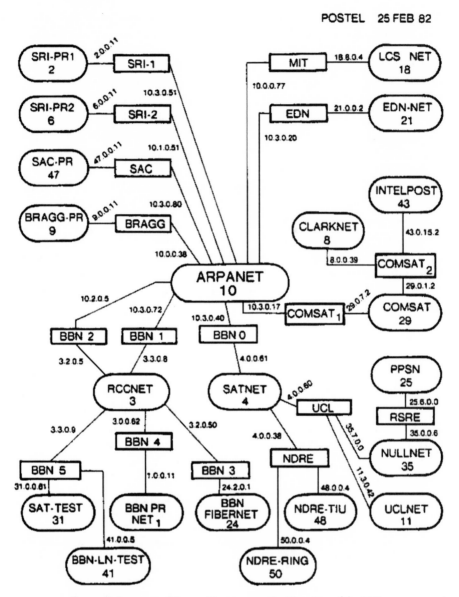

FIGURE 1.1. POSTEL'S INTERNET MAP OF FEBRUARY 1982. Courtesy of the U.S. government and the Information Sciences Institute.

between all of the different networks' communication systems, TCP/IP created a simplified, foundational protocol layer with which any communications systems

Research Projects Agency (DARPA), which became the world's first packet-switching network in 1969. *See* NAT'L SCI. FOUND., SCIENCE AND ENGINEERING INDICATORS 8–6 (1998), http://www.nsf .gov/statistics/seind98/access/c8/c8s1.htm.

could work.[128] This "Transport Layer" functions by its own very simple rules: it does the absolute minimum required to route and transport messages and does not need to understand any of the communication systems.[129] In fact, it only needs to know the IP address to which the message is being sent.[130] TCP/IP was revolutionary in part because of the way it was developed – it was brainstormed during a break at a meeting using sketches on cardboard.[131] In contrast, OSI had been an effort by hundreds of scientists at an intergovernmental agency with a budget at that time of more than 100 million Swiss francs.[132] This demonstrates the adage, "Standards should be discovered, not decreed."[133] This is one example of the many forms that cyber regulation can take and how it is possible to address a functionality problem through polycentric action. Despite support for OSI, use of TCP/IP increased along with supporting infrastructure, making it the winning protocol in large part because of "end-to-end" design, which revolutionized the early Internet.[134]

Columbia Professor Tim Wu helpfully compares end-to-end design to attorneys mailing letters through the postal service.[135] Lawyers compose letters by following their own grammatical or composition rules. Then, they send those letters by complying with a few simple requests from the post office: correctly format a delivery address, stamp it, and put it in the post. Lawyers do not need to know how the system works. Likewise, the post office working at the Transport Layer does not need to understand lawyers' grammar to deliver the letters; so while the lawyers are dependent on the postal service, the postal service is not dependent on the lawyers.[136] Similarly, nothing matters about a packet-switching network except that it uses IP addresses; networks can change without the Transport Layer needing to take note.

Thus, unlike other networks of networks, TCP/IP had the capacity – in terms of efficiency and flexibility – to eventually accommodate the thousands of different networks that form the Internet.[137] Nevertheless, this scaling feat would have meant little without a similarly scaled physical system to package and transport so many diffused packets of information.[138] To accomplish this, TCP/IP uses "distributed routing" to construct packets of the same size so that any network may handle them

---

[128] *Id.* at 67.

[129] Post, *supra* note 123, at 83.

[130] An Internet Protocol (IP) address is a numerical label assigned to every device participating in a computer network. *See* DOD STANDARD INTERNET PROTOCOL, IETF REQUEST FOR COMMENT (RFC) 760, (1980), http://tools.ietf.org/html/rfc760.

[131] *See* MURRAY, *supra* note 115, at 70.

[132] *Id.* at 64–70.

[133] HAFNER & LYON, *supra* note 119, at 254.

[134] *See, e.g.,* J. KEMPF & R. AUSTEIN, THE RISE OF THE MIDDLE AND THE FUTURE OF END-TO-END: REFLECTIONS ON THE EVOLUTION OF THE INTERNET ARCHITECTURE, IETF RFC 3724, (Mar. 2004), http://www.faqs.org/rfcs/rfc3724.html (last visited Oct. 1, 2011).

[135] *See* Tim Wu, *Application-Centered Internet Analysis,* 85 VA. L. REV. 1163, 1189–91 (1999).

[136] *Id.*

[137] *See* DOUGLAS E. COMER, COMPUTER NETWORKS AND INTERNETS 615 (3d ed. 2001).

[138] Post, *supra* note 123, at 77, 89.

and allow the packets to take any route to their destination.[139] This innovation frees up busy networks and enhances efficiency,[140] while also setting the stage for cyber attackers masking attribution.

Rather than having one centralized machine process all data, early Internet engineers allowed for data to be routed along linked networks until it arrived at the correct address.[141] This is the heart of distributed routing, and the routing rules that move information along are straightforward: (1) if you are the designated network or machine – stop, (2) if you are not – send.[142] But if a centralized server is not following these rules, what is? Kahn and Cerf devised a system of "gateways," similar to today's routers, which connect two or more networks and act as entrances.[143] In short, they are computer way stations that "receive and forward messages" by reading the destination computer's IP address.[144] As such, in some ways, the legacy of the 1970s lives on in the form of many different networks connected by routers to form the Internet.

Routers maintain routing tables and use algorithms to indicate where to send data packets to machines along each of their member networks,[145] akin to air traffic controllers directing incoming and outgoing flights. No single network or router has to keep track of changes; every router just stays informed of local changes to its own networks and unique tables. Without this system, it would have taken too long to process and move information online, thus impeding the growth of cyberspace. Unlike a centralized machine, however, distributed routing also means that the Internet can accommodate more data sent by more users from more locations[146] – its capacity to incorporate changes and route information increases alongside its size and regulatory complexity.

Ultimately, resolving issues through packet switching, end-to-end design, and distributed routing meant that the TCP/IP inter-network could and did expand at a phenomenal pace.[147] By the early 1990s, all the ingredients were in place for explosive growth: a robust and open network, a free and user-friendly protocol in the form of TCP/IP, and an increase in the number of personal computers underscoring strong demand.[148] The amount of servers grew quickly, from one based out of the Stanford Linear Accelerator Center in 1990 to more than 250 in 1993, and after a

---

[139] *Id.* at 73.
[140] MURRAY, *supra* note 115, at 67.
[141] *See* POST, *supra* note 123, at 74.
[142] *Id.*
[143] *See* MURRAY, *supra* note 115, at 67–69.
[144] GRAHAM J. H. SMITH, INTERNET LAW AND REGULATION 10 (3d ed. 2000).
[145] *See* ABBATE, *supra* note 126, at 128–29.
[146] *See* POST, *supra* note 123, at 76.
[147] *Id.* at 141; *ISC Domain Survey*, INTERNET SYSTEMS CONSORTIUM, http://www.isc.org/solutions/survey (last visited June 28, 2012).
[148] *See* MURRAY, *supra* note 115, at 72.

series of technical milestones by 1995 the "World Wide Web" became equated with the Internet, boasting more than 73,500 servers.[149]

In contrast to the TCP/IP inter-network, the designers of OSI networks imagined that each country would contribute a similarly structured network to the Internet, so there was no need to create a foundational Transport Layer or protocol whereby all of the differently structured networks could be linked.[150] They, and many others, did not foresee the evolution of a global Internet but, perhaps prophetically, a state-centric vision of cyberspace in which countries control domestic networks, a concept that is discussed further in Chapter 2. The failure of OSI also largely sidelined the ITU, which is responsible for publishing technical standards for global information and communication technologies such as radios, satellites, and telephones, but not to the same extent Internet-related technologies, though this may be changing.[151]

As opposed to OSI, little consideration was initially given to how TCP/IP networks should be governed or how they should be made more secure. Uncontrollable growth was encouraged by the protocol design,[152] and those who worked on the network of networks in its early days began informally managing it. Without a particular form of governance stipulated, structures materialized on an ad hoc basis.[153] The next two sections discuss how two of these structures, ICANN and IETF, emerged as different models of governance to guide the Internet's address and communication systems, and analyze what the implications have been for cybersecurity.[154]

Institutionalized Governance: ICANN and the Precarious Root

The context from which ICANN has evolved is similar to a dramatized version of dialing 4-1-1 for information. Imagine that the sole means of communicating is by telephone, and that there is no way to memorize a phone number. To get in touch

---

[149] *See id.*; Robert Cailliau, *A Short History of the Web*, Speech Delivered at the Launching of European Branch of the W3 Consortium (Nov. 2, 1995), http://www.netvalley.com/archives/mirrors/robert_cailliau_speech.htm.

[150] *See* POST, *supra* note 123, at 89, 140.

[151] *See, e.g., What We Do*, INTERNET SOC'Y, http://www.internetsociety.org/what-we-do/education-and-leadership-programmes/ietf-and-ois-programmes/internet-society-fellowship (last visited Jan. 24, 2014) (discussing the IETF as being "the world's premier open Internet standards-development body."); Carolyn Duffy Marsan, *IETF vs. ITU: Internet Standards Face-Off*, NETWORK WORLD (Dec. 3, 2012), http://www.networkworld.com/news/2012/120312-argument-ietf-itu-264594.html; Internet of Things Global Standards Initiative, ITU, http://www.itu.int/en/ITU-T/gsi/iot/Pages/default.aspx (last visited Jan. 24, 2014).

[152] *See* POST, *supra* note 123, at 141.

[153] *See* MURRAY, *supra* note 115, at 92, 97.

[154] *See Internet Governance Routing it Right*, ECONOMIST, Dec. 2, 2010, http://www.economist.com/node/17627815 [hereinafter *Routing it Right*].

with anyone for anything, you must consult the phone book – of which there is only one copy that is managed by one person. Naturally, you are hesitant to trust this person because he could remove or change a number in the phone book on a whim and without any legal consequences. Not long ago, this is not unlike how the Internet functioned.

If machines are connected to each other on the Internet via a name and address index akin to a phone book, then its editor was Jon Postel, whom techies call the "God" of the Internet.[155] As a graduate student in the 1970s, Postel was enlisted as the caretaker of the master copy of the "hosts.txt" file, which listed ARPANET's IP addresses and corresponding domain names.[156] Then, during much of the 1980s and 1990s, he managed the "root" file of the new Domain Name System (DNS).[157] This section details the development of the Internet's address system and Postel's early role in it, focusing on the emergence of the DNS and the major changes in Internet governance that domain names provoked leading to the formation of ICANN itself and with it Phase Two of Internet governance.

The Early Internet's Address System and the Man Who Could Have Erased It

In the beginning, before there were domain names such as www.rotary.org that correspond to IP addresses, users navigated networks by typing in actual IP addresses – dotted decimal notations such as 132.9.107.14.[158] The four parts of this number are used like a mailing address to identify networks or hosts, just as certain lines of a mailing address correspond to a street, city, or state.[159] This system efficiently moves information, but can be cumbersome for users. Domain names such as www.rotary .org were created so that users would not have to remember long IP addresses. Early on, for every new machine added to the network, Postel updated the hosts.txt file with new domain names and their corresponding IP addresses.[160] As the Internet grew, however, the system became unmanageable.

Enter the DNS, which was created in 1983 and functions by spreading this task across many coordinating files and servers.[161] Each domain name holds a uniquely coded address. For example, www.rotary.org is a three-part address located in three

---

[155] SciTech 'God of the Internet' is Dead, BBC NEWS, Oct. 19, 1998, http://news.bbc.co.uk/2/hi/science/nature/196487.stm.

[156] See POST, *supra* note 123, at 148.

[157] See MURRAY, *supra* note 115, at 103–06.

[158] *Id.* at 95.

[159] IP addresses are made up of 32-bit binary strings. "Bits" are the 1s and 0s (electronic pulses and non-pulses) of computer-speak. An IPv4 address is the equivalent representation of a 32-bit binary string, which is split into four eight-bit sequences known as "bytes" that also correspond to one of the decimal strings. *Internet History*, COMPUTER HIST. MUSEUM, http://www.computerhistory.org/internet_history/#1964 (last visited Jan. 24, 2014); *Internet Protocol, DARPA Internet Program Protocol Specification*, UNIV. SOUTHERN CAL. INFO. SCI. INST. (Sept. 1981), http://tools.ietf.org/html/rfc791.

[160] See MURRAY, *supra* note 115, at 96–97.

[161] *Id.* at 100–01.

separate index files. The end of each domain name (i.e., dot-org or dot-com) indicates the top-level domain (TLD).[162] As of October 2013, there were more than 270 country-code TLDs (such as dot-uk), while the list of generic TLDs was expanding from 22 "to possibly 1,400 new names."[163] The files are located on one or more "DNS servers," or name servers, which are "queried," or asked, to resolve the question of which IP address corresponds to a given domain name.[164] There are many thousands of DNS servers on the Internet resolving billions of queries daily.[165]

How a DNS query is resolved is best illustrated by example. Suppose a host computer's resolver queries www.indiana.edu, which is located at the address 12.34.56.78. The resolver will first check its "cache," or short-term memory, in case it has recently queried this domain name and has the stored IP address information ready.[166] If the host has requested this address recently enough, the process is over. If not, the host then forwards its query to a local DNS server, which then checks its own cache.[167] If the information is not there, or has expired, then the query is forwarded up a line of servers until one has the answer.[168] For each index, there are "authoritative" servers, which have the most updated versions of address records for their indexes, and there are servers that periodically receive updated information from authoritative servers and cache answers that they can pass along in response to client queries. At the end of the line are authoritative root name servers.[169] The process is not unlike stopping to ask for directions – if a driver can find someone local who knows the area well, their question is answered; if not, they might have to ask others or eventually contact some authoritative service to find their way.

Despite the multiple steps involved, this system is fast. With its hierarchical structure and ability to resolve queries by caching, the DNS effectively scaled the Internet's address system so much so that the fundamental operation of the DNS has hardly changed since 1983.[170] The same is not true for governance. Postel, who had been responsible for updating the DNS's equivalent of the hosts.txt file, otherwise known as the "authoritative root zone file," or root, no longer manually updates the

---

[162] *See* POST, *supra* note 123, at 144.

[163] *First New Generic Top-Level Domains Delegated*, ICANN (Oct. 23, 2013), http://www.icann.org/en/news/press/releases/release-23oct13-en; *New Generic Top-Level Domains* , ICANN, http://newgtlds.icann.org/en/announcements-and-media/video/overview-en (last visited Jan. 24, 2014). There are more country codes than countries because country-code TLDs are sometimes given to disputed territories. For a list of current TLDs, see *Root Zone Database*, IANA, http://www.iana.org/domains/root/db/ (last visited Sept. 23, 2012).

[164] CHARLES M. KOZIEROK, THE TCP/IP GUIDE: A COMPREHENSIVE, ILLUSTRATED INTERNET PROTOCOLS REFERENCE 887 (2005).

[165] *See* POST, *supra* note 123, at 148.

[166] *Id.*

[167] *Id.*

[168] *See, e.g., How DNS Query Works*, MICROSOFT TECHNET (Jan. 21, 2005), http://technet.microsoft.com/en-us/library/cc775637%28WS.10%29.aspx (last visited Sept. 23, 2012).

[169] *See* POST, *supra* note 123, at 152.

[170] *See id.* at 148; J. KLENSIN, ROLE OF THE DOMAIN NAME SYSTEM, IETF RFC 3467, (2003), http://tools.ietf.org/html/rfc3467#page-4.

FIGURE 1.2. JON POSTEL ("GOD" OF THE INTERNET). Photo courtesy of Irene Fertik, USC News Service. Copyright 1994, USC.

DNS.[171] When Postel was its manager, if someone would have erased the root, then the TLDs would have disappeared and DNS servers would not have known how to resolve queries and direct Internet traffic.[172] In short, the Internet's addressing system would have crashed. Computers would still be connected to other machines on the network, but there would be no way to find them – as with the previously mentioned example, phones would still exist without a phone book, but no one would know how to place a call.

Because the TCP/IP network was not yet geopolitically or economically vital in the 1980s and early 1990s, few challenged Postel's personal authority over the root.[173] Similarly, when the U.S. government gave operational control of the root to a small start-up called Network Solutions, Inc. (NSI) in 1992, it went largely unreported in the mainstream news.[174] However, that apathy soon ended. By the mid-1990s, fortunes were at stake, and people became more concerned with who controlled the

---

[171] The root is a text file that lists all of the TLDs and the IP addresses of their authoritative name servers. When compressed, the file is a mere twenty kilobytes – about the size of a long email – but contains "the Internet's most strategic point of control." Craig Simon, *The Privatization of the Internet's Domain Name System and the Implications for Global Politics*, ROOTS OF POWER (2008), www.rootsofpower .com. TLDs exist only because the root says they do. *See DNS Root Name Servers FAQ*, INTERNET SOC'Y, http://www.isoc.org/briefings/020/ (last visited Nov. 1, 2012).

[172] *See* POST, *supra* note 123, at 152.

[173] *See* Hans Klein, *ICANN and Internet Governance: Leveraging Technical Coordination to Realize Global Public Policy*, INFO. SOC'Y 193, 198–99 (2002).

[174] *See* POST, *supra* note 123, at 149.

root and had the legal authority to change it and the DNS,[175] foreshadowing larger debates about governance and cybersecurity to follow.

DNS Wars: The U.S. Government Strikes Back

In the early 1990s, the U.S. Congress opened up the TCP/IP network to the general public and to commercial activity,[176] but relatively little consideration had been given to governance. Postel was still determining which TLDs could be added to the root,[177] and many businesses were not yet savvy about the commercial opportunities available online. Overlapping jurisdictions, for example, led to trademarks being abused such as through cybersquatting; that is, occupying a known trademark in the hope of selling it back to the rightful owner for a profit later.[178] These issues created legal disputes, but there was no system yet in place to decide such disputes.[179] "The dot-com boom had begun[,]"[180] and by the mid-to late-1990s, interested parties were seeking to influence Internet governance, resulting in the growth of the cyber regime complex that has direct implications for enhancing global cybersecurity.

Controlling the root held financial implications for stakeholders. Theoretically, whoever controlled the root could charge whatever they wished of anyone adding a TLD, and anyone running a TLD could charge for registering a new domain name.[181] Geopolitical and legal questions loomed. For one, who should decide which disputed territories received country codes and whether trademark owners should have a right to domains containing their trademarked names?[182] So began the "DNS Wars," during which an array of private companies, nonprofits, individuals, governments, and civil society organizations emerged to vie for a stake in Internet governance.[183] Nonprofits like the Internet Society (ISOC), an umbrella organization focused on Internet technologies and policies, consulted with foreign governments, which were questioning their exclusion from decision-making in this

---

[175] *Id.* at 149–52.

[176] *Id.* at 149–50.

[177] *See* MURRAY, *supra* note 115, at 103–04.

[178] *See, e.g.,* Oliver R. Gutierrez, *Get Off My URL: Congress Outlaws Cybersquatting in the Wild West of the Internet*, 17(1) SANTA CLARA COMPUTER & HIGH TECH. L.J. 139, 142–43 (2001).

[179] *See, e.g., Ethics in Computing*, NC ST. UNIV., http://ethics.csc.ncsu.edu/commerce/cybersquatting/ (last visited Jan. 24, 2014) (providing an overview of ethics in computing including recent cases).

[180] POST, *supra* note 123, at 149.

[181] *See* Scott P. Sonbuchner, *Master of Your Domain: Should the U.S. Government Maintain Control over the Internet's Root?*, 17 MINN. J. INT'L L. 183, 186 (2008).

[182] *See Overview*, ICANN: NEW GENERIC TOP-LEVEL DOMAINS http://newgtlds.icann.org/en/ announcements-and-media/video/overview-en (last visited Mar. 28, 2013) (answering questions about registering country code domains and resolving registration disputes); *Trademark Clearinghouse*, ICANN: NEW GENERIC TOP-LEVEL DOMAINS, http://newgtlds.icann.org/en/about/ trademark-clearinghouse (last visited Mar. 28, 2013) (noting ICANN's role in developing mechanisms to protect the rights of trademark holders).

[183] *See* Jessica Litman, *The DNS Wars: Trademarks and the Internet Domain Name System*, 4 J. SMALL & EMERGING BUS. L. 149, 158 (2000).

newly global network.[184] Undeterred, the U.S. government began asserting its authority over the root and DNS, underscoring the Internet's status as a pseudo commons at best, as is discussed in Chapter 2.[185]

Amidst the DNS crisis, Postel overplayed his hand.[186] On January 28, 1998, he copied the root and redirected many of its queries from the authoritative root server to a second server – his computer at the University of Southern California (USC) – conducting what he called a "test" and others called a "hijacking."[187] Few people noticed, but with just a few keystrokes, Postel could have implemented a new set of TLDs or even eliminated dot-com for much of the world.[188] His test was reversed within a week, as an irate Ira Magaziner, then-President Clinton's senior science advisor, called Postel and said that both he and USC would be liable if he continued compromising the root.[189] Magaziner also said that the United States would consider future unauthorized changes to the root a criminal offense – although it was unclear at the time what law, if any, Postel had broken by his actions, demonstrating an early example of legal ambiguity in the dynamic arena of cyberspace.[190]

To further complicate matters, in early 1998, the U.S. government's five-year contracts with Postel and NSI were set to expire.[191] Postel's test heightened concerns, and on January 30, 1998, the U.S. government issued a green paper that called for a new private-sector organization to manage the DNS and the root and in so doing arguably brought to a close Phase One of Internet governance.[192] Enter ICANN,[193] which eventually would become the closest thing the web has to a governing body responsible for operational stability: it manages IP address space, domain names, and the DNS root server system.[194]

ICANN and the Cyber Regime Complex

Creating a new institution to manage the DNS amidst the dot-com boom was no simple matter. Because vesting authority had not been a key concern when TCP/IP

---

[184] *See* MURRAY, *supra* note 115, at 89, 91 (noting that the main goal of ISOC is to host and support standards-making bodies such as IETF).

[185] *See* JACK GOLDSMITH & TIM WU, WHO CONTROLS THE INTERNET?: ILLUSIONS OF A BORDERLESS WORLD 42 (2006).

[186] *Id.* at 42–44.

[187] POST, *supra* note 123, at 154; LAURA LAMBERT, THE INTERNET: A HISTORICAL ENCYCLOPEDIA 200–02 (2005).

[188] GOLDSMITH & WU, *supra* note 185, at 45.

[189] *Id.* at 46.

[190] POST, *supra* note 123, at 154.

[191] *See* MURRAY, *supra* note 115, at 105.

[192] *Id.* at 106.

[193] ICANN's power, however, is limited because its contract may be terminated within 120 days by the U.S. government. *See* DOD-ICANN Understanding § VII.

[194] *See* ICANN Bylaws, ICANN (June 24, 2011), http://www.icann.org/en/about/governance/bylaws; *The Internet: A Peace of Sorts: No One Controls the Internet, but Many are Determined to Try*, ECONOMIST (Nov. 17, 2005), http://www.economist.com/node/5178973 [hereinafter *A Peace of Sorts*].

was still experimental, most Internet engineering and policy projects were simply contracted out by the U.S. government. Cerf, the "father" of the Internet and co-creator of TCP/IP,[195] has said that those contracted with were mostly graduate students who went about developing the Internet's architecture as they saw fit.[196] As the Internet grew, research positions of "the ARPANET elite" – including Kahn, Cerf, and Postel – began to blur into management roles.[197] These managers tried to institutionalize their duties through an alphabet soup of new organizations, including: the Internet Activities Board, which became the Internet Architecture Board (IAB) in 1983; the IETF in 1986; the Internet Assigned Numbers Authority (IANA) in 1988; the Internet Research Task Force (IRTF) in 1989; the ISOC in 1992; and the World Wide Web Consortium (W3C) in 1994.[198] Whereas IANA, which is housed under ICANN as of February 2014, was headed by Postel and was in charge of maintaining the root and managing IP address allocation,[199] ISOC was created in part to protect IETF from lawsuits and solicit funding for the other organizations.[200] But then, as the DNS Wars broke out in the late 1990s, ISOC asserted itself as an appropriate body for determining the "highest questions of Internet policy" – putting it at odds with the U.S. government.[201] In 1996, ISOC and IANA organized an ad hoc committee to resolve DNS issues, enlisting in their cause foreign governments, the World Intellectual Property Organization, and the ITU, among other institutions.[202] This committee laid out a proposal for a new Internet governance structure, but the U.S. government rejected it in January 1998, prompting, some suggest,Postel's "test."[203]

The United States' rejection of the committee's proposal was a turning point, wherein the U.S. government asserted its authority over the ARPANET elite, although critics of the proposal also included IBM, AT&T, and U.S. civil society groups citing concerns about power grabbing.[204] But the U.S. government began bargaining with corporate interests and significant international stakeholders; still, many developing countries were only involved at the periphery.[205] Throughout the summer of 1998, negotiators crafted a plan backed by the U.S. government and a powerful coalition of stakeholders.[206] The result of this process was ICANN, a non-profit corporation headquartered in the United States with a board of directors from

---

[195] GOLDSMITH & WU, *supra* note 185, at 36, 58.
[196] *See* JOYCE REYNOLDS & JON POSTEL, NETWORK WORKING GROUP, IETF RFC 1000 (1987), http://www.rfc-editor.org/rfc/rfc1000.txt.
[197] MUELLER, *supra* note 2, at 89.
[198] *Id.* at 90–97.
[199] *Id.* at 93.
[200] *Id.* at 95–96.
[201] GOLDSMITH & WU, *supra* note 185, at 37.
[202] *See* MURRAY, *supra* note 115, at 104–07.
[203] GOLDSMITH & WU, *supra* note 185, at 42–44.
[204] *Id.* at 147–50; MUELLER, *supra* note 2, at 151.
[205] MUELLER, *supra* note 2, at 170–72.
[206] *Id.* at 170–74.

TABLE 1.1. *Internet organizations and their functions*

Organization	Structure	Areas of Responsibility	Strengths	Criticisms
ICANN	Nonprofit	Manages core Internet functions, including IP addresses and the DNS	Centrality to Internet functionality and track record	Historic ties to U.S. government
ISOC	Nonprofit	"Organizational home" for various Internet management groups	Recognized authority and influence	Acts through members
IETF	Collaborative Forum of Volunteers	Develops and improves core technologies, standards, and protocols	Recognized technical leadership	Avoids policy influence
IRTF	Collaborative Forum of Volunteers	Identifies areas for future research and development	Industry independence	Competes with other bodies for policy influence
W3C	Collaborative Committees	Focuses on technical development of web standards	Expertise in specific standards	Narrow focus on web issues

Courtesy of The Center for a New American Security: David A. Gross et al., *Cyber Security Governance: Existing Structures, International Approaches and the Private Sector, in* AMERICA'S CYBER FUTURE: SECURITY AND PROSPERITY IN THE INFORMATION AGE 105, 115 tbl. 2 (Kristin M. Lord & Travis Sharp eds., 2011).

the private and public sectors drawn from around the world, but without a significant role for foreign governments.[207] Thus began Phase Two of Internet governance, which included efforts aimed at globalizing Internet policymaking.

ICANN had few supporters when the U.S. government formally entered into a contract with it in February 1999, since by then many nations were clamoring for a greater role in Internet governance.[208] This increased attention grew partly from rapid increases in cybercrime and espionage, as well as the potential of cyber warfare, illustrating the link between cyber insecurity and the evolution of Internet governance.[209] Whereas IETF evolved organically within an engineering network, the U.S. government created ICANN, engendering questions of legitimacy that continue to plague the institution.[210] Moreover, Postel's sudden death in October

---

[207] *See* MURRAY, *supra* note 115, at 106; ICANN Bylaws, ICANN, http://www.icann.org/en/about/governance/bylaws (last visited Oct. 15, 2013).

[208] *See* MUELLER, *supra* note 2, at 175, 183–84; *Management of Internet Names and Addresses,* U.S. DEP'T COM. (1998), http://www.icann.org/en/general/white-paper-05jun98.htm.

[209] KNAKE, *supra* note 7, at 5.

[210] *See* MURRAY, *supra* note 115, at 106 (commenting that ICANN was created by the United States "artificially"). However, even though the U.S. government decided to form ICANN, there was a period of open discussion regarding what form the new organization should take. Indeed, one criticism is that ICANN incorporates *too many* democratic mechanisms in its decision-making. *See* Philip Corwin, *The ICANN Policy and Decision Making Process Is Seriously Flawed,* INTERNET COM. ASSOC. (Aug. 15, 2012),

1998 "robbed the organization of its moral center, [and] a good part of its institutional memory. . . . "[211] Nevertheless, even with this troubled start, ICANN has persisted, if not always with solid footing.

ICANN: Walking the Virtual Tightrope

Those involved with the creation of ICANN knew that domain names and IP addresses were at the core of the Internet's operation, and that the transition of Internet governance to a nonprofit organization "would be risky and controversial."[212] However, few might have imagined the coming controversies over ICANN's policymaking, or that the organization would long retain so much power despite near continuous challenges to its legitimacy. This feat is especially impressive given that beyond its general managing of the Internet's address system, ICANN's work has also had a lasting effect on international legal, political, economic, and security issues.

Regarding ICANN's legal relevance, as was previously mentioned, the organization has been active in resolving cybersquatting disputes. In twelve years, it has adjudicated more than 10,000 cases in which domain names were either "confusingly similar to" or illegitimately misused trademarks.[213] Only in contentious cases involving parties legitimately competing to use a name did ICANN defer to the courts.[214] ICANN also has the authority to approve or disapprove the addition of new country code and other TLDs,[215] meaning that it plays an important role in the development of e-commerce and touches on geopolitics.

The degree to which ICANN should be able to pursue and enforce its guidelines depends in part on who directs ICANN. This is an important aspect of the larger debate on ICANN's authority and relates to perceptions of U.S. control over core

---

http://internetcommerce.org/Registration_Abuse_Time_to-Fish_or_Cut_Bait (arguing that the extended duration of deliberation results in a lengthy process without yielding concrete action). Thus, it is too simplistic to state, for example, that IETF is a bottom-up organization while ICANN utilizes top-down management processes. Rather, given that ICANN does have some limited enforcement authority to make decisions, regarding TLDs for instance, and that it is a nonprofit representing multiple stakeholders but as of 2014 with authority ultimately vested in the U.S. Department of Commerce, it is more accurate to consider a continuum with IETF at one end, and ICANN near the center. The other extreme of the Internet governance spectrum may be considered a more state-centric, top-down model favored by some nations as discussed in Chapters 2 and 7. *See, e.g.,* Ellery Roberts Biddle & Emma Llansó, *WCIT Watch Day 11: We Cannot Compromise on the Internet*, Ctr. Democracy & Tech. (Dec. 13, 2012), www.cdt.org/blogs/1312wcit-watch-day-11-we-cannot-compromise-internet (describing the frustration of some countries with the ITU's decision-making approach).

[211] *See* Mueller, *supra* note 2, at 181.

[212] *Id.* at 2.

[213] Post, *supra* note 123, at 159; *see also* Kathy Bowrey, Law and Internet Cultures 51 (2005) (discussing ICANN's trademark dispute resolution policy).

[214] *See* Christopher G. Clark, Note, *The Truth in Domain Names Act of 2003 and a Preventative Measure to Combat Typosquatting*, 89 Cornell L. Rev. 1476, 1479–80, 1486–87 (2003); Bowrey, *supra* note 213, at 51.

[215] *See* Post, *supra* note 123, at 152.

functions of the Internet.[216] Calls for a more multilateral approach have not abated since the organization's founding as more countries have recognized the importance of the Internet,[217] and have only become louder post-Snowden.[218]

Doubts about ICANN's legitimacy began crystallizing in the summer of 2000 when ICANN's original bylaws required the election of a new "At Large" Board of Directors.[219] Elections allowed any Internet user who had joined ICANN's At Large community to vote for five regional board members.[220] The first At Large elections in October 2000 resulted in an outright "rejection of the current board and its policies."[221] However, instead of stepping down, the board passed its powers to an executive committee that excluded the new directors from key decisions, further tarnishing its legitimacy.[222]

ICANN's regulatory failures began attracting increased attention by the international community along with calls for reform to include more public- and private-sector stakeholders outside of the United States.[223] For example, some stakeholders were hoping that the United Nations would take over some or all of ICANN's responsibilities in the early 2000s, but that plan was cancelled amidst a negative reaction by the U.S. government.[224] One episode of this ongoing debate involved the 2005 UN World Summit on the Information Society (WSIS).[225] Geopolitical divides were on display during these meetings: the U.S., Canadian, Japanese, and E.U. negotiators were suspicious of other governments wishing to restrict content, even as developing countries were wary of multi-stakeholder governance involving the private sector, among other issues.[226] In the end, however, multi-stakeholder governance, understood here as "the coming together of different interest groups on an equal footing,"[227] was affirmed, as was a broad definition of Internet governance that included cybersecurity.[228] To put its proposals into practice, WSIS created a Working Group on Internet Governance that suggested the creation of an Internet Governance Forum where public and private stakeholders could meet and discuss issues of Internet governance.[229] This was done at a UN-sponsored forum in 2006

---

[216] *See* Loek Essers, *ICANN Keeps Control Over IANA Internet Root*, PC WORLD (July 3, 2012), http://www.pcworld.com/article/258722/icann_keeps_control_over_iana_internet_root.html.

[217] *A Peace of Sorts, supra* note 194.

[218] *See* Mueller & Wagner, *supra* note 47, at 1.

[219] MURRAY, *supra* note 115, at 114.

[220] *Id.* at 115.

[221] *Id.*

[222] *Id.* at 116–17.

[223] *Id.* at 118–22.

[224] *Id.* at 123.

[225] *Id.* at 118.

[226] *Id.* at 120.

[227] Milton Mueller et al., *Democratizing Global Communication? Global Civil Society and the Campaign for Communication Rights in the Information Age*, INT'L J. COMM. 267, 268 (2007).

[228] *See* Report of the Working Group on Internet Governance, *supra* note 4, at para. 12.

[229] *See* MURRAY, *supra* note 115, at 122–23 (noting that some proposals would have made ICANN accountable to the IGF, turning it into an international NGO under the oversight of a UN body).

helping to usher in the third phase of Internet governance with concerns over polit-ical representation coming increasingly to the fore.[230] Many developing nations saw the IGF as a vehicle to make Internet governance a more multilateral endeavor.[231] Since its creation, the IGF has been criticized as a toothless talking shop, but its members continue to meet and receive international support.[232] However, accord-ing to Professor Milton Mueller, since 2005 there has also been "a proliferation of national and regional Internet Governance Forums at various levels and [address-ing] various topics."[233] Thus, rather than the IGF forestalling the globalization of Internet governance, it seems to have fueled the rise of what could be termed poly-centric Internet governance forums that are further challenging the perceived U.S. led status quo in this domain.[234]

There are signs that the U.S. government may be changing tack in light of increased international pressure to globalize Internet governance. In September 2009, when the U.S. government's contract with ICANN was again set to expire, the two parties released an Affirmation of Commitments (AOC) in which the United States agreed to transfer some authority to advisory committees "made up of gov-ernment and private-sector representatives around the world" that would review decisions about TLD and domain name availability, languages, and costs.[235] At the UN-backed IGF forum in November 2009, members of the international commu-nity commented on the AOC and the U.S. government's changing relationship with ICANN positively, but with some reservations.[236] Other avenues to enhance legitimacy through structural reform include enhancing accountability from the top-down (subjecting ICANN to a "higher, established authority"), bottom-up (mak-ing ICANN "directly accountable to users and other stakeholders[]"), and through peer-to-peer mechanisms (providing users with "a choice among coordinated gover-nance arrangements.").[237] But the U.S. government still maintains a dominant role in Internet governance. The U.S. Department of Commerce owns the authoritative root name server and contracts the root's management to a U.S. company called

---

[230] *See id.*

[231] *Id.* (citing D. McCullogh, *US Endorses Internet Governance Forum*, CNET (Nov. 16, 2005), http://www.freerepublic.com/focus/f-news/1523112/posts).

[232] *See* Kieren McCarthy, *United Nations Lauds Internet's 'Arranged Marriage': Internet Governance Forum Ends on a High Note*, REGISTER (Nov. 2, 2006), http://www.theregister.co.uk/2006/11/02/igf_meeting_ends/; INTERNET GOVERNANCE FORUM, http://www.intgovforum.org/cms/ (last visited Jan. 29, 2013).

[233] Mueller & Wagner, *supra* note 47, at 8.

[234] *See id.* at 8–10.

[235] *U.S. Moves to Lessen Its Oversight of Internet*, ASSOC. PRESS (AP) (Sept. 30, 2009), http://www.nytimes.com/2009/10/01/technology/internet/01icann.html [hereinafter *Oversight*]; *see Affirmation of Commitments by the United States and the Internet Corporation for Assigned Names and Num-bers*, ICANN (Sept. 30, 2009), http://www.icann.org/en/announcements/announcement-30sep09-en.htm.

[236] *Oversight, supra* note 235.

[237] *What to Do About ICANN: A Proposal for Structural Reform*, INTERNET GOVERNANCE PROJECT (Apr. 5, 2005), at 3–7 , www.internetgovernance.org/pdf/igp-icannreform.pdf.

VeriSign, which is "contractually obligated to secure written approval" from the Department before making any TLD changes.[238] Plans to transfer control of the root had not been implemented as of February 2014. Still, challenges to U.S. control do exist. Consider that the physical locations of root name servers used to be either in the United States or under the control of U.S. allies, but now copies of this "strategic international asset" exist all over the world.[239]

Despite its U.S. ties, ICANN has evolved, presenting a more genuinely global face. In 2010, it expanded the role of the Governmental Advisory Committee, which had previously been derided for its lack of influence.[240] This development helped bring both China and Russia back into ICANN's Governmental Advisory Committee, although the Committee's recommendations remain just that – advisory.[241] Likewise, in June 2011, ICANN decided to allow internationalized TLDs in non-Latin scripts, including Arabic, Mandarin, Hindi, Japanese, and Russian. These efforts are likely part of a larger strategy to enhance its international legitimacy.[242] Soon after the AOC was published, former director of the U.S. Department of Homeland Security's National Cyber Security Center and current ICANN President Rod Beckstrom stated, "the Internet is on a long-term arch from being 100 percent American to being 100 percent global."[243] That process may be accelerated by NSA revelations that have catalyzed ICANN, along with IETF and other leading Internet governance organizations, to call for the "'globalization' of ICANN and the IANA functions," underscoring a public break with the U.S. government.[244]

---

[238] Markus Müller, *Who Owns the Internet? Ownership as a Legal Basis for American Control of the Internet*, 15(3) Fordham Intell. Prop. Media & Ent. L.J. 709, 717 (2005) ("This gives the United States the capacity to threaten a country with the prospect of taking away its country-code TLD."); *see also* Phillip Corwin, *The ICANN-U.S. AOC: What It Really Means*, Internet Com. (Oct. 1, 2009), http://www.internetcommerce.org/ICANN-U.S._AOC (discussing the changes in oversight wrought by the 2009 AOC).

[239] Knake, *supra* note 7, at 24; *see also* Root Servers, http://www.root-servers.org/ (last visited June 22, 2012) (laying out details of the root servers' locations).

[240] *See* Rebecca Wanjiku, *Government Role in ICANN Increases*, PC World (Mar. 13, 2010), http://www.pcworld.com/article/191470/government_role_in_icann_increases.html.

[241] *See A Peace of Sorts*, *supra* note 194; Lennard G. Kruger, *Internet Governance and the Domain Name System: Issues for Congress*, Cong. Res. Serv., R42351, at 2 (2013), www.fas.org/sgp/crs/misc/R42351.pdf; *Internet Infrastructure: Chinese Walls*, Economist (Mar. 2, 2006), http://www.economist.com/node/5582257 [hereinafter *Chinese Walls*] (discussing the reasons for China's creation of new Mandarin Internet-address suffixes).

[242] *See, e.g.*, *'Historic' Day as First Non-Latin Web Addresses Go Live*, BBC News (May 6, 2010), http://www.bbc.co.uk/news/10100108; Carla Thornton, *ICANN to Allow Chinese, Arabic, Russian Domain Names*, PC World (Mar. 4, 2009), http://www.pcworld.com/article/160718/icann_to_allow_chinese_arabic_russian_domain_names.html.

[243] *Oversight*, *supra* note 235.

[244] Mueller & Wagner, *supra* note 47, at 1 (citing *Montevideo Statement on the Future of Internet Cooperation*, ICANN (Oct. 7, 2013), http://www.icann.org/en/news/announcements/announcement-07oct13-en.htm (calling for the acceleration of "the globalization of ICANN and IANA functions, towards an environment in which all stakeholders, including all governments, participate on an equal footing."); *The Core Internet Institutions Abandon the US Government*, Internet Governance Project (Oct. 11, 2013), http://www.internetgovernance.org/2013/10/11/the-core-internet-institutions-abandon-the-us-government/.

The future of ICANN as an Internet governance forum remains unsettled and depends at least in part on how ICANN deals with pressure from skeptical stakeholders, especially emerging markets. If ICANN poorly manages many contrasting viewpoints by moving difficult issues such as privacy to the periphery for the sake of short-term gain, the organization's long-term authority may be undermined.[245] ICANN could establish more institutional trust and political capital by addressing common problems such as cybersecurity more explicitly. For instance, the organization made some progress in enhancing security, particularly for the DNS, by formalizing the ICANN Computer Incidence Response Team in September 2010.[246] Much more remains to be done, however, especially in allaying concerns over plans for allowing hundreds more TLDs,[247] which could increase the prevalence of cyber attacks as discussed in Chapter 3.[248]

At this stage, no one can definitively say whether or in what capacity ICANN will continue to be a key governing body of tomorrow's Internet.[249] The U.S. Department of Commerce, for example, announced plans not to renew its contract with ICANN in 2014, further unsettling the status quo and potentially paving the way for the U.S. government "to relinquish federal . . . control over the administration of the Internet. . . . ").[250] However, perhaps the most important question looking ahead concerns who or what *should* manage the DNS, and how? The process of working out rules and procedures has necessarily been complex and will be ongoing. Yet for an organization at risk of obsolescence since its formation, it is no small feat that ICANN has thrived despite entrenched opposition, even at times from the U.S. government itself.[251] To reapply Churchill's mantra, this may demonstrate that an

---

[245] BOWREY, *supra* note 213, at 14 (noting that ICANN has so far avoided engaging with the contentious issue of privacy, instead hoping that "cultural differences and the reality of competing priorities will disappear. . . . This strategy makes political sense in terms of ICANN's own governance problems. It does not however provide a method for actually resolving disputes. . . . ").

[246] *See* Patrick Jones, *An Update on ICANN Security Efforts*, ICANN BLOG (Nov. 12, 2010), http://blog .icann.org/2010/11/an-update-on-icann-security-efforts/ (formalizing cybersecurity best practices based on firms including Microsoft).

[247] *ANA Cites Major Flaws in ICANN's Proposed Top-Level Internet Domain Program*, ASS'N NAT'L ADVERTISERS (Aug. 4, 2011), http://www.ana.net/content/show/id/21790.

[248] *See, e.g.*, Antone Gonsalves, *China DDoS Attack Shows Not All TLD Servers Equally Secure*, CSO (Aug. 27, 2013), http://www.csoonline.com/article/738803/china-ddos-attack-shows-not-all-tld-servers-equally-secure.

[249] *See Routing it Right, supra* note 154.

[250] Craig Timberg, *U.S. to Relinquish Remaining Control Over the Internet*, WASH. POST (Mar. 14, 2014), http://www.washingtonpost.com/business/technology/us-to-relinquish-remaining-control-over-the-internet/2014/03/14/0c7472d0-abb5-11e3-adbc-888c8010c799_story.html?wpmk=MK0000200; *see* Muelle & Wagner, *supra* note 47, at 27; *ICANN's Major Agreements and Related Reports*, ICANN, http://www.icann.org/en/about/agreements (last visited June 3, 2013); Eric Engleman, *Commerce Department Keeps ICANN as Web's Address Manager*, BLOOMBERG (July 3, 2012), http://www.bloomberg.com/news/2012-07-02/u-s-commerce-department-retains-icann-as-web-s-address-manager.html.

[251] *See International Groups Want Off Internet Name Expansion*, REUTERS (Dec. 13, 2011), http:// www.reuters.com/article/2011/12/13/us-internet-names-idUSTRE7BC2KZ20111213; Mueller & Wagner, *supra* note 47, at 20 (noting that in fact "ICANN's President is positioning his organization

institution like ICANN is "the worst system of internet governance, apart from all the others."[252]

ICANN, however, is not the only institutional model of Internet governance. One of the organizations responsible for governing the Internet's communication system is IETF, which, unlike ICANN, is a true bottom-up informal institution. One of the biggest questions in Internet governance remains the future of the Internet's communication system – especially if we consider the Internet to be a domain constituted by code.[253] The next section explores the relevance of code to governance – a theme returned to in Chapter 3 – and analyzes IETF's approach to managing the communications system along with its relevance to polycentric regulation.

BOTTOM-UP GOVERNANCE AND THE INFORMAL IETF

While a great deal of attention is given to the Internet's address system and the future of ICANN, relatively few people are aware of how the Internet's communication system is governed. Indeed, its policy and commercial implications are less visible and direct than those of the address system, so it has, for the most part, avoided the controversies that have plagued ICANN. IETF is an open access forum "of network designers, operators, vendors, and researchers concerned with the evolution of the Internet architecture" that helps coordinate interoperability in the Internet's communication system.[254] IETF has been engineering new and updating old protocols since 1986 by maintaining and publishing Internet standards. These are sets of documents put out by working groups that comprise the official protocol set of the global TCP/IP network; in other words, they contain the code that defines the Internet's architecture. [255] If it is obvious why domain names require governance, though, it may be less clear why standards and code need oversight. While domain names exist in the foreground, standards stay in the background; no money is exchanged. So why do they matter to governance, and what lessons does the IETF model hold for reconceptualizing Internet governance and enhancing cybersecurity?

"Code is Law"

In order to grasp the role and importance of IETF, it is first essential to understand why code itself is so central to Internet governance. Harvard Law Professor

to be engaged in areas of Internet governance that go far beyond its narrow focus on domain names and IP addresses.").

[252] Maija Palmer, *ICANN Chairman Urges Patience*, FIN. TIMES TECH BLOG (July 8, 2011), http://blogs .ft.com/tech-blog/2011/07/icann-chairman-urges-patience/.

[253] *See* Lawrence B. Solum, *Models of Internet Governance, in* INTERNET GOVERNANCE: INFRASTRUCTURE AND INSTITUTIONS 48, 52 (Lee A. Bygrave & Jon Bing eds., 2009).

[254] *Glossary*, ICANN, http://www.icann.org/en/about/learning/glossary (last visited Jan. 26, 2014).

[255] *See* MURRAY, *supra* note 115, at 91.

Lawrence Lessig was the first to succinctly say: "Code is Law" (referring to software and hardware code, not a cryptographic code).[256] Professor Lessig argues that code, or architecture, regulates cyberspace by "set[ting] the terms" on which it is experienced.[257] "The basic code [that] . . . the Internet implements" is the TCP/IP protocols,[258] which, as has been described, makes attribution difficult. This has both benefits and drawbacks in that it protects free speech by enhancing anonymity,[259] but complicates the cyber threat because it is difficult to locate attackers.[260] Additionally, as code changes – driven by both private- and public-sector actors – so, too, does regulation.[261] For example, certification schemes that allow websites to confirm details about users can be both narrow (such as confirming a user's age) and broad (raising larger privacy concerns).[262]

Professor Lessig offers a story to help explain this notion. Consider that there is something called "Avatar space," a "virtual space" where real people interact, in which a woman grows beautiful but poisonous flowers.[263] Her neighbor's dog dies after eating them, and a fight between the woman and her neighbor ensues until they realize a mutually beneficial solution: change things so that the flowers' poison could become impotent if anyone steals them.[264] But how do they implement such a systemic change? With the help of code, they reprogram the flowers' behavior.[265] Professor Lessig writes: "The rules in Avatar space are imposed, not through sanctions, and not by the state, but by the very architecture of the particular space. A law is defined, not through a statute, but through the code that governs the space."[266] As this example makes clear, code is law in the virtual world because it regulates, just as statutes do in the real world: "Regulability is thus a function of design."[267] What made Avatar space different is what makes cyberspace unique, specifically "that regulation is imposed primarily through code."[268] Engineers write code using programming languages to tell computers what to do.[269] Code is everywhere, including at the foundational level of the Internet's design. Thus, code is a

---

[256] LAWRENCE LESSIG, CODE AND OTHER LAWS OF CYBERSPACE 6 (1999).

[257] Lawrence Lessig, *Code is Law: On Liberty in Cyberspace*, HARV. MAG. (Jan.–Feb. 2000), http://harvardmagazine.com/2000/01/code-is-law.html.

[258] *Id.*

[259] *Id.*

[260] *See* HOWARD F. LIPSON, CARNEGIE MELON UNIV., TRACKING AND TRACING CYBER-ATTACKS: TECHNICAL CHALLENGES AND GLOBAL POLICY ISSUES, at ix (2002), http://www.sei.cmu.edu/reports/02sr009 .pdf.

[261] LESSIG, *supra* note 256, at 9.

[262] *Id.* at 33–34.

[263] *Id.* at 9–10.

[264] *Id.* at 12–13.

[265] *Id.* at 13.

[266] *Id.* at 20.

[267] LAWRENCE LESSIG, CODE: VERSION 2.0 34 (2006).

[268] *Id.* at 24; LESSIG, *supra* note 256, at 20.

[269] There are thousands of types of programming languages, including C, C++, Java, Perl, PHP, Python, and SQL. *See* ANTHONY AABY, INTRODUCTION TO PROGRAMMING LANGUAGES 1–3, 17–18 (2004).

critical factor in determining what is and is not possible in cyberspace,[270] including cybersecurity.

Governments, though, can and do influence code. As Professor Lessig has argued, this may be beneficial in the United States when we regularly critique the status quo to help ensure the continuation of core constitutional values in this new domain.[271] But other nations with different traditions are also shaping code, and those effects can spill across borders. Consider the development of wireless networking standards. The Institute of Electronic and Electrical Engineers developed the first wireless networking standard, Wireless Local Area Network (WLAN); most countries have implemented it or a standard from the same family.[272] China, on the other hand, disliking the anonymity and anarchy of this U.S. standard,[273] designed its own wireless networking standard called WLAN Authentication and Privacy Infrastructure (WAPI), which requires both wireless devices and access points to authenticate themselves.[274] The Chinese government has said that the WAPI standard must be incorporated into every Wi-Fi device used within its borders, although black-market mobiles without WAPI have made it into China.[275] As of May 2010, Dell and Apple began to sell smartphones with WAPI wireless technology to Chinese consumers.[276] This example demonstrates how governments can mandate code and regulate through law, here with privacy and cybersecurity implications.[277] It also highlights the complex and changing collection of stakeholders shaping Internet governance. One stakeholder – especially one as significant as China, which is creating its own "network center of gravity[]" – can significantly affect the interconnected regulatory environment of cyberspace.[278] As more nations weigh in on Internet governance, this situation will only become more complex, as was demonstrated with the ICANN saga. China's insistence on attempting to implement WAPI, even though it was rejected as an international standard,[279] indicates a larger shift. As China gains power to control network standards – the most basic building blocks of network design[280] – it, along

---

[270] See LESSIG, *supra* note 267, at 33–34.

[271] Lessig, *supra* note 257.

[272] See *History of Institute of Electrical and Electronic Engineers (IEEE) Standards*, IEEE GLOBAL HISTORY NETWORK, http://www.ieeeghn.org/wiki/index.php/History_of_Institute_of_Electrical_and_Electronic_Engineers_%28IEEE%29_Standards (last visited Jan. 26, 2014).

[273] GOLDSMITH & WU, *supra* note 185, at 101.

[274] See Owen Fletcher, *Years on, China Pushes WAPI in Mobile Phones*, IDG NEWS SERV. (May 8, 2009), http://www.cio.com/article/492084/Years_on_China_Pushes_WAPI_in_Mobile_Phones.

[275] See Sumner Lemon, *China's WAPI Will Not Go Down Without A Fight*, NETWORK WORLD (May 30, 2006), http://www.networkworld.com/news/2006/053006-chinas-wapi-protocol.html.

[276] See Owen Fletcher, *Apple Tweaks Wi-Fi in IPhone to Use China Protocol*, PC WORLD (May 3, 2010), http://www.pcworld.com/article/195524/article.html.

[277] See Nigel Inkster, *China in Cyberspace*, in CYBERSPACE AND NATIONAL SECURITY: THREATS, OPPORTUNITIES, AND POWER IN A VIRTUAL WORLD 191, 200 (Derek S. Reveron ed., 2012) (detailing Chinese attempts to regulate code); JODY R. WESTBY, INTERNATIONAL GUIDE TO CYBER SECURITY 42–43 (2004) (discussing the security shortcomings of wireless systems).

[278] GOLDSMITH & WU, *supra* note 185, at 101.

[279] See Lemon, *supra* note 275.

[280] Id.

with other nations, can design and implement different systems replete with varying values and security features.[281] As Professor Lessig argues, "We are just beginning to see why the architecture of the space matters – in particular, why the *ownership* of that architecture matters."[282] This question of who controls the Internet is further unraveled in Chapter 2, but for now, let us turn to a related question: who exactly makes design decisions about the Internet's communication system, composed of code and standards, and what impact does this have on governance and security?

The Digital World is Flat: Self-Organization through the IETF

In comparison to ICANN's development, IETF evolved naturally from technical communities to deal with particular problems, and as a result, it enjoys greater legitimacy though it, too, is not without its critics.[283] In the beginning, as with Postel's IANA, the IETF was a means for U.S. government-funded researchers to coordinate with one another.[284] No one was obligated to attend IETF meetings, but it seemed to be in everyone's best interest to do so.[285] In a sign of IETF's growing importance, its first meeting in January 1986 consisted of twenty-one researchers.[286] As of 2011, VeriSign and the NSA funded the chairperson.[287]

The basic administrative framework of IETF was settled by the early 1990s. It is comprised of working groups and directors of seven functional areas, including applications, routing, and security.[288] There is also a general area director who functions as IETF's chair.[289] These structures developed organically, and IETF has a reputation for being a relatively flat organization, adopting ideas when justified by results rather than rank.[290] Indeed, an early IETF mantra coined in 1992 survives: "We reject: kings, presidents, and voting. We believe in: rough consensus and running code."[291]

---

[281] *See* Lawrence Lessig, *The Law of the Horse: What Cyberlaw Might Teach*, 113 HARV. L. REV. 501, 532–33 (1999) (discussing examples – primarily in the U.S. context – of law regulating code, and warning that "a competition could develop. Authors of code might develop code that displaces law; authors of law might respond with law that displaces code.").

[282] LESSIG, *supra* note 256, at 7.

[283] *See* MURRAY, *supra* note 115, at 92, 234.

[284] BOWREY, *supra* note 213, at 56.

[285] *See* MURRAY, *supra* note 115, at 91.

[286] *See* MUELLER, *supra* note 2, at 90–92 (chronicling the growth of IETF meetings from 50 people in 1987 to more than 650 in 1992).

[287] *See* Carolyn Duffy Marsan, *Q&A: Security Top Concern for New IETF Chair*, NETWORK WORLD (July 26, 2007), http://www.networkworld.com/news/2007/073007-ietf-qa.html (reporting attendance in 2007 at the IETF meeting was 1,146 people).

[288] *See* MURRAY, *supra* note 115, at 91.

[289] *See* Brian Carpenter, *The Internet Engineering Task Force: Overview, Activities, Priorities*, INTERNET SOC'Y (Feb. 10, 2006), http://www.isoc.org/isoc/general/trustees/docs/Feb2006/IETF-BoT-20060210 .pdf; *Overview of the IETF*, INTERNET ENG'G TASK FORCE, http://www.ietf.org/old/2009/overview .html (last visited Mar. 28, 2013).

[290] BOWREY, *supra* note 213, at 56.

[291] *Id.*

Anyone who wants to can join the IETF at any time for free, and everyone who is a "member" is a volunteer who is welcome to join in the discussion and submit a proposal for a new standard or an alteration to an existing standard in the form of a request for comment (RFC).[292] These comments cover a world of conversations, from better protocols to April Fools' Day jokes. Postel's obituary, which begins "A long time ago, in a network, far far away, a great adventure took place!" is published as RFC comment 2468.[293] Standards-track RFCs go through a process of review.[294]

Much of the time, IETF standards are built into our systems without our knowledge and are chosen for the simple reason that they work well.[295] As such, IETF is only in charge to the extent that people act like it is – a model of consensus governance, although one with its share of corporate and governmental control.[296] The notion of bottom-up governance that has been created in IETF is an example of one facet of polycentric regulation that is briefly discussed here and examined more fully in the Chapter 2. This theory, pioneered by Nobel Laureate Elinor Ostrom and others at The Vincent and Elinor Ostrom Workshop in Political Theory and Policy Analysis at Indiana University and elsewhere, asserts that local participation is key to efficiently and sustainably managing common pool resources.[297] Proponents assert that self-regulation is flexible, has a greater capacity to adapt to technological advancements than centralized hierarchies, and can be more efficient than the exclusive exercise of governmental authority.[298] However, such a regime requires active user engagement based on "shared responsibility" and accountability throughout development and implementation,[299] as well as recognizing a role for higher-level coordination.[300] The Internet governance context requires balancing new polycentric initiatives with existing laws to create an adaptable and efficient system to mitigate cybersecurity challenges. That is difficult both to conceptualize

---

[292] See MURRAY, *supra* note 115, at 68; *Getting Started in the IETF*, IETF, http://www.ietf.org/newcomers .html (last visited Jan. 26, 2014).

[293] VINT CERF, I REMEMBER IANA, IETF RFC 2468 (Oct. 17, 1998), www.ietf.org/rfc/rfc2468.txt (last visited Oct. 17, 2011).

[294] S. BRADNER, THE INTERNET STANDARDS PROCESS – REVISION 3, IETF RFC 2026 (Oct. 1996), www.ietf.org/rfc/rfc2026.txt (last visited Oct. 17, 2011).

[295] See *The IETF Standards Process*, IETF, http://www.ietf.org/about/standards-process.html (last visited Jan. 26, 2014).

[296] See POST, *supra* note 123, at 135–39.

[297] Interview with Elinor Ostrom, distinguished professor, Indiana University-Bloomington, in Bloomington, Ind. (Oct. 13, 2010).

[298] See Elinor Ostrom, *Polycentric Systems: Multilevel Governance Involving a Diversity of Organizations*, in GLOBAL ENVIRONMENTAL COMMONS: ANALYTICAL AND POLITICAL CHALLENGES INVOLVING A DIVERSITY OF ORGANIZATIONS, 105, 107–09 (Eric Brousseau et al. eds., 2012); Elinor Ostrom, *Polycentric Systems as One Approach for Solving Collective-Action Problems* 1–2, 4, 6–8 (Vincent & Elinor Ostrom Workshop in Political Theory & Policy Analysis, Ind. Univ., Working Paper No. 08–6, 2008). http://dlc.dlib.indiana.edu/dlc/bitstream/handle/10535/4417/W08-6_Ostrom_DLC.pdf/sequence=1.

[299] MONROE E. PRICE & STEFAN G. VERHULST, SELF-REGULATION AND THE INTERNET 21–22 (2005); Ostrom 2012, *supra* note 298, at 118.

[300] See Michael D. McGinnis, *An Introduction to IAD and the Language of the Ostrom Workshop: A Simple Guide to a Complex Framework*, 39(1) POL'Y STUD. J. 163, 171–72 (2011).

and to put into practice, as is explored in Parts II and III of this book. But as an example of a community engaging in the equivalent of local participation to maintain the Internet as a common resource, IETF helps illustrate some of the benefits and drawbacks of polycentric governance. On the one hand, a polycentric approach maximizes flexibility and adaptability;[301] on the other, a lack of a defined hierarchy and enforcement mechanisms makes ensuring the uptake of best practices difficult, especially on a global scale.[302] Exploring these distinctions and finding an appropriate balance between bottom-up and top-down mechanisms is critical as both the future of Internet governance and cybersecurity hinge on diverse organizations working well together for the public benefit.[303]

Similar to DNS, governance of the Internet's communication system was catalyzed once commercial interests became significant. For example, the "text/html" that forms the backbone of today's web was defined by an IETF working group in 1995.[304] This design allows for the pay-per-click scheme of Google AdWords, which is at the core of Google's business plan.[305] Similarly, the code and standards that IETF adopts often favor certain technologies and may align more with some companies' products, giving those firms a commercial advantage and strong interest in the IETF drafting process. As global telecom competition has shifted toward China, the possibility of such commercial advantages has become more pronounced. China's Huawei Telecom, which in 2012 became the world's largest telecom provider, has pushed this debate forward through the ITU, which has traditionally been a central player in writing standards for communication technologies.[306] In 2010 and 2011, IETF and the ITU had a public standards dispute over multiprotocol label switching (MPLS) network extensions, which direct data from one network node to the next. Talks collapsed in early 2011,[307] but there was some progress in 2012.[308] Over time, the continued vitality of IETF might well hinge in part on how well it can

---

[301] *See* Robert O. Keohane & David G. Victor, *The Regime Complex for Climate Change* 9 PERSP. ON POL. 7, 8–9 (2011); *see also* Cole, *supra* note 9, at 412.

[302] *See* Robert O. Keohane & David G. Victor, *The Regime Complex for Climate Change* at 3–4 (Harv. Proj. on Int'l Climate Agreements Discussion Paper No. 10-33, 2010) (discussing regime complexes).

[303] *See* Ostrom 2012, *supra* note 298, at 107 ("Many policy analysts presume that without major external resources and top-down planning by national officials, public goods and sustainable common-pool resources cannot be provided. This presumption is wrong. The opposite presumption that local communities will *always* solve collective-action problems is also wrong.").

[304] *See* D. CONNOLLY & L. MASINTER, THE 'TEXT/HTML' MEDIA TYPE, IETF RFC 2854, (June 2000), http://www.ietf.org/rfc/rfc2854.

[305] *See, e.g.*, Claire Cain Miller, *Google's Income Rises 32%, Topping Forecast*, N.Y. TIMES (Oct. 14, 2010), http://www.nytimes.com/2010/10/15/technology/15google.html.

[306] *See ITU-T Recommendations*, INTERNET TELECOMM. UNION, http://www.itu.int/en/ITU-T/publications/Pages/recs.aspx (last visited Jan. 26, 2014) (noting that ITU standards are often employed in voice-over IP (VoIP), videoconferencing, and video compression, which are useful for YouTube, the iTunes store, and Adobe Flash Player, among other services).

[307] *See* A. SPRECHER & A. FARREL, MLPS TRANSPORT FILE (MLPS-TP) SURVIVABILITY FRAMEWORK, IETF RFC 6372 (2011), http://www.ietf.org/mail-archive/web/ietf-announce/current/msg09381.html.

[308] *See* R. WINTER ET AL., DRAFT RFC ON MPLS-TP IDENTIFIERS FOLLOWING ITU-T CONVENTIONS, IETF (Aug. 29, 2012), http://tools.ietf.org/html/draft-ietf-mpls-tp-itu-t-identifiers-04.

navigate the increasing attention being paid to it by the public and private sectors especially as it begins to take more public stances on the future shape of Internet governance.[309]

Aside from commercial interests,[310] security concerns have also prompted more interest in IETF's processes and decisions. IETF has acknowledged that its standards may create vulnerabilities. Indeed, many of IETF's early protocols "were designed without built-in security."[311] In 2007, former IETF chair Russ Housley said his chief concern was improving cybersecurity through new or altered Internet standards.[312] But in November 2010, Robert Knake wrote that if IETF did not come up with more secure standards soon, the U.S. government may need to get involved to push the process forward.[313] This comment underscores the extent to which cybersecurity is a growing concern to both the public and private sectors, and the necessity of finding new conceptual models to hasten improvements.[314] As Knake has argued, optimal Internet governance should include representatives from diverse communities including the private sector, consumer groups, the technical community, and intergovernmental forums working at multiple regulatory levels to enhance cybersecurity.[315] This is, in essence, calling for a polycentric framework.[316] However, the challenge comes in conceptualizing the myriad facets of such a complex system so as to maximize benefits and minimize costs, which is addressed further in Chapter 6.

As with ICANN, IETF's authority as a private regulatory body of the Internet's communications system has been challenged. Different communities have various expectations, and in the case of IETF, the organization only sets standards and has little interest in resolving disputes over the ways these standards are used downstream.[317] According to Temple Professor David Post, "That is not their game.

---

[309] *See* Mueller & Wagner, *supra* note 47, at 1.

[310] *See* *ITU-T In Brief*, INTERNET TELECOMM. UNION, http://www.itu.int/en/ITU-T/about/Pages/default .aspx (last visited Jan. 26, 2014).

[311] Marsan, *supra* note 287.

[312] *See id.* (listing three specific goals of rolling out IPv6, DNS security, and the SIDR [Secure Inter-Domain Routing] working group).

[313] KNAKE, *supra* note 7, at 27.

[314] *See id.* at vii.

[315] *Id.* at 12–13, 18.

[316] *Cf. id.* at vii (placing the emphasis on legal and technological solutions rather than analyzing the full gamut of available tools available including laws, norms, markets, code, and self-regulation that are discussed in Parts II and III). *See also* Bruce Schneier, *The US Government Has Betrayed the Internet. We Need to Take it Back*, GUARDIAN (Sept. 5, 2013), http://www.theguardian.com/commentisfree/ 2013/sep/05/government-betrayed-internet-nsa-spying ("We need to demand that real technologists be involved in any key government decision making on these issues. We've had enough of lawyers and politicians not fully understanding technology; we need technologists at the table when we build tech policy.").

[317] *See* Mueller & Wagner, *supra* note 47, at 20 (noting that the "inability of many IETF veterans to come to grips with the whole concept of 'governance' illustrates the wide gaps in the mentalities of" Internet governance stakeholders).

But given the way the network has evolved to date, nor is it anyone else's."[318] The challenges that IETF is facing illustrate the extent to which geopolitics, technological advancements, commerce, and code are influencing Internet governance, and as a result, the ways in which the cyber threat may be managed.

NETWORKED, FLAT, AND CROWDED: THE EVOLUTION OF INTERNET GOVERNANCE

The governing schemes of both ICANN and IETF have strengths and weaknesses.[319] ICANN's legal status benefits the address system by providing it with a formalized governance structure and sense of stability. Despite this, the ability of ICANN to legitimatize itself and implement policies remains contested.[320] Alternatively, IETF's suggestions may be less scrutinized because it has never asserted any governing status, while its lack of formal institutionalization and open access underpinnings have provided the space for innovation and earned it greater legitimacy.[321] IETF, however, lacks the authority to mandate technical standards, including cybersecurity policies – hence the slow deployment of IPv6 and the continued prevalence of technical vulnerabilities discussed in Chapter 3.[322] Still, both ICANN and IETF have emerged as centers of governance as the Internet has developed and required someone or something to both ensure predictability to DNS for e-commerce and create new Internet standards to maintain interoperability between diverse systems.

No one body or organization governs cyberspace; rather, a host of organizations with overlapping functions form a regime complex that has both benefits and drawbacks to Internet governance and cybersecurity. On the benefits side, elements of this regime complex can act as checks and balances on one another, promoting regulatory accountability as well as flexibility in this dynamic space.[323] Organizations, firms, and even states become laboratories for identifying and testing best practices. The history of management by bottom-up consensus begun in the 1960s

---

[318] BOWREY, *supra* note 213, at 6.

[319] Klein, *supra* note 173, at 195–98; MURRAY, *supra* note 115, at 92.

[320] *See* Julia Black, *Constructing and Contesting Legitimacy and Accountability in Polycentric Regulatory Regimes*, 2 REG. & GOVERNANCE 137, 145, 147, 154 (2008).

[321] *See* POST, *supra* note 123, at 138–39 (noting that the IETF is "in charge only because, and only to the extent, everyone treats it as being in charge[]" and that the IETF has no enforcement powers).

[322] Created in 1981, IP version 4 (IPv4) allowed for more than four billion IP addresses, which early Internet architects thought would be sufficient for expansion. They were wrong. So, since 1992, engineers have been designing and attempting to implement a new system called IP version 6 (IPv6), which features a larger address space – on the order of billions of IP addresses for each person alive in 2013. Architects again imagine this scale to be inexhaustible. *See Top 10 Features that Make IPv6 'Greater' than IPv4*, http://ipv6.com/articles/general/Top-10-Features-that-make-IPv6-greater-than-IPv4.htm (last visited Jan. 26, 2014).

[323] *See* Keohane & Victor, *supra* note 302, at 3, 19–20 (listing six criteria for effective regime complexes: "coherence, effectiveness, determinacy, sustainability, accountability, and epistemic quality").

continues to be prevalent in both ICANN and IETF, though more so in the latter. However, because no one body has authority to mandate an Internet standard or cybersecurity initiative, governance can be ad hoc and face gridlock,[324] resulting in the haphazard uptake of best practices to manage cybersecurity challenges. Meanwhile, the intergovernmental organization poised to take on a greater role in global Internet governance through its Member States during this third phase of Internet governance, the ITU, also has its critics given in part that it has historically been a state-centric organization,[325] though its relevance as an umbrella forum to discuss the highest issues of Internet governance and cybersecurity is becoming better established as discussed in Chapter 7.[326]

As the Internet continues to evolve, so, too, will Internet governance. After all, even though the Internet could theoretically survive a nuclear war, nothing can protect it from geopolitics.[327] If the technical underpinnings of the Internet have been based on an informal consensus among engineers and scientists since its inception, governments have come to appreciate the importance of the Internet and are taking on a greater regulatory role.[328] Cyber attacks, which affect both the Internet's address and communication systems, have also added to demands for governance models that foster security. This brings to the fore old questions that have surrounded ICANN and IETF: who has the authority to decide which interests should be prioritized? In short, who governs, and how is this changing? These questions are harder to answer today than they were in the mid-1980s or even late 1990s when IETF and ICANN respectively emerged. Today, the Internet is truly global, with every continent except Australia and Antarctica having more than 100 million users.[329] Determining how governance affects security and vice versa should be a matter of common interest for all stakeholders, whereas increasing national regulation and the evolving cyber threat suggests the need for dynamic conceptual models that promote coordinated responses. Without greater regulatory clarity, jurisdictional confusion will ensue, as seen in courts that have interpreted legal ambiguities to resolve disputes and indirectly redefine the role of the state in Internet governance.

---

[324] *Id.* at 17.

[325] *See* KNAKE, *supra* note 7, at 8; *Global Internet Governance and the ITU*, CTR. DEMOCRACY & TECH. (Aug. 2012), https://www.cdt.org/files/file/Global%20Internet%20Governance%20and%20the%20ITU .pdf; *Signatories of the Final Acts*, WCIT 2012, http://www.itu.int/osg/wcit-12/highlights/signatories .html [hereinafter *Signatories of the Final Acts*].

[326] *See* Mueller & Wagner, *supra* note 47, at 26.

[327] MURRAY, *supra* note 115, at 63 (noting that the idea that ARPANET was created as a military communications network designed to withstand a nuclear strike is an urban myth, and that that goal in fact came from a Rand study, which is a global policy nonprofit).

[328] POST, *supra* note 123, at 126–27.

[329] *See Internet World Stats: Usage and Population Statistics*, INTERNET WORLD STATS (June 30, 2012), http://www.internetworldstats.com/stats.htm (reporting that the world average growth rate of Internet use went up more than 500 percent since 2000, with the most rapid growth occurring in Africa, the Middle East, and Latin America).

Consider the groundbreaking Yahoo! case in 2001.[330] A group in France sued Yahoo! because its auction site was selling Nazi gear and paraphernalia in violation of French law.[331] Yahoo! based its defense on the fact that it would be impossible to control all requests to access its many sites and servers.[332] The company managed a French-language site, yahoo.fr, which conformed to French law, but yahoo.com, the company's U.S. server, was also accessible to users in France.[333] If Yahoo! was forced to remove the Nazi items from yahoo.com, users everywhere would not be able to purchase the items, essentially "making French law the effective rule for the world."[334] However, the French court rejected Yahoo!'s impossibility argument, undermining assumptions about a borderless Internet and demonstrating the extent to which actions taken by regulators can have ramifications across the cyber regime complex.[335] Instead of paying a fine, Yahoo! removed the Nazi items from its website.[336] Then it sued the French organization in a U.S. court, arguing that Yahoo!'s First Amendment rights to free speech had been violated.[337] The company lost on the French organization's appeal in 2006.[338] By 2005, with less confidence and capital, Yahoo! had also bowed to Chinese national laws by censoring search results and monitoring chat rooms.[339]

Yahoo!'s transformation reflects that of the broader Internet "from a technology that resists territorial law to one that facilitates its enforcement."[340] Other more recent cases reinforce this trend. Take the aftermath of the WikiLeaks episode, in which a combination of political pressure and cyber attacks purportedly incentivized Amazon to stop hosting the WikiLeaks website, forcing it to relocate to servers in Europe.[341]

---

[330] *See* Yahoo!, Inc. v. La Ligue Contre le Racisme et L'Antisemitisme, 169 F. Supp. 2d 1181 (N.D. Cal. 2001), *rev'd*, 379 F.3d 1120 (9th Cir. 2005), *rev'd en banc*, 433 F.3d 1199 (9th Cir. 2006).

[331] *See* Elissa A. Okoniewski, *Yahoo!, Inc. v. LICRA: The French Challenge to Free Expression on the Internet*, 18(1) AM. UNIV. INT'L L. REV. 295, 296–97 (2002) (recounting how Yahoo!'s sale of Nazi memorabilia in France contravened French Penal Code R. 645-1, and acted as the basis of the private suit in the *Yahoo!* case).

[332] *See* GOLDSMITH & WU, *supra* note 185, at 5.

[333] *Id.*

[334] *Id.*

[335] *See id.* at 6 (discussing the "race to the bottom" that may result from such a "tyranny of unreasonable governments.").

[336] *Id.* at 8.

[337] *See* Yahoo! Inc. vs. La Ligue Contre Le Racisme et L'Antisemitisme, 433 F.3d 1199, 1206 (9th Cir. 2006) (en banc) (describing Yahoo!'s claim that its First Amendment rights prevented the French interim order from being enforced); Juan Carlos Perez, *Yahoo Loses Appeal in Nazi Memorabilia Case*, PC WORLD, (Jan. 12, 2006), http://www.pcworld.com/article/124367/yahoo_loses_appeal_in_nazi_memorabilia_case.html.

[338] *Id.*

[339] *See* GOLDSMITH & WU, *supra* note 185, at 10.

[340] *Id.*

[341] *See, e.g., Cyber Attacks Force WikiLeaks to Move Web Address*, FR. 24 (Mar. 12, 2010), http://www.france24.com/en/20101203-wikileaks-website-address-server-cyber-attacks-switzerland-france-usa (reporting that WikiLeaks had published "hundreds of confidential diplomatic cables that have given unvarnished and sometimes embarrassing insights into the foreign policy of the United States and its allies.").

Or consider the 2012 arrest of a Google executive in Brazil for refusing to take down videos from YouTube.[342] As these episodes help demonstrate, Internet governance is transforming to cater more to the interest of states, and many countries have developed laws that are reshaping the global cyber regulatory environment.[343] Yet many questions about Internet governance remain unresolved. How can the cyber regime complex be better coordinated to promote cyber peace? Should the United States take a more assertive role in enhancing global cybersecurity, or, alternatively, should it more actively share authority with the ITU or another intergovernmental body? Many governments increasingly favor the latter approach, as discussed in Chapter 7.[344] Take, for example, the IANA (now housed under ICANN). Since its inception, it has been in charge of dispersing IP address space to five regional Internet registries. Many countries have complained that IANA's IPv4 allocation unfairly favored the United States, a view shared by Houlin Zhao, the ITU deputy secretary general.[345] There has been a movement to ensure that IPv6 allocations are more equitable.[346] As with the dispute between the ITU and IETF about extensions to the MPLS standard, it is hard to predict how stakeholders might resolve this question over the management of IPv6 address space.[347]

The United States enjoys a central role in Internet governance,[348] but as the cyber regime complex evolves its primacy will continue to be challenged, a phenomenon producing profound implications for managing the cyber threat. In the

---

[342] *See Internet Freedom: Free to Choose*, ECONOMIST (Oct. 6, 2012), http://www.economist.com/node/ 21564198 ("Brazilian authorities briefly detained Google's country boss on September 26th for refusing to remove videos from its YouTube subsidiary that appeared to breach electoral laws.").

[343] *Id.* (reporting on national approaches to Internet regulation, and highlighting the fact that "[s]ites in countries with fierce or costly libel laws often censor content the moment they receive a complaint, regardless of its merit."). In response, Professor Tim Wu has suggested that user committees may be created by video-hosting services to help ensure that sensitive content is in line with local norms. *Id.* If this were to happen, it could help ratchet back one component of encroaching state control of the Internet and reinforce self-governance practices that are critical to successful polycentric governance. The role of user communities in the cybersecurity context is explored further in Chapter 7.

[344] *See Signatories of the Final Acts*, *supra* note 325; *cf.* Mueller & Wagner, *supra* note 47, at 9–10 (discussing the formation of the "Freedom Online coalition" that was created in 2011 and "led by the Netherlands, the United States and Sweden[]" with the goal of promoting "international co-operation to promote freedom and human rights on the Internet. . . . ").

[345] *See* Yang Jingde & Liu Yang, *Interview: Internet IP Addresses Not Exhausted: ITU Official*, XINHUA (Feb. 14, 2011), http://news.xinhuanet.com/english2010/business/2011-02/14/c_13730415.htm. The Asia Pacific Network Information Centre, one of the five regional Internet registries, was the first to run out of IPv4 addresses in April 2011. Deputy Secretary Zhao has noted that the IANA only distributed about "300 million IP addresses to China, accounting for less than 10 percent of the global total," even though China has more than "400 million Internet users. . . . " *Internet IP Addresses not Exhausted: ITU Official*, CHINA DAILY (Feb. 14, 2011), http://www.chinadaily.com.cn/world/2011-02/14/content_ 12004139.htm.

[346] *See ITU and IPv6*, http://www.itu.int/net/ITU-T/ipv6/ (last visited Jan. 26, 2014).

[347] *Cf.* Jennifer L. Schenker, *Nations Chafe at U.S. Influence over Internet*, N.Y. TIMES (Dec. 8, 2003), http://www.nytimes.com/2003/12/08/business/nations-chafe-at-us-influence-over-the-internet .html (discussing the historic tensions associated with U.S. influence over Internet governance, some of which may apply in determining the outcome of this dispute).

[348] *See* David R. Johnson & David G. Post, *Law and Borders – The Rise of Law in Cyberspace*, 48 STAN. L. REV. 1367, 1393 (1996).

wake of revelations regarding NSA surveillance programs, the alliance between Internet organizations such as ICANN and IETF and emerging markets including Brazil is advocating for decreased U.S. control of Internet governance, which, in the worst-case scenario, threatens further fragmentation.[349] Promoting polycentric regulation could help reframe Internet governance into a more efficient, flexible, and representative system increasing accountability and fostering cyber peace; but determining how best to accomplish this is no easy feat, as is explored in Chapter 2.

SUMMARY

This chapter has described the evolution of Internet governance from "a network built by government researchers and computer scientists who had no CEO, no master business plan, no paying subscribers, [and] no investment in content"[350] into a cyber regime complex. The history of this evolution was considered in three phases. Phase One was defined by the emergence of TCP/IP and informal organizations such as IETF, in which researchers worked together to support the nascent network. By Phase Two, TCP/IP had become the Internet that we know today, and a rush of stakeholders emerged to play a role in Internet governance from ICANN in 1998 to the Internet Governance Forum in 2006, underscoring the growing globalization of governance structures and the pivot from concerns of Internet access and economic fairness pushed by international organizations such as the ITU to questions of political representation. Phase Three may be considered a reaction to the unfinished business of Phase Two with efforts underway to formalize a global system of Internet governance lead predominantly by nations, address latent cyber insecurity, and find common ground to ward off a "'new digital divide."[351]

Cyber attacks have been ineffectively managed throughout the history of Internet governance. The address and communication systems, along with other technologies, need to scale security to better manage the cyber threat. As Knake has argued, the focus must shift from interoperability to cybersecurity.[352] With more nations vying for a say in Internet governance in part because of the rise in cybercrime and espionage, and the specters of cyber terrorism and war, the time is ripe for questioning the status quo and seeking out new frameworks that both protect the innovative nature of cyberspace and also enhance cybersecurity.

On a small scale, the story of eBay illustrates the evolution of Internet governance as well as possible paths forward. When eBay launched in 1995 as "AuctionWeb,"

---

[349] *See* Tom Gjelten, *Are We Moving to a World With More Online Surveillance?*, NPR (Oct. 16, 2013), http://www.npr.org/blogs/parallels/2013/10/16/232181204/are-we-moving-to-a-world-with-more-online-surveillance?sc=17&f=1001; *After NSA Leaks, ICANN and W3C Don't Want the US to Control the Internet Anymore*, SOFTPEDIA (Oct. 11, 2013), http://news.softpedia.com/news/After-NSA-Leaks-ICANN-and-W3C-Gon-t-Want-the-US-to-Control-the-Internet-Anymore-390541.shtml.

[350] JONATHAN ZITTRAIN, THE FUTURE OF THE INTERNET AND HOW TO STOP IT 7 (2008).

[351] Downes, *supra* note 118. ICANN's relationship with the U.S. government remained unsettled as this book went to press. For more up-to-date information, see Internet Governance Project, http://www.internetgovernance.org/; and cyber-peace.com.

[352] KNAKE, *supra* note 7, at 25.

it was rather small and known to relatively few users, so buyers and sellers mostly interacted like friends in a community.[353] The creator, Pierre Omidyar, established a "Feedback Forum," telling readers to "[g]ive praise where it is due; make complaints where appropriate. . . . "[354] To his surprise, it worked. But by 1999, eBay had more than five million users, and problems with fraud and pranks began negatively impacting its reputation and calling into question some of the self-governance mechanisms Omidyar had devised.[355] The eBay management decided to hire two former law enforcement officials to run a fraud investigation team; its purpose was to search for signs of fraud on eBay and coordinate with law enforcement.[356] By 2011, eBay had approximately 100 million active users and more than 30,000 employees including hundreds of security personnel.[357] In short, eBay's security system scaled, and by prosecuting the small number of users who abused its system in federal courts, eBay thrived. The auction system depended on an engaged user community as well as government power exercised through the courts (a strategy that Facebook is also employing, as discussed in Chapter 5), which became necessary as malicious actors multiplied.[358]

Similarly, the Internet was largely self-governing for much of its early history, which has had myriad benefits and drawbacks, including in the arena of cybersecurity. Now as cyberspace arguably becomes more state-centric, benefits lie in sovereign governments clarifying governance and promoting security features, but this risks sacrificing innovation, complicates the regulatory environment of cyberspace, and may threaten a positive vision of cyber peace. As with eBay, neither public nor private sector power alone is sufficient to manage the cyber threat. The question thus looms of how Internet governance in particular and cyberspace in general should be conceptualized to provide a more robust framework for managing cyber attacks and promoting cyber peace. The creation of a supranational centralized authority with enforcement powers is unlikely as states take a more assertive role in Internet governance. Rather, reframing oversimplified bottom-up and top-down visions of Internet governance into a more accurate discussion of the burgeoning cyber regime complex offers a potential avenue to coordinate polycentric action without negatively impacting the Internet's status as an innovation engine. As countries, companies, and the international community seek to assert greater power online in the name of security, the future of the Internet as a generative web hangs in

---

[353] *See* GOLDSMITH & WU, *supra* note 185, at 130.

[354] *Id.* at 131.

[355] *Id.* at 132.

[356] *Id.* at 134.

[357] *See eBay: Investor FAQs*, EBAY INC., http://investor.ebayinc.com/faq.cfm (last visited June 7, 2013); Kevin Maney, *10 Years Ago, eBay Changed the World*, USA TODAY (Mar. 22, 2005), http://usatoday30.usatoday.com/tech/news/2005-03-21-ebay-cover_x.htm; Zak Strambor, *EBay's U.S. Sales Rise 14% in Q3*, INTERNET RETAILER (Oct. 19, 2011), http://www.internetretailer.com/2011/10/19/ebays-us-sales-rise-14-q3.

[358] *See* GOLDSMITH & WU, *supra* note 185, at 135.

the balance.[359] The remainder of this book analyzes the potential of polycentric governance to help lay the foundation for cyber peace by addressing the technical vulnerabilities, national security concerns, economic considerations, legal ambiguities, and geopolitical issues replete in the interdisciplinary field of cybersecurity, beginning in Chapter 2 with an analysis of sovereignty in cyberspace.

[359] ZITTRAIN, *supra* note 350, at 42, 176.

2

Who Controls Cyberspace? Analyzing Cyber Regulation through Polycentric Governance

Connection technologies can benefit the human-rights activist and the terrorist alike. But whether these technologies will be used for good or ill is not the most important question. The most important question is how they will affect relationships between individuals and states. Not all governments will manage the turbulence of declining state authority the same way.

> – Google Chairman Eric Schmidt and Google Ideas Director Jared Cohen[1]

The Net interprets censorship as damage and routes around it.

> – Electronic Frontier Foundation Co-Founder John Gilmore[2]

The central question that this chapter poses is at once simple and preposterous. On the one hand, cyberspace is a complex and dynamic space, so unlike in the days of Postel, no one person or entity controls cyberspace; as Richard Clarke and Robert Knake argue "[n]o one is really in charge."[3] On the other hand, as Professor Seymour Goodman put it, "cyberspace comes to ground somewhere."[4] The physical infrastructure of the Internet is owned by governments, private citizens, and corporations such as Internet Service Providers (ISPs). But the flow of information that constitutes the content of cyberspace may be thought of as a type of commons potentially accessible to any Internet user. Some proponents of this view, like those supporting the net-neutrality movement, maintain that government regulation is needed to protect cyberspace and to ensure that ISPs do not discriminate

---

[1] Eric Schmidt & Jared Cohen, *The Digital Disruption*, N.Y. TIMES (Oct. 25, 2010), http://www.nytimes.com/2010/10/26/opinion/26iht-edschmidt.html.

[2] Philip Elmer-De Witt, David S. Jackson, & Wendy King, *First Nation in Cyberspace*, TIME (Dec. 6, 1993), http://www.chemie.fu-berlin.de/outerspace/internet-article.html.

[3] RICHARD A. CLARKE & ROBERT K. KNAKE, CYBER WAR: THE NEXT THREAT TO NATIONAL SECURITY AND WHAT TO DO ABOUT IT 79 (2010).

[4] *See* Seymour E. Goodman, Jessica C. Kirk, & Megan H. Kirk, *Cyberspace as a Medium for Terrorists*, 74 TECH. FORECASTING & SOC. CHANGE 193, 196–97 (2007).

between different types of content.[5] Yet, as we will see, national regulation over the Internet is a double-edged sword with censorship on the rise.[6] This point of contention may seem esoteric to newcomers, but it is critical because the openness of the Internet has both contributed to innovation and is a component of the cyber threat.

Against those who seek greater government regulation – so-called "cyber paternalists," some of whom advocate for enhanced national Internet sovereignty – the "cyber-libertarians" favor Internet freedom and believe that the market should largely be left to regulate cyberspace.[7] Elements within the latter school also maintain that the decentralized nature of cyberspace means that the best regulatory system is one that develops organically, such as the IETF.[8] An array of organizations discussed in Chapter 1 contributes to the functioning of the Internet, but none has the power to manage the entirety of cyberspace. Simply put, elements of cyberspace are owned by everyone, and no one. Derived from the Greek word for "governor," cyberspace "couples the idea of communication and control with *space*, a domain previously unknown and unoccupied, where 'territory' can be claimed, controlled, and exploited."[9] However, unlike the physical world in which the Internet's infrastructure exists and over which nations may exercise control, cyberspace is a virtual

[5] For an overview of the net neutrality movement, see Timothy B. Lee, *The Durable Internet: Preserving Network Neutrality Without Regulation*, CATO INST. (Nov. 12, 2008), http://www.cato .org/sites/cato.org/files/pubs/pdf/pa-626.pdf; Jon M. Peha et al., *The State of the Debate on Network Neutrality*, 1 INT'L J. COMM. 709 (2007). *See also* Gautham Nagesh & Brent Kendall, *Court Tosses FCC's 'Net Neutrality' Rules*, WALL ST. J. (Jan. 14, 2014), http://online.wsj.com/news/articles/ SB10001424052702304049704579320500441593462?mg=reno64-wsj&url=http%3A%2F%2Fonline.wsj .com%2Farticle%2FSB10001424052702304049704579320500441593462.html (reporting on "[a] U.S. appeals court on Tuesday threw out federal rules requiring broadband providers to treat all Internet traffic equally...."); Susan Crawford, *Crawford: Why Net Neutrality Matters to You*, NEWSDAY (Jan. 15, 2014), http://www.newsday.com/opinion/oped/crawford-why-net-neutrality-matters-to-you-1.6807160 (arguing that "Internet service providers are common carriers, and as such they need government oversight and regulation.").

[6] *See* Ronald Deibert, *Cybersecurity: The New Frontier*, in FOREIGN POL'Y ASS'N GREAT DECISIONS 2012, at 45, 56–57 (2012). Although there are many types of national regulation over the Internet, this chapter focuses on censorship as a means of illustrating the connection between Internet governance and a positive vision of cyber peace that includes human rights. Other arenas of regulatory action, such as regarding critical national infrastructure, are explored in Chapter 4.

[7] *See, e.g.*, ANITA L. ALLEN, UNPOPULAR PRIVACY: WHAT MUST WE HIDE? 183 (2011) (suggesting that Internet accessibility has undermined the arguments against "cyber-paternalism" made by civil libertarians); Nathan Jurgenson & P.J. Rey, *Cyber-Libertarianism*, P2P FOUND., http://p2pfoundation .net/Cyber-Libertarianism (last visited Mar. 27, 2013) (describing the common ideology and history of cyber-libertarianism). Although presented here as a black and white distinction, in actuality there are varying shades of gray between these competing camps as is explored later in this chapter.

[8] *See* David R. Johnson & David G. Post, *Law and Borders – The Rise of Law in Cyberspace*, 48 STAN. L. REV. 1367, 1400–02 (1996) (discussing some of the legal challenges associated with regulating cyberspace); Jurgenson & Rey, *supra* note 7.

[9] Stephen J. Lukasik, *Protecting the Global Information Commons*, 24 TELECOMM. POL'Y 519, 525 (2000).

space, but one that is emerging as a domain of human endeavor that is in many ways no less significant than the real world.[10]

The pseudo commons represents a compromise position between competing models of cyber regulation, namely those espousing Internet sovereignty and Internet freedom.[11] The regime complex that has evolved to govern the cyber pseudo commons might well be conceptualized within a polycentric framework, which recognizes the multi-level, multi-purpose, multi-functional, and multi-sectoral regulatory relationships at work in cyberspace.[12] Professor Ronald Deibert, among others, has pointed out that Professor Ostrom's work in this arena may well have some application to cybersecurity.[13] Analyzing the cyber pseudo commons through the lens of polycentricism may provide new insights on how to enhance cybersecurity and foster cyber peace.

Chapter 1 introduced the multifaceted cyber threat and how Internet governance has evolved to manage, or in some cases mismanage, cyber attacks. Chapter 2 builds from this foundation by conceptualizing cyberspace as a pseudo commons in an effort to see which, if any, elements of polycentric governance may apply to enhance cybersecurity. Even as many nations are asserting greater control over cyberspace, other stakeholders, including the U.S. Department of Defense, continue to refer to cyberspace as part of the "global commons."[14] However, is cyberspace really still a commons, and for that matter, was it ever? Or is it being enclosed to such an extent that it is becoming a form of private property, or even an extension of national territory? Fundamentally, who enjoys sovereignty in cyberspace, and how might it be exercised? And why do these distinctions matter for cybersecurity? The goal of this chapter is to explore possible answers to these questions as well as the overarching one: "who controls cyberspace in the twenty-first century?"

The chapter is structured as follows. First, we investigate the nature of cyberspace and how it is evolving. We then introduce the concept of the global commons and the theory and implications of the cyber pseudo commons, examining both the degree of national and private control of cyberspace. Next, the tragedy of the

---

[10] *See, e.g.,* Dan Hunter, *Cyberspace as Place and the Tragedy of the Digital Anticommons,* 91 CAL. L. REV. 439, 442–443 (2003) (discussing the extent to which cyberspace is being enclosed).

[11] *See* Johnson & Post, *supra* note 8, at 1367–69; Lawrence Lessig, *The Law of the Horse: What Cyberlaw Might Teach,* 113(2) HARV. L. REV. 501, 502 (1999); *see also* Joseph S. Nye, Jr., *Cyber Power,* HARV. KENNEDY SCH. 15 (May 2010) (referring to cyberspace as an "imperfect commons."); Press Release, Ind. Univ., London Conference Reveals 'Fault Lines' in Global Cyberspace and Cybersecurity Governance (Nov. 7, 2011), http://newsinfo.iu.edu/news/page/normal/20236.html.

[12] *See* Michael D. McGinnis, *An Introduction to IAD and the Language of the Ostrom Workshop: A Simple Guide to a Complex Framework,* 39(1) POL'Y STUD. J. 163, 171–72 (Feb. 2011) (discussing polycentrism generally); ANDREW W. MURRAY, THE REGULATION OF CYBERSPACE: CONTROL IN THE ONLINE ENVIRONMENT xi (2006).

[13] *See* Deibert, *supra* note 6, at 57.

[14] *See* DEP'T OF DEF., STRATEGY FOR HOMELAND DEFENSE AND CIVIL SUPPORT 12 (2005), http://www.defense.gov/news/jun2005/d20050630homeland.pdf [hereinafter STRATEGY FOR HOMELAND DEFENSE]; DEP'T OF DEF., NATIONAL DEFENSE STRATEGY 16 (2008), http://www.defense.gov/pubs/2008nationaldefensestrategy.pdf.

cyber commons is examined,[15] and solutions to the tragedy are discussed, including nationalization, privatization, and common-property joint-management. Finally, we analyze the veracity of applying polycentric governance to cyberspace as a means of reconceptualizing cybersecurity by considering the application of the theory to another global collective-action problem – climate change.

WHAT IS CYBERSPACE?

The complexity of this question can first be demonstrated by highlighting what cyberspace is *not*: it is neither the Internet nor the web. The Internet is merely the networked physical infrastructure of interconnected computer networks that allows information to move through cyberspace, and the web is simply a service that runs on the Internet. The relationship between the web, the Internet, and cyberspace is illustrated in Figure 2.1.

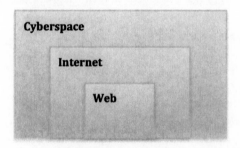

FIGURE 2.1. THE WEB, INTERNET, AND CYBERSPACE

Academics, the popular press, and governments around the world have tried to define cyberspace. None have fully succeeded, although governmental definitions often share at least two common features. First, cyberspace is commonly conflated with the Internet as a global network of hardware,[16] emphasizing the critical infrastructure concerns of governments. Second, cyberspace has been conceptualized as an information domain, one that at least some cyber powers wish to dominate.[17]

---

[15] *See, e.g.,* Antonio Lambino, *Impending Tragedy of the Digital Commons?,* WORLD BANK (Oct. 25, 2010), http://blogs.worldbank.org/publicsphere/node/5562.

[16] *See, e.g.,* DAVID BELL, AN INTRODUCTION TO CYBERCULTURES 6–7 (2001); *see also* Damir Rajnovic, *Cyberspace – What Is It?,* CISCO BLOG (July 26, 2012), http://blogs.cisco.com/security/cyberspace-what-is-it (reviewing some of the similarities and differences between how a subset of countries define "cyberspace").

[17] *See, e.g.,* Robert A. Miller & Daniel T. Kuehl, *Cyberspace and the "First Battle" in 21st-Century War,* 68 DEF. HORIZONS 1, 1–3 (2009), http://www.ndu.edu/CTNSP/docUploaded/DH68.pdf (revealing that the arena of cyberwarfare resembles traditional warfare in that nations compete for superiority and control); *Army Cyber,* U.S. ARMY CYBER COMMAND, http://www.arcyber.army.mil/org-arcyber.html (last visited Mar. 21, 2013) (discussing network dominance and stating that "[i]t is in cyberspace that we must use our strategic vision to dominate the information environment throughout interdependencies and independent systems").

What most of these definitions have in common, however, is also what they ignore – users. Along with technology, e-commerce, and geopolitics, people are the ultimate driving force in the evolution of cyberspace, from Postel to the present. Without people, there would be no content to translate into bits and send throughout the networks. And without people, there would be no cyber attacks. Consequently, understanding the motivations of hacktivists (hacker activists), criminals, terrorists, patriotic hackers, and warriors in cyberspace is a critical component to forming effective cybersecurity policies. Yet defining intent and attributing attacks is both technically and legally difficult, as is explored in Chapters 3 and 6.

The task of defining cyberspace is made more complicated given the fact that it is always evolving. Its content is consolidating because of the influence of semi-closed platforms just as its reach is expanding.[18] Compete, a web analytics company, found that "the top ten Web sites accounted for 31 percent of U.S. pageviews in 2001, 40 percent in 2006, and about 75 percent in 2010."[19] Consumers favor semi-closed, proprietary networks, like those common in many smart phones, due to their ease of use, while companies favor these networks since they can make it simpler to make a profit.[20] According to *Wired Magazine*, fast is beating flexible.[21]

As cyberspace evolves, it is also becoming "flat,"[22] and many organizations are working to make it flatter still. The United Nations, for example, is helping to spread Internet technology to Africa, while Secretary General of the ITU Dr. Hamadoun Touré has argued that governments must "regard the [I]nternet as basic infrastructure – just like roads, waste, and water."[23] A 2011 UN report argued – as have the countries of Spain, France, and Finland – that Internet access is a basic human right even though practitioners, including Vinton Cerf, the "Father of the Internet," have taken umbrage with this position.[24] Moreover, combining broadband

---

[18] *See* Jonathan Zittrain, The Future of the Internet and How to Stop It 3 (2008) (discussing the "rise and stall" of the generative Internet).

[19] Chris Anderson & Michael Wolff, *The Web is Dead: Long Live the Internet*, Wired Mag. (Aug. 17, 2010), http://www.wired.com/magazine/2010/08/ff_webrip/all/1 (citing Compete Pulse, http://blog .compete.com/ (last visited Jan. 31, 2013)).

[20] *Id.*

[21] *Id.*

[22] Thomas L. Friedman, Hot, Flat, and Crowded: Why We Need a Green Revolution – and How It Can Renew America 29–30 (2008) (describing how the spread of networked personal computers allow people to work together and have led to a dramatic flattening of the world); *see also* Thomas L. Friedman, The World is Flat: A Brief History of the Twenty-First Century 163 (2005) (explaining how the capabilities, power, and speed of computing have increased dramatically over a relatively short period of time).

[23] *Internet Access Is 'a Fundamental Right,'* BBC News (Mar. 8, 2010), http://news.bbc.co.uk/2/hi/ 8548190.stm.

[24] *See* Vinton G. Cerf, Op-Ed, *Internet Access Is Not a Human Right*, N.Y. Times, Jan. 5, 2012, at A25 (arguing that the Internet enables people to seek their human rights, but access to the Internet in and of itself is not a human right). For a discussion of the link between spreading Internet access, human rights, and the promotion of positive cyber peace, see Henning Wegener, *Government Internet Censorship: Cyber Repression*, in The Quest for Cyber Peace 43, 51 n.85 (Int'l Telecomm. Union & Permanent Monitoring Panel on Info. Sec. eds., 2011), http://www.itu.int/dms_pub/itu-s/opb/gen/S-GEN-WFS.01-1-2011-PDF-E.pdf (citing Recommendations Concerning the Promotion and Use of

Internet connections in nations with weak governance increases the risk that they will become havens for cybercriminals,[25] showcasing both the benefits and drawbacks of the strong growth in online services on cybersecurity.[26] As access spreads, cyberspace itself, which is defined here as "a time-dependent set of interconnected information systems and the human users that interact with these systems,"[27] remains malleable. But important questions remain unanswered. For example, is cyberspace a commons?[28] If so, what are the implications for cybersecurity policymaking?

INTRODUCING THE GLOBAL COMMONS

A "commons" is a general term meaning "a resource shared by a group of people...."[29] The notion of the commons can mean either a "resource system" or "a property rights regime[,]" depending on context.[30] As the term is used here, the notion is that certain areas (such as the sky) belong to all and should be preserved

Multilingualism and Universal Access to Cyberspace, UNESCO, Oct. 15, 2003, ¶ 6, http://portal .unesco.org/ci/en/ev.php-URL_ID=13475&URL_DO=DO_TOPIC&URL_SECTION=201.html (arguing for "universal access to the Internet as an instrument for promoting the realization of the human rights....")); Geneva Declaration of Principles, World Summit on the Information Society, Dec. 2003, ¶ 4, www.itu.int/dms_pub/itu-s/md/03/wsis/doc/S03-WSIS-DOC-0004!!PDF-E .pdf (reaffirming "that everyone has the right to freedom of opinion and expression....").

[25] *See* Marthie Grobler & Joey Jansen van Vuuren, *Broadband Broadens Scope for Cyber Crime in Africa, in* INFO. SEC. SOUTH AFRICA CONF. PROC. (Hein S. Venter et al. eds., 2010), http://icsa.cs.up .ac.za/issa/2010/Proceedings/Full/28_Paper.pdf; *Cybercriminals in Developing Nations Targeted*, BBC NEWS, (July 20, 2012), http://www.bbc.co.uk/news/technology-18930953 (pointing out that enhanced interconnectivity often means increased criminal activity); Tamisin Ford, *Ivory Coast Cracks Down on Cyber Crime*, BBC (Jan. 16, 2014), http://www.bbc.co.uk/news/business-25735305 ("According to the Ivorian government, it received more complaints about cyber criminality in the first half of 2013 than any other country on the continent, making it Africa's unlikely capital of 'brouteurs' – Ivorian slang for cyber criminals.").

[26] One correlation in this vein that deserves further research is the link between the expansion of cyberspace and associated positive network effects caused by norm entrepeneurs spreading cybersecurity best practices. *See* Neal K. Katyal, *The Dark Side of Private Ordering: The Network/Community Harm of Crime, in* THE LAW AND ECONOMICS OF CYBERSECURITY 193, 193–94 (Mark F. Grady & Francesco Parisi eds., 2006).

[27] Rain Ottis & Peeter Lorents, *Cyberspace: Definition and Implications*, 2010 INT'L CONF. ON INFO. WARFARE & SEC. 267, 268 (emphasis omitted); *see also* Reno v. ACLU, 521 U.S. 844, 890 (1997) (O'Connor, J., concurring in the judgment in part and dissenting in part) (describing how cyberspace differs from the physical world, specifically noting its "malleable" nature); *Cyberspace as a Warfighting Domain: Policy, Management and Technical Challenges to Mission Assurance: Hearing Before the Terrorism, Unconventional Threats, & Capabilities Subcomm. of the H. Comm. on Armed Servs.*, 111th Cong. 96 n.1 (2009) (statement of Lt. Gen. Keith Alexander, Commander, Joint Functional Component Command for Network Warfare) (explaining that cyberspace is "the interdependent network of information technology infrastructures, and includes the Internet, telecommunications networks, computer systems, and embedded processors and controllers in critical industries" (quoting National Security Presidential Directive 54/Homeland Security Presidential Directive 23 (Jan. 8, 2008))).

[28] *See* Deibert, *supra* note 6, at 56–57.

[29] Charlotte Hess & Elinor Ostrom, *Introduction: An Overview of the Knowledge Commons, in* UNDERSTANDING KNOWLEDGE AS A COMMONS: FROM THEORY TO PRACTICE 3, 3 (Charlotte Hess & Elinor Ostrom eds., 2006).

[30] *Id.* at 5.

for posterity instead of private persons or the state exclusively managing a resource.[31] Under international law, "commons" are the exception, not the rule, given that territorial sovereignty has in large part defined international relations and international law since the 1648 Treaty of Westphalia, which ushered in the modern nation-state system.[32] The notion of the global commons posits that there are limits to national sovereignty in certain parts of the world, and that these areas should be "open to use by the [international] community but closed to exclusive appropriation" by treaty or custom.[33] At its height, the global commons comprised nearly 75 percent of the Earth's surface, including the high seas and Antarctica, as well as outer space, the atmosphere, and some argue, cyberspace.[34] Some of these regions were gradually regulated to a greater or lesser extent not by individual countries, but by the international community at times through the vague Common Heritage of Mankind (CHM) concept that will be discussed later in this chapter.[35] More recently, this trend has reversed itself; for instance, individual coastal nations, rather than the international community, now control the vast majority of readily accessible offshore resources.[36] The same trend might be playing out in cyberspace where many nations are seeking to assert greater control online, challenging the notion of cyberspace as a commons.[37]

Commons exist at both the domestic and international levels. Domestically, in economic terms, the commons may be defined as an area in which "common pool resources" are found.[38] Such common pool resources are exhaustible, and are managed through a property regime in which enforcing the exclusion of a "defined

---

[31] *See, e.g.,* J. E. S. Fawcett, *How Free Are the Seas?*, 49 INT'L AFF. 14, 14 (1973).

[32] *See* Leo Gross, *The Peace of Westphalia, 1648–1948*, 42 AM. J. INT'L L. 20, 20, 26 (1948).

[33] CHRISTOPHER C. JOYNER, GOVERNING THE FROZEN COMMONS: THE ANTARCTIC REGIME AND ENVIRONMENTAL PROTECTION 222 (1998) (defining a global commons and positing that Antarctica may qualify as a global commons suitable to the application of the CHM concept); Geert van Calster, *International Law and Sovereignty in the Age of Globalization*, INT'L L. & INST., at 2–3, http://www.eolss.net/Sample-Chapters/C14/E1-36-01-04.pdf.

[34] *See, e.g.,* STRATEGY FOR HOMELAND DEFENSE, *supra* note 14, at 12; Mark E. Redden & Michael P. Hughes, NAT'L DEF. UNIV., SF NO. 259, GLOBAL COMMONS AND DOMAIN INTERRELATIONSHIPS: TIME FOR A NEW CONCEPTUAL FRAMEWORK?, 1–3 (2010), http://www.ndu.edu/press/lib/pdf/StrForum/SF-259.pdf (merging the traditional civilian definition of global commons, which includes Antarctica, and emphasizing the importance to the U.S. military of operating throughout the global commons).

[35] *See* KEMAL BASLAR, THE CONCEPT OF THE COMMON HERITAGE OF MANKIND IN INTERNATIONAL LAW xix–xx (1998) (describing the history of international efforts to bring the seabed, ocean floor, and outer space resources, such as the moon, within the CHM).

[36] *Id.* at 225–26.

[37] *See* Deibert, *supra* note 6, at 46 (analyzing the trend in the past decade of nations abandoning a laissez-faire approach to Internet governance and asserting themselves in cyberspace); Paul Tassi, *The Philippines Passes a Cybercrime Prevention Act that Makes SOPA Look Reasonable*, FORBES (Oct. 2, 2012), http://www.forbes.com/sites/insertcoin/2012/10/02/the-philippines-passes-the-cybercrime-prevention-act-that-makes-sopa-look-reasonable/.

[38] SUSAN J. BUCK, THE GLOBAL COMMONS: AN INTRODUCTION 2–5 (1998) (explaining that common pool resources implicate property rights and are defined as "subtractable resources managed under a property regime in which a legally defined user pool cannot be efficiently excluded from the resource domain").

user pool" is difficult.[39] Examples include some fisheries, pastures, and forests. What do fisheries have to do with cybersecurity? It is the difficulties of enforcement and overuse that binds these areas together. The possibility of overuse, however, differs across domains. Information itself cannot be overused in the same way that a fishery can be overfished, so long as the information is non-rivalrous, meaning that one person's use does not take away available goods from others.[40] Cyberspace, however, as has been stated is more than information or computer networks.[41] Overuse can occur in cyberspace, such as when spam messages consume limited bandwidth, which have been called a form of "information pollution,"[42] and during distributed denial of service (DDoS) attacks, which can cause targeted websites to crash through too many requests for site access.[43]

At the international level, the expansive areas that "do not fall within the jurisdiction of any one country are termed international or global commons."[44] These are regions to which all nations enjoy legal access but in which enforcement is difficult. Each area of the commons is unique, with its own "geographical, economic, legal, and administrative attributes."[45] The different domains of the global commons existing beyond national jurisdiction are not states because they lack the requirements of statehood, such as a permanent population.[46] Instead, the commons are governed through a mixture of regulations at multiple levels, including multilateral treaty regimes, regional accords, and national regulations. There is no

---

[39] *Id.* at 5; *see also* Joseph S. Nye Jr., *Cyber Power*, HARV. BELFER CTR. 15 (2010), http://belfercenter.ksg.harvard.edu/files/cyber-power.pdf (making the case that cyberspace may be considered a type of common pool resource, and as such "self-organization is possible under certain conditions.'").

[40] *See* NIVA ELKIN-KOREN & ELI M. SALZBERGER, LAW, ECONOMICS AND CYBERSPACE: THE EFFECTS OF CYBERSPACE ON THE ECONOMIC ANALYSIS OF LAW 53 (2004); Hess & Ostrom, *supra* note 29, at 9.

[41] *See, e.g.,* David T. Fahrenkrug, *Cyberspace Defined*, NAT'L MILITARY STRAT. CYBERSPACE OPERATIONS, http://www.au.af.mil/au/awc/awcgate/wrightstuff/cyberspace_defined_wrightstuff_17may07.htm (last visited May 22, 2013).

[42] David A. Bray, *Information Pollution, Knowledge Overload, Limited Attention Spans, and Our Responsibilities as IS Professionals*, GLOBAL INFO. TECH. MGMT. ASSOC. WORLD CONF. (June 2008), http://ssrn.com/abstract=962732; *see also* Roger Hurwitz, *The Prospects for Regulating Cyberspace: A Schematic Analysis on the Basis of Elinor Ostrom, "General Framework for Analyzing Sustainability of Social Ecological Systems,"* 325 SCI. 419, 419–22 (2009) (arguing that aside from bandwidth, "the more important common pool resource is public or shared trust" that may be breached through cyber insecurities).

[43] *See, e.g.,* Jonathan A. Ophardt, *Cyber Warfare and the Crime of Aggression: The Need for Individual Accountability on Tomorrow's Battlefield*, 2010 DUKE L. & TECH. REV. 3, ¶¶ 2–6, ¶10 n.35 (describing how DDoS attacks have been used in conjunction with more conventional warfare tools, such as in the 2008 conflict between Russia and Georgia in South Ossetia, but arguing that such nation-wide tactics would be more difficult in countries with greater interconnectivity such as the United States).

[44] BUCK, *supra* note 38, at 5–6.

[45] JOYNER, *supra* note 33, at 27.

[46] *See* JAMES CRAWFORD, THE CREATION OF STATES IN INTERNATIONAL LAW 45–46 (2d ed. 2006) (referring to the traditional criteria of statehood in the Montevideo Convention on the Rights and Duties of States of 1933, which includes a permanent population, defined territory, government, and the ability to enter into relations with other states).

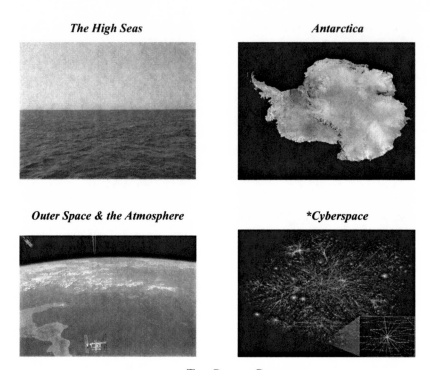

FIGURE 2.2. THE GLOBAL COMMONS

binding legal principle uniting these disparate regimes, but the closest candidate historically has been the CHM concept, which arose from two observations.[47] First, certain natural resources in the global commons were becoming increasingly valuable, and developing nations wanted their share before the resources were depleted.[48] Second, the technological gaps between developing and developed nations kept developing nations from accessing these resources.[49] Nevertheless, despite its adoption in the deep seabed and outer space, there is still no consensus about how to define the CHM concept, or broader agreement on how to govern the global commons.[50] Cyberspace is the most recent and contested addition, and as a result, "regulation," understood here as "all mechanisms of social control – including unintentional and non-state processes,"[51] over this area is still evolving.

A number of scholarly works and U.S. government reports maintain contradictory opinions as to whether cyberspace is part of the global commons. On the one

---

[47] *See* BUCK, *supra* note 38, at 29.
[48] *Id.*
[49] *Id.*
[50] *See* C. A. Fleischer, *The International Concern for the Environment: The Concept of the Common Heritage, in* TRENDS IN ENVIRONMENTAL POLICY AND LAW 321, 330–32 (M. Bothe ed., 1980); BASLAR, *supra* note 35, at 2.
[51] ROBERT BALDWIN ET AL., A READER ON REGULATION 4 (1998).

hand, for example, the 2005 U.S. Strategy for Homeland Defense and Civil Support states, "the global commons consist of international waters and airspace, space, and cyberspace."[52] The 2008 National Defense Strategy does not explicitly reference cyberspace, but it does include "information transmitted under the ocean or through space" when analyzing the global commons.[53] This global view of cyberspace is shared by others, such as Nemanja Malisevic of the Organization for Security and Cooperation in Europe, who has argued that "[a]n attack on this cyberspace, any attack, whatever its background or motivation is an attack on all of us . . . collectively as Internet users. A comprehensive approach to enhancing cyber security is therefore the only reasonable way forward."[54] Yet on the other hand, former DHS Deputy Secretary Jane Holl Lute has argued that cyberspace is not a global commons: "It's more like light than like air or water. There are no perfect metaphors . . . or historical analogies."[55] Opinions about the nature and control of cyberspace abound. A Google search returns more than 14.2 million hits on the subject, whereas LexisNexis, a research database, lists more than 3,000 relevant articles. This underscores both the importance of and widespread interest in the topic, as well as the necessity of paying attention to all sides of the debate to find common ground. To that end, and given the realities of private and governmental control, the following section analyzes cyberspace as, at best, a pseudo commons and discusses why this distinction matters for managing cyber attacks.

THE CYBER PSEUDO COMMONS

Cyberspace does share certain aspects with other areas of the global commons. It is in some ways an open-access system, the traditional components of which include:

---

[52] Patrick W. Franzese, *Sovereignty in Cyberspace: Can it Exist?*, 64 A.F. L. Rev. 1, 41 (2009) (quoting Strategy for Homeland Defense, *supra* note 14, at 12).

[53] *Id.* (quoting National Defense Strategy, *supra* note 14, at 16). The 2013 Strategy also references "global commons." Dep't of Def., Strategy for Homeland Defense and Defense Support of Civil Authorities 25 (2013), http://www.defense.gov/news/homelanddefensestrategy.pdf ("The Department relies on an active, layered defense – a global defense in-depth in all domains – to prevent attacks on the homeland by denying and defeating aggressors abroad, in the global commons, and in the approaches to the United States.").

[54] Presentation by Nemanja Malisevic, *Combating Terrorist Use of the Internet: Comprehensive Approach to Cyber Security – The OSCE Perspective*, NATO CCDCOE Conf. Cyber Conflict, in Tallinn, Est. (June 17, 2010).

[55] Jane Holl Lute, Deputy Sec'y, Dep't of Homeland Sec., Remarks at the Black Hat Conf. (July 29, 2010), http://www.dhs.gov/ynews/speeches/sp_1280437519818.shtm. James Lewis also considers the use of the term "global commons" in reference to cyberspace to be inadequate due to prevalent security and governance concerns. *Cybersecurity: Next Steps to Protect Our Critical Infrastructure: Hearing Before the S. Comm. on Commerce, Sci., & Transp.*, 111th Cong. 16 (2010) (statement of James A. Lewis, Director and Senior Fellow, Technology and Public Policy Program, Center for Strategic and International Studies) [hereinafter *Cybersecurity: Next Steps*] ("The vision was that cyberspace would be a global commons led and shaped by private action, where a self-organizing community could invent and create. This ideology of a self-organizing global commons has shaped internet architecture and policy, but we must now recognize its inadequacy.").

unregulated areas featuring relatively undefined property rights, enforcement problems, and overuse issues (as with spam and DDoS attacks).[56] The open-source "creative commons" movement, and even the TCP/IP framework itself, are testaments to the commons features of cyberspace.[57] However, much of the Internet's infrastructure is owned and operated by private firms and subject to the jurisdiction of myriad laws and regulations around the world.[58] Thus, cyberspace does not fit within the classic definition of a global commons existing beyond national jurisdiction. At best, then, cyberspace may be considered a pseudo commons comprised of a "shared global infrastructure" that is controlled by public and private entities subject to national and international regulations.[59] Fully understanding the unique status of cyberspace and its implications for cybersecurity policymaking requires analyzing the nature and extent of public and private sector regulation. First however, assuming cyberspace is a pseudo commons, then it may be amenable to some derivation of the tragedy of the commons scenario.[60] That scenario is addressed next to ascertain the applicability of classic solutions to this policy problem, namely nationalization and privatization.

Tragedy of the Cyber Pseudo Commons

The first step in understanding cyberspace as a commons susceptible to a tragedy is to review collective action problems, which are classic "social dilemma[s]."[61] People tend to maximize their short-term personal interests ahead of the collective good. This is a dilemma, in economic terms, because an outcome exists that would make everyone better off if only people cooperated.[62] Similar problems in which lack of cooperation leads to less than optimal results for the participants are the

---

[56] *See* David Feeny et al., *The Tragedy of the Commons: Twenty-Two Years Later,* 18 HUM. ECOLOGY 1, 4 (1990) (describing the open access system of property rights as one in which access to the resource is available to everyone, free, and unregulated). Feeny also explains that open access systems lead to degradation of the resource due to overuse and an inability to enforce regulations or exclusion mechanisms. *Id.* at 6, 9.

[57] Deibert, *supra* note 6, at 56–57.

[58] *Id.*

[59] *Cybersecurity: Next Steps, supra* note 55 (rejecting the idea that cyberspace is a global commons because the resources used in cyberspace are often privately owned by entities located in different jurisdictions). Lewis reinforces this conclusion by highlighting the observations that "private efforts to secure networks will be always be overwhelmed by professional military and criminal action[,]" and that "absent government intervention, security may be unachievable" due in part to the fact that "[c]ybersecurity is a public good that the market has failed to produce in sufficient quantities." *Id.* This topic is returned to in Chapter 5.

[60] *See* MURRAY, *supra* note 12, at 81 (explaining Professor Lessig's two alternative regulatory models of the commons).

[61] Elinor Ostrom, *A Polycentric Approach for Coping with Climate Change* 6 (World Bank, Policy Research Working Paper No. 5095, 2009), http://www.iadb.org/intal/intalcdi/pe/2009/04268.pdf.

[62] *Id.* (explaining that there is "at least one outcome [that] yields higher returns for *all* who are involved, but participants ... maximizing short-term benefits make independent decisions and are not predicated to achieve this outcome.").

prisoner's dilemma and free riding.[63] According to Professor Ostrom, free riders "enjoy the benefit of others' restraint in using shared resources or others' contribution to collective action."[64] But if many individuals decide to free ride in this manner, "eventually no one contributes" resulting in "collective *inaction*."[65] The common benefits, then, are not achieved. In managing cyber attacks, for example, nations that work to police the Internet and catch cyber criminals enjoy many of the same benefits from their actions as those that do not. This can, in turn, result in a "tragedy."

The tragedy of the commons model predicts the gradual overexploitation of all common pool resources – including oceans and the atmosphere.[66] This model does not apply to cyberspace in a traditional way. At the most basic level, cyberspace itself can expand through the addition of new networks,[67] but increased use also multiplies threat vectors along with the potential supply of malicious actors who are able to launch attacks against a greater array of networks.[68] Former DHS Secretary Michael Chertoff, for example, has argued that the cyber threat constitutes "a potential tragedy of the commons scenario" given "[o]ur reliance on cyberspace."[69] Without concerted action, vulnerabilities may ultimately degrade the resource of cyberspace on which companies, countries, and the international community depend.[70]

Vulnerabilities may take many forms, including spam and cyber attacks. A spammer incurs minor costs but can impose large costs on individuals and organizations, resulting in a negative externality analogous to environmental pollution.[71] Similar

---

[63] *Id.* at 7–8.

[64] *Id.* at 8.

[65] *Id.*

[66] *See* Feeny et al., *supra* note 56, at 1.

[67] *See* TIM JORDAN, CYBERPOWER: THE CULTURE AND POLITICS OF CYBERSPACE AND THE INTERNET 120 (1999) (describing the increase in Internet access as well as information overload); *cf.* RON DEIBERT, CAN. DEF. & FOREIGN AFF. INST., DISTRIBUTED SECURITY AS CYBER STRATEGY: OUTLINING A COMPREHENSIVE APPROACH FOR CANADA IN CYBERSPACE 6–11 (2012), https://citizenlab.org/wp-content/uploads/2012/08/CDFAI-Distributed-Security-as-Cyber-Strategy_-outlining-a-comprehensive-approach-for-Canada-in-Cyber.pdf (discussing the expansion of cyberspace to more countries and regions of the world, yet noting the increasing use of censorship practices within some of these nations).

[68] *See* Nick Nykodym et al., *Criminal Profiling and Insider Cyber Crime*, 2 DIGITAL INVESTIGATION 261, 264–65 (2005) (explaining how the Internet's expanding role in business has correspondingly increased the threat of cybercrime and made criminals more difficult to catch); Richard Chirgwin, *AusCERT Wrap-Up, Day 2: Attack Vectors Will Multiply Faster than Defences*, CSO (May 17, 2012), http://www.cso.com.au/article/424868/auscert-wrap-up_day_2_attack_vectors_will_multiply_faster_than_defences/ (declaring that it is "hard to escape the conclusion that the 'Internet of Things' will create a host of new attack vectors that will probably only become clear after we have enthusiastically adopted a new technology: that's the way it always goes.").

[69] Michael Chertoff, *Foreword*, 4 J. NAT'L SEC. L. & POL'Y 1, 2 (2010).

[70] *See, e.g., Cybersecurity Strategy of the European Union: An Open, Safe and Secure Cyberspace*, EUR. COMM'N at 2 (Feb. 7, 2013) (reporting that "a 2012 Eurobarometer survey showed that almost a third of Europeans are not confident in their ability to use the internet for banking or purchases.") [hereinafter *EU Cybersecurity Strategy*].

[71] *See* Dennis D. Hirsch, *Protecting the Inner Environment: What Privacy Regulation Can Learn from Environmental Law*, 41 GA. L. REV. 1, 25–26 (2006) (comparing the negative externalities created

to the classic tragedy of the commons involving overgrazing on a village green, here the spammer fully benefits from each email, but gets to share the cost with the rest of society.[72] Acting rationally, spammers will not refrain from spamming since others will take their place, which helps explain the phenomenal growth in spam messages.[73] The U.S. Congress has recognized this potential tragedy, stating in a Senate report that "[l]eft unchecked at its present rate of increase, spam may soon undermine the usefulness and efficiency of e-mail as a communications tool,"[74] effectively depleting the resource that spammers are targeting. Cyber attacks similarly have the potential to degrade the cyber pseudo commons. For example, cyber criminals targeting e-commerce have become so successful that they are, in some cases, shaking consumer confidence, which could be degraded to such an extent that users sacrifice convenience for security.[75] A similar scenario could unfold as a result of espionage,[76] or during a cyber war. Thus, the tragedy of the cyber pseudo commons predicts the degradation of a resource, namely cyberspace, because of environmental (spam) and security (cyber attacks) challenges potentially resulting in further enclosure and displacement of the public benefit.[77]

A similar scenario unfolds by considering cyberspace as an anti-commons. The tragedy of the anti-commons situation is one "in which private ownership leads to underuse or development that is detrimental to both individual owners and the public[]"[78] – the opposite of the tragedy of the commons. Under this conceptualization, "multiple owners each have a right to exclude others . . . and no one has an effective privilege of use," stifling innovation.[79] This situation

---

by spammers by forcing recipients to spend more time filtering and reading emails to the negative externalities polluters create in forcing others to deal with emissions).

[72] *Id.* at 27–29.

[73] *See* Lily Zhang, Note, *The CAN-SPAM Act: An Insufficient Response to the Growing Spam Problem,* 20 Berkeley Tech. L.J. 301, 304 (2005) (reporting that in 2004, an estimated two trillion spam emails were sent, outnumbering traditional mail advertising 100 to 1). *But see* Symantec, Internet Security Threat Report: 2011 Trends 29 (2011), http://www.symantec.com/content/en/us/enterprise/other_resources/b-istr_main_report_2011_21239364.en-us.pdf (reporting that the amount of spam has decreased to "42 billion spam messages a day in global circulation in 2011" from "61.6 billion in 2010."). Note, though, that these figures are merely estimates and are in dispute.

[74] S. Rep. No. 108-102, at 6 (2003).

[75] *See, e.g.,* Alan D. Smith, *Cybercriminal Impacts on Online Business and Consumer Confidence,* 28 Online Info. Rev. 224, 225–26 (2004) (examining the effect that cybercrime has on consumer confidence while noting that companies must balance increasing security with maintaining maximum convenience for the consumer); *EU Cybersecurity Strategy, supra* note 70, at 2.

[76] *See* David E. Sanger & Nicole Perlroth, *Hackers From China Resume Attacks on U.S. Targets,* N.Y. Times, May 19, 2013, at A1 (reporting on alleged Chinese cyber espionage targeting U.S. interests).

[77] *Cf.* Lawrence Lessig, The Future of Ideas: The Fate of the Commons in a Connected World 167 (2001) (explaining the tragedy of the commons in terms of inhibiting innovation through increasing control over content).

[78] Marc A. Rodwin, *Patient Data: Property, Privacy & the Public Interest,* 36 Am. J. L. & Med. 586, 603 (2010).

[79] *Id.* at 603–04 (quoting Michael A. Heller, *The Tragedy of the Anticommons: Property in the Transition from Marx to Markets,* 111 Harv. L. Rev. 621, 624 (1998)).

is rare, though, because property owners can oftentimes buy one another out and develop the resource.[80] A tragedy of the anti-commons could unfold in cyberspace due to the fractured nature of Internet governance and splintering of property rights and responsibilities, potentially hampering both innovation and cybersecurity.[81]

To secure cyberspace and ward off the tragedies of the commons or anti-commons, there are four main approaches that are discussed throughout the remainder of this chapter: national regulation, privatization, common property solutions, and polycentric governance.[82] All of these solutions have strengths and weaknesses, and exploring them fully goes beyond the scope of this book. The challenge faced by governments around the world is to reallocate incentives such that it is in the best interest of companies and countries not to free ride, but to cooperate to secure their networks, and clarify governance to spur innovation and better manage the cyber threat. That is one reason why national regulation in cyberspace is such a critical topic, and the one that we turn to next.

National Regulation in Cyberspace

Analyzing national regulation in cyberspace is important for at least three reasons: (1) national control of cyberspace is increasing and is a critical aspect of its status as a pseudo commons, (2) enclosure through nationalization is one of the classic solutions to the tragedy of the commons, and (3) national regulations form an important component of polycentric governance, even though states do not enjoy a "general regulatory monopoly" in cyberspace.[83] Proponents see such regulation as being "fully consistent with a state's rule-making authority under international law,"[84] subject to certain domestic protections like privacy in the U.S.

---

[80] *See* Richard A. Epstein & Bruce N. Kuhlik, *Is There a Biomedical Anticommons?*, REG. Summer 2004, at 54–56 (arguing against a biomedical anti-commons, but noting that an anti-commons scenario can arise such as in situations of sequential monopoloists).

[81] Consistent with Professor Richard Epstein and Bruce Kuhlik's conception of the anti-commons, this scenario could also arise in cyberspace if property rights became "too strong." *Id.* at 54. For example, if the movement toward state-centric control was further crystallized.

[82] *See* Garrett Hardin, *The Tragedy of the Commons*, 162 SCI. 1243, 1248 (1968); GLENN G. STEVENSON, COMMON PROPERTY ECONOMICS: A GENERAL THEORY AND LAND USE APPLICATIONS 1–5 (1991) (distinguishing between open access resources and common property); Elinor Ostrom, *Polycentric Systems as One Approach for Solving Collective-Action Problems* 2 (Vincent & Elinor Ostrom Workshop in Political Theory & Policy Analysis, Ind. Univ., Working Paper No. 08–6, 2008), http://dlc.dlib .indiana.edu/dlc/bitstream/handle/10535/4417/W08-6_Ostrom_DLC.pdf?sequence=1 (advocating that a polycentric approach is best suited to managing the collective action problem of climate change).

[83] MURRAY, *supra* note 12, at 47.

[84] Kelly A. Gable, *Cyber-Apocalypse Now: Securing the Internet Against Cyberterrorism and Using Universal Jurisdiction as a Deterrent*, 58 VAND. J. TRANSNAT'L L. 57, 102 n.235 (2010) (citing Sanjay S. Mody, *National Cyberspace Regulation: Unbundling the Concept of Jurisdiction*, 37 STAN. J. INT'L L. 365, 366 (2001)).

context.[85] Critics question national regulators' ability to shape the regulatory environment.[86]

This subsection briefly examines current national Internet regulations from around the world, focusing on the censorship practices of the cyber superpowers, the United States and China. This investigation illustrates how such laws are shaping the regulatory environment of cyberspace while at the same time beginning to ascertain the role states can and should play in a system of polycentric governance aimed at promoting positive cyber peace. Indeed, some governments such as China and Russia prefer the term "information security" to cybersecurity and focus on censorship as an important part of their security strategies.[87] But these nations are by no means alone in engaging in Internet censorship. As Professor Deibert has argued, "there is a growing norm worldwide for national Internet filtering. . . . "[88] What impact does such widespread filtering have on cyberspace and conceptions of Internet governance that includes human rights protections, and are these and other enclosures of the pseudo commons essential to enhancing cybersecurity, or merely being used as a way to prop up regimes?[89]

The Origins and Purpose of Cyber Censorship

According to Professor Yulia Timofeeva, the term "censorship" began in Rome "when 'censors' collecting citizens' information . . . for tax purposes, eventually came to be general moral judges."[90] Today, censorship has many forms, including inspecting, altering, or suppressing objectionable content. Yet what is objectionable is often in the eye of the beholder. As Justice Potter Stewart famously wrote in trying to define the threshold between art and obscenity, "I know it when I see it. . . . "[91] In the early days of cyberspace, state censorship and surveillance was thought to be difficult due to the decentralized design of the Internet.[92] This attribute caused cyber libertarians

---

[85] For an early accounting of the impact of electronically stored data on privacy in the U.S. context, see A. Michael Froomkin, *Flood Control on the Information Ocean: Living with Anonymity, Digital Cash, and Distributed Databases*, 15 J.L. & COM. 395, 505–06 (1996) (arguing that the growth of electronic data stored on networks may have profound impacts on personal privacy). Differing conceptions about privacy in the era of big data have not abated in the interim. See Sam Schehner, *Online Privacy Could Spark U.S.-EU Trade Rift*, WALL ST. J. (Jan. 8, 2014), http://online.wsj.com/news/articles/SB10001424052702304361604579291041878017398.

[86] See Johnson & Post, *supra* note 8, at 1370.

[87] See Neal Ungerleider, *The Chinese Way of Hacking*, FAST CO. (July 12, 2011), http://www.fastcompany.com/1766812/inside-the-chinese-way-of-hacking (transcribing an interview with Adam Segal, the Ira A. Lipman Fellow at the Council on Foreign Relations, in which Mr. Segal discusses how the Chinese differentiate between information security and cybersecurity). The distinction between information security and cybersecurity is discussed further in Chapter 4.

[88] Deibert, *supra* note 6, at 48.

[89] *Id.* at 46.

[90] YULIA TIMOFEEVA, CENSORSHIP IN CYBERSPACE: NEW REGULATORY STRATEGIES IN THE DIGITAL AGE ON THE EXAMPLE OF FREEDOM OF EXPRESSION 17 (2006).

[91] Jacobellis v. Ohio, 378 U.S. 184, 197 (1964) (Stewart, J., concurring).

[92] See Ronald J. Deibert & Nart Villeneuve, *Firewalls and Power: An Overview of Global State Censorship of the Internet*, in HUMAN RIGHTS IN THE DIGITAL AGE 111, 111 (Mathias Klang & Andrew Murray eds.,

to herald cyberspace as a tool to help spread liberalization, challenge the control of authoritarian governments, help build civil society, and indirectly further a positive cyber peace. However, far from being beyond state control, time has shown that cyberspace is increasingly enclosed and regulated by public and private sector actors. The technology to allow for such practices is advancing, again demonstrating the influence of technological advancement on Internet governance and further straining the link between Internet use and liberalization.[93]

Types of Content Filtering

There are at least three forms of Internet content filtering mechanisms: black lists, content analysis, and white lists.[94] First, black lists (also called "exclusion filtering"), may be used to deny access to certain IP addresses, such as when the Chinese government blocked access to 18,931 websites that it did not want its citizens viewing.[95] Second, "content analysis" can filter the results of certain keywords or graphics.[96] Third, depending on the goals of the government in question, results may be limited to a white list of only certain websites, which is also called "inclusion filtering."[97] These varied approaches may also be used together.[98] Perhaps even more complex, though, than how content is filtered are the varied reasons for censorship.

Governmental rationales for filtering content often differ from country to country. In the United States, these reasons include protecting children.[99] Whereas in Myanmar, until August 2012 when censorship practices were relaxed, filtering had long been used to help control restive populations.[100] However, Britain also engages in widespread censorship "along with more than three dozen other states around the world...."[101] Governments may work with corporations to build black lists on top of commercially developed software platforms at local, organizational, or national levels. For example, local censorship, also known as "client-based filtering," is legally

---

2005) (suggesting that, while many believed the Internet to be "immune" from state censorship, recent technological advances prove that this is no longer the case).

[93] *See* Alexis C. Madrigal, *The Inside Story of How Facebook Responded to Tunisian Hacks*, ATLANTIC (Jan. 24, 2011), http://www.theatlantic.com/technology/archive/2011/01/the-inside-story-of-how-facebook-responded-tog-tunisian-hacks/70044 (explaining the Tunisian government's successful attack on Facebook in which it was allegedly able to steal "an entire country's worth of passwords" and hack political protest pages).

[94] *See* Deibert & Villeneuve, *supra* note 92, at 112–13.

[95] *See* Jonathan Zittrain & Benjamin Edelman, *Empirical Analysis of Internet Filtering in China*, BERKMAN CTR. INTERNET & SOC'Y (2003), http://cyber.law.harvard.edu/filtering/china/.

[96] Deibert & Villeneuve, *supra* note 92, at 112.

[97] *Id.* at 112–13.

[98] *Id.*

[99] *See id.* at 117.

[100] *See Burma Abolishes Media Censorship*, BBC NEWS (Aug. 20, 2012), http://www.bbc.co.uk/news/world-asia-19315806.

[101] Dawn C. Nunziato, *How (Not) to Censor: Procedural First Amendment Values and Internet Censorship Worldwide*, 42(4) GEO. J. INT'L L. 1123, 1126 (2011).

required in cyber cafés in many nations, such as Cuba.[102] This is important, especially in many developing nations, because cyber cafés are a primary point of public access to cyberspace.[103] Organizational content filtering, or "server-based filtering," can also be used to censor within the network infrastructure itself.[104] Other censorship strategies include singling out particular IP addresses as well as intermittent filtering, the latter of which, according to Professor Deibert and Nart Villeneuve, "is perhaps the most difficult to detect."[105] Low-volume filtering is also used by some nations that wish to make a symbolic point that they can censor cyberspace such as by focusing on high-value targets.[106] Yet national content filtering is difficult, as may be seen when India decided to block access to one Yahoo! Group, Kynhun, which advocated independence from India. The Indian government was technologically unable at the time to enforce this directive, and instead mistakenly blocked access to approximately 12,000 Yahoo! Groups.[107] Suffice it to say, there is not only one technology used for censorship, or rationale to restrict results – any router or proxy server can be turned into a tool for surveillance in the right hands.[108]

National Approaches to Censorship

Freedom of expression is a treasured right in the United States, but it is culturally relative and infused with differing meanings around the world. Cyberspace has promoted the largely unrestricted flow of information since its inception, challenging many nations and their legal systems to rethink – and in some cases reassert – censorship practices. As Professor Lessig has noted, "[t]he architecture of the Internet, as it is right now, is perhaps the most important model of free speech since the founding [of the republic]."[109] Many nations, however, choose to maintain law and order, protect their citizens from exploitation, and control content to stay in power rather than promote freedom of speech or other human rights integral to positive cyber peace.[110] As a result, censorship is occurring around the world arguably contributing to cyber insecurity.[111] Reporters Without Borders has noted that "[a]ll authoritarian regimes are now working to censor the Web, even countries in sub-Saharan Africa."[112]

---

[102] Deibert & Villeneuve, *supra* note 92, at 114; *see Dictatorships Get to Grips with Web 2.0*, REPORTERS WITHOUT BORDERS (Feb. 1, 2007), http://en.rsf.org/dictatorships-get-to-grips-with-01-02-2007,20839 .html [hereinafter *Dictatorships*].

[103] Deibert & Villeneuve, *supra* note 92, at 116–17.

[104] *Id.* at 114.

[105] *Id.* at 118.

[106] *Id.*

[107] *Id.* at 119.

[108] *Id.* at 111.

[109] LAWRENCE LESSIG, CODE: AND OTHER LAWS OF CYBERSPACE, VERSION 2.0 at 237 (2006).

[110] *See* Milton Mueller & Ben Wagner, *Finding a Formula for Brazil: Representation and Legitimacy in Internet Governance*, INTERNET GOVERNANCE FORUM 9–10 (2014), http://www.internetgovernance .org/wordpress/wp-content/uploads/MiltonBenWPdraft_Final.pdf.

[111] *See* TIMOFEEVA, *supra* note 90, at 14.

[112] *Dictatorships*, *supra* note 102.

Pakistan has been intent on developing a "web wall" to censor content nationwide.[113] Many nations engaging in these practices may be doing so in contravention of the Universal Declaration of Human Rights (UDHR), which includes Article 19's protections on freedom of speech, communication, and access to information.[114] This apparent disregard for UDHR highlights the difficulty of relying on non-binding international law to check assertive national governments online and foster cyber peace, which is explored further in Chapter 6.

Common types of filtered content include sensitive cultural, social, and security issues such as homosexuality, pornography, and instructions for illegal activities. Violent manuals and materials have also been banned, as in the Nuremberg files case wherein information available online may have been linked to the murder of several doctors who were providing abortions.[115] Even though national censorship is common, however, it is not all-encompassing. The experience of the Arab Spring demonstrates both the power of the Internet as a tool for social mobilization, such as in Tunisia, as well as the readiness of governments to shut down Internet connections to control unrest, as in Egypt and Syria.[116] Moreover, the private sector also plays an important role in both enabling and frustrating national cyber censorship beyond its status as a technology supplier to governments. Google, for example, announced services in late 2013 that would make it easier to circumvent censors and even protect human rights groups from cyber attacks as part of "Project Shield."[117] However, when Facebook chooses to censor its results, it has significant knock-on effects given its more than one billion users as of September 2013, making it the digital equivalent of the third most-populous nation on Earth.[118] In addition, private censorship can also occur at the behest of governments. Several nations, including the United Kingdom and Canada, have imposed content filtering not directly through

[113] *See* Eric Pfanner, *Pakistan Builds Web Wall Out in the Open*, N.Y. Times (Mar. 2, 2012), http://www.nytimes.com/2012/03/03/technology/pakistan-builds-web-wall-out-in-the-open.html (describing Pakistan's public request for proposals to help it build a "URL filtering and blocking system" that would allow for systematic Internet censorship). *But see The New Politics of the Internet: Everything is Connected*, Economist (Jan. 5, 2013), http://www.economist.com/news/briefing/21569041-can-internet-activism-turn-real-political-movement-everything-connected (reporting that Pakistan's plans for a national firewall have been delayed).

[114] Universal Declaration of Human Rights, G.A. Res. 217 (III) A art. 19, UN Doc. A/RES/217(III) (Dec. 10, 1948).

[115] *See* Planned Parenthood of Columbia/Willamette, Inc. v. American Coalition of Life Activists, 290 F.3d 1058 (9th Cir. 2002).

[116] *See, e.g., Google Chairman Warns of Censorship After Arab Spring*, BBC News (June 27, 2011), http://www.bbc.co.uk/news/world-us-canada-13935470; Christopher Rhoads, *Syria's Internet Blockage Brings Risk of Backfire*, Wall St. J. (June 3, 2011), http://online.wsj.com/article/SB10001424052702304563104577637637637722080144.html.

[117] *Google Unveils Service to Bypass Government Censorship, Surveillance*, Al Jazeera (Oct. 21, 2013), http://america.aljazeera.com/articles/2013/10/21/google-inc-unveilsservicetobypassgovernmentcensorshipsurveillanc.html [hereinafter *Google Unveils Service*].

[118] *Facebook: Key Facts*, Facebook, http://newsroom.fb.com/Key-Facts (last visited Jan. 10, 2014); *Facebook Censorship*, Huff. Post, http://www.huffingtonpost.com/tag/facebook-censorship (last visited Jan. 10, 2014).

a government mandate, but instead have indirectly required their country's ISPs to use filters, which has been criticized as a means to push censorship "outside the law. . . . "[119]

Online content that may be found objectionable in one part of the world can be acceptable in another, and vice versa. International agreement on what constitutes illegal content, with the exception of child pornography, is often lacking.[120] But despite technological advances, it seems thus far that the Internet is not "too big to censor," and as the Web becomes "more social, nothing prevents governments or" the private sector "from building censorship engines powered by recommendation technology similar to that of Amazon and Netflix."[121] China is one of the most well-known practitioners of national censorship and the centralized regulation of cyberspace. The following subsections focus on China's Internet policies briefly juxtaposed against those of the United States to illustrate both of their respective approaches to cyber regulation and also the polycentric nature of cyber regulation that holds lessons for enhancing cybersecurity.

Internet Sovereignty? An Internet with Chinese Characteristics

There are few places on Earth where censorship is undertaken more often and in such an array of forms as it is in the People's Republic of China (PRC). Take Amazon.com. At one level, Amazon.cn, supposedly "the world's largest Chinese online bookstore[,]"[122] resembles its American counterpart, selling everything from the *Twilight* series to *Battlestar Galactica*. But dig deeper and differences multiply. A search conducted in early 2011 revealed only a single hit for the search "human rights in China": Alexandra Harney's *The China Price*. Perhaps most tellingly, a search performed by the *New York Times* in 2010 for "censorship" and "China" returned a result for a book entitled, *When China Rules the World*.[123]

The PRC has an elaborate set of policies and bureaucratic structures in place regulating the online experience in China. An estimated 30,000 personnel spread across twelve government agencies enforce more than sixty Internet regulations

---

[119] Nunziato, *supra* note 101, at 1137. This also puts developed nations including the UK in the difficult position of advocating Internet freedom on the one hand, while at the same time censoring search results in the name of limiting "objectionable" content and protecting vulnerable citizens. Ben Rooney, *U.K. Debates Internet Freedom*, WALL ST. J. (July 31, 2013), http://online.wsj.com/article/SB10001424127887323681904578639821400334756.html.

[120] *See Internet Censorship: Law & Policy Around the World*, ELEC. FRONTIERS AUSTL., http://www.efa.org.au/Issues/Censor/cens3.html (last updated Mar. 28, 2002) [hereinafter EFA] (explaining that since 1995 a number of governments around the world have been trying to coordinate bans and restrictions on access to certain materials such as pornography, racial hatred, and political speech); *Internet Censorship Listed: How Does Each Country Compare?*, GUARDIAN, http://www.guardian.co.uk/technology/datablog/2012/apr/16/internet-censorship-country-list (last visited June 10, 2013) (reporting on an Open Net Initiative study providing more recent information on worldwide censorship practices).

[121] EVGENY MOROZOV, THE NET DELUSION: THE DARK SIDE OF INTERNET FREEDOM 100 (2011).

[122] Dan Levin, *New Scrutiny on Censorship Issues for U.S. Companies in China*, N.Y. TIMES (Mar. 1, 2010), http://www.nytimes.com/2010/03/02/technology/02internet.html.

[123] *Id.*

and censorship systems implemented by state-owned Chinese ISPs, businesses, and organizations.[124] These laws have helped define the online experience in China, although many are not applicable to special status areas like Hong Kong or Macau, explaining Google's 2010 decision to relocate its Chinese operations to Hong Kong.[125] The bureaucracy that supports such regulations is opaque, but Chinese Communist Party organs including the Politburo, high-level state offices, and numerous ministries such as the Ministry of Industry and Information Technology shape and enforce censorship laws.[126] Collectively China's strict control over the Internet is often referred to colloquially as the "Great Firewall," referencing the government's ability to both filter content arriving from servers outside the PRC, and to control the flow of information between routers within its borders.[127]

"[A]s the Internet's economic, social, and political importance has grown,"[128] so too has the PRC's interest in cyberspace. However, there are relatively few official statements describing government-maintained Internet filtering or content control. As was expressed on the radio program *This American Life*: "The full set of rules the censors use are known only to the government, and the rules change constantly without notice."[129] Professors Jonathan Zittrain and Benjamin Edelman conducted an extensive study in 2003 to quantify the true extent and nature of the Chinese censorship apparatus. They did this by requesting "204,012 distinct websites," finding that "more than 50,000 were inaccessible from at least one point in China on at least one occasion."[130] This information, which is summarized in Table 2.1, led Zittrain and Edelman to conclude that the PRC blocks a wide range of web content, including information about "news, health, education, and entertainment."[131]

---

[124] *See, e.g.,* Jinqiu Zhao, *A Snapshot of Internet Regulation in Contemporary China: Censorship, Profitability and Responsibility, in* FROM EARLY TANG COURT DEBATES TO CHINA'S PEACEFUL RISE 141, 141–42 (Friederike Assandri & Dora Martins eds., 2009) (tying China's rapid economic development to its increase in the use of the Internet and the government's subsequent regulatory efforts to censor online speech); Jonathan Watts, *China's Secret Internet Police Target Critics with Web of Propaganda,* GUARDIAN (June 13, 2005), http://www.guardian.co.uk/technology/2005/jun/14/newmedia .china (describing China's use of part-time "commentators" who are tasked with guiding online discussions away from "politically sensitive topics").

[125] *See* Miguel Helft and David Barboza, *Google Shuts China Site in Dispute Over Censorship,* N.Y. TIMES (Mar. 22, 2010), http://www.nytimes.com/2010/03/23/technology/23google.html?_r=0.

[126] *See* Heng He, *Google Exits Censorship but Chinese Regime Exports It,* EPOCH TIMES (May 10, 2010), http://www.theepochtimes.com/n2/opinion/google-exits-censorship-but-chinese-regime-32461 .html (chronicling the history of the Internet in China and the government's decision to control availability of content instead of building an entirely separate Chinese Intranet).

[127] *See* Robert McMahon & Isabella Bennett, *U.S. Internet Providers and the 'Great Firewall of China,'* COUNCIL ON FOREIGN REL. (Feb. 23, 2011), http://www.cfr.org/china/us-internet-providers- great-firewall-china/p9856.

[128] *An Internet with Chinese Characteristics,* ECONOMIST (July 30, 2011), http://www.economist.com/node/ 21524821.

[129] Evan Osnos, *Americans in China,* THIS AM. LIFE (June 22, 2012), http://www.thisamericanlife.org/ radio-archives/episode/467/transcript (last visited Feb. 20, 2013).

[130] Zittrain & Edelman, *supra* note 95.

[131] *Id.*

TABLE 2.1. *Measuring the extent of Chinese censorship*[132]

Type of content blocked	Proportion of tested sites blocked (% of top 100 sites)	Examples
Dissident/Democracy Sites	34.8 (average of data collected)	Amnesty International, Human Rights Watch, Hong Kong Voice of Democracy
Health	20.2 (average of data collected)	AIDS Healthcare Foundation, Health in China
Education	N/A (nearly 700 sites blocked)	Columbia, Caltech, MIT, University of Michigan
News	42	BBC News, CNN, Time Magazine, PBS
Government Sites	N/A (more than 500 sites blocked)	Voice of America, U.S. Department of Defense, Australian Federal Government
Taiwanese and Tibet Sites	9.3 (overall)	Voice of Tibet, Taiwanese Parliamentary Library, Taiwan Health Clinic
Entertainment	N/A (more than 450 sites blocked)	Deep Impact, Taiwanese site of MTV
Religion	N/A (more than 1,700 sites blocked)	Atheist Network, Catholic Civil Rights League, Feng Shui

The PRC's national content filtering and censorship systems work by configuring the routers that connect China's domestic networks to the global Internet to contain black lists of banned domain names. If a user requests one of these blocked websites, the router responsible does not forward on the request, resulting in an error message ("This Page Cannot be Displayed").[133] Email is also filtered both nationally and through ISPs in China.[134] Beyond content filtering, the PRC has attempted to regulate the Chinese Internet in two ways. First, the government has implemented preventative regulation.[135] Such regulation separates Internet content providers from service providers, blocks certain websites, and analyzes the content on individual bulletin boards, chat rooms, and news sites.[136] Internet cafés are also required to install surveillance and firewalls to keep track of their users.[137] Second, the threat of

---

[132] Table redrawn from Zittrain & Edelman, *supra* note 95.

[133] Deibert & Villeneuve, *supra* note 92, at 120.

[134] *See id.*; *How Censorship Works in China: A Brief Overview*, HUMAN RIGHTS WATCH, http://www.hrw .org/reports/2006/china0806/3.htm (last visited June 21, 2012).

[135] *See* Francoise Mengin, *The Changing Role of the State in Greater China in the Age of Information*, *in* CYBER CHINA: RESHAPING NATIONAL IDENTITIES IN THE AGE OF INFORMATION 51, 53 (Francoise Mengin ed., 2004) [hereinafter CYBER CHINA].

[136] *Id.* at 53–54.

[137] *See* Christopher Hughes, *Controlling the Internet Architecture within Greater China, in* CYBER CHINA, *supra* note 135, at 71, 71–73.

"repressive actions" encourages self-regulation.[138] Internet police have been established in multiple Chinese provinces, and arrested Internet users have been tried for crimes ranging from the dissemination of pornography to committing fraud.[139] Activities that "damage national unification" and "endanger social stability" have also been targeted,[140] highlighting China's socio-political challenges ranging from Taiwan and Tibet to the religious movement Falun Gong.[141] Chinese citizens are also encouraged to self-censor consistent with the "Public Pledge of Self-Regulation and Professional Ethics for China Internet Industry," which is issued by the Internet Society of China.[142] Since being rolled out on March 16, 2001, hundreds of organizations, including Yahoo!, have signed the Pledge.[143]

Critics have been scathing in their denunciations of Yahoo! and other complicit companies in China's censorship practices, arguing that they will assist the PRC in committing human rights violations.[144] Google has not been spared. Stephen Colbert, a television host and political satirist, interviewed Eric Schmidt, Google's CEO, and accused him of taking four years to become principled and move out from under "China's communist yoke."[145] Despite this popular backlash, however, many multinational firms continue to be complicit in censorship. Skype, for example, signed an agreement with China to block certain keywords, undermining its encryption and privacy protocols.[146] Censorship software supporting such initiatives in many cases has been developed by companies based in the United States, putting the U.S. government in the dubious position of advocating for freedom of speech online, while U.S. companies in some cases develop the technology to undermine

---

[138] *See* Francoise Mengin, *New Information Technologies and the Reshaping of Power Relations: An Approach to Greater China's Political Economy*, *in* CYBER CHINA, *supra* note 135, at 1, 7.

[139] *See Chinese Police to Continue Internet Crime Crackdown*, XINHUANET (Aug. 13, 2012), http://news.xinhuanet.com/english/china/2012-08/13/c_123578541.htm (reporting that Chinese police "have arrested more than 19,000 suspects and deleted more than 3.85 million pieces of information concerning illegal trade and pornography on the Internet.").

[140] *See* Christopher R. Hughes, *China and the Globalization of ICTs: Implications for International Relations*, 4(2) NEW MEDIA & SOC. 205, 205–09 (2002).

[141] *Id.*; *see also* Craig S. Smith, *Rooting Out Falun Gong; China Makes War on Mysticism*, N.Y. TIMES (Apr. 30, 2000), http://www.nytimes.com/2000/04/30/weekinreview/the-world-rooting-out-falun-gong-china-makes-war-on-mysticism.html?sec=&spon=&pagewanted=all (reporting on China's campaign against Falun Gong).

[142] Internet Soc'y of China, Public Pledge of Self-Regulation and Professional Ethics for China Internet Industry, Art. 5, 20 (2011), http://www.isc.org.cn/english/Specails/Self-regulation/listinfo-15321.html; Deibert & Villeneuve, *supra* note 92, at 115.

[143] Deibert & Villeneuve, *supra* note 92, at 115.

[144] *See* Kenneth Roth, *Yahoo! Risks Abusing Rights in China*, HUMAN RIGHTS WATCH (July 31, 2002), http://hrw.org/press/2002/08/yahoo-ltr073002.htm.

[145] Eric Schmidt Interview, COLBERT NATION (Sept. 21, 2010), http://www.colbertnation.com/the-colbert-report-videos/359744/september-21–2010/eric-schmidt.

[146] *See Big Blog: Skype President Addresses Chinese Privacy Breach*, SKYPE (Oct. 2, 2008), http://blogs.skype.com/en/2008/10/skype_president_addresses_chin.html; *cf.* Paul Carsten, *Microsoft Blocks Censorship of Skype in China: Advocacy Group*, REUTERS (Nov. 27, 2013), http://www.reuters.com/article/2013/11/27/us-microsoft-china-censorship-idUSBRE9AQ0Q520131127 (reporting that "Microsoft Corp. has made it harder to monitor calls and chats over its Skype phone service in China.").

that goal.[147] Recognizing this fact, in April 2012, the Obama Administration instituted economic sanctions against tech firms whose technologies enable repressive regimes to target their own citizens.[148] But domestic Chinese firms have also continued to develop content filtering software. An example is Filter King, which "claims to block more than 500,000 websites" by using "keyword-filtering options [that] . . . can be set up to transmit users' attempts to reach banned information to a centralized police database."[149]

Chinese leaders have long had an ambivalent relationship with the Internet. The Internet in China will likely continue to have distinctly Chinese characteristics, including a comparatively large role for the state. In fact, during the Arab Spring in early 2011, China reorganized its censorship bureaucracy, reportedly creating a new office under the State Council Information Office to "regulate every corner of the nation's vast Internet community. . . . "[150] Policies instituted by the PRC, which some have likened to an "IT menace,"[151] also have significant impact beyond the borders of China. If current trends continue, Mandarin could well be the dominant language on the Internet by 2017.[152] The open question is whether China's censorship will close it off from the wider innovations happening in cyberspace, and if its policy of "Internet sovereignty" is self-defeating.[153] In the fifteenth century, the Chinese turned their back on the sea with catastrophic consequences for Chinese society, ushering in the "century of humiliation" and a lingering distrust of the West.[154] Could the same thing now be happening to some degree in the new frontier of cyberspace?[155] Yet encouraging homegrown Internet firms through

---

[147] *See* McMahon & Bennett, *supra* note 127.

[148] *See, e.g.,* George A. Lopez, *Will Obama Move Thwart Murderous Regimes?*, CNN (Apr. 25, 2012), http://www.cnn.com/2012/04/25/opinion/lopez-sanctions-tech/index.html (lauding the new policy's potential to impede high-tech companies from aiding in the commission of mass atrocities).

[149] Deibert & Villeneuve, *supra* note 92, at 117.

[150] Michael Wines, *China Creates New Agency for Patrolling the Internet*, N.Y. TIMES (May 4, 2011), http://www.nytimes.com/2011/05/05/world/asia/05china.html?_r=1.

[151] *Google Boss Schmidt Labels China an 'IT Menace,'* BBC NEWS (Feb. 2, 2013), http://www.bbc.co.uk/news/technology-21307212.

[152] *See* Deibert, *supra* note 6, at 54.

[153] *See* Paul Mozur, *China's Self-Defeating Censorship*, N.Y. TIMES (Feb. 16, 2010), http://www.nytimes.com/2010/02/16/opinion/16iht-edmozur.html (speculating that China's censorship will have a destabilizing impact in the long term, impeding economic development and undermining government credibility); *see also* CHINA INFO. OFF. OF THE STATE COUNCIL, THE INTERNET IN CHINA (2010), http://english.gov.cn/2010-06/08/content_1622956.htm (describing some of the laws and policies regulating the Chinese Internet).

[154] Michelle (Qian) Yang, Effective Censorship: Maintaining Control In China 26 (Jan. 1, 2010) (unpublished B.A. thesis, University of Pennsylvania), http://repository.upenn.edu/cgi/viewcontent.cgi?article=1138&context=curej (arguing that Chinese nationalism is "still a reaction to Western infringements on Chinese sovereignty and Western biases"); *see also* Thomas F. Christensen, *Chinese Realpolitik: Reading Beijing's World-View*, FOREIGN AFF., Sept./Oct. 1996, at 37, 45–46 (characterizing the redress of the century of humiliation as a "core nationalist goal" for Chinese citizens).

[155] *See China's Internet: A Giant Cage*, ECONOMIST (Apr. 6, 2013), http://www.economist.com/news/special-report/21574628-internet-was-expected-help-democratise-china-instead-it-has-enabled (discussing the evolution and challenges facing China's censors).

banning foreign competitors such as Facebook has been a boon for domestic Chinese industry.[156]

To put Chinese Internet regulations in context, it is useful to compare and contrast Chinese censorship practices with what is occurring in the United States. Although the PRC's censorship system is sophisticated, it does not exist in isolation. Regulations from other jurisdictions, including the United States, impact the Internet in China and illustrate the polycentric system emerging in cyberspace.[157] The United States is not the most Internet-connected country on Earth – that distinction goes to South Korea by some estimates as of February 2014[158] – nor is it the freest country online according to Freedom House, which gave that honor to Iceland in 2013.[159] Yet given that the United States arguably remains the world's leading cyber superpower and is a proponent of a "global networked commons,"[160] according to former U.S. Secretary of State Hillary Clinton, it is critical to assess its approach to cyber regulation.

Internet Freedom? U.S. Cyber Censorship

There is a key distinction between how the United States and other countries, such as China, claim to view cyberspace. The United States has a stated policy of promoting a single "global networked commons" where freedom of speech is sacrosanct, so long as it has the ability to monitor that speech when needed through stepped-up wiretapping and surveillance.[161] China on the other hand, along with many other nations, is viewed as building digital barriers in the name of Internet

---

[156] One example is the firm RenRen, which has become China's leading social networking firm. *See* RenRen: Home, http://www.renren-inc.com/en/ (last visited June 10, 2013).

[157] *See* MURRAY, *supra* note 12, at 47–49.

[158] *See* Tim Hornyak, *Getting Online in Super-Wired South Korea*, CNET (July 16, 2012), http://news.cnet .com/8301-17938-105-57473480-1/getting-online-in-super-wired-south-korea/; Joel Strauch, *Greetings from the Most Connected Place on Earth*, PC WORLD (Feb. 21, 2005), http://www.pcworld.com/ article/119741/greetings_from_the_most_connected_place_on_earth.html. *Cf. Countries*, INTERNET WORLD STATS, http://www.internetworldstats.com/list2.htm (last visited Feb. 9, 2014) (listing Australia as the nation with the highest proportion of Internet penetration at 89.5 percent).

[159] FREEDOM HOUSE, FREEDOM ON THE NET 2013: A GLOBAL ASSESSMENT OF INTERNET AND DIGITAL MEDIA 16 (Sanja Kelly et al. eds., 2013), http://freedomhouse.org/sites/default/files/resources/FOTN %202013_Full%20Report_0.pdf (the designation of "free" is determined in reference to three categories: "obstacles to access, limits on content, and violation of user rights."); *see also* Alex Pearlman, *The World's 7 Worst Internet Censorship Offenders*, GLOBAL POST (Apr. 4, 2012), http://www.globalpost .com/dispatches/globalpost-blogs/rights/the-worlds-7-worst-internet-censorship-offenders (discussing the result of an annual report conducted by Reporters without Borders, Freedom House, and the United Nations Democracy).

[160] Hillary Rodham Clinton, U.S. Sec'y of State, Remarks on Internet Freedom (Jan. 21, 2010), http://www .state.gov/secretary/rm/2010/01/135519.htm (emphasizing the need for behavioral norms and respect among states to encourage the free flow of information and protect against cyber attacks).

[161] *See* Ian Black, *NSA Spying Scandal: What We Have Learned*, GUARDIAN (June 10, 2013), http:// www.theguardian.com/world/2013/jun/10/nsa-spying-scandal-what-we-have-learned (reporting on an NSA wiretapping program code-named PRISM); Charlie Savage, *Officials Push to Bolster Law on Wiretapping*, N.Y. TIMES (Oct. 18, 2010), http://www.nytimes.com/2010/10/19/us/19wiretap.html? pagewanted=all.

sovereignty.[162] The debate between Internet freedom and sovereignty, however, is an oversimplification, and ultimately a false choice. The United States has national regulations that filter content, if to far less of an extent than China,[163] whereas its policy of Internet freedom has been accused of being hypocritical given revelations about its spying programs as well as historic U.S. support for targeted dictators in the Arab Spring.[164] Some have even called for the United States to declare sovereignty over its virtual borders by blocking traffic from ISPs or even entire nations where cyber attacks originate.[165]

Although it is true that China goes further than many nations in curtailing free speech on the Internet, its government is not alone in enacting laws to control cyberspace.[166] Consider the case of Iran, which has been reported to be building a national network separate from the global Internet to enhance governmental control of information and potentially better manage cyber attacks.[167] In fact, Ethiopia, Cuba, and more than 40 other nations now routinely monitor Internet traffic.[168] This process will not likely result in a balkanization into 193 separate intranets,[169] or

---

[162] *See, e.g.,* Evan Osnos, *Can China Maintain "Sovereignty" Over the Internet?*, NEW YORKER (June 11, 2010), http://www.newyorker.com/online/blogs/evanosnos/2010/06/what-is-internet-sovereignty-in-china.html (noting that originally, Internet sovereignty was used by U.S. academics in the 1990s to propose that the Internet itself should be thought of as a kind of sovereign entity with its own rules and citizens); L. Gordon Crovitz, *America's First Big Digital Defeat*, WALL ST. J. (Dec. 16, 2012), http://online.wsj.com/article/SB10001424127887323981504578181533577508260.html (arguing that the Internet is being progressively enclosed by authoritarian governments).

[163] *See Internet Censorship Listed, supra* note 120.

[164] *See, e.g.,* Conor Friedersdorf, *Google, Apple, and Microsoft Agree: NSA Spying Undermines Freedom*, ATLANTIC (Dec. 9, 2013), http://www.theatlantic.com/politics/archive/2013/12/google-apple-and-microsoft-agree-nsa-spying-undermines-freedom/282143/ (reporting that leading U.S. tech companies believe that NSA surveillance programs "threaten[] constitutional rights, individuals rights, and freedom."); Evgeny Morozov, *The Real Challenge for Internet Freedom? US Hypocrisy. And There's No App for That.*, CHRISTIAN SCI. MONITOR (Feb. 17, 2011), http://www.csmonitor.com/Commentary/Global-Viewpoint/2011/0217/The-real-challenge-for-Internet-freedom-US-hypocrisy.-And-there-s-no-app-for-that (fearing that the U.S. government's historical support of Arab dictators and local police may prove to be the most substantial challenge to the "Internet Freedom Agenda").

[165] *See* Franzese, *supra* note 52, at 41.

[166] *See* Osnos, *supra* note 162.

[167] *See* James Ball & Benjamin Gottlieb, *Iran Preparing Internal Version of Internet*, WASH. POST (Sept. 19, 2012), http://www.washingtonpost.com/world/national-security/iran-preparing-internal-version-of-internet/2012/09/19/79458194-01c3-11e2-b260-32f4a8db9b7e_story.html?wpmk=MK0000200; Timothy B. Lee, *Here's How Iran Censors the Internet*, WASH. POST (Aug. 15, 2013), http://www.washingtonpost.com/blogs/the-switch/wp/2013/08/15/heres-how-iran-censors-the-internet/. *Cf.* Golnaz Esfandiari, *Iran Official Slams Ahmadinejad-Era Censorship*, RADIO FREE EUR. (Oct. 9, 2013), http://www.rferl.org/content/iran-censorship-rights-ahmadinejad/25131517.html (reporting on a more moderate tone regarding censorship being set by the new Iranian administration).

[168] *See* DEIBERT, *supra* note 67, at 7; Marietje Schaake, *Stop Balkanizing the Internet*, HUFF. POST (July 17, 2012), http://www.huffingtonpost.com/marietje-schaake/stop-balkanizing-the-internet_b_1661164.html.

[169] This figure is based on the number of UN Member States, though the estimate varies depending on political factors. The U.S. Department of State, for example, recognizes 195 independent countries. *See Independent States in the World*, U.S. DEP'T ST., http://www.state.gov/s/inr/rls/4250.htm (last updated Dec. 9, 2013).

private computer networks, but the movement toward an increased role for national regulation in cyberspace will help define the future of Internet governance and the ways in which cybersecurity may be enhanced. Indeed, growing global backlash to NSA programs may have the perverse effect of pushing Internet governance more rapidly in a state-centric direction, undermining the Internet freedom agenda.[170]

The United States has been somewhat successful in advancing its view of cyberspace encapsulated in the International Strategy for Cyberspace and echoed in the 2011 G-8 summit communiqué, as discussed in Chapter 7.[171] Yet, despite its advocacy of an open and free global networked commons, as has been stated, censorship does happen even in the United States. For example, Google publishes information about governments that have requested information about its users or asked it to remove content.[172] According to a June 2012 Global Transparency Report, between July and December 2011, Google received 1,000 such requests total and complied with more than half of them.[173] These figures may be compared to the period from January to June 2013, in which Google received nearly 4,000 requests to remove almost 25,000 pieces of content – a quadrupling since 2011 and a 68 percent increase since late 2012.[174] Dorothy Chou, a senior policy analyst at Google, has written that governments asking the company to remove political content has become a trend in recent years.[175] This includes Western democracies like the United States, from which Google received more requests than any other country.[176]

Numerous statutes codify U.S. censorship practices. The Children's Online Protection Act, which subsidizes Internet access for schools, for example, requires content filtering in schools and public libraries.[177] The Supreme Court upheld the law on June 23, 2003.[178] The United States also attempted to control Internet pornography through the Communications Decency Act (CDA), which was

---

[170] *See, e.g.,* Amar Toor, *Will the Global NSA Backlash Break the Internet?*, VERGE (Nov. 8, 2013), http://www.theverge.com/2013/11/8/5080554/nsa-backlash-brazil-germany-raises-fears-of-internet-balkanization.

[171] *See* INTERNATIONAL STRATEGY FOR CYBERSPACE: PROSPERITY, SECURITY, AND OPENNESS IN A NETWORKED WORLD, WHITE HOUSE (2011), http://www.whitehouse.gov/sites/default/files/rss_viewer/international_strategy_for_cyberspace.pdf.

[172] *Government Removal Requests*, GOOGLE TRANSPARENCY REP., http://www.google.com/transparency report/removals/government (last visited Jan. 11, 2014).

[173] Nicole Perlroth, *Google Getting More Requests from Democracies to Censor*, N.Y. TIMES BITS BLOG (June 18, 2012, 6:30 PM), http://bits.blogs.nytimes.com/2012/06/18/google-getting-more-requests-from-democracies-to-censor.

[174] *Government Removal Requests Continue to Rise*, GOOGLE TRANSPARENCY REP. (Dec. 19, 2013), http://googleblog.blogspot.com/2013/12/transparency-report-government-removal.html.

[175] *Id.;* Dorothy Chou, *More Transparency into Government Requests*, GOOGLE (June 17, 2012), http://googleblog.blogspot.com/2012/06/more-transparency-into-government.html.

[176] *See* Perlroth, *supra* note 173; GOOGLE TRANSPARENCY REP., *supra* note 172 (noting that "[t]he number of content removal requests we received [from the United States] increased by 70% compared to the previous reporting period.").

[177] 20 U.S.C. § 9134(f) (2006); 47 U.S.C. § 254(h)(5).

[178] *See* United States v. Am. Library Ass'n, 539 U.S. 194, 214 (2003) (plurality opinion) (holding that required filtering under CIPA is not a violation of users' constitutional right to free speech).

passed by the U.S. Congress in 1996, but was struck down by the Supreme Court on First Amendment grounds in 1997.[179] From 1996 to 2002, four U.S. states – New York, New Mexico, Michigan, and Virginia – "have passed Internet censorship legislation restricting/banning online distribution of material deemed 'harmful to minors[,]'" but all this legislation was subsequently deemed unconstitutional.[180] However, other types of filtering designed to protect children and morality, national security, or enhance cybersecurity are commonplace,[181] though many controversies remain. A contemporary example is the live debate over the Cyber Intelligence Sharing and Protection Act (CISPA).[182] Another overarching issue is whether the Federal Communications Commission should regulate the Internet as it does radio and television.[183] The EU Commission has similarly grappled with how to approach net neutrality.[184] And aside from censorship, there is the contentious question over what role national governments should play in protecting critical infrastructure, which is addressed in Chapter 4. How these debates play out will affect both the degree and type of U.S. regulation in cyberspace, which in turn has an impact around the world given the interconnected regulatory landscape of cyberspace.

The Cost and Future of Internet Censorship

Before the question of whether some form of government regulation is the best way to enhance cybersecurity may be discussed, it is first important to consider if any government *can* effectively regulate cyberspace. Consider our current example of censorship. There are numerous ways to circumvent censorship practices.[185] Yet today politicians around the world are focusing on the Internet as an arena to be controlled,[186] ranging from the draconian policies in North Korea to more subtle

---

[179] Communications Decency Act of 1996, Pub. L. No. 104-104, tit. V, 110 Stat. 133, *invalidated by* Reno v. ACLU, 521 U.S. 844, 849 (1997).

[180] EFA, *supra* note 120.

[181] *See* Ronald Deibert, *Internet Filtering in the United States and Canada*, *in* ACCESS DENIED: THE PRACTICE AND POLICY OF GLOBAL INTERNET FILTERING 226, 226 (Ronald Deibert et al. eds., 2008).

[182] *See, e.g.*, Julian Sanchez, *CISPA Is Dead. Now Let's Do a Cybersecurity Bill Right*, WIRED (Apr. 26, 2013), http://www.wired.com/opinion/2013/04/cispas-dead-now-lets-resurrect-it/; *Even Worse Than SOPA: New CISPA Cybersecurity Bill Will Censor the Web*, RT (Apr. 20, 2012), http://rt.com/usa/news/cispa-bill-sopa-internet-175 (reporting on congressional efforts to draft legislation allowing greater government access to online data and the harsh response such efforts have received from open Internet advocacy groups).

[183] *See* Amy Schatz, *FCC Seeks Deal on Internet Rules*, WALL ST. J. (June 22, 2010), http://online.wsj.com/article/SB10001424052748704256304575321273903045994.html (describing how phone and cable companies are urging Congress to amend the Communications Act to prevent the FCC from regulating broadband lines); Nagesh & Kendall, *supra* note 5.

[184] *See Commission Communication, The Open Internet and Net Neutrality in Europe*, COM (2011) 222 final (Apr. 19, 2011), http://eur-lex.europa.eu/LexUriServ/LexUriServ.do?uri=COM:2011:0222:FIN:EN:PDF.

[185] *See, e.g.*, PEACE FIRE, http://www.peacefire.org/ (last visited Sept. 26, 2012) (self-described as "The world's largest distribution network for proxy sites to circumvent Internet censorship."); *Google Unveils Service*, *supra* note 117.

[186] *See* Guobin Yang, *China: Defending its Core Interests in the World – Part II*, YALE GLOBAL (Apr. 7, 2010), http://yaleglobal.yale.edu/content/china-defending-its-core-interest-world-part-ii.

censorship and filtering controls in countries like Thailand.[187] It is neither the case, then, that cyberspace is free and unregulated, nor that cyber regulation is always effective at reaching the desired ends.

Pervasive censorship comes with political and economic costs. Nations such as China may even suffer some long-term economic damage due to strict Internet policies.[188] Yet so far there is little sign of the wave of Internet censorship abating.[189] As states begin to further enclose the cyber pseudo commons, the "network effects," or the benefits generated by the interaction of individuals and organizations worldwide online, may diminish hampering prospects for cyber peace.[190] Ultimately, relying exclusively on governmental action, even where it is effective, risks prioritizing short-term national gains ahead of the long-term interest of the international community. As such, national regulation, far from being a domestic concern, becomes a global issue affecting the well-being of individuals and potentially the wealth of nations.

Cybersecurity is transnational by its nature, requiring international cooperation to thwart the tragedy of the cyber pseudo commons or anti-commons. Cyber threats are global threats, but nations do have a role in shaping the regulatory landscape. Predicting how these regimes will shape cyberspace, however, is difficult given the dynamic nature of the environment. The task is made harder still by the lack of verifiable data, as well as the multifaceted role played by the private sector in both Internet governance and cybersecurity. The next section builds from Chapter 1 in analyzing the role of the private sector in managing cyberspace, focusing on cybersecurity and whether the second classic solution to the tragedy of the commons, privatization, may be applicable in cyberspace.

THE ROLE OF THE PRIVATE SECTOR IN MANAGING CYBERSPACE

Although nations are increasingly asserting their regulatory authority in cyberspace, so too is the private sector, which remains in de facto control of much of the Internet infrastructure, including in the United States;[191] in fact, more than 90 percent of U.S. critical national infrastructure is in private hands.[192] Thus, *The Economist* is

---

[187] *See* Dave Lee, *North Korea: On the Net in World's Most Secretive Nation*, BBC (Dec. 10, 2012), http://www.bbc.co.uk/news/technology-20445632; Malcolm Crompton, *Big Data: Our Future or Censor?*, OPEN FORUM (May 17, 2011), http://www.openforum.com.au/content/big-data-our-future-or-censor.

[188] *See* Michael Wines, *Internet Censorship: China May Suffer Long-Term Economic Damage From Closing Down Google*, N.Y. TIMES (Mar. 25, 2010), http://www.nytimes.com/2010/03/24/world/asia/24china.html.

[189] *Cf.* Esfandiari, *supra* note 167.

[190] *See, e.g.*, Mark A. Lemley & David McGowan, *Legal Implications of Network Economic Effects*, 86(3) CAL. L. REV. 479, 480–82, 494–95 (1998); Toor, *supra* note 170.

[191] *See, e.g.*, Rajiv C. Shah & Jay P. Kesan, *The Privatization of the Internet's Backbone Network*, 51 J. BROADCASTING & ELECTRONIC MEDIA 93, 93–95 (2007) (chronicling a "transition of control from the government to the private sector," consistent with the historic prominence of private telecommunications networks in the United States).

[192] *See, e.g.*, ALFRED R. BERKELEY, III ET AL., NAT'L INFRASTRUCTURE ADVISORY COUNCIL, CRITICAL INFRASTRUCTURE PARTNERSHIP STRATEGIC ASSESSMENT: FINAL REPORT AND RECOMMENDATIONS

not entirely incorrect in describing the Internet as "a network of networks that are mostly privately owned."[193] There has been an ongoing debate about the enclosure of cyberspace and the imposition of private property rights to help improve security and respect these private relationships that form the foundation of Internet functionality.[194] But before the validity of that argument may be assessed, we must first lay down a foundation for analyzing property rights in cyberspace.

Little agreement exists as to the nature of property, and even less about what positive and negative rights property holders may enjoy – making the task of determining rights and responsibilities in cyberspace all the more difficult. However, it is nonetheless useful to consider some of the many views on property rights to determine whether the imposition of such rights can help address the tragedy of the cyber pseudo commons and enhance cybersecurity. According to Professor O. Lee Reed, theorists from Cicero to John Locke have failed to reach a common definition of "property."[195] Dictionary entries "define property as a thing or collection of things that one owns," or as "a bundle of 'sticklike rights.'"[196] The positive rights making up this bundle include the rights to possess, use, or to alienate property.[197] Yet it is not even agreed whether property is a natural right or an artificial creation of the state, or whether property rights lead to environmental degradation or are a primary way to stave off collective harm.[198] These vague, contradictory definitions of property help demonstrate the difficulty of reaching agreement on clarifying property rights in cyberspace. For the present purposes, however, property is defined as "an aggregate of rights that are guaranteed and protected by the government."[199] To exemplify, consider a toolbox. A person can reach in and pick out one or another of the available tools to build something that they want. In this analogy, each tool is a category of property rights, with the wrenches, screwdrivers, and hammers constituting the various rights, duties, and liabilities that together comprise property.[200]

---

3 (2008), http://www.dhs.gov/xlibrary/assets/niac/niac_critical_infrastructure_protection_assessment_final_report.pdf (arguing that the United States will be "safer, more secure, and resilient" as a result of increased cooperation between the public and private sectors).

[193] *The Threat From the Internet: Cyberwar*, ECONOMIST (July 1, 2010), http://www.economist.com/node/16481504.

[194] *See* Hunter, *supra* note 10, at 446. There is an analogy in this conceptualization of cyberspace to the nature of the firm, e.g., whether it is merely a "nexus of contracts" or a distinct "legal entity" with emergent properties that are greater than the sum of its parts. *See* TIMOTHY L. FORT, BUSINESS, INTEGRITY, AND PEACE: BEYOND GEOPOLITICAL AND DISCIPLINARY BOUNDARIES 79 (2011). Emergence is discussed further later in this chapter while the role that businesses can and should play in furthering cyber peace is analyzed in Chapter 5.

[195] O. Lee Reed, *What Is "Property"?*, 41 AM. BUS. L.J. 459, 459 n.34 (2004).

[196] *Id.* at 459 (citing WEBSTER'S THIRD NEW INTERNATIONAL DICTIONARY 1818 (Philip Babcock Gove ed., 1986)).

[197] *See* A. M. Honore, *Ownership, in* OXFORD ESSAYS IN JURISPRUDENCE 107, 113–20 (A. G. Guest ed., 1st ser., 1961).

[198] Reed, *supra* note 195, at 461–62.

[199] BLACK'S LAW DICTIONARY 1216 (6th ed. 1990).

[200] *See* STEVENSON, *supra* note 82, at 50 (discussing property rights from an economics perspective).

Property, like cyberspace itself, is an important and complex concept. But how and when do property rights emerge in cyberspace, and what role might they play in enhancing cybersecurity? Some economists argue that property rights begin when benefits exceed costs.[201] The extent to which property rights may be enforced varies with competing claims to communal rights, as well as diverging cultural norms. "Tragedy" can occur whenever institutions are ill-suited to the environment or are outpaced by social changes, creating governance gaps. Proponents of privatization assert that it can forestall such a tragedy by incentivizing the rational exploitation of a resource.[202] In theory, private property rights give the owner a pecuniary interest in refraining from destructive practices.[203] In the cyber context, however, property rights are malleable. Applying property laws originally created to govern fox hunting to cyber attacks can be "unnecessary, harmful, and wrong."[204] For example, fully privatizing cyberspace through the granting of property rights risks turning it into a medium like television, sacrificing innovation even as it clarifies ownership.[205] Yet private-sector representatives have been successful at convincing judges that property rights do exist online such as through extending the law of trespass, and so by "tiny, almost imperceptible steps, commercial operators are enclosing cyberspace"[206] – potentially leading to the creation of a cyber anti-commons previously discussed. As a compromise position, some scholars call for the creation of collaborative cybersecurity partnerships, in which limited property rights are granted to realize appropriate returns from private security expenditures and ward off free riders.[207] This approach recognizes elements of cybersecurity as a public good, but implementing it requires an analysis of public-private partnerships, which are introduced in this chapter and examined more fully in Chapter 5.

The subject of property rights in cyberspace is a book in itself, but the purpose here is merely to introduce the topic and demonstrate the extent to which property rights can and do exist in cyberspace. Ralph Waldo Emerson remarked,

---

[201] Harold Demsetz, *Toward a Theory of Property Rights*, 57(2) AM. ECON. REV. 347, 348 (1967).

[202] *See* Minjeong Kim, *The Representation of Two Competing Visions on the Fundamentals of Copyright: A Content Analysis of Associated Press News Coverage on Copyright, 2004–2009*, 16 COMM. L. & POL'Y 49, 62 (2011).

[203] *See* David Lebang, *Property Rights, Democracy, and Economic Growth*, 49 POL. RES. Q. 5, 5 (1996) (arguing that "economies of nations that protect property rights grow more rapidly than those of nations that do not protect property rights.").

[204] Hunter, *supra* note 10, at 518–19 (making reference to cyber attacks in the Article but primarily discussing the imposition of property rights as being an incorrect policy choice given the potential for creating an anti-commons).

[205] *See* News Release, Stanford Univ. News Serv., Law Professor Examines Property Rights in Cyberspace (Apr. 3, 1995), http://news.stanford.edu/pr/95/950403Arc5300.html (classifying audience commodification as a consequence of private ownership).

[206] Hunter, *supra* note 10, at 445, 519.

[207] *See* Bruce H. Kobayashi, *An Economic Analysis of the Private and Social Costs of the Provision of Cybersecurity and Other Public Security Goods*, 14 SUP. CT. ECON. REV. 261, 276–78 (2006) (citing the exclusion of non-payers attempting to "free ride" as essential to the formation of successful security expenditures); *Cybersecurity: Next Steps*, *supra* note 55.

"As long as our civilization is essentially one of property, of fences, of exclusiveness, it will be mocked by delusions."[208] Whether establishing more property rights in the name of better security is such a delusion depends on the ability of the private sector to enhance cybersecurity. Thus, the question becomes: has a relatively privatized Internet increased or decreased cybersecurity? And can the situation be improved through partnering with governments? It is essential that government be both a regulator and a resource to at-risk companies. However, there is an argment to be made that neither the government nor the private sector should be put in exclusive control of managing cyberspace because this could sacrifice both liberty and innovation on the mantle of security, potentially leading to neither.

The history of the Internet is full of companies that tried to dominate different aspects of cyberspace: "Netscape tried to own the homepage; Amazon.com tried to dominate retail; Yahoo, the navigation of the Web."[209] Google is the culmination and irony of this process, both promoting and partially presiding over an open web.[210] This follows a well-established trend from other industries, such as telecommunications. After thousands of companies vied for market share in the early twentieth century, Bell (AT&T) controlled nearly all U.S. long distance lines and 79 percent of its telephones by 1909.[211] Now the Internet has matured and a small cohort of companies is similarly influencing its operation and evolution. Take Facebook, which decides what content is appropriate for its user community through a governance regime that handles more than two million reports per week.[212] According to Jud Hoffman, Facebook's global policy manager, creating and managing rules for the reporting process "is not that different from a legislative and judicial process all rolled up into one[.]"[213] In some ways, this top-down "technocratic, developer-king" model is beating out a democratic bottom-up management approach as demonstrated by the fact that Facebook took away the right for its users to vote on changes to the firm's policies in December 2012,[214] leading to calls of nationalizing

---

[208] RALPH WALDO EMERSON & FRANK DAVIDSON, NAPOLEON; OR, THE MAN OF THE WORLD 63 (1947), http://user.xmission.com/~seldom74/emerson/napoleon.html.

[209] Anderson & Wolff, *supra* note 19.

[210] *Id.*; *Google Unveils Service, supra* note 117.

[211] *See* MILTON L. MUELLER, JR. & MILTON MUELLER, UNIVERSAL SERVICE: COMPETITION, INTERCONNECTION, AND MONOPOLY IN THE MAKING 68, 73, 110 (1997).

[212] *See* Alexis Madrigal, *The Perfect Technocracy: Facebook's Attempt To Create Good Government for 900 Million People*, ATLANTIC, (June 19, 2012), http://www.theatlantic.com/technology/archive/2012/06/governing-the-social-network/258484 (outlining the intricacies of Facebook's reporting system, which channels reports through a series of processes to create refined "categories of problems"); *cf.* Janet Tavokoli, *Facebook's Fake Numbers: 'One Billion Users' May Be Less Than 500 Million*, HUFF POST (Dec. 11, 2012), http://www.huffingtonpost.com/janet-tavakoli/facebooks-fake-numbers-on_b_2276515 .html (critiquing the published number of Facebook statistis as unrealistic given the high volume of fraudulent accounts).

[213] Madrigal, *supra* note 212.

[214] *Id.* (reasoning that a lack of "digital citizenship" allows Facebook to side-step the democratic process in favor of efficiency); Jessica Guynn, *Facebook Polls Close: Facebook Wins Privacy Vote*

the social network.[215] Google is similarly seeking to consolidate its power by protecting its search engine results as First Amendment speech akin to editorial decisions made by newspaper staff. [216] If such decisions are "speech," Professor Tim Wu wrote in a *New York Times* editorial, then this risks "making the First Amendment . . . a formidable anti-regulation tool."[217] As Chapter 5 will argue, private companies taking on some responsibility for self-governance is an important step in better managing cyber attacks. Successful polycentric governance, though, requires balance lest one stakeholder, be it nations or the private sector, reshape the Internet to suit its own interests.

The question of how best to handle the private sector's role in cyberspace is one of the hardest challenges in Internet governance. Part of the problem is that, in the quest for maximum profit, some businesses sometimes do not take necessary security precautions, thereby leaving them open to attacks that exploit old vulnerabilities, as is explored in Chapters 3 and 5. This may be especially evident when the cost of cyber attacks are not internalized. But it is not that simple given that, even with an array of cybersecurity best practices in place, firms in some cases face state and state-sponsored cyber attackers with deep pockets, time, and patience.[218] As a result, some are skeptical about the free market's ability to enhance cybersecurity and call for increased national regulation, even as others question regulators' ability to keep pace with the rapidly changing cyber threat matrix. A divide persists between those favoring a regulatory regime, requiring firms to enhance their cybersecurity, and proponents of a voluntary scheme, featuring potentially an expanded R&D tax credit, information sharing, and cyber risk insurance.[219] The use of public-private partnerships (P3) to identify and implement security best practices is an important aspect of either a free market or a regulatory approach. Such P3s are commonly seen as part of the solution to cyber threat management and involve the federal government and private sector sharing information, while also encouraging companies to guard their networks.[220] The Obama administration has embraced the

---

    by a Landslide, L.A. TIMES, Dec. 10, 2012, http://www.latimes.com/business/technology/la-fi-tn-facebook-polls-close-facebook-wins-privacy-vote-by-a-landslide-20121210,0,2513523.story.

[215] *See* Philip N. Noward, *Let's Nationalize Facebook*, SLATE (Aug. 16, 2012), http://www.slate.com/articles/technology/future_tense/2012/08/facebook_should_be_nationalized_to_protect_user_rights_.html.

[216] Eugene Volokh & Donald M. Falk, *First Amendment Protection for Search Engine Search Results – White Paper Commissioned by Google* (SSRN Working Paper, 2012), http://papers.ssrn.com/sol3/papers.cfm?abstract_id=2055364.

[217] Tim Wu, *Free Speech for Computers?* N.Y. TIMES, June 19, 2012, at A29.

[218] *See, e.g., Cybersecurity: Next Steps, supra* note 55.

[219] *See* H. Republican Cybersecurity Task Force, 112th Cong., Recommendations of the House Republican Cybersecurity Task Force 5, 8, 14 (2011) (recommending the use of voluntary incentives to improve cybersecurity, such as expanded tax credits and insurance programs).

[220] *See* INTELLIGENCE & NAT'L SEC. ALLIANCE, ADDRESSING CYBER SECURITY THROUGH PUBLIC-PRIVATE PARTNERSHIP: AN ANALYSIS OF EXISTING MODELS 3, 12 (2009), http://www.insaonline.org/CMDownload.aspx?ContentKey=e1f31be3-e110-41b2-aa0c-966020051f5c&ContentItemKey=161e015c-670f-449a-8753-689cbc3de85e [hereinafter ADDRESSING CYBER SECURITY] (presenting government

P3 concept, although it is largely up to Congress to shape how such relationships evolve, as discussed in Chapter 5.

Given the extent of private regulation and control, the issue of private-sector management in cyberspace is a critical topic. Property rights exist online and are a potential solution to the tragedy of the cyber pseudo commons, so long as free riding and enforcement concerns can be overcome. However, both privatization and nationalization have drawbacks and benefits as applied to enhancing cybersecurity. A third, often overlooked solution to the tragedy of the commons is common property, which involves well-defined "group control over the resource" leading to "the balancing of benefits and costs" through rules regulating joint use.[221] Such a system has been applied to the deep seabed to an extent through the CMH concept.[222] We next consider the applicability of this approach to enhancing cybersecurity, couched within a broader discussion of sovereignty in cyberspace.

SOVEREIGNTY IN THE CYBER PSEUDO COMMONS

Cyberspace is not an untamed wilderness. Enclosure is increasing with several dozen nations now routinely filtering traffic, threatening the dawn of a new age of Internet sovereignty.[223] Similarly, Internet freedom is often honored more in the breach than in the observance, even in the United States. Thus, John Perry Barlow's maxim in his *Declaration of the Independence of Cyberspace*, "Governments of the Industrial World, you weary giants of flesh and steel . . . [,] [y]ou have no sovereignty where we gather,"[224] seems to have been debunked. Or has it? Cyberspace retains elements of the knowledge commons from which it originated, even as technology works to both enable and undermine censors. The choice between Internet sovereignty and Internet freedom, then, is a false one. There is a middle ground of conceptualizing cyberspace as a dynamic pseudo commons in which many public and private regulators compete and cooperate at multiple levels. Yet if the cyber pseudo commons is to thrive and cybersecurity is to be strengthened, then multilateral collaboration must play an important part. The justifications for regulating cyberspace globally need to be considered as a prerequisite.

---

involvement, in addition to private-sector participation, as essential to the legitimacy and effectiveness of a public-private partnership for cybersecurity) [hereinafter *Addressing Cyber Security*].

[221] *See* STEVENSON, *supra* note 82, at 3.

[222] *See* Anne L. Hollick & R. N. Cooper, *Global Commons: Can They Be Managed?, in* THE ECONOMICS OF TRANSNATIONAL COMMONS 141, 143–44 (Partha Dasgupta et al. eds., 1997).

[223] *See* Johathan Zittrain & John Palfrey, *Introduction, in* ACCESS DENIED: THE PRACTICE AND POLICY OF GLOBAL INTERNET FILTERING 1, 2 (John G. Palfrey et al. eds., 2008); James A. Lewis, *Why Privacy and Cyber Security Clash, in* AMERICA'S CYBER FUTURE: SECURITY AND PROSPERITY IN THE INFORMATION AGE 123, 138 (Kristin M. Lord & Travis Sharp eds., CNAS, 2011) (predicting the extension of sovereign control by governments into cyberspace).

[224] Christopher Shea, *Sovereignty in Cyberspace*, BOSTON GLOBE (Jan. 15, 2006), http://worldtradelaw .typepad.com/ielpblog/2006/01/sovereigntyjuri.html.

At least two options exist. First, the international community could reach an understanding that cyberspace is an arena over which nations can and should exercise sovereignty, such as through the effects doctrine.[225] Second, the international community could treat cyberspace as a true global commons.[226] The former interpretation provides a firm legal grounding on which an international regime could be built. The latter notion is increasingly unlikely given state practice, but a compromise position may be found by examining the CHM concept.

Option 1: Regulating Cyberspace through the Effects Doctrine

The general principle of sovereignty – that territorial integrity be upheld and a state maintain its monopoly on coercive violence – is fundamental to international law and relations as previously mentioned,[227] but does not apply as directly to IT. That would seem to hinder the regulation of cyberspace. As a practical matter, however, concerns over sovereignty should not forestall international action on cyber attacks for at least two reasons. First, at least one entity controls the physical infrastructure of the Internet at any given point since the networks that comprise the Interent are located in or fall under the jurisdiction of one nation or another.[228] Sovereignty then "exists for all of the networks that a cyber attack may use to reach its target . . . [if] only [for] a few milliseconds."[229] Second, an array of national and international laws already apply to cyberspace as explored in Chapter 6. For example, it is well established in international law that the effects doctrine permits the regulation of activities that impact a state's territory.[230] Taken to its extreme, some argue that this notion should be expanded to include discussions of a Cyber Monroe Doctrine.[231] Yet even those who favor a state-centric approach to cybersecurity have noted the

---

[225] *See* 22 U.S.C. § 6081(9) (2006) (recognizing the international norm that a nation can "provide for rules of law with respect to conduct outside its territory that has or is intended to have substantial effect within its territory").

[226] *See e.g.*, James Boyle, *The Second Enclosure Movement and the Construction of the Public Domain*, 66 LAW & CONTEMP. PROBS. 33, 37 (2003) (exploring the CHM concept through the example of the human genome project).

[227] *See* S. A. Korff, *The Problem of Sovereignty*, 17 AM. POL. SCI. REV. 404 (1923); John Jackson, *Sovereignty-Modern: A New Approach to an Outdated Concept*, 97 AM. J. INT'L L 782, 782–85 (2003).

[228] *See* James A. Lewis, *The "Korean" Cyber Attacks and Their Implications for Cyber Conflict*, CTR. STRATEGIC & INT'L STUD. (Oct. 2009), at 3.

[229] *Id.*

[230] *See* 22 U.S.C. § 6081(9) (2006).

[231] *See Reviewing the Federal Cybersecurity Mission: Hearing Before the Subcomm. on Emerging Threats, Cybersecurity, & Sci. & Tech. of the H. Comm. on Homeland Sec.*, 111th Cong. 32 (2009) (statement of Mary Ann Davidson, Chief Security Officer, Oracle Corp.) (calling for a policy analogous to the Monroe Doctrine, because "we need a doctrine for how we intercede in cyberspace that covers both offense and defense and maps to existing legal and societal principles in the offline world."). The Monroe Doctrine announced that the Americas were closed to further European colonization and that any such attempt by a European power would negatively impact U.S. national security. *See* GADDIS SMITH, THE LAST YEARS OF THE MONROE DOCTRINE, 1945–1993, at 3 (1995) (explaining the purpose of the Monroe Doctrine and noting that it was a "warning against foreign intrusion").

important role the international community plays in enhancing cybersecurity.[232] To that end, cyberspace may also be regulated to a greater degree through common property concepts such as the CHM, but to the extent that cyberspace is a commons, it is one facing unique challenges and thus requiring novel regulatory solutions.

Option 2: Regulating Cyberspace through the CHM Concept

There is arguably insufficient state practice to support the view that cyberspace is a single networked global commons belonging to all users. Nevertheless, it is a popular sentiment, even in China. The Internet is "the common wealth of humankind," according to the *China Daily*.[233] Because there is not yet widespread agreement on the nature of cyberspace,[234] it stands to reason that deciding on a legal framework for governing cyberspace is a challenge to say the least. That is why a nuanced approach is important. The Internet infrastructure located within a state's territory is subject to that state's territorial sovereignty, as is infrastructure located on the deep seabed or in outer space.[235] However, control over the content of cyberspace is another matter, but even there some overlap may be inevitable.[236]

Some have advocated for applying the common property CHM concept to help manage the cyber pseudo commons. Neither scholars nor policymakers have agreed on a common understanding of the CHM, but drawing from the available literature, a working definition would likely comprise five main elements.[237] First, there can be no private or public appropriation; no one legally owns common heritage spaces.[238] As applied to cyberspace, this could mean that although both the private and public sectors control Internet infrastructure, they cannot actually own Internet content. However, there is evidence in the form of scholarly commentary and state practice that this prohibition on appropriation should not be viewed as a significant impediment to regulation, and that instead "non-exclusive use" may be "better [suited] to the practical reality."[239] Second, "representatives from all nations" must work together to manage global common pool resources.[240] As collective management is unfeasible, a specialized agency must be set up "to coordinate shared management policies,"[241] such as the International Seabed Authority that manages deep seabed

---

[232] Interview with Richard Clarke, chairman for Good Harbor Consulting, in Wash., D.C. (Jan. 4, 2011).

[233] Tang Lan, *Reality of the Virtual World*, CHINA DAILY (July 16, 2011), www.chinadaily.com.cn/opinion/2011-07/16/content_12915072.htm.

[234] *See* Rajnovic, *supra* note 16.

[235] *See* Lewis, *supra* note 228, at 3.

[236] *See id.*

[237] *See* Jennifer Frakes, *The Common Heritage of Mankind Principle and the Deep Seabed, Outer Space, and Antarctica: Will Developed and Developing Nations Reach a Compromise?*, 21 WIS. INT'L L.J. 409, 411–13 (2003).

[238] *Id.* at 411.

[239] *See* BASLAR, *supra* note 35, at 90, 235 (arguing that the CHM concept should not be applicable "in certain circumstances where the object . . . is a resource rather than an area.").

[240] Frakes, *supra* note 237, at 412.

[241] *Id.* at 412.

mining.[242] The closest analogues in the cyber context would be ICANN, the IGF, or possibly the ITU, but expanding the mandate of these organizations or creating a new body is politically divisive, as is explored in Chapter 7.[243] Third, all nations must "actively share" in the "benefits acquired from exploitation of the resources from the common heritage region."[244] This aspect could arguably be fulfilled through the nonprofit characteristic of the current system as embodied in ICANN combined with efforts to spread Internet access and encourage multi-stakeholder governance. Fourth, there can be no weaponry or military installations established in common heritage areas as they should be used for "peaceful purposes."[245] Cyber weapons and conflicts, however, are already widespread, though what constitutes "peaceful" differs depending on the common heritage region in question helping to inform the concept of cyber peace.[246] Finally, the commons "must be preserved for the benefit of future generations."[247] IPv6 is being rolled out to assist in this regard, given that IPv4 addresses are rapidly running out with rationing underway in Europe as of September 2012.[248] Consequently, while the CHM concept does have some utility as an organizing concept in Internet governance, its practical use is limited in light of its relative decline in popularity and continuing ambiguity.[249]

Although cyberspace has shaken the connection between territory and sovereignty, it is clear that nations are shaping cyberspace. In a "networked world, no island is an island[,]" meaning "that threats to [the] social order are [no longer easily] identifiable as "either internal (crime/terrorism) or external (war)."[250] Concerns over sovereignty should not preclude regulation.[251] Nations have the right to protect

---

[242] *See* United Nations Convention on the Law of the Sea, art. 137, Dec. 10, 1982, 1833 U.N.T.S. 397; David Shukman, *Deep Sea Mining 'Gold Rush' Moves Closer*, BBC (May 17, 2013), http://www.bbc.co .uk/news/science-environment-22546875 (reporting on a UN plan to regulate deep seabed mining).

[243] *Cf.* Toor, *supra* note 170 (noting the increased likelihood of a change in Internet governance structures subsequent to NSA spying revelations).

[244] Frakes, *supra* note 237, at 412.

[245] *Id.* at 413.

[246] *See* Antarctic Treaty art. 1(1), Dec. 1, 1959, 12 U.S.T. 794, 402 U.N.T.S. 72 (defining "peaceful use" in Antarctica as banning "any measures of a military nature. . . ."); Treaty on Principles Governing the Activities of States in the Exploration and Use of Outer Space, Including the Moon and Other Celestial Bodies, art. 4, Jan. 27, 1967, 18 U.S.T. 2410, 610 U.N.T.S. 205 (entered into force Oct. 10, 1967); BASLAR, *supra* note 35, at 106.

[247] Frakes, *supra* note 237, at 413.

[248] *See* Mark Ward, *Europe Hits Old Internet Address Limits*, BBC (Sept. 14, 2012), http://www.bbc .com/news/technology-19600718.

[249] *See, e.g.*, Antonio Segura-Serrano, *Internet Regulation and the Role of International Law*, 10 MAX PLANCK UNYB 192, 260 (2006) (arguing that the CHM concept applies "reasonably well to the Internet's core resources" but noting that it "has not even been mentioned to date" in the context of Internet governance negotiations). *But see* AHMAD KAMAL, THE LAW OF CYBER-SPACE: AN INVITATION TO THE TABLE OF NEGOTIATIONS 4 (2013) (arguing that "cyber-space is part of the common heritage of mankind."). However, the CHM concept could be given new life if emerging markets such as Brazil that have historically favored the CHM concept in certain contexts embrace it during coming rounds of Internet governance negotiations. *See* BASLAR, *supra* note 35, at 129.

[250] Susan Brenner, *At Light Speed: Attribution and Response to Cybercrime/Terrorism/Warfare*, 97 J. CRIM. L. & CRIMINOLOGY 379, 382 (2007).

[251] *See* Jackson, *supra* note 227, at 790.

their sovereign interests through the effects doctrine. Yet, given the interconnected nature of cyberspace, it would be prudent to also deepen multilateral collaboration and foster cyber peace such as through a modified CHM concept built on the emerging tenants of sustainable development.[252] This system is reminiscent of John Herz's notion of "neoterritorality," whereby sovereign states recognize their common interests, such as the public good of cybersecurity, while also mutually respecting one another's independence and the increasing importance of non-state actors.[253] The Obama administrations' Cyberspace Strategy's inclusion of multi-stakeholder governance may be a step toward this approach,[254] and discussed in Chapter 7. Under this interpretation, sovereignty should be conceived not as an application of "state *control*" but of "state *authority*."[255] In the context of cyberspace, this authority is relatively widespread including private, national, and international actors, all of which must work together to regulate cyberspace and enhance cybersecurity.

In summary, the choice between Internet sovereignty and freedom is indeed a false one. The cyber pseudo commons is neither a simple extension of national territory, nor a global commons free from state control. Conceptualizing such a dynamic environment requires an equally complex model of governance. Thus, this chapter concludes by analyzing the applicability of polycentric governance in the cyber pseudo commons and its capacity to promote cyber peace.

POLYCENTRIC REGULATION IN CYBERSPACE: A FRAMEWORK FOR ANALYZING CYBERSECURITY CHALLENGES

According to Professor Andrew Murray, cyberspace is a uniquely malleable environment and its "stratified . . . structure [underscores] a particularly complex regulatory environment, making . . . mapping or forecasting" the effects of regulations "especially difficult."[256] Commentators such as Professors David Post and David

---

[252] For example, the International Law Association's New Delhi Declaration on Principles of International Law Relating to Sustainable Development resembles the principles comprising the CHM concept. Both endorse non-appropriation, common management, equitable benefit sharing, peaceful use, and preservation. *See* Int'l Law Ass'n, *New Delhi Declaration on Principles of International Law Relating to Sustainable Development* CISDL (Apr. 2, 2002), www.cisdl.org/tribunals/pdf/NewDelhiDeclaration .pdf. This underscores the degree to which the core features of the CHM are alive and well in the sustainable development movement, which in turn enjoys comparative popularity across a broad spectrum of stakeholders and could be used as a foundation for new multilateral Internet governance and cybersecurity insturments. *See* Gabcikovo-Nagymaros Project (Hung. v. Slovk.) 1997 I.C.J. 88, 92 (Sept. 25) (separate opinion of Vice-President Weeramantry) (noting the "wide and general acceptance by the global community" of sustainable development).

[253] *See* Mark W. Zacher, *The Decaying Pillars of the Westphalian Temple: Implications for International Order and Governance, in* GOVERNANCE WITHOUT GOVERNMENT: ORDER AND CHANGE IN WORLD POLITICS 58, 100 (James N. Rosenau & Ernst-Otto Czempiel eds., 1992).

[254] *See* INTERNATIONAL STRATEGY FOR CYBERSPACE, *supra* note 171, at 10, 12, 23–24.

[255] Janice Thomson, *State Sovereignty in International Relations: Bridging the Gap Between Theory and Empirical Research*, 39 INT'L STUDIES Q. 213, 216 (1995) (emphasis added).

[256] MURRAY, *supra* note 12, at 52.

Johnson have turned to abstract models to help map cyberspace because a change in one regulatory framework can have unintended repercussions elsewhere given the "astronomical number of different configurations. . . ."[257] Many of these consequences may be minimal in the physical world, but not so in cyberspace given that layering creates "an exponentially complex system. . . ."[258] Does this mean that Internet freedom advocates are then correct? Is effective cyber regulation impossible? Not necessarily. In fact, the malleability of cyberspace can help make it regulatable.[259] Mapping cyber regulation, however, has proven challenging given that it requires not only recording the status quo, but also allowing for regulatory flux stemming from myriad variables including advancing technology.[260] For regulators, this suggests that they can never be sure of the outcome of an intervention, making already complex tasks such as enhancing cybersecurity all the more difficult.[261]

In response, some commentators, including Professor Murray, have argued for adopting dynamic regulatory models such as symbiotic regulation to help better understand this complex environment, suggesting that "harmony . . . may be harnessed" in even a chaotic regulatory system.[262] Other scholars have turned to complexity theory as well as systems theory, the latter of which was developed in the biological context to describe the relationships between parts of a system, such as the human body.[263] Even under these approaches, however, changing one element of the system can have "ripple effects" throughout,[264] a phenonemon also noted by Professor Lon Fuller, an advocate of taking a polycentric approach to better understand such issues.[265]

Most definitions of law, including Professor Fuller's description of law as "the enterprise of subjecting human conduct to the governance of rules,"[266] allow for overlapping regulatory systems. Professor Fuller himself noted: "Multiple systems do exist and have in history been more common than unitary systems."[267] This is a critical aspect of understanding polycentric regulation in cyberspace since it is not the case that states, nor any other entity, enjoy sole rulemaking powers online.[268]

---

[257] David G. Post & David R. Johnson, *Chaos Prevailing on Every Continent: Toward a New Theory of Decentralized Decision-Making in Complex Systems*, 73 CHI.-KENT L. REV. 1055, 1059, 1070–71, n. 36 (1998) (citing F. A. HAYEK, STUDIES IN PHILOSOPHY, POLITICS AND ECONOMICS 27 (1967)).

[258] MURRAY, *supra* note 12, at 53.

[259] *Id.* at 52–53.

[260] *See id.* at 27 (citing W. ROSS ASHBY, AN INTRODUCTION TO CYBERNETICS 251 (1956)); LESSIG, *supra* note 77, at 71 (arguing for the greater inclusion of technology into regulatory discourse).

[261] *See* MURRAY, *supra* note 12, at 27.

[262] *Id.* at xii, 250.

[263] *See id.* at 26–26 (citing Post & Johnson, *supra* note 257).

[264] Post & Johnson, *supra* note 257, at 1070–71.

[265] *See* MURRAY, *supra* note 12, at 27 (citing Lon Fuller, *The Forms and Limits of Adjudication*, 92 HARV. L. REV. 353 (1978)).

[266] *Id.* at 47 (quoting LON FULLER, THE MORALITY OF LAWS 106 (1964)).

[267] *Id.* (quoting FULLER, *supra* note 266, at 123).

[268] *Id.*

Some commentators define polycentric as analogous to "non-statist law,"[269] while others consider it as "the enterprise of subjecting human conduct to the governance of external controls whether state or non-state, intended or unintended."[270] However, such definitions miss some of the unique aspects of polycentric governance as the term is used here, including its emphasis on self-organization and the notion that "diverse organizations" and governments working at "multiple levels" can create policies that "increase levels of cooperation . . . [and] compliance. . . ."[271] In order to understand the benefits and drawbacks of a polycentric approach in conceptualizing cybersecurity, however, it is first necessary to briefly review the literature on regimes.

Regulatory Approaches in Cyberspace

Commons are not necessarily anarchic systems, but instead are often complex social systems featuring their own norms, rules, and laws.[272] Regulatory theorists have identified an array of modalities that may be used to control patterns of behavior within such complex systems, including cyberspace.[273] These include strategies ranging from command and control to self-regulation including relying on markets to reach a desired outcome,[274] such as enhancing cybersecurity. Professor Lessig identifies four modalities of cyber regulation: architecture, law, the market, and norms that "may be used individually or collectively" by policymakers.[275] These modalities roughly mirror the remaining structure of this book, focusing on architecture in Chapter 3, the market in Chapter 5, and laws and norms in Chapters 4, 6, and 7.[276] Another more general model of regulation is also among the oldest – the public interest approach – which recognizes that state action is needed to correct market failures and manage public goods such as cybersecurity.[277] Despite their utility, though, each of these approaches has drawbacks. The public interest approach, for example, assumes that

---

[269] *Id.* at 7 n.15 (citing Tom W. Bell, *Polycentric Law*, 7(1) HUMANE STUD. REV. 4 (1991–1992).

[270] *Id.* at 47.

[271] Ostrom, *supra* note 61, at 12–13 (listing four broad characteristics for when cooperation governing the global commons is most likely to occur, including when: "(1) Many of those affected have agreed on the need for changes in behavior and see themselves as jointly sharing responsibility for future outcomes; (2) The reliability and frequency of information about the phenonena of concern are relatively high; (3) Participants know who else has agreed to change behavior and that their conformance is being monitored; and (4) Communication occurs among at least subsets of participants"); Robert O. Keohane & David G. Victor, *The Regime Complex for Climate Change*, 9 PERSP. ON POL. 7, 7–9 (2011).

[272] *See* Johnson & Post, *supra* note 8, at 1393.

[273] *See* MURRAY, *supra* note 12, at 29, 37.

[274] *See id.* at 28 (comparing how the regulatory strategies modeled by professors Baldwin and Cave, Thatcher, and Lessig might be applied to cyberspace); ROBERT BALDWIN & MARTIN CAVE, UNDERSTANDING REGULATION 34 (1999) (categorizing regulatory strategies based on whether governments use resources to command, to deploy wealth, to harness markets, to inform, to act directly, or to confer protected rights).

[275] MURRAY, *supra* note 12, at 28; *see* LESSIG, *supra* note 77, at 71.

[276] MURRAY, *supra* note 12, at 35–42.

[277] *Id.* at 35–36.

governments enjoy "more information than other actors[,]"[278] which is not always the case in the cybersecurity context given issues of disclosure and information sharing. Other theories mistakenly assume that a single actor may effectively regulate cyberspace. But as has been shown, national regulation by itself, for example, can be ineffective given the global nature and environmental malleability of cyberspace. Consider the EU Directive on Privacy and Electronic Communications, which has had only a "limited impact on the number of spam messages," as has the U.S. CAN-SPAM Act.[279] The question then becomes how to fashion a regime by which the best of these diverse approaches could be used to better manage cyber attacks.

According to Professor Oran Young, "[r]egimes are social institutions governing the actions of those involved . . . [T]hey are practices consisting of recognized roles linked together by clusters of rules or conventions governing relations among the occupants of these roles."[280] Regimes thus have two primary and at times contradictory effects. First, they "constrain [the] policy options" of actors.[281] Second, they create rights,[282] such as the right to maintain a domain name. Nations respond first and foremost to the concerns of domestic politics when deciding the composition of a new regime,[283] although scientific uncertainty and advancing technology also play important roles in shaping regimes.[284] Yet even with a high degree of scientific and political agreement, regulatory action may still be delayed as a result of differing incentive structures among diverse stakeholders including states, non-governmental organizations, and "epistemic communities," which are "policy networks formed by . . . experts . . . specializing in a particular policy area."[285] This can lead to deadlock, and even if these diverse groups can agree on a new regime, the result may still be suboptimal for at least three reasons. First, within the UN system, consensus is often required in practice by agreements, although not as a matter of UN procedural law.[286] This can lead to codification of the lowest common denominator regulatory scheme given that a minority, or even a single nation, can stall progress indefinitely. Second, nations may fail to ratify the treaties even in situations of strong domestic support.[287] Third, even if ratification occurs, treaty enforcement remains a problem

[278] *Id.* at 35.

[279] *Id.* at 33; Council Directive 2002/58, 2002 O.J. (L 201) (EC); CAN-SPAM Act, 15 U.S.C. §§ 7701–7713 (2006). *Cf.* Gareth Morgan, *Global Spam E-mail Levels Suddenly Fall*, BBC (Jan. 6, 2011), http://www .bbc.co.uk/news/technology-12126880 (noting a decline in global spam messaging, but reporting that "the reasons for the decline are not fully understood. . . . ").

[280] ORAN R. YOUNG, INTERNATIONAL COOPERATION: BUILDING REGIMES FOR NATIONAL RESOURCES AND THE ENVIRONMENT 12–13 (1989).

[281] *See* BUCK, *supra* note 38, at 30.

[282] *See id.*

[283] *See* Keohane & Victor, *supra* note 271, at 16.

[284] *See* BUCK, *supra* note 38, at 7.

[285] *Id.* at 8.

[286] *See* Eilene Galloway, *Consensus Decisionmaking by the United Nations Committee on the Peaceful Uses of Outer Space*, 7 J. SPACE L. 3, 3–4 (1979).

[287] *See, e.g.*, Liz Kilmas, *Republicans Defeat Ratification of the U.N.'s 'Rights of Persons with Disabilities' Treaty in Senate*, BLAZE (Dec. 4, 2012), http://www.theblaze.com/stories/2012/12/04/republicans-defeat-ratification-of-the-u-n-s-rights-of-persons-with-disabilities-treaty-in-senate/ (reporting on the

across many fields of international law.[288] Various strategies may be employed to address these problems, such as negotiating treaties with incentives or sanctions to promote compliance, but such strategies can be politically unpopular or insufficient. Instead, regime complexes are formed as interim responses to help manage global collective action problems such as cyber attacks.[289]

Regime complexes are created when several different regimes "coexist in the same issue area without clear hierarchy," which can be caused by different and continuously evolving political coalitions.[290] Given the multipolar state of international relations, "loosely coupled" regime complexes enjoy advantages over unitary regimes such as some UN consensus-driven multilateral treaties.[291] Building institutions is costly, and thus, leaders who invest in such efforts often find it easier to work in smaller "clubs," such as the Major Emitters Forum comprised of the largest greenhouse gas emitters,[292] rather than through forums with universal membership like the UN Framework Convention on Climate Change.[293] Under these varying frameworks, the United Nations may play the role of an umbrella organization, or one component within a regime complex, rather than being at the center of regulatory efforts.[294] As interests, power, technology, and information diffuse and evolve over time, comprehensive regimes are difficult to form, and once formed, can be unstable.[295] According to Professor Young, international regimes emerge as a result of "codifying informal rights and rules that have evolved over time through a process of converging expectations or tacit bargaining."[296] Sufficient time has arguably not yet elapsed for this process to play out in the cybersecurity context. Consequently, regime complexes are becoming relatively more popular, which may have some benefits if negotiations for multilateral treaties "divert attention from more practical efforts to create" flexible regimes.[297] In a worst case scenario, an inflexible comprehensive regime could actually stifle innovation by crowding out smaller-scale efforts that might be more effective at enhancing cybersecurity as discussed further

---

U.S. Senate's failure to ratify a disability rights treaty that was "modeled after the Americans with Disabilities Act."); *Treaties Pending in Senate*, U.S. Dep't St., http://www.state.gov/s/l/treaty/pending/ (last updated Apr. 23, 2013).

[288] *See* Buck, *supra* note 38, at 31.

[289] *See* Keohane & Victor, *supra* note 271, at 10–11 (discussing regime complexes in the climate change context).

[290] *See* Robert O. Keohane & David G. Victor, *The Regime Complex for Climate Change* at 2, 4 (Harv. Proj. on Int'l Climate Agreements Discussion Paper No. 10-33, 2010).

[291] *Id.* at 2.

[292] *Major Economies Forum on Energy and Climate*, U.S. Dep't St. (2011), http://www.state.gov/r/pa/prs/ps/2011/09/172527.htm; Keohane & Victor, *supra* note 271, at 9–11.

[293] *See* Keohane & Victor, *supra* note 271, at 9–10.

[294] *See id.* at 19.

[295] *Id.* at 7.

[296] Oran R. Young, Global Governance: Drawing Insights from the Environmental Experience 10 (1997).

[297] Keohane & Victor, *supra* note 271, at 8.

in Chapter 7.[298] However, there are also the costs of regime complexes to consider, including enforcement, sustainability, and legal inconsistencies.[299] Consequently, regime complexes must be critically assessed.

When analyzing regimes, according to Professors Robert Keohane and David Victor, "it is helpful to imagine a continuum. At one extreme are" thick, comprehensive treaty systems such as the World Trade Organization, and "at the other extreme are highly fragmented collections of institutions with no identifiable core and weak or nonexistent linkages. . . . "[300] In between is a range of semi-hierarchical regimes with "loosely coupled systems of institutions."[301] Comprehensive regimes are most common when the interests of powerful actors are aligned "across a broad issue area,"[302] such as what arguably may be occurring in the arenas of cybercrime and data privacy.[303] Such a level of agreement and cooperation is rare in the international community, particularly in an era increasingly defined by multipolar politics.[304] This has led to a greater emphasis on targeted, issue-specific regimes that are discussed next in the context of polycentric analysis.

Polycentric Institutional Analysis and Climate Change

Polycentrism has arisen across an array of disciplines, from law to urban studies, and involves the study of multiple power centers in a given environment.[305] Professor Vincent Ostrom defined a "polycentric" order as "one where many elements are capable of making mutual adjustments for ordering their relationships with one another within a general system of rules where each element acts with independence of other elements."[306] Proponents claim that top-down planning by officials may

---

[298] *See, e.g.,* Elinor Ostrom, *Beyond Markets and States: Polycentric Governance of Complex Economic Systems,* 100 AM. ECON. REV. 641, 656 (2010) (citing Andrew F. Reeson & John G. Tisdell, *Institutions, Motivations and Public Goods: An Experimental Test of Motivational Crowding,* 68 J. ECON. BEHAVIOR & ORG. 273 (2008) (finding "externally imposed regulation that would theoretically lead to higher joint returns 'crowded out' voluntary behavior to cooperate.")).

[299] *See* Kal Raustiala & David G. Victor, *The Regime Complex for Plant Genetic Resources,* 58 INT'L ORG. 277, 277–78 (2004); Keohane & Victor, *supra* note 271, at 3–4.

[300] Keohane & Victor, *supra* note 290, at 3–4.

[301] Raustiala & Victor, *supra* note 299, at 278.

[302] Keohane & Victor, *supra* note 290, at 4.

[303] *See, e.g.,* Jeremy Kirk, *Russia Pushes for Online Code of Conduct at United Nations General Assembly,* COMPUTER WORLD UK (Oct. 3, 2011), http://www.computerworlduk.com/news/public-sector/3307976/russia-pushes-for-online-code-of--conduct-at-united-nations-general-assembly/; *General Assembly Backs Right to Privacy in Digital Age,* UN NEWS CTR. (Dec. 19, 2013), http://www.un.org/apps/news/story.asp?NewsID=46780&Cr=privacy&Cr1=#.UtKxrPYjBkU.

[304] *See* Abraham M. Denmark, *Managing the Global Commons,* WASH. Q. 165, 167 (July 2010).

[305] *See, e.g.,* SURYA PRAKASH SINHA, LEGAL POLYCENTRICITY AND INTERNATIONAL LAW 1 (1996); Robert C. Kloosterman & Sako Musterd, *The Polycentric Urban Region: Toward a Research Agenda,* 38(4) URBAN STUD. 623, 623 (2001).

[306] Vincent Ostrom, *Polycentricity (Part 1),* in POLYCENTRICITY AND LOCAL PUBLIC ECONOMIES: READINGS FROM THE WORKSHOP IN POLITICAL THEORY AND POLICY ANALYSIS 52, 57 (Michael Dean McGinnis ed., 2009).

be unnecessary to build efficient regimes to govern common-pool resources.[307] In fact, the state is only one of many actors in a polycentric system.[308] It is the desire to address a common concern that ties together the various state and non-state actors in a system of polycentric governance, which can then enjoy "mutual monitoring, learning, and adaptation of better strategies over time."[309]

Professor Ostrom and other scholars have argued for the adoption of polycentric management solutions to collective action problems stemming from the global commons in situations where the international community is either unable or unwilling to take the necessary action.[310] The basic notion in this context is that "a single governmental unit" may be incapable of managing "global collective action problems" due in part to free riders discouraging "trust and reciprocity" between stakeholders.[311] Nations that are not bound, in other words, enjoy the benefits of other nations' sacrifices without realizing the costs; solutions "negotiated at a global level, if not backed by a variety of efforts at national, regional, and local levels, are not guaranteed to work well."[312] Those advocating for a polycentric approach argue that instead of the creation of a centralized artificial organization, such as in the vein of ICANN, local institutions relying to the extent possible on organic self-organization should be created to promote trust and bottom-up governance.[313] "You don't need big brother to step in to protect the commons," explains the imminent late Stanford climate scientist Professor Steve Schneider.[314] Such a polycentric approach would enjoy active oversight at multiple scales. Polycentric governance then builds from the regime complex literature by recognizing both the benefits and drawbacks of multilevel regulation, the importance of norm building and self-organization, the critical governance role played by non-state actors, and the need for some degree of hierarchy to avoid help gridlock. Originally developed in other contexts, Professor Ostrom and others have worked to extend these principles to atmospheric governance.[315] For the purposes of introducing polycentrism, it is helpful to briefly summarize this work to

---

[307] *See* Ostrom, *supra* note 82, at 2.

[308] *See* Julia Black, *Constructing and Contesting Legitimacy and Accountability in Polycentric Regulatory Regimes*, 2(2) REG. & GOVERNANCE 137, 138–40 (2008).

[309] Elinor Ostrom, *Polycentric Systems for Coping with Collective Action and Global Environmental Change*, 20(1) GLOBAL ENVT'L CHANGE 550, 552 (2010) ("Polycentric systems are characterized by multiple governing authorities at differing scales rather than a monocentric unit.").

[310] *See* Ostrom, *supra* note 61, at 3–4, 32.

[311] *Id.* at 35; *see* Keohane & Victor, *supra* note 290, at 9 (discussing the feasibility of managing climate change context through diverse institutions).

[312] Ostrom, *supra* note 61, at 4.

[313] *Id.* at 4–5, 35.

[314] Interview with Steve Schneider, Professor of Biology, Stanford University, in Copenhagen, Den. (Dec. 8, 2009).

[315] Ostrom, *supra* note 61; *see also* Daniel H. Cole, *From Global to Polycentric Climate Governance*, 2 CLIMATE L. 395, 412 (2011) (arguing that certain "regime complexes" that exist as a "middle ground" between fully hierarchical and fragmented systems are analogous to polycentric governance); Keohane & Victor, *supra* note 290, at 2 (exploring "the continuum between comprehensive international regulatory institutions, which are usually focused on a single integrated legal instrument, at one end

see whether and how it may be applied to cyberspace generally and cybersecurity specifically, as some such as Professor Deibert have advocated.[316]

Although the atmosphere is global, the effects of climate change vary from region to region. Actions taken by a multiplicity of actors on a small scale can impact on the global climate change problem; insulating housing or buying more fuel-efficient cars alone could reduce energy consumption worldwide by 30 percent.[317] "Millions of actors affect the global atmosphere[,]"[318] just as they do the Internet. With weather patterns changing, global sea levels rising, and temperatures set to increase by more than 1.5 degrees Celsius by 2100, climate change is a problem affecting the entire world, but one in which benefits are dispersed and the harms are often concentrated.[319] As such, it is a classic collective-action problem in which it is in the best interest of individual nations to free ride.[320] This behavior was on display at the 15th Conference of the Parties (COP15) to the United Nations Framework Convention on Climate Change (UNFCCC), held in Copenhagen in December 2009, when delegations from 192 nations came together to address the mounting problem of global climate change.[321] During COP15, the actions of a few nations were able to block progress for days, thereby underscoring the difficulties of reaching consensus in a multipolar world discussed earlier in the chapter.[322] At the heart of the issue was how the atmosphere should be governed – what form should regulation take, what is the most appropriate level for regulation, and how can compliance be enforced? In the end, COP15 proved unable to answer these questions, although some progress was made at subsequent meetings.[323] The struggle to reach agreement across such an

of a spectrum and highly fragmented arrangements at the other. In-between these two extremes are nested regimes and regime complexes, which are loosely coupled sets of specific regimes.").

[316] *See* Deibert, *supra* note 6, at 57.

[317] Ostrom, *supra* note 61, at 4–5 (citing Michael P. Vandenberg & Anne C. Steinemann, *The Carbon-Neutral Individual*, 82 N.Y.U. L. Rev. 1673, 1674 (2007)).

[318] *Id.* at 5.

[319] *See id.* at 8; Jonathan M. Harris & Brian Roach, *The Economics of Climate Change*, Global Dev. & Env't Inst. at 8 (2009); Intergovernmental Panel on Climate Change Special Report on Climate Change, http://www.ipcc.ch/ipccreports/tar/wg2/index.php?idp=55; Intergovernmental Panel on Climate Change, Climate Change 2013: The Physical Science Basis Summary for Policymakers, at 18 (2013), *available at* http://www.climatechange2013.org/images/uploads/WGI_AR5_SPM_brochure.pdf.

[320] *See* Ostrom, *supra* note 61, at 1, 8.

[321] *See* Emma Duncan, *Getting Warmer*, Economist (Dec. 3, 2009), http://www.economist.com/node/14994872.

[322] *See Key Powers Reach Compromise at Climate Summit*, BBC (Dec. 19, 2009), http://news.bbc.co.uk/2/hi/europe/8421935.stm.

[323] *See, e.g.*, Roger Harrabin, *UN Climate Talks Extend Kyoto Protocol, Promise Compensation*, BBC (Dec. 8, 2012), http://www.bbc.co.uk/news/science-environment-20653018 (noting that the Russian delegation tried to slow progress at COP18 but ultimately their objections were put down by the Chairman); Matt McGrath, *Last-Minute Deal Saves Fractious UN Climate Talks*, BBC (Nov. 23, 2013), http://www.bbc.co.uk/news/science-environment-25067180. COP15 also illustrated the extent to which negotiations over implementing the CHM concept have changed over time, according to Professor Michael Oppenheimer, lead author of the Third and Fourth Intergovernmental Panel on Climate Change assessments. "[P]ragmatism and efficiency has led to the uptake of emissions

array of interests has led to the development of more targeted forums since COP15, both in terms of membership and subject matter, in what could be considered a shift toward a polycentric approach to atmospheric management.[324] The U.S. Conference of Mayors climate protection efforts are an example of this movement, with more than 500 U.S. mayors signing on to voluntary efforts aimed at reduce emissions and for their cities.[325] Such initiatives have met with some success, which is why Professor Ostrom argued that polycentric regulation is "the best way to address transboundary problems . . . since the complexity of these problems lends itself well to many small, issue-specific units working autonomously as part of a network that is addressing collective action problems. It is an application of the maxim, 'think globally, but act locally.'"[326]

A prime example of a successful targeted treaty in the climate-change context is the Montreal Protocol, in which an initially small group of nations worked to ban the use of chlorofluorocarbons (CFCs) that destroy ozone.[327] However, such a regime is not easily translated into other contexts given differences in the science, chemicals, and manufacturing sectors. Ozone heals itself. So, too, does the climate, but on a much longer timescale. The science linking CFCs and the hole in the ozone was also well established whereas in the climate-change context, climate scientist Schneider asks, "What's the climate hole? How many more heat waves would constitute a climate hole?" [328] Similarly, how many and what type of cyber attacks will it take to reach a tipping point? Richard Clarke, for example, envisions a scenario in which the tipping point is never reached, but instead small-scale losses in IP mount to result in a "death of a thousand cuts."[329] A clear substitute to CFCs was also available,[330] unlike for all carbon emissions or the Internet.[331] It

trading, which some view as privatization of the commons," argues Professor Oppenheimer. Electronic interview with Michael Oppenheimer, Albert G. Milbank Professor of Geosciences and International Affairs, Princeton Univ. (Jan. 23, 2012). "What has fallen by the wayside is that the principle of equity (for example, equal per capita emissions) is seen as a very distant objective." *Id.*

[324] *See* Cole, *supra* note 315, at 395 (discussing the potential of polycentric governance to better address climate change given the failures of multilateral efforts).

[325] *See* About the Mayors Climate Protection Center, http://usmayors.org/climateprotection/about.htm (last visited Oct. 11, 2013).

[326] Interview with Elinor Ostrom, Distinguished Professor, Indiana University-Bloomington, in Bloomington, Ind. (Oct. 13, 2010).

[327] *See* Daniel Bodansky, *The History of the Global Cliamte Change Regime, in* INTERNATIONAL RELATIONS AND GLOBAL CLIMATE CHANGE 23, 29–35 (Urs Luterbacher & Detlef F. Sprinz eds., 2001) (noting that the Montreal Protocol was precipitated by national regulation).

[328] Schneider, *supra* note 314.

[329] Ron Rosenbaum, *Richard Clarke on Who Was Behind the Stuxnet Attack,* SMITHSONIAN (Apr. 2012), http://www.smithsonianmag.com/history-archaeology/Richard-Clarke-on-Who-Was-Behind-the-Stuxnet-Attack.html?c=y&story=fullstory.

[330] *See* Kal Raustiala, Nonstate Actors in the Global Climate Regime, in INTERNATIONAL RELATIONS AND GLOBAL CLIMATE CHANGE, *supra* note 327, at 95, 102.

[331] *See* Michael V. Copeland, *The Internet Needs a Plan B,* WIRED (Feb. 27, 2013), http://www.wired.com/business/2013/02/the-internet-needs-a-plan-b/ (reporting on Danny Hillis, an early Internet pioneer, who argues that we need to build a Plan B for if and when the public Internet crashes).

was just a matter of incentivizing the switch to the substitute in nations with new industries, which required payments. However, these payments were small relative to the problem of climate change – the United States has paid some $21 billion during the life of the Montreal Protocol.[332] Finally, the magnitude of the affected industry was vastly different. Instead of a multi-billion dollar CFC industry in a handful of countries, global climate change impacts multi-trillion dollar industries across myriad sectors and economies. The scale of the problem thus makes climate change exceedingly more difficult to manage than the ozone hole – similar to the multifaceted cyber threat. Nevertheless, there is a potential for targeted measures in both the climate change and cyber contexts to put us on the path to binding multilateral agreements,[333] as discussed in Chapter 7.

There is no perfect forum in a multipolar world; both top-down and bottom-up regulatory approaches have benefits and drawbacks. In the cyber context, focusing exclusively on multilateral treaties would help manage free riders but risks stalling progress given geopolitical divides, whereas relying on bottom-up regulations in the vein of the IETF promises informality, flexibility, and promotes experimentation even as the absence of hierarchical control threatens gridlock. A true polycentric approach would be an all-of-the-above effort that includes the best of both worlds, but determining how this could work in practice first requires an analysis of the literature on polycentric governance.

Introducing Polycentric Governance

Few have done more to develop the tools of polycentric governance than Professors Elinor and Vincent Ostrom and others affiliated at the Indiana University Vincent and Elinor Ostrom Workshop in Political Theory and Policy Analysis. For example, Vincent Ostrom's early work in the 1970s and 1980s challenged the conventional wisdom that advocated consolidation as a way to cut costs and improve services from schools to police departments, showing that in fact "[n]o systematic empirical evidence supported reform proposals related to moving the provision of public goods from smaller-scale units to larger governments."[334] Elinor Ostrom built from this foundation and applied polycentric governance to the regulation of common pool resources, demonstrating with her colleagues in a series of field studies that many groups at the small-to-medium scale do in fact cooperate to mitigate collective action problems.[335] In fact, these studies indicated that polycentric systems

---

[332] Cass R. Sunstein, *Montreal vs. Kyoto: A Tale of Two Protocols* at 15 (John M. Olin L. & Econ. Working Paper No. 302 (2d series), Aug. 2006), www.law.uchicago.edu/files/files/302.pdf.

[333] *See, e.g.*, Christopher Joyce, *Climate Strategists: To Cut Emissions, Focus On Forests*, NPR (Dec. 10, 2011), http://www.npr.org/2011/12/10/143454111/climate-activists-to-cut-emissions-focus-on-forests?sc=17&f=1001 (reporting that some nations such as Norway are looking outside the UN framework for action on climate change).

[334] *See* Ostrom, *supra* note 61, at 50 (emphasis omitted).

[335] *Id.* at 10.

frequently enjoyed better outcomes than those of central governments, benefiting from local investment and expertise that improved flexibility and promoted innovation.[336]

Polycentric self-organization can be a powerful tool to solve collective action problems, but doing so requires "public entrepreneurs working closely with citizens frequently to find new ways of putting services together using a mixture of local talent and resources."[337] The ability to self-organize in the cyberspace context thus may depend to an extent on the technical savvy of the user, network operator, and network owner. If done correctly, by incentivizing systems where "large, medium, and small governmental and nongovernmental enterprises engage in diverse cooperative as well as competitive relationships," such a bottom-up approach can lower transaction costs, leaving people better off.[338] Indeed, communities can establish and enforce norms of behavior, as was explored in the eBay example of Chapter 1. Yet self-regulation has its limits in cyberspace given the worldwide Internet community, free riders, and enforcement problems, among other issues discussed in Chapter 7.

Polycentric networks are susceptible to institutional fragmentation and gridlock caused by overlapping authority that must still "meet standards of coherence, effectiveness, [and] . . . sustainability. . . . "[339] In other words, because no one person or organization is ultimately in control, confusion and delay may result.[340] There are also moral and political problems at play. First, polycentric regulation may result in what Garrett Hardin called "lifeboat ethics," which holds that when it is impossible to equitably preserve access to the commons for all, the poor are left behind.[341] In the cyber context, this could take the form of developing nations being unable to make needed cybersecurity gains in the absence of a multilateral framework without

---

[336] *See id.* at 53; Elinor Ostrom, *Polycentric Systems: Multilevel Governance Involving a Diversity of Organizations, in* GLOBAL ENVIRONMENTAL COMMONS: ANALYTICAL AND POLITICAL CHALLENGES INVOLVING A DIVERSITY OF ORGANIZATIONS 105, 117 (Eric Brousseau et al. eds., 2012).

[337] Elinor Ostrom, *Unlocking Public Entrepreneurship and Public Economies* 2 (UN Univ. World Inst. for Dev. Econ. Research, Discussion Paper No. 2005/01, 2005), http://www.wider.unu.edu/publications/ working-papers/discussion-papers/2005/en_GB/dp2005-01/_files/78091749378753796/default/dp2005 %2001%20Ostrom.pdf.

[338] Ostrom, *supra* note 82, at 3–4 (discussing the distinction between polycentric systems and a "monocentric hierarchy") (citing Bruno S. Frey & Reiner Eichenberger, *FOCJ: Competitive Governments for Europe,* 16(3) INT'L REV. L. ECON. 315, 315 (1996)); *see also* Cole, *supra* note 315, at 405 (arguing that "[i]nstead of a 'monocentric hierarchy,' where governmental units at higher levels make all the decisions, and units at lower levels simply follow commands from above, a truly polycentric system is one in which governmental units both compete and cooperate, interact and learn from one another, and responsibilities at different governmental levels are tailored to match the scale of the public services they provide.") (citing Ostrom, *supra* note 61, at 33).

[339] Keohane & Victor, *supra* note 290, at 3, 18–19, 25.

[340] *See* Ostrom, *supra* note 309, at 554–55 (reviewing some of the objections to relying on polycentric governance to address global climate change, including "leakage, inconsistent policies, inadequate certification, gaming the system, and free riding.").

[341] *See* Garrett Hardin, *Lifeboat Ethics: The Case Against Helping the Poor,* PSYCHOLOGY TODAY (Sept. 1974), at 38–40, 123–124, 126 (examining, from an ethical viewpoint, when swimmers surrounding a lifeboat should be taken aboard as an analogy for analyzing resource distribution policies given the divide between developed and developing nations).

resource and technology transfers from developed nations. Second, the cyber powers are reluctant to negotiate thorny verification and attribution issues, among other concerns, in a small forum given their current asymmetric advantages.[342] That is why it is vital to couple multilateral progress with bottom-up initiatives to effectively manage global collective-action problems such as cyber attacks.

Although polycentric governance is consistent with long-held doctrines in Catholic social thought such as subsidiarity and emergence,[343] along with findings in biological anthropology about the desirability of small groups in promoting positive group dynamics,[344] it is distinct from the other theories of regulation. International law, for example, has long operated on the premise of the matching principle requiring that nations and ultimately localities implement customary international law principles as well as ratified treaties.[345] However, the matching principle assumes the desirability of matching a particular jurisdiction with the scope of a given problem, which may be appropriate in some contexts but goes against the literature on polycentric governance as applied to the global commons insofar as the latter argues for the desirability of multisector action at multiple scales.[346] Moreover, although the importance of individuals and non-state actors is increasingly recognized within the corpus of international law, it arguably remains state-centric.[347] Political scientists

---

[342] Cf. Kirk, *supra* note 303 (reporting on the push for an online code of conduct).

[343] William Byron, a Jesuit priest and former President of Catholic University, summarized subsidiarity as: "[N]o higher level of organization should perform any function that can be handled efficiently and effectively at a lower level of organization by human persons, who individually or in groups, are close to the problem and close to the ground." William J. Bryon, *Ten Building Blocks of Catholic Social Teaching*, AM. MAG. (Oct. 31, 1998), http://americamagazine.org/issue/100/ten-building-blocks-catholic-social-teaching. For a thorough grounding in emergence and its application to our daily lives, see CHRISTIAN SMITH, WHAT IS A PERSON?: RETHINKING HUMANITY, SOCIAL LIFE, AND THE MORAL GOOD FROM THE PERSON UP 25–26 (2010) ("Emergence refers to the process of constituting a new entity with its own particular characteristics through the interactive combination of other, different entities that are necessary to create the new entity but that do not contain the characteristics present in the new entity.").

[344] See TIMOTHY L. FORT, ETHICS AND GOVERNANCE: BUSINESS AS MEDIATING INSTITUTION 50–51 (2001).

[345] See, e.g., Ramses Wessel & Jan Wouters, *The Phenomenon of Multilevel Regulation: Interactions Between Global, EU and National Regulatory Spheres*, in MULTILEVEL REGULATION AND THE EU: THE INTERPLAY BETWEEN GLOBAL, EUROPEAN AND NATIONAL NORMATIVE PROCESS 9, 20 (Andreas Follesdal et al. eds., 2008) (noting how regulations promulgated by international organizations like the WTO have a binding effect on other legal orders like the EU, its member states, and even individuals); Jonathan R. Macey & Henry N. Butler, *Externalities and the Matching Principle: The Case for Reallocating Environmetnal Regulatory Authority*, 14 YALE L. & POL'Y REV. 23, 25 (1996) (developing the matching principle).

[346] Cf. Jonathan H. Adler, *Jurisdictional Mismatch in Environmental Federalism*, 14 N.Y.U. ENVTL. L.J. 130, 133 (2005) ("By matching jurisdiction with the scope of a given problem, the institutional structure can ensure the greatest 'match' between a given problem and the institutional response."); *with* Ostrom, *supra* note 61, at 4 (arguing in the climate change context that "given the importance of technological change, without numerous innovative technological and institutional efforts at multiple scales, we may not even begin to learn which combined sets of actions are the most effective in reducing the long-term threat of massive climate change.").

[347] See, e.g., Anne-Marie Slaughter Burley, *International Law and Relations Theory: A Dual Agenda*, 87(2) AM. J. INT'L L. 205, 231 (1993) (demonstrating how international law has been largely built on the application of laws of sovereign states in foreign contexts). Professor Slaughter has also pioneered

such as Professors Keohane and Joseph Nye developed a model of "complex inter-dependence" that sought to supplement state action with a greater study of non-state actors that is perhaps more applicable to cyber regulation.[348] These efforts have led more recently to greater study of global governance and so-called "regime clusters" in the international relations literature, which have been used to explain uneven rates of development among other phenomena.[349] Yet this contributes relatively little to addressing global collective action problems. "Global governance," on the other hand, refers to the need for governance and rule making at the global level because of intensifying connections between states and peoples.[350] Proponents argue that without global governance, states will "retreat behind protective barriers" laying the groundwork for enduring conflicts.[351] Although this concept plays an important role for both policymakers and scholars in understanding the current state of interna-tional relations, its study has been critiqued for becoming so broad that the term has come to mean "virtually anything."[352] The confusion in part lies in the multitude of contexts in which the term "governance" has been evoked. Although definitions vary, a broad understanding of the term is offered by Professor Gerry Stoker, who defines governance as that part of human activity "concerned with creating the conditions for ordered rule and collective action."[353] Global governance is more concerned with norms and rules "rather than actors and [the] relations between them."[354] In contrast, a polycentric approach envisions more than simply competing systems of multilevel regulations, or "a collective of partially overlapping and non-hierarchical

---

network theory studying transnational regulatory networks and its progeny. However, this work pri-marily focuses on states, making it less useful for analyzing cybersecurity. *See* Anne-Marie Slaughter, *Sovereignty and Power in a Networked World Order*, 40 Stan. J. Int'l L. 283, 283 (2004).

[348] *See* Robert O. Keohane & Joseph S. Nye, Power and Interdependence: World Politics in Transition 23–24 (1977) (contrasting traditionally state-centric "realist" paradigms of world politics with a "complex interdependence" theory, which considers how non-state actors may participate in and help shape world politics). *See also* David Armstrong et al., International Law and International Relations 99 (2d ed. 2012) (discussing the views of realists and liberals regarding the success of institutions, such as the realist viewpoint that "institutions will only be effective . . . when they serve and hence are supported by powerful states.").

[349] Miriam Abu Sharkh, *Global Welfare Mixes and Wellbeing: Cluster, Factor and Regression Analyses from 1990 to 2000*, at 21–23 (Stanford Univ. Ctr. on Democracy, Dev., & the Rule of Law, Working Paper No. 94, 2009), http://iis-db.stanford.edu/pubs/22388/No.94_Sharkh_Global_welfare.pdf.

[350] *See, e.g.*, Michael Barnett & Raymond Duvall, *Power in Global Governance*, in Power in Global Governance 1, 1 (Michael Barnett & Raymond Duvall eds., 2005).

[351] *Id.*

[352] Klaus Dingwerth & Philipp Pattberg, *Global Governance as a Perspective on World Politics*, 12 Global Governance 185, 185 (2006).

[353] Gerry Stoker, *Governance as Theory: Five Propositions*, 155 Int'l Social Sci. J. 17, 17 (1998).

[354] Dingwerth & Pattberg, *supra* note 352, at 199. *See also* Michael D. McGinnis, *Updated Guide to IAD and the Language of the Ostrom Workshop: A Simplified Overview of a Complex Framework for the Analysis of Institutions and their Development*, at 8 (Working Paper Ver. 2c, 2013), http://php.indiana .edu/~mcginnis/iad_guide.pdf (contrasting polycentricity with federalism and noting that the latter "as typically understood does not necessarily incorporate or recognize the critical role of cross-border special-purpose jurisdictions.").

regimes" that vary in extent and purpose.[355] Instead, it may be understood as an effort to marry elements of these interdisciplinary concepts of regime complexes and clusters, multilevel governance, and global governance together under a single conceptual framework so as to better study multidimensional problems such as cybersecurity.[356]

Polycentric governance is important for its capacity to embrace self-regulation and bottom-up initiatives, its focus on multi-stakeholder governance to foster collaboration across multiple regulatory scales, as well as its emphasis on targeted measures to address global collective action problems. By "ordering and structuring our perception of the world," concepts such as polycentricism help us relate certain phenomena to one another, "make judgments about the relevance and significance of information, to analyze specific situations, and to create new ideas."[357] Thus, concepts are among the most important tools of social science,[358] and represent a critical starting point for analyzing subjects as complex as cybersecurity. Having introduced polycentrism and understanding some of how it differs from other theories of multilevel regulation, it is now possible to apply this conceptual framework to cybersecurity challenges.

Applying Polycentric Governance to Cybersecurity

Polycentric governance seems to be gaining popularity across the global commons, either as an incremental step or potentially an alternative to multilateral treaty making. What are the benefits of polycentric regulation in cyberspace specifically? On the positive side, the concept encourages regulatory innovation and competition between regimes as well as "flexibility across issues and adaptability over time."[359] This flexibility may be seen in the dynamic role played by the IETF in Internet governance. It also avoids the necessity of centralized, supranational control because: "better, one might think, 192 sovereigns than one or a few."[360] This networked, distributed approach exemplifies a key insight of polycentric governance applied to cyberspace – "no one regulator may impose their will on any subject of regulation without the agreement of competing regulators (and the support of regulatees)."[361] For example, in the case of the PRC, content is regulated by the government as

---

[355] Raustiala & Victor, *supra* note 299, at 277.

[356] However, we must be careful not to make polycentric governance such a broad proposition that it falls victim to the same critiques as global governance. To help address such concerns, it will be important to model and further refine the core features of polycentric governance discussed above.

[357] Dingwerth & Pattberg, *supra* note 352, at 186.

[358] *Id.* at 198.

[359] Keohane & Victor, *supra* note 290, at 18; *see also* Constantine Michalopoulos, *WTO Accession, in* DEVELOPMENT, TRADE AND THE WTO: A HANDBOOK 61, 61–70 (Bernard M. Hoekman et al. eds., 2002) (discussing the benefits of polycentric regulation in the context of WTO accession).

[360] CRAWFORD, *supra* note 46, at 32 (discussing the creation of states in international law).

[361] MURRAY, *supra* note 12, at 49.

well as external agencies such as the International Broadcasting Bureau and the private sector.[362] Loosely linked regime complexes that avoid fragmentation consequently "can be much more flexible and adaptable than integrated-comprehensive regimes."[363] This is especially important in cyberspace where technology is rapidly advancing, creating new environmental pressures and security concerns. Given that the only constant is "technological change, without numerous innovative technological and institutional efforts at multiple scales, we may never be able to learn which combined sets of actions are the most effective"[364] in mitigating collective action problems like cyber attacks.

Successful examples of polycentric governance such as the IETF have led Professor Ostrom to argue, "Cyberspace governance is more or less a success. It is a domain in which private governance has evolved. Yes, there are still significant problems, but they are problems of complexity and not necessarily scale."[365] Indeed, polycentric regulation has the potential to address the shortcomings of current conceptual approaches often favored by policymakers such as categorizing cyber attacks loosely according to scale and motive. Instead, the concept embraces multilevel governance and involvement by both the public and private sectors to create targeted measures that better address the full range of cyber threats. But is such praise justified? And how can we move from a conceptual framework to real-world solutions to outstanding cybersecurity challenges? This is the million-dollar question that is unpacked throughout the rest of this book and summarized in Chapter 7. However, Professor Ostrom created an informative framework of eight design principles for the management of common pool resources that helps to guide discussion. These include the importance of: (1) "clearly defined boundaries for the user pool . . . and the resource domain";[366] (2) "proportional equivalence between benefits and costs";[367] (3) "collective choice arrangements" ensuring "that the resource users participate in setting . . . rules";[368] (4) "monitoring . . . by the appropriators or by their agents";[369] (5) "graduated sanctions" for rule violators;[370] (6) "conflict-resolution mechanisms [that] are readily available, low cost, and legitimate";[371] (7) "minimal recognition of rights to organize";[372] and (8) "governance activities [being] . . . organized in multiple layers of nested enterprises."[373] Not all of Professor Ostrom's design principles

---

[362] *Id.*

[363] Keohane & Victor, *supra* note 290, at 25.

[364] Ostrom, *supra* note 61, at 4.

[365] Ostrom, *supra* note 326.

[366] Buck, *supra* note 38, at 32.

[367] Ostrom, *supra* note 336, at 118 tbl. 5.3 (citing Elinor Ostrom, Governing the Commons: The Evolution of Institutions for Collective Action 90 (1990)).

[368] Buck, *supra* note 38, at 32.

[369] *Id.*

[370] *Id.*

[371] *Id.*

[372] Ostrom, *supra* note 336, at 118 tbl. 5.3.

[373] *Id.*

are applicable in cyberspace given that they were designed primarily for managing small-scale resources, such as forests and lakes. However, some do have salience, and are addressed in turn.

Defined Boundaries

According to Professor Ostrom, "The boundary rules relate to who can enter, harvest, manage, and potentially exclude others' impacts. Participants then have more assurance about trustworthiness and cooperation of the others involved."[374] Boundaries in cyberspace, though, can be difficult to draw, though it does happen through legal mechanisms such as enclosure and the Internet sovereignty movement discussed earlier in this chapter, and organically, including the creation of micro communities discussed in Chapter 7. The literature here suggests that group-defined boundaries can help foster trust and collaboration, but that narrowly focused communities can also ignore other interests, stakeholders, and the wider impact of their actions.[375] To overcome such apathy, communities must have a defined stake in the outcome to effectuate good governance, which can in part be accomplished by educating users about the cyber threat and their power to help manage it.

Proportionality

This design principle underscores the need for equity in a system so that some of the "users [do not] get all the benefits and pay few of the costs...."[376] Proportionality emphasizes why the creation of a level playing field for firms is so important, as is explored in Chapter 5. It also evokes the debate over the CHM concept at the international level and why equity is still so vital to a functioning global legal system in an era of competing national cybersecurity strategies and the offensive use of cyber attacks, which are topics returned to in Chapters 4 and 6.

Collective-Choice Arrangements and Minimal Recognition of Rights

Professor Ostrom's third design principle states "that most of the individuals affected by a resource regime are authorized to participate in making and modifying the rules related to boundaries, assessment of costs..., etc."[377] This principle arguably implies the importance of engaged and proactive rulemaking by stakeholders including technical communities, the private sector, and the international community.[378] For example, external authorities like the U.S. government could formally recognize the importance of defined communities such as the IETF to develop and

---

[374] *Id.* at 119.
[375] *See* Murray, *supra* note 12, at 164.
[376] Ostrom, *supra* note 336, at 120.
[377] *Id.*
[378] *See* George J. Siedel & Helena Haapio, *Law as a Source of Strategic Advantage: Using Proactive Law for Competitive Advantage*, 47 Am. Bus. L.J. 641, 656–57 (2010) (discussing the origins of the proactive law movement, which may be considered "a future-oriented approach to law placing an emphasis on legal knowledge to be applied before things go wrong.").

implement best practices to help address technical vulnerabilities. Alternatively, the Internet Governance Forum discussed in Chapter 1 could be formalized and empowered to help codify global multi-stakeholder Internet governance.[379] Moreover, this principle recognizes the need to modify rules as the technological environment changes.[380] As we have seen, the cyber threat matrix is continuously evolving, making it vital for local rules in the form of industry best practices to proactively evolve along with cyberspace, and providing a cautionary tale against heavy-handed government regulation.

Monitoring

As Professor Ostrom posits, trust can typically only do so much to mitigate rule-breaking behavior.[381] Eventually, some level of monitoring becomes important. In self-organized communities, typically monitors are chosen among the members to ensure "the conformance of others to local rules."[382] One manifestation of this in the cybersecurity context are information sharing organizations described in Chapter 5, which is a step down from industry councils that may have the authority to punish rulebreakers. Legislation has been proposed to create such industry councils in the United States and empower them "to develop and coordinate the enforcement of cybersecurity guidelines for key U.S. sectors."[383] Similarly, more robust information sharing about cyber attacks could be enacted domestically, regionally, and globally, though this could be a double-edged sword with increased monitoring leading to privacy concerns. Whether such initiatives prove sufficient to manage the multifaceted cyber threat remains to be seen.

Graduated Sanctions and Dispute Resolution

Other insights from Professor Ostrom's principles such as the need for graduated sanctions for rule violators and effective dispute resolution speak to the importance of addressing legal ambiguities and establishing norms of behavior in the cybersecurity context. The former point underscores the significance of not "[l]etting an infraction pass unnoticed,"[384] meaning that the cost of cyber attacks need to be more internalized to firms through some combination of market reaction and governmental supervision. The latter point is a key component of creating a functioning body of international cybersecurity law in which the rules of the road are clear for companies, countries, and the international community. These principles are unpacked further in Chapters 6 and 7.

---

[379] *See Montevideo Statement on the Future of Internet Cooperation*, ICANN (Oct. 7, 2013), http://www.icann.org/en/news/announcements/announcement-07oct13-en.htm.

[380] Ostrom, *supra* note 336, at 120.

[381] *Id.*

[382] *Id.*

[383] *House Homeland Security Leaders Said Close to Unveiling Cybersecurity Bill*, BLOOMBERG BNA (June 10, 2013), http://www.bna.com/house-homeland-security-n17179874424/.

[384] Ostrom, *supra* note 336, at 121.

Nested Enterprises

According to Professor Ostrom, "When common-pool resources that are being man-aged by a group are part of a larger set of resource systems, an eighth design principle is usually present in robust systems. The nested enterprise principle states that gover-nance activities are organized in multiple layers of related governance regimes."[385] Just as this multilevel system is imperative for environmental governance in large ecological systems with distinct local dynamics,[386] so too is it essential for enhanc-ing cybersecurity given the local, national, and global impact of cyber attacks on economic development and security. This principle posits that larger institutions are important for "govern[ing] the interdependencies among smaller [governance] units,"[387] highlighting the need for effective multi-stakeholder governance given the extensive private-sector control of the Internet's infrastructure. Such a system would assist in "handling some problems at a very small scale," such as data breaches of low-value information, "and other problems at ever larger scales"[388] potentially including prized trade and state secrets.

Polycentricity and Cybersecurity

Thus far, the emerging system of polycentric governance in cyberspace has proven relatively adept at technical governance, but it has so far been unable to arrest the proliferation of cyber attacks. And the situation seems to be getting worse, as is shown in the non-comprehensive data assembled by the U.S. Cyber Emergency Response Team (US-CERT), an arm of DHS, in Figure 2.3. US-CERT has estimated that a significant cyber intrusion occurs every five minutes and that the number of attacks on critical infrastructure jumped some 2,000 percent from 2009 to 2011,[389] while Trend Micro has determined that new pieces of malware are being created at the rate of two per second.[390] The open question is what additional regulatory mechanisms should be added to the cyber regime complex to better manage cyber attacks. In other words, how can we maximize the benefits while limiting the drawbacks of polycentric management?

An effective polycentric management system for cyberspace would embody a system of nested enterprises using the tools of law and norms, code, market-based incentives, self-regulation, public-private partnerships, and multilateral

[385] *Id.* at 122.
[386] *Id.*
[387] *Id.*
[388] *Id.*
[389] *See* Amber Corrin, *Cyber Incident Reports Skyrocketed Over Three-Year Period*, FCW (July 2, 2012), http://fcw.com/articles/2012/07/02/ics-cert-report-cyber-attacks-skyrocket.aspx.
[390] *See Solutions for Federal Agencies*, TREND MICRO, http://www.trendmicro.com/us/business/industries/government/index.html (last visited Oct. 30, 2012); Dan Dunkel, *Finding The Cure for Cyber Blind-ness & Missed Opportunities*, SDM (Oct. 17, 2012), http://www.sdmmag.com/articles/88361-finding-the-cure-for-cyber-blindness-missed-opportunities.

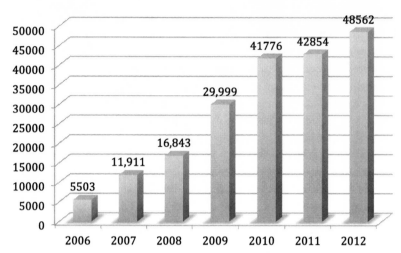

FIGURE 2.3. A FAILURE OF COLLECTIVE ACTION – NUMBER OF CYBER INCIDENTS CATA-LOGED BY CERT FROM 2006 TO 2012. *Source*: GAO, CYBERSECURITY: A BETTER DEFINED AND IMPLEMENTED NATIONAL STRATEGY IS NEEDED TO ADDRESS PERSISTENT CHALLENGES 6 fig. 1 (2013), http://www.gao.gov/products/GAO-13-462T.

collaboration – some of which are alluded to in Professor Ostrom's design principles – to enhance cybersecurity.[391] Crafting such a dynamic set of regimes given the malleability and complexity inherent in cyberspace is no small feat. Action is required from each stakeholder, including companies, countries, the international community, and ultimately users. Part II addresses how polycentrism may be applied through the regulatory modalities of the Internet architecture and code, national regulation, and market-based incentives to help address technical vulnerabilities, better protect critical national infrastructure, and assist companies in managing cyber attacks. Chapters 6 and 7 then analyze the utility of international law and norms in fostering cyber peace. In brief, mixtures of regulatory modalities working at multiple levels will be required to enhance cybersecurity. Relevant agencies should enforce self-generated community codes and industry best practices.[392]

[391] This list was inspired by LESSIG, *supra* note 109, at 94. Professor Ostrom and her colleagues also elucidated a list of ten variables that they have found are vital to the likelihood of self-organization, which Professor Roger Hurwitz has applied to cyberspace. *See* Hurwitz, *supra* note 42, at 419–22 (noting that these variables include the "size of [the] resource, productivity of the system, predictability of system dynamics, resource unit mobility, number of users, leadership, norms/social capital, knowledge of the SES, importance of resource to users, [and] collective choice rules."). Professor Hurwitz concludes that the balance of these variables "do not particularly support effective self-regulation of cyberspace...." However, he believes that progress may be made in that direction by the "acknowledgement by states that security breaches on the Internet undermines the public trust...; [and that] technologically informed, politically astute leadership that is committed to working at a global level to provide cyber security" is needed such as to address the attribution problem discussed in Chapters 3 and 6. *Id.*

[392] MONROE E. PRICE & STEFAN G. VERHULST, SELF-REGULATION AND THE INTERNET 22 (2005).

Norms for Internet content, service providers, and nations should be negotiated and adopted.[393] Companies should adopt proactive cybersecurity models, and governments should secure critical national infrastructure by forming more robust cybersecurity partnerships to share intelligence and better manage the multifaceted cyber threat.

In conclusion, "[t]he advantage[s] of a polycentric approach [are] that it encourages experimental efforts by multiple actors,"[394] embraces self-regulation, focuses on multi-stakeholder governance including both the public and private sectors, and emphasizes targeted measures to begin to address global collective action problems lest inaction hasten a worst-case scenario. Just as the states are laboratories for democracy in the U.S. federal system, as Justice Louis D. Brandeis famously observed,[395] so too are firms and nations laboratories for polycentric governance in cyberspace. This is important because, according to Professor Ostrom, "simply recommending a single governmental unit to solve global collective action problems – because of global impacts – needs to be seriously rethought and the important role of smaller-scale effects recognized."[396] There is no supranational authority at the global level in charge of cyberspace. Nor is there likely to be in the near future.[397] Cyberspace has already become too geopolitically important for the cyber powers to limit their sovereignty lightly. The likely outcome is a regime complex in which a number of national and international regulations continue to govern cyberspace, potentially fostered by a club of "like-minded" nations and industry players as is envisioned in the Obama administration's International Strategy for Cyberspace discussed in Chapter 7.[398] However, effective polycentric governance is predicated on the difficult task of getting diverse stakeholders to work well together across sectors and borders. Polycentric regulation has its faults, but so too does waiting for a consensual cybersecurity treaty that may come too late, if at

---

[393] See Kirk, *supra* note 303; Matthew J. Schwartz, *U.S.-Chinese Summit: 4 Information Security Take-aways*, INFO. WK. SEC. (June 11, 2013), www.informationweek.com/security/government/us-chinese-summit-4-information-security/240156396.

[394] Ostrom, *supra* note 61, at 32.

[395] See New State Ice Co. v. Liebmann, 285 U.S. 262, 311 (1932) (Brandeis, J., dissenting).

[396] Ostrom, *supra* note 61, at 35; *see, e.g.,* Christopher Joyce, *Climate Strategists: To Cut Emissions, Focus On Forests*, NPR (Dec. 10, 2011), http://www.npr.org/2011/12/10/143454111/climate-activists-to-cut-emissions-focus-on-forests?sc=17&f=1001 (reporting that some nations such as Norway are looking outside the UN framework for action on climate change). *But see EU Freezes Aviation Carbon Tax*, SYDNEY MORNING HERALD (Nov. 13, 2012), http://www.smh.com.au/travel/travel-news/eu-freezes-aviation-carbon-tax-20121113-2999v.html (reporting that the EU caved in to pressure from China and other countries over its aviation carbon tax, demonstrating the political blowback and false starts that can happen from taking bottom-up action to address global collective action problems).

[397] Nye, Jr., *supra* note 223, at 19 (arguing that "large-scale formal treaties regulating cyberspace seem unlikely.").

[398] See INTERNATIONAL STRATEGY FOR CYBERSPACE, *supra* note 171, at 9 (constructing a strategy that heavily builds on U.S. partnerships with other nations and private industry; *see also* Richard A. Clarke, *A Global Cyber-Crisis in Waiting*, WASH. POST (Feb. 7, 2013), http://articles.washingtonpost.com/2013-02-07/opinions/36973008_1_cybercrime-fly-away-teams-espionage (discussing the desirability of a like-minded approach to help build consensus toward enhancing cybersecurity).

all. It is necessary to analyze the best and worst of both bottom-up and top-down approaches to see how cybersecurity may be better enhanced; a task that we begin next in Part II.

SUMMARY

Cyberspace is a dynamic domain that may best be understood as a pseudo commons replete with public and private sector regulations occurring at multiple levels. If this depiction is accurate, then a modification of the tragedy of the commons or anti-commons scenarios might play out in cyberspace because of the proliferation of vulnerabilities and the rise of enclosure. To address these outcomes and enhance cybersecurity generally, national, private, common property, and polycentric approaches to cyber regulation were examined. Ultimately, a polycentric conceptualization was favored and some of the implications of examining the cyber threat through this lens were considered. This chapter is emblematic of the rest of the book in that it attempts to take a nuanced approach to cyber regulation. Now that the foundation of polycentric management in cyberspace has been laid, it is possible to analyze how this concept may be applied to foster cyber peace.

PART II

Managing Vulnerabilities

If you spend more on coffee than on IT security, then you will be hacked. What's more, you deserve to be hacked.

– Former Presidential Cybersecurity Advisor Richard Clarke[1]

The only truly secure system is one that is powered off, cast in a block of concrete and sealed in a lead-lined room with armed guards – and even then I have my doubts.

– Purdue Professor Gene Spafford[2]

---

[1] Robert Lemos, *Security Czar: Button Up or Get Hacked*, CNET (Feb. 19, 2002), http://news.cnet.com/ Security-czar-Button-up-or-get-hacked/2100-1002_3-840335.html. This chapter was first published as *Hacking the Planet, the Dalai Lama, and You: Managing Technical Vulnerabilities in the Internet through Polycentric Governance*, Copyright © 2014 Fordham Intellectual Property, Media & Entertainment Law Journal and Scott J. Shackelford and Amanda N. Craig.

[2] Quotable Spaf, http://spaf.cerias.purdue.edu/quotes.html (last visited Jan. 14, 2014) (citing A. K. Dewdney, *Computer Recreations: Of Worms, Viruses and Core War*, 260 SCI. AM., Mar. 1989, at 110, 110).

3

Hacking the Planet, the Dalai Lama, and You

Managing Technical Vulnerabilities in the Internet

'The Internet was designed without any contemplation of national boundaries. The actual traffic in the Net is totally unbounded with respect to geography.' Vint[on] Cerf, who uttered those words, should know; he helped design the computer protocols that made the Internet possible. And yet the 'father of the Internet' is only partially right. Yes, the Internet he designed did not contemplate national boundaries. But no . . . the Internet is not 'unbound with respect to geography.' Cerf's central mistake, a mistake typically made about the Internet, is to believe that there was something necessary or unchangeable about the Net's original architecture.

– Harvard Professor Jack Goldsmith and Columbia Professor Tim Wu[3]

Dr. Charlie Miller says that he can crash the Internet and take control of some of the most protected computer systems in the world.[4] Miller, now a cybersecurity analyst at Twitter,[5] was the first person to break into Apple's iPhone; he discovered a software flaw that would have allowed him to take control of every iPhone on the planet.[6] He has won the prestigious Black Hat cybersecurity competition, among numerous other awards, and worked for the NSA for five years.[7] In 2010, while presenting at a NATO Committee of Excellence conference on cyber conflict in Tallinn, Estonia, Miller conducted a thought experiment – if he was forced to, how would he go about crashing the Internet and taking control of well-defended computer systems?[8]

---

[3] JACK GOLDSMITH & TIM WU, WHO CONTROLS THE INTERNET? ILLUSIONS OF A BORDERLESS WORLD 58 (2006).

[4] Charlie Miller, Presentation at the NATO Cooperative Cyber Defence Centre of Excellence (CCD-COE) Conference, in Tallinn, Est. (June 17, 2010), http://ccdcoe.org/conference2010/materials/app .html.

[5] *See* Andy Greenberg, *Twitter Hires Elite Apple Hacker Charlie Miller To Beef Up Its Security Team*, FORBES (Sept. 14, 2012), http://www.forbes.com/sites/andygreenberg/2012/09/14/twitter-snags-elite-apple-hacker-charlie-miller-to-beef-up-its-security-team/.

[6] *See* Andy Greenberg, *How to Hijack 'Every iPhone in the World'*, FORBES (July 28, 2009), http://www .forbes.com/2009/07/28/hackers-iphone-apple-technology-security-hackers.html.

[7] *See* Kelly J. Higgins, *Apple 'Ban' Gives Miller Time To Hack Other Things*, SEC. DARK READING (July 10, 2012), http://www.darkreading.com/end-user/apple-ban-gives-miller-time-to-hack-othe/240003490.

[8] Miller, *supra* note 4.

In the scenario that he imagined, former North Korean leader Kim Jong-Il had kidnapped and induced him to "hack the planet" – to control as many protected systems and Internet hosts as possible so as to dominate cyberspace. Miller then catalogued all of the steps that would be required to meet this audacious and dastardly goal.

He would need people – roughly 600 working throughout the world, and a way to communicate with them.[9] The trick would be identifying them – a task made easier if Miller or another expert in the field was a willing co-conspirator with a North Korean intelligence agency like the Cabinet General Intelligence Bureau.[10] Assuming that he could gather the necessary talent, Table 3.1 describes how Miller would divide tasks among his "army."

Miller's cyber army would need funding and "weapons" like botnets, distributed denial of service attacks, and – above all – zero-day exploits, all of which are described in this chapter. These weapons would often use the Internet, but to complete his hack, Miller would also need to compromise hard, protected targets that are often "air gapped," or not connected to the Internet. High-profile attacks like Stuxnet, the exfiltrated documents published by WikiLeaks, and the 2008 breach of classified U.S. government systems are examples of these types of attacks on supposedly isolated targets.[11] Attackers look for entry points that are poorly defended with the goal of using one host to infect others on the closed network.[12] This could be accomplished by low-tech means, such as through a simple flash drive.[13]

Lastly, Miller would need time. For the first three months, his cyber army would search for vulnerabilities. From three to nine months, zero-day exploits would be identified and used to take over routers. After one year, some hard, protected targets would be compromised. At eighteen months, sufficient zero-day exploits would be found and air-gapped systems compromised to begin final planning. Finally, after two years, the attack could start manifesting itself assuming that no law enforcement agency or other group identified the attackers in the meantime, which is a rather large assumption.

The bottom line, according to Miller, is that the Internet and even air-gapped computer systems may be controlled or crashed for roughly $50 million, which is

---

[9] *Id.*

[10] *See North Korean Intelligence Agencies*, FAS, www.fas.org/irp/world/dprk/index.html (last visited June 12, 2013).

[11] *See, e.g.*, Tom Gjelten, *For Recent Cyberattacks, Motivations Vary*, NPR (June 16, 2011), http://www.npr.org/2011/06/16/137210246/for-recent-cyberattacks-motivations-vary (reporting on a subset of cyber attacks and discussing the varying motivations of attackers); *Protecting SCADA Systems with Air Gaps is a Myth*, INFOSEC ISLAND, May 21, 2012, http://www.infosecisland.com/blogview/21388-Protecting-SCADA-Systems-with-Air-Gaps-is-a-Myth.html (discussing air gapping).

[12] Miller, *supra* note 4.

[13] *See, e.g.*, Farhad Manjoo, *Don't Stick It In: The Dangers of USB Drives*, SLATE (Oct. 5, 2010), http://www.slate.com/articles/technology/technology/2010/10/dont_stick_it_in.html.

TABLE 3.1. *Charlie Miller's hypothetical cyber army*[14]

Job title	Brief job description	Approximate number of hackers required	Total cost (in millions, USD)
Vulnerability analyst	Find bugs in code: need to be world-class programmers	20	$2.9
Exploit developers	Research and exploit vulnerabilities across a range of platforms	70	$7.3
Botnet collectors	Collect hosts (i.e., take over millions of computers)	60	$4.15
Botnet maintainers	Monitor size and health of botnets	220	$12.9
Operators	Exploit hard and soft targets	60	$5.4
Remote personnel	Set up operations around the world and access "air-gapped systems"	20	$.4
Developers	Develop custom software, including bots	40	$2.85
Testers	Test exploits for functionality and reliability	15	$.8
Technical consultants	Offer expertise in specific systems, like SCADA and medical devices	20	$2
System administrators	Keep systems running and updated	10	$.5
Managers	Manage the army	52	$6.2

reportedly less than what North Korea spends on cybersecurity annually.[15] Richard Clarke, among others, has warned that North Korea will not shy away from using its cyber warfare capabilities in a conflict.[16] This danger is posed by other isolated

[14] Miller, *supra* note 4.

[15] *Id. see also* SEC'Y OF DEF., MILITARY AND SECURITY DEVELOPMENTS INVOLVING THE DEMOCRATIC PEOPLE'S REPUBLIC OF KOREA 9 (2012) (an annual report to Congress discussing North Korea's cyber warfare capabilities).

[16] *See* Andy Greenberg, *Security Guru Richard Clarke Talks Cyberwar*, FORBES (Apr. 8, 2010), http://www.forbes.com/2010/04/08/cyberwar-obama-korea-technology-security-clarke.html.

regimes as well, and there is "anecdotal evidence that unknown parties have explored the possibility of disrupting the global network."[17] Sound ripe for a spy thriller? What is good for genre-writing enthusiasts is rarely an ideal starting point for policymakers. According to some commentators, such narratives merely serve to inflate fears and undermine constructive efforts to enhance cybersecurity,[18] and it is true that such a scenario is highly unlikely. But there is some value to be extracted from this tale. The vulnerabilities that Miller points to are real and require our attention if we are to ensure that fiction does not become reality.

This chapter fills in the analytical background to Miller's narrative by analyzing the key vulnerabilities in the Internet's infrastructure, protocols, and code, and how they may be better managed through targeted interventions at multiple levels. First, though, we begin by investigating how it is possible to regulate through architecture to enhance cybersecurity, building from the work of Professors Lessig and Murray, as well as other regulatory theorists.[19] Afterward, the Internet's systemic vulnerabilities are explored along with how cyber attackers are exploiting them, using case studies such as *GhostNet*. Finally, we address the extent to which the prospects for cyber peace may be improved through a polycentric approach to addressing technical vulnerabilities.

REGULATING THROUGH NETWORK ARCHITECTURE
TO ENHANCE CYBERSECURITY

Technology is a critical component of managing vulnerabilities in the cyber regulatory environment, but implementing fixes and enhancing cybersecurity requires an understanding of the multiple layers that comprise cyberspace.[20] Sir Tim Berners-Lee analyzes four distinct layers of Internet architecture: the transmission, computer, software, and content layers.[21] Critically, each layer "only uses functions from the layer below, and only exports functionality to the layer above."[22] This means that mitigation strategies are most efficiently introduced from the bottom-up, leading to both opportunities and challenges for regulators and illustrating the potential for polycentric governance in this context.[23]

---

[17] James A. Lewis, *The "Korean" Cyber Attacks and Their Implications for Cyber Conflict*, CSIS 6 n.7 (2009), http://csis.org/files/publication/091023_Korean_Cyber_Attacks_and_Their_Implications_for_Cyber_Conflict.pdf.

[18] *See, e.g.*, *Cyberwar: War in the Fifth Domain*, ECONOMIST, July 3, 2010, at 25 (reporting on the unlikelihood of a cyber apocalypse) [hereinafter *Cyberwar*].

[19] *See* ANDREW W. MURRAY, THE REGULATION OF CYBERSPACE: CONTROL IN THE ONLINE ENVIRONMENT 43 (2006).

[20] *Id.*

[21] *Id.* (citing TIM BERNERS-LEE, WEAVING THE WEB: THE ORIGINAL DESIGN AND ULTIMATE DESTINY OF THE WORLD WIDE WEB BY ITS INVENTOR 129–30 (2000)).

[22] *Id.*

[23] *Id.* at 44–45.

To help translate these insights into a regulatory framework for policymakers, Harvard Professor Yochai Benkler has introduced a simplified three-layer structure composed of: (1) the "physical infrastructure," including the fiber-optic cables and routers making up the physical aspect of cyberspace; (2) the "logical infrastructure," comprising necessary "software such as the TCP/IP protocol"; and (3) the "content layer," which includes data and, indirectly, users.[24] This model has also been adopted with some modifications by Professor Lessig to help explain how code regulates content and becomes law,[25] and to advocate for protecting openness so as to incentivize "decentralized innovation" through codifying such architecture in the supporting layers.[26] However, Professor Murray has argued that such an approach is "idealistic" and could create conflict, observing that, "the harnessing of one regulatory modality through the application of another is more likely to lead to further regulatory competition, due to the complexity of the network environment."[27] Instead of solely relying on code, then, laws, norms, and markets also have important roles to play in shaping this polycentric regulatory environment as discussed throughout the remainder of this book.[28] Because of its emphasis on targeted measures, self-organization, and collaborative bottom-up governance, polycentric governance may provide an avenue to better understand this regulatory complexity and how it can be harnessed to enhance cybersecurity. Yet in order to conceptualize such a dynamic environment operating at multiple scales, it is first necessary to analyze the Internet's architecture along with efforts to make it more secure at all levels.

Securing the Internet's Physical Infrastructure

Recall the last time you logged on to check your personal email. The way you did so is probably very similar to the way someone halfway across the world would do so. We tend to access the Internet in similar ways; we request IP addresses through the same sorts of servers and send messages along the same types of routers. This means that we all use the same Internet protocols, or standards, which are written and published by bodies such as the IETF as discussed in Chapter 1. Then, we use the same sorts of devices, operating systems, applications, and programs to create documents, open attachments, and send emails. And, we are all human, which means we have

[24] *Id.* (citing Yochai Benkler, *From Consumers to Users: Shifting the Deeper Structure of Regulation Toward Sustainable Commons and User Access*, 52 FED. COMM. L.J. 561, 562 (2000)).

[25] *See* LAWRENCE LESSIG, FREE CULTURE: HOW BIG MEDIA USES TECHNOLOGY AND THE LAW TO LOCK DOWN CULTURE AND CONTROL CREATIVITY 160 (2004) (describing "the interaction between architecture and law" in the context of copyright regulation).

[26] LAWRENCE LESSIG, THE FUTURE OF IDEAS: THE FATE OF THE COMMONS IN A CONNECTED WORLD 85 (2002); MURRAY, *supra* note 19, at 46.

[27] MURRAY, *supra* note 19, at 46 ("It is highly unlikely that content producers, media corporations and other copyright holders will allow for a neutral system designed to protect cultural property and creativity at the cost of loss of control over their products.").

[28] *Id.* at 46–47, 124.

common experiences while using this hardware and software. Shared vulnerabilities exist at each of these levels contributing to the cyber threat, beginning with the Internet's physical infrastructure.

At its most basic level, the Internet is composed of a series of cables, computers, and routers.[29] Innocent or malicious hardware flaws in this physical infrastructure can give rise to myriad vulnerabilities. As Clarke and Knake explain, "What can be done to millions of lines of code can also be done with millions of circuits imprinted on computer chips inside computers, routers, and servers."[30] Circuits leave physical trapdoors, but as with code, most experts cannot easily identify flaws in a computer chip.[31] Indeed, producing a microchip requires some 400 steps.[32] Aside from manufacturing or design defects, some bugs may be purposefully implanted. A 2012 Microsoft report found malware being installed in PCs at factories in China, highlighting the insecurity of production lines.[33] U.S. government reports have also cited supply chain concerns for hardware, finding components embedded with security flaws.[34] In a worst-case scenario, kill switches could be installed in Pentagon networks to power down critical systems by remote control as a prelude to an attack. Yet revelations from Edward Snowden have revealed that the NSA has also been intercepting computer shipments to install backdoors in hardware and even spy on Microsoft's internal communications system.[35]

The U.S. Department of Defense's commercial-off-the-shelf (COTS) program was intended to help drive down costs for proven technologies by using state-of-the-art commercial systems in lieu of the cost-plus-award-fee method that covered contractors costs and paid them a profit.[36] The advantages of COTS are self-evident, but with a COTS item – such as Dell computer hardware, which has been widely used by the Department of Defense – the government cannot monitor the manufacturing process.[37] Thus, the true cost of COTS lies in the vulnerabilities that it introduces

---

[29] *Id.* at 44.
[30] Richard A. Clarke & Robert K. Knake, Cyber War: The Next Threat to National Security and What to Do About It 95 (2010).
[31] *Id.*
[32] *See* Wesley K. Clark & Peter L. Levin, *Securing the Information Highway*, Foreign Aff. (Nov.–Dec. 2009), http://www.afa.org/edop/2009/edop_10-23-09.asp.
[33] *Malware Inserted on PC Production Lines, Says Study*, BBC (Sept. 13, 2012), http://www.bbc.com/news/technology-19585433.
[34] *See* Clarke & Knake, *supra* note 30, at 95; Aliya Sternstein, *Threat of Destructive Coding on Foreign-Manufactured Technology is Real*, NextGov (July 7, 2011), http://www.nextgov.com/cybersecurity/2011/07/threat-of-destructive-coding-on-foreign-manufactured-technology-is-real/49363/.
[35] *See, e.g.*, Raphael Satter, *Report: NSA Intercepts Computer Deliveries*, AP (Dec. 29, 2013), http://hosted.ap.org/dynamic/stories/E/EU_NSA_SURVEILLANCE?SITE=AP&SECTION=HOME&TEMPLATE=DEFAULT.
[36] *See, e.g.*, Press Release, Frost & Sullivan, U.S. Department of Defense to Increasingly Rely on Commercial Off-the-Shelf Aircraft, Notes Frost & Sullivan, (June 6, 2013), http://www.frost.com/prod/servlet/press-release.pag?docid=279378546 (reporting on spending increases on the DOD's COTS aircraft purchase program).
[37] *See* Clarke & Knake, *supra* note 30, at 86 (discussing the production process of a Dell laptop).

into critical national infrastructure.[38] Grasping how to best contain the issue of hardware flaws is difficult because the supply chain involves many companies operating in myriad countries. According to some experts like Clarke, buying hardware that has been manufactured abroad leaves U.S. systems vulnerable to attacks.[39] However, there are not enough U.S. manufacturers to allow the Pentagon to buy domestically, as shown by the DOD's purchase of 2,200 Sony PlayStation 3s in 2009 to provide processing power for a military supercomputer.[40] These systems are often manufactured abroad in nations including China that have track records of supply chain insecurity.[41] Once compromised, hardware is often in the hands of an unknowing user. Few hardware vulnerabilities are likely to be discovered and fixed – and even fewer are likely to be attributed to a particular cyber attacker.

More can be done to secure the Internet's physical infrastructure. New add-on security features are needed to safeguard systems,[42] as are quality control and, in the U.S. context, more domestic sources of key components. The DOD, for example, could revise COTS and make a long-standing commitment to U.S. firms to purchase critical components domestically. This would have the dual benefits of being both a boon to the U.S. electronics industry by creating good U.S. jobs as well as promoting cybersecurity. Though far from a perfect solution since domestically produced hardware may still be vulnerable to insider attacks and such protectionism would need to be targeted, transparent, and justifiable to assuage concerns over touching off a trade war,[43] it could be an improvement on the status quo. Securing the physical layer, though, is merely the first step toward enhancing cybersecurity and ultimately fostering cyber peace.

[38] *See also* Elizabeth Montalbano, *DOD Approves Dell Android Tablet For Use*, INFO. WK. (Oct. 31, 2011), http://www.informationweek.com/government/mobile/dod-approves-dell-android-tablet-for-use/231901988 (reporting on an example of DOD purchases of Dell products).

[39] *See* Adrian Kingsley-Hughes, *Hardware Imported from China Could Leave U.S. Open to Cyber-Threats*, ZDNET (Mar. 30, 2012), http://www.zdnet.com/blog/hardware/hardware-imported-from-china-could-leave-us-open-to-cyber-threats/19400.

[40] *See Military Purchases 2,200 PS3s*, CNN (Dec. 9, 2009), http://scitech.blogs.cnn.com/2009/12/09/military-purchases-2200-ps3s/.

[41] *See* WHITE HOUSE, CYBERSPACE POLICY REVIEW: ASSURING A TRUSTED AND RESILIENT INFORMATION AND COMMUNICATIONS INFRASTRUCTURE 34 (2011) (noting that "the emergence of new centers for manufacturing, design, and research across the globe raises concerns about the potential for easier subversion of computers and networks through subtle hardware or software manipulations.") [hereinafter CYBERSPACE POLICY REVIEW]; *Sony to Manufacture PS3 in China to Ensure Supply (SNE)*, SEEKING ALPHA (May 16, 2006), http://seekingalpha.com/article/10729-sony-to-manufacture-ps3-in-china-to-ensure-supply-sne.

[42] *See* NATIONAL INFORMATION ASSURANCE (IA) GLOSSARY, COMM. NAT'L SEC. SYS. 2 (CNSS No. 4009, 2010), http://www.cnss.gov/Assets/pdf/cnssi_4009.pdf.

[43] *See* CYBERSPACE POLICY REVIEW, *supra* note 41, at 34 ("Foreign manufacturing does present easier opportunities for nation-state adversaries to subvert products; however, the same goals could be achieved through the recruitment of key insiders or other espionage activities."); Allan A. Friedman, *Cybersecurity and Trade: National Policies, Global and Local Consequences*, BROOKINGS INST. 4–5 (2013), http://www.brookings.edu/~/media/research/files/papers/2013/09/19%20cybersecurity%20and%20trade%20global%20local%20friedman/brookingscybersecuritynew.pdf.

Managing Vulnerabilities in the Logical Infrastructure

As Chapter 1 described, security has not scaled along with the expanding Internet. Early networks such as ARPANET, used by a relatively small population of engineers and academics, had little need for built-in security. Cybersecurity concerns grew as the Internet evolved, but technologies that brought interoperability and efficiency were favored over better security, which could slow systems down or make them incompatible. As a result, many potential measures that could enhance cybersecurity became mired in debate.[44] In particular, there are four protocols that represent key aspects of the Internet's architecture and present significant vulnerabilities in the logical infrastructure: the Transport Control Protocol (TCP), the Internet Protocol (IP), the Domain Name System (DNS) protocol, and the Border Gateway Protocol (BGP). TCP, IP, and DNS were introduced in Chapter 1; TCP/IP is the set of protocols that Kahn and Cerf designed, easing interconnection and laying the groundwork for the Internet.[45] DNS is the Internet's address system, created by Postel and others, that works as a phone book to map domain names to IP addresses. BGP tells routers how and where to send information and is the protocol that enables distributed routing. Each of these protocols and their vulnerabilities are addressed in turn, along with efforts to make them more secure within a polycentric framework.

TCP/IP

Together, TCP and IP describe how the Internet transmits information from one place to another by addressing, fragmenting, and reassembling packets of data between two reliable hosts[46] – not completely unlike the transporters on *Star Trek*. IP, however, is an unreliable, "best effort" protocol, meaning that packets are not inherently secure.[47] There is no easy way to verify who sent an IP packet, determine whether it has been modified, or even ascertain if anyone has viewed it en route. It is the job of TCP to add reliability by monitoring the delivery of IP packets.[48] As the layer of the Internet Protocol Suite situated between the Internet layer and the applications layer, TCP acts as a go-between. It turns fragmented data into a coherent stream. Many applications, like the web and email, use TCP because of its reliability.

Although TCP provides some protection against packets going astray, it was never intended to provide security against a malicious adversary modifying or inserting

---

44 *See* Robert K. Knake, Council on Foreign Rel., Internet Governance in an Age of Cyber Insecurity vii (2010).

45 *See* Murray, *supra* note 19, at 67–68.

46 Internet Protocol: Darpa Internet Program Protocol Specification, Info. Scis. Inst. (1981) http://tools.ietf.org/html/rfc791.

47 *Id.*; *TCP/IP Core Protocols*, Microsoft TechNet, http://technet.microsoft.com/en-us/library/cc958827.aspx (last visited Jan. 14, 2014).

48 Transmission Control Protocol: Darpa Internet Program Protocol Specification, Info. Scis. Inst. (1981), http://tools.ietf.org/html/rfc793.

packets into communications between two parties.[49] For example, before data can be transferred between two hosts, TCP must first establish a connection between them through a process that is often referred to as a "three-way handshake," akin to the exchange of "hellos" to start a telephone conversation.[50] These "hello" messages in technical parlance are called SYN messages, or synchronized packets. A malicious attacker posing as a client can use a "SYN flood" by falsifying or omitting information to render a server unable to complete its part of the handshake,[51] an experience that may be likened to tying up a switchboard with incoming callers who refuse to hang up.

As with IP, TCP was recognized by the mid-1990s as insecure.[52] Extra security was introduced into the three-way handshake, such as IETF randomizing certain information to guard against sequence number spoofing.[53] Although this limited attacks against TCP, it has not eliminated all vulnerabilities. In part, TCP remains vulnerable because IP is vulnerable: by hijacking IP packets, an attacker can eavesdrop on a TCP session, record the sequence of numbers being used, and forge a set of false IP packets that trick TCP.[54] This allows for spying, a starting point for cyber espionage and crime, which are both core threats to cyber peace.

DNS

In August 2013, the *New York Times* online operations, along with an array of other organizations such as Twitter, were hacked, allegedly by the Syrian Electronic Army.[55] These and other sites have been compromised as a result of insecurities in the DNS, allowing attackers to, for example, "limit access" to the *New York Times*

---

[49] *See Security Threats*, MICROSOFT TECHNET, http://technet.microsoft.com/en-us/library/cc723507 .aspx (last visited June 12, 2013) (providing an overview of cybersecurity threats including those targeting TCP) [hereinafter *Security Threats*].

[50] Randall Stewart & Chris Metz, *SCTP: New Transport Protocol for TCP/IP*, 5(6) IEEE INTERNET COMPUTING 64, 67 (2001).

[51] *See id.* at 65, 67; WESLEY EDDY, TCP SYN FLOODING ATTACKS AND COMMON MITIGATIONS, IETF RFC 4987 (2007), http://tools.ietf.org/html/rfc4987. For further discussion of SYN functionality, see Hossein Falaki et al., *A First Look at Traffic on Smartphones*, IMC INTERNET MEASUREMENT CONF. PROC. 281, 285 (2010), https://research.microsoft.com/en-us/um/people/ratul/papers/imc2010-smartphone-traffic .pdf.

[52] *See* Chris Chambers, Justin Dolske, & Jayaraman Iyer, *TCP/IP Security*, DEP'T COMP. SCI. OHIO ST. UNIV., http://www.linuxsecurity.com/resource_files/documentation/tcpip-security.html (last visited Jan. 14, 2014) ("Although it is not possible to go back in time and change history, we can look forward to the future. In the 1990s, TCP/IP security is a concern, and a newer version of the protocol has been developed[,]" namely IPv6).

[53] *See* STEVEN M. BELLOVIN, DEFENDING AGAINST SEQUENCE NUMBER ATTACKS, IETF RFC 1948 (1996), http://tools.ietf.org/html/rfc1948.

[54] *See Security Threats, supra* note 49.

[55] *See* Hayley Tsukayama & Timothy B. Lee, *How the Syrian Electronic Army and Other Hacker Groups are Attacking News Web Sites*, WASH. POST (Aug. 28, 2013), http://www.washingtonpost.com/business/ economy/how-the-syrian-electronic-army-and-other-hacker-groups-are-attacking-news-web-sites/ 2013/08/28/bda8f464-1032-11e3-8cdd-bcdc09410972_story.html?wpmk=MK0000200.

website "for nearly than 48 hours."[56] In this case, attackers hacked into an Australian domain name registry and managed to alter stored information there allowing them to redirect users to a webpage sporting whatever information the Syrian Electronic Army wished to post.[57]

Unfortunately, such attacks are far from the exception since, like IP and TCP, DNS was recognized as being insecure in the mid-1990s, but fixes stalled.[58] Then, in 2008, hacker Dan Kaminsky found a bug that demonstrated the full extent of the DNS Protocol's vulnerability,[59] in essence demonstrating the concept years before the Syrian Electronic Army's attacks. In short, the system could be manipulated so that the wrong IP addresses could be linked to a domain name, tricking users into visiting the wrong website. For example, users could write their banks' web addresses into their browsers and end up at fake sites where they might unknowingly enter their credentials. Thus, the process of matching a domain name to its correct IP address – the main job of the DNS protocol – was unreliable and insecure.[60] This is because the DNS, like many other protocols, was designed to work despite accidental failures but not malicious attacks. According to Von Welch, deputy director of the Indiana University Center for Applied Cybersecurity Research, "What we've been seeing is the slow hardening of the protocols to try and turn their failure protections into attack protections."[61]

Kaminsky's bug is not the simplest of things to understand, so consider the following analogy. Imagine you live in an alternate universe, wherein every day you must search for the location of your bank. The address of your bank never changes, but you cannot remember the address – you only know it by its name, Susie's Wonderful Bank (SWB). The place that maintains address information for your local branch of SWB would be too busy to function effectively if everyone lined up outside of its doors every day, so most of the time, you just go to a local shop to ask for directions. When you walk into any such shop, all you have to do is write down your request for "Susie's Wonderful Bank" on a piece of paper, submit it at the front counter, and wait.

The person at the front counter will give you the address of SWB immediately if the person in line before you requested it as well; otherwise, you will have to wait a bit longer until a front counter attendant can connect with a bank representative to find an address. Many of the representatives are simultaneously responding to your query as well as others' requests for different banks, so the attendant will have to sift through many pieces of paper to find the response that matches your request. In doing so, the attendant is looking for two things. One: the name of the corporation.

---

[56] *Id.*

[57] *See id.*

[58] *See* Chambers, *supra* note 52.

[59] *See, e.g.,* Cory Wright, *Understanding Kaminsky's DNS Bug*, LINUX J. (July 25, 2008), http://www.linuxjournal.com/content/understanding-kaminskys-dns-bug (detailing the Kaminsky bug).

[60] *See id.*

[61] Electronic Interview with Von Welch, deputy director, Indiana University Center for Applied Cybersecurity Research (Sept. 23, 2011).

In order to prove that they have the right address, bank representatives must show that they obtained their information from an authoritative source. Two: a code. Every morning, front desk attendants are told codes of the day for each local bank; these will be a number between zero and 65536. When attendants pass your request along to all of the representatives, they label it with the day's code. Bank representatives that respond to your request will have noted the day's code, and will include it on their responses. As such, the first piece of paper that the attendant comes across that has some form of "Susie's" and the right code is the one that he or she will hand to you. You will trust that the response is correct and will proceed to that address without fear of being misled.

Except recall that the local shops are open to the public, and people are milling around. Some people will go to the shops every day, acting like representatives and hoping to throw a bank's clients off course because front desk attendants do not always have time to verify that representatives are who they say they are. Every day, these imposters will write many responses for places like SWB, but instead of including the right address they will make one up. On the many copies that they write, they will include faked code numbers. They will do this for many banks and submit these papers to attendants in many shops, and occasionally, they will get lucky and overload an attendant with responses. All it takes is one correct guess to lead a bank client astray to a fake bank that looks like that person's normal bank. Once arriving at the fake bank, that person will hand over all of their credit card and bank account numbers, which the fake representative can then misuse.

This scavenger hunt-like process parallels what happens on the Internet every time you want to travel to an IP address for which you only remember the domain name. Just as your local branch address information center could not manage traffic if everyone requested information from it daily, the DNS can get overloaded if it is repeatedly queried for an IP address. As a result, the DNS has a hierarchy wherein domains and sub-domains only have to keep track of their own IP addresses. DNS servers mirror the DNS hierarchy, and only a limited number of servers at each level of the hierarchy keep track of their particular set of IP addresses. This is like Susie's Bank being part of a multinational corporation, wherein an international office only keeps track of the addresses of national offices, which only record the addresses of regional offices, and so on. Thus you, the bank client, cannot visit any number of offices around the world to find out your local branch's address; there are a limited number of places that hold the official records. But nor do you always have to look it up with the official record holder; "recursive DNS servers" store and help to find IP addresses, especially those that we visit often.[62] There are typically three players in the process of resolving a DNS request: "your computer, your ISP[']s recursive DNS servers, and a website's authoritative DNS servers."[63] Authoritative

---

[62] Wright, *supra* note 59.
[63] *Id.*

DNS servers are responsible for maintaining accurate records of IP addresses for their particular domains, like Susie's regional offices, whereas recursive DNS servers serve as go-betweens, like the local shops.[64]

When you type a domain name like www.susieswonderfulbank.com into your web browser, your computer asks a recursive DNS server to return the IP address of that domain. Sometimes, recursive DNS servers know the address that you have requested immediately because they cache answers to address queries for a length of time – just as the front desk attendant at the local shop remembers an address when the person in line before you has requested it. However, when recursive DNS servers do not have an answer ready, they must ask authoritative DNS servers to resolve the query.[65] The response even tells the recursive DNS server how long to store this information in its cache[66]; for example, it might say 300,000 seconds, which is roughly three and a half days. If an authoritative DNS server sends back information about an unrelated domain name, like www.lisasbank.com, recursive DNS servers and your computer will ignore it using a technique called "bailiwick checking."[67] Since the late 1990s, most recursive DNS servers and computers, also called "resolvers," have used bailiwick checking to keep servers from "poisoning" a cache with such misleading information.[68] In effect, bailiwick checking means that records representing a different domain from that which was queried are ignored.[69] Moreover, the authoritative DNS server's response will have a code that tells the recursive DNS server that the authoritative server is legitimate.[70] Like bailiwick checking, this was intended to add security to the DNS protocol. However, hackers work around these security measures by guessing codes, oftentimes through the use of bots discussed later in the chapter.[71]

With all of this background, we can return to Kaminsky's bug. To take advantage of it, an attacker would likely plant fake web pages that are extensions of the same domain. Then, when users click on links with the same authority record, their browsers would ask a resolver which web page to display by using different codes. If an attacker constantly sends answers to all of the users' resolvers with the help of a bot, he or she will eventually guess the right code. The recursive DNS server will then think that the response was from an authoritative DNS server, and the response will be accepted. Because the wrong answer will be stored in that resolver's cache, everyone using the poisoned ISP is at risk until the specified time expires. In 2009, a Brazilian bank reported that its ISP was poisoned and "that some of its customers

---

[64] *Id.*

[65] *Id.*

[66] See *How DNS Query Works*, Microsoft (Jan. 21, 2005), http://technet.microsoft.com/en-us/library/cc775637%28v=ws.10%29.aspx.

[67] Wright, *supra* note 59.

[68] *Id.*

[69] *Id.*

[70] *Id.*

[71] See Yurie Ito, Making the Internet DNS More Secure and Resilient: An ICANN Perspective, http://www.cu.IPv6tf.org/lacnic13/04-lacNIC-yurieito.pdf (last visited Jan. 14, 2014).

were redirected to websites" that were designed "to steal their passwords[.]"[72] *Linux Journal* blogger Cory Wright wrote of Kaminsky's bug: "Yes, the exploit is real, and it is severe." He also suggested it "may be the biggest DNS security issue in the history of the Internet.... "[73]

BGP

The Border Gateway Protocol is the core routing protocol of all of the networks that comprise the Internet.[74] Like the other protocols discussed in this section, it is charged with a fundamental task – telling information how to move. When an email, for example, is sent from one network to another, it passes through routers. When a router receives an IP packet, BGP uses an algorithm to make decisions about where to route it next.[75] BGP keeps routers up-to-date with information they need to receive and correctly transmit traffic.[76] As such, it is important that the information BGP provides is accurate and reliable. However, like IP, BGP offers insufficient ways to confirm accuracy. Rather, sets of routers under a single administration, which are known as "autonomous systems," trade data that is taken at face value enabling fast and scaled growth, but less control.[77] There were more than 25,000 registered autonomous systems comprising the Internet as of 2007,[78] but BGP does not have an authentication mechanism to ensure that updates really are from where they purport to be.[79] It does not have anything equivalent to a recursive DNS server's code to double-check. BGP simply trusts the updates, which has earned it the euphemism, "routing by rumor."[80] More and more, however, this trust is

---

[72] See Bill Snyder, *What You Missed: A Major Internet Security Hole was Finally Plugged*, INFOWORLD (Dec. 31, 2010), http://www.infoworld.com/t/authentication-and-authorization/what-you-missed-major-internet-security-hole-was-finally-plugged-896.

[73] Wright, *supra* note 59.

[74] See Y. RECHTER ET AL., A BORDER GATEWAY PROTOCOL 4 (BGP-4), IETF RFC 4271 (2006), http://www.ietf.org/rfc/rfc4271.

[75] RICK KUHN, KOTIKALAPUDI SRIRAM, & DOUG MONTGOMERY, NAT'L INST. STANDARDS & TECH., BORDER GATEWAY PROTOCOL SECURITY, at 1-1, 2-3-1 (2007), http://csrc.nist.gov/publications/nistpubs/800-54/SP800-54.pdf.

[76] *Id.* at 2-1.

[77] See Fariba Khan & Carl A. Gunter, *Tiered Incentives for Integrity Based Queuing*, PROC. WORKSHOP ECON. NETWORKS, SYSTEMS, & COMPUTATION 1, 1 (2010), http://netecon.seas.harvard.edu/NetEcon10/Papers/Khan10.pdf.

[78] *Id.* at 6.

[79] KUHN, SRIRAM, & MONTGOMERY, *supra* note 75, at 3-1.

[80] JAMES MACFARLANE, NETWORK ROUTING BASICS: UNDERSTANDING IP ROUTING IN CISCO SYSTEMS 109 (2006); H. Shokrzadeh et al., *Improving Directional Rumor Routing in Wireless Sensor Networks*, IEEE INT'L CONF. 1, 1 (2007). There are six types, or principles, of security that enable users to have increasing "trust" in their hardware and software, including: confidentiality, integrity, availability, consistency, control, and audit. *See* SIMSON GARFINKEL ET AL., PRACTICAL UNIX AND INTERNET SECURITY 33–35 (3d ed. 2003) (noting that often, security professionals "use the word *trust* to describe their level of confidence that a computer system will behave as expected."). Confidentiality, like privacy, means "[p]rotecting information from being read or copied by anyone who has not been authorized by the owner of that information," whereas integrity signifies protecting information from being altered or deleted without authorization. *Id.* at 33. Availability involves protecting services from being degraded.

being broken as "Internet disruptions due to corrupt or improperly formatted or assigned BGP announcements are becoming more prevalent."[81] In 2004, thousands of U.S. networks "were misdirected to Turkey"; in 2005, "AT&T, XO and Bell South networks were misdirected to Bolivia"; and in 2007, "Yahoo was unreachable for an hour due to a routing problem."[82] Some of these incidents may have been accidental, but all likely were not. For example, in 2008, Pakistan Telecom purportedly "hijacked all traffic aimed at YouTube[,]" taking the website offline for several hours.[83] In 2010, a Chinese state-controlled telecommunications company commandeered 15 percent of the Internet's routers, intercepting data from the U.S. military for eighteen minutes without anyone seeming to notice the service disruption.[84] Dmitri Alperovitch, vice president of threat research at the anti-virus firm McAfee, said that the incident represented "one of the biggest – if not the biggest – hijacks – we have ever seen" while noting that "it could happen again, anywhere and anytime."[85]

"BGP eavesdropping" is a threat that "has long been considered a theoretical weakness" by intelligence agencies such as NSA, which has reportedly been given private demonstrations of the capability.[86] Besides disruptive hijacking and imperceptible eavesdropping, however, the BGP vulnerability also enables many other exploits, including "network overloading," which reduces the bandwidth available for other traffic, "black holes," which involves sending traffic to routers that "drop some or all" IP packets, and "looping," wherein IP packets "enter a looping path" and are never delivered but use up bandwidth.[87] In short, the BGP is the most scalable of all routing protocols, but it is also at the "greatest risk of being the target of attacks designed to disrupt or degrade service on a large scale."[88] The question then becomes, how can we better manage this and other protocol vulnerabilities?

Protocol Fixes

Efforts aimed at securing vulnerabilities in IP, TCP, DNS, and BGP are ongoing, as are debates about the Internet's design and how security might be enhanced. One

---

Id. Consistency implies ensuring that a system behaves as expected, control involves "[r]egulating access," and audit means system owners have "record[s] of activity" that allow them to trace mistakes or malicious acts. *Id.* at 33–34. Vulnerabilities lie in these principles' non-achievement, stemming from problems with Internet Protocols to flaws in code and the bad practices of users.

[81] Derek Gabbard, *Do Recent BGP Anomalies Shed a Light on What's to Come?*, SEC. WK. (Sept. 29, 2010), http://www.securityweek.com/do-recent-bgp-anomalies-shed-light-whats-come.

[82] Ram Mohan, *Routing on The Internet: A Disaster Waiting to Happen?*, SEC. WK. (Dec. 1, 2010), http://www.securityweek.com/routing-internet-disaster-waiting-happen.

[83] *Id.*

[84] *See* Stew Magnuson, *Cyber Experts Have Proof That China Has Hijacked U.S.-based Internet Traffic*, NAT'L DEF. MAG. (Nov. 12, 2010), http://www.nationaldefensemagazine.org/blog/Lists/Posts/Post.aspx?ID=249.

[85] *Id.*

[86] Kim Zetter, *Revealed: The Internet's Biggest Security Hole*, WIRED (Aug. 26, 2008), http://www.wired.com/threatlevel/2008/08/revealed-the-in/.

[87] KUHN, SRIRAM, & MONTGOMERY, *supra* note 75, at 3–2.

[88] U.S. DEP'T HOMELAND SEC., THE NATIONAL STRATEGY TO SECURE CYBERSPACE 30 (2003).

major issue is over where defenses should be focused – throughout the system or at the "endpoints" (that is, applications closest to the user). Some think that IP, TCP, DNS, and BGP need to be significantly altered so that security is brought in at a fundamental level.[89] Others, however, think that this kind of security would change the nature of the Internet too much by undermining anonymity or be impossible to achieve, preferring instead that security be built into applications like the web or email.[90] Currently, efforts in both veins are being undertaken. For example, IETF editors have written Internet Protocol Security (IPsec), which intends to improve integrity, confidentiality, and control by providing "interoperable, high quality, cryptographically-based" security at the IP layer.[91] IPsec is available for IPv4 and was originally made mandatory by the IETF on all standards-compliant IPv6 networks, but its "actual use . . . is optional."[92] For DNS, a Domain Name Security Extensions (DNSSEC) protocol, which was proposed by IETF in 1997 and revised in 2005, has been receiving attention since Kaminsky's 2008 bug.[93] Nevertheless, like IPsec, implementation has been haphazard, and skepticism remains about whether these solutions actually resolve security problems.

IPsec

Despite IPsec's deployment on all major operating systems, it is still not widely used.[94] Why? Part of the problem lies in market reluctance to bear the cost of enhancing security such as by encrypting traffic. Moreover, IPv6 has not been universally deployed as of 2013 and IPsec is only an optional extension on IPv4[95] – it is still "not the first choice for many security needs."[96] Instead, application-level solutions such as Secure Sockets Layer (SSL), Transport Layer Security (TLS), and Secure Shell (SSH) are sometimes favored as they are easier to deploy.[97] Instead of changing how IP-addressed packets will act on the Internet, SSL/TLS and SSH

---

[89] *See, e.g.,* Tyson Macaulay, *Upstream Intelligence: A New Layer of Cybersecurity,* 13 IA NEWSLETTER 22, 23 (2010) (Def. Technical Info. Ctr., U.S. Dep't of Def.) (discussing a layered cybersecurity approach designed to better manage protocol vulnerabilities).

[90] *See, e.g.,* Clyde Wayne Crews, Jr., *Cybersecurity and Authentication: The Marketplace Role in Rethinking Anonymity – Before Regulators Intervene,* 20(2) KNOW. TECH. & POL. 97, 97–98 (2007) ("Over the coming tumultuous period of dealing with online threats, policymakers should allow the experimentation necessary to cope with today's lack of online authentication to proceed with minimal interference.").

[91] S. KENT & K. SEO, SECURITY ARCHITECTURE FOR THE INTERNET PROTOCOL, IETF RFC 4301 (2005), http://tools.ietf.org/html/rfc4301.

[92] *IPv6 Security Brief,* CISCO 1 (2011), http://www.cisco.com/en/US/prod/collateral/iosswrel/ps6537/ps6553/white_paper_c11-678658.pdf; *see* KENT & SEO, *supra* note 91.

[93] *See* D. EASTLAKE, DOMAIN NAME SYSTEM SECURITY EXTENSIONS, IETF RFC 2535 (1999), http://www.ietf.org/rfc/rfc2535.

[94] Electronic Interview, Yaron Sheffer, chief technology officer, Porticor Cloud Security (Jan. 23, 2011).

[95] *See* J. LOUGHNEY, IPv6 NODE REQUIREMENTS, IETF RFC 4294 (2006), http://tools.ietf.org/html/rfc4294.

[96] Sheffer, *supra* note 94.

[97] *See* B. BRISCOE, TUNNELING OF EXPLICIT CONGESTION NOTIFICATION, IETF RFC 6040 (2010), http://tools.ietf.org/html/rfc6040.

create secure channels of communication that act like private networks built on top of the Internet.[98] SSH, for example, forms a secure shell around data transferred between two particular IP addresses across the open Internet.[99] Remote users and servers are identified at each end of the shell, allowing encrypted messages to be sent and received.[100] Similarly, SSL/TLS uses identification, authentication, and encryption to engender confidentiality and control, enabling it to transmit private information between particular IP addresses on top of the open Internet.[101] To do so, SSL/TLS identifies and "authenticates clients" and servers and then encrypts messages sent between them, such as to create a secure Virtual Private Network (VPN).[102] Because it can protect messages sent between websites and their own servers, SSL/TLS is also often associated with more secure web browsing, or Hypertext Transfer Protocol Secure (HTTPS) rather than Hypertext Transfer Protocol (HTTP).[103] By providing clients with a trustworthy channel by which to communicate, SSL/TLS enables consumers to shop, bank, and otherwise take risks online, although even this technology has been compromised; in 2011, for example, hackers stole credentials, allowing them to spy on 300,000 Gmail accounts.[104]

HTTPS also presents certain security problems that help illustrate the drawbacks of SSL/TLS, including the fact that SSL/TLS certificate authorities, which are third parties that companies and website owners use to implement encryption, are sometimes not themselves trustworthy.[105] Companies like Google or Facebook implicitly trust these certificate authorities even though they can lie about users' identities or be hacked, resulting in an attacker obtaining false certificates.[106] For example, in early 2011, nearly 200 different certificate authorities fulfilled Mozilla policies and thus could be used to find websites on Firefox, including the China Internet Network Information Center (CNNIC), which is run by the Chinese government.[107] In mid-2011, fraudulent certificates were obtained from the servers of Comodo, a popular certificate authority that creates certificates for the likes of Gmail and Yahoo! Mail,

---

[98] *See* Mark Hachman, *IPv4 to IPv6 IP Address Transition Becoming Critical*, PC MAG. (Oct. 18, 2010), http://www.pcmag.com/article2/0,2817,2371036,00.asp; *SSL VPN Security*, CISCO SYS., http://www.cisco.com/web/about/security/intelligence/05_08_SSL-VPN-Security.html.

[99] *See SSL VPN Security, supra* note 98.

[100] *Id.*

[101] *See What is TLS/SSL?*, MICROSOFT TECHNET (Mar. 28, 2003), http://technet.microsoft.com/en-us/library/cc784450(WS.10).aspx.

[102] *Id.*

[103] *Id.* (discussing how HTTPS is the result of layering HTTP with the additional security capabilities of SSL/TLS).

[104] *See Web Commerce Hack Attack May 'Happen Again'*, BBC (Oct. 18, 2011), http://www.bbc.co.uk/news/technology-15348821.

[105] Interview with Chris Palmer, Google engineer and former technology director, Electronic Frontier Foundation, in San Francisco, Cal. (Feb. 25, 2011).

[106] *See, e.g.*, Danny O'Brien, *The Internet's Secret Back Door*, SLATE (Aug. 27, 2010), http://www.slate.com/articles/technology/webhead/2010/08/the_internets_secret_back_door.html (reporting on the vulnerabilities created by these certificate authorities).

[107] *See Add China Internet Network Information Center (CNNIC) CA Root Certificate*, Bugzilla@Mozilla, https://bugzilla.mozilla.org/show_bug.cgi?id=476766; *Mozilla Included CA Certificate List*, MOZILLA, http://www.mozilla.org/projects/security/certs/included/ (last visited Nov. 12, 2013).

allegedly by an Iranian hacker.[108] These episodes help demonstrate that although SSL/TLS has been effective in creating valuable channels of trust on the Internet, this fix cannot compare with IPsec given that SSH and SSL/TLS operate at the application layer of the IP, whereas IPsec works below the application "layer and secures everything [built] . . . on top of the IP network" from the bottom-up.[109] An analogy is going to each parking lot in the United States and installing an anti-theft system on every car versus requiring the factory to do so. Both options have the same effect, but the latter is likely far more efficient.

Nevertheless, IPsec is not a magic bullet. According to Yaron Sheffer – co-chair of IP Security Maintenance and Extensions at the IETF – the success of IPsec has been mixed.[110] Moreover, new standards, such as those involving deep packet inspection, could also undermine the viability of IPsec as a security tool.[111] Those in favor of more endpoint-based security might argue that resources would be better spent on implementing HTTPS and other application-level improvements to IP. However, this could still be a second-best solution to a bottom-up fix such as IPsec, although opinions are mixed. The roll out of IPv6 should help speed uptake of IPsec, but more must be done to incentivize and enhance IPsec as well as application-level security technologies to better manage vulnerabilities. IPv6, for example, boasts strong encryption, but also makes it easier for third parties to use traffic analysis to determine "who is communicating with whom."[112] Although online communities and standards bodies such as the IETF play an important role in developing technical fixes for vulnerabilities, speeding uptake requires market-based incentives and potentially polycentric regulation, as discussed in Chapter 5.

DNSSEC

Like IPsec, DNSSEC is complex, and opinions about its importance and effectiveness vary. By the early 2000s, it became clear that DNSSEC would not scale for large networks like the Internet. Then in 2005, IETF updated the DNSSEC protocol and Sweden became the first country-code top-level domain (TLD) to deploy it.[113] However, like IPsec, no organization mandated that DNSSEC be implemented, and

---

[108] *See* Peter Bright, *Another Fraudulent Certificate Raises the Same Old Questions About Certificate Authorities*, ARSTECHNICA (Aug. 29, 2011), http://arstechnica.com/security/2011/08/earlier-this-year-an-iranian/. However, several firms, including Google, Microsoft, and Mozilla, have more recently taken some steps in clamping down on fraudulent certificate authorities. *See* Ms. Smith, *Chrome, Firefox, IE to Block Fraudulent Digital Certificate*, NETWORKWORLD (Jan. 4, 2013), http://www.networkworld.com/community/blog/chrome-firefox-ie-block-fraudulent-digital-certificate.

[109] U.S. DEP'T COMM., CYBERSECURITY, INNOVATION, AND THE INTERNET ECONOMY 59 (2011).

[110] *See* Sheffer, *supra* note 94.

[111] *See* Juha Saarinen, *ITU Sparks Internet Privacy Fears*, IT NEWS (Dec. 7, 2012), http://www.itnews.com.au/News/325490,itu-sparks-internet-privacy-fears.aspx (reporting that "[e]ncrypted, compressed and transcoded data can . . . [be] identified by the [ITU] standard, including IPsec traffic. . . . ").

[112] KENNETH GEERS, NATO CCDCOE, STRATEGIC CYBER SECURITY 91 (2011).

[113] *See* R. ARENDS ET AL., PROTOCOL MODIFICATIONS FOR THE DNS SECURITY EXTENSIONS, IETF RFC 4035, (2005), http://www.ietf.org/rfc/rfc4035.txt; *DNSSEC – The Path to a Secure Domain*, INT'L INFRASTRUCTURE FOUNDATION, www.iis.se/english/domains/tech/dnssec/ (last visited Jan. 15, 2014).

few large domain name registries did so. Privacy concerns arose along with a lack of confidence in DNSSEC generally.[114] As Paul Vixie, president of Internet Systems Consortium, wrote in 2008, "It's been thirteen years since the first DNSSEC mailing list was set up and about four times in those thirteen years IETF has declared victory only to discover that the stuff didn't work well outside the lab."[115] Classic collective action problems have also emerged that slowed deployment because DNSSEC works best if it is supported throughout the DNS hierarchy as well as the application layer.[116] Confusion about deploying DNSSEC at the root added another disincentive.

Kaminsky's bug discovery wrenched DNSSEC out of its malaise. Upon learning about the vulnerability from Kaminsky, Microsoft, Cisco Systems, Sun Microsystems, and BIND coordinated efforts and simultaneously released a security patch in July 2008.[117] The patch did not fix the problem overnight, but it did begin the process of effectively addressing the vulnerability. However, progress remains slow on DNSSEC writ large. Pre-2008 implementation problems have not disappeared, and adoption of DNSSEC remains imperfect. It was deployed in the root zone in July 2010 and has now been implemented in the dot-gov, dot-net, dot-edu, dot-org, and dot-com domains.[118] Yet few organizations have deployed DNSSEC,[119] which is in part because of the fact that industry is not used to investing resources in the DNS. In the past, it had been considered a "highly resilient" system.[120] DNSSEC adds complexity and costs, at least at the outset. Moreover, not all security professionals have confidence that DNSSEC will solve DNS problems without creating new issues;[121] at best, it would fix a narrow problem around which attackers can navigate. And there is yet another collective action problem to consider. If ISPs and similar

[114] *See* DNSSEC Privacy Policy Statement, Dnssec.net, http://www.dnssec.net/pp (last visited Jan. 15, 2014).

[115] Paul Vixie, *Why You Should Deploy DNSSEC*, Dnssec.net (Aug. 2008), http://www.dnssec.net/why-deploy-dnssec.

[116] Rod Rasmussen, *Application Layers – The DNSSEC Chicken and Egg Challenge*, Sec. Wk. (Dec. 20, 2010), http://www.securityweek.com/application-layers-dnssec-chicken-and-egg-challenge.

[117] *See* Ellen Messmer, *Major DNS Flaw Could Disrupt the Internet*, Network World (July 8, 2008), http://www.networkworld.com/news/2008/070808-dns-flaw-disrupts-internet.html.

[118] *See* Root DNSSEC, http://www.root-dnssec.org/ (last visited Jan. 15, 2014).

[119] *See* Carolyn D. Marsan, *5 Years After Major DNS Flaw is Discovered, Few US companies Have Deployed Long-Term Fix*, Network World (Jan. 29, 2013), http://www.networkworld.com/news/2013/012913-dnssec-266197.html (reporting that "DNSSEC adoption [has] stall[ed] outside of federal [the] government.").

[120] Roland van Rijswijk, *DNSSEC: Checking if DNS Points in the Right Direction*, DNSSEC.NET (Jan. 2010), http://www.dnssec.net/why-deploy-dnssec.

[121] *See* Ron Altchison, *The Case Against DNSSEC*, CircleID (Aug. 14, 2007), http://www.circleid.com/posts/070814_case_against_dnssec/; Albert Sweigart, *Controversial DNSSEC Could Solve Pernicious Internet Security Issues*, Zone Alarm, http://www.zonealarm.com/blog/index.php/2009/03/controversial-dnssec-could-solve-pernicious-internet-security-issues (last visited June 13, 2013) (arguing that "[t]he DNSSEC protocol would place the root authority to authenticate the entire domain name system with the U.S. Department of Commerce, including the domain name system of 187 different countries[,]" raising potential geopolitical concerns).

infrastructure players adopt DNSSEC but others do not and DNS requests stop resolving, end users may get frustrated and take their business elsewhere.[122] Thus, uncertainty abounds both about the quality of DNSSEC itself and the feasibility of deploying it universally absent regulatory intervention.[123]

Securing TCP and BGP

In contrast to the confusion surrounding security for IP and DNS, security for TCP and BGP remains somewhat ad hoc. For TCP, some effective countermeasures have been developed, although there are trade-offs. For example, IP packet filtering disallows IP address spoofing and serves as a counter to SYN floods, but universal deployment is unlikely.[124] Alternatively, SYN cache and SYN cookies have been described as among the best ways to defend against SYN floods,[125] but these methods may undermine broader network performance.[126] For BGP, however, there are few effective solutions. Several alternative BGP protocols have been proposed, but it has not yet been resolved which, if any, of these protocols should be adopted.[127] However, like SSL/TLS for IP or bailiwick checking for DNS, filtering may thwart some eavesdroppers by allowing "only authorized peers to draw traffic from their routers, and is only for specific IP prefixes."[128] Unfortunately, though, filtering can be inefficient and only effective if every ISP participates, underscoring another collective action problem potentially amenable to polycentric regulation. A more systemic approach to addressing BGP vulnerabilities has been developed by Stephen Kent, chief scientist for information security at BBN Technologies, but the scheme would only authenticate the "first hop" in a BGP route.[129]

IPsec and DNSSEC demonstrate that fixes to key Internet protocols are being developed, and adoption of endpoint-based solutions such as HTTPS and VPNs is increasing. However, overall progress has been slow considering that many of these vulnerabilities were identified in the mid-1990s. There is little consensus about which solutions are best and how to incentivize implementation. For example, can security extensions to key protocols even be effective? Are endpoint-based solutions

---

[122] *See Why Not Convergence?*, IMPERIAL VIOLET (Sept. 7, 2011), http://www.imperialviolet.org/2011/09/07/convergence.html; DNSSEC, http://epic.org/privacy/dnssec (last visited June 12, 2013).

[123] *See* CYBERSECURITY, INNOVATION, AND THE INTERNET ECONOMY, *supra* note 109, at 61.

[124] *See* Rod Rasmussen, *The Implementation Challenges for DNSSEC*, SEC. WK. (Nov. 24, 2010), http://www.securityweek.com/implementation-challenges-dnssec; EDDY, *supra* note 51 (predicting that "global deployment of filters is neither guaranteed nor likely.").

[125] *See* Wesley M. Eddy, *Defenses Against TCP SYN Flooding Attacks*, 9(4) INTERNET PROTOCOL J. (2006), http://www.cisco.com/web/about/ac123/ac147/archived_issues/ipj_9-4/syn_flooding_attacks.html.

[126] *See id.*; *TCP Maintenance and Minor Extensions*, IETF, https://datatracker.ietf.org/wg/tcpm/charter/ (last visited Jan. 15, 2014); EDDY, *supra* note 51.

[127] *See* Stephen Kent et al., *Secure Border Gateway Protocol*, 18 IEEE J. SELECTED AREAS COMM. 582, 582 (2000).

[128] Zetter, *supra* note 86.

[129] *Id.*

preferable, and if so, how can we be sure that end users will adopt them? Is there a role for law here, and what are the regulatory, economic, and political implications?

The Internet's architecture contributes to its insecurity, which presents complex challenges for stakeholders including engineers, governments, businesses, and users. Every day, the Internet delivers DNS responses that are not reliably authenticated and sends unverified IP packets between hosts and through routers that are running on trust, which is sometimes misplaced. For example, although bank ATMs, air traffic control systems, and electrical grids can run on private networks, many systems still send information via the public Internet, even if they are protected by VPNs and HTTPS, which can introduce new vulnerabilities.[130] Cyber peace requires addressing these technical vulnerabilities and incentivizing the adoption of solutions from the bottom-up once scientific consensus is achieved, such as incentives to support the uptake of IPsec, DNSSEC, and IP packet filtering, as well as the creation of a National Science Foundation (NSF) grant competition, or even a Cybersecurity X Prize, to research alternatives to the BGP.[131] The main barriers to doing so include the cost of implementing DNSSEC and IPsec, and uncertainty about whether these and other fixes are effective or will simply shift the locus of the problem. This debate may be compared to the Montreal Protocol analogy from Chapter 2 in which the science linking CFCs to the ozone hole was clear and a relatively small subset of industry was affected, as opposed to the UNFCCC climate-change negotiations.[132] As with the ozone hole, Kaminsky's bug showed a common problem to which there was an available solution in the form of security patches and DNSSEC. The differences here lies in the greater number and diversity of stakeholders required to take action – making that aspect more similar to the UNFCCC process – as well as continuing scientific uncertainty. Until these issues are overcome, targeted measures should be taken even if they do not solve all protocol vulnerabilities. The extension of DNSSEC to the root and TLDs is an example of successful public-private polycentric governance in which the U.S. government, IETF, and private firms came together to address a common problem and in so doing, enhanced the public good of cybersecurity. Such partnerships should be broadened and strengthened, but securing the logical infrastructure is just the second layer of vulnerability requiring attention. Cyber peace also requires securing the software built on top of these networking protocols.

Debugging and Regulating through Code

Architectural vulnerabilities of the Internet lay the groundwork for explaining the cyber threat, but there is more to it than that. If everything built on top of the Internet

[130] See *Tracking* Ghostnet: *Investigating a Cyber Espionage Network*, INFO. WARFARE MONITOR (Mar. 29, 2009), http://www.scribd.com/doc/13731776/Tracking-GhostNet-Investigating-a-Cyber-Espionage-Network; Rose Tsang, *Cyberthreats, Vulnerabilities and Attacks on SCADA Networks* 13 (Goldman School, Univ. of Cal. Working Paper, 2009).

[131] See KNAKE, *supra* note 44, at 26–27 (calling for the creation of such a NSF program).

[132] See Daniel Bodansky, *The History of the Global Climate Change Regime*, in INTERNATIONAL RELATIONS AND GLOBAL CLIMATE CHANGE 23, 29–35 (Urs Luterbacher & Detlef F. Sprinz eds., 2001).

was secure or if all users behaved with perfect insight into cyber risks, the threats posed by the Internet's protocols might be contained. Unfortunately, this is not the case. Users rarely excel at security assessment, as is illustrated in the cybersecurity survey results in Chapter 7. Similarly, what is built on top of the Internet, including operating systems and applications, is far from ironclad. This substantiates a third fundamental vulnerability: code.

A programming error is but a recent incarnation of a vulnerability that is even older than Internet protocols. It is an error in craftsmanship, like a poorly secured board that would never have been discovered but for a tornado. In this case, however, the crafters of software are laying lines of code rather than framing a house, and hackers are the storm. As was described in Chapter 1, "code is law," but even though code has such a vital role to play in Internet governance, it is written and tested by fallible human beings who make errors, creating "bugs."[133] Back in 1949, Maurice Wilkes, a British computer scientist, wrote:

> As soon as we started programming, we found to our surprise that it wasn't as easy to get programs right as we had thought. Debugging had to be discovered. I can remember the exact instant when I realized that a large part of my life from then on was going to be spent in finding mistakes in my own programs.[134]

Debugging is not an easy process, mostly because programs often run adequately with bugs – just as a house does not often collapse because of a few loose nails. Moreover, bugs are seemingly endless. A popular programming song jokes:

> 99 *little bugs in the code,*
> 99 *little bugs in the code,*
> *Fix one bug, compile it again,*
> 101 *little bugs in the code.*[135]

Code, then, is subject to human error as well as malicious intent because some programmers may purposefully insert bugs so that they or others can reenter the code later. Either way, sophisticated hackers may also exploit these bugs. And this problem may get worse before it gets better. As programs grow increasingly complex, more lines of code are often used to get the job done. Microsoft's Windows 95 had 10 million lines of code; Windows XP has approximately 40 million.[136] More lines of code mean more opportunities to make mistakes and more targets to defend against attackers. As was described by Clarke and Knake in *Cyber War*, "even experts cannot usually identify coding errors or intentional vulnerabilities in a few lines of code, let alone in millions."[137]

---

[133] Lawrence Lessig, Code and other laws of cyberspace 28 (1999).
[134] Peter van der Linden, Expert C Programming: Deep C Secrets 109 (1994).
[135] Quotes for Software Engineers, Anonymous, http://cseweb.ucsd.edu/~wgg/quotes.html (last visited Jan. 15, 2014).
[136] *See* Guy Hart-Davis, Mastering Windows XP Home Edition 26 (2006).
[137] Clarke & Knake, *supra* note 30, at 90.

Targets abound because code underlies everything, meaning that attackers can shift their focus as some systems improve or others gain popularity. For example, whereas operating system vulnerabilities are reportedly declining, application vulnerabilities are increasing.[138] More hackers are also targeting Apple products as they gain market share. In October 2010, Apple reported that there are approximately "5,000 'strains' of malware that target the Mac and . . . that [some] 500 new Mac-specific samples [are] appearing every month."[139] In 2012, a single Trojan virus infected more than 550,000 Apple computers.[140] In addition, because developers like Microsoft and Apple are often unaware of coding mistakes when they release new products, bugs can go undiscovered for some time.[141] This gives attackers time to find and exploit bugs and to damage strategically important targets.

According to Professor Murray, leveraging control of the Internet's physical infrastructure could lead the market to "route around this anomaly in the same way the network routes around damaged nodes."[142] Instead, he advocates for designing interventions to manage vulnerabilities in the logical infrastructure,[143] which in turn shapes the regulatory environment of cyberspace. Indeed, the common reliance on basically "a single protocol" makes regulating through code an appealing proposition.[144] For example, code-based controls could be introduced to promote enhanced privacy, data management,[145] and cybersecurity. But code-based cybersecurity solutions face at least two problems: (1) code-based controls would have to be leveraged into the carrier layer of the logical infrastructure, and (2) the carrier layer is founded on TCP/IP, which "was designed as an end-to-end protocol" lacking intelligence.[146] In other words, code is only as secure as the underlying systems on which it is running, which as has been discussed are far from perfect. Nevertheless, this underscores the importance of standards-setting bodies "with the ability to leverage comprehensive code-based controls . . . [namely] technical 'consortia of interested persons and companies'"[147] such as the IETF. The question then becomes how best to encourage

---

[138] *From the Eye of the Storm: 2011 Information Security Predictions*, INFO. SEC. (Jan. 6, 2011), http://www.infosecurity-us.com/view/14954/from-the-eye-of-the-storm-2011-information-security-predictions/.

[139] John E. Dunn, *Mac Users Warned of Growing Virus Threat*, TECH. WORLD (Oct. 21, 2010), http://news.techworld.com/security/3245158/mac-users-warned-of-growing-virus-threat/.

[140] *See* Rob Waugh, *'Rude Awakening' for Mac Users as Cyber Attack Infects 550,000 of Apple's 'Virus Free' Machines – with UK and U.S. Worst Hit*, MAIL ONLINE (Apr. 5, 2012), http://www.dailymail.co.uk/sciencetech/article-2125496/Apple-computers-infected-Flashback-Trojan-virus-rude-awakening-Mac-users.html.

[141] *See* Haroon Meer, THINKST APPLIED RESEARCH, *Cyber Warfare: Beyond the "Beyond the Hype" Approach*, CCDCOE NATO Conf. Cyber Conflict, in Tallinn, Est. (June 16, 2010); Leyla Bilge & Tudor Dumitras, *Before We Knew It: An Empirical Study of Zero-Day Attacks in the Real World*, PROC. 2012 ACM CONF. COMPUTER & COMPUTER SEC. 833, 835–36 (2012).

[142] *See* MURRAY, *supra* note 19, at 85.

[143] *Id.*

[144] *Id.* at 86.

[145] *Id.* (citing Joel Reidenberg, *Lex Informatica: The Formation of Information Policy Rules Through Technology*, 76 TEX. L. REV. 553, 556–65 (1998)).

[146] *Id.* at 87–88.

[147] *Id.* at 88 (quoting Reidenberg, *supra* note 145, at 582–83 n.35).

the uptake of cybersecurity best practices published by these bodies as consensus emerges while also addressing underlying vulnerabilities, which will be discussed.

Like the Internet protocols, programming flaws are spread throughout the system, permeating hardware and software and often bringing to light vulnerabilities at the application layer. Yet the fourth and final major vulnerability discussed in this section – social platforms – represents an even wider and more dispersed problem: you and me. The phrase "social engineering" describes a method that takes advantage of the fact that, ultimately, it is humans who run software on hardware on networks, and it is we who are often considered to be the most insecure link in an insecure system.

The Threat of Social Engineering to the Content Layer

Social engineering is merely one type of threat facing the content layer, but this variety of cyber attack is increasingly popular and most often occurs when an attacker sends a user a malware-infected email or message that is uniquely targeted to an individual or organization.[148] It is merely an updated version of an age-old scam that manipulates people into divulging sensitive information, but those updates make it cutting edge. Today, attackers often do their homework before attempting a scam. They can search your cache to see which websites you have visited. Or they might be able to access your Facebook, Twitter, or LinkedIn accounts where they can learn about your friends, interests, and professional networks to tailor attacks.[149]

Social engineering began as "phishing" emails as exemplified in Figure 3.1, which were sent out en masse,[150] but early phishing emails were relatively easy to spot. Most people knew not to click on a link in an email purportedly from "Bank of America" when, for example, the red and blue flag image looked odd. More recently, though, phishing emails have become more sophisticated and successful. For example, "spear phishing" is becoming increasingly common, which involves sending targeted messages of the kind that even fooled Google employees in 2009, as discussed in Chapter 5.[151] "Whaling" messages are, forgive the pun, sent to the "big fish" of an organization (apologies to biological taxonomists).[152] According to *The Economist*, "The amount of information now available online about individuals makes it ever easier to attack a computer by crafting a personalized email that is

---

[148] See Angela Hennessy, *This Social Engineer 'Hacks' People to Infiltrate Multi-Million Dollar Companies*, VICE (July 10, 2013), http://www.vice.com/en_uk/read/we-spoke-to-a-social-engineer-about-how-he-hacks-people-and-infiltrates-secure-companies.

[149] See, e.g., Michael Cobb, *Heading Off Advanced Social Engineering Attacks*, DARK READING (Mar. 18, 2013), http://www.darkreading.com/vulnerability/heading-off-advanced-social-engineering/240150975 (describing the development of social engineering attacks); Stacy Cowley, *LinkedIn is a Hacker's Dream Tool*, CNN MONEY (Mar. 12, 2012), http://money.cnn.com/2012/03/12/technology/linkedin-hackers/index.htm (reporting on the desirability of using LinkedIn as a hacking tool).

[150] Tom N. Jagatic et al., *Social Phishing*, 50(10) COMM. ACM 94, 94–95 (Oct. 2007).

[151] *Spear Phishers: Angling to Steal Your Financial Info*, FBI (Apr. 1, 2009), http://www.fbi.gov/news/stories/2009/april/spearphishing_040109.

[152] See *Scam Watch*, AUSTL. COMP. & CONSUMER COMM'N, http://www.scamwatch.gov.au/content/index.phtml/itemId/829460 (last visited Jan. 15, 2014).

Dear valued customer of TrustedBank,

We have recieved notice that you have recently attempted to withdraw the following amount from your checking account while in another country: $135.25.

If this information is not correct, someone unknown may have access to your account. As a safety measure, please visit our website via the link below to verify your personal information:

http://www.trustedbank.com/general/custverifyinfo.asp

Once you have done this, our fraud department will work to resolve this discrepency. We are happy you have chosen us to do business with.

Thank you,
TrustedBank

Member FDIC © 2005 TrustedBank, Inc.

FIGURE 3.1. EXAMPLE OF PHISHING EMAIL

more likely to be trusted and opened."[153] In other words, if an attacker can learn that you are a 35-year-old male from Indiana who works at a pharmaceutical company, are friends with Tom, and likes science fiction, then it is far easier to craft a message that you would open. And typically it is possible to get far more information than that through a public records search. Attached to either sort of message may be a link to a malicious website to open, or file to download. Such messages will often purportedly be from someone you know or an organization with which you do business. This tactic capitalizes on the inherent trust in your relationships. And it works.

A study conducted at Indiana University documents the usefulness of social media in social engineering. As Fred Cate, a distinguished professor at Indiana University Maurer School of Law and director of the Center for Applied Cybersecurity Research, wrote in comments submitted to the White House, "the percentage of recipients of a phishing message persuaded to provide their account name and password increased from 16 to 72 percent when researchers made it appear that the fraudulent message originated from a Facebook friend."[154] Such an instance may create a spiraling problem, as many people reuse passwords for their social platforms, personal or work email, and bank accounts. In fact, a study done by Internet security

[153] *Cyberwar, supra* note 18.
[154] Fred Cate, *Comments to the White House 60-Day Cybersecurity Review*, WHITE HOUSE 3 (Mar. 27, 2009), http://www.whitehouse.gov/files/documents/cyber/Center%20for%20Applied%20Cybersecurity%20Research%20-%20Cybersecurity%20Comments.Cate.pdf.

company Bitdefender in 2010 "found that 75 percent of users had one common password for social networking and accessing their email."[55] Additionally, because there is growing evidence of wrongdoers collaborating, one attacker's Facebook profile hacking may be another's ticket to committing crime or espionage. Imagine, for example, that you have been emailing your boss about where to open a new bank account, and an attacker inserts an account into the thread and tells you to transfer the money into it. Most often you would probably confirm the change with your boss, but if it is five o'clock on a Friday, you might just do it. And you would not be alone. A version of this sort of hack happened to Lockheed Martin employees.[56] The U.S.-based defense contractor designs and builds sophisticated jet fighters for the U.S. military; the jets' blueprints include more than 7.5 million lines of code and intricate hardware designs.[57] Attackers after this information might once have spent significant time and resources attempting to crack encryption, and break down firewalls. But instead, this time they tried social engineering, and it reportedly worked. Emails purportedly sent by Chinese hackers were crafted to look like they were being sent from the Pentagon. They requested blueprints for the F-35 Lightning Joint Strike Fighter, and Lockheed Martin employees obliged.[58]

At this point, you may be thinking it probably takes sophistication to conduct these sorts of attacks, and sophistication is rare. True, but sophistication can go on sale. In recent years, attackers have been able to buy kits that support social engineering attacks online. According to one report, in the first six months of 2007 fully 42 percent of all phishing messages originated from three toolkits sold on the web.[59] To some researchers, including those who investigated *GhostNet*, the widespread use of social engineering tactics and the availability of tools for executing such attacks are equally concerning and help explain the rise in cybercrime and espionage.[60]

Summary

This section on physical, logical, and content vulnerabilities has demonstrated how every layer of cyberspace is insecure. Because of IP, TCP, DNS, and BGP protocol

---

[55] *Study Reveals 75 Percent of Individuals Use Same Password for Social Networking and Email*, Sec. Wk. (Aug. 16, 2010), http://www.securityweek.com/study-reveals-75-percent-individuals-use-same-password-social-networking-and-email.

[56] *See* Henry Severs, *'The Greatest Transfer of Wealth in History': How Significant is the Cyber-Espionage Threat?*, TheRiskyShift (Jan. 17, 2013), http://theriskyshift.com/2013/01/cyber-espionage-the-greatest-transfer-of-wealth-in-history/ (noting that "[o]ne of the most renowned cyber-espionage cases, the breach of global aerospace, defence, and advanced technology company Lockheed Martin, is also an excellent example of social engineering.").

[57] *See id.*; Siobhan Gorman, August Cole, & Yochi Dreazen, *Computer Spies Breach Fighter-Jet Project*, Wall St. J. (Apr. 21, 2009), http://online.wsj.com/news/articles/SB124027491029837401.

[58] *See What Should we Learn from the Lockheed Martin Attack*, Hot Sec. (June 10, 2011), http://www.hotforsecurity.com/blog/what-should-we-learn-from-the-lockheed-martin-attack-1093.html.

[59] *See* Cate, *supra* note 154, at 2 (citing Stephanie Hoffman, *Storm Warning*, VARBus., at 32, Jan. 28, 2008).

[60] *Tracking* Ghostnet, *supra* note 130, at 18, 47.

vulnerabilities, the Internet itself is vulnerable. Bugs in hardware and software make systems running on the Internet exploitable. And humans who use the hardware and software can make a bad situation worse. Even if all the bugs were fixed and protocols were secured, according to Johnny Long, co-author of *No Tech Hacking*, there is always going to be a human somewhere who "holds the keys to the kingdom" and may be scammed or bribed into giving them up.[161] Cyber peace requires then not only technical innovation to counter the growing number of cyber weapons and their proliferation, but also education and better management practices to help counter insider threats. Although technical fixes in the form of IPsec, DNSSEC, and anti-social engineering campaigns are not panaceas for these vulnerabilities, they do represent targeted measures developed by consortia that can be implemented from the bottom-up. Before discussing how this may be conceptualized within a polycentric framework, however, it is first necessary to analyze the types of cyber attacks and how they may be better managed.

CYBERSECURITY 101: UNDERSTANDING THE WEAPONS

The vulnerabilities previously outlined help explain the cyber threat, but these vulnerabilities would mean little if they were not being exploited. This section takes the next logical step by accounting for the attack tools: cyber weapons. However, just as analyzing the cyber threat had to begin with the difficult question of defining cyber attacks, so must we first contextualize "cyber weapons." This is difficult because, at their root, cyber weapons are merely lines of code. However, these "weapons" can take advantage of different vulnerabilities in hardware, protocols, and software to hack, probe, spy on, and steal information.[162] Cyber weapons may be defined as any purposefully inserted exploit that is developed or utilized for the destruction of "confidentiality, integrity, and availability of computer data and systems. . . ."[163] However, some common types of weapons are more prevalent than others; for instance, as Charlie Miller explained in the opening to this chapter, to "hack the planet" one would need numerous tools, from DDoS attacks to zero-day exploits. This section lays out these and other categories of malware before moving on to discuss how they may be better managed by using *GhostNet* and *Shadow Network* as case studies.

---

[161] Ivo Vegter, *Hacking into Hollywood*, ITWEB (Apr. 15, 2008), http://www.itweb.co.za/index.php?option=com_content&view=article&id=1886.

[162] *See, e.g.*, Ellen Nakashima, *List of Cyber-Weapons Developed by Pentagon to Streamline Computer Warfare*, WASH. POST (May 31, 2011), http://articles.washingtonpost.com/2011-05-31/national/35264250_1_cyber-computer-warfare-stuxnet (reporting on the Pentagon's cyber arms development efforts).

[163] COUNCIL OF EUR., CRIMINAL MONEY FLOWS ON THE INTERNET: METHODS, TRENDS AND MULTI-STAKEHOLDER COUNTERACTION 6 (2012) (defining cybercrime). *See Department of Cyber Defense*, TECHNOLYTICS at 5 (2007); JOHN R. VACCA, COMPUTER AND INFORMATION SECURITY HANDBOOK 982 (2012) (arguing that "cyber weapons, in many circumstances, are called viruses, Trojans and the like when deployed by criminals or fraudsters.").

Spyware

The cyber weapons with which many of us are most familiar are collectively referred to as malware, which is malicious software that infects systems and can be used to spy on or damage computers, servers, or networks.[164] Common forms of malware include spyware, viruses, worms, and Trojan horses.[165] Spyware, which is useful for social engineering attacks, is a computer program that "transmits personal information to a third party without the user's knowledge or consent."[166] It is often installed along with free software (shareware) from malicious websites that allows its authors to monitor which websites users visit or even their general computer use. Spyware use is rampant.[167] It has provoked an entire industry of anti-spyware software such as Spy Sweeper, which is designed to scan a computer's memory and disk drives and clean or delete whatever has been affected by malicious code. Despite these efforts, some estimate that as of 2005 more than 80 percent of computers were infected with spyware,[168] although the real number is impossible to estimate. Indeed, it has become so commonplace that some groups are lobbying governments to legalize it.[169]

Trojan Horses

Trojan horses are a means for delivering and propagating malicious code such as spyware and are known for masquerading (like their ancient namesake) as something else, such as an image or joke. They are often delivered as attachments in emails or as downloads on websites and facilitate unauthorized access to a user's computer.[170] With this access, hackers can deliver malware to perform any number of tasks, including downloading or uploading files.[171] Often, however, Trojans are used to

---

[164] *See* Robert Moir, *Defining Malware: FAQ*, Microsoft (Oct. 1, 2003), http://technet.microsoft.com/en-us/library/dd632948.aspx.

[165] *Viruses/Contaminant/Destructive Transmission Statutes*, Nat'l Conf. St. Legislatures, http://www.ncsl.org/IssuesResearch/TelecommunicationsInformationTechnology/StateVirusandComputerContaminantLaws/tabid/13487/Default.aspx (last updated Feb. 14, 2012).

[166] *McAfee Threat Glossary*, http://www.mcafee.com/us/threat-center/resources/threat-glossary.aspx (last visited Jan. 16, 2014).

[167] *See* Qing Hu & Tamara Dinev, *Is Spyware an Internet Nuisance or Public Menace?*, 48(8) Comm. ACM, Aug. 2005, at 61; Erik Kain, *Report: NSA Intercepting Laptops Ordered Online, Installing Spyware*, Forbes (Dec. 29, 2013), http://www.forbes.com/sites/erikkain/2013/12/29/report-nsa-intercepting-laptops-ordered-online-installing-spyware/.

[168] *See* Matt Hines, *Research: Spyware Industry Worth Billions*, CNET (May 3, 2005), http://news.cnet.com/Research-Spyware-industry-worth-billions/2100-1029_3-5693730.html.

[169] *See* Mark Gibbs, *Canadian Industry Groups Want to Legalize Spyware*, Forbes (Feb. 7, 2013), http://www.forbes.com/sites/markgibbs/2013/02/07/canadian-industry-groups-want-to-legalize-spyware/.

[170] *See McAfee Threat Glossary*, *supra* note 166 ("A malicious program that pretends to be a benign application. It does not replicate but causes damage or compromises the security of your computer.").

[171] *See* Symantec, Windows Rootkit Overview 4–6 (2010), http://www.symantec.com/avcenter/reference/windows.rootkit.overview.pdf.

gather information like passwords or credit card information.[172] Once a Trojan is installed, attackers can use it to find out information by keystroke logging (capturing the keys you strike on a keyboard), or screen or clipboard logging (taking periodic screen shots).[173] Trojans are also increasingly being used as the first stage of a broader cyber attack. They can stay hidden while installing another threat, such as a bot,[174] which may help explain the exploding popularity of Trojans – a 2009 survey found that Trojan-type attacks accounted for 83 percent of detected total global malware.[175]

Viruses

Like Trojans, viruses are spread by infected websites and email attachments that are often opened as a result of hackers using social engineering techniques. They attach to programs, documents, and files.[176] After reaching a host machine, a virus is designed to alter a computer's functionality by placing "its own code in the path of execution of another program" – the opening of which unleashes the virus.[177] They are aptly named, acting like a biological virus that invades a host cell in your body and directs the cellular machinery to replicate more viruses. As such, unlike Trojans, once they are executed, viruses can self-replicate. Although some viruses are designed to damage computers by "damaging programs, deleting files, or reformatting the hard disk[,]" most viruses tend to use up computer memory and "cause erratic behavior. . . . "[178] Types of viruses range widely: some infect the boot sector, which is in charge of powering up your computer; others target applications like Microsoft Office.[179] Free anti-virus software is available, such as Ad-Aware Free Internet Security and Avira, to help eliminate this malware variant.

---

[172] *See, e.g.*, Hines, *supra* note 168; Lucian Constantin, *Computer Trojan Horse Steals Credit Card Details from Hotel Reception Software*, PC WORLD AUSTL. (Apr. 19, 2012), http://www.pcworld.idg.com.au/article/421947/computer_trojan_horse_steals_credit_card_details_from_hotel_reception_software/.

[173] *See* RACHAEL LININGER & RUSSELL DEAN VINES, PHISHING: CUTTING THE IDENTITY THEFT LINE 110-11 (2005); Nigel Lewis, SANS INFOSEC, FIRST STEP DATA CAPTURE – KEY STROKE LOGGERS 6 (2001), http://www.sans.org/reading_room/whitepapers/monitoring/first-step-data-capture-key-stroke-loggers_4.

[174] *See Norton by Symantec: Crimeware: Trojans and Spyware*, http://securityresponse.symantec.com/en/uk/norton/cybercrime/trojansspyware.jsp (last visited June 16, 2013).

[175] *BitDefender Malware and Spam Survey finds E-Threats Adapting to Online Behavioral Trends*, BIT DEFENDER (Aug. 3, 2009), http://www.bitdefender.com/news/bitdefender-malware-and-spam-survey-finds-e-threats-adapting-to-online-behavioral-trends-1094.html.

[176] *See McAfee Threat Glossary, supra* note 166.

[177] *Norton by Symantec: What is the Difference Between Viruses, Worms, and Trojans?*, http://www.symantec.com/business/support/index?page=content&id=TECH98539 (last visited Jan. 16, 2014).

[178] *Id.*

[179] *See* JOSEPH F. GUSTIN, CYBER TERRORISM: A GUIDE FOR FACILITY MANAGERS 25 (2004).

Worms

Worms are similar to viruses, but whereas viruses can only self-replicate once they are executed, worms can self-replicate of their own accord.[180] Because of this trait, worms are among the most virulent type of malware.[181] For example, even if you never open your email account, a worm might send a copy of itself by email to everyone in your address book. This allows worms to spread quickly. Recent worms, like Conficker, not only replicate, but also change their appearance, making them harder to patch and contain. A variant of the Conficker worm infected as many as nine million PCs in only four months.[182] And unlike most Trojans or viruses, all worms need is a single unpatched system to infect an entire network.[183]

Logic Bombs

Worms, viruses, and Trojans might also contain logic bombs as a means of effectuating an attacker's intent.[184] Logic bombs appear as either malware or some coded lines of nefarious instructions inserted into software. The story that began this study – of the 1982 explosion of a Siberian gas pipeline – is an example of what an early logic bomb could do.[185] Logic bombs set off a malicious function when certain conditions are met – like a time, date, or an employee's departure.[186] They can cause systems or even entire networks to crash. The full extent of logic bomb infiltration on existing networks is unknown but likely widespread. There may even be logic bombs implanted in U.S. critical national infrastructure.[187]

DDoS Attacks

Like logic bombs, Distributed Denial of Service (DDoS) attacks are a mechanism for achieving an attacker's intent. These attacks not only take advantage of bugs in code, but also act on vulnerabilities in TCP, DNS, and BGP protocols to overload servers and crash or disrupt websites. At the heart of DDoS attacks are denial of

---

[180] *See* McAfee *Threat Glossary, supra* note 166.
[181] *See* STEPHEN J. BIGELOW, TROUBLESHOOTING, MAINTAINING & REPAIRING NETWORKS 551 (2002).
[182] *See* Mark Soper, *Conficker Worm's Infected Over 9 Million PCs – is Your Work or Home PC One of Them?*, MAXIMUM PC (Jan. 21, 2009), http://www.maximumpc.com/article/news/conficker_worms_infected_over_9_million_pcs_is_your_work_or_home_pc_one_them.
[183] *See* TREND MICRO, 2009's MOST PERSISTENT MALWARE THREATS 5–6 (2010), https://imperia.trend micro-europe.com/imperia/md/content/us/trendwatch/researchandanalysis/2009s_most_persistent_malware_threats__march_2010_.pdf.
[184] *See* McAfee *Threat Glossary, supra* note 166 ("Also known as time bomb, a program that allows a Trojan to lie dormant and then attack when the conditions are just right.").
[185] *See Cyberwar, supra* note 18.
[186] McAfee *Threat Glossary, supra* note 166.
[187] *See* CLARKE & KNAKE, *supra* note 30, at 92.

service (DoS) attacks, which are launched from a single computer and Internet connection.[188] Like viruses, DoS attacks represent their namesake: they seek to limit or halt normal services. However, it is difficult to slow down or crash entire systems or servers with one computer by overwhelming it with traffic. Thus, DoS attacks work on the premise of doing something that costs individuals little but costs their targets a lot, similar to spam. According to Miller, "the attacker only has to send one packet, and the recipient has to do a lot of work."[189] SYN flooding attacks, which were referred to previously as a vulnerability of the TCP, are an example of this kind of weapon.[190] By sending along more and more spoofed IP packets to a server, an attacker causes that server to devote a disproportionate amount of memory to one individual request. It is as if David can play mind tricks on Goliath by making him believe that David has been cloned; Goliath's attention is diverted, and he may be more easily overwhelmed.

If DoS attacks wreak havoc by causing maximum disruption with minimum effort, DDoS take this approach to its logical extreme. DDoS attacks are like DoS attacks, except that they come not from one computer and network, but from many. DDoS attacks crash websites by using all the bandwidth to a server, overloading a specific application. Many commercial websites have been brought down by DDoS attacks, and they also featured prominently in the attacks on Estonia and Georgia discussed in Chapter 4.[191] Networks of "zombie" computers called botnets, short for networks of software robots, can repeat network requests more quickly than a human user and often carry out DDoS attacks.[192] Bots are not all bad; some are even helpful, such as Einstein@Home, BOINC, and SETI, which take advantage of distributed computing to engage the public in helping scientists conduct research projects. Others can be mischievous. In 2006, Stephen Colbert's supporters developed a bot to help him (temporarily) win a naming contest for a Hungarian bridge.[193] However, they also can be used maliciously.[194] Botnets can be difficult to disrupt since botnet operators can accomplish their goals without users even necessarily being aware that their systems have been compromised since often computer performance is barely impacted. In the second quarter of 2010, Microsoft reported that its anti-malware programs removed bots from some 6.5 million PCs worldwide.[195]

[188] *See McAfee Threat Glossary, supra* note 166 (defining DDoS attacks as "[a] type of denial-of-service (DoS) attack in which more than one traffic generator directs traffic to a targeted URL.").

[189] Electronic Interview with Charlie Miller, Twitter cybersecurity analyst (Oct. 18, 2010).

[190] *See SYN Flood Attack Explained,* http://www.ddosprotection.net/syn-flood/ (last visited June 16, 2013).

[191] *See* Dave Dittrich, Distributed Denial of Service (DDoS) Attacks/Tools, http://staff.washington.edu/dittrich/misc/ddos/ (last updated July 4, 2013) (compiling news reports of DDoS attacks).

[192] *See McAfee Threat Glossary, supra* note 166; T. Luis de Guzman, Comment, *Unleashing a Cure for the Botnet Zombie Plague: Cybertorts, Counterstrikes, and Privileges,* 59 CATH. U.L. REV. 527, 528 (2010).

[193] *See Stephen Colbert Salutes Hungary,* COLBERT REPORT (Aug. 22, 2006), http://www.colbertnation.com/the-colbert-report-videos/73378/august-22-2006/stephen-colbert-salutes-hungary.

[194] *See* CLARKE & KNAKE, *supra* note 30, at 292; *Bitcoin: Bitcoin Mining by Botnet,* KREBSONSECURITY (July 18, 2013), http://krebsonsecurity.com/2013/07/botcoin-bitcoin-mining-by-botnet/.

[195] 9 MICROSOFT, *Battling Botnets for Control of Computers, in* SEC. INTELLIGENCE REP. 23 (2010).

Zero-Day Exploits

Although DDoS attacks have been a mainstay for hackers, Miller equates them to "clubs and rocks."[196] They are effective as a brute force method to crash systems, but they often do not destroy resources or do permanent damage. Zero-day exploits, on the other hand, are in another league from other cyber weapons. In a traditional exploit scenario, a vendor releases a patch for coding errors and then a hacker creates an exploit that will affect users who have not yet installed software patches.[197] However, launching a large- scale attack then requires something more, like coding errors that have no available software patch. This something more is a zero-day exploit, which numerous computer experts have called the "the Holy Grail" of exploits.[198] In a zero-day attack, a hacker creates an exploit before the vendor knows about the vulnerability, so the attack base is broader.[199] There is little that users can do to slow down zero-days once they are unleashed, so an attacker "can wreak maximum havoc."[200] In 2009, several zero-day exploits were unleashed, including those targeting Internet Explorer and Adobe Acrobat.[201] They were also featured in the Stuxnet attacks.[202] Even after they are discovered and patches are released, zero-days often continue to be used because of the slow deployment of patches.

Summary

This section has analyzed both the intent of attackers, such as DDoS attacks, spyware, and logic bombs, as well as the mechanisms used to launch cyber attacks, including zero-day exploits, viruses, worms, and Trojan horses. These cyber weapons and others comprise the arsenal available to attackers to take advantage of vulnerabilities in the physical, logical, and content layers of the Internet. Such malware is becoming more sophisticated, targeted, and automated. However, before analyzing how to better manage these attacks, it is first necessary to examine how and why attackers are using this arsenal.

CYBERSECURITY 102: USING THE WEAPONS

Botnets and other cyber weapons are readily accessible as online toolkits and are relatively inexpensive. Coupled with the facts that the Internet is global, access is

---

[196] Miller, *supra* note 189.

[197] TREND MICRO, *supra* note 183, at 23–24.

[198] Gregg Keizer, *Microsoft's Reaction to Flame Shows Seriousness of 'Holy Grail' Hack*, COMPUTER-WORLD (June 7, 2012), http://www.computerworld.com/s/article/9227860/Microsoft_s_reaction_to_Flame_shows_seriousness_of_Holy_Grail_hack.

[199] *Id.* (describing one zero-day exploit targeting Office 2000 and Office XP).

[200] Tony Bradley, *Zero Day Exploits*, ABOUT.COM, http://netsecurity.about.com/od/newsandeditorial1/a/aazeroday.htm (last visited Mar. 10, 2014).

[201] TREND MICRO, *supra* note 183, at 23–24.

[202] *See, e.g.*, Liam Murchu, *Stuxnet Using Three Additional Zero-Day Vulnerabilities*, SYMANTEC (Sept. 14, 2010), http://www.symantec.com/connect/blogs/stuxnet-using-three-additional-zero-day-vulnerabilities (reporting that Stuxnet used four zero-day vulnerabilities).

widespread, and the benefits to attackers are concentrated while costs are diffused, a worrying scenario unfolds. As Scott Charney, Microsoft's vice president for trust-worthy computing, wrote of the cyber threat in 2009: "There are many malicious actors [including criminals, terrorists, and states]. . . . Indeed, the Internet is a great place to commit crime because it provides global connectivity, anonymity, lack of traceability, and rich targets."[203] Unpacking the cyber threat thus not only requires exploring the evolution of cyber weapons, but also an analysis of motive and attri-bution.

According to a 2009 Trend Micro report, cybercrime kits are now widely available online, and they are getting cheaper.[204] Prices can range from a few cents up to hundreds of dollars or more for sophisticated malware.[205] According to a 2005 Symantec study, $300 will rent a 150,000-strong botnet.[206] Some reports have found that it is even possible to sign up for a free three-minute botnet trial,[207] while Zeus, the prolific Trojan horse mentioned in Chapter 1, can be purchased for as little as $700.[208] And it can be freely traded.[209] *GhostNet* researchers report that "[t]oday, pirated cyber-crime kits circulate extensively on the Internet and can be downloaded by anyone about as easily as the latest pirated DVD."[210] Whereas Miller says that he needs about $50 million to hack the planet, according to Haroon Meer, a cybersecurity specialist at Thinkst, you could put together a team that could break in just about anywhere, that is, win a battle if not a war, for a fraction of that cost.[211] This is according to informal surveys conducted by Meer with his fellow cybersecurity specialists, who self-report a high success rate at breaking into targeted systems. A total cost of less than $500,000 to break into nearly any system worries Meer: "It's a scary number. That wouldn't even pay for the annual anti-virus subscription of a big multinational company."[212]

An explosion in both the white and black markets has led to the increased availabil-ity of cyber weapons. For example, software that allows remote access to or control of

---

[203] Scott Charney, Microsoft, Rethinking the Cyber Threat: A Framework and Path Forward 5 (2009).

[204] *Tracking* Ghostnet, *supra* note 130, at 47; *Threat Reports*, Trend Micro, https://imperia.trend micro-europe.com/us/trendwatch/research-and-analysis/threat-reports/ (last visited Dec. 16, 2012).

[205] *See* Michael Cross & Debra Littlejohn Shinder, Scene of a Cybercrime 499 (2008); Byron Acohido, *DIY Cybercrime Kits Power Growth in Net Phishing Attacks*, USA Today (Jan. 18, 2010), http://usatoday30.usatoday.com/money/industries/technology/2010-01-17-internet-scams-phishing_n.htm.

[206] *See* VII Symantec, Internet Security Threat Report 63 (2005).

[207] *See* Gunter Ollman, *Want to Rent an 80–120k DDoS Botnet?*, Day Before Zero, http://blog.damballa .com/?p=330 (last visited June 16, 2013).

[208] Nicolas Falliere & Eric Chien, Symantec, Zeus: King of the Bots 1 (2009), http://www.syman tec.com/content/en/us/enterprise/media/security_response/whitepapers/zeus_king_of_bots.pdf.

[209] *Id.*

[210] *Tracking* Ghostnet, *supra* note 130, at 51 (footnote omitted).

[211] Meer, *supra* note 141.

[212] *Id.*

a Blackberry is being sold commercially.[213] Similarly, a company that made and sold spyware had to be taken to court before they would take if off the market.[214] Lines can be difficult to draw since spyware enables users to send infected attachments, but it can also allow parents to monitor their children's web activities.[215] In addition, according to Lewis of CSIS, the turnaround time on exploitative tools from the NSA to the black market is not long – perhaps "three to eight years" – although the evidence relied upon in making this estimate is "partial and anecdotal."[216]

Whether available on the white or black markets, cyber weapons have evolved quickly to attack social networking platforms and mobile devices.[217] According to one 2011 report, "The pace of change in this technology is quite dramatic. Only a few years ago, malware for smartphones and cellular devices was unheard of."[218] By 2010, however, it was relatively commonplace.[219] In November 2010 alone, for example, a virus that stole contact information to commit fraud had reportedly hit more than one million mobile phones in China.[220] Such attacks are concerning not only because they are becoming easier to launch, but also because they point to criminal organizations getting involved. As Scott Charney noted, a variety of actors are taking advantage of these weapons.[221] With the help of vulnerable Internet platforms like mobile phones, according to National White Collar Crime Center Director Donald Brackman, "Internet crime is evolving in ways we couldn't have imagined just five years ago."[222] Monetary interests alone may not be driving this evolution. Rather, state-sponsored attacks may be partly to blame because states can combine a hacker's tricks with "the intelligence apparatus to reconnoiter a target, the computing power to break codes and passwords, and the patience to probe a system until it finds a weakness – usually a fallible human being."[223] Elements within the private sector are taking note. Google, for example, has begun posting warnings if its security

---

[213] *See* KEN DUNHAM, MOBILE MALWARE ATTACKS AND DEFENSE 240–42 (2009).

[214] *See* DirectRevenue LLC, FTC File No. 052–3131 (June 26, 2007), http://ftc.gov/os/caselist/0523131/0523131cmp070629.pdf.

[215] *See* David Crary, *Parental Dilemma: Whether to Spy on Their Kids*, USA TODAY (Sept. 5, 2011), http://usatoday30.usatoday.com/news/health/wellness/teen-ya/story/2011-09-05/Parental-dilemma-Whether-to-spy-on-their-kids/50262316/1; Mike Lennon, *New Tool Reveals Internet Passwords*, SEC. WK. (July 1, 2010), http://www.securityweek.com/new-tool-reveals-internet-passwords.

[216] Lewis, *supra* note 17, at 9.

[217] *See generally* DUNHAM, *supra* note 213 (exploring many of the myriad vulnerabilities prevalent on mobile devices).

[218] *From the Eye of the Storm*, *supra* note 138.

[219] *See* MCAFEE LABS, MCAFEE THREATS REPORT: THIRD QUARTER 2010 at 15–16 (2010), http://www.mcafee.com/us/resources/reports/rp-quarterly-threat-q3-2010.pdf.

[220] *See* Warwick Ashford, *Over a Million Mobile Phones Hit by Virus in China*, COMPUTER WKL'Y (Nov. 12, 2010), http://www.computerweekly.com/Articles/2010/11/12/243921/Over-a-million-mobile-phones-hit-by-virus-in-China.htm.

[221] CHARNEY, *supra* note 203, at 5.

[222] Mary Jean Babic, *The Evolution of Cyber Crime*, UNIV. MICH. LSA MAG., Spring 2011 at 29, http://issuu.com/lsamagazine/docs/11spr-entiremag/1.

[223] *Cyberwar*, *supra* note 18.

team believes that a state-sponsored attack could compromise users' accounts.[224] The involvement of states in sponsoring cyber attacks is also altering the nature of cyber conflict – just as the growing involvement of states in Internet governance is impacting its trajectory. As such, considering states' use of cyber weapons is critical to understanding attempts to manage them. The next section begins this discussion continued in Chapter 4 by analyzing the technical dimension of a cyber espionage network that has allegedly been traced back to China. Attribution problems and other topics discussed throughout Part II – such as the use of social engineering and the roles of the private and public sectors in enhancing cybersecurity – are contextualized.

FROM THE FOOTHILLS OF THE HIMALAYAS TO THE FRONTIERS OF CYBERSPACE: CYBER WEAPONS, STATES, AND THE PROBLEM OF ATTRIBUTION

The attack was first traced from northern India, where Tibet's spiritual leader resides. "[T]he private office of the Dalai Lama" had been targeted and sensitive documentation extracted, according to *GhostNet* investigator Greg Walton.[225] However, from that starting point, the investigation expanded. Between 2007 and 2009, Walton and others at the Information Warfare Monitor (IWM) discovered that more than 1,295 computers "located at ministries of foreign affairs, embassies, international organizations, news media offices, and NGOs[]" in 103 countries had been compromised.[226] The resulting report found that roughly 70 percent of the control servers implicated in the attacks were located at IP addresses that resolved to China.[227] In April 2010, IWM released a follow-up report entitled *Shadows in the Cloud*, which analyzed data systematically stolen from governments, businesses, academia, and computer networks in the United Nations, India, the United States, "and several other countries."[228] Investigators of the so-called *Shadow* network were able to view documents that cyber attackers had exfiltrated. Whereas the command and control structure of

---

[224] *See* Jason Ryan, *Google to Warn Users of Possible State-Sponsored Cyber Attacks*, ABC NEWS (June 5, 2012), http://abcnews.go.com/blogs/politics/2012/06/google-to-warn-users-of-possible-state-sponsored-cyber-attacks/. These warnings began in June 2012. Since then, thousands of Gmail users have been alerted that their accounts may have been compromised by alleged state-sponsored attacks. Nicole Perlroth, *Google Warns of New State-Sponsored Cyberattack Targets*, N.Y. TIMES BITS (Oct. 2, 2012, 6:44PM), http://bits.blogs.nytimes.com/2012/10/02/google-warns-new-state-sponsored-cyberattack-targets/.

[225] *Canadian Researchers Uncover Spy Plot Against Dalai Lama*, GLOBE & MAIL (Mar. 29, 2009), http://www.theglobeandmail.com/news/world/canadian-researchers-uncover-spy-plot-against-dalai-lama/article1366560/.

[226] *Tracking Ghostnet, supra* note 130, at 1.

[227] *Id.* at 22.

[228] INFO. WARFARE MONITOR & SHADOWSERVER FOUNDATION, SHADOWS IN THE CLOUD: INVESTIGATING CYBER ESPIONAGE 2.0, at iv, 32–35, 46 (2010), http://www.scribd.com/doc/29435784/SHADOWS-IN-THE-CLOUD-Investigating-Cyber-Espionage-2-0 [hereinafter *Shadow*].

Shadow was arguably more intricate than that of *GhostNet*, investigators found that all of the core servers that appeared to be at the center of the network were hosted on domain names in China.[229] Ultimately however, the IWM team wrote: "Although we are able to piece together circumstantial evidence that provides the location and possible associations of the attackers, their actual identities and locations remain illusory. We [only] catch a glimpse of a shadow of attribution in the cloud. . . ."[230]

Even without being able to positively attribute the attacks, the *GhostNet* and *Shadow* investigations provide evidence that hackers' motives and weapons are evolving. The *Shadow* report confirms what *GhostNet* hypothesizes: the hackers that created these networks appear to be moving up the information value chain in that they are more interested in intelligence gathering than in stealing credit card numbers.[231] Further, although attackers are using the same old vulnerabilities, their methods are improving, such as by using sophisticated social engineering techniques.[232]

The IWM investigators did not prove that the Chinese government was in fact behind the attacks despite circumstantial evidence such as the networks' targets and the nature of the data being stolen.[233] The sort of documents exfiltrated range widely, from business plans to confidential information regarding India's foreign relations.[234] Nevertheless, there was a common thread: "attackers managed to compromise those with a keen interest in the PRC."[235] Beyond data about those targeted, investigators also found another piece of evidence: an email address. Losttemp33@hotmail.com, which was used to register one of the core server domains used by attackers in *Shadow*, is associated with the "Godfather of the Chinese Trojan."[236] This led investigators to identify an individual who reportedly was born on July 24, 1982, and lives in Chengdu, China, which is a hub of the People's Liberation Army's signals intelligence efforts.[237] Still, investigators determined that these correlations do not amount to attribution.[238] What would hard evidence look like? It could potentially require a forensic analysis of the system(s) used, which would require PRC cooperation – something that is unlikely, to say the least. The most plausible explanation then, according to IWM, "is that the *Shadow* network is based out of the PRC by one or more individuals with strong connections to the Chinese criminal

---

[229] *Id.* at iv, 1.

[230] *Id.* at 2–3 ("Although there was circumstantial evidence pointing to elements within the People's Republic of China, our investigation concluded that there was not enough evidence to implicate the Chinese government itself and attribution behind *GhostNet* remains a mystery.").

[231] *Id.* at 38.

[232] *Id.* at 17.

[233] *Id.* at 3.

[234] *Id.* at 9, 35.

[235] *Id.* at 33.

[236] *Id.* at 37; Top Chinese Hackers, DARK VISITOR (Dec. 11, 2007), http://www.thedarkvisitor.com/top-chinese-hackers/.

[237] *Shadow, supra* note 228, at 37–38.

[238] *Id.* at 3.

underground . . . [information attained by which] may end up in the possession of some entity of the Chinese government."239

As is demonstrated by *Shadow*, attribution is difficult because attackers can mask their identities, dispersing themselves across platforms and jurisdictions.240 This may be done because of at least three reasons: the first is conceptual, the second is technical, and the third (discussed in Chapter 6) is legal. Conceptually, attribution means different things to different people. To some, it might just mean identifying an IP address; to others, a state or an organization; and to others, a human being with a motive.241 Technically, sophisticated attacks by knowledgeable hackers, whether private or state sponsored, are difficult to trace definitively to their source.242 The science of tracing cyber attacks has been somewhat slow to develop in part because of TCP/IP.243 If an IP packet can be grabbed or spoofed mid-route, it becomes difficult to trace it back to where it actually began. Thus, whereas in theory it is possible to locate the IP address of cyber attackers and use that information to identify individual hackers, sophisticated attackers are able to re-route or otherwise confuse programs designed to locate them. Similarly, if a hacker is using a botnet to carry out attacks, the process of tracing IP packets becomes much more involved and time consuming.

Can the cyber infrastructure be modernized to enhance tracing? The short answer is yes, but not easily or cheaply. Overhauling protocols once they are implemented is no simple matter. Some, like Admiral McConnell, remain adamant: "[W]e need to reengineer the Internet to make attribution, geolocation, intelligence analysis, and impact assessment . . . more manageable."244 However, this is unlikely – at least in

---

239 *Id.* at 40.

240 *See, e.g., China IP Address Link to South Korea Cyber-Attack*, BBC (Mar. 21, 2013), http://www .bbc.co.uk/news/world-asia-21873017 (reporting on a series of cyber attacks targeting South Korean firms that have been traced back to China but potentially originated with North Korean hackers). The same holds true for Mandiant's 2013 report on China's cyber espionage activities. *See* Dan Mcwhorter, *Mandiant Exposes APT1 – One of China's Cyber Espionage Units & Releases 3,000 Indicators*, M-Unition (Feb. 18, 2013), www.mandiant.com/blog/mandiant-exposes-apt1-chinas-cyber-espionage-units-releases-3000-indicators/; *cf.* Jeffrey Carr, *Mandiant APT1 Report Has Critical Analytical Flaws*, Digital Dao (Feb. 19, 2013), http://jeffreycarr.blogspot.com/2013/02/ mandiant-apt1-report-has-critical.html (arguing that "if you're going to make a claim for attribution, then you must be both fair and thorough in your analysis and, through the application of a scientific method like ACH, rule out competing hypotheses and then use estimative language in your finding. Mandiant simply did not succeed" in this regard.).

241 *See* Nat'l Res. Council of the Nat'l Acads., Technology, Policy, Law, and Ethics Regarding U.S. Acquisition and Use of Cyberattack Capabilities 138–141 (William A. Owens, Kenneth W. Dam, & Herbert S. Lin eds., 2009) [hereinafter National Academies].

242 *See id.* at 139; Howard F. Lipson, CERT Coordination Ctr., Tracking and Tracing Cyber-Attacks: Technical Challenges and Global Policy Issues 4–5 (2002), http://www.dtic.mil/ cgi-bin/ GetTRDoc?AD=ADA408853&Location=U2&doc=GetTRDoc.pdf.

243 *See* Lipson, *supra* note 242, at 27; Larry Greenemeier, *Seeking Address: Why Cyber Attacks Are So Difficult to Trace Back to Hackers*, Sci. Am. (June 11, 2011), www.scientificamerican.com/article.cfm? id=tracking-cyber-hackers.

244 Mike McConnell, *McConnell on How to Win the Cyber-War We're Losing*, Wash. Post (Feb. 28, 2010), http://www.washingtonpost.com/wp-dyn/content/article/2010/02/ 25/AR2010022502493.html.

the short term – and many people are not convinced that the architecture should be overhauled because it would mean limiting anonymity online.[245] Compromise may take the form of encouraging the use of VPNs and focusing on improving security for certain cyber transactions such as those involving critical national infrastructure, which could be made more traceable without ending anonymity as we know it.

Alternative technical strategies do exist, however, for managing the attribution problem, though legitimate disagreements persist on this point. Those strategies pioneered by the U.S. Cyber Emergency Response Team (US-CERT), an element within the Department of Homeland Security that "proactively manage[s] cyber risks to the Nation,"[246] for example, are promising. These include the use of probabilistic trace-back techniques to audit a small percentage of packets, making it easier to find the source of DDoS attacks,[247] as well as securing code and encouraging users to practice good cyber hygiene.[248] There is also the possibility of tracing back single IP packets, although this is more difficult and raises privacy concerns.[249] For example, in the aftermath of DDoS attacks that Estonia suffered in 2007, experts "followed attacking pings to specific zombie computers, and then watched to see when the infected machines 'phoned home'... [eventually finding the] higher-level controlling devices."[250] Charney also has written that it is possible to increase attribution through deploying "strong authentication technologies ... more effective technical trace-back mechanisms," and multilateral collaboration.[251] Regarding the latter point, cooperative intrusion detection in which nations work together to help increase transparency for where packets originate would be a boon to cybercrime investigators and aid in "all-source attribution" in which information is integrated from a variety of sources in order to identify an attacker.[252]

As these technologies and techniques develop, it is useful to reassess our paradigm. Some argue, for example, that we should forget about attribution and focus on defense strategies, whereas others insist that attribution must be front and center – in short, that a "probability threshold" for attributing attacks should be devised.[253]

---

[245] *But see* Jonathan Mayer, *There's Anonymity on the Internet. Get Over It.*, FREEDOM TO TINKER (Oct. 27, 2009), https://freedom-to-tinker.com/blog/jrmayer/theres-anonymity-internet-get-over-it/ (making the case that anonymity will continue on the Internet).

[246] United States Computer Emergency Readiness Team (US-CERT), *About Us*, http://www.us-cert.gov/about-us (last visited June 16, 2013).

[247] *See* LIPSON, *supra* note 242, at 41–46.

[248] *See* Greenemeier, *supra* note 243; *cf.* Jathan Sadowski, *Why We Should Wash Our Hands of 'Cyber Hygiene,'* SLATE (June 19, 2013), http://www.slate.com/blogs/future_tense/2013/06/19/cyber_hygiene_vint_cerf_s_concept_of_personal_cybersecurity_is_problematic.html (arguing that the concept of cyber hygiene "is a wrong and shallow way to think about the topic, one that puts an undue onus on the individual.").

[249] LIPSON, *supra* note 242, at 27, 43.

[250] *See* CLARKE & KNAKE, *supra* note 30, at 15.

[251] CHARNEY, *supra* note 203, at 8.

[252] NATIONAL ACADEMIES, *supra* note 241, at 139; Greenemeier, *supra* note 243.

[253] CHARNEY, *supra* note 203, at 9.

The latter approach, though, requires a legal analysis of applicable (if unsettled) international law, which is undertaken in Chapter 6.

Attribution presents technical, legal, and policy-related challenges, much like many of the other vulnerabilities and malware recently discussed. In documenting these instances of espionage, this section has applied the science of tracing cyber attacks and some of the larger principles examined thus far, including sovereignty, state sponsorship, and attribution, to show both the challenges and urgency of managing vulnerabilities. The final step is to determine whether such attacks may be better conceptualized within a polycentric framework.

UNDERSTANDING THE CYBER THREAT ECOSYSTEM WITHIN
A POLYCENTRIC FRAMEWORK

To substantiate discussions of cyber weapons and vulnerabilities at multiple levels and explore some of the difficulties inherent in achieving cyber peace, this chapter has discussed two cyber espionage networks documented by the IWM: *GhostNet* and *Shadow*. These networks demonstrate how cyber attacks are evolving and suggest that there are now many malicious actors in cyberspace – including states. As was explored in Chapter 1, since the early 2000s, states have become more interested in the Internet in terms of governance, as a tool for espionage,[254] and as a way to control restive populations. "These days even the website of China's Defense Ministry has a section with music downloads[,]" notes Evgeny Morozov.[255] However, while states are an important aspect of the evolving cyber threat, cyber attacks, like most kinds of threats, are the result of a more complex ecosystem. Protocols, programming, and people all contribute to its structure and give form to its vulnerabilities. And as cyberspace expands, these problems may get worse before they get better. Every day our digital lives are enhanced, but each new program, app, or cloud computing service also "creates an opportunity for this ecosystem to morph, adapt, and exploit" because "these new technologies [develop] faster than procedures and rules have been created to deal with the . . . vulnerabilities they introduce."[256] Because of the manner in which Internet governance has evolved, as Chapters 1 and 2 depicted, no single entity has a mandate to enhance security in the system, and perhaps

---

[254] *See, e.g.,* Matthew M. Aid, *Inside the NSA's Ultra-Secret China Hacking Group,* FOREIGN POL'Y (June 10, 2013), http://www.foreignpolicy.com/articles/2013/06/10/inside_the_nsa_s_ultra_secret_china_hacking_group ("According to a number of confidential sources, a highly secretive unit of the National Security Agency . . . called the Office of Tailored Access Operations . . . has successfully penetrated Chinese computer and telecommunications systems for almost 15 years, generating some of the best and most reliable intelligence information about what is going on inside the People's Republic of China.").

[255] EVGENY MOROZOV, THE NET DELUSION: THE DARK SIDE OF INTERNET FREEDOM 138 (2011).

[256] *Shadow, supra* note 228, at 1; *see also* Joshua McGee, *A Cybersecurity Assessment of Cloud Computing,* CSIS, June 9, 2011, http://csis.org/blog/cybersecurity-assessment-cloud-computing (summarizing some of the upsides and downsides of cloud computing applied to cybersecurity).

that is how it should be since if a single entity did occupy the field, such as the U.S. government or an intergovernmental organization, it could risk crowding out innovative bottom-up efforts.[257]

This chapter has shown that vulnerabilities exist at the physical, logical, and content layers of the Internet's architecture, and that an array of cyber weapons are being deployed by attackers with varying motives to take advantage of these vulnerabilities. Whether it is problems in IP or DNS, these vulnerabilities are best managed from the bottom-up through cybersecurity education, market-based incentives, and, if necessary, regulatory intervention. Such efforts will benefit from coordination among dispersed power centers; for example, the extension of DNSSEC to the root and TLDs is an example of a successful polycentric measure that has improved on the status quo, even if it has not fully resolved the underlying problem. Lessons should be taken from protocols, which must fill a real need, be incrementally deployable, and enjoy open source availability to be successful.[258]

In short, instead of waiting for scientific and political consensus for how best to comprehensively solve the cyber threat, action should be taken through nested enterprises at multiple levels taking into account the layering of the Internet's infrastructure and Professor Ostrom's design principles, such as the need for monitoring and information sharing to help ensure good governance.[259] This effort may be conceptualized as a polycentric undertaking given that it "encourages experimentation at multiple levels,"[260] self-regulation and bottom-up governance, as well as targeted measures to address global collective action problems. For example, empowering communities with defined boundaries of responsibility and authority recognized by state actors is one component of mitigating technical vulnerabilities under the "collective-choice arrangements and minimal recognition of rights" principle.[261] However, because of the limits of regulating exclusively through code and the risk of regulatory competition,[262] as well as the multifaceted nature of cyber attacks extending beyond technical vulnerabilities, laws, norms, and markets also have a key role to play in shaping the regulatory environment and fostering cyber peace. The way

---

[257] *See* Elinor Ostrom, *Beyond Markets and States: Polycentric Governance of Complex Economic Systems,* 100 Am. Econ. Rev. 641, 656 (2010) (citing Andrew F. Reeson & John G. Tisdell, *Institutions, Motivations and Public Goods: An Experimental Test of Motivational Crowding,* 68 J. Econ. Behavior & Org. 273 (2008) (finding "externally imposed regulation that would theoretically lead to higher joint returns 'crowded out' voluntary behavior to cooperate.")).

[258] D. Thaler & B. Aboba, What Makes for a Successful Protocol? 11, IETF RFC 5218, (2008), http://tools.ietf.org/html/rfc5218#page-11.

[259] *See* Elinor Ostrom, *Polycentric Systems: Multilevel Governance Involving a Diversity of Organizations, in* Global Environmental Commons: Analytical and Political Challenges Involving a Diversity of Organizations 105, 118–120 (Eric Brousseau et al. eds., 2012) (citing Elinor Ostrom, Governing the Commons: The Evolution of Institutions for Collective Action 90 (1990)).

[260] Elinor Ostrom, *A Polycentric Approach for Coping with Climate Change* 39 (World Bank Policy Research Working Paper No. 5095, 2009).

[261] *See* Ostrom, *supra* note 259, at 120.

[262] *See* Murray, *supra* note 19, at 46.

forward, then, involves taking incremental steps to address the multiple layers and dimensions of this threat ecosystem, focusing first on the physical and logical infrastructures given that these layers comprise the foundation of cybersecurity. Potential solutions to TCP, IP, DNS, and BGP vulnerabilities such as IPsec, DNSSEC, and IP packet filtering should be further refined and, after achieving broader consensus, widely implemented; hardware and software must be improved, such as through securing supply chains or creating liability structures; and users must be incentivized to become better educated and responsible. Managing technical vulnerabilities, though, is just the first step in the journey to a positive cyber peace. Securing critical national infrastructure, for example, requires proactive private-sector engagement built on the analysis begun here and extended in Chapters 4 and 5.

4

The New Cyber Warfare

Securing Critical National Infrastructure in the Digital Age

The world is only just beginning to see glimpses of cyber war.... It is time for states to sit down and discuss how to limit this threat to world peace.

– Professor Joseph S. Nye[1]

During the winter of 2013–14, amidst the school delays and extreme weather conditions in much of the United States, the federal Emergency Alert System issued a warning, but perhaps not the one people expected: "Civil authorities in your area have reported that the bodies of the dead are rising from their graves and attacking the living.... Do not attempt to approach or apprehend these bodies, as they are considered extremely dangerous."[2] Hackers had penetrated the system to issue a "bogus zombie alert" in yet another "disturbingly common" episode showcasing the myriad vulnerabilities buried in "critical systems throughout [U.S.] government...."[3] Aside from being fodder for bored hackers, such weaknesses can be exploited by cyber criminals, terrorists, and nation-states, which makes securing critical infrastructure a key test of effective cybersecurity policymaking. Thus far, though, it is a test that many nations, including the United States, are failing.

According to Carl von Clausewitz, as a new domain becomes a "hub of all power and movement on which everything depends" – like cyberspace has – the possibility of conflict within that domain becomes a core issue of international peace

---

[1] Joseph S. Nye, *Cyber War and Peace*, PROJECT SYNDICATE (Apr. 10, 2012), http://www.project-syndicate .org/commentary/cyber-war-and-peace. Portions of this chapter are scheduled to appear in the *Stanford Journal of International Law* at 50 STAN. J. INT'L L. __ (forthcoming) (2014). When possible and appropriate, please cite to that version.

[2] Craig Timberg & Lisa Rein, *Senate Cybersecurity Report Finds Agencies Often Fail to Take Basic Preventive Measures*, WASH. POST (Feb. 4, 2014), http://www.washingtonpost.com/business/ technology/senate-cybersecurity-report-finds-agencies-often-fail-to-take-basic-preventive-measures/ 2014/02/03/493390c2-8ab6-11e3-833c-33098f9e5267_story.html?wpmk=MK0000200.

[3] Id.

and security.[4] This insight is especially relevant as cyber attacks have become an increasingly invaluable weapon in national arsenals. From *GhostNet* to Stuxnet and its progeny, cyber weapons have evolved from being considered a supporting component in military operations to systems that are capable of causing actual damage in the real world, including to critical infrastructure.[5] Understanding the many facets of this new domain of conflict is central to promoting global cybersecurity – in order to attain cyber peace, then, it is necessary to study cyber war.

The goal of this chapter is to analyze the scope and evolution of cyber war doctrines and what steps the cyber powers are taking to prepare for and mitigate the threat of cyber conflict, focusing on securing critical national infrastructure. To accomplish this, it is necessary to first examine theories of "cyber power" and investigate some of the main theatres of cyber conflict to extrapolate what trends are prevalent and how they may be addressed to enhance cybersecurity. Next, the revolution in cyber affairs is assessed in reference to the leading cyber powers – including the United States, the United Kingdom, China, Russia, and Israel – both to identify best practices that could, over time, give rise to norms and eventually be codified in international law, and begin to determine how well state-centric approaches are managing the cyber threat.[6] This will help determine the role that nations can and should play as a component of a polycentric approach to enhancing cybersecurity.

DEFINING THE NEW CYBER WARFARE

War and conflict are inherently asymmetric – as Clausewitz noted, mutual destruction assures that "true peer competitors . . . rarely engage in conflict . . . ."[7] This lesson played out during much of the twentieth century with the rise in proxy wars featuring increasingly sophisticated technology, from jet fighters to cyber attacks.[8] Sophisticated offensive cyber attack capabilities vary between countries even though near ubiquitous technology would seem to level the playing field. This means that an asymmetric structure of opportunity persists, providing an opening for non-state groups. In order to better understand the dynamics present at the dawn of a new

---

[4] Steven H. McPherson & Glenn Zimmerman, *Cyberspace Control, in* SECURING FREEDOM IN THE GLOBAL COMMONS 83, 84 (Scott Jasper ed., 2010).

[5] *See* THOMAS RID, CYBER WAR WILL NOT TAKE PLACE 37–38 (2013); DAVID E. SANGER, CONFRONT AND CONCEAL: OBAMA'S SECRET WARS AND SURPRISING USE OF AMERICAN POWER ix–xi (2012); Eric Schmitt & Thom Shanker, *U.S. Debated Cyberwarfare in Attack Plan on Libya*, N.Y. TIMES (Oct. 17, 2011), http://www.nytimes.com/2011/10/18/world/africa/cyber-warfare-against-libya-was-debated-by-us.html.

[6] *See* ELINOR C. SLOAN, THE REVOLUTION IN MILITARY AFFAIRS ix, 116–17 (2002) (discussing the extent to which information technology is transforming modern warfare, as well as framing the U.S. response to cyber terrorism as part of the revolution in military affairs).

[7] *See* Samuel Liles, *Cyber Warfare: As a Form of Low-Intensity Conflict and Insurgency*, NATO CCDCOE PROC. 47, 47 (2010), http://www.ccdcoe.org/publications/2010proceedings/Liles%20-%20 Cyber%20warfare%20%20As%20a%20form%20of%20low-intensity%20conflict%20and%20insurgency .pdf.

[8] *See id.*

age of cyber conflict it is first necessary to reexamine classic cyber warfare and the history of cyber conflict.

Cyber warfare generally refers to an attack by one nation against the computers or networks of another to cause "disruption or damage."[9] Cyber war doctrines vary, as discussed in Chapter 1, but generally require maintaining "freedom of access to and use of" cyberspace while denying that freedom to adversaries.[10] Achieving this vision requires robust offensive and defensive capabilities to protect critical national infrastructure and manage cyber threats.[11] According to Dr. Lani Kass, former director of the U.S. Air Force Cyberspace Task Force, "[c]yber, as a war-fighting domain . . . favors the offense"[12] because, as explored in Chapter 3, it is generally easier to detect and exploit a vulnerability than to protect against one. As General Hayden notes, "We have built the Internet in such a way that it's very hard to defend it. It's built on openness. It's built on access. It's built on agility. None of those things help the defense[,]"[13] an insight equally applicable to military commanders and business managers.

According to the U.S. DOD, information operations "shall be employed to support full spectrum dominance . . . with the goal of achieving information superiority for the United States."[14] Under this heading, the U.S. DOD is using "computer network operations" to "attack, deceive, degrade, disrupt, deny, exploit, and defend electronic information and infrastructure."[15] Simply put, nothing is off the table to prevent war by securing "U.S. military strategic superiority in the [cyberspace] domain."[16] However, achieving strategic superiority in an increasingly crowded environment is no easy feat, made even more difficult by the explosion of cybercrime and espionage. These facets of the cyber threat may seem like minimal concerns in a national

---

[9] RICHARD A. CLARKE & ROBERT K. KNAKE, CYBER WAR: THE NEXT THREAT TO NATIONAL SECURITY AND WHAT TO DO ABOUT IT 6 (2010).

[10] NAT'L RES. COUNCIL OF THE NAT'L ACADS., TECHNOLOGY, POLICY, LAW, AND ETHICS REGARDING U.S. ACQUISITION AND USE OF CYBERATTACK CAPABILITIES 162 (William A. Owens, Kenneth W. Dam & Herbert S. Lin eds., 2009) [hereinafter NATIONAL ACADEMIES].

[11] *See* Clay Wilson, *Information Operations, Electronic Warfare, and Cyberwar: Capabilities and Related Policy Issues*, CONG. RES. SERV., RL31787 at 4–6 (2007).

[12] Noah Shachtman, *Air Force Readying Cyber Strikes*, WIRED (Oct. 9, 2007), http://www.wired.com/dangerroom/2007/10/also-nsa-target/; *see also The National Military Strategy for Cyberspace Operations*, U.S. JOINT CHIEFS STAFF, Dec. 2006, at 2, http://www.dod.mil/pubs/foi/joint_staff/jointStaff_jointOperations/07-F-2105doc1.pdf [hereinafter *Joint Chiefs*] (discussing U.S. doctrines of cyber defense and offense).

[13] Transcript of *Hayden: Hackers Force Internet Users to Learn Self-Defense*, PBS NEWS HOUR (Aug. 21, 2010), http://www.pbs.org/newshour/bb/science/july-dec10/cyber_08-11.html [hereinafter PBS NEWS HOUR].

[14] DOD Directive 3600.01 (May 23, 2011), http://openanthropology.org/libya/infoops.pdf. Note that this language has been revised in the May 2, 2013 Directive, which instead refers to integrating information operations "into the full spectrum of military operations." DOD Directive 3600.01 (May 2, 2013), http://www.dtic.mil/whs/directives/corres/pdf/360001p.pdf.

[15] *Information Dominance Corps*, U.S. NAVY, at 8 (2010), www.usna.edu/Cyber/documents/IDC/IDC_Overview.pdf.

[16] *Joint Chiefs*, *supra* note 12, at vii.

---

*Low Risk of Escalation

→ Reconnaissance, espionage, crime
   → Attack preparations (leave-behind weapons)
     → Disruption and damage of military targets outside national territory
      → Disruption and damage of military targets inside national territory
       → Disruption and damage of critical infrastructure
        → Disruption and damage of other civilian targets

*High Risk of Escalation

FIGURE 4.1. CYBER CONFLICT THRESHOLDS. *Source:* James A. Lewis, *The "Korean" Cyber Attacks and Their Implications for Cyber Conflict*, CTR. STRATEGIC & INT'L STUD. (CSIS) (Oct. 2009), at 6.

security context but they create opportunities for attackers to stay below certain cyber conflict thresholds while still inflicting damage. Former Deputy Defense Secretary Lynn, for example, notes that "the vast majority of malicious cyber activity today does not cross [the] threshold" of being a national security concern but promotes caution because ultimately "bits and bytes can be as threatening as bullets and bombs."[7]

Further along the escalation threshold from cybercrime and espionage as shown in Figure 4.1 is disruption and damage to critical national infrastructure (CNI),[18] which is especially problematic for policymakers given extensive private-sector control. The potential of cyber weapons to cripple CNI has brought the public into the cyber war arena, much like air power brought public attention to aerial combat during the twentieth century. Even though securing CNI is only one aspect of cyber war doctrines, the multi-sector nature of the policy problem lends itself to polycentric analysis and so is a primary focus of this chapter for three reasons. First, CNI regulation will likely shape many evolving areas of cybersecurity policymaking and international engagement. Because it is linked with military, civilian, and supply chain concerns, CNI policy may ultimately impact cybersecurity confidence-building measures and norms related to the laws of war, along with national regulation, government procurement, and international trade. On the one hand, this complicates CNI policymaking, but on the other hand, it demonstrates wide possibilities for engagement between the cyber powers and beyond. Second, as ABI Research, a New York-based market research firm, has stated, "Cyber security for critical infrastructure has become an issue of primary importance to nation

---

[17] William J. Lynn III, *Remarks on the Department of Defense Cyber Strategy*, U.S. DEP'T DEF. (July 14, 2011), http://www.defense.gov/speeches/speech.aspx?speechid=1593.

[18] James A. Lewis, *The "Korean" Cyber Attacks and Their Implications for Cyber Conflict*, CTR. STRATEGIC & INT'L STUD. (Oct. 2009), at 6.

states."[19] As such, intense forms of imitation and learning are occurring, which may prompt norms discussions that could help states to forestall further policy divergence on such a substantial issue.[20] Third and finally, despite the complex nature of CNI policymaking, many states share comparable goals, perhaps reflecting the fact that securing CNI has been a state responsibility since Roman times.[21] Cultural and political differences will still make CNI norms development difficult, but at least states can acknowledge that they are struggling with similar challenges and are aiming to achieve related goals, opening up a potential avenue to further cyber peace.

The task of securing CNI is daunting, and only seems to be becoming more so as events unfold. Cyber attacks on U.S. Central Command, Estonia, Georgia, and Iran, among many others, have intensified concerns that hostile foreign governments or non-state actors could preemptively launch cyber attacks on CNI, including companies that support energy distribution, telecommunications, and financial services.[22] An array of U.S. natural gas pipeline companies and nuclear power plants were reportedly hit in 2013 alone.[23] Because modern societies – as well as large and small companies alike – rely heavily on networked systems and IT to do tasks like payroll, inventory tracking, and research and development, even small-scale cyber operations have the potential to disrupt services and harm public welfare,[24] whereas more substantial exploits could cause paralysis or worse.[25] According to Professors Christopher Joyner and Catherine Lotrionte, "Western societies have spent years building information infrastructures [in ways] that are interoperable, easy to access and easy to use."[26] Yet the open philosophy of this system

---

[19] *National Policies for Protecting Critical Infrastructure to Drive Billions in Cyber Security Spending*, ABI Res. (June 18, 2013), www.abiresearch.com/press/national-policies-for-protecting-critical-infrastr.

[20] *See* Ronald J. Deibert & Masachi Crete-Nishihata, *Global Governance and the Spread of Cyberspace Controls*, 18 Global Governance 339, 339 (2012).

[21] In Rome, the government became increasingly concerned with protecting aqueducts as it realized how extensively Roman society relied on them to provide such an "essential service." Michael J. Assante, *Infrastructure Protection in the Ancient World*, Proc. of the 42nd Haw. Int'l Conf. on Sys. Sci. at 2 (2009), http://www.hicss.hawaii.edu/HICSS_42/BestPapers42/ElectricalPower/ReliabilityAndCyberSecurity.pdf.

[22] *See, e.g., Researchers Warn of New Stuxnet Worm*, BBC News (Oct. 19, 2011), http://www.bbc.co.uk/news/technology-15367816 [hereinafter *New Stuxnet*] (reporting on the Duqu exploit and its capacity to attack firms that manufacture industrial control systems).

[23] David Goldman, *Hacker Hits on U.S. Power and Nuclear Targets Spiked in 2012*, CNN Money (Jan. 9, 2013), http://money.cnn.com/2013/01/09/technology/security/infrastructure-cyberattacks/ (reporting that "[t]he number of attacks reported to a U.S. Department of Homeland Security cybersecurity response team grew by 52% in 2012" to 198).

[24] *See* Christopher C. Joyner & Catherine Lotrionte, *Information Warfare as International Coercion: Elements of a Legal Framework*, 12 Eur. J. Int'l L. 825, 829–30, 858 (2001); John Reed, *The White House: Cyber Attacks Against Critical Infrastructure Are Way Up*, FP Nat'l Sec. (May 24, 2013), http://killerapps.foreignpolicy.com/posts/2013/05/24/the_white_house_cyber_attacks_against_critical_infrastructure_are_way_up.

[25] *See Cybersecurity Today and Tomorrow: Pay Now or Pay Later*, Computer Sci. & Telecomm. Bd., Nat'l Res Council 3 (2002) [hereinafter *Cybersecurity Today*].

[26] Joyner & Lotrionte, *supra* note 24, at 826.

is also its Achilles' heel because one infected system can compromise an entire network.

Securing CNI is a far more daunting proposition than safeguarding all of a nation's ports or power plants against physical intruders. Even defining what CNI is in the cyber context is difficult. When the U.S. DOD unveiled declassified portions of its strategy for cyberspace, former Deputy Defense Secretary Lynn announced that everything from the electric grid to telecommunications and transportation systems constitute CNI, stating that "a cyber attack against more than one [of these networks] could be devastating."[27] The U.S. DHS defines "critical infrastructure" as "the assets, systems, and networks, whether physical or virtual, so vital to the United States that their incapacitation or destruction would have a debilitating effect on security, national economic security, national public health or safety, or any combination thereof."[28] Proposed legislation such as the U.S. Cybersecurity Act of 2012 would have given the DHS the authority to decide which systems are critical and set cybersecurity performance requirements for covered entities, as will be discussed.[29] Other countries have different approaches. The UK Center for the Protection of Critical National Infrastructure (CPNI) includes nine industries as comprising critical infrastructure: "communications, emergency services, energy, financial services, food, government, health, transport, and water."[30] These varying definitions are helping to animate national approaches to securing vulnerable CNI with certain areas of convergence and divergence that are explored later in this chapter.

Identifying a cyber attack on CNI from the normal transnational data flows is daunting and not unlike picking out a single, disguised person from the some 180,000 passengers that pass through Chicago's O'Hare airport daily. As computer systems become more prevalent, sophisticated, and interconnected, society is becoming increasingly vulnerable to poor system design, accidents, and cyber attacks. The global scale and interconnection of computer networks multiplies these vulnerabilities. The President's Commission on Critical Infrastructure Protection has noted that more than nineteen million individuals around the world have the knowledge

---

[27] Lynn, *supra* note 17.

[28] *What is Critical Infrastructure*, DHS, http://www.dhs.gov/what-critical-infrastructure (last visited Jan. 16, 2014); *see What is the ICS-CERT Mission?*, http://ics-cert.us-cert.gov/Frequently-Asked-Questions (last visited Jan. 17, 2014) (The U.S. Cyber Emergency Response Team, which is part of DHS, identifies sixteen critical infrastructure sectors consistent with Homeland Security Presidential Directive 7, including: agriculture, banking and finance, chemical, commercial facilities, dams, defense industrial base, drinking water and water treatment systems, emergency systems, energy, government facilities, information technology, nuclear systems, public health and healthcare, telecommunications, and transportation systems).

[29] *See* Cybersecurity Act of 2012, S. 2105, 112th Cong. § 103(b)(1)(C) (2012).

[30] *The National Infrastructure*, CPNI, http://www.cpni.gov.uk/about/cni/ (last visited Jan. 16, 2014); *see* Paul Cornish et al., *Cyber Security and the UK's Critical National Infrastructure*, CHATHAM HOUSE REP., at 2 (Sept. 2011), http://www.chathamhouse.org/publications/papers/view/178171.

necessary to launch cyber attacks,[31] and that was in 1997, well before the uptick in malware kit use. As Chapter 3 explored, little specialized equipment is needed, and Interpol has estimated that there are as many as 30,000 websites providing automated hacking tools.[32] The goods and ills of the Internet are bound together through billions of optic fibers.

Cyber conflict, including cyber war, is a complex strategic problem lacking an appropriate policy framework with outstanding issues ranging from deterrence, to preemption, to proportional response. Given the relative ease of offense, difficulty of defense, and strategic importance of securing CNI that is largely under the control of the private sector in many nations, cyber war raises a host of difficult challenges to policymakers that may be conceptualized within a polycentric framework. That said, there has not yet been a genuine cyber war, and there is reason to hope that one will not occur in the future, hence the focus in this chapter on one pressing facet of cyber conflict: CNI. As with managing technical vulnerabilities, securing CNI requires targeted measures by non-state actors, states, and groups of nations working together to address the collective action problem of cyber attacks. Generally accepted international norms in cyber conflict are slowly emerging that could help "limit the scope of conflict and shape behavior," as is explored in Chapters 6 and 7, such as "the line between reconnaissance or exploitation (espionage and crime) and disruption and damage" (terrorism and war).[33] A secondary threshold is the one between damaging or disrupting military infrastructure and CNI.[34] Baseline norms that protect CNI or minimize damage to noncombatants could provide an important jumping-off point for establishing more formalized thresholds of cyber conflict.[35] Such norms are required to help hold in check a new era of cyber conflict, which differs from classic conceptions based on three trends that will be explored: (1) the list of cyber powers continues to lengthen, (2) more states seem to be sponsoring cyber attacks through non-state actors targeting both public and private entities, and (3) the growing sophistication of attackers' techniques coupled with advancing technology risks escalation. A brief, non-comprehensive history of cyber conflict is offered to help couch these trends in greater context and to explore what they might portend for clarifying norms and promoting cyber peace.

---

[31] PRESIDENT'S COMM'N ON CRITICAL INFRASTRUCTURE PROTECTION, CRITICAL FOUNDATIONS: PROTECTING AMERICA'S INFRASTRUCTURE x, 9 (1997), http://www.fas.org/sgp/library/pccip.pdf.

[32] *See* Sumit Gosh, *Evolutionary History of Critical Infrastructure Protection in the USA, in* CYBERCRIMES: A MULTIDISCIPLINARY ANALYSIS 173, 178 (Sumit Ghosh & Elliot Turrini eds., 2010).

[33] Lewis, *supra* note 18, at 5. Simply put, "[n]orms are shared expectations about appropriate behavior." Roger Hurwitz, *An Augmented Summary of The Harvard, MIT and U. of Toronto Cyber Norms Workshop* 5 (2012), http://citizenlab.org/cybernorms/augmented-summary.pdf. They may be descriptive of current best practices or prescriptive, meaning they specify behaviors that norm accepters should adopt. *Id.*

[34] Hurwitz, *supra* note 33, at 6.

[35] *Id.* at 7.

A Short History of Cyber Conflict

Clarke and Knake argue that cyber war "happens at the speed of light... is global... skips the battlefield... and has begun."[36] Not everyone agrees with this assessment, though, with some such as Dr. Thomas Rid of King's College London arguing that cyber war has not occurred and likely will not in the future.[37] Part of the reason for these differing perceptions is that the history behind the hype of cyber war is shrouded in secrecy. This subsection attempts to bring some of this cloak-and-dagger world to light by focusing on several of the best- and least-known examples of cyber conflict, extending from 1998 to 2012. Before we begin, however, it is first necessary to introduce the concept of "cyber power" because the history of cyber conflict is in many ways the quest for cyber power.

To put cyber power in context, consider an analogy: air power. There is a long-running debate over the independent war-winning capability of air power, which has been long promised but has not yet fully materialized.[38] A similar debate is raging in the cyber context.[39] How might "cyber power" be defined? Books on military doctrine discuss other types of power, like sea power, in terms of inputs and outputs.[40] Inputs include things like how big of a fleet a country maintains, whereas outputs "influence the behavior" of another country.[41] Under this conceptualization, practicing cyber power might require using soft power persuasion techniques such as offering incentives like grants for improving cybersecurity in some contexts over hard power public shaming to limit trade secrets theft or even having a standing cyber army that can assert operational control over a given network as a mission dictates.[42] However, cyberspace is in many ways a "unique hybrid regime" unlike the ocean with which it is so often compared.[43] Information is intangible and difficult to control, so barriers to entry are low, diffusing power. Ownership of technology is also fungible, in part because of the defenders' dilemma; that is, an intruder only needs to locate one entry point, whereas a defender must protect all points from attack simultaneously.[44]

---

[36] *See* CLARKE & KNAKE, *supra* note 9, at 31.

[37] RID, *supra* note 5, at 10 ("So far there is no known act of cyber 'war,' when war is properly defined.").

[38] *See* MARK CLODFELTER, THE LIMITS OF AIR POWER: THE AMERICAN BOMBING OF NORTH VIETNAM ix (1989).

[39] *See* RID, *supra* note 5, at 178.

[40] *See* GEOFFREY TILL, SEAPOWER: A GUIDE FOR THE TWENTY-FIRST CENTURY 21 (2009).

[41] *Id.*

[42] *See* Kathrin Hille, *China Claims 'Mountains of Data' on Cyber Attacks by US*, FIN. TIMES (June 5, 2013), http://www.ft.com/cms/s/0/921f47cc-cdce-11e2-a13e-00144feab7de.html#axzz2WbuSB803 (reporting on the back and forth U.S.-Sino "name and shame" game relating to cyber attacks); Joseph S. Nye, Jr., *Power and National Security in Cyberspace*, in AMERICA'S CYBER FUTURE: SECURITY AND PROSPERITY IN THE INFORMATION AGE 7, 8 (Kristin M. Lord & Travis Sharp eds., CNAS, 2011) ("Power is the ability to influence others to obtain the outcomes one wants through hard power behavior (coercion and payments) and soft power behavior (framing agendas, attraction and persuasion). Different resources support power behavior in different contexts, and cyberspace is a new context.").

[43] Nye, *supra* note 42, at 7, 8.

[44] *See* Steve Riley & Jesper M. Johansson, *The Defender's Dilemma*, INFORMIT (Aug. 5, 2005), http://www.informit.com/articles/article.aspx?p=397659&seqNum=4.

In addition, virtual communities are transnational by their nature, lacking the equivalent of territorial seas, although states may exercise sovereignty over the Internet's physical infrastructure located in their territory, as was explored in Chapter 2.[45]

Defining cyber power is difficult, then, as it was for A. T. Mahan with sea power, which he left undefined in his classic work, *The Influence of Sea Power Upon History*.[46] For our purposes, however, cyber power is defined consistent with Professor Nye's approach as "the ability to obtain preferred outcomes through use of the electronically interconnected information resources of the cyber domain."[47] This is less state-centric than the U.S. Joint Chiefs of Staff definition of "space power," which is described as "the total strength of a nation's capabilities to conduct and influence activities to, in, through, and from space to achieve its objectives."[48] As such, Professor Nye's approach recognizes the myriad actors engaged in and facets to enhancing global cybersecurity, including the need for international cooperation and empowering institutions at multiple scales to better manage the cyber threat.[49] Accomplishing this goal, though, is difficult because of the need for collaboration between numerous established and emerging power centers,[50] as well as the problems of attribution and the defenders' dilemma among other issues facing states that will be discussed in this chapter and have been present to varying degrees since the dawn of cyber conflict.

The Opening Cyber Salvos

It is difficult to say when the first cyber attacks on states began. Part of the reason for this is the overlapping nature of cyber war with cybercrime, cyber espionage, and cyber terrorism discussed in Chapter 1. A further complication is the covert nature of cyber war, perpetuating a lack of integrated communication and reporting. Some studies into cyber conflict begin with the 1982 Soviet gas pipeline explosion mentioned in the Preface. Others, including NATO's, start with the November 1988 Morris worm that infected MIT's network and is often credited as the first hack.[51]

---

[45] See Wolff Heintschel von Heinegg, *Legal Implications of Territorial Sovereignty in Cyberspace*, NATO CCDCOE PROC. 7, 11 (2012), http://www.ccdcoe.org/publications/2012proceedings/1_1_von_Heinegg_LegalImplicationsOfTerritorialSovereigntyInCyberspace.pdf (arguing that "[t]he basic applicability of the principle of territorial sovereignty to cyberspace entails that the cyber infrastructure located on the land territory, in the internal waters, in the territorial sea, and, where applicable, in the archipelagic waters, or in the national airspace is covered by the respective State's territorial sovereignty.").

[46] See generally A. T. MAHAN, THE INFLUENCE OF SEA POWER UPON HISTORY, 1660–1783 (2004).

[47] Nye, *supra* note 42, at 7, 8.

[48] Eric Sterner, *Beyond the Stalemate in the Space Commons, in* THE CONTESTED COMMONS 107, 111 (CNAS ed., 2010) (citing DEP'T OF DEF., JOINT PUBLICATION 3–14, SPACE OPERATIONS GL-9 (Jan. 6, 2009)).

[49] See Nye, *supra* note 42, at 7, 12–13, 19.

[50] *Id.* at 21.

[51] See *Cyber Timeline*, NATO REV. MAG., http://www.nato.int/docu/review/2013/Cyber/timeline/EN/index.htm (last visited Jan. 16, 2014) (noting that the Morris worm was named after its creator, Robert Tapan Morris, who "became the first person to be convicted under the US' computer fraud and abuse act. He now works as a professor at MIT."); JONATHAN ZITTRAIN, THE FUTURE OF THE INTERNET AND HOW TO STOP IT 36–37 (2008).

But the prevalence of cyber attacks and the realization by governments and non-state actors of their potential use as a weapon did not materialize in a meaningful and widely appreciated way until the late 1990s. It is useful to review the history of these early cyber attacks against states chronologically from the 1998 "Solar Sunrise" attack to the 2010 Stuxnet incident to demonstrate the increasing sophistication and prevalence of cyber attacks on states, and what that means for hopes of cyber peace.

In the February 1998 "Solar Sunrise" attack, hackers that appeared to be based in the United Arab Emirates (UAE) managed to breach DOD's security.[52] The attack exploited known operating system vulnerabilities and was a precursor to further sorties appearing to come from Israel, the UAE, France, Taiwan, and Germany targeting U.S. Air Force, Navy, and Marine Corps computers worldwide.[53] However, it was not the UAE government behind the initial attacks, but an Israeli teenager and two high school students from Cloverdale, California, who took advantage of the global integration of the Internet to mask their true location and identities.[54] This episode recalls an earlier, informal era of cyber attackers prior to organized crime and other more sophisticated state and non-state actors regularly launching cyber attacks.[55]

The United States was far from the sole victim of cyber attacks in the late 1990s. Between 1999 and 2000, India, for example, experienced a nearly 600 percent increase in website defacements, partly because of ongoing hostilities with Pakistan over the disputed territory of Kashmir.[56] Similarly, between 2000 and 2001, Israel saw spikes and troughs in cyber attacks corresponding with key events of the second intifada.[57] These attacks began in response to "the kidnapping of three Israeli soldiers on October 6, 2000," when "pro-Israeli hackers launched sustained DDoS attacks against sites of the Palestinian Authority . . . Hezbollah and Hamas."[58] This initial volley lead pro-Palestinian hackers to retaliate in what some argue constituted a cyber jihad, "taking down sites belonging to the Israeli Parliament (Knesset), the Israeli Defense Forces . . . and the Tel Aviv Stock Exchange," among others.[59] None of these incidents constituted uses of force equivalent to an armed attack as discussed in

---

[52] *See* Bradley Graham, *U.S. Studies a New Threat: Cyber Attack*, Wash. Post (May 24, 1998), http://www.washingtonpost.com/wp-srv/washtech/daily/may98/cyberattack052498.htm.

[53] *See* Joyner & Lotrionte, *supra* note 24, at 839.

[54] *Id.* at 840; The Honorable Porter Goss, *An Introduction to the Impact of Information Technology on National Security*, 9 Duke J. Comp. & Int'l L. 391, 396 (1999).

[55] *See, e.g.*, Kenneth Geers, *Cyberspace and the Changing Nature of Warfare*, SC Mag. (Aug. 27, 2008), http://www.scmagazine.com/cyberspace-and-the-changing-nature-of-warfare/article/115929/ (reporting on the development of cyberwarfare and noting that then Prime Minister Vladimir Putin stated in the aftermath of an anti-Russian Chechen Internet campaign that "we surrendered this terrain some time ago . . . but now we are entering the game again.").

[56] *See* Michael A. Vatis, *Cyber Attacks During the War on Terrorism: A Predictive Analysis*, Dartmouth Univ. Inst. Sec. Tec. Stud. 5, 7 (2001), http://www.ists.dartmouth.edu/docs/cyber_a1.pdf.

[57] *See id.* at 6; Dorothy E. Denning, *A View of Cyberterrorism 5 Years Later*, in Internet Security: Hacking, Counterhacking, and Society 123, 129–30 (Kenneth Einar Himma ed., 2007).

[58] Vatis, *supra* note 56, at 7.

[59] *Id.*

Chapter 6, but the growing potential of using cyber attacks to disrupt economies and play a part in conflicts was becoming more ingrained, as was reinforced in Kosovo.

Days after NATO bombings began during the Kosovo Crisis, on March 30, 1999, NATO web servers were hit by sustained cyber attacks, including of the DDoS variety, by what were suspected to be hackers from the former Yugoslavia.[60] During this same period, a number of U.S. military, NATO, and commercial websites experienced website defacement, allegedly at the hands of Serbian, Russian, and Chinese hackers.[61] The conflict also saw myriad U.S. efforts to disrupt former Serbian President Slobodan Milosevic's command and control systems,[62] and was important for the involvement of non-state actors in the conflict along with a growing number of states, heralding campaigns to come.

Later, the "Moonlight Maze" attacks of 2001 became among the most extensive cyber attacks aimed at the U.S. government to that point, involving attackers gaining access to thousands of classified files.[63] According to U.S. officials, state-sponsored Russian hackers penetrated DOD computers for more than a year, stealing data from U.S. agencies such as the Department of Energy and NASA, as well as from military contractors and universities.[64] Damage from the attacks was limited and some, including Richard Clarke, have likened it to pre-war reconnaissance.[65] However, Moonlight Maze did help solidify the rise of state-sponsored attacks targeting the intellectual property of an array of public- and private-sector organizations, but it would soon be dwarfed by later events.

On April 1, 2001, a U.S. surveillance aircraft and a Chinese fighter jet collided over Hainan Island in the South China Sea.[66] In the aftermath of this event, a number of Chinese hacker groups organized a weeklong patriotic hacker campaign against U.S. targets, hitting some 1,200 sites, including the White House and U.S. Air Force.[67] How involved the Chinese government was in these attacks remains unclear.[68] However, since the events of 2001, China has been suspected to be responsible for many other intrusions of U.S. networks, including "Titan Rain."[69] Ongoing since 2003, Titan Rain involves a series of attacks on U.S. computer systems, including

---

[60] *See* Geers, *supra* note 55.

[61] *See* ANTHONY H. CORDESMAN & JUSTIN G. CORDESMAN, CYBER-THREATS, INFORMATION WARFARE, AND CRITICAL INFRASTRUCTURE 16–17 (2002) [hereinafter CORDESMAN & CORDESMAN].

[62] *See id.* at 16–17, 35–39.

[63] *See* Major Arie J. Schaap, *Cyber Warfare Operations: Development and Use Under International Law,* 64 A.F. L. REV. 121, 141 (2009).

[64] *See id.* (citing Joyner & Lotrionte, *supra* note 24, at 841 n.60).

[65] *Id.*

[66] *See U.S. Spy Plane, Chinese Fighter Collide,* CNN (Apr. 1, 2001), http://articles.cnn.com/2001-04-01/us/us.china.plane.02_1_spy-plane-chinese-fighter-chinese-island?_s=PM:US.

[67] *See* Daniel M. Creekman, *A Helpless America? An Examination of the Legal Options Available to the United States in Response to Varying Types of Cyber Attacks from China,* 17 AM. U. INT'L L. REV. 641, 642–44 (2002).

[68] *See id.* at 645.

[69] Schaap, *supra* note 63, at 141–42.

those of Lockheed-Martin and NASA.[70] According to the SANS Institute, a computer security training company, these attacks seemed to come from China and were the results of military hackers trying to garner information on U.S. defense systems.[71] Such attacks helped usher in an era of cyber attacks on states, including Estonia, Georgia, and Iran. Given their importance for jumpstarting popular and academic attention in the field, the cyber attacks on Estonia will be discussed next in some detail.

Web War I? The Cyber Attacks on Estonia

On April 27, 2007, Estonia was attacked. In a matter of hours, the online portals of Estonia's leading banks crashed, along with the principal newspaper websites.[72] Government communications were compromised: "An enemy had invaded and was assaulting dozens of targets."[73] This, however, was not the result of a weapon of mass destruction or a kinetic attack. A botnet was to blame.[74]

Nevertheless, the effects of this assault were in some ways just as destabilizing as a conventional offensive on this, at the time the most wired country in Europe, popularly known as "eStonia."[75] By 2007, Estonia had instituted an e-government in which all bank services, and even parliamentary elections, were carried out via the Internet.[76] Estonians file their taxes online, and use their cell phones to shop and pay for parking. "The country is saturated in free Wi-Fi" and is home to Skype, among other leading IT companies.[77] Thus, in many ways, this small Baltic nation is like a "window into the future."[78] Someday, "the rest of the world will be as wired" as "eStonia."[79] That day is fast approaching, and is what made the cyber attacks against Estonia all the more effective and prescient for study.

In a matter of days, the cyber attacks brought down many critical websites amidst widespread social unrest and rioting, which left 150 people injured and one Russian national dead.[80] This was the first time that so many critical sectors within a country had been targeted all at once. At the time, the Russian government was suspected to

---

[70] Id.
[71] Id.; Tom Espiner, *Security Experts Lift Lid on Chinese Hack Attacks*, ZDNET (Nov. 23, 2005), http://www.zdnet.com/security-experts-lift-lid-on-chinese-hack-attacks-3039237492/.
[72] Joshua Davis, *Hackers Take Down the Most Wired Country in Europe*, WIRED (Aug. 21, 2007), http://www.wired.com/politics/security/magazine/15-09/ff_estonia.
[73] Id.
[74] Id.
[75] Id.
[76] *Estonia Hit by 'Moscow Cyber War'*, BBC NEWS (May 17, 2007), http://news.bbc.co.uk/2/hi/europe/6665145.stm [hereinafter BBC NEWS, *Estonia Hit*].
[77] Davis, *supra* note 72; *see also Estonia and Slovenia: When Small is Beautifully Successful*, ECONOMIST (Oct. 13, 2005), http://www.economist.com/displayStory.cfm?Story_ID=E1_VDNVSPS (reporting more broadly on Estonia's economy).
[78] Davis, *supra* note 72.
[79] Id.
[80] *See Putin Warns Against Belittling War Effort*, RADIO FREE EUR. (May 9, 2007), http://www.rferl.org/content/article/1076356.html.

FIGURE 4.2. MAP OF ESTONIA. *Source:* CIA World Factbook: Estonia, https://www.cia
.gov/library/publications/the-world-factbook/geos/en.html (last visited Jan. 26, 2014).

have sponsored the attacks.[81] Regardless of who was actually to blame, the scale of
these attacks makes studying them a useful case study to determine how even worse
cyber attacks may affect other victim nations in the future.

Timeline of the Cyber Attacks on Estonia
The cyber attacks on Estonia occurred in the context of a larger dispute between
Estonia and Russia over the removal of a Soviet-era statue and war graves from
the center of Estonia's capital, Tallinn.[82] The monument had been built by the

[81] *See* BBC NEWS, *Estonia Hit, supra* note 76.
[82] *See* Davis, *supra* note 72.

Soviets in 1947 to commemorate their victory over the Nazis in this region during World War II.[83] Although the majority of Estonians viewed the statue as a symbol of a hated foreign occupation, thousands of ethnic Russians in Estonia rioted over the removal of what they viewed as "a cherished memorial to wartime sacrifice."[84] In Moscow, a Kremlin-youth movement surrounded and attacked the Estonian embassy, causing it to temporarily close, which prompted protests from the United States, NATO, and the European Union.[85] The main group reportedly behind the protests in Russia was the government-funded pro-Kremlin "Nashi su" ("Youth Movement, Ours!"), which was created in 2005 as an anti-fascist student group that has since grown to more than 100,000 members.[86] Feeling the Western pressure and following a German-brokered deal between Russia and Estonia, the blockade soon ended.[87] Even though the embassy battle was lost, though, the "cyber riot" was just beginning.[88]

The Estonian public and private sector came under a prolonged cyber campaign beginning on April 28, 2007, that lasted for several weeks. The primary weapon deployed against the state was DDoS attacks. Data from Arbor Networks Active Threat Level Analysis System shows that there were "some 128 unique DDoS attacks targeting IPs within Estonia" during this period.[89] National Internet traffic increased from 20,000 packets to more than 4 million packets per second.[90] The attacks lasted for hours and appeared to originate in diverse countries, including Egypt, Peru, the United States, and Russia.[91]

The cyber campaign against Estonia took many forms. Some involved defacing websites with Russian propaganda. Most attacks, however, concentrated on shutting the sites down outright. By May 9, when Russia and its allies commemorated the defeat of Nazi Germany in Red Square, at least six Estonian state websites crashed.[92] These included the foreign and justice ministries, as well as Estonian organizations, newspapers, and broadcasters. The main news outlet was forced to sever its international Internet connections to stay online, effectively gagging

---

[83] *Id.*

[84] *A Cyber Riot: Estonia and Russia*, ECONOMIST (May 12, 2007), http://www.economist.com/node/ 9163598 [hereinafter *A Cyber Riot*].

[85] *U.S. House Passes Resolution Supporting Estonia*, BALTIC TIMES (June 06, 2007), http://www .baltictimes.com/news/articles/18002/.

[86] *See* Charles Clover, *Kremlin-Backed Group Behind Estonia Cyber Blitz*, FIN. TIMES (Mar. 11, 2009), http://www.ft.com/cms/s/0/57536d5a-0ddc-11de-8ea3-0000779fd2ac.html#axzz29Ku3my1w; *Pro-Kremlin Activist Claims Responsibility for Estonia Cyberattack*, FOX NEWS (Mar. 13, 2009), http://www.foxnews.com/story/0,2933,509143,00.html.

[87] *A Cyber Riot, supra* note 84.

[88] *Id.*

[89] Sean Kerner, *Estonia Under Russian Cyber Attack?*, INTERNET NEWS (May 18, 2007), http://www .internetnews.com/security/article.php/3678606/Estonia+Under+Russian+Cyber+Attack.htm.

[90] Davis, *supra* note 72.

[91] *Id.*

[92] *Id.*

FIGURE 4.3. SOVIET-ERA VICTORY STATUE IN TALLINN

the former Estonian news service from telling the world about the attacks on its country.[93] The attacks also targeted "mission-critical computers," including those used in telephone exchanges.[94] Estonia was nearing a digital collapse on May 10, but Estonia's Cyber Emergency Response Team (CERT-EE) prevailed, helping Estonia avoid the worst-case scenario that many feared.[95] The Estonian Defense Minister, Jaak Aaviksoo, has argued that the cyber attacks amounted to a national security emergency, likening the situation to a complete blockade, what some have called an "infoblockade."[96] Linton Wells II, the former deputy assistant secretary of

---

[93] Id.

[94] See Jeffrey Kelsey, Hacking into International Humanitarian Law: The Principles of Distinction and Neutrality in the Age of Cyber Warfare, 106 MICH. L. REV. 1427, 1429 (2008).

[95] See Davis, supra note 72.

[96] Estonia Has No Evidence of Kremlin Involvement in Cyber Attacks, RIA NOVOSTI (RUSSIAN NEWS & INFO. AGENCY) (June 9, 2007), http://en.rian.ru/world/20070906/76959190.html.

defense, said after the attacks, "This may well turn out to be a watershed in terms of widespread awareness of the vulnerability of modern society."[97] But who was really to blame for the attacks, and what can or should be done about it? The legal dimension of attribution is introduced next as it pertains to the investigation of state-sponsored cyber attacks against Estonia.

Determining Responsibility for the Cyber Attack on Estonia

Finding those responsible for the cyber attacks on Estonia was among the murkiest problems facing authorities in the aftermath of the onslaught. Estonian officials were met with opposition from their Russian counterparts as they investigated whether the salvos originated from Russian government computing centers or affiliated facilities run by Nashi su and other similar organizations.[98] Yet, as Chapter 3 explained, it is exceedingly difficult to prove from where these attacks originated. Thousands of attacks appeared to come from computer systems around the world. However, early on there was circumstantial evidence of Russian involvement given that at least some of these were hackers were goaded into attacking Estonian websites in Russian-language chat rooms, which posted detailed instructions on how to launch botnet attacks.[99] In addition, this was not "the first time [that] the Russian government had been accused of" orchestrating cyber conflict for political purposes.[100] Prior to the cyber attacks on Estonia, "a similar assault had been launched against an alliance of Russian opposition parties led by chess grandmaster Garry Kasparov[,]" which was designed to make it more difficult for Kasparov to communicate with his followers; Kasparov was later arrested.[101]

The Russian government volunteered no cooperation to Estonia in tracking down the true source of these botnets.[102] Still, Estonia opened criminal investigations into the attacks under felonies of computer sabotage, and because many alleged hackers were Russian, submitted a request for bilateral investigation under the Mutual Legal Assistance Treaty (MLAT) between Estonia and Russia.[103] Despite earlier promises, however, the Russian Supreme Procurature refused assistance to Estonia

---

[97] Mark Landler & John Markoff, *Digital Fears Emerge after Data Siege in Estonia*, N. Y. TIMES (May 29, 2007), http://www.nytimes.com/2007/05/29/technology/29estonia.html?pagewanted=all.

[98] *See* Peter Finn, *Cyber Assaults on Estonia Typify a New Battle Tactic*, WASH. POST (May 19, 2007), http://www.washingtonpost.com/wp-dyn/content/article/2007/05/18/AR2007051802122.html.

[99] *See* Davis, *supra* note 72; Landler & Markoff, *supra* note 97.

[100] Davis, *supra* note 72.

[101] *Id.*; Ilya Mouzykantskii & Robert Mackey, *Moscow Court Finds Kasparov Not Guilty of Illegal Protest During Pussy Riot Trial*, N.Y. TIMES (Aug. 24, 2012), http://thelede.blogs.nytimes.com/2012/08/24/moscow-court-finds-kasparov-not-guilty-of-illegal-protest-during-pussy-riot-trial/; *Opposition Protesters Arrested as Putin's Party Suffers Losses*, CNN (Dec. 4, 2011), http://articles.cnn.com/2011-12-04/world/world_europe_russia-elections_1_ruling-party-united-russia-party-parliamentary-election?_s=PM:EUROPE.

[102] *See* Finn, *supra* note 98.

[103] *Russia Refused Legal Assistance in Cyber Attacks Investigation*, 17 EST. REV. 3, 4 (2007).

under the treaty.[104] This demonstrates the weaknesses of applying MLATs to enhance cybersecurity, especially given that such agreements often lack mandatory enforcement mechanisms. Ultimately, the only conviction from the cyber attacks was on January 24, 2008 when an ethnic Russian student living in Tallinn was found guilty of launching an assault on the Reform Party's website of Prime Minister Andrus Ansip. He was fined $1,642.[105] To put that figure in perspective, though a complete accounting of the losses because of these cyber attack is not available, the one Estonian bank that reported losses from this episode for this period "estimated around $1 million in damages . . . ."[106]

A month after the attacks, "assessments conducted by the U.S. government and" several private-sector contractors determined that the cyber attacks were most "likely carried out by politically motivated hacker gangs [such as Nashi su]," not directly by Russian security agencies.[107] In one report, Mike Witt, former deputy director of US-CERT, concluded that the attacks against Estonia lacked the sophistication of the cyber powers, including Russia.[108] This does not necessarily mean, though, that the Russian government did not have a role in inciting the attacks. One Russian hacker, for example, believes that at least some hackers acted under recommendations from parties in higher positions.[109] Indeed, in March 2009, hackers affiliated with Nashi su formally claimed responsibility for the attacks.[110] The saga of determining attribution for the 2007 attacks on Estonia highlights the range of issues that arise when considering how best to form a legal regime to better manage cyber attacks. It also provides lessons about how to enhance cybersecurity given that Estonia has been rated as being among the most "prepared [countries] against cyberattacks" in the world,[111] and shows how the "boundaries between crime, warfare, and terrorism[]" can be blurred as discussed in Chapter 1.[112] The episode also raises questions of proving state sponsorship that are further explored in Chapter 6.

---

[104] *See* MILTON L. MUELLER, NETWORKS AND STATES: THE GLOBAL POLITICS OF INTERNET GOVERNANCE 23 n.19 (2010).

[105] *See* Jeremy T. G. Kirk, *Student Convicted in Attack Against Estonian Web Site*, PC WORLD (Jan. 24, 2008), http://www.pcworld.com/article/141730/student_convicted_in_attack_against_estonian_web_site .html.

[106] Stephen Herzog, *Revisiting the Estonian Cyber Attacks: Digital Threats and Multinational Responses*, 4 J. STRATEGIC SEC. 49, 51–52 (2011).

[107] Shaun Waterman, *Who Cyber Smacked Estonia?*, UNITED PRESS INT'L (June 11, 2007), http:// www.upi.com/Business_News/Security-Industry/2007/06/11/Analysis-Who-cyber-smacked-Estonia/ UPI-26831181580439/; *see* Clay Wilson, *Botnets, Cybercrime, and Cyberterrorism: Vulnerabilities and Policy Issues for Congress*, CONG. RES. SERV., RL32114 at 7–9 (2008).

[108] *See* Waterman, *supra* note 107.

[109] *See* Landler & Markoff, *supra* note 97.

[110] *See* Clover, *supra* note 86; Noah Shachtman, *Kremlin Kids: We Launched the Estonian Cyber War*, WIRED (Mar. 11, 2009), http://www.wired.com/dangerroom/2009/03/pro-kremlin-gro/.

[111] Kalev Aasmae, *The Poster Child for Cybersecurity Done Right: How Estonia Learnt from Being Under Attack*, ZDNET (Feb. 5, 2013), http://www.zdnet.com/the-poster-child-for-cybersecurity-done-right-how-estonia-learnt-from-being-under-attack-7000010628/.

[112] Wilson, *supra* note 107, at 8.

The Reaction of the United States to the Cyber Attacks on Estonia

What looked initially to be a near-disastrous attack for Estonia was met with relative ambivalence from many U.S. officials. A former Defense Advanced Research Projects Agency chief scientist characterized the incident as "more like a cyber riot than a military attack."[113] The episode, nevertheless, does paint a picture for what future cyber conflicts may look like. It makes little sense for an opponent to challenge the U.S. military directly through the use of armed force. As was discussed earlier in this chapter, much more likely are asymmetric contests that exploit potential U.S. vulnerabilities, including cyberspace.[114] Defense assessments have laid out myriad challenges to protecting U.S. networks, including interoperability, information systems security, and the culture of the intelligence community itself.[115] The United States, like Estonia, is right, then, to be concerned about the continuing proliferation of cyber attacks. Laying out a framework for deterrence is critical to enhancing states' cybersecurity and the prospects for cyber peace, though that is easier said than done.

Cyber Deterrence

Devastating cyber attacks could be deterred if attacking nations, groups, or individuals knew that they would face retaliation. Deterrence, simply put, is the credible threat of violent or non-violent retaliation.[116] A defender counts on this threat to "change the opponent's calculus of the benefits and costs of an attack."[117] In cyber conflicts, however, deterrence is difficult.[118] The United States, for example, is "widely recognized to have pre-eminent offensive cyber capabilities, but it obtains little deterrent effect from this."[119] The same is arguably true for China, which may have "leaped ahead of the United States" in terms of its cyber espionage capabilities.[120]

---

[113] Waterman, *supra* note 107.

[114] STEVEN LAMBAKIS ET AL., UNDERSTANDING 'ASYMMETRIC' THREATS TO THE UNITED STATES 10, 18 (NAT'L INST. PUB. POL'Y, 2002), http://missilethreat.wpengine.netdna-cdn.com/wp-content/uploads/ 2012/11/20021000-NIPP-asymmetricthreats.pdf; *cf.* Courtney Coren, *PACOM Chief Says US Losing Military Dominance to China in Asian-Pacific*, NEWSMAX (Jan. 17, 2014), http://www.newsmax.com/ Newsfront/PACOM-china-locklear-dominance/2014/01/17/id/547656 ("'Our historic dominance [of the Pacific] that most of us in this room have enjoyed is diminishing, no question,' said Locklear, chief of the United States Pacific Command (PACOM).").

[115] U.S. DEP'T DEF., OFF. GEN. COUNS., AN ASSESSMENT OF INTERNATIONAL LEGAL ISSUES IN INFORMATION OPERATIONS 2 (2d ed. 1999), http://www.au.af.mil/au/awc/awcgate/dod-io-legal/dod-io-legal .pdf [hereinafter DOD ASSESSMENT]; Tom Gjelten, *Cyberattack: U.S. Unready for Future Face of War*, NPR (Apr. 7, 2010), http://www.npr.org/templates/story/story.php?storyId=125598665.

[116] *See* Elbridge A. Colby, *Expanded Deterrence*, HOOVER POL'Y REV. NO. 149 (June 2, 2008), http://www .hoover.org/publications/policy-review/article/5717.

[117] Lewis, *supra* note 18, at 4.

[118] *See* PETER W. SINGER & ALLAN FRIEDMAN, CYBERSECURITY AND CYBERWAR: WHAT EVERYONE NEEDS TO KNOW 147 (2014).

[119] Lewis, *supra* note 18, at 4.

[120] Brian Grow & Mark Hosenball, *Special Report: In Cyberspy vs. Cyberspy, China Has the Edge*, REUTERS (Apr. 14, 2011), http://www.reuters.com/article/2011/04/14/us-china-usa-cyberespionage-idUSTRE73D24220110414.

Part of the reason for this is the fact that traditional deterrent concepts, such as the threat of counterstrike, are hard to apply in cyberspace. As Lewis explains:

> In the Cold War, there was symmetry in vulnerabilities – each side had cities and populations that the other could hold hostage. That symmetry no longer exists. The United States is far more dependent on digital networks than its opponents and this asymmetric vulnerability means that the United States would come out worse in any cyber exchange.[121]

Moreover, deterrence requires accepting a certain amount of collateral damage, but uncertainty over the extent of such collateral damage in cyberspace can make political leaders unwilling to take the risk of retaliatory responses, lest they widen conflicts.[122] Like a biological weapon, cyber attacks could get out of the control of an attacker.[123] And, ultimately, effective cyber deterrence requires identifying and prosecuting attackers, or raising the cost to perpetrators in other ways such as through countermeasures and sanctions as discussed in Chapters 6 and 7.

In summary, a "combination of asymmetric vulnerability, weak attribution and unpredictable collateral damage limit our ability to make a credible threat against an opponent in cyberspace."[124] According to Lewis, "Given the limitations of deterrence, a nation like the United States, which is uniquely vulnerable [to cyber attacks], would gain . . . [by helping to craft] international norms" of state conduct in cyberspace,[125] a theme returned to later in this chapter and in Chapter 7. Before delving more deeply into the national security strategies of the cyber powers, though, it is first important to conclude this brief history of cyber conflict with a discussion of the Georgian war and Stuxnet.

The Use of Cyber Attacks in the 2008 Invasion of Georgia

A year and a half after the cyber riot in Estonia, a major cyber conflict erupted in the country of Georgia, a nation that is slightly smaller than South Carolina with a population of approximately five million people as of 2013.[126] Despite its small size and proximity to Russia, or perhaps because of it, Georgians have long sought their

---

[121] Lewis, *supra* note 18, at 5.

[122] *Id.* However, the argument may also be made that such collateral damage may be ethically preferable to the casualties resulting from the use of kinetic weapons. *See* NATIONAL ACADEMIES, *supra* note 10, at 69 (making the case that cyber attack tools should be available to policymakers under certain circumstances); RID, *supra* note 5, at 171 ("This analysis has also argued that the most sophisticated cyber attacks are highly targeted, and that cyber weapons are unlikely to cause collateral damage in the same way as conventional weapons.").

[123] *See New Stuxnet, supra* note 22.

[124] Lewis, *supra* note 18, at 5.

[125] *Id.* at 6.

[126] *See CIA World Factbook: Georgia*, https://www.cia.gov/library/publications/the-world-factbook/geos/gg.html (last visited Jan. 17, 2014) [hereinafter *CIA World Factbook*]. Between the Estonian and Georgian cyber conflicts, Russian hacker groups also allegedly targeted the country of Lithuania in July 2008. *See* Brian Krebs, *Lithuania Weathers Cyber Attack, Braces for Round 2*, WASH. POST (July 8, 2008), http://voices.washingtonpost.com/securityfix/2008/07/lithuania_weathers_cyber_attac_1.html.

FIGURE 4.4. MAP OF GEORGIA

independence, which they declared during the Russian Revolution in 1918 and again following the breakup of the Soviet Union in 1991. Nevertheless, South Ossetia and Abkhazia, two regions of Georgia, have long been supported by Russia and have set up autonomous governments that have led some nations to recognize them as breakaway republics despite remaining ostensibly part of Georgia.[127] To maintain order, a peacekeeping force of Russian, Georgian, and South Ossetian troops was formed in 1992 under a Russian commander, but they failed to quell ongoing tensions.[128]

The fragile peace ended when South Ossetian separatists launched a series of missile attacks on Georgian villages in July 2008. The Georgian army responded by bombarding the capital of South Ossetia, Tshkhinvali, following on August 7 with an attack on the region.[129] The Russian army invaded the next day, expelling the Georgians as a series of cyber attacks were launched, including DDoS attacks that disrupted Georgian media and blocked the CNN and BBC websites.[130] Attacks also defaced Georgian government websites and effectively severed the Georgian government's Internet connection to the rest of the world.[131] The Georgian Ministry of Foreign Affairs was forced to move to a BlogSpot account in an attempt to report what was happening in the country.[132] The Georgian President's website was moved to a router located somewhat ironically in Atlanta, Georgia.[133] When the Georgians

---

[127] *CIA World Factbook, supra* note 126.

[128] *See* Eneken Tikk et al., *Cyber Attacks Against Georgia: Legal Lessons Identified*, NATO 4 (Ver. 1, 2008), http://www.carlisle.army.mil/DIME/documents/Georgia%201%200.pdf; Roy Allison, *Russia Resurgent? Moscow's Campaign to 'Coerce Georgia to Peace'*, 84(6) INT'L AFF. 1145, 1146 (Nov. 2008).

[129] *See* Tikk et al., *supra* note 128, at 4.

[130] CLARKE & KNAKE, *supra* note 9, at 18.

[131] Tikk et al., *supra* note 128, at 7, 15.

[132] *Id.* at 14, 37.

[133] *Id.* at 14.

tried to stop the attacks by blocking Russian access, the attack vector was switched to routers in China, Canada, Turkey, and even Estonia.[134]

Some combination of the Kremlin, organized crime, and even citizen groups could have been behind the cyber attacks on Georgia.[135] But "there is no conclusive proof" on who was to blame.[136] However, the attacks were also noteworthy as a demonstration of how the sophistication and strategy of cyber attackers has evolved. First, attackers hit a widely distributed and static list of targets, hobbling centralized coordination and making it even more difficult to determine state responsibility and shut down the offending hosts.[137] Second, building off the cyber attacks on Estonia and even earlier to the Kosovo campaign, this conflict engaged criminal gangs along with regular Internet users and reinforced the murky nature of attributing state-sponsored cyber attacks.[138] Third, this episode helped demonstrate the viability of using cyber weapons alongside traditional military forces as part of an international armed conflict.[139] These tactics and others hindered the Georgian government's communication capabilities, increasing the effectiveness of Russia's forces.

The cyber attacks on Georgia were part of a complex, blended campaign, but the attacks included many of the same hallmarks as the 2007 attacks on Estonia, including: defacement of websites, DDoS attacks to degrade communications and disrupt civil society, the involvement of non-state actors, and the distribution of malicious software with instructions for use.[140] This incident is important from a cyber war doctrinal perspective as it illustrates the direction in which future cyber conflicts may evolve – engaging non-state actors along with the citizenry online as part of a blended campaign, raising questions of proportional response and the line between combatants and non-combatants explored in Chapter 6. The Georgia attacks also point to the continuing difficulty of determining state responsibility for cyber attacks, and the necessity of securing critical infrastructure during a cyber conflict. These trends may be further illustrated, and in some cases contrasted, by examining Stuxnet.

Stuxnet: The Cyber Shot Heard around the World

In October 2010, Stuxnet was launched, a kind of "cyber-missile" that targeted Iranian nuclear facilities, specifically the centrifuges at the nuclear refinery at Natanz used

---

[134] *Id.* at 6–11; *see also* Stephen W. Koms & Joshua E. Kastenberg, *Georgia's Cyber Left Hook*, 38 PARAMETERS – U.S. ARMY WAR C. Q. 60, 71 (2008) (arguing that under the Budapest Convention and U.S. law these attacks amounted to cybercrime, not cyber warfare).

[135] *See* John Markoff, *Before the Gunfire, Cyberattacks*, N.Y. TIMES (Aug. 12, 2008), http://www.nytimes.com/2008/08/13/technology/13cyber.html; Noah Shachtman, *Top Georgian Official: Moscow Cyber Attacked Us – We Just Can't Prove It*, WIRED (Mar. 11, 2009), http://www.wired.com/dangerroom/2009/03/georgia-blames/.

[136] Tikk et al., *supra* note 128, at 12.

[137] *Id.* at 38.

[138] *Id.*

[139] *See id.* at 19.

[140] *See id.*

to enrich uranium.[141] The worm took advantage of flaws in Microsoft Windows and Siemens systems to disrupt the operation of specific plant processes and delay Iran's nuclear program,[142] in the process causing collateral damage around the world. Its complexity led some to conclude that the attackers had the backing of one or more national governments.[143] This puts Stuxnet in contrast to the cyber attacks on Estonia and Georgia; this was no mass DDoS assault involving unsophisticated hackers, but a deftly targeted attack utilizing stolen digital certificates to mask its code, and modified software to cause the Iranian centrifuges to malfunction.[144] In total, more than 20 percent of Iran's nuclear centrifuges were reportedly damaged or destroyed.[145]

The tale of how digital detectives deciphered Stuxnet reveals how extraordinary this cyber weapon truly is. The investigation began when International Atomic Energy Agency inspectors noticed an increase in the number of centrifuges that the Natanz plant was decommissioning, jumping from 800 in a given year to more than 1,000 in a month.[146] Why? As it turned out, it was because of Stuxnet 3.0. The developer(s) had been refining it since its initial deployment in June 2009 into a sophisticated weapon more than fifty times larger than typical malware,[147] using four zero-day exploits in the code, which, as discussed in Chapter 3, are quite rare and difficult to uncover.[148] Out of the millions of varieties of malware that antivirus researchers discover each year, only a handful use zero-day exploits.[149] If it had been criminals behind Stuxnet, they likely would have used the exploits earlier to make money. The fact that the attack used so many such exploits means that whoever was behind it had the resources to find the flaws, and had the time, patience, and motive

---

[141] *A Cyber-Missile Aimed at Iran?*, ECONOMIST (Sept. 24, 2010), http://www.economist.com/blogs/babbage/2010/09/stuxnet_worm; Kim Zetter, *How Digital Detectives Deciphered Stuxnet, the Most Menacing Malware in History*, WIRED (July 11, 2011), http://www.wired.com/threatlevel/2011/07/how-digital-detectives-deciphered-stuxnet/all/1.

[142] *See* William J. Broad et al., *Israeli Test on Worm Called Crucial in Iran Nuclear Delay*, N.Y. TIMES (Jan. 15, 2011), http://www.nytimes.com/2011/01/16/world/middleeast/16stuxnet.html?pagewanted=all &_r=0; Sharon Weinberger, *Computer Security: Is This the Start of Cyberwarfare?*, 474 NATURE 142, 142–45 (2011).

[143] *See* Transcript of Debate, *Deterrence in Cyberspace: Debating the Right Strategy with Ralph Langner and Dmitri Alperovitch*, BROOKINGS INST. 15 (Sept. 27, 2011), http://www.brookings-tsinghua.cn/sitecore/content/Home/events/2011/0920_cyberspace_deterrence.aspx.

[144] *See* Nicolas Falliere, Liam O. Murchu & Eric Chien, *W32: Stuxnet Dossier*, SYMANTEC (Symantec Security Response, Version 1.4, Feb. 2011), http://www.symantec.com/content/en/us/enterprise/media/security_response/whitepapers/w32_stuxnet_dossier.pdf.

[145] *See Assessing Five Cyber Incidents: Legal and Operational Perspectives on Response Options*, CSIS: GLOBAL SECURITY FORUM 2011, at 6, csis.org/files/attachments/110607_GSF_slides_cyber_final.pdf.

[146] Zetter, *supra* note 141.

[147] *Id.*

[148] *Id.*

[149] *Id. But see Iran to 'Speed Up' Uranium Enrichment at Nuclear Plants*, BBC NEWS (July 19, 2011), http://www.bbc.co.uk/news/world-middle-east-14196882 (reporting on the extent to which Iran's nuclear efforts are accelerating); *Iran 'Has Tripled' Uranium-Enriching Centrifuges at Natanz Plant*, RT (Apr. 17, 2013), http://rt.com/news/iran-nuclear-centrifuges-natanz-016/.

to disrupt the Iranian nuclear enrichment facilities, which is partly why the United States and Israel are suspected of being behind the attacks.[150] However, several elements of Stuxnet that could help definitively settle the question of sponsorship remain encrypted despite the efforts of investigators.[151]

Whether Stuxnet was a warning shot, a cyber weapons test, or even an act of cyber war remains unclear. It does, however, highlight the benefits and drawbacks of offensive cyber operations, namely avoiding physical harm but permitting unpredictable collateral damage and the release of dangerous code that can be repurposed.[152] There were reports in late 2011 that Son of Stuxnet, named Duqu by Symantec, has already been developed.[153] This should not come as a surprise; after all, it took a team of geniuses to create the first nuclear weapon, but only average engineers to copy it.[154] This is worrisome given that there is a growing list of nations that have the capability of and interest in joining the cyber arms race, which arguably "is already going on" and "is very intense," according to Michael Nacht, former assistant secretary of defense for Global Strategic Affairs.[155] Besides the United States, Russia, China, and Israel, "Taiwan, Iran, Australia, South Korea, India, Pakistan, and several NATO" allies join a growing array of countries in having cyber attack capabilities.[156] Iran, for example, has been blamed by the U.S. government for the 2012 cyber attack on the "world's most valuable company" – Saudi Aramco – that sabotaged more than 30,000 of Aramco's PCs, an episode that former Defense Secretary Panetta has

---

[150] See SANGER, *supra* note 5, at ix–xiii (reporting on U.S. government involvement with Stuxnet, code-named "Operation Olympic Games").

[151] Zetter, *supra* note 141.

[152] See SINGER & FRIEDMAN, *supra* note 118, at 119 (arguing that Stuxnet "neither hurt nor killed anyone. By comparison, when Israel attempted to obstruct Iraqi nuclear research in 1981, its forces dropped sixteen 2,000-pound bombs on a research site during 'Operation Opera,' leveling it and killing eleven soldiers and civilians.").

[153] See New Stuxnet, *supra* note 22; Kim Zetter, *Son of Stuxnet Found in the Wild on Systems in Europe*, WIRED (Oct. 18, 2011), http://www.wired.com/threatlevel/2011/10/son-of-stuxnet-in-the-wild/.

[154] *Enumerating Stuxnet's Exploits*, LANGNER (Jun. 7, 2011), http://www.langner.com/en/2011/06/07/enumerating-stuxnet%E2%80%99s-exploits/.

[155] Kristin M. Lord & Travis Sharp, Executive Summary, *in* AMERICA'S CYBER FUTURE, *supra* note 42, at 7, 28.

[156] CLARKE & KNAKE, *supra* note 9, at 64. For example, in July 2013, India published its first cyber policy explicitly devoted to protecting critical information infrastructure: the National Cyber Security Policy 2013 (NCSP). National Cyber Security Policy 2013, http://deity.gov.in/sites/upload_files/dit/files/National%20Cyber%20Security%20Policy%20(1)_0.pdf (India). While many commentators applauded this step forward, others have criticized it for sidestepping tough issues in favor of providing a broader framework for cybersecurity policy development. *See, e.g., National Cyber Security Policy*, TIMES OF INDIA, http://timesofindia.indiatimes.com/topic/National-Cyber-Security-Policy (comprising a repository of a collection of essays and articles relating to the NCSP) (last visited Jan. 17, 2014). Still, certain provisions of the NCSP such as section IV(B) do promote the adoption of global best practices "in information security and compliance" and "in formal risk assessment and risk management processes." *Id.* at art. IV(B). The NCSP has evolved to become more reminiscent of U.S. efforts at establishing voluntary cybersecurity best practices than the more heavy-handed Chinese proposed approach discussed later in the chapter.

described as a "significant escalation of the cyber threat."[157] Non-state actors are also getting into the game; in 2009, Iraqi-based militants reportedly used software that cost $26 to access unencrypted imagery from U.S. drones.[158] Yet for the time being, states still seem to dominate the digital battlefield.[159]

Summary

Cyber attacks have been used by states since the late 1990s during conflicts as well as to gather intelligence as in the cases of Moonlight Maze and Titan Rain. Over time, these attacks have become increasingly sophisticated and are now true cyber weapons, as illustrated by Stuxnet. As the doctrine of cyber war matures, a new era of conflict is dawning. This new chapter represents a crystallization of trends identified throughout this section, including that: (1) the list of cyber powers continues to lengthen, (2) states are sponsoring cyber attacks through non-state actors targeting the public and private sectors and further masking attribution, and (3) the growing use of cyber attacks risks increased collateral damage to noncombatants and critical infrastructure.[160] Achieving cyber peace in this new era of cyber conflict requires addressing each of these trends, such as by enhancing multilateral collaboration among the cyber powers potentially within a polycentric framework. This in turn requires an analysis of national approaches to cybersecurity policymaking to identify areas of convergence and divergence.

NATIONAL CYBERSECURITY STRATEGIES OF THE CYBER POWERS

An array of strategies are being employed to manage cyber attacks at the national level where cybersecurity doctrines are fast evolving, divergent, and oftentimes opaque.[161] These strategies vary according to resource endowments, political calculus, and technological sophistication. Progress toward enhancing national-level cybersecurity has been mixed. Some states, like Singapore, have only relatively recently created new

---

[157] Nicole Perlroth, *In Cyberattack on Saudi Firm, U.S. Sees Iran Firing Back*, N.Y. TIMES (Oct. 23, 2012), http://www.nytimes.com/2012/10/24/business/global/cyberattack-on-saudi-oil-firm-disquiets-us .html?pagewanted=all&gwh=1F4FC0B318FBFE315234ADE86576CBA2; *see also US General Warns over Iranian Cyber-Soldiers*, BBC TECH. (Jan. 18, 2013), http://www.bbc.co.uk/news/technology-21075781 (reporting that Iran is developing cyber warfare capabilities that are making it a "force to be reckoned with").

[158] *See* Siobhan Gorman, Yochi J. Dreazen, & August Cole, *Insurgents Hack U.S. Drones*, WALL ST. J. (Dec. 17, 2009), http://online.wsj.com/article/SB126102247889095011.html.

[159] This compilation of cyber attacks on states is far from exhaustive. For further entries see the Appendix, and *Cyber Timeline, supra* note 51.

[160] However, the growing sophistication of attackers and advancing technology illustrates the ethical potential of cyber weapons to limit physical damage on civilians during military operations. *See* SINGER & FRIEDMAN, *supra* note 118, at 119.

[161] *See* OECD, CYBERSECURITY POLICY MAKING AT A TURNING POINT: ANALYZING A NEW GENERATION OF NATIONAL CYBERSECURITY STRATEGIES 3 (2012) (summarizing the national cybersecurity strategies of ten nations, and noting that "'[s]overeignty considerations' have become increasingly important.") [hereinafter OECD].

cybersecurity authorities responsible for safeguarding critical national infrastructure, whereas other nations, including the United States, United Kingdom, Israel, China, and Russia, are developing advanced cyber warfare capabilities.[162] However, there does seem to be a growing recognition of the need to safeguard critical infrastructure that could give rise to norm-building opportunities.[163] Although it would be useful to examine all of the states with cyber attack capabilities, space constraints require that we focus here on the strategies of arguably the leading cyber powers: the United States, United Kingdom, China, Russia, and Israel. Each of these nations is developing national policies to secure cyberspace generally, and CNI in particular. These regulations form an important component of polycentric governance.[164]

Among the challenges faced by national regulators is the difficulty of protecting civil liberties while also providing public safety. This may be seen in the U.S. context with the public debate over the NSA's PRISM program following leaks from former CIA-employee Edward Snowden revealing the extent of U.S. government surveillance activities.[165] Civil libertarians push for preserving some degree of Internet freedom, whereas many countries are anxious to protect CNI, curtail cyber espionage and cybercrime, and prepare for cyber war.[166] Each nation has to strike a balance between these competing priorities of cybersecurity and civil rights, especially privacy. The manner in which nations accomplish this balancing act will shape the cyber regulatory environment, as well as the tools available to enhance cybersecurity both within and between states. Thus, it is important to analyze national approaches to cybersecurity to attain a more complete picture of the emerging cyber regime complex and how it may be conceptualized to enjoy the benefits while limiting the drawbacks of polycentric governance.

United States

The United States in many ways pioneered cybersecurity at the national level, beginning with the creation of the first CERT at Carnegie Mellon University in 1988 in response to a growing number of network intrusions.[167] The number of

---

[162] PBS News Hour, *supra* note 13.

[163] OECD, *supra* note 161, at 12 ("Most countries include the concept of critical information infrastructures in the scope of their [national cybersecurity] strategy . . . .").

[164] *See* Andrew W. Murray, The Regulation of Cyberspace: Control in the Online Environment 47 (2006).

[165] *See* Glenn Greenwald, Ewen MacAskill, & Laura Poitras, *Edward Snowden: The Whistleblower Behind the NSA Surveillance Revelations*, Guardian (June 9, 2013), http://www.guardian.co.uk/world/2013/jun/09/edward-snowden-nsa-whistleblower-surveillance; Matt Apuzzo, *What's the Problem with PRISM?*, AP (June 11, 2013), http://news.yahoo.com/whats-problem-prism-203441280.html (reporting on the scope and development of PRISM).

[166] *See* Tom Cohen, Jim Acosta, & Mariano Castillo, *Obama Announces Modest Changes to NSA Data Collection*, CNN (Jan. 17, 2014), http://www.cnn.com/2014/01/17/politics/obama-nsa-changes/index.html?utm_source=feedburner&utm_medium=feed&utm_campaign=Feed%3A+rss%2Fcnn_allpolitics+%28RSS%3A+Politics%29; Tom Gjelten, *Does Averting Cyberwar Mean Giving Up Web Privacy?*, NPR (June 9, 2010), http://www.npr.org/templates/story/story.php?storyId=127575960.

[167] *See* About Us, US-CERT, www.us-cert.gov/about-us (last visited Jan. 17, 2014).

"computer security incidents" that US-CERT investigates has grown from six in 1988 to more than 106,000 by some estimates in 2011.[168] However, US-CERT, which is now part of DHS, is only the beginning of the confused world of U.S. cybersecurity policymaking.[169] The FBI investigates cyber attacks, especially those involving cybercrime. If the attack source is foreign, then the CIA is involved (though, as we have seen, attribution can be difficult). If the cyber attack involves financial intrusions, the Secret Service is the primary service on point. The DOD, DHS, State Department, and NSA[170] also have cybersecurity expertise; in fact, the DOD alone operates more than 15,000 networks in 4,000 installations spread across 88 countries.[171]

Modern efforts toward increasing cybersecurity for CNI in particular can be traced to the aftermath of the April 1995 bombing of the Murrah Federal Building in Oklahoma City.[172] President Clinton responded to the bombings by issuing Presidential Decision Directive 39 (PDD 39),[173] creating a Critical Infrastructure Working Group and "establish[ing] infrastructure protection as a national priority."[174] In May 1998, combining work product that had emerged out of PDD 39, the Clinton administration issued Presidential Decision Directive 63,[175] which contemplated critical infrastructure as "those physical and cyber-based systems essential to the minimum operations of the economy and the government[,]"[176] and representing a broader effort to respond to threats on U.S. CNI.[177] Indeed, regulation of cybersecurity has frequently come from executive action. In addition to the Clinton Directives, President Bush and President Obama have both issued directives taking aim at securing CNI.[178] Yet more than fifty U.S. statutes also influence national cybersecurity in one capacity or another, though none of these constitute an overarching framework.[179]

---

[168] See *Cybersecurity Results*, HOMELAND SEC., http://www.dhs.gov/cybersecurity-results (last visited Jan. 17, 2014); HOWARD F. LIPSON, TRACKING AND TRACING CYBER-ATTACKS: TECHNICAL CHALLENGES AND GLOBAL POLICY ISSUES 5 (CERT COORDINATION CTR., 2002); *CERT Statistics (Historical)*, CERT, http://www.cert.org/stats/ (last visited Oct. 2, 2012).

[169] See *U.S. Federal Cybersecurity Market Forecast 2010–2015*, MARKET RES. MEDIA (Mar. 2011), http://www.scribd.com/doc/15849095/US-Federal-Cyber-Security-Market-Forecast-20102015.

[170] See Glenn Greenwald & Ewen MacAskill, *Obama Orders US to Draw Up Overseas Target List for Cyber-Attacks*, GUARDIAN (June 7, 2013), http://www.guardian.co.uk/world/2013/jun/07/obama-china-targets-cyber-overseas.

[171] Kristin M. Lord & Travis Sharp, Executive Summary, *in* AMERICA'S CYBER FUTURE, *supra* note 42, at 7, 12; see JOSEPH F. GUSTIN, CYBER TERRORISM: A GUIDE FOR FACILITY MANAGERS 158–59 (2007).

[172] Eric A. Greenwald, *History Repeats Itself: The 60-Day Cyberspace Policy Review in Context*, 4 J. NAT'L SEC. L. & POL'Y 41, 43 (2010).

[173] Presidential Decision Directive 39 (June 21, 1995), http://www.fas.org/irp/offdocs/pdd39.htm.

[174] Greenwald, *supra* note 172, at 43.

[175] Presidential Decision Directive 63 (May 22, 1998), http://www.fas.org/irp/offdocs/pdd/pdd-63.htm.

[176] *Id.*; Stephanie A. Devos, *The Google-NSA Alliance: Developing Cybersecurity Policy at Internet Speed*, 21 FORDHAM INTELL. PROP. MEDIA & ENT. L.J. 173, 179 (2010).

[177] Greenwald, *supra* note 172, at 45.

[178] See Eric A. Fischer, *Federal Laws Relating to Cybersecurity: Overview and Discussion of Proposed Revisions*, CONG. RES. SERV., R42114 at 3 (2013), http://www.fas.org/sgp/crs/natsec/R42114.pdf.

[179] *Id.* at 2.

Perhaps indicative of this fragmented approach, it cannot actually be said that the federal government has a single definition of what constitutes CNI in all cases, to say nothing of how it should be secured, though some progress is being made.[180]

Further demonstrating the increasing complexity of CNI regulation, in 2009, President Obama, shortly after taking office, commanded a review of the federal government's cybersecurity plans and activities, aiming to take inventory of current operations and to make plans for the future.[181] After the review was completed, President Obama declared U.S. CNI to be a "strategic national asset,"[182] and U.S. Cyber Command (CYBERCOM) was tasked with centralizing command of U.S. cyber operations. It is now operational for "full spectrum" operations, including defensive and offensive capabilities.[183] However, the Pentagon has not yet publicly clarified doctrines defining how and when U.S. forces will respond to cyber attacks,[184] and questions remain about whether CYBERCOM should continue its close ties with NSA.[185] Regardless, CYBERCOM is only responsible for the dot-mil domain; the government domain, dot-gov, and the corporate domain, dot-com, remain the responsibilities of DHS and private firms, respectively.[186] Given the difficulty of developing clear, effective guidelines for enhancing national cybersecurity and protecting CNI, CYBERCOM's place vis-à-vis other U.S. agencies and departments remains somewhat undefined, even as it adds functionality.[187]

---

[180] *See Cybersecurity Update: Key US and EU Regulatory Developments*, SKADDEN, ARPS, SLATE, MEAGHER & FLOM LLP (June 25, 2013), www.skadden.com/insights/cybersecurity-update; *see also* JÖRN BRÖMMELHÖRSTER, SANDRA FABRY, & NICO WIRTZ, CRITICAL INFRASTRUCTURE PROTECTION: SURVEY OF WORLDWIDE ACTIVITIES 3 (2002) (noting the lack of an "all embracing" U.S. CNI strategy, but noting significant progress in securing CNI).

[181] *See* Roy Mark, *Obama Orders 60-Day Cyber-Security Review*, EWEEK (Feb. 2, 2010), http://www.eweek.com/c/a/Security/Obama-Orders-60Day-Cyber-Security-Review/.

[182] Barack Obama, President of the United States, Remarks by the President on Securing Our Nation's Cyber Infrastructure, White House, Office of the Press Secretary, May 29, 2009, http://www.whitehouse.gov/the-press-office/remarks-president-securing-our-nations-cyber-infrastructure.

[183] *See Cyberwar: War in the Fifth Domain*, ECONOMIST, July 3, 2010, at 25, http://www.economist.com/node/16478792 [hereinafter *Cyberwar*]; U.S. *Cyber Command*, UNITED STATES STRATEGIC COMMAND, http://www.stratcom.mil/factsheets/Cyber_Command/ (last visited May 22, 2013); Jim Garamone, *Cybercom Chief Details Cyberspace Defense*, U.S. DEP'T DEF. (Sept. 23, 2010), http://www.defense.gov/news/newsarticle.aspx?id=60987.

[184] *See* Jim Michaels, *Pentagon Seeking 'Rules of Engagement' for Cyber War*, USA TODAY (Apr. 4, 2013), http://www.usatoday.com/story/news/nation/2013/04/04/pentagon-wants-cyber-war-rules-of-engagement/2054055/.

[185] *See* SINGER & FRIEDMAN, *supra* note 118, at 134.

[186] *See* Remarks by Secretary Janet Napolitano at San Jose State Univ., DHS (Apr. 16, 2012), http://www.dhs.gov/news/2012/04/16/remarks-secretary-janet-napolitano-san-jose-state-university.

[187] *See* Ellen Nakashima, *Pentagon Creating Teams to Launch Cyberattacks as Threat Grows*, WASH. POST (Mar. 13, 2013), http://www.washingtonpost.com/world/national-security/pentagon-creating-teams-to-launch-cyberattacks-as-threat-grows/2013/03/12/35aa94da-8b3c-11e2-9838-d62f083ba93f_story.html?wpmk=MK0000200 (reporting the creation of thirteen offensive CYBERCOM teams that will be operational by 2014); Ellen Nakashima, *Pentagon to Boost Cybersecurity Force*, WASH. POST (Jan. 27, 2013), http://www.washingtonpost.com/world/national-security/pentagon-to-boost-cybersecurity-force/2013/01/19/d87d9dc2-5fec-11e2-b05a-605528f6b712_story.html?wpmk=MK0000200 (reporting that CYBERCOM will expand its forces from 900 to 4,900 troops and civilians).

The Obama administration has implemented several initiatives to create a more integrated cybersecurity policy, including appointing a cybersecurity coordinator. But the position does not require Senate approval and has been described as being heavy on responsibility but light on real authority.[188] A fully integrated U.S. cybersecurity policy has yet to be established, as was described earlier.[189] Outstanding issues include whether the DHS should be a regulator or a resource for at-risk companies and institutions, how best to reform information-sharing practices and protect critical national infrastructure, and how much power the President should have over the Internet.[190]

Dueling legislation appeared in 2012 in the form of the Cybersecurity Act favored by Senate democrats, and the SECURE IT Act supported by Senate republicans. The former bill would grant new powers to DHS to oversee government cybersecurity, set "cybersecurity performance requirements" for firms operating what DHS deems to be "critical infrastructure," and create "exchanges" to promote information sharing, but would not settle cybersecurity turf battles between agencies.[191] The Cybersecurity Act designates an industry as "critical" by deciding whether "damage or unauthorized access to that system or asset could reasonably result in the interruption of life-sustaining services . . . ; catastrophic economic damages to the United States . . . ; [or] severe degradation of national security."[192] But it explicitly omits "commercial information technology product[s], including hardware and software."[193] The latter bill favors a more voluntary approach and relies on the NSA; a politically disfavored strategy in the wake of continuing revelations about NSA surveillance programs for the foreseeable future.[194] Neither bill nor other cybersecurity reform package had been

---

[188] *See* Ellen Nakashima, *Obama to Name Howard Schmidt as Cybersecurity Coordinator*, WASH. POST (Dec. 22, 2009), http://www.washingtonpost.com/wp-dyn/content/article/2009/12/21/AR2009122103055 .html.

[189] *See* Lieberman, Collins, Carper Statement on Cybersecurity, Sen. Comm. Homeland Sec. & Gov. Aff., July 19, 2012, http://www.hsgac.senate.gov/media/majority-media/lieberman-collins-rockefeller-feinstein-carper_offer-revised-legislation-to-improve-security---of-our-most-critical-private-sector-cyber-systems-.

[190] *Id.*

[191] *Cybersecurity* Act of 2012, S. 2105, 112th Cong. § 103(b)(1)(C) (2012). The theory underlying the Cybersecurity Act of 2012 is that risk is no longer being borne by the risk takers in the event of a cyber attack on CNI, since a successful attack could affect a wide range of individuals and firms. Proponents argue that the government should take on a greater role in protecting CNI and enhancing cybersecurity for the public good. *But see* Eli Dourado, *Is There a Cybersecurity Market Failure?* (George Mason Univ. Mercatus Ctr., Working Paper No. 12-05, 2012), http://mercatus.org/publication/there-cybersecurity-market-failure-0 (arguing that market failures are not so common in the cyber-security realm).

[192] Cybersecurity Act of 2012, *supra* note 191, at § 103(b)(1)(C).

[193] *Id.* at § 103(b)(2)(C).

[194] *See* Diana Bartz, *SECURE IT Act: Senate Republicans Introduce Softer Cybersecurity Bill*, HUFF. POST (Mar. 1, 2012), http://www.huffingtonpost.com/2012/03/01/secure-it-act_n_1314213.html. Proponents argue that SECURE IT is preferable to the Cybersecurity Act of 2012 because it creates less new regulation, relying instead on voluntary information sharing and focusing on federal contractors. The debate continues, especially given concerns of overregulation, privacy, and civil liberties

enacted as of February 2013,[195] leaving President Obama to issue an executive order that, among other things, expanded public-private information sharing and established a voluntary "Cybersecurity Framework" comprised partly of private-sector best practices that companies could adopt to better secure CNI.[196] Many commentators, though, have gauged this effort as falling short of what is required,[197] though it is a promising step forward and could in time help define a cybersecurity duty of care.[198]

Although resources are increasingly being put toward enhancing cybersecurity, much work remains to be done.[199] For example, despite years of trying, still only 2 percent of the integrated circuits purchased by the Pentagon are made in the United States, with the majority coming from Asian nations with track records of "'unambiguous, deliberate subversions' of computer hardware[,]" as discussed in Chapter 3.[200] Such practices, along with a growing list of sophisticated cyber attackers taking advantage of latent vulnerabilities, have led to the loss of terabytes of sensitive information, according to former Deputy Defense Secretary Lynn.[201] In response, and in addition to the previously mentioned legislation, the Obama administration has sought new regulations that would require all communications services, including Skype, BlackBerry, and Facebook, to be "capable of complying"

protections, though some of these concerns are tempered by procedures that the DHS is charged with developing under the Cybersecurity Act. *See* Ellen Nakashima, *NSA Thwarted in Cybersecurity Initiative*, WASH. POST (Feb. 28, 2012), http://www.washingtonpost.com/world/national-security/white-house-nsa-weigh-cyber-security-personal-privacy/2012/02/07/gIQA8HmKeR_story.html (reporting on privacy concerns held by the Obama administration concerning the NSA's attempts to take a more active role in protecting CNI); Paul Rosenzweig, *Information Sharing and the Cybersecurity Act of 2012*, LAWFARE (Feb. 14, 2012, 6:43 PM EST), http://www.lawfareblog.com/2012/02/information-sharing-and-the-cybersecurity-act-of-2012.

[195] *See* Alexei Alexis, *House Homeland Security Leaders Said Close to Unveiling Cybersecurity Bill*, BLOOMBERG BNA (June 10, 2013), http://www.bna.com/house-homeland-security-n17179874424/ (reporting on cybersecurity reform efforts in the House and Senate as of June 2013).

[196] *See* WHITE HOUSE PRESS SEC'Y, EXECUTIVE ORDER ON IMPROVING CRITICAL INFRASTRUCTURE CYBERSECURITY (Feb. 12, 2013), http://www.whitehouse.gov/the-press-office/2013/02/12/executive-order-improving-critical-infrastructure-cybersecurity-0; Mark Clayton, *Why Obama's Executive Order on Cybersecurity Doesn't Satisfy Most Experts*, CHRISTIAN SCI. MONITOR (Feb. 13, 2013), http://www.csmonitor.com/USA/Politics/2013/0213/Why-Obama-s-executive-order-on-cybersecurity-doesn-t-satisfy-most-experts.

[197] *See* Clayton, *supra* note 196.

[198] *See Pieces in Place for Industry to 'Get Started' on Cyber Framework Adoption*, INSIDE CYBERSECURITY (Nov. 20, 2013), http://insidecybersecurity.com/index.php?option=com_user&view=login&return=aHRocDovL2luc2lkZWN5YmVyc2VjdXJpdHkuY29tL0N5YmVyLURhaWx5LU5ld3MvRGFpbHktTmV3cy9uaXNoLXBpZWNlcy1pbi1wbGFjZS1mb3ItaW5kdXN0cnktdG8tZ2VoLXN0YXJ0ZWQtG8tZ2VoLXNhcnktcXNmcnktZXJ2aWNhb2V5ZGFpbHktTmV3cy9uaXNoLXBpZWNlcy1pbi1wbGFjZS1mb3ItaW5kdXN0cnktdG8tZ2VoLXN0YXJ0ZWQtMTA3NS5odG1s ("The telecommunications industry and the Federal Communications Commission plan to use an emerging framework of cybersecurity standards to assess and prioritize best practices for the sector as it works to address evolving cyber threats . . . .").

[199] *See* Amber Corrin, *Budget Shows How Cyber Programs are Spreading*, FCW (Apr. 12, 2013), http://fcw.com/Articles/2013/04/12/budget-cybersecurity.aspx.

[200] John Markoff, *Old Trick Threatens the Newest Weapons*, N.Y. Times (Oct. 26, 2009), http://www.nytimes.com/2009/10/27/science/27trojan.html?pagewanted=all&_r=0.

[201] Lynn, *supra* note 17.

with a wiretap order by intercepting and unscrambling encrypted messages.[202] Critics of such actions point to John Barlow's verse: "Relying on the government to protect your privacy is like asking a peeping tom to install your window blinds."[203]

Despite its notable cybersecurity lapses, the United States has proven adroit at using cyberspace to accomplish certain national security goals. For example, U.S. cyber attacks successfully penetrated Iraqi security systems prior to the second invasion of Iraq, reportedly sending emails with surrender instructions that "many Iraqi officers obeyed . . . ."[204] The Pentagon also forced the Somalian Internet to shut down under the pretext that the providers were supporting terrorism.[205] Nevertheless, even these successes are a double-edged sword, incentivizing competitors to ratchet up their own efforts to match U.S. capabilities and therefore increase global cyber insecurity. As Clarke and Knake note, "The biggest secret in the world about cyber war may be that at the very same time the U.S. prepares for offensive cyber war, it is continuing policies that make it impossible to defend the nation effectively from cyber attack."[206] The question that few want to ask is: what happens if the United States loses a cyber war? What would the implications be to broader U.S. national security, as well as to international peace and stability?

United Kingdom

Similar to the United States, where a 2014 poll of defense officials found cyber attacks to be "the greatest threat to U.S. national security,"[207] the United Kingdom has identified terrorism and cyber attacks as the two greatest threats in the twenty-first century.[208] Specifically, British Foreign Secretary William Hague has called the epidemic of cybercrime "one of the greatest global and strategic challenges of our time."[209] Yet British cybersecurity regulation is still developing, and a doctrine of cyber power remains largely undefined, even as new revelations about U.K.-U.S.

---

[202] *See* Charlie Savage, *U.S. Tries to Make it Easier to Wiretap the Internet*, N.Y. Times, Sept. 27, 2010, at A1.

[203] John Perry Barlow, *Decrypting the Puzzle Palace*, 35(7) Comm. ACM 25 (July 1992).

[204] Clarke & Knake, *supra* note 9, at 11.

[205] *See* Sasha Costanza-Chock, *The Whole World is Watching: Online Surveillance of Social Movement Organizations*, *in* Who Owns the Media?: Global Trends and Local Resistances 271, 271 (Pradip Thomas & Zaharom Nain eds., 2004); *US Shuts Down Somalia Internet*, BBC News (Nov. 23, 2001), http://news.bbc.co.uk/2/hi/africa/1672220.stm.

[206] Clarke & Knake, *supra* note 9, at xi.

[207] *Poll: Cyber Attacks Biggest Threat to National Security*, Def. One (Jan. 6, 2014), http://www.defense one.com/threats/2014/01/poll-cyber-attacks-biggest-threat-national-security/76253/?oref=d-interstitial-continue.

[208] *See* J. Nicholas Hoover, *Cyber Attacks Becoming Top Terror Threat, FBI Says*, Info. Wk. (Feb. 1, 2012), http://www.informationweek.com/government/security/cyber-attacks-becoming-top-terror-threat/232600046; *Cyber Attacks and Terrorism Head Threats Facing UK*, BBC News (Oct. 18, 2010), http://www.bbc.co.uk/news/uk-11562969.

[209] *Hague Gives Cybercrime Warning*, BBC News (Oct. 4, 2012), http://www.bbc.co.uk/news/uk-19824188.

cyber espionage campaigns come to light.[210] Through the Center for the Protection of National Infrastructure (CPNI), the UK engages in the protection of infrastructure by using a "criticality scale" to gauge priorities and tout the benefits of public-private partnerships to enhance cybersecurity, though few details are publicly available.[211]

In the United Kingdom, as in the United States, voluntary industry strategies and law enforcement regulations are intended to enhance CNI protection. The 2011 UK Cyber Security Strategy, which focuses on government contractors, states that the British government "will work with industry to develop rigorous cyber security . . . standards" similar to the U.S. NIST Cybersecurity Framework,[212] but does not lay out how the largely voluntary approach it envisions of creating a "trusted environment" represents a change to the status quo sufficient to effectively meet this threat to British national security.[213] Nor does the strategy spell out how the awareness of individuals and businesses about the cyber threat will be raised,[214] or offer specifics about how the CPNI will help enhance cybersecurity for the "wider group of companies not currently deemed part of the critical infrastructure"[215] but which are nevertheless essential to Britain's long-term economic competitiveness.

Unlike the regulation of CNI, the United Kingdom has been making some progress in reorganizing its cyber warfare capabilities, including at the Government Communications Headquarters, which is the center for Her Majesty's Government's Signal Intelligence.[216] A new office, the UK Cyber Security Operations Center, has also been created within the Cabinet Office to liaise with a host of British trade associations and industry groups such as the Information Assurance Advisory Council, and governmental departments, as well as to provide strategic oversight.[217] In late 2010, the Ministry of Defense (MOD) was reported to be forming a Defense Cyber Operations Group responsible for "developing, testing and validating cyber techniques as a complement to traditional military capabilities."[218] Then, in 2011, the MOD announced that cyber warriors would be "put alongside conventional troops"

---

[210] *See, e.g.*, Matthew Kalman, *Israeli PM Condemns US and UK Spying on Predecessor as 'Unacceptable*,' GUARDIAN (Dec. 23, 2013), http://www.theguardian.com/world/2013/dec/23/netanyahu-condemns-spying-nsa-gchq-unacceptable.

[211] *The National Infrastructure*, CPNI, http://www.cpni.gov.uk/about/cni/ (last visited Oct. 21, 2011); *see* BRÖMMELHÖRSTER, FABRY, & WIRTZ, *supra* note 180, at 3 (noting the lack of a clear organizational structure for securing British CNI).

[212] UK CYBER SECURITY STRATEGY: PROTECTING AND PROMOTING THE UK IN A DIGITAL WORLD 27 (2011), http://www.carlisle.army.mil/dime/documents/UK%20Cyber%20Security%20Strategy.pdf.

[213] *Id.* at 28.

[214] *Id.* at 26–27.

[215] *Id.* at 28.

[216] *See Who We Are*, GCHQ, http://www.gchq.gov.uk/who_we_are/Pages/index.aspx (last visited Jan. 28, 2014).

[217] *See UK Government Cyber Security Operations Centre Going Live Soon*, INFO. SEC. MAG. (Mar. 12, 2010), http://www.infosecurity-magazine.com/view/8020/uk-government-cyber-security-operations-centre-going-live-soon/.

[218] Matt Grainger, *UK Government to Create Cyber Warfare Division*, PCR (Nov. 15, 2010), http://www.pcr-online.biz/news/35145/UK-to-create-cyber-warfare-division.

and that hundreds of cyber experts would be recruited as part of a £650 million campaign to enhance UK cybersecurity.[219] The UK government has even gone so far as to publicly announce that it is developing offensive cyber attack capabilities, illustrating that arguably "[t]he cultural norms against waging war in cyberspace are slowly eroding."[220] Urgent action is needed in part to better manage the "'astonishing' levels of cyber-attacks on UK industry" being perpetuated by criminals and states, according to the British Military Intelligence, Section 5 (MI5).[221]

On the regulatory side, the UK government has endorsed bills allowing police and security services to legally demand ISPs and Internet users to reveal passwords and privacy encryption codes,[222] as well as singling out foreign firms with "perceived links to the Chinese State[,]" such as Huawei, for extra scrutiny to ensure that their products do not pose a threat to national security.[223] Such initiatives are due at least in part to the concerns of domestic firms and "the damage [cybercrime] does to the financial and social fabric of the country,"[224] and are also perhaps a response to the growing capabilities of other allied and antagonistic cyber powers, including China, Russia, and Israel.

China

Numerous reports have been published about China's complicity in, and active state sponsorship of, cyber attacks against a huge array of targets.[225] These attacks seem to

---

[219] *UK Beefs Up Cyber Warfare Plans*, BBC News (May 31, 2011), http://www.bbc.co.uk/news/technology-13599916.

[220] Brian Fung, *How Britain's New Cyberarmy Could Reshape the Laws of War*, Wash. Post (Sept. 30, 2013), http://www.washingtonpost.com/blogs/the-switch/wp/2013/09/30/how-britains-new-cyberarmy-could-reshape-the-laws-of-war/?wprss=rss_business&tid=pp_widget.

[221] Gordon Corera, *MI5 Fighting 'Astonishing' Level of Cyber-Attacks*, BBC News (June 25, 2012), http://www.bbc.co.uk/news/uk-18586681.

[222] *See* Liat Clark, *Cybersecurity Academics: UK 'Web Snooping' Bill is Naïve and Dangerous*, Wired (Apr. 23, 2013), http://www.wired.co.uk/news/archive/2013-04/23/uk-isps-privacy. The UK is also subject to the February 2013 EU cybersecurity directive discussed in Chapter 5.

[223] *See* Intelligence & Sec. Comm., Foreign Involvement in the Critical National Infrastructure: The Implications for National Security 4–5 (2013), www.gov.uk/government/uploads/system/uploads/attachment_data/file/205680/ISC-Report-Foreign-Investment-in-the-Critical-National-Infrastructure.pdf. Similarly, In October 2012, a U.S. House of Representatives report recommended that government systems "should not include" equipment from Huawei or ZTE, two leading Chinese companies, and "strongly encouraged" U.S. private sector entities to "consider the long-term security risks associated with doing business with either ZTE or Huawei." Mike Rogers & C.A. Dutch Ruppersberger, *Investigative Report on the U.S. National Security Issues Posed by Chinese Telecommunications Companies Huawei and ZTE*, U.S. House of Representatives, vi (Oct. 8, 2012), http://intelligence.house.gov/sites/intelligence.house.gov/files/Huawei-ZTE%20Investigative%20Report%20(FINAL).pdf.

[224] Dave Clemente, *UK Cybersecurity Plan a 'Promising Step' But with Risks*, BBC (Nov. 25, 2011), http://www.bbc.com/news/technology-15893773.

[225] *See* Dan Mcwhorter, *Mandiant Exposes APT1 – One of China's Cyber Espionage Units & Releases 3,000 Indicators*, M-Unition (Feb. 18, 2013), www.mandiant.com/blog/mandiant-exposes-apt1-chinas-cyber-espionage-units-releases-3000-indicators/; Ben Worthen, *Wide Cyber Attack is Linked to China*, Wall St. J. (Mar. 30, 2009), http://online.wsj.com/article/SB123834671171466791.html.

be getting more frequent, spiking "from one or two per week in 2005" to more than fifty per day in 2008, according to Symantec, though it remains unclear how many of these attacks actually originated in China due to the attribution problem.[226] For example, Chinese hackers have been widely reported to "have successfully penetrated the U.S. electrical grid...."[227] This is especially worrying because in March 2007, the Department of Energy conducted an experiment to see whether a power plant could be damaged by a cyber attack. Researchers were reportedly able to "cause a generator to shake, smoke, and shut down with a few keystrokes."[228]

China has disavowed charges of sponsoring cyber attacks, but the PRC's "own stated military goals include improving the country's ability to wage information warfare."[229] Although little public data exist, China is known to be aggressively hiring young, tech-savvy cyber warriors to carry out cyber attacks against a variety of targets, including Taiwan.[230] This force is being trained under a policy of Local War Under Informationized Conditions (LWUIC). LWUIC is the People's Liberation Army's "effort to develop a fully networked architecture capable of coordinating military operations on land, in air, at sea, in space and across the electromagnetic spectrum."[231] The DOD has long confirmed that China is enhancing its cyber warfare capabilities, with an emphasis on weakening potential adversaries' command and control systems.[232] In light of China's relative conventional military weakness compared to the United States for the foreseeable future,[233] China is making use of cyber attacks to secure an asymmetric advantage.[234] China, then, like the United States, is pursuing an aggressive cyber warfare program, and may now be the world leader in economic espionage.

The rapid expansion of China's cyber warfare capabilities began after the defeat of Iraq in Desert Storm; the Chinese government concluded that their approach of

---

[226] Worthen, *supra* note 225.

[227] Reese Nguyen, *Navigating Jus Ad Bellum in the Age of Cyber Warfare*, 101 Cal. L. Rev. 1079, 1011 (2013); *see* James Burgess, *Chinese Military Renews Cyber-Attacks, Focusing on US Electrical Grid*, Oilprice.com (May 23, 2013), http://oilprice.com/Latest-Energy-News/World-News/Chinese-Military-Renews-Cyber-Attacks-Focusing-on-US-Electrical-Grid.html.

[228] James D. Zirin, *Abdicating on a 'Cyber Czar'?*, L.A. Times (Oct. 14, 2009), http://articles.latimes.com/2009/oct/14/opinion/oe-zirin14.

[229] Larry Greenmeier, *China's Cyber Attacks Signal New Battlefield is Online*, Sci. Am. (Sept. 18, 2007), http://www.scientificamerican.com/article.cfm?id=chinas-cyber-attacks-sign.

[230] Mac William Bishop, *China's Cyberwarriors*, Foreign Pol'y (Sept. 2006), http://www.foreignpolicy.com/articles/2006/08/08/chinas_cyberwarriors.

[231] Steve DeWeese, *Capability of the People's Republic of China to Conduct Cyber Warfare and Computer Network Exploitation*, Northrup Grumman at 6 (Oct. 9, 2009), http://www.domain-b.com/defence/general/NorthropGrumman_domain-b.pdf; *see also* Dennis J. Blasko, *Chinese Strategic Thinking: People's War in the 21st Century*, Jamestown Found. (Mar. 18, 2010), http://www.jamestown.org/single/?no_cache=1&tx_ttnews[tt_news]=36166 (discussing the wider application of LWUIC in Chinese strategic thinking).

[232] *See* FY2013 Annual Report to Congress on the Military Power of the People's Republic of China at 36, http://www.defense.gov/pubs/2013_China_Report_FINAL.pdf.

[233] *Cf.* Coren, *supra* note 114.

[234] Robert McMillan, *Report Says China Ready for Cyber-war, Espionage*, PC World (Oct. 23, 2009), http://www.pcworld.com/article/174210/report_says_china_ready_for_cyberwar_espionage.html.

amassing an army to challenge advanced Western nations would not work. Instead, they embarked on a process of enhancing their asymmetric warfare capabilities, including cyber war.[235] By 2003, China had announced the creation of cyber warfare units, which conduct reconnaissance, infiltrate networks, and disseminate propaganda.[236] Soon after, the Titan Rain attacks were planned and executed, and China is now reportedly spending between $50 billion and $100 billion annually on developing new cyber capabilities.[237] These figures may be compared with total British defense spending planned for 2014 of approximately £45 billion.[238] Such state support has allowed China to undergo one of the most dramatic and rapid military cyber transformations in modern history.[239]

Beyond hard cyber power, China has been more aggressive than the United States in regulating software that could compromise its systems, including reportedly banning government computers from running certain Microsoft programs because the PRC government assumed these might include a "backdoor" that would allow the U.S. government to infiltrate Chinese systems.[240] At least one 2013 report indicates that such fears may in fact be justified.[241] Indeed, China is taking an array of steps to protect its CNI, calling for "dynamic monitoring of the Internet" and "strengthening [security for] industrial control systems," potentially in response to the success of Stuxnet.[242] These efforts have been underway since at least since 1994, when Decree No. 147 was issued by the State Council,[243] the country's highest state-run (rather than party-run) executive and administrative organ.[244]

Chinese policymakers do not use CNI terminology under the scheme developed to enforce Decree No. 147.[245] Rather, the PRC ranks industry systems on a scale of

[235] *See* Timothy L. Thomas, *China's Electronic Strategies*, 47 MILITARY REV. (May-June 2001), http://www.au.af.mil/au/awc/awcgate/milreview/thomas.htm.

[236] *See* J. P. "Jack" London, *Made in China*, 137(4) PROC. MAG. 1,298 (Apr. 2011), http://www.usni.org/magazines/proceedings/2011-04/made-china.

[237] Jack London's Speech on American Cybersecurity and China's Increasing Threat, CACI, Nov. 14, 2012, http://www.caci.com/speeches/jpl_2011-11-10.shtml.

[238] *See UK Public Spending Details for 2014*, UK PUBLIC SPENDING, http://www.ukpublicspending.co.uk/uk_budget_pie_chart (last visited May 22, 2013).

[239] *Cyberwar, supra* note 183.

[240] Rana Foroohar & Melinda Liu, *When China Rules the World*, NEWSWEEK, Mar. 22, 2010, at 26.

[241] *See* F. Michael Maloof, *NSA Has Total Access Via Microsoft Windows*, WND (June 23, 2013), http://www.wnd.com/2013/06/nsa-has-total-access-via-microsoft-windows/ (reporting that "[t]he National Security Agency has backdoor access to all Windows software since the release of Windows 95 . . . .").

[242] Adam Segal, *China Moves Forward on Cybersecurity Policy*, COUNCIL FOREIGN REL. (July 14, 2012), http://blogs.cfr.org/asia/2012/07/24/china-moves-forward-on-cybersecurity-policy/.

[243] *China's Protection for Critical Information Infrastructure*, BLUE PAPER, XJTU INFO. SEC. L. RES. CTR. 3–4 (2012), http://infseclaw.net/ (hereinafter XJTU Blue Paper).

[244] The State Council, *People Daily (English)*, http://english.peopledaily.com.cn/data/organs/statecouncil.shtml. Decree No. 147 required Chinese information systems to be protected, particularly in the fields of "state affairs, economic construction, national defense, and the most advanced science and technology." XJTU Blue Paper, *supra* note 243, at 18–19.

[245] *See* CIIP, Xjtu Inf. Sec. L. Res. Ctr., China's Protection for Critical Information Infrastructure 1 (2012) [hereinafter *Blue Paper*] (noting that "[c]oncepts like 'critical infrastructure' (CI) and 'critical information infrastructure' can be found nowhere in China's laws and regulations.").

1 to 5 (5 representing the most substantial risk and importance to national security), based on a system that originated in the United States.[246] Whole industries are not categorized in this manner; rather, the Ministry of Public Security (MPS), the Ministry of Industry and Information Technology (MIIT), and other governmental organizations focus on systems within these industries since certain systems, such as a telecommunications network, are more important to national security than others, such as a mobile phone company's website.[247] Even so, it is sometimes difficult to distinguish between security levels – especially 3, 4, and 5, which all effectively outlaw foreign technology products in favor of domestic industry.[248] Moreover, once made these classifications are difficult to put into practice. For instance, GB17859 did not specify which government entities should be tasked with ensuring compliance with a level's technical demands.

To help clarify the situation in 2007, new administrative regulations were issued known as MLPS,[249] short for "multi-level protection scheme."[250] MLPS filled in the gaps left by Decree No. 147 and GB17859 by describing in greater detail how the five-level system should be applied and which government entities should be in charge of the various aspects of implementation. Of the highest concern to many foreign companies and governments, MLPS also imposes elevated requirements "on security products destined for use in Level 3 or above information

---

[246] *See* GB/T 17859: Classified Criteria for Securing Protection of Computer Information System 1 (1999) (noting, in a rough translation from the original Mandarin, that "[t]his standard references the United States trusted computer systems evaluation criteria."). This system differentiates between levels by focusing on technical criteria, like identification and authentication. *See* Yi Mao, Xiaohua Chen, & Yan Liu, *Comparative Study Between the Chinese Standards and the Common Criteria*, ATSEC, at 10 (2011), www.atsec.com/downloads/presentations/comparative_study_between_chinese_standards_and_the_common_criteria.pdf. For example, at level one, users must be asked to authenticate their identities (by using, for instance, a password). By level five, computer information systems must be able to identify unique users, authorize their access to certain data, and hold them accountable for their actions. *See id.* at 9–11; GB/T 17859.

[247] As an aside, these agencies are experiencing similar turf battles to what has been common in the United States, and along similar lines with MPS being a security ministry boasting robust cybersecurity capabilities analogues to the DOD, and MIIT as a more recently created organization tasked with regulating civilian communications somewhat similar to DHS. *See* DIETER ERNST, INDIGENOUS INNOVATION AND GLOBALIZATION: THE CHALLENGE FOR CHINA'S STANDARDIZATION STRATEGY 38 (2011) (discussing some of "the turf wars between the MPS and the MIIT"); CHINA AND CYBERSECURITY: POLITICAL, ECONOMIC, AND STRATEGIC DIMENSIONS 6 (2012), http://igcc.ucsd.edu/assets/001/503568 .pdf.

[248] *See, e.g.*, GB/T 28449: Information System Classified Security Protection Assessment Process Guidelines (2012); GB/T 20269: Security Management of Information System Requirements (2006).

[249] This book uses the English-language acronym MLPS due to its popular use in English-language academic papers. However, as Nathaniel Ahrens wrote in 2012, "the term *MLPS* was coined by the United States Information Technology Office, an industry trade association. . . . The Chinese Representative to the Committee on the Technical Barriers to Trade in the WTO stated that RCPIS is the correct name during a meeting on March 24–25, 2011." Nathaniel Ahrens, *National Security and China's Information Security Standards: Of Shoes, Buttons, and Routers*, Ctr. STRATEGIC & INT'L STUD. 2 n.7 (2012), http://csis.org/files/publication/121108_Ahrens_NationalSecurityChina_web.pdf.

[250] 信息安全等级保护管理办法 43 号: Administrative Measures for the Graded Protection of Information Security, No. 43 (2007).

systems . . . ."[251] MLPS not only mandates the use of Chinese IP but also requires that such products be researched, developed, and manufactured by an entity "invested or controlled by Chinese citizens, legal persons or the state, and have independent legal representation in China[.]"[252] In late 2011, Japanese and European delegations to the World Trade Organization's Committee on the Technical Barriers to Trade stated that the commercial impact of strictly enforcing MLPS "might be tremendous" and pointed out that MLPS has gradually taken "over sectors of the economy not regarded as critical to national security anywhere else in the world . . . ."[253]

Going forward, the challenge facing Chinese policymakers is to seek common ground with other leading cyber powers in relation to protecting CNI. Elements within the Chinese and U.S. governments also seem to recognize to varying degrees that a protracted cyber conflict focusing on CNI would leave all concerned worse off and may even be unwinnable, prompting bilateral dialogue. But although relatively little information is publicly available, both nations are also likely trying to ensure that the first salvo in a true cyber war is also the last.[254]

Russia

Like China, Russia has been committed to developing its cyber warfare capabilities since the mid-1990s.[255] Although never proven due to the difficulty of attribution, Russia has been linked to the cyber attacks on Estonia in 2007, Georgia and

---

[251] SCOTT CHARNEY & ERIC T. WERNER, MICROSOFT, CYBER SUPPLY CHAIN RISK MANAGEMENT: TOWARD A GLOBAL VISION OF TRANSPARENCY AND TRUST 5 (2011).

[252] *Id.* at 6 (noting that "the core technology and key components of products must have independent Chinese or indigenous intellectual property rights[.]").

[253] Ahrens, *supra* note 249, at 7. Unlike in China, India's IT, electricity, and telecom sectors experienced substantial private sector investments in the 1990s, diffusing responsibility for disasters among diverse operators similar to the status quo in the United States. M.M. Chaturvedi, M.P. Gupta, & Jaijit Bhattacharya, *Cyber Security Infrastructure in India: A Study*, *in* EMERGING TECHNOLOGIES IN E-GOVERNMENT 70, 73 (G.P. Sahu ed., 2008), http://www.csi-sigegov.org/emerging_pdf/9_70-84.pdf. As a result – and again, as in the United States – regulation varies among sectors; for instance, while the Reserve Bank of India has regulated the cybersecurity of the Indian banking system, other industries have not been similarly impacted. *India's National Cyber Security Policy–Implications for the Private Sector*, CHECKMATE (July 21, 2013), http://niiconsulting.com/checkmate/2013/07/indias-national-cyber-security-policy-implications-for-the-private-sector/ (last visited Jan. 17, 2014). India's most significant cyber law is arguably the Indian IT Act of 2000. The IT Act has been amended since 2000; for instance, in 2006, the law made companies liable for not following "reasonable security practices and procedures" and identified the need to protect "Critical Information Infrastructure." Chaturvedi, Gupta, & Battacharya, *supra* note 253, at 74. This Act gives the Indian government widespread authority to regulate CNI and enhance cybersecurity, for example by defining a duty of cybersecurity care – perhaps not an authority as extensive as the powers Chinese regulators enjoy, but more robust than comparable U.S. efforts, though the NIST Cybersecurity Framework may be considered as a step in this direction.

[254] *See* David Gewirtz, *For China, Hacking May Be All About Sun Tzu and World War III*, ZDNET (May 29, 2013), http://www.zdnet.com/for-china-hacking-may-be-all-about-sun-tzu-and-world-war-iii-7000015988/.

[255] *See* JEFFERY CARR, INSIDE CYBER WARFARE: MAPPING THE CYBER UNDERWORLD 162 (2009).

Lithuania in 2008, and Poland in 2009, among others.[256] Indeed, Russian sponsorship stretches back to the original Moonlight Maze attacks of the late 1990s, and arguably even before that, beginning with "their Revolution in Military Affairs in the 1980s."[257] Over this time period, Russian cyber military doctrines have evolved "from computer network exploitation to computer network attack during the latter days of the second Chechen war from 1997 to 2001 . . . ."[258] However, while perhaps slightly more transparent than Chinese cybersecurity strategy, the true extent and organization of Russia's cyber army – and especially its sponsorship of cyber criminals and patriotic hackers – remains a hotly debated topic. For example, despite criticism of its cyber warfare operations in Georgia, Russia has not established a corps of "information troops," preferring instead to rely on civilian volunteers who may lack the skill and dedication of regular soldiers but have the benefits of anonymity and affordability.[259] However, the Russian government has laid out the goal of changing the status quo by 2020 by creating a centralized system to detect and prevent cyber attacks, including those on CNI, giving over many functions to the Federal Security Service (FSB).[260]

Also like China, Russia uses the broader term "information security," rather than cybersecurity. Why the difference? Information security arguably includes content. In essence, some claim that these countries are not only concerned about cyber attacks on networks, but also the information being carried on them. "The worry is that Twitter, Facebook, and other social networks could be used for political reasons[,]" explains Adam Segal of the Council on Foreign Relations.[261] In these nations' views, cyberspace should be free from Western value labels, including free speech. In Russia, this perspective dates back to the birth of the Russian Internet, and even before that to the Foundation for Effective Politics, which is a Russian organization that has been accused of supporting government power online.[262] This emphasis on information security broadens the term "cybersecurity" to include the impact of the Internet on national security and freedom of expression, which may help to explain the different approaches taken by Russia and China in regulating the Internet. It also underscores the difficulty of reaching consensus on enhancing cybersecurity through multilateral channels, and could shed some light on why Russia and China have been allegedly willing to sponsor cyber attacks, unlike,

---

[256] *See* Davis, *supra* note 72; Tikk et al., *supra* note 128, at 4; Krebs, *supra* note 126; John Leyden, *Polish Government Cyberattack Blamed on Russia*, REGISTER (Oct. 13, 2009), http://www.theregister.co.uk/2009/10/13/poland_cyberattacks/.

[257] CARR, *supra* note 255, at 162.

[258] *Id.*

[259] *See* Keir Giles, *"Information Troops" – a Russian Cyber Command?*, NATO CCDCOE PROC. 45, 45 (2011), http://www.ccdcoe.org/publications/2011proceedings/InformationTroopsARussianCyberCommand-Giles.pdf.

[260] *See Russia has Developed a National Cyber Security Policy*, FISMA NEWS, http://www.thecre.com/fnews/?p=1481 (last visited Jan. 17, 2014).

[261] Neal Ungerleider, *The Chinese Way of Hacking*, FASTCOMPANY (July 13, 2011), http://www.fastcompany.com/1766812/inside-the-chinese-way-of-hacking.

[262] *See* CARR, *supra* note 255, at 17–18, 163.

for example, the United States, which prefers developing sophisticated cyber weapons in-house.[263]

There are at least three institutions "responsible for information security in Russia . . . ."[264] First, the Security Council of Russia, which is chaired by the Russian President, is tasked with protecting national interests that could be compromised through cyber attacks, presumably including CNI.[265] Second, the FSB and the Ministry of Defense are "responsible for ensuring the security of state communications . . . ."[266] Third, the Russian armed forces are in charge of "studying the impact of information operations on" the military and preparing for cyber war,[267] a task that may be reorganized into a centralized cybersecurity command.[268] Since the breakup of the Soviet Union, Russia, like China, has viewed cyber warfare as a means of challenging NATO military dominance asymmetrically and likely will continue to do so for the foreseeable future.

Israel

Geopolitical concerns and several wars have put Israel at the forefront of cybersecurity, with tools reportedly rivaling U.S. capabilities.[269] As the most wired nation in the Middle East, Israel is uniquely vulnerable to cyber attacks.[270] Given its technological prowess, however, it is also at the cutting edge of offensive cyber warfare capabilities. For example, Israel reportedly used cyber attacks to cripple Syrian air defense systems prior to launching airstrikes on a nuclear facility in September 2007.[271] The attacks disrupted Syrian radar systems, showing empty sky where squadrons of Israeli attack planes flew overhead.[272]

---

[263] However, in the Chinese context at least, the differences in terminology may be driven by linguistic variations such as the fact that "the term cybersecurity doesn't really exist in the Chinese language" (rather, the literal translation of the character used for "cyber" means "network"). Piin-Fen Kok, *EastWest Direct: U.S.-China Cyber Tensions*, EAST-WEST INST. (Apr. 18, 2013), http://www.ewi.info/eastwest-direct-us-china-cyber-tensions.

[264] Timothy I. Thomas, *Russia's Information Warfare Structure: Understanding the Roles of the Security Council, Fapsi, the State Technical Commission and the Military*, 7(1) EUR. SEC. 156, 156 (1998).

[265] *Id.*

[266] *Id.* at 170.

[267] *Id.* at 156.

[268] *See Russia Considering Cyber-Security Command*, RIA NOVOSTI (Mar. 21, 2012), http://en.rian.ru/russia/20120321/172301330.html.

[269] *See* David E. Sanger, *Obama Order Sped Up Wave of Cyberattacks Against Iran*, N.Y. TIMES (June 1, 2012), http://www.nytimes.com/2012/06/01/world/middleeast/obama-ordered-wave-of-cyberattacks-against-iran.html?pagewanted=all; Daniel Eshel, *Cyber-Attack Deploys in Israel's Order of Battle*, AVIATION WK. (Sept. 15, 2010).

[270] *See* Hamoud Salhi, *Assessing Theories of Information Technology and Security for the Middle East*, in INTERNATIONAL RELATIONS AND SECURITY IN THE DIGITAL AGE 106, 109 (Johan Eriksson & Giampiero Giacomello eds., 2007).

[271] *See* CLARKE & KNAKE, *supra* note 9, at 1–5.

[272] *Id.* at 5.

Israel's impressive cyber warfare capabilities reflect its military's recognition of, and actions to, manage the dangers and opportunities replete in cyberspace. In the 1990s, it "established a special authority to supervise" many aspects of Israeli cybersecurity.[273] This first-mover competitive advantage of being among the first nations to achieve cyber sophistication led Israeli cybersecurity firms to become market leaders, helping the Israeli Defense Forces (IDF), for example, to fend off a 2009 attack by Hamas on its Amos 3 spy satellite.[274] Other countries are taking note of Israel's successes. Former Royal Air Force Chief Marshal Sir Stephen Dalton has said, "Britain should take lessons from the Israeli military in Gaza in the use of sophisticated measures to engage in 21st century cyberwarfare."[275] Yet Israel has not always come out on top during cyber conflicts. During the Second Lebanon War in 2006, Hezbollah agents attacked Israeli communications systems, giving them an unprecedented real-time picture of Israeli troop movements, which according to one former Israeli general had "'disastrous' consequences for the Israeli offensive."[276] In response, the IDF has deployed a new computer network that is operating independently of the public Internet – the cyber arms race continues.

To help buttress its cyber defenses, Israel established an eGovernment initiative housed under the Ministry of Finance, which protects Israeli government systems. As of 2010, Israeli eGovernment consisted of approximately 250 people, 50 of whom were devoted to security matters.[277] One of these Israeli cybersecurity specialists, Assaf Keren, provided a window into Israeli cybersecurity during a 2010 NATO conference.[278] First, he laid out the difficult environment in which eGovernment operates. For example, after Israeli commandos raided a Turkish relief ship en route to the Gaza Strip, Keren reported: "[t]wo weeks of cyber attacks followed the flotilla incident, and that's typical."[279] To help meet this and similar onslaughts, Keren next noted that Israeli eGovernment has deployed a number of strategies. To illustrate one approach, consider how eGovernment dealt with the defacing of the Bank of Israel's homepage with a jihadist statement. After the attacks, the Bank's website was moved to eGovernment servers, where it has never since been defaced despite more than 250,000 reported attempts.[280] Because of its success at protecting Israel's government networks, Keren reported that Israeli eGovernment is now responsible for 95 percent of Israeli government websites. But how does Israel possess such detailed information

---

[273] Eshel, *supra* note 269.

[274] *Id.*

[275] *Id.*

[276] Mohamad Bazzi, *Hezbollah Cracked the Code; Technology Likely Supplied by Iran Allowed Guerilla to Stop Israeli Tank Assaults*, N.Y. NEWSDAY (Sept. 19, 2006), http://intelligence-summit.blogspot.com/2006/09/hezbollah-cracked-code.html.

[277] Assaf Keren, *E-Government Israel, Israeli Government Information Security Overview: Architecture, Attacks and Incident Response*, NATO CCDCOE Conf. Cyber Conflict, in Tallinn, Est. (June 16, 2010).

[278] *Id.*

[279] *Id.*

[280] *Id.*

on which systems are being compromised, and by whom? According to Keren, Israeli eGovernment has logged all data packets and Internet connections inside the Israeli government since 1997, and often each packet is analyzed several times to locate any malware.[281] In some ways then, Israeli cybersecurity could be a model for other nations. Indeed, its efforts at securing CNI began in the early 2000s, and in 2011 Israel established "a national cyber headquarters in the Prime Minister's Office."[282] However, despite Israel's impressive track record, it cannot secure cyber peace alone. No nation is an island in cyberspace. Multilateral cooperation is needed, yet this is difficult not only between antagonists, but also among close allies, as seen in the successes and failures of NATO's cybersecurity efforts.

Regional Cyber Defense: NATO Cybersecurity

During the cyber attack on Estonia, elements within Estonia's government discussed whether to consider invoking "NATO Article 5, which states that an assault on one allied country obligates the alliance to attack the aggressor[.]"[283] NATO Articles 4, 5, and 7 are the collective security mechanisms that underpin the alliance, and constitute NATO's key legal basis for engaging in the use of force, including armed attacks.[284] Eventually, Estonia did seek help – although not through Article 5 – initiating "the first time [in NATO history] that a member state had formally requested emergency assistance in the defense of its digital assets."[285] Among much else, the episode illustrated the lack of a coherent NATO cyber doctrine and strategy, which the alliance has since taken some steps to ameliorate.

Among the first times NATO formally grappled with how to respond to cyber attacks was in May 2008 during the Bucharest Summit.[286] Specifically, paragraph 47 of the Bucharest Summit Declaration states, "Our Policy on Cyber Defense emphasizes the need for NATO and nations to protect key information systems in accordance with their respective responsibilities; share best practices; and provide a capability to assist Allied nations, upon request, to counter a cyber attack."[287] There have so far been two tangible results from the Bucharest Summit. The first occurred when seven NATO nations and the Allied Command signed documents formalizing the creation of a Cooperative Cyber Defense (CCD) Centre of Excellence (COE)

---

[281] *Id.*

[282] Lior Tabansky, *Critical Infrastructure Protection Against Cyber Threats*, 3 MILITARY & STRATEGIC AFF. 61, 73 (Nov. 2011).

[283] Davis, *supra* note 72.

[284] North Atlantic Treaty, arts. 4, 5, 7, Apr. 4, 1949, 63 Stat. 2241, 34 U.N.T.S. 243, http://www.nato.int/cps/en/natolive/official_texts_17120.htm.

[285] Rex B. Hughes, *NATO and Cyber Defence: Mission Accomplished?*, NATO-OTAN, Apr. 2009, at 1, http://www.atlcom.nl/site/english/nieuws/wp-content/Hughes.pdf.

[286] *See id.*; NATO Topics: Defending Against Cyber Attacks, What Does This Mean in Practice?, http://www.nato.int/cps/en/natolive/75747.htm (last visited Dec. 21, 2012).

[287] Bucharest Summit Declaration, Sec. 47, North Atlantic Treaty Organization, Apr. 3, 2008, http://www.nato.int/cps/en/natolive/official_texts_8443.htm.

in Tallinn, Estonia.[288] This is the tenth NATO COE in existence, and the only one focused solely on cybersecurity. The second result of the Bucharest Summit was the creation of a new Cyber Defense Management Authority (CDMA) in Brussels, which is a NATO effort to centralize cyber defense capabilities.[289] The goal of the CDMA is to merge public- and private-sector cyber defense elements with an eye toward preventing, detecting, and deterring attacks from either state or non-state sources. Little public data exists as to the precise capabilities of the CDMA, but "it is thought to contain advanced real-time electronic monitoring capabilities for pinpointing threats and sharing critical cyber intelligence...."[290] Thus far, however, the organization has made relatively little public impact on the cybersecurity landscape.

Ultimately, the North Atlantic Council remains in overall control of NATO's cybersecurity policies. At this point, cyber attacks activate only Article 4 of the NATO treaty, requiring members only to "consult together" in cases of cyber attacks but not assist one another as required under Article 5.[291] Further steps need to be taken before NATO can effectively manage cyber attacks. These include coordinating the CERTs of NATO nations and ensuring that every CERT is fully staffed and trained.[292] National criminal laws relating to cyber attacks should also be further harmonized, norms created, and proposals such as the development of redundant networks of backup servers implemented. NATO will likely face blended attacks incorporating a cyber component in the future. So far, however, NATO has not been an appropriate forum for multilateral cooperation to enhance cybersecurity. Instead, regional – and particularly bilateral – relationships between close allies, such as the "five eyes" of the United States, United Kingdom, Canada, Australia, and New Zealand, are more robust – although the DOD signaled in its cyberspace strategy rollout that it might be seeking to expand this inner circle by reaching out to new partners.[293] This is consistent with the application of polycentric theory to cybersecurity to the extent that small groups prefer to undertake targeted measures in the face of multipolar opposition to a consensual approach.

"A panel of experts headed by" former U.S. Secretary of State Madeleine Albright "reported in May [2010] that cyber-attacks are among the three 'most probable threats

---

[288] See N. Atl. Treaty Org. Press Release, *NATO Opens New Centre of Excellence on Cyber Defence,* May 14, 2008, http://www.nato.int/docu/update/2008/05-may/e0514a.html.

[289] See Hughes, *supra* note 285; Kelly A. Gable, *Cyber-Apocalypse Now: Securing the Internet Against Cyberterrorism and Using Universal Jurisdiction as a Deterrent,* 43 VAND. J. TRANSNAT'L L. 57, 91 (2010).

[290] Hughes, *supra* note 285, at 2.

[291] Joshua McGee, *NATO and Cyber Defense: A Brief Overview and Recent Events,* CTR. STRAT. INT'L STUD. (July 8, 2011), http://csis.org/blog/nato-and-cyber-defense-brief-overview-and-recent-events.

[292] See Hughes, *supra* note 285, at 2–3, 5.

[293] See Hillary Rodham Clinton, *Remarks on the Release of President Obama Administration's International Strategy for Cyberspace,* U.S. DEP'T ST., May 16, 2011, http://www.state.gov/secretary/rm/2011/05/163523.htm; cf. Howard LaFranchi, *US Spying Scandal: Why Germany and France Won't Get Britain's Deal,* CHRISTAIN SCI. MONITOR (Oct. 28, 2013), http://www.csmonitor.com/World/Security-Watch/2013/1028/US-spying-scandal-Why-Germany-and-France-won-t-get-Britain-s-deal-video.

to the alliance[,]" and that a cyber attack "may be serious enough to merit a response under" Article 5.[294] Nevertheless, there is not yet a consensus on the question of whether or not Article 5 should be activated in the event of a true cyber attack. The only time that Article 5 has been invoked to date was after the 9/11 attacks. So far, the alliance has made the determination that "cyber attacks against NATO systems occur frequently, but most often below the threshold of political concern."[295] The question remains, then, how NATO will respond to cyber attacks falling above or close to that threshold.

Rex Hughes, a cybersecurity researcher at the University of Cambridge and the University of Toronto, effectively sums up the current status of NATO's cybersecurity strategy when he argues, "NATO is not ready to fight the first cyber conflict."[296] Indeed, there was only one paragraph on cybersecurity in the 2010 NATO Lisbon Summit Declaration.[297] CDMA is no CYBERCOM. There is still no defined NATO cyber defense strategy, or list of norms codifying best practices.

Other regional organizations are not faring much better. As one anonymous observer noted: "The EU is wearing a blindfold – we don't know how many teams we're playing against, and we don't even know the impact of the football if it goes in." However, the February 2013 EU draft cybersecurity strategy provides some cause for hope both at the national level, by requiring nations to establish cybersecurity performance standards and limit turf battles between agencies, and at the regional level, by clarifying the roles of CERT-EU, the European Network and Information Security Agency, and the European Cybercrime Center, among other agencies, to respond to different categories of cyber attacks up to a major incident potentially activating the EU Solidarity Clause.[298] Cecilia Malmström, EU Commissioner for Home Affairs, has summed the strategy up as follows: "The strategy has two overarching purposes. It provides a basis for greater cooperation between the different actors and, most importantly, shows the direction for future work[.]"[299] Impetus for the 2013 EU strategy stemmed from a growing lack of confidence on the part of EU

---

[294] James Joyner, *Cyber Attacks and Article 5*, NATO COUNCIL (July 2, 2010), http://www.acus.org/new_atlanticist/cyber-attacks-and-article-5.

[295] NATO 2020: ASSURED SECURITY; DYNAMIC ENGAGEMENT 45 (May 17, 2010), http://www.nato.int/cps/en/natolive/official_texts_63654.htm.

[296] Stmt. by Rex Hughes, NATO and Cyber Conflicts, NATO CCDCOE Conf. Cyber Conflict, in Tallinn, Est. (June 17, 2010).

[297] *See* NATO Lisbon Summit Declaration, Nov. 20, 2010, para. 40, http://www.nato.int/cps/en/natolive/official_texts_68828.htm.

[298] *See Joint Communication to the European Parliament, the Council, the European Economic and Social Committee and the Committee of the Regions: Cybersecurity Strategy of the European Union: An Open, Safe and Secure Cyberspace* 4–5, 17–19 (Feb. 7, 2013) [hereinafter *EU Cybersecurity Strategy*] (the proposal includes five strategic priorities: (1) to "achiev[e] cyber resilience"; (2) to "[d]rastically reduc[e] cybercrime; (3) to "develop[] [a new] cyberdefense policy"; (4) to "[d]evelop the industrial and technological resources for cybersecurity"; and (5) to "[e]stablish a coherent international cyberspace policy for the European Union and promote core EU values.").

[299] Nerea Rial, *What Comes after the Cyber Security Strategy?*, NEWEUROPE ONLINE (May 16, 2013), http://www.neurope.eu/article/what-comes-after-cyber-security-strategy.

citizens in the security of e-commerce platforms, as well as the interconnected nature of the EU market opening up familiar free rider and collective action problems.[300]

To sum up, an early international Internet regime came into being during the 1990s with the widespread adoption of the TCP/IP protocol.[301] In the years since, the notion of minimal national government involvement in Internet governance has been challenged. There are now more than 250 CERTs operating worldwide, but cooperation between them remains limited, forming an impediment to information sharing that organizations such as IMPACT are attempting to address.[302] Instead, the strategies of each cyber power demonstrate that they are pursuing a largely state-centric approach to cybersecurity, though this may be changing to an extent with the renewed focus on international engagement by the Obama administration and within the EU. Indeed, there seems to be a governance spectrum emerging in relation to securing CNI in particular with nations such as the U.S. and the UK preferring a more voluntary approach and other cyber powers including Russia and China opting for a larger role for the state. The 2013 EU cybersecurity strategy seems to fall toward the middle of the spectrum, with calls for establishing "appropriate cybersecurity performance requirements" as well as mandatory reporting for cyber attacks having a "significant impact" on firms operating across a broad array of sectors.[303]

Time and experience will tell which approach is more effective at securing CNI, but at least three trends are prevalent. First, states are reorganizing old and creating new government entities to regulate and develop policy for CNI. As states shift responsibility for CNI to clarify turf battles, they may look to one another to determine best practices, such as the benefits and drawbacks of centralizing cybersecurity command authority. Second, states are struggling to determine which systems and industries should be considered the *most* "critical" infrastructures.[304] Third, governments are increasingly concerned about the extent to which they can trust global IT hardware and software supply chains,[305] leading to efforts aimed at mitigating supply chain risk such as through the exclusion of certain vendors and the encouragement of domestic innovation. Ultimately cyber peace requires not only that nations take responsibility for the security of their own networks, but also that they work together

---

[300] *EU Cybersecurity Strategy, supra* note 298, at 2, 17 (suggesting that national responses to certain cyber attacks will likely involve direct EU-level involvement to a degree).

[301] *See* MARKUS FRANDA, GOVERNING THE INTERNET: THE EMERGENCE OF AN INTERNATIONAL REGIME 203 (2001).

[302] *See Roles and Functions,* IMPACT, http://certlite.impact-alliance.org/portal/about-us/roles-functions/ (last visited June 19, 2013).

[303] *EU Cybersecurity Strategy, supra* note 298, at 2, 12.

[304] Though the United States has maintained a core list of CNI industries for more than a decade, the list evolves; for example, prisons and industrial capacity have been crossed off, special events and national monuments were added and then dropped, and the defense industrial base was added. *See* John Moteff & Paul Parfomak, *Critical Infrastructure and Key Assets: Definition and Identification,* CONG. RES. SERV., RL32631 at 1–3 (2004), http://www.fas.org/sgp/crs/RL32631.pdf.

[305] *See, e.g.,* CHARNEY & WERNER, *supra* note 251, at 4–6.

to build robust regimes that promote the public good of global cybersecurity. Doing so requires agreeing on the detriments of the prevailing status quo, such as the danger of false attribution and escalation, while focusing on areas of common concern, as is explored in Chapter 7.

A POLYCENTRIC APPROACH TO SECURING CRITICAL NATIONAL INFRASTRUCTURE

The central premise of this chapter is that in order to attain cyber peace, it is necessary to study cyber war. A vital component of both cyber war and peace is CNI. Nations define CNI differently based on an array of socioeconomic and political factors,[306] and use varying regulatory mechanisms to enhance cybersecurity.[307] The unsatisfactory status quo in the United States has led some to argue that the U.S. government must do more to secure CNI,[308] a path also being followed by European, Chinese, and Russian authorities, among others. But protecting CNI should not only be of interest to national regulators given that network effects spill across borders.[309] Many private sector CNI companies operate across jurisdictions, and some infrastructure – such as the finance sector – is by its nature international, further complicating the international legal environment.[310] Some, though, have questioned the ability of legal controls in cyberspace to enhance cybersecurity, a topic returned to in Chapters 5 and 6.

Efforts to regulate CNI through the law alone may be insufficient, as seen in the experience of countries attempting to erase obscene content in cyberspace.[311] To date, no country has successfully eradicated obscene materials from its domestic Internet without comprehensive filtering.[312] Supporters of legal intervention point to the early successes of the Budapest Convention, but the continued prevalence of cybercrime has prompted a new round of international negotiations.[313] Nevertheless,

---

[306] Tabansky, *supra* note 282, at 62 ("Infrastructure is defined as critical when it is believed that disrupting its function would lead to a significant socio-economic crisis with the potential to undermine the stability of a society and thereby cause political, strategic, and security consequences.").

[307] *See* Moteff & Parfomak, *supra* note 304, at 8, 12.

[308] *See* Sean M. Condron, *Getting It Right: Protecting American Critical Infrastructure in Cyberspace*, 20(2) HARV. J. L. & TECH. 404, 422 (2007).

[309] *See* MURRAY, *supra* note 164, at 53; Stewart Baker, Shaun Waterman, & George Ivanov, *In the Crossfire: Critical Infrastructure in the Age of Cyber War*, MCAFEE 24–31 (2009), http://www.mcafee.com/us/resources/reports/rp-in-crossfire-critical-infrastructure-cyber-war.pdf; *National Policies for Protecting Critical Infrastructure to Drive Billions in Cyber Security Spending*, ABI RES. (June 18, 2013), http://www.abiresearch.com/press/national-policies-for-protecting-critical-infrastr.

[310] *See, e.g.*, Taylor Armerding, *Critical Infrastructure Protection: Are We Prepared for a Massive Cyberattack on U.S. Systems?*, CSO (July 1, 2013), http://www.csoonline.com/article/735736/critical-infrastructure-protection-are-we-prepared-for-a-massive-cyberattack-on-u.s.-systems-.

[311] *See* MURRAY, *supra* note 164, at 227.

[312] *Id.*

[313] *See* Brian Harley, *A Global Convention on Cybercrime?*, COLUM. SCI. & TECH. L. REV. (2010), http://www.stlr.org/2010/03/a-global-convention-on-cybercrime/.

as technology advances along with the geopolitical importance of cyberspace, more nations are expanding the scope of data monitoring and domestic regulation as was introduced in Chapter 2.[314] Some of these efforts take the form of crafting national cybersecurity strategies aimed at winning cyber wars and securing CNI. The United States has taken steps in this direction with the establishment of CYBERCOM, as have the United Kingdom, China, Russia, and Israel. Cybersecurity best practices identified as a result of these efforts, and informed by private-sector expertise as is discussed in the next chapter, should be followed with states acting as norm entrepreneurs.[315] Yet enforcement remains a daunting problem,[316] as does addressing the identified trends in cyber conflict, including checking the growing prevalence of sophisticated state-sponsored cyber attacks.

Nations do not have a monopoly in cyber regulation.[317] Nor can any nation acting alone achieve cyber peace. Regulations must be supported by other nations, beginning with close allies, but eventually expanding outwards to include the wider international community so as to avoid the creation of safe harbors.[318] Because of the interconnected status of the cyberspace regulatory environment, it is useful to consider a polycentric approach to securing CNI. As with managing the technical vulnerabilities in the Internet, securing CNI requires targeted measures by individual nations and groups of nations to address the global collective action problem of cyber attacks. The beginnings of this may be seen in NATO, although there is much room for improvement. Like the IETF model, there is scope for both bottom-up governance in the form of industries creating norms of conduct enshrining best practices, as well as a role for governments in regulating at-risk CNI for the public good. Although there are some benefits in government involvement in cybersecurity such as to promote equity and proportionality between actors as well as providing for effective monitoring and graduated sanctions consistent with Professor Ostrom's design principles,[319] the heavy-handed approach favored by such nations as Russia and China should be critically assessed lest innovation and civil liberties

---

[314] *See* Ronald J. Deibert & Nart Villeneuve, *Firewalls and Power: An Overview of Global State Censorship of the Internet*, *in* HUMAN RIGHTS IN THE DIGITAL AGE 111, 111 (Mathias Klang & Andrew Murray eds., 2005).

[315] *See* TIM MAURER, CYBER NORM EMERGENCE AT THE UNITED NATIONS: AN ANALYSIS OF THE ACTIVITIES AT THE UN REGARDING CYBER-SECURITY 47 (2011).

[316] *See* SUSAN J. BUCK, THE GLOBAL COMMONS: AN INTRODUCTION 78–79 (1998).

[317] *See* MURRAY, *supra* note 164, at 47.

[318] *Id.* at 228; Marthie Grobler & Joey Jansen van Vuuren, *Broadband Broadens Scope for Cyber Crime in Africa*, PROC. 2010 INFO. SEC. SOUTH AFRICA CONF., in Sandton, South Africa (Aug. 2–4, 2010), http://researchspace.csir.co.za/dspace/bitstream/10204/4338/1/Grobler1_2010.pdf.

[319] *See* Elinor Ostrom, *Polycentric Systems: Multilevel Governance Involving a Diversity of Organizations*, *in* GLOBAL ENVIRONMENTAL COMMONS: ANALYTICAL AND POLITICAL CHALLENGES INVOLVING A DIVERSITY OF ORGANIZATIONS 105, 118–20 (Eric Brousseau et al. eds., 2012) (citing ELINOR OSTROM, GOVERNING THE COMMONS: THE EVOLUTION OF INSTITUTIONS FOR COLLECTIVE ACTION 90 (1990)).

suffer. As FCC commissioner Robert McDowell has said, "No government . . . can make . . . decisions in lightning-fast Internet time."[320]

This chapter has analyzed the development and history of cyber conflict as well as the cybersecurity strategies of the cyber powers. Results have been mixed. Whereas some nations have made significant progress in managing the cyber threat, others have lagged behind. Israel, for example, has distinguished itself as a leader in cybersecurity by recognizing the threat early on and taking steps to mount an effective defense. How difficult it has been for the cyber powers to secure their own systems from attack illustrates why relying on an exclusively state-centric approach to cybersecurity may be problematic, underscoring the need for polycentric governance that includes private-sector engagement along with multilateral collaboration.

This was far from an exhaustive review of the voluminous literature on cyber war and CNI security. Rather, the primary goal here was to present the scope of the problems facing states when strategizing about how best ways to manage cyber conflict, as well as analyze how the cyber powers are approaching this challenge with special reference to CNI. Yet the only way to truly secure CNI along with some measure of cyber peace is by managing the cyber risk to the private sector, which is the subject we turn to next.

---

[320] Jerry Brito, *The Case Against Letting the U.N. Govern the Internet*, Time (Feb. 13, 2012), http://techland .time.com/2012/02/13/the-case-against-letting-the-united-nations-govern-the-internet/#ixzz28OQI UoDs.

5

Risky Business

Enhancing Private-Sector Cybersecurity

We're an information-based society now. Information is everything. That makes ... company executives, the front line – not the support mechanism, the front line – in [determining] what comes.

– Director of the Office of National Counterintelligence Executive Frank Montoya, Jr.[1]

For a firm possessing something of value, security is merely a deterrent, not a guarantee. Consider the Louvre, which has long been one of the largest, most visited, and sophisticated art museums in the world.[2] Yet in 1911, Vincenzo Peruggia walked out of the Louvre with the Mona Lisa under his jacket.[3] Every institution is fallible, but we do tend to expect more from those at the top of their field. Google, for example, has been so successful that its trademarked name has been repurposed as an oft-used verb.[4] So it stands to reason that Google would have security to match its reputation. However, Google's engineers cannot make vulnerability vanish any more than the security officers at the Louvre did in 1911; like every other company that uses computer systems or the Internet, it is susceptible to cyber attacks. How businesses manage these attacks and the role that government and other stakeholders should play in enhancing private-sector cybersecurity is another key component to fostering cyber peace.

Consider what was reported on January 12, 2010. Cyber attacks allegedly emanating from within China were directed at stealing Google's intellectual property along

---

[1] Tom Gjelten, *Bill Would Have Businesses Foot Cost of Cyberwar*, NPR (May 8, 2012), http://www.npr.org/2012/05/08/152219617/bill-would-have-businesses-foot-cost-of-cyber-war.

[2] *See* 2011 *Exhibition and Museum Attendance Figures*, ART NEWSPAPER Apr. 2012, at 35, www.theartnewspaper.com/attfig/attfig11.pdf.

[3] *See* HUGH MCLEAVE, ROGUES IN THE GALLERY: THE MODERN PLAGUE OF ART THEFTS 6, 25 (2003).

[4] *See* Nick Bilton, *For Start-Ups, the Ultimate Goal: Becoming a Verb*, N.Y. TIMES (Nov. 30, 2010), http://bits.blogs.nytimes.com/2010/11/30/for-start-ups-the-ultimate-goal-becoming-a-verb/.

with at least thirty other corporations.[5] These attacks, dubbed "Operation Aurora" by McAfee, were part of a sophisticated campaign using spear phishing attacks and at least one zero-day exploit.[6] In Google's case, the attacks were noteworthy for at least three reasons. First is who the attackers targeted, which included Chinese human rights activists' Gmail accounts.[7] Second is the type of IP that was targeted: the companies' source code; that is, its "crown jewels."[8] Such an attack was largely unprecedented and indicative of changes in the cyber threat matrix. "We have never ever, outside of the defense industry, seen commercial industrial companies come under that level of sophisticated attack," said Dmitri Alperovitch, vice president of threat research for McAfee, in the wake of Aurora.[9]

Attacks like Aurora have been termed "advanced persistent threats" (APTs),[10] and although governments and defense industries have long been addressing these sorts of threats, corporate entities are now becoming targets of APTs as well.[11] This leads us to the third reason for why Auroa was noteworthy: the campaign illustrated the extent to which state-sponsored attacks – in this case allegedly emanating from China – are targeting private firms.[12] Hackers are oftentimes no longer "kids having fun[,]"[13] though individual hackers can still pose significant challenges to companies as appears to be the case in the Christmas 2013 hack of Target affecting some 110 million customers,[14] illustrating the evolution of cyber attacks from Solar Sunrise

---

[5]   *See, e.g., Operation Aurora,* INFOSEC DAILY (Jan. 15, 2010), http://www.isdpodcast.com/episode-47-operation-aurora/; Kim Zetter, *Google Hack Attack Was Ultra Sophisticated, New Details Show,* WIRED (Jan. 14, 2010), http://www.wired.com/threatlevel/2010/01/operation-aurora/.

[6]   *See* Michael J. Gross, *Enter the Cyber-dragon,* VANITY FAIR (Sept. 2011), http://www.vanityfair.com/culture/features/2011/09/chinese-hacking-201109; Brian Grow & Mark Hosenball, *Special Report: In Cyberspy vs. Cyberspy, China Has the Edge,* REUTERS (Apr. 14, 2011), http://www.reuters.com/article/2011/04/14/us-china-usa-cyberespionage-idUSTRE73D24220110414; Kim Zetter, *'Google' Hackers Had Ability to Alter Source Code,* WIRED (Mar. 3, 2010), http://www.wired.com/threatlevel/2010/03/source-code-hacks/.

[7]   *A New Approach to China,* OFFICIAL GOOGLE BLOG (Jan. 12, 2010), http://googleblog.blogspot.com/2010/01/new-approach-to-china.html.

[8]   Zetter, *supra* note 6.

[9]   Zetter, *supra* note 5.

[10]   *Protecting Your Critical Assets: Lessons Learned From "Operation Aurora,"* MCAFEE, at 3 (Mar. 1, 2010), http://www.mcafee.com/us/resources/white-papers/wp-protecting-critical-assets.pdf.

[11]   *Id.*

[12]   *See Report to Congress,* U.S.-CHINA ECON. & SEC. REV. COMMISSION 168 (U.S. Naval Inst., 2012) ("In 2012, Chinese state-sponsored actors continued to exploit government, military, indsutrial, and nongovernmental computer systems."); VERIZON, DATA BREACH INVESTIGATIONS REPORT 5, 21–22 (2013), http://www.verizonenterprise.com/DBIR/2013/ [hereinafter DBIR 2013] (reporting that state-sponsored attacks accounted for 19 percent of all reported attacks, with organized crime being the biggest external source at 55 percent).

[13]   Interview with Chris Palmer, Google engineer and former technology director, Electronic Frontier Foundation, in San Francisco, Cal. (Feb. 25, 2011).

[14]   *See* Marie-Louise Gumuchian & David Goldman, *Security Firm Traces Target Malware to Russia,* CNN (Jan. 21, 2014), http://www.cnn.com/2014/01/20/us/money-target-breach/ ("A security firm that had pointed the finger at a 17-year-old Russian last week updated its report Monday to identify a different Russian resident as being responsible for writing the malware used in an attack compromised the credit card numbers and other personal information of up to 110 million Target customers.").

to Stuxnet as discussed in Chapter 4. Instead, companies need to be defending against whoever their most sophisticated attacker is likely to be. In the case of large corporations like Google, that includes governments.

As groundbreaking as Operation Aurora was to the commercial and security communities, soon thereafter the "Night Dragon" attacks resulted in global oil, gas, and petrochemical companies also losing sensitive data and intellectual property that "can make or break multibillion dollar deals. . . . "[15] Like Aurora, these attacks were reportedly launched by servers located within China, although "hosted services in the United States and compromised servers in the Netherlands" were also used to breach energy firms located "in Kazakhstan, Taiwan, Greece, and the United States. . . . "[16] Unlike Aurora, however, Night Dragon was not particularly sophisticated,[17] though targeted attacks like Night Dragon are on the rise across an array of industries.[18] For example, more than seventy different governments and organizations, including the United Nations, India, the International Olympic Committee, and defense and security firms were the targets of cyber attacks dubbed "Operation Shady RAT" by McAfee.[19] Unlike the Night Dragon attacks, these attacks were not confined to a particular sector,[20] but like Night Dragon, there is speculation that elements within China were behind them.[21] This lends some credence to the U.S. Office of the National Counterintelligence Executive's conclusion that "Chinese actors are the world's most active and persistent perpetrators of economic espionage."[22]

However, cyber attacks on the private sector did not suddenly emerge in 2010; indeed, there is evidence that the Night Dragon and Shady RAT attacks themselves

---

[15] George Kurtz, *Global Energy Industry Hit in "Night Dragon" Attacks*, McAfee (Feb. 10, 2011), http://blogs.mcafee.com/corporate/cto/global-energy-industry-hit-in-night-dragon-attacks.

[16] *Global Energy Cyberattacks: "Night Dragon,"* McAfee, at 4 (2011), http://www.mcafee.com/us/resources/white-papers/wp-global-energy-cyberattacks-night-dragon.pdf.

[17] *Id.* at 7.

[18] *Id.* at 13; Charlie Sherlock, *Industrial Control Systems: Cyber Attack and Operational Security Solution Overview*, Cypro Software, Oct. 2012, at 22 (stating that "[w]ell coordinated, targeted attacks such as Night Dragon, orchestrated by a growing number of malicious attackers . . . are rapidly on the rise.").

[19] *See* Dmitri Alperovitch, *Revealed: Operation Shady RAT*, McAfee, at 6–9 (2011), http://www.mcafee .com/us/resources/white-papers/wp-operation-shady-rat.pdf.

[20] *See* Drew Amorosi, *You Dirty, Shady RAT*, Info Sec. (Oct. 19, 2011), http://www.infosecurity-magazine.com/view/21462/you-dirty-shady-rat/.

[21] *See, e.g.*, Ellen Nakashima, *Report on 'Operation Shady RAT' Identifies Widespread Cyber-Spying*, Wash. Post (Aug. 2, 2011), http://www.washingtonpost.com/national/national-security/report-identifies-widespread-cyber-spying/2011/07/29/gIQAoTUmqI_story.html. *But see* Amorosi, *supra* note 20 (discussing some of the controversies surrounding the Shady RAT report); *China Refutes McAfee Claims It was Behind Shady RAT Attacks*, Info. Sec. (Aug. 5, 2011), http://www.infosecurity-magazine .com/view/19908/china-refutes-mcafee-claims-it-was-behind-shady-rat-attacks/ (reporting on the PRC's response denying McAfee's allegations involving Shady RAT).

[22] Off. Nat'l Counterintelligence Exec., Report to Congress on Foreign Economic Collection and Industrial Espionage: Foreign Spies Stealing U.S. Economic Secrets in Cyberspace, 2009–2011 at i (Oct. 2011) [hereinafter Foreign Spies]; *see also* DBIR 2013, *supra* note 12, at 21 (maintaining that "96 percent of espionage cases were attributed to threat actors in China and the remaining 4 percent were unknown.").

may have been ongoing since 2006.[23] Many companies and countries alike have been experiencing cyber attacks since at least the 1990s. But how has the cyber threat to the private sector evolved, and how might it be characterized today? Are particular industry sectors at increased risk? What role should governments play alongside firms in securing CNI? And how can markets – together with laws, norms, and code – be used to help shape the regulatory landscape and promote cyber peace?

This chapter analyzes how cyber attacks have affected the private sector, focusing on the decade from 2001 to 2011, and summarizes what challenges may be on the horizon. It argues that firms must take a proactive strategy to manage cyber attacks for their own competitive wellbeing as well as to enhance overall cybersecurity and help secure CNI. Leaving cybersecurity solely to the market may well be insufficient to foster cyber peace,[24] so an analysis is undertaken of market-based incentives and regulatory interventions. The chapter is divided into three sections. First, survey data are analyzed to help reveal the frequency and cost associated with cyber attacks, describing how these statistics have changed over time, and which industry sectors are particularly at risk. The sources and limitations of these data are also considered, and new data is presented from one large organization with more than 500 employees. Next, best practices that may be used to manage cyber threats are evaluated, providing examples of proactive and reactive strategies, budgetary limitations, operational strategies, risk assessment, technical debt, and policy development. Individual case studies include Microsoft, Google, and Facebook, as well as examples from smaller firms.[25] Finally, various regulatory mechanisms are analyzed to consider their potential for enhancing private-sector cybersecurity within a polycentric framework.

DEFINING THE CYBER THREAT TO THE PRIVATE SECTOR

Given the effectiveness of Aurora and Night Dragon, among other recent cyber attacks including those on Target and Neiman Marcus, more firms are becoming aware of the need for better cybersecurity.[26] In an international survey conducted

---

[23] *See* Alperovitch, *supra* note 19, at 6; Michael Joseph Gross, *Operation Shady RAT – Unprecedented Cyber-espionage Campaign and Intellectual-Property Bonanza*, VANITY FAIR (Aug. 2, 2011), http://www.vanityfair.com/culture/features/2011/09/operation-shady-rat-201109.

[24] *See* ANDREW W. MURRAY, THE REGULATION OF CYBERSPACE: CONTROL IN THE ONLINE ENVIRONMENT 168, 176 (2006); *Developing Cyber Security Synergy*, CYBER SEC. POL'Y & RES. INST. 14 (2011).

[25] These exampes and case studies were selected merely to help introduce the role that businesses can play in promoting cyber peace. There are an array of other firms and organizations deserving of further study in this regard, including the Global Network Initiative. *See* Global Network Initiative, www.globalnetworkinitiative.org/ (last visited Feb. 10, 2014).

[26] *Cf.* Lily Hay Newman, *A 17-Year-Old Was Behind the Target, Neiman Marcus Credit Card Hacks*, SLATE (Jan. 20, 2014), http://www.slate.com/blogs/future_tense/2014/01/20/target_neiman_marcus_credit_card_number_hacks_were_caused_by_a_17_year_old.html (noting that "with so many reports that other companies have been hacked but have not yet come forward, it seems to be time for a discussion about security breach disclosures for retailers.").

by Symantec in 2010, cyber attacks or data loss topped a majority of the surveyed companies' list of concerns.[27] In fact, 42 percent of respondents ranked cyber attacks as their organizations' most significant risk, trumping natural disasters, terrorism, and traditional crime.[28] Nevertheless, this general concern is not always followed by prompt or effective action. As such, this section attempts to quantify and qualify the cyber threat to the private sector to encourage risk-based analysis while noting some of the constraints on cyber threat data gathering. Employing publicly available information, four questions are considered: How often do cyber attacks happen? Which industries are most at risk? What types of attacks occur most frequently? And how much do they cost?

The Trouble with Data

At the outset, there are at least two elements required to assess a problem: a clear definition of the difficulty, and a shared, reliable way to measure outcomes. Consider how the risk of experiencing street crime is gauged. If you walked down the street somewhere in Detroit, Michigan, or St. Louis, Missouri, in 2008 – two of the U.S. cities with the highest violent crime statistics – there was roughly a 2 percent chance that you would have witnessed a violent crime.[29] The FBI warns that such simplistic statistical analyses "provide no insight into the many variables that mold . . . crime" in a particular place, and "create misleading perceptions. . . . "[30] Still, there are some variables that make crime statistics generally useful and reliable. For one, the FBI's Uniform Crime Reporting program has a common definition of violent crime as "murder and nonnegligent manslaughter, forcible rape, robbery, and aggravated assault."[31] Second, we can attach monetary value to violent crime because we have some understanding of its financial consequences.[32] Finally, numbers are available and reliable because cities must report such statistics annually.[33]

Unfortunately, the elements that have made crime statistics relatively meaningful are not in place for cyber attacks. Consensus on what constitutes a cyber attack has been slow to emerge, as was introduced in the Preface. Without greater clarification, firms are disincentivized from information sharing. For example, Jim Hutchins, the

[27] *See* STATE OF ENTERPRISE SECURITY STUDY, SYMANTEC, at 6 (2010), http://www.symantec.com/about/news/resources/press_kits/detail.jsp?pkid=sesreport2010 [hereinafter STATE OF ENTERPRISE SECURITY].

[28] *See id.; Survey: SMBs are Getting Serious about Information Protection,* SYMANTEC (2010), http://www.symantec.com/about/news/resources/press_kits/detail.jsp?pkid=smbsurvey2010.

[29] *2009 Uniform Crime Reports,* FBI (Sept. 2010), http://www.fbi.gov/about-us/cjis/ucr/crime-in-the-u.s/2009.

[30] *Variables Affecting Crime,* FBI, http://www2.fbi.gov/ucr/cius2009/about/variables_affecting_crime.html (last visited Jan. 21, 2014).

[31] *Violent Crime: Crime in the United States,* FBI, http://www2.fbi.gov/ucr/cius2009/offenses/violent_crime/index.html (last visited Jan. 21, 2014).

[32] *See, e.g.,* Michael Shank, *New Study Shows Violence Costing America Over $460 Billion,* HUFF. POST (Apr. 24, 2012), http://www.huffingtonpost.com/michael-shank/cost-of-violence_b_1450173.html.

[33] *See Uniform Crime Reports,* FBI, http://www.fbi.gov/about-us/cjis/ucr/ucr (last visited Jan. 21, 2014).

chief technology officer at T2 Systems, an Indianapolis-based company that provides data management and integrated software and hardware technology for parking systems, said that he would not bother reporting regular DDoS attacks because if the government "got reports on all of those attacks, then they'd be overwhelmed."[34] Attaching value is also a challenge because it can be difficult to assess the consequences of cyber attacks for users and firms. If malware is slowing down your computer, you may not feel compelled to address it; however, if you knew it was also stealing your passwords, you would likely act fast to remove it.

Assessing cyber attack data in the United States are difficult for three main reasons. First, almost no one is demanding and few are asking for it, though this is beginning to change. Information-sharing organizations do exist, but most are not publicly available and are often devoted to particular industry sectors. For example, whereas institutions might internally track attacks or provide data to industry groups like the Financial Services Roundtable or government partnerships such as InfraGard and the Information Sharing and Analysis Centers (ISACs), there is "no common information sharing model" and no single authority with a clear mandate to collect or keep track of cyber attack information.[35] The Securities and Exchange Commission (SEC) published its views on disclosure requirements in 2011, and although it stopped short of requiring publicly traded firms to disclose all cyber attacks, it interpreted existing regulations broadly, for example, in requiring disclosure of "material" attacks leading to financial losses,[36] and hinted that additional reporting requirements may be coming.[37] Second, companies rarely feel compelled to voluntarily compile, organize, and transmit data about breaches in part because of liability concerns. In responding to a request for comments from the U.S. Department of Commerce in September 2010, Microsoft wrote that past voluntary gathering methods have "largely been ineffective" due to personnel costs

---

[34] Telephone Interview with Jim Hutchins, CIO, T2 Systems, in Indianapolis, Ind. (May 23, 2011).

[35] Joe Waldron, *Comments of VeriSign, Inc, VeriSign Response to NOI 100721305–0305-01*, DEP'T COMM. INTERNET POL'Y TASK FORCE (Sept. 13, 2010), at 2, http://www.nist.gov/itl/upload/VeriSign_Cybersecurity-NOI-Comments-9-13-10.pdf.

[36] DIV. OF CORP. FIN., U.S. SEC. & EXCH. COMM'N, CF DISCLOSURE GUIDANCE: TOPIC NO. 2 CYBERSECURITY 9 (Oct. 13, 2011), https://www.sec.gov/divisions/corpfin/guidance/cfguidance-topic2.htm; Joel Bronstein, *The Balance Between Informing Investors and Protecting Companies: A Look at the Division of Corporation Finance's Recent Guidelines on Cybersecurity Disclosure Requirements*, 13 N.C. J.L. & TECH. ON. 257, 271 (2012) (citing TSC Indus., Inc. v. Northway, Inc., 426 U.S. 438, 449 (1976), which defined "material" as "a substantial likelihood that the disclosure of the omitted fact would have been viewed by the reasonable investor as having significantly altered the 'total mix' of information made available.").

[37] *See, e.g., SEC Staff Provides Guidance on Disclosure Obligations Relating to Cybersecurity Risks and Cyber Incidents*, WSGR ALERT (Oct. 18, 2011), http://www.wsgr.com/WSGR/Display.aspx?Section Name=publications/PDFSearch/wsgralert-cybersecurity-risks.htm [hereinafter WSGR ALERT]; Chris Strohm, *SEC Chairman Reviewing Company Cybersecurity Disclosures*, BLOOMBERG (May 13, 2013), http://www.bloomberg.com/news/2013-05-13/sec-chairman-reviewing-company-cybersecurity-disclosures.html (reporting that the SEC is exploring strenthening cyber attack disclosure requirements).

and a lack of trust in how shared information will be managed.[38] In other words, the process is time-consuming, and if the data are somehow released to the public, it could affect companies' reputations and bottom lines. This is in spite of the fact that studies that have shown that cybersecurity should be viewed as a "value creator" supporting e-business, not as merely a "cost of doing business."[39] This is an argument for treating cybersecurity as one element of corporate social responsibility, or perhaps even corporate foreign policy.[40] It is in corporations' own long-term self-interest (as well as that of national security) to take such a wider view of private-sector risk management, as former U.S. Cybersecurity Coordinator Howard Schmidt, among others, has argued.[41] According to Professor Lawrence Gordon, "the most powerful incentive for an organization in the private sector to invest in cybersecurity activities is the motivation to increase the organization's value to its owners."[42] Assessing that value, though, can be difficult due to misaligned incentives; for example, LinkedIn's "stock price actually rose days after" a cyberattacker breached its system and stole more than "six million of its customers' passwords."[43] Indeed, studies have found that, if anything, investors seem to be less concerned about cybersecurity incidents than they were before 9/11.[44]

Third, there may be insufficient perceived benefit in reporting cyber attacks owing to a lack of confidence in law enforcement. The Computer Security Institute (CSI) surveys hundreds of U.S. cybersecurity practitioners annually to determine the extent to which they share information about cyber attacks. It found that less

[38] Microsoft Response to the Department of Commerce Notice of Inquiry on Cybersecurity, Innovation and the Information Economy, NIST Docket No.: 100721305–0305-01 (Sept. 20, 2010), at 3, http://www.nist.gov/itl/upload/Microsoft_Cybersecurity-NOI-Comments_9-20-10.pdf.

[39] Huseyin Cavusoglu, *Economics of IT Security Management, in* ECONOMICS OF INFORMATION SECURITY 71, 73 (L. Jean Camp & Stephen Lewis eds., 2004).

[40] *See* Jody R. Westby, *Governance of Enterprise Security*, CYLAB 2012 REPORT, May 16, 2012, at 26 ("Organizations can enhance their reputation by valuing cybersecurity and the protection of privacy and viewing it as a corporate social responsibility."); Timothy L. Fort, *Corporate Foreign Policy*, Q. FIN. (forthcoming, 2014).

[41] Howard A. Schmidt, *Price of Inaction Will Be Onerous*, N.Y. TIMES (Oct. 17, 2012), http://www.nytimes.com/roomfordebate/2012/10/17/should-industry-face-more-cybersecurity-mandates/price-of-inaction-on-cybersecurity-will-be-the-greatest ("[w]hile there is a cost to doing more to improve cybersecurity, there is a bigger cost if we do not and that cost is measured not only in dollars, but in national security and public safety.").

[42] *Incentives for Improving Cybersecurity in the Private Sector: A Cost-Benefit Perspective, H. Comm. on Homeland Security*, 110th Cong. 1, 1 (2007) (statement of Lawrence. A. Gordon, professor, University of Maryland), http://hsc-democrats.house.gov/SiteDocuments/20071031155020-22632.pdf.

[43] Nicole Perlroth, *Lax Security at LinkedIn Is Laid Bare*, N.Y. TIMES (June 10, 2012), http://www.nytimes.com/2012/06/11/technology/linkedin-breach-exposes-light-security-even-at-data-companies.html (claiming that companies like LinkedIn have little incentive to bolster security efforts due to an absence of "legal penalties" and low risk of customer defection).

[44] *See* Lawrence A. Gordon, Martin P. Loeb, & Lei Zhou, *The Impact of Information Security Breaches: Has There Been a Downward Shift in Costs?*, 19 J. COMPUTER SEC. 33, 33 (2011) (aruing that "[t]wo possible reasons for this downward shift are (1) more effective remediation and disaster recovery and (2) a perceived decrease in the tendency of customers to refrain from doing business with firms experiencing an information security breach.").

than one third reported intrusions to law enforcement or legal counsel from 2004 to 2008.[45] In short, Google's handling of Aurora notwithstanding, many firms are reticent to report breaches to the authorities. Admitting to imperfect security may undermine consumer trust, which is one reason why information sharing has been a key component of proposed U.S. cybersecurity reform legislation.[46]

Gathering data to quantify the cyber threat to the private sector is only the beginning. Calculating the costs of attacks is also challenging, especially the impact on brand reputation, the price of downtime,[47] legal liability, and costs associated with a "competitor's access to confidential or proprietary information."[48] Some have gone so far as to argue that financial information about cybercrime reflects only "approximate guesses."[49]

If calculating losses is difficult, mitigating risk is even more complex. Partly in recognition of the immature "state of cybersecurity metrics as a practical art," the Index of Cyber Security – a website that intends to be a resource for information security professionals – employs "sentiment-based" surveys.[50] Rather than asking IT security professionals for their data, the survey asks about their perceptions of risk. Because those perceptions are based on experience, being aware of such sentiments provides some worthwhile guidance to other professionals. However, it does little to address the challenge of accumulating reliable data to develop robust metrics.

Without clear definitions, shared and meaningful values, or reliable data, information about cyber attacks affecting the private sector and analyses of their organizational or financial impacts remains limited and unsophisticated. Despite the complexity of the problem, though, some resources do exist for at-risk firms, including surveys and reports by the U.S. government and security vendors like McAfee, as well as research centers like CSI. These surveys and reports, which are relied on throughout this chapter along with interviews and new empirical data, have attempted to work around some the difficulties identified. However, due to the previously described limitations, contextual information about these sources is

---

[45] *See* Lawrence A. Gordon et al., 2006 *CSI/FBI Computer Crime and Security Survey*, COMPUTER SEC. INST. (CSI), at 2, http://i.cmpnet.com/gocsi/db_area/pdfs/fbi/FBI2006.pdf [hereinafter 2006 CSI Survey]; Robert Richardson, *CSI Computer Crime & Security Survey*, CSI at 13 (2008), http://i.cmpnet.com/v2.gocsi.com/pdf/CSIsurvey2008.pdf [hereinafter 2008 CSI Survey].

[46] *See, e.g.*, Emil Protalinski, *Senate Blocks Cybersecurity Act*, ZDNET (Aug. 2, 2012), http://www.zdnet.com/senate-blocks-cybersecurity-act-7000002051/ (discussing the failure of the Cybersecurity Act of 2012).

[47] *See, e.g.*, Katherine O'Callaghan et al., *Managing Unplanned IT Outages*, CIO (Jan. 26, 2010), http://cio.co.nz/cio.nsf/depth/6ADE938F9B29DB40CC2576B600673837.

[48] Cavusoglu, *supra* note 39, at 74.

[49] Robert Richardson, 2007 *CSI Computer Crime and Security Survey*, CSI, at 3, http://gocsi.com/sites/default/files/uploads/2007_CSI_Survey_full-color_no%20marks.indd_.pdf [hereinafter 2007 CSI Survey].

[50] INDEX OF CYBERSECURITY, http://www.cybersecurityindex.org/ (last visited Jan. 21, 2014) (reporting a perceived risk value of 1,966 in December 2013, with the baseline of 1,000 being March 2011).

provided, and incompatibilities are highlighted. Still, these data offer a patchwork of insights about the frequency, nature, and cost of cyber attacks to the private sector.

Analyzing the Cyber Threat to the Private Sector

Do you remember the first time you ordered something online? It might have been as early as 1995 when eBay's predecessor, AuctionWeb, launched. Or maybe you stumbled onto e-commerce in 1994 when Pizza Hut began online ordering.[51] If so, you probably were not looking over your shoulder when you were deciding between pepperoni and eggplant. By the dot-com boom of the late 1990s, many U.S. and European companies had realized the commercial opportunities of e-commerce, but few took the time to address the vulnerabilities that they were introducing into their systems. That free pass was temporary. In the interim, firms have racked up "technical debt," an industry term for the legacy costs of rolling out new products without first improving security.[52] But like any debt, we need information to best manage repayment. To that end, this subsection analyzes the available data, addressing the four recently posed questions, beginning with frequency.

How Often Do Cyber Attacks Affect the Private Sector?

Epsilon and its customers, including JPMorgan Chase, Verizon, Sony, the International Monetary Fund, Sega, Citigroup, and more, were hit by cyber attacks in a span of just three months, from April to June 2011.[53] Yet together these breaches merely constitute one episode in an ongoing series of successful attacks. For example, in March 2013 what has been billed as the "biggest cyberattack in history" impacted service for millions of Internet users around the world.[54] It is difficult to say, though, how the number and type of attacks on the private sector have risen or fallen over time because few surveys are consistent. However, as the "longest-running survey in the information security field," the annual CSI/FBI and CSI surveys provide a useful starting point for analysis.[55] Annually since 1996, and in occasional partnership with the FBI, CSI has surveyed hundreds of information security practitioners with some surprising results.[56]

---

[51] *See* MURRAY, *supra* note 24, at 63.

[52] Palmer, *supra* note 13.

[53] *See, e.g.,* David Goldman, *Mass E-mail Breach: Just How Bad Is It?,* CNN MONEY (Apr. 6, 2011), http://money.cnn.com/2011/04/06/technology/epsilon_breach/index.htm (listing the prominent companies impacted by a data breach that leaked customers' email addresses); Johnathan Davis, *Hackers Gone Wild: Sega Joins Growing List of Victims,* INT'L BUS. TIMES (June 18, 2011), http://www.ibtimes .com/hackers-gone-wild-sega-joins-growing-list-victims-291765.

[54] Doug Gross, *Massive Cyberattack Hits Internet Users,* CNN (Mar. 29, 2013), http://www.cnn.com/ 2013/03/27/tech/massive-internet-attack.

[55] 2007 CSI Survey, *supra* note 49, at 1.

[56] *Id.* at 3.

From 2000 to 2008, the CSI and CSI/FBI surveys found that the proportion of organizations reporting an attack ranged from 43 to 70 percent.[57] That percentage was highest in 2000, which may be partially explained by technology shifting the threat model, as will be discussed. Data presented in U.S. government surveys from the 2000s are comparable to these figures.[58] For example, the National Computer Security Survey (NCSS) was conducted in 2005 to document "the nature, prevalence, and impact of cyber intrusions against businesses in the United States."[59] As part of that effort, nearly 36,000 businesses (out of some 23 million active U.S. businesses) were surveyed,[60] making the NCSS a uniquely large and systematically inclusive survey.[61] According to the 2005 NCSS, 67 percent of businesses detected at least one attack in 2005, with 43 percent detecting ten or more incidents.[62] Moreover, surveys suggest that the number of employees a business has impacts its threat matrix, with smaller firms being more likely to experience attacks from external agents for financial or personal gain, whereas larger businesses are more likely to be targeted because of a disagreement or protest undescoring the rise of "hacktivism."[63]

McAfee and Symantec have also published numerous global reports, finding that cyber attacks are increasingly hitting firms of all sizes. According to a 2010 Symantec report, 75 percent of surveyed IT executives in 27 countries stated that they had detected one or more attacks, and 41 percent characterized such attacks as "somewhat/highly effective."[64] Likewise, in a 2011 McAfee survey, 85 percent of two hundred IT executives in fourteen countries reported experiencing "network infiltrations[,]" and 80 percent had dealt with a "large-scale denial-of-service attack."[65] Even more dramatically, *Perceptions About Network Security*, a 2011 survey published by the Ponemon Institute, found that 90 percent of surveyed firms said that they had detected at least one cyber attack in the past year.[66]

Smaller firms are at risk, too. A May 2011 article in the *Los Angeles Times* described how Village View Escrow Inc., a small escrow and title company, suffered a cyber

---

[57] *See* 2008 CSI Survey, *supra* note 45, at 13.

[58] *See* Ramona R. Rantala, *Cybercrime Against Businesses*, 2005, U.S. Dep't Justice, Bureau Justice Stat. Special Rep., at 1, 4 (Sept. 2008), http://bjs.ojp.usdoj.gov/content/pub/pdf/cbo5.pdf; Lois M. Davis et al., The National Computer Security Survey (NCSS) 45 (2005), http://www.rand.org/pubs/technical_reports/2008/RAND_TR544.pdf.

[59] Rantala, *supra* note 58, at 2.

[60] *Id.* at 3; *Small Business Trends*, Small Bus. Admin., http://www.sba.gov/content/small-business-trends (last visited Jan. 22, 2014).

[61] Rantala, *supra* note 58, at 2.

[62] *Id.* at 1.

[63] *See* Verizon, Data Breach Investigations Report 19 (2012), http://www.verizonbusiness.com/resources/reports/rp_data-breach-investigations-report-2012_en_xg.pdf [hereinafter DBIR 2012].

[64] State of Enterprise Security, *supra* note 27, at 7.

[65] McAfee & CSIS, In the Dark: Critical Industries Confronting Cyberattacks 6 (2011), http://www.mcafee.com/us/resources/reports/rp-critical-infrastructure-protection.pdf [hereinafter In the Dark].

[66] *See* Ponemon Inst., Perceptions About Network Security: Survey of IT & IT Security Practitioners in the U.S. 3 (June 2011), http://www.juniper.net/us/en/local/pdf/additional-resources/ponemon-perceptions-network-security.pdf.

attack that cost the company $465,000.[67] According to Symantec's June 2010 *SMB Information Protection Survey*, 75 percent of small and medium-sized businesses (SMB) surveyed in May 2009 reported being hit by cyber attacks, which is the same percentage experienced by all enterprises in Symantec's 2010 *State of Enterprise Security* survey.[68] A Verizon survey also found that, despite seeing fewer compromised records in total, there was a "virtual explosion of breaches involving smaller organizations" in 2010 partly because of better information sharing.[69] However, fewer businesses in Symantec's 2010 SMB survey rated cyber attacks as "somewhat/extremely effective."[70] It is also important to keep in mind that these figures represent businesses *detecting* attacks, not necessarily *being* attacked.

What these statistics highlight is that both large and small enterprises suffer a significant number of attacks, although the types and frequency vary. Since the mid-2000s, anywhere between 43 to 90 percent of private-sector firms have annually reported detecting attacks. Overall risk likely lies somewhere in-between, but, in addition to size, many other factors influence risk assessments and estimates. For one, geographical location is important. A McAfee/CSIS survey highlights risk differentials between different countries regarding various kinds of attacks; for example, it suggests that Brazilian and Mexican businesses are at a greater risk from DDoS attacks than East Asian firms.[71] Other risk factors include company cybersecurity policies as well as industry sector.

Which Industries are Being Targeted?
The fear of cyber attacks on CNI has grown with reports of cyber attacks on U.S. utilities.[72] The consequences of such attacks are potentially devastating. For example, a report by the U.S. Cyber Consequences Unit estimates losses from a major attack on U.S. CNI at roughly $700 billion.[73] Stuxnet demonstrated how industrial control systems can be compromised. According to a 2009 McAfee/CSIS report, "Critical infrastructure owners and operators report that their networks and control

---

[67] Cyndia Zwahlen, *Small Firms Learn Size Doesn't Matter to Hackers*, L.A. TIMES (May 23, 2011), http://www.latimes.com/business/la-fi-smallbiz-security-20110523,0,5494792.story.

[68] SYMANTEC, SMB INFORMATION PROTECTION SURVEY 7 (June 2010), http://www.symantec.com/content/en/us/about/media/pdfs/SMB_ProtectionSurvey_2010.pdf?om_ext_cid=biz_socmed_twitter_2010Jun_worldwide_SMB [hereinafter SMB SURVEY]; STATE OF ENTERPRISE SECURITY, *supra* note 27, at 8.

[69] VERIZON, DATA BREACH INVESTIGATIONS REPORT 14 (2011), http://www.verizonbusiness.com/resources/reports/rp_data-breach-investigations-report-2011_en_xg.pdf [hereinafter DBIR 2011].

[70] SMB SURVEY, *supra* note 68, at 7 (though this survey does not define what constitutes "somewhat/extremely effective," it lists "the average annual cost of . . . cyber attacks" as $188,242).

[71] *See* IN THE DARK, *supra* note 65, at 23–24.

[72] *See* Douglas Birch, *Cyber Attacks on Utilities, Industries Rise*, NAVY TIMES (Sept. 29, 2011), http://www.navytimes.com/news/2011/09/ap-cyber-attacks-on-utilities-industries-rise-092911/.

[73] *See* JAYSON M. SPADE, INFORMATION AS POWER: CHINA'S CYBER POWER AND AMERICA'S NATIONAL SECURITY 26 (Jeffrey L. Caton ed., 2012) (citing Eugene Habiger, *Cyberwarfare and Cyberterrorism: The Need for a New U.S. Strategic Approach*, CYBER SECURE INST., Feb. 1, 2010, at 15–17).

systems are under repeated cyberattack, often by high-level adversaries [such as foreign governments]."[74] Indeed, some electric companies have reported being probed thousands of times each month.[75] Survey findings also suggest anecdotal evidence that "militaries in several countries have done reconnaissance and planning for cyberattacks on other nations' power grids. . . ."[76]

Certain industries, including those related to CNI, seem to be particularly at risk. According to the U.S. Department of Justice, companies in the telecommunications, computer system design, and chemical and drug manufacturing sectors experienced the most incidents.[77] On the other end of the spectrum, forestry, agriculture, and the food service industries reported the lowest prevalence of cybercrime.[78] However, there are some inconsistencies between reports. For example, according to Verizon's 2011 *Data Breach Investigation Report*, the hospitality and retail industries were the most at risk of a data breach.[79]

In a more specific investigation of data breaches, McAfee, along with the Science Applications International Corporation, published a survey focusing on the theft of intellectual property and other sensitive corporate data.[80] It found that the sectors most at risk of such data theft included car manufacturing, renewable energies, and materials research.[81] The survey also reported that cybercriminals have targeted research and development, marketing strategies, as well as product development data among other trade secrets.[82] These findings align with other research on economic espionage.[83]

In short, whereas critical infrastructure industries do seem to be particularly at risk, some softer targets are also vulnerable. Few industries seem to be out of the woods, not even forestry, fishing, and hunting.[84] To further assess cyber risk, the next two subsections examine the frequency of different types of attacks and their costs.

Which Types of Attacks Occur Most Frequently?

Certain types of cyber attacks – especially cyber theft and DDoS attacks – have become front-page news. In May 2011, Sony's PlayStation network was attacked, and

---

[74] IN THE CROSSFIRE: CRITICAL INFRASTRUCTURE IN THE AGE OF CYBER WAR, McAFEE/CSIS 1 (2009), http://iom.invensys.com/EN/pdfLibrary/McAfee/WP_McAfee_In_The_Crossfire_03-10.pdf [hereinafter IN THE CROSSFIRE].

[75] IN THE DARK, *supra* note 65, at 5.

[76] *Id.*

[77] *See* Rantala, *supra* note 58, at 1, 16–17.

[78] *Id.* at 1.

[79] DBIR 2011, *supra* note 69, at 12, 27.

[80] UNDERGROUND ECONOMIES: INTELLECTUAL CAPITAL AND SENSITIVE CORPORATE DATA NOW THE LATEST CYBERCRIME CURRENCY (2011), http://www.ndia.org/Divisions/Divisions/Cyber/Documents/rp-underground-economies.pdf [hereinafter UNDERGROUND ECONOMIES].

[81] *Id.* at 7.

[82] *Id.* at 7, 16.

[83] *See* HEDIEH NASHERI, ECONOMIC ESPIONAGE AND INDUSTRIAL SPYING 1–2, 93 (2004).

[84] *See* Rantala, *supra* note 58, at 1.

hackers reportedly compromised more than 100 million gamers' names, addresses, emails, user names, and passwords.[85] Forty-five "million credit and debit card" numbers were taken, potentially by using wireless data poaching or "wardriving," during the T.J. Maxx data theft.[86] Booz Allen, a U.S. defense contractor, was attacked by the hacktivist group Anonymous, which targeted a server that "basically had no security measures in place," according to one report.[87] Although the ends of these attacks are similar, the means differ.

As Chapter 3 illustrated, there are many different types of cyber attacks. NCSS uses three descriptive categories for cybercrime alone: cyber attacks, including viruses and worms; cyber theft, such as fraud and embezzlement; and computer security incidents, which includes spyware and spoofing.[88] However, these categories do overlap, meaning that incidents can double or even triple count. With that caveat, NCSS data reveal at least two trends about the types of attacks experienced by respondents. First, cyber theft appears to be the least prevalent type of incident, and cyber attacks the most prevalent under this categorization.[89] Second, among the 11 percent of businesses reporting cyber theft, fraud was the most common, followed by embezzlement, then intellectual property theft.[90] Within the subset of theft of intellectual property, trade secrets were most commonly stolen.[91] Viruses were by far the most frequently reported type of cyber attack, although 40 percent of respondents reported being able to block virus infections.[92]

---

[85] *See* Ian Sherr & Amy Schatz, *Sony Details Hacker Attack*, WALL ST. J. (May 5, 2011), http://online.wsj .com/article/SB10001424052748703849204576302970153688918.html; Hayley Tsukayama, *Cyber Attack Was Large-Scale, Sony Says*, WASH. POST (May 4, 2011), http://www.washingtonpost.com/blogs/ faster-forward/post/cyber-attack-was-large-scale-sony-says/2011/05/04/AF78yDpF_blog.html; Nick Bilton, *Sony Explains PlayStation Attack to Congress*, N.Y. TIMES (May 4, 2011), http://bits.blogs .nytimes.com/2011/05/04/sony-responds-to-lawmakers-citing-large-scale-cyberattack/.

[86] Larry Greenemeier, *T.J. Maxx Data Theft Likely Due to Wireless 'Wardriving'*, INFO. WK. (May 9, 2007), http://www.informationweek.com/news/199500385.

[87] *Hacked Off: Hitting the Booz*, ECONOMIST (July 14, 2011), http://www.economist.com/node/18958759.

[88] *See* Rantala, *supra* note 58, at 2. Spoofing is an attack in which one program falsifies data to masquerade as another. *See, e.g.,* Divya Pal Singh, Pankaj Sharma, & Ashish Kumar, *Detection of Spoofing Attacks in Wireless Networks and Their Remedies*, 1 INT'L J. RES. REV. IN ENGINEERING SCI. & TECH. 1, 1–2 (2012).

[89] Rantala, *supra* note 58, at 2–3.

[90] *Id.* at 3.

[91] *Id.* At its most basic level, a trade secret may be defined in the U.S. context as "any confidential business information which provides an enterprise a competitive edge" and is not publicly known. *What is a Trade Secret?*, WIPO, http://www.wipo.int/sme/en/ip_business/trade_secrets/trade_secrets .htm (last visited Sept. 24, 2013). *See also* 18 U.S.C. 1839(3)("[T]he term 'trade secret' means all forms and types of financial, business, scientific, technical, economic, or engineering information, including patterns, plans, compilations, program devices, formulas, designs, prototypes, methods, techniques, processes, procedures, programs, or codes, whether tangible or intangible, and whether or how stored, compiled, or memorialized physically, electronically, graphically, photographically, or in writing if - (A) the owner thereof has taken reasonable measures to keep such information secret; and (B) the information derives independent economic value, actual or potential, from not being generally known to, and not being readily ascertainable through proper means by, the public.... ").

[92] Rantala, *supra* note 58, at 3.

There is some disparity between the figures presented in these surveys. Most significantly, the McAfee/CSIS reports suggest that the occurrence of phishing, extortion, and theft are far more widespread than CSI/FBI and CSI surveys or the NCSS findings indicate. Extortion is not even a category used by the NCSS, although the number of critical infrastructure enterprises that reported being the victim of extortion in the 2011 McAfee/CSIS report rose by 25 percent.[93] According to Allan Paller, director of the SANS Institute, "Hundreds of millions of dollars have been extorted [from various companies], and maybe more . . . This kind of extortion is the biggest untold story of the cybercrime industry."[94]

What are the cyber criminals extorting, and from whom? The most common target is financial information, whereas "[t]he least common . . . [is] password and login information"[95] – likely because they are so easy to obtain by other means. Still, as with DDoS attacks, victimization rates vary significantly by country. Extortion was reportedly especially common in Mexico and India.[96] Although extortion cases are fairly equally distributed across CNI sectors, the highest rates seem to occur in the power, oil, and gas sectors.[97] Power sector cases in particular are worrisome because of attackers' ability to create outages, such as reportedly occurred in Brazil in 2005 and 2007.[98] Moreover, attackers are making use of "ransomware" to blackmail firms and individuals, with some attackers allegedly even posing as law enforcement officials.[99]

Finally, like extortion, data breaches were more commonly reported in McAfee/CSIS reports than in the other surveys. More than 60 percent of businesses reported data loss in the 2009 McAfee/CSIS survey,[100] a figure ranging from 25 percent to more than 90 percent in other studies. To illustrate the variety of competing estimates, consider that more than 40 million customer accounts were compromised in an eight-month stretch in 2005 alone, according to one study.[101] However, a Verizon report highlights a downward trend in the number of total records compromised "from 361 million in 2008 to 144 million in 2009 to just" four million in 2010.[102] Nevertheless, the same report recorded more actual instances of data breaches in 2010, so the number of records lost likely decreased because of the

---

[93] In the Dark, *supra* note 65, at 6.

[94] *Id.*

[95] In the Crossfire, *supra* note 74, at 9.

[96] In the Dark, *supra* note 65, at 6–7.

[97] In the Crossfire, *supra* note 74, at 7.

[98] *Id.* at 8.

[99] *See* Will Oremus, *Pay Up or the Hard Drive Gets It*, Slate (Oct. 9, 2012), http://www.slate.com/articles/technology/technology/2012/10/ransomware_hackers_new_trick_to_take_over_your_computer_and_blackmail_you_for_cash_.html.

[100] *See* In the Crossfire, *supra* note 74, at 6, 9.

[101] *See* Sean C. Honeywill, *Data Security and Data Breach Notification for Financial Institutions*, 10 N.C. Banking Inst. 269, 270 (2006).

[102] *Are Megabreaches Out? E-Thefts Downsized in 2010*, Krebs on Sec. (Apr. 19, 2011), http://krebsonsecurity.com/2011/04/are-megabreaches-out-e-thefts-downsized-in-2010/; *see* DBIR 2011, *supra* note 69, at 2.

size of compromised companies' databases rather than the number of organizations affected.[103] In any case, Verizon's 2012 Data Breach Investigations Report found that "174 million records were compromised in 2011, the second-highest total since the company began tracking breaches in 2004."[104] Even that figure was surpassed in 2013.[105]

Other data breach trends are also visible in the Verizon reports.[106] For example, in the 2011 report, the lower number of compromised records might be indicative of a change in the type of data being stolen.[107] In descending order from most to least common, these data include personal information, sensitive organizational data, bank account data, classified information, and medical records.[108] This trend continued in the 2012 Verizon report.[109]

These data illustrate that the cybercrime threat matrix is continuously evolving even as some vulnerabilities may be stabilizing, providing new challenges to law enforcement. Cybercriminals have taken advantage of the interconnected Internet to launch attacks, such as now-infamous hacking episodes like Code Red, Nimda, and MyDoom that infiltrated millions of computers, causing billions of dollars in damage.[110] As anti-virus programs and other means of computer security evolved, attackers determined how to better target specific systems. This growing sophistication has underscored vulnerabilities revealed in these surveys, such as regarding IP.[111]

Both Verizon reports highlight that IP is becoming the "new goal of cyber-criminals."[112] The number and size of breaches involving IP, particularly trade secrets, are difficult to quantify because of problems related to tracking and information sharing.[113] Some institutions, however, are getting better at protecting their IP. Consider the experience of one large organization of more than 500 employees. From May 2005 to June 2011, this organization experienced a range of system abuses and compromises laid out in Figure 5.1. However, it began introducing safeguards in

---

[103] *Id.* at 6.

[104] Joel Griffin, *Report Sheds Light on Intellectual Property Theft*, Sec. Infowatch (Oct. 24, 2012), http://www.securityinfowatch.com/article/10819280/report-sheds-light-on-intellectual-property-theft; *see* DBIR 2012, *supra* note 63, at 1.

[105] *See* DBIR 2013, *supra* note 12, at 3; Hadley Malcolm, *Target: Data Stolen From Up to 70 Million Customers*, USA Today (Jan. 10, 2014), http://www.usatoday.com/story/money/business/2014/01/10/target-customers-data-breach/4404467/.

[106] *See* DBIR 2011, *supra* note 69, at 2 (summarizing data breach trends).

[107] *Id.* at 13.

[108] *Id.* at 50.

[109] DBIR 2012, *supra* note 63, at 42.

[110] *See* Miranda Marquit, *The 12 Costliest Computer Viruses Ever*, Fine Print (Aug. 3, 2010), http://blog.insure.com/2010/08/03/the-12-costliest-computer-viruses-ever/ (estimating losses to the top three worst viruses up to 2010 at approximately $90 billion).

[111] *See, e.g.*, Debra Wong Yang & Brian M. Hoffstadt, *Countering the Cyber-Crime Threat*, 43 Am. Crim. L. Rev. 201, 201–02, 206 (2006).

[112] DBIR 2011, *supra* note 69, at 50; DBIR 2012, *supra* note 63, at 6.

[113] *See* DBIR 2012, *supra* note 63, at 44.

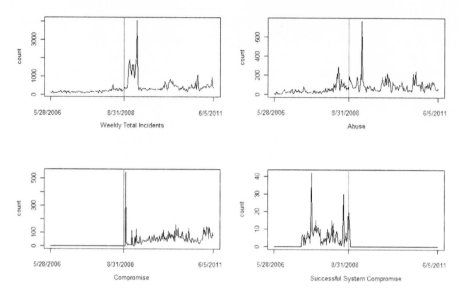

FIGURE 5.1.   CYBER ATTACKS AFFECTING ONE LARGE ORGANIZATION, 2006 TO 2011

August 2008 by undertaking some of the reforms discussed in the next section, which helped better manage cyber attacks. These data both offer an illustration of what is possible in enhancing cybersecurity, and provide a counterexample to the worst-case cyber threat thesis of both attacks and vulnerabilities compounding without end.

A complex picture of the cyber threat to the private sector has begun to emerge. However, conclusions about these data should be tempered with at least two caveats. First, as previously noted, these numbers reflect what businesses or organizations have detected and reported, not what they have actually experienced. Second, recall that cyber attacks are not limited to the neat categories presented here. Rather, they are multifaceted. How businesses and surveys categorize attacks varies. Also, understanding the frequency of attacks only reveals part of the story. To isolate attack vectors and better assess how organizations assess cyber risk, we need to know something about how businesses attach costs to different types of cyber attacks.

How Much Do Cyber Attacks Cost?

Cyber attacks often go unnoticed or unattributed, leading firms to underreport both incidents and losses. As ZDNet reports, "In a perfect world," compromised enterprises would confess their losses, but "[i]n the real world, a Conficker infected international company would try to stay beneath the radar if it can. . . . "[114] Returning to the stories of T.J. Maxx and Sony helps illustrate the confusion over calculating costs associated with different types of cyber attacks. In the mid-2000s, T.J. Maxx

[114] Dancho Danchev, *Conficker's Estimated Economic Cost? $9.1 Billion*, ZDNET (Apr. 23, 2009), http://www.zdnet.com/blog/security/confickers-estimated-economic-cost-91-billion/3207.

paid out tens of millions in settlement claims to states and consumers after a cyber attack resulted in it losing more than 45 million debit and credit card numbers.[115] Although initial cost estimates for the breach were on the order of $25 million, eventually the damage to TJX, the parent company of T.J. Maxx, reportedly reached more than $250 million in settling claims, litigating lawsuits, and fixing the security flaws that allowed the breach in the first place.[116] Compare these figures with the 2011 PlayStation Network breaches that may ultimately cost Sony between $1 and $2 billion directly, and potentially billions more indirectly because of reputational harm as well as costs to consumers and credit card companies.[117] These figures should not be surprising given that data breaches have been reported to cost U.S. companies as much as $204 per lost consumer record as of 2009, according to Betterley Consultants, a research and consulting firm.[118] However, estimates vary, which makes calculating the true cost of cyber attacks difficult. As a representative from TechAmerica, an advocacy group for the U.S. technology industry, wrote in late 2010, such "calculations are incomplete estimates at best, and sorely understated at worst."[119] Businesses often either do not have information about losses or hesitate to share it. How much do cyber attacks cost? No one really knows, but the following analysis summarizes and critiques some of the best available estimates.

According to the NCSS survey, in 2005, more than 90 percent of respondents that were affected by cybercrime sustained some actual financial loss, estimated at $867 million in total.[120] Theft was the most expensive, representing less than 1 percent of the total incidents but accounting for more than half of the total losses.[121]

---

[115] *See T.J. Maxx: Pays Millions for Poor Cybersecurity*, NEW INTERNET (July 21, 2011), http://www .thenewnewinternet.com/2009/06/24/tj-maxx-pays-millions-for-poor-cyber-security/.

[116] *See* Mary Helen Miller, *Data Theft: Top 5 Most Expensive Data Breaches*, CHRISTIAN SCI. MONITOR, http://www.csmonitor.com/Business/2011/0504/Data-theft-Top-5-most-expensive-data-breaches/ 3.-TJX-256-million-or-more (last visited Jan. 22, 2014); Jaikumar Vijayan, *One Year Later: Five Take-Aways From the TJX Breach*, COMPUTERWORLD (Jan. 17, 2008), http://www.computerworld.com/s/ article/9057758/One_year_later_Five_takeaways_from_the_TJX_breach.

[117] *See* Ryan Nakashima & Jordan Robertson, *Sony: Credit Data Risked in PlayStation Outage*, AP (Apr. 26, 2011), http://www.businessweek.com/ap/financialnews/D9MRP4R03.htm (reporting that total losses could eventually exceed $24 billion); *Sony Monetary Penalty Notice*, UK 1998 DATA PROTECTION ACT (Jan. 14, 2013), http://www.ico.org.uk/news/latest_news/2013/~/media/documents/library/Data_ Protection/Notices/sony_monetary_penalty_notice.ashx (discussing British authorities charging Sony with a £250,000 fine for placing private data at risk in 2013). *But see* Dara Kerr, *Sony PSN Hacking Lawsuit Dismissed by Judge*, CNET (Oct. 23, 2012), http://news.cnet.com/8301-1023-3-57538716-93/ sony-psn-hacking-lawsuit-dismissed-by-judge/ (reporting on a judge dismissing a resulting lawsuit against Sony).

[118] *See Understanding the Cyber Risk Insurance and Remediation Services Marketplace*, BETTERLEY RISK RES. (Sept. 2010), at 4, http://betterley.com/samples/crmm_10_nt.pdf [hereinafter BETTERLEY 2010].

[119] Liesyl I. Franz, *Comments of TechAmerica*, IN THE MATTER OF CYBERSECURITY, INNOVATION AND THE INTERNET ECONOMY, NIST DOCKET NO., 100721305–0305-01, at 3–4 (Sept. 20, 2010), http://www.nist .gov/itl/upload/TechAmerica_Cybersecurity-NOI-Comments_9-20-10.pdf.

[120] *See* Rantala, *supra* note 58, at 1, 5.

[121] *Id.*

Furthermore, a 2009 McAfee/CSIS report found that, on average, respondents suffered some system downtime because of attacks, and that 24 hours of downtime cost approximately $6.3 million.[122] Other surveys yielded different results, especially regarding the cost of different types of attacks. According to CSI/FBI and CSI surveys, in the early to mid-2000s, viruses were among the most expensive variety of cyber attacks, costing survey respondents $55 million in 2004 and nearly $43 million in 2005.[123] Reflecting more than the fact that fewer respondents are providing financial information, these costs have continued to drop; CSI survey respondents said viruses cost them just $40,141 on average in 2008.[124] Although the frequency of viruses remains high, the anti-virus and anti-malware industries have been successful at safeguarding system integrity.

Other types of attacks have also seen significant cost shifts. According to CSI/FBI and CSI surveys, total losses from denial of service attacks, for example, have decreased from $26 million in 2004 to between $2 and $7 million in 2005 to 2007, although the frequency of DDoS attacks has remained more consistent.[125] Conversely, the cost of reported financial fraud has increased from about $2.5 million in 2005 to more than $21 million in 2007, replacing viruses as the source of the greatest financial losses to affected firms.[126] These numbers seem low when compared to NCSS's total of $450 million in losses to cyber theft,[127] but keep in mind that NCSS includes more respondents, and the definition of cyber theft includes embezzlement and fraud, which are considered separately in the CSI/FBI and CSI surveys.

Survey variance has been an important caveat throughout this analysis, helping to underscore the difficulty of determining the true cost of cyber attacks. Costs may balloon when respondents consider labor costs, overhead, business disruption, and revenue losses. A 2010 Symantec study, which aggregated the cost of theft of customer information and IP, downtime, and loss of productivity, revenue, and customer trust, found an average cost of $2 million annually for all businesses, and $2.8 million for large businesses.[128] However, the cost of data breaches varies, with one McAfee report finding an average cost per affected organization to be "less than $700,000 in 2008" and "more than $1.2 million" in 2010.[129] The previously mentioned Ponemon Institute has noted that the average cost of a data breach was

---

[122] *See* IN THE CROSSFIRE, *supra* note 74, at 10.

[123] *See* Lawrence A. Gordon et al., *2004 CSI/FBI Computer Crime and Security Survey*, CSI at 1, https://gocsi.com/sites/default/files/uploads/FBI2004.pdf [hereinafter 2004 CSI Survey]; Lawrence A. Gordon et al., *2005 CSI/FBI Computer Crime and Security Survey*, CSI, at 15, https://gocsi.com/sites/default/files/uploads/FBI2005.pdf [hereinafter 2005 CSI Survey].

[124] *See* 2008 CSI Survey, *supra* note 45, at 17.

[125] *See* 2004 CSI Survey, *supra* note 123, at 10; 2005 CSI Survey, *supra* note 123, at 15; 2006 CSI Survey, *supra* note 45, at 13–14; 2007 CSI Survey, *supra* note 49, at 2, 15.

[126] *See* 2005 CSI Survey, *supra* note 123, at 15; 2006 CSI Survey, *supra* note 45; 2007 CSI Survey, *supra* note 49, at 19.

[127] *See* Rantala, *supra* note 58, at 5.

[128] STATE OF ENTERPRISE SECURITY STUDY, *supra* note 27, at 9.

[129] UNDERGROUND ECONOMIES, *supra* note 80, at 15.

$6.8 million in 2009 and $7.2 million in 2010.[130] Ponemon attributes this cost increase to the evolution of attack sources, especially the rise of cybercrime, the cost of which increased nearly 50 percent per record from 2009 to 2010.[131] These figures highlight the fact that cybercriminals are becoming more sophisticated. Rather than only stealing credit card numbers, they are also targeting intellectual property, which is far more profitable and can potentially be sold to competitors or even foreign governments.[132]

Corporate intellectual property may be considered "the new currency of cybercrime."[133] Even in 2008, the average respondent to a McAfee survey lost an estimated "$4.6 million worth of intellectual property. . . . "[134] Although they may be unable to quantify it, many firms are aware that the loss of IP poses a risk to long-term competitiveness. According to Ponemon, companies rank theft of information assets like IP first, followed by a disruption to their business operations, which can have a longer-term effect on their customer base.[135] The theft of IP, particularly trade secrets, is a long-term economic and national security challenge that may intensify as social engineering attacks become more sophisticated.[136] Insurance, which is further discussed in this chapter, is one way that the private sector is managing escalating costs, but this does relatively little to meet longer-term strategic challenges. Moreover, uncertainty about the available data makes creating a complete and accurate picture difficult. For example, despite the high cost of data breaches and theft in the Ponemon and McAfee reports, other surveys show a downward trend in average cost for all cyber attacks since 2001. Why is there such variation in the numbers, and what should we do about it?

Managing Uncertainty in the Cyber Threat Matrix

There are numerous reasons why the statistics used in various cybersecurity reports may be misleading, such as small sample sizes replete with "enormous, unverified outliers" that can skew results.[137] Former CSI Director Robert Richardson speculates that there are several other reasons why uncertainty abounds in assessing

---

[130] PONEMON INST., ANNUAL STUDY: U.S. COST OF A DATA BREACH 5 (2010), http://www.fbiic.gov/public/2011/mar/2010_Annual_Study_Data_Breach.pdf [hereinafter DATA BREACH].

[131] *Id.* at 4.

[132] McAFEE, UNSECURED ECONOMIES: PROTECTING VITAL INFORMATION 1 (2009), www.cerias.purdue.edu/assets/pdf/mfe_unsec_econ_pr_rpt_fnl_online_012109.pdf [hereinafter UNSECURED ECONOMIES].

[133] UNDERGROUND ECONOMIES, *supra* note 80, at 3.

[134] *See* UNSECURED ECONOMIES, *supra* note 132, at 1, 3, 7.

[135] PERCEPTIONS ABOUT NETWORK SECURITY, *supra* note 66, at 10.

[136] *See* UNDERGROUND ECONOMIES, *supra* note 80, at 23.

[137] Dinei Florêncio & Cormac Herley, *The Cybercrime Wave That Wasn't*, N.Y. TIMES (Apr. 14, 2012), http://www.nytimes.com/2012/04/15/opinion/sunday/the-cybercrime-wave-that-wasnt.html.

private-sector cybersecurity vulnerabilities.[138] First, costs per respondent in CSI/FBI and CSI surveys may increase or decrease because of response rates.[139] Second, with few exceptions, firms often do not quantify indirect costs like the impact on brand reputation because of the uncertainty involved.[140] As explained by Ashish Arora, a Duke University professor specializing in intellectual property, "We have measures such as cost per square foot to generally assess the value of a house in a specific neighborhood. There is no such standardized way to assess the value of patents and other intellectual properties."[141] Third, the costs of some types of attacks may be coming under control. The most significant example of this, according to Richardson, is, as was discussed, computer viruses,[142] with anti-virus vendors and their products becoming more effective,[143] thus reshaping the cyber threat matrix.

However, the overall cost of cyber attacks was on the rise in the late 2000s in part because of the increase in "targeted attacks," which CSI defines as attacks aimed at an organization or a subset of the population (i.e., a type of APT).[144] "Five years ago, the notion of targeted malware was hypothetical; today [writing in 2007] it is a significant reality," according to Richardson.[145] Yet the rising proportion of targeted attacks might also be attributed to a lack of clarity in defining APTs. As Verizon suggests, "APT hysteria" may be a bit overblown, and although it is true that some organizations are the target of state-sponsored attacks, "[i]t is also undoubtedly true . . . that *some* who think they are victims of APTs are really the victims of organized criminals, hacktivists, glorified script kiddies, and their own mistakes."[146] That does not mean that APTs should be ignored. Quite the opposite: more organizations need to improve at defining, detecting, and defending against such attacks. Anti-virus software and firewalls offer little resistance. Perhaps worryingly, Verizon has found that two-thirds of malware it investigated – the highest percentage it has ever seen – was "customized," meaning anything "from a simple repack of existing malware" created to avoid detection to "code written from the ground up for a specific attack."[147] Organizations must guard against such sophisticated threats. Although a lack of information and collective action problems prevail, firms need to own up to the fact that technical debt in all its forms, like any other debt, must be paid back. Until it is, the private sector and the larger economy will continue to suffer.

The threat of cyber attacks to the private sector is significant and ranges from well-known malware to customized APTs. The cost of cyber attacks has varied over time

[138] 2007 CSI Survey, *supra* note 49, at 2–3.
[139] Id.
[140] See 2005 CSI Survey, *supra* note 123, at 15.
[141] Unsecured Economies, *supra* note 132, at 26.
[142] See 2007 CSI Survey, *supra* note 49, at 16.
[143] Id.
[144] Id. at 2, 17.
[145] Id. at 17.
[146] DBIR 2011, *supra* note 69, at 5.
[147] Id. at 30.

depending on the industry sector, size of the firm, and type of attack. As has been demonstrated, however, data is inconsistent. This represents an inherent limitation in assessing cybersecurity risk. Thus, although this section has sketched out the problem of cyber attacks to the private sector, the challenge of adding color and depth to form a more complete picture that would help guide responses remains. This is attempted next by identifying industry best practices and examining the extent to which the competitive market is capable of enhancing cybersecurity.

ENHANCING CYBERSECURITY THROUGH THE COMPETITIVE MARKET

Those, such as Judge Frank Easterbrook, who advocate "that efficiency is the desired outcome" of the law and that the free "market is the most desirable route to such efficiency," believe that regulation displaces competition and can even "defeat the market altogether."[148] However, some regulatory room is left even among free-market proponents to correct market imperfections.[149] The questions, then, as applied to cybersecurity are two-fold. First, can the free market effectively enhance private-sector cybersecurity? Many commentators, such as Harris Miller, president of the Information Technology Association of America, argue in favor of this proposition and assert that regulation inhibits innovation.[150] Second, if market imperfections do exist, what types of regulations should be imposed on firms to enhance security while minimizing resulting market distortions? The first question is addressed in this section by analyzing how the market has incentivized private-sector best practices to date in terms of technology, organization, and budgeting using Microsoft, Google, and Facebook as case studies, leaving the second question of regulatory intervention to enhance private-sector cybersecurity for the final section of the chapter.

Managing the Cyber Threat at Microsoft

In the early 2000s, cybersecurity for Microsoft was arguably not a priority.[151] Because the company has enjoyed such market dominance,[152] though, its products have been natural targets for hackers. As a result, Microsoft bore the brunt of the first wave of

---

[148] MURRAY, *supra* note 24, at 165–66.
[149] *Id.* at 166. *But see* Eli Dourado, *Is There a Cybersecurity Market Failure?* (George Mason Univ. Mercatus Ctr., Working Paper No. 12–05, 2012), http://mercatus.org/publication/there-cyber security-market-failure-o (arguing that market failures are not so common in the cybersecurity realm); Jerry Brito & Tate Watkins, *Loving the Cyber Bomb? The Dangers of Threat Inflation in Cybersecurity Policy*, 3 HARV. NAT'L SEC. J. 39, 82 (2011) (making the case against there being a cybersecurity market failure).
[150] *See* Dawn Kawamoto, *Time to Regulate the Software Industry?*, CNET (Feb. 16, 2005), http://news .cnet.com/Time-to-regulate-the-software-industry/2100-7348_3-5579963.html.
[151] *See, e.g., Microsoft Discloses Windows Security Flaw*, KOMONEWS (Nov. 20, 2002), http://www .komonews.com/news/archive/4076601.html.
[152] *See, e.g.,* Richard MacManus, *Microsoft has 97% of OS Market, Says OneStat.com*, ZDNET (Aug. 21, 2006), http://www.zdnet.com/blog/web2explorer/microsoft-has-97-of-os-market-says-onestatcom/262.

cyber attacks, and its reputation was tainted by its security lapses beginning during this period. Since then, however, the company has invested considerable resources in enhancing its cybersecurity. Mark Dowd, who is an expert in application security and is famous for hacking into secure systems,[153] gave a talk about how he managed to break into Microsoft's software, which might seem to suggest that the focus on security has been for naught. However, as Chris Palmer notes, "[I]t took him three months, and he had a team. So it took a super genius and his team three months; in the old days, it took him three hours."[154] That is progress, and it did not happen overnight.

Much of the credit for Microsoft's success is given to its Security Development Lifecycle (SDL), which mandates security standards in software.[155] Work on the SDL began in the late 1990s, but the cyber attacks of the early 2000s provided the impetus needed to accelerate the project. Microsoft then "started a set of very rapid response measures that we called security pushes," according to Steve Lipner, senior director of security engineering strategy in Microsoft's Trustworthy Computing Group.[156] In short, product teams for Windows, Office 2003, and other software stopped normal development activities to focus wholly on improving security. But "it was an ad-hoc process," according to Lipner. "We took techniques that we understood and applied them in relatively unstructured ways."[157] Then, in late 2003, a new proposal began taking shape. Lipner recalls its evolution: "We [Microsoft employees] think we understand something about secure development; the need for it isn't going to go away; we need to mandate a process for all Microsoft products."[158] A meeting was called, and the SDL mandate was born. After July 2004, the SDL was made mandatory for all Microsoft products, and since then, the process has been regularly updated. Microsoft has also taken the initiative to share the SDL with others in the software industry, and many companies use its standards to help direct their own software development processes.

How well is SDL working? "The industry as a whole doesn't have a lot of good metrics to measure security, so we tend to go back to measuring vulnerability," according to Lipner.[159] Under this rubric, Microsoft has found that "newer products have fewer vulnerabilities, and the vulnerabilities that remain are less severe and harder to exploit, so that to us is an indication that we're doing the right thing."[160] This was confirmed in a series of tests that Dan Kaminsky among others

---

[153] Palmer, *supra* note 13.

[154] *Id.*

[155] *See Microsoft's Security Development Lifecycle*, MICROSOFT, http://www.microsoft.com/security/sdl/default.aspx (last visited Oct. 8, 2012).

[156] Telephone Interview with Steve Lipner, senior director of Security Engineering Strategy, Microsoft's Trustworthy Computing Group (Apr. 13, 2011).

[157] *Id.*

[158] *Id.*

[159] *Id.*

[160] *Id.*

ran against Microsoft Office in 2011 finding that "flaws and exploitable vulnerabilities in . . . Microsoft Office ha[ve] fallen dramatically. . . . "[161]

Problems persisted, however, so Microsoft has developed a means of fixing security flaws as they arise that engages the wider community of users. A "white hat" (ethical) security researcher finds a vulnerability and emails it to the company at secure@microsoft.com. Some firms, like Mozilla Firefox and Google, provide financial incentives for researchers to send private email for vulnerabilities that they discover; Google, for example, raised its bug bounty in 2012 to $20,000 for vulnerabilities that allow high-level attacks.[162] Microsoft does not have a bug payment program, although it has begun offering a $200,000 BlueHat Prize contest challenging researchers to design novel cybersecurity solutions.[163] The firm also hosts internal conferences to bring together internal and external security researchers to evaluate the threat landscape, according to Paul Nicholas, senior director of Global Security Strategy and Diplomacy at Microsoft.[164] Microsoft's focus has been on creating a "culture of responsibility" and a more coordinated approach to sharing data.[165] In other words, Microsoft has recognized that it needs serious and long-term collaboration to discover vulnerabilities and secure its products in an increasingly complex cyber threat landscape.

After a vulnerability is located, Microsoft researchers take a well-defined series of steps, the timing of which varies by the scope and impact of the vulnerability and whether or not it has been made public or is "in the wild."[166] First, researchers determine whether it is a real vulnerability; for example, while something may technically be a "vulnerability" it may not actually be exploitable.[167] Next, if it meets the requirements of being real, new, and plausible, it is assigned to product and specialist teams associated with Microsoft's Security Response Center, which tests whether or not the vulnerability is something that needs to be addressed.[168] If the reported vulnerability checks out, then Microsoft starts an in-depth investigation to see if there are any additional vulnerabilities that may involve building new tools, threat modeling, or writing new software. Then, the fix is tested on internal systems and widely used consumer software. If necessary, the fix is also tried with a subset of commercial customers who have agreed to such testing to ensure that an update does

[161] *Vulnerabilities in Microsoft Office and OpenOffice Compared*, LINUX TODAY (Apr. 21, 2011), http://www.linuxtoday.com/security/2011042100941SCDT.

[162] *See* Gregg Keizer, *Google Raises Bug Bounties to $20,000*, COMPUTERWORLD (May 7, 2012), www.computerworld.com/s/article/9226895/Google_Raises_Bug_Bounties_to_20_000.

[163] *See Microsoft BlueHat Prize*, MICROSOFT, http://www.microsoft.com/security/bluehatprize/ (last visited Jan. 21, 2014).

[164] Telephone Interview with Paul Nicholas, director, Global Security Strategy and Diplomacy, Microsoft (Apr. 11, 2011).

[165] *Id.*

[166] *Id.*

[167] *Id.*

[168] *Id.*

not disrupt customers' line of business applications.[169] Finally, a package update is released on the first Tuesday of each month, known as "update Tuesday." Most Microsoft consumers have their systems set up with automatic updates enabled.[170] However, Microsoft more recently stepped up its emphasis on rapid updating to limit the amount of time that hackers can reverse engineer updates to find the exploit,[171] and has also rolled out an array of additional services such as its Digital Crimes Unit that help to solidify its status as a cybersecurity norm entrepeneur as discussed later in this chapter.[172]

The previous section sketched out how big of a problem cyber attacks are for the private sector by describing how often they happen, the particular risks that certain industries face, and the range of associated costs. Although the statistics and figures cited contribute to a better understanding of those issues, uncertainty remains. That uncertainty is magnified by varying corporate cybersecurity policies and practices. As has been illustrated, Microsoft has been working on enhancing cybersecurity for more than a decade and still has no silver bullet, though it has made substantial progress through the SDL. Many other firms are just beginning to catch up. As such, this section analyzes private-sector best practices while connecting them to a larger discussion about the effectiveness of the competitive market in enhancing cybersecurity. Building off of the Microsoft case study, we begin by investigating both reactive and proactive cybersecurity approaches. Then, the inquiry proceeds by examining some of the best and worst staffing and budgeting strategies. Finally, some of the pitfalls of existing strategies are analyzed, focusing on the perceived disconnect between investing in cybersecurity and protecting the bottom line.

Cyber Insecurity: Proactive and Reactive Cybersecurity Strategies

Imagine the feeling of excitement and opportunity that the Model T Ford represented to consumers in the early twentieth century. That newfound freedom came at a price, however, with early cars lacking safety features such as seatbelts, adjustable mirrors, and crumple zones to absorb impact, to say nothing of airbags. Despite the fact that many of these safety features seem intuitive in retrospect, it took some time to standardize them. Formal studies were needed to assess risk, and then stakeholders – including companies, consumers, and governments – needed to perceive risks as important and devote resources to implementing fixes. One of the first popular reports pushing the improvement of car safety was published by *Popular Science* in 1950, featuring the attention-grabbing title, "Making the Death Seat Safer," and

---

[169] Lipner, *supra* note 156.

[170] *Id.*

[171] Nicholas, *supra* note 164.

[172] *See Microsoft Digital Crimes Unit*, MICROSOFT http://www.microsoft.com/government/ww/safety-defense/initiatives/pages/digital-crimes-unit.aspx (last visited Feb. 10, 2014); Jan Neutze, *Cybersecurity Norms for a Secure Cyber-Future*, MICROSOFT SEC. BLOG (May 23, 2012, 11:49AM), http://blogs.technet.com/b/security/archive/2012/05/23/cybersecurity-norms-for-a-secure-cyber-future.aspx.

highlighting the potential of seatbelts and padded dashboards.[173] However, it was not until 1958 that a Volvo engineer invented the three-point lap and shoulder seatbelt. It then took nearly two decades before the results of crash tests were published to inform consumers of cars' variable safety performances. The first U.S. law mandating the use of seat belts was not passed until 1984.

Making vehicles safer has been a long and convoluted process, and they still are not perfect – 34,080 people died on U.S. roadways in 2012.[174] Still, the situation is improving with fatality rates per registered vehicle and distance travelled decreasing steadily, though there was an uptick in 2012.[175] As recently as 1994, there were 40,716 traffic fatalities.[176] However, it has been more than a century since the first Model T rolled off the production line in 1908. Part of the problem early on was ignorance of safety issues. Later, as safety concerns became better documented, there was uncertainty about how best to address them. Thus, developing the technology took time, and eventually, the advent of crash tests, safety standards, regulation and subsequent litigation all played important roles in creating safer cars.

Similarly, the Internet has been viewed as an engine for economic growth and freedom, but the security concerns surrounding its misuse have only relatively recently come to the fore. To continue the automobile analogy, we are arguably now in the 1960s in terms of cybersecurity. Some secure technologies like the seat belt have been developed, but more are needed, and many of the details of assessing risk and the shape of the regulatory environment remain to be defined. Unfortunately, though, we do not have another fifty years to get it right. Like the automobile industry, IT has largely been a private-sector-driven project, so much of the work of developing more secure technology and better business practices has been private. For now, the digital buck often stops at the boardroom, not the President's desk, as was alluded to in Frank Montoya's quote at the beginning of the chapter. It is thus essential to secure the boardroom as much as possible, which is increasingly difficult given the rise of sophisticated malware such as proximity attacks that can compromise the hardware of surrounding users, turning managers' smartphones into microphones.[177] Companies have reacted in various ways to cyber insecurity, resulting in differing approaches to developing and implementing corporate cybersecurity strategies.

At a general level, corporate cybersecurity approaches may be understood to exist along a proactivity spectrum. Many firms remain predominantly reactive – more so in developed countries like the United States and United Kingdom than

---

[173] See George H. Waltz, Jr., *Making the Death Seat Safer*, 157(1) POP. SCI. 82 (July 1950).

[174] See *In a Sharp Trend Reversal, Highway Fatalities Rise*, USA TODAY (May 3, 2013), http://www.usatoday.com/story/news/nation/2013/05/03/us-highway-road-deaths-increase/2132457/.

[175] *Id.; Traffic Fatalities in 2010 Drop to Lowest Level in Recorded History*, NHTSA (Apr. 1, 2011), http://www.nhtsa.gov/PR/NHTSA-05-11 (reporting that 32,788 people were killed in traffic collisions in 2010).

[176] *Traffic Safety Facts: 2004 Data*, NHTSA at 2, http://www.nhtsa.gov/PR/NHTSA-05-11 (last visited Oct. 8, 2012).

[177] See Tom Kellermann, *The Evolution of Targeted Attacks in a Web 3.0 World*, TREND MICRO (July 2, 2012), http://cloud.trendmicro.com/the-evolution-of-targeted-attacks-in-a-web-3-0-world/.

in emerging markets like India or China, which have been shown to be more proactive.[178] The one area in which companies across the board are commonly more proactive is in response to data breaches because of the short-term expense and potential for long-term reputational harm.[179] Firms diverge, though, in how narrowly or broadly they define IT security. For example, although two firms may consider protecting infrastructure a chief goal of their IT security efforts, one may approach this by focusing only on hardware, whereas another might think about business processes. As such, Scott Dynes, an expert in the economics of information security, has placed companies on proactive-reactive continuums to describe four basic approaches to implementing IT security: the "sore thumb," "IT risk," "business risk," and "systemic" paradigms.[180] Reviewing these approaches helps to identify industry best practices, which in turn informs the larger question of the potential for the competitive market to enhance cybersecurity as one component in an emerging polycentric system to foster cyber peace.

First, the sore-thumb paradigm is the most reactive and disconnected from business management. It is a "tactical response to Infosec [information security] events such as a virus infection."[181] Although only one of the manufacturing firms that Dynes interviewed for his study fell wholly into this category, many firms have likely taken such an approach at some point in their histories.[182] According to the Ponemon Institute's annual data breach studies, the first breach a company faces tends to be more expensive than later breaches.[183] Some firms thus may fall into this category because, even if they are aware of risks, they cannot justify the necessary investments to mitigate a hypothetical.[184] However, firms in this category are not necessarily unwilling to invest in better security. Rather, it suggests that the firm has insufficient information or, for whatever reason, has not taken the initiative to proactively manage and develop policies related to potential cybersecurity risks. This underscores Dynes's conclusion that the sore-thumb approach "provides many opportunities for improvement."[185]

Unlike the sore-thumb approach, the IT risk and business risk paradigms can be either proactive or reactive. What makes the IT risk paradigm unique from the business risk paradigm is how information security is conceptualized. In the IT risk

---

[178] *See* UNSECURED ECONOMIES, *supra* note 132, at 6 (comparing cybersecurity investment rates across countries and concluding that "[i]t appears that decision makers in many countries, particularly developed ones, are reactive rather than proactive.").

[179] *See* DATA BREACH, *supra* note 130, at 12, 17.

[180] Scott Dynes, *Information Security Investment Case Study: The Manufacturing Sector*, CTR. DIGITAL STRATEGIES at 9 (2006), http://www.tuck.dartmouth.edu/cds-uploads/research-projects/pdf/InfoSec Manufacturing.pdf.

[181] *Id.* at 10.

[182] *Id.*

[183] *See* DATA BREACH, *supra* note 130, at 6–7.

[184] Scott Dynes et al., *Cyber Security: Are Economic Incentives Adequate?*, *in* CRITICAL INFRASTRUCTURE PROTECTION 15, 23–25 (Eric Goestz & Sujeet Shenoi eds., 2008).

[185] Dynes, *supra* note 180, at 9.

paradigm, cybersecurity directors work toward the goal of "protecting hardware."[186] Alternatively, the business risk paradigm looks at how cybersecurity risks could impact the business, with continuity of "business processes" being the chief goal.[187] In both cases, there is also some level of risk-management methodology implied.[188] Cybersecurity initiatives are ranked, and a director then "prioritize[s] responses based on estimates of the likelihood and cost of a successful attack, and the cost to mitigate the vulnerability."[189]

The fourth approach, the systemic paradigm, is proactive and considers IT risk comprehensively.[190] Cybersecurity efforts are built-in from the start like Microsoft's SDL. As the director of a manufacturing firm in Dynes's study put it, just as it "makes no sense to even think about IT-enabled business without having information security baked in; it also makes no sense to have 'naked' Infosec [information security] initiatives that are not developed as part of some business process."[191] This strategy also streamlines security funding because the cost is included as part of an overall project.[192]

These four paradigms represent a wide spectrum of engagement, both with information security itself and with the business strategies that often enable IT security efforts. Yet there are at least two areas where firms' strategies seem to overlap. First, most enterprises gather information from similar sources, including trade magazines, vendors, and peers.[193] Second, the more dependent on IT the firm is and the more breaches it experiences, the more likely business managers are to be receptive to efforts aimed at enhancing cybersecurity.[194] Overall, however, a range of variables shape firms' strategies, from an engaged IT security director or CEO, to data breaches or even insurance coverage, as will be explored.

Data are not available to assess where the majority of firms fall on the proactivity spectrum, but as companies weigh new security investments, Dynes's studies have shown that organizations may be rewarded for more proactively managing cybersecurity.[195] The *Wall Street Journal* reports that "an industry of experts – including attorneys, public-relations specialists, and forensic investigators – has emerged to help" firms navigate cyber attack responses.[196] As these incidents become more

---

[186] *Id.*

[187] *Id.*

[188] *Id.*

[189] *Id.*

[190] *Id.*

[191] *Id.* at 10.

[192] *Id.*

[193] *Id.* at 8.

[194] *Id.* at 11; *cf. id.* at 10 ("The firms that were the most proactive were not necessarily the biggest or the most dependent on IT; the firms that were the most reactive were not necessarily the smallest, but did tend to be the least IT dependent.").

[195] *See id.* at 20–21.

[196] Ben Worthen & Anton Troianovski, *Firms Adjust to Hacks*, WALL ST. J. (June 17, 2011), http://online .wsj.com/article/SB10001424052702303499204576389773023983518.html.

commonplace, a breach handled well – as in quickly detected, disrupted, and disclosed – can actually improve customer loyalty and a company's brand.[197] To see such firm-level improvements and enhance overall cybersecurity though, many companies will need to become more proactive by implementing technological, budgetary, and organizational best practices.

Technological and Budgetary Cybersecurity Best Practices

Many organizations could stand to invest more in cybersecurity, but deciding how much and which technologies to prioritize are areas open to debate. Cybersecurity surveys regularly rank firewalls and anti-virus software as the security technologies most often used, but fewer companies regularly update such software.[198] After that, percentages drop off. Roughly 65 percent of companies use encryption for data in transit, according to CSI and Verizon surveys.[199] About half use intrusion prevention systems and encryption for data in storage, while approximately one-third use public-key encryption, specialized wireless security systems, or content-monitoring systems to prevent data loss.[200] Deep-packet inspection is increasingly the technology that organizations are most likely to install post-breach because it is able to identity cyber threats, but it connotes a reactive focus and is also the technology allowing Iran to keep a tight grip on its domestic web.[201] Network assessment and biometrics such as fingerprinting are also becoming more popular, especially in Asian markets.[202]

The technology of data encryption is continuing to improve.[203] One form of encryption that many people use daily is HTTPS, which combines the traditional web protocol HTTP with SSL/TLS, an encryption protocol. For years, banking and e-commerce have been made more secure by HTTPS, but other types of websites are also turning to it. In 2010 and 2011, Google and Facebook made HTTPS an opt-in option and Mozilla's Firefox, in conjunction with the Tor Project and the

---

[197] *See id.*

[198] *See, e.g.,* 2007 CSI Survey, *supra* note 49, at 18; 2008 CSI Survey, *supra* note 45, at 19; DBIR 2011, *supra* note 69, at 63.

[199] *See* 2007 CSI Survey, *supra* note 49, at 18; 2008 CSI Survey, *supra* note 45, at 19; DBIR 2011, *supra* note 69, at 63.

[200] *See* 2007 CSI Survey, *supra* note 49, at 18; 2008 CSI Survey, *supra* note 45, at 19; DBIR 2011, *supra* note 69, at 63.

[201] UNDERGROUND ECONOMIES, *supra* note 80, at 12; EVGENY MOROZOV, THE NET DELUSION: THE DARK SIDE OF INTERNET FREEDOM 221 (2011).

[202] *See* UNDERGROUND ECONOMIES, *supra* note 80, at 12; 2007 CSI Survey, *supra* note 49, at 18; 2008 CSI Survey, *supra* note 45, at 19; *Trial by Fire: What Global Executives Expect of Information Security*, PwC at 18, 35 (2010), http://www.pwc.com/en_GX/gx/information-security-survey/pdf/pwcsurvey2010_report.pdf [hereinafter *Trial by Fire*]; Selena Mann, *Biometrics Growing in Popularity, Analyst Says*, IT WORLD CAN. (Feb. 7, 2011), http://www.itworldcanada.com/news/biometrics-growing-in-popularity/142401.

[203] *See* UNDERGROUND ECONOMIES, *supra* note 80, at 18.

Electronic Frontier Foundation, began offering HTTPS everywhere.[204] Additionally, although encrypting at-rest data (i.e., not in transit) is slowly catching on, it may become an especially important option for firms as they transition from reactive to proactive cybersecurity approaches.[205] Only 7 percent of companies reported being dissatisfied with encryption in the 2005 NCSS survey,[206] though the popularity of encryption has taken a hit owing to revelations about the NSA installing backdoors in various encryption algorithms.[207] But by guarding data internally and forcing thieves to decrypt it, encryption can help protect both corporate IP and the long-run competitiveness of economies.[208] It is a vital best practice in the campaign to enhance private-sector cybersecurity.

Implementing technological fixes, though, takes investment. According to CSI surveys, the majority of respondents "said that their organizations allocated 5 percent or less of their overall IT budget to information security. . . ."[209] The U.S. government, for comparison's sake, spends roughly 11 percent of its public IT budget on information security, according to Booz Allen.[210] A 2008 McAfee survey found that only 19 percent of U.S. company respondents spend "20 percent or more of . . . [their] IT budgets on security. . . ."[211] These numbers, of course, may not reflect the whole picture. For one, firms keep track of their IT security budgets differently. Although there is a central security team at Microsoft, for example, most work on improving security, according to Lipner, is done by engineers in product groups on a regular basis and so the cost is distributed and not separately itemized.[212] In addition, investment varies significantly by company size and geography. Larger companies have been reported to spend more overall on security but less per employee, except for the largest organizations of more than $1 billion in revenue, at which point the trend reportedly seems to reverse.[213] And companies in emerging economies tend to spend relatively more than their developed-nation counterparts, according to a 2009 Price

---

[204] See *HTTPS Everywhere*, ELECTRONIC FRONTIER FOUND., https://www.eff.org/https-everywhere (last visited Oct. 8, 2012).

[205] See, e.g., Alexander Rothacker, *Encrypting Data at Rest*, INFOSEC ISLAND (Nov. 18, 2010), https://www.infosecisland.com/blogview/9625-Encrypting-Data-at-Rest.html.

[206] See Rantala, *supra* note 58, at 9.

[207] See, e.g., Michael Lee, *NSA Encryption Backdoor Proof of Concept Published*, ZDNet (Jan. 6, 2014), http://www.zdnet.com/nsa-encryption-backdoor-proof-of-concept-published-7000024793/.

[208] See Ryan Gallagher, *Latest Snowden Leak Reveals NSA War on Encryption, But It's Not Yet Dead*, SLATE (Sept. 5, 2013), http://www.slate.com/blogs/future_tense/2013/09/05/nsa_surveillance_snowden_leak_reveals_nsa_war_on_encryption.html.

[209] 2008 CSI Survey, *supra* note 45, at 8; see 2005 CSI Survey, *supra* note 123, at 5.

[210] See *Cyber Management*, BOOZ ALLEN HAMILTON, at 1, www.boozallen.com/media/file/cyber-management.pdf (last visited Jan. 9, 2013) (reporting that "[t]he U.S. spends $80 billion per year on information and communications technology – $9 billion of which goes into information technology (IT) security.").

[211] See UNSECURED ECONOMIES, *supra* note 132, at 6.

[212] Lipner, *supra* note 156.

[213] See 2006 CSI Survey, *supra* note 45, at 6–7.

Waterhouse Coopers (PwC) survey.[214] Still, few respondents are actually reducing security budgets or deferring capital or operating outlays,[215] although the Ponemon Institute estimates that more than $46 billion in investments are needed to secure private firms operating CNI.[216]

Firms are taking an array of approaches to improve cybersecurity. Just as there is no flawless safety technology for cars, there is no perfect cybersecurity technology – but some, like encryption, are becoming increasingly important. However, firms seem to be largely underinvesting in these technologies, with the private sector in the developed world reportedly lagging behind. These developments are important because they underscore the need for smart investments in cybersecurity technologies, as well as the importance of operational cybersecurity involving the efficient structuring of people and processes to assess and manage cyber risk. Identifying organizational best practices, then, is another critical component to private-sector led cybersecurity improvements.

Organizational Cybersecurity Best Practices: People and Processes

When Sony was hacked in early 2011, it did not have a chief information security officer (CISO) or senior manager devoted wholly to information security.[217] This is an example of Dynes's sore-thumb paradigm because Sony reactively acquired a CISO in the ensuing public relations disaster. It is also an example of the importance of regularly reviewing operational practices within enterprises, which could lead not only to increased awareness but also better representation, targeted investments, and more accountability. New best practices cannot typically be uniformly applied; they must be tailored to fit with each business's existing culture. Nevertheless, some general operational guidelines exist to help optimize organizational cybersecurity.

The first step is leadership. CEOs may not be well versed in or receptive to discussions about cybersecurity, but managers should advocate for and implement "centralized management of IT security solutions so they" have an automatic mechanism for measuring and enforcing IT security best practices throughout their organizations.[218] CISOs are one way to achieve such coordination as they enable "enterprises to align information protection with corporate security policies and regulatory or business-partner mandates."[219] This has resulted in companies with CISOs saving more than

---

[214] *See Trial by Fire, supra* note 202, at 32–33.

[215] *Id.*

[216] See, e.g., Eric Engleman & Chris Strohm, *Cybersecurity Disaster Seen in U.S. Survey Citing Spending Gaps*, BLOOMBERG (Jan. 31, 2012), http://www.bloomberg.com/news/2012-01-31/cybersecurity-disaster-seen-in-u-s-survey-citing-spending-gaps.html.

[217] *See, e.g.,* Isabel Reynolds, *Sony Recruits Information Security Boss After Hacking*, REUTERS (Sept. 6, 2011), http://www.reuters.com/article/2011/09/06/us-sony-idUSTRE7851PH20110906.

[218] DATA BREACH, *supra* note 130, at 8.

[219] *Id.*

20 percent on data breach costs over those that do not, according to one Symantec survey.[220] Firms are increasingly recognizing this need. In 2006, only 43 percent of respondents to a PwC survey said that they had a CISO or other similar security executive, but by 2009, that rate had increased to 85 percent.[221]

However, merely having a CISO or other senior leader to manage data breaches is not enough. It also matters to whom that CISO reports and to what extent he or she coordinates with other managers. Just 13 percent of respondents to a 2012 PwC survey made the survey's "leader cut," a label used to identify respondents that measured and reviewed their cybersecurity policies annually, had "an overall information security strategy in place[,]" analyzed the types of cyber attacks hitting their networks, and had a CISO or equivalent reporting to "the top of the house[.]"[222] Those organizations that made the cut reported half as many incidents as those that did not.[223]

There are many other organizational hurdles to overcome even if a CISO is in place, ranging from establishing an actionable vision for cybersecurity to securing funding and effectively communicating with others in the C-suite.[224] Tensions with the chief information officer (CIO) can occur because part of the CISO's job is to critique "from a security angle" how staffs deploy products and services.[225] When CIOs and CISOs are not on the same page, it may be indicative of a disconnect between IT security and IT developed for business processes.[226]

Although leadership and high-level coordination are imperative, cybersecurity is also the responsibility of every employee. Thus, it is vital that firms help educate and assess employees' cybersecurity habits, which could also have positive knock-on effects in employees' personal lives, further contributing to cyber peace. Surveys reveal that the majority of firms recognize that security awareness training is important, but many respondents believe either that their organizations do not invest enough in it or do not do enough to assess the effectiveness of programs.[227] According to the 2008 CSI survey, for example, only 32 percent of respondents with security training programs said that their companies tested the training's utility.[228] It is critical

[220] *Id.* at 32.
[221] Ralph DeFragesco, *Chief Information Security Officer: A New Spin on an Old Job*, IT Bus. EDGE (Nov. 2, 2009), http://www.itbusinessedge.com/cm/blogs/defrangesco/chief-information-security-officer-a-new-spin-on-an-old-job/?cs=37172.
[222] *See Eye of the Storm: Key Findings from the 2012 Global State of Information Security Survey*, PwC at 33, http://www.pwc.co.nz/global-state-of-information-survey.aspx [hereinafter *Eye of the Storm*].
[223] *Id.*
[224] *Id.* at 8, 20–21.
[225] Ellen Messmer, *Can a New CISO Improve Sony Playstation Network Security?*, NETWORK WORLD (May 2, 2011), http://www.networkworld.com/news/2011/050211-playstation-ciso.html.
[226] *See* Bill Brenner, *A Disturbing Disconnect Between CSOs and CIOs*, CSO ONLINE (Sept. 28, 2010), http://www.csoonline.com/article/619767/a-disturbing-disconnect-between-csos-and-cios?page=1.
[227] *See Eye of the Storm, supra* note 222, at 15, 23.
[228] *See* 2008 CSI Survey, *supra* note 45, at 20.

that training programs are evaluated early and often, and that their message is con-stantly reinforced as part of a larger firm-wide cybersecurity awareness initiative.[229]

Having a centralized and well-communicated cybersecurity policy with an effec-tive training component is critical to organizational cybersecurity. However, up to 80 percent of small firms reportedly lack cybersecurity policies.[230] The consequences of not having such a plan have been documented in the healthcare sector. In one study by Dynes, different hospital departments experienced varying degrees of dis-ruption because each was ostensibly left to develop its own contingency plans.[231] The materials acquisition department had developed such a plan; radiology had not.[232] Unsurprisingly, when a worm attacked the hospital's systems, one of the largest dis-ruptions occurred in the radiology department, leaving clinicians unable to make diagnoses.[233] Alternatively, Facebook's proactive cybersecurity policy has meant that it was ready to act decisively during the beginning of the Arab Spring when protesters across the Middle East and North Africa demanded political change.[234] On Christ-mas Day, the company's security staff began receiving complaints from activists in Tunisia that Tunisian ISPs "were injecting malicious code into users' Facebook log-in pages," meaning that users' passwords were being compromised.[235] Facebook was able to manage this event because of a well-articulated cybersecurity policy: the Facebook Immune System (FIS),[236] which has "built an offensive capability."[237] As part of this program, Facebook has a "scalps wall," a life-size scrapbook immortaliz-ing the spammers, child predators, fraudsters, and other criminals that the company has gone after, often through litigation.[238] Facebook could not haul the Tunisian ISPs into a U.S. court, but they did have a ready group of consultants to protect users.

Facebook's security is by no means perfect – malware often spreads through the site, negatively affecting many users.[239] However, in this case, Facebook was able to roll out a technical solution, and within a week the site saw a 15 percent jump in

---

[229] See UNSECURED ECONOMIES, *supra* note 132, at 26.

[230] See *80% of U.S. Small Businesses Have No Cyber Security Policies in Place*, HOMELAND SEC. NEWS WIRE (Oct. 25, 2011), http://www.homelandsecuritynewswire.com/80-us-small-businesses-have-no-cyber-security-policies-place?page=0,1.

[231] See Scott Dynes, *Information Security and Health Care – A Field Study of a Hospital After A Worm Event*, CTR. DIGITAL STRATEGIES (Aug. 22, 2006), at 16, http://digitalstrategies.tuck.dartmouth.edu/cds-uploads/research-projects/pdf/InfoSecHealthCare.pdf.

[232] *Id.* at 9, 17.

[233] *Id.* at 16.

[234] Elinor Mills, *At Facebook, Defense is Offense*, CNET (Jan. 31, 2011), http://news.cnet.com/8301-27080-3-20029954-245.html#ixzz1Sbm4KNe8.

[235] *Id.*

[236] See Jim Giles, *Inside Facebook's Massive Cyber-Security System*, INFO. POL'Y (Oct. 28, 2011), http://www.i-policy.org/2011/10/inside-facebooks-massive-cyber-security-system-.html.

[237] Mills, *supra* note 234.

[238] *Id.*

[239] See, e.g., Sharon Vaknin, *How to Avoid, Remove Facebook Malware*, CNET (June 14, 2011), http://howto.cnet.com/8301-11310_39-20070931-285/how-to-avoid-remove-facebook-malware/.

Tunisian traffic.[240] According to one 2010 survey, 65 percent of companies had "an overall information security strategy" in 2009, up from 59 percent in 2008.[241] However, unlike Facebook, even where they exist many firms are lagging in transferring these broad policies into more specific areas of planning and technical capacity, such as having an identity management strategy, a business continuity plan, or an accurate inventory of where sensitive data is stored.[242] Similarly, many firms may hold on to data longer than they need to, unnecessarily increasing the possibility that it will be compromised. In 2012, according to a PwC survey, just 43 percent of organizations with strategies called those strategies "effective" and themselves "proactive" at implementing their plans.[243]

Before planning and policies can be effectively developed, risk must be assessed. As was noted earlier in this chapter, this is exceptionally difficult; according to Palmer, "everyone wants [risk assessment], and nobody has it."[244] Many businesses have instead turned to risk management.[245] But as Michal Zalewski, a security researcher at Google, attests, the idea of risk management simply does not make sense in the cybersecurity context.[246] Zalewski notes, "The doctrine says that if having some unimportant workstation compromised every year is not going to cost the company more than $1,000 in lost productivity, maybe they should just budget this much and move on rather than spending $10,000 on additional security measures. . . . "[247] Such prioritization of security efforts is natural, but it does deceptively little to actually manage cyber threats for at least three reasons. First, in interconnected systems like a company's intranet, losses are "not tied to an [individual] asset."[248] In fact, "many of the most spectacular security breaches in history started in relatively unimportant and neglected entry points. . . . "[249] This is in part because security is focused on the networks' periphery – after penetration, internal security is minimal.[250] Second, statistical forecasting can only take us so far; it does not, for example, "tell you much about your individual risks[.]"[251] Third, and relatedly, risk management works well when insurance companies "can use statistical modeling to offset capped claims,"

[240] Mills, *supra* note 234.
[241] *Trial by Fire*, *supra* note 202, at 18–19.
[242] *Id.* at 33, 35.
[243] *Eye of the Storm*, *supra* note 222, at 6.
[244] Palmer, *supra* note 13.
[245] *See* Jacques Bus, *Societal Dependencies and Trust*, *in* THE QUEST FOR CYBER PEACE 14, 23 (Int'l Telecomm. Union & Permanent Monitoring Panel on Info. Sec. eds., 2011), http://www.itu.int/dms_pub/itu-s/opb/gen/S-GEN-WFS.01-1-2011-PDF-E.pdf (defining risk management "as processes involving risk identification and analysis and decision-making including maximization of positive and minimization of negative implications of risk event occurrence.").
[246] Michal Zalewski, *Security Engineering: Broken Promises*, ZDNET (May 20, 2010), http://www.zdnet.com/blog/security/security-engineering-broken-promises/6503.
[247] *Id.*
[248] *Id.*
[249] *Id.*
[250] Palmer, *supra* note 13.
[251] Zalewski, *supra* note 246.

but this is difficult in the context of cybersecurity.[252] These caveats should push firms to rethink risk management and to assess cyber risk as comprehensively as possible.

Risk assessment is an important dimension to developing organizational cybersecurity, both in the long-term project of improving private-sector cybersecurity and in the short-term to help guide limited investment. Effective risk assessment requires having a well-developed understanding of both technical threats and vulnerabilities. However, many firms do not regularly assess their cyber risk,[253] and most reportedly do not rely on third parties to conduct audits.[254] Without formal assessments it can be difficult to offer a business case before a group of managers to go beyond baseline anti-virus suites.[255]

The extent to which an industry sector uses an explicit risk-analysis methodology varies widely. The financial sector has developed its own standards and means of evaluating best practices. This reflects the diversity of organizational approaches to cybersecurity, although firms with coordinated, centralized, and proactive cybersecurity policies managed by effective leaders fare better than those with a more reactive stance. This may broadly be considered as an application of the power of negative thinking to cybersecurity, e.g., plan for every possible type of cyber attack and thereby gain knowledge about the strengths and weaknesses in a firm's cybersecurity strategy.[256] Even as organizational cybersecurity varies, however, firms face common challenges that affect the ability of the competitive market to enhance cybersecurity on its own.

Challenges to Corporate Cybersecurity

Three of the most significant cybersecurity challenges faced by the private sector are inadequate information sharing, linking business to IT security resources, and enhancing coordination as management becomes further removed from data supervision. Regarding the first issue, there is insufficient data available to reliably assess risk, as was previously discussed. Some of the best assets are sector-based and information-sharing organizations. For example, the financial sector has organizations like the Financial Services Roundtable mentioned earlier in the chapter. Membership organizations like CSI and TechAmerica also share information within their communities. Meanwhile, there are several U.S. government organizations that

---

[252] *Id.*

[253] *See* Underground Economies, *supra* note 80, at 11; *Trial by Fire*, *supra* note 202, at 32–33 (noting that only 30 percent of surveyed North American firms conducted "enterprise risk assessment[s] at least twice a year[,]" compared to 43 percent of South American firms).

[254] *Trial by Fire*, *supra* note 202, at 18–19.

[255] *See* Dynes, *supra* note 180, at 11.

[256] *See* Chris Hadfield, An Astronaut's Guide to Life on Earth: What Going to Space Taught Me About Ingenuity, Determination, and Being Prepared for Anything 53–54, 72 (2013) ("Like most astronauts, I'm pretty sure that I can deal with what life throws at me because I've thought about what to do if things go wrong, as well as right. That's the power of negative thinking.").

encourage information sharing, such as InfraGard, which serves as a platform for the FBI, "businesses, academic institutions, and law enforcement to . . . share information to prevent" cyber attacks.[257] Additionally, Information Sharing and Analysis Centers were created in 1998 to encourage companies in important industries to engage with the government. There are now some sixteen ISACs devoted to many different sectors, including water, electric, nuclear, IT, and financial services.[258] However, most firms do not share data through information-sharing organizations. In 2007, just 19 percent of the respondents to a CSI survey reported that they belong to an ISAC.[259] Two of the most significant reasons for not reporting incidents to law enforcement officials include fear that competitors or cybercriminals might use leaked information to their advantage, and a belief that nothing will be gained.[260] However, information sharing will be important to improving private-sector cybersecurity capacities as well as enabling effective policymaking. This may serve as motivation for the government to invest in improving public-private partnerships, as is discussed in the next section.

Effective cybersecurity requires collaboration and that programs and systems be infused with best practices from the beginning. As the U.S. publisher Henry R. Luce wrote, "Business, more than any other occupation, is a continual dealing with the future; it is a continual calculation, an instinctive exercise in foresight."[261] It requires that companies stay on top of new problems, know their own capacity, and invest early. For example, in promoting its cloud services technology in early 2011, Google released a white paper explaining its approach to security, stating that security is a "key component" of its development process.[262] This exemplifies Dynes's systemic paradigm and may be compared to Microsoft's SDL. And Google did not get there by accident; it has a formal corporate cybersecurity policy enforced through regular audits, an ongoing employee education program, and an embedded cybersecurity team.[263] The impact of these efforts can be seen in the Google Chrome browser, which is now among the most secure in its class.[264] Palmer points to Chrome as showing that "defensive security engineering can work, at least within certain

---

[257] U.S. Chamber Comm., Internet Security Essentials for Business 2.0 at 32 (2012), https://www.uschamber.com/sites/default/files/legacy/issues/defense/files/020956_PDF_web.pdf; *see About Infra-Gard*, InfraGard, https://www.infragard.org/ (last visited Jan. 22, 2014).

[258] *See, e.g., About Us*, Nat'l Council of ISACs, http://www.isaccouncil.org/aboutus.html (last visited June 21, 2013).

[259] *See* 2008 CSI Survey, *supra* note 45, at 22.

[260] *See* Rantala, *supra* note 58, at 7.

[261] Leslie Pockell & Adrienne Avila, The 101 Greatest Business Principles of All Time 74 (2004).

[262] *Security Whitepaper: Google Apps Messaging and Collaboration Products*, Google (2010), at 2, http://static.googleusercontent.com/external_content/untrusted_dlcp/www.google.com/en/us/a/help/intl/en-GB/admins/pdf/ds_gsa_apps_whitepaper_0207.pdf.

[263] *Id.* at 2–3, 6, 11.

[264] *See* Palmer, *supra* note 13; Gregg Keizer, *German Gov't Endorses Chrome as Most Secure Browser*, Computerworld (Feb. 3, 2012), http://www.computerworld.com/s/article/9223957/German_gov_t_endorses_Chrome_as_most_secure_browser.

bounds, even in extremely difficult cases like web browsers. That has implications for how we handle cyber war and peace: it shows that security-as-quality-engineering is viable. . . ."[265] These proactive policies have not kept Google from getting attacked, but they have likely lessened the instances and severity of breaches. In addition, Google's partnerships with the U.S. government has allowed for more effective information sharing, making the firm better able to manage sophisticated cyber attacks.[266] Fundamentally, this reflects a proactive and business-minded approach to cybersecurity where security is not only part of the technology development process, but also the management's general strategy. Instilling this quality in more private-sector cybersecurity strategies is pivotal to the ability of the competitive marketplace to foster cyber peace.

Taking a proactive approach to cybersecurity will be increasingly important as companies are becoming more integrated globally and management is further removed from direct data supervision. Mark Lobel of PwC has noted that this is especially important for companies that, unlike Google, may not have the capacity to manage all of their data.[267] According to Michael Versace, senior advisor at the Financial Services Technology Consortium, companies should "expand their view of information governance and security policy beyond the perimeter [of their net-works] and think strategically about the value of information assets in the extended enterprise. . . ."[268] Unfortunately, firms too often think of security like building castle walls in the Middle Ages: they devote all of their resources to the perimeter and are defenseless once an attacker sneaks inside, as Palmer noted earlier in the chapter. The same goes for firewalls. Perimeter security is important, but oftentimes, businesses not only leave portions of their vital internal networks undefended, but also forget that their own castle walls do not wrap around their allies with which they may share supply lines. Taken to an extreme, just as marauding bands of Vikings and Mongols incentivized European cities to build walls cutting them off from one another, cyber attacks could eventually shape business decisions to such an extent that they might limit partnerships and impede growth.[269]

Thus, firms need to not only consider how they will protect valuable information on their own networks, but also how they will manage the associated risks of storing their data on another company's system. Hutchins, CIO at T2 Systems, reports that only about 5 to 10 percent of the companies with which his firm works understand

---

[265] Palmer, *supra* note 13.

[266] *See* Ellen Nakashima, *Google to Enlist NSA to Help it Ward off Cyberattacks*, WASH. POST (Feb. 4, 2010), http://www.washingtonpost.com/wp-dyn/content/article/2010/02/03/AR2010020304057.html?hpid=topnews.

[267] Bill Brenner, *Business Partners a Growing Security Concern*, CSO SEC. & RISK (Sept. 29, 2010), http://www.csoonline.com/article/620074/business-partners-a-growing-security-concern.

[268] UNSECURED ECONOMIES, *supra* note 132, at 25.

[269] *See* Cheng Li & Ryan McElveen, *NSA Revelations Have Irreparably Hurt U.S. Corporations in China*, BROOKINGS INST. (Dec. 12, 2013), http://www.brookings.edu/research/opinions/2013/12/12-nsa-revelations-hurt-corporations-china-li-mcelveen.

how their data is being secured.[270] This is especially troubling because peer companies are often best at informing and influencing one another.[271] Beyond that, companies can hold vendors or third parties accountable contractually or operationally. Companies consequently should follow President Ronald Reagan's tactics in enforcing nuclear arms treaties: "Trust but verify."[272] This includes vetting potential vendors, limiting what third parties can access, and escorting them when they visit in person. As of 2011, according to a 2012 PwC survey, 56 percent of North American respondents "have established security baselines for partners and customers."[273] Thus, many firms are increasingly concerned about their affiliates' security.[274] The U.S. government has also become more engaged with ensuring supplier security, taking the step in a 2012 House Intelligence Report of instructing U.S. firms not to do business with Huawei, a leading Chinese telecom company, lest malware be more easily introduced into U.S. CNI.[275]

There are additional positive signs, however, that corporate leaders may be starting to understand cybersecurity challenges and how they may be better managed.[276] According to PwC, "Asked to select from a list of seventeen possible strategies for meeting security objectives" in 2010, "CEOs pointed to a priority often overlooked by . . . business[es] in years past and frequently championed by CIOs and CISOs: increasing the focus on data protection."[277] CISOs are making some headway in the boardroom. For example, Hutchins notes that he has finally gotten through to his bosses. Board meetings used to go something like this: "Okay, so if you get the funding for this security measure, that will make us 100 percent secure?"[278] "No," Hutchins would respond, "it will make us *more* secure."[279] But now the Board better recognizes how cybersecurity works. Still, Hutchins knows that every company could invest more than it currently does and perhaps be no more secure as a result.[280] That is a paradox of IT security: there is both near infinite risk and room for investment, and each carries the other forward. In that way, cybersecurity is like plumbing insofar as few people notice it until it stops working, and then it is worth paying whatever it takes to fix. The major challenge this paradox presents to businesses, then, is defining the threat matrix and making smart investments to proactively protect their customers and reputations.

---

[270] Hutchins, *supra* note 34.

[271] *See, e.g.,* Dynes, *supra* note 184, at 8.

[272] *See, e.g.,* Kenneth W. Abbott, *'Trust But Verify': The Production of Information in Arms Control Treaties and Other International Agreements,* 26 CORNELL INT'L L.J. 1, 2 (1993).

[273] *See Trial by Fire, supra* note 202, at 14, 32–33 fig. 12.

[274] *Id.*

[275] *See* Mike Rogers & Dutch Ruppersberger, *Investigative Report on the U.S. National Security Issues Posed by Chinese Telecommunications Companies Huawei and ZTE,* 112th Cong. vi (2012).

[276] *Trial by Fire, supra* note 202, at 16–17.

[277] *Id.* at 16.

[278] Hutchins, *supra* note 34.

[279] *Id.*

[280] *Id.*

There are immediate and long-term benefits for taking such a proactive cyberse-curity stance, that is, building it in rather than bolting it on after the fact. Surveys have shown that firms that invest in "a more favorable security posture" pay less per compromised record, for example, than do other companies.[281] However, the type and extent of investment must be analyzed using robust information-sharing mechanisms to instill technical, budgetary, and organizational best practices. Given the private sector's dominant role in securing CNI, it will often need to take the lead. However, automobile safety did not arrive by the will of Henry Ford and his cohorts alone. There were many other stakeholders affecting the strategies of companies in that century-long (and ongoing) project, just as there will be in cybersecurity. It is in the private sector's best interest to enhance security, but the competitive market is not a panacea. Industry leaders such as Microsoft, Google, and Facebook have built proactive methods for threat management and there has been movement to improve organization and investments, but, as seen in the strategic management literature, voluntary mechanisms have inherent limitations, especially given the rapid pace of technological change. As Professor Murray argues, "The market functions – but only so far!"[282] Governments also have a role to play in helping the private sector meet cybersecurity challenges, but what form should regulation take, and how can any adverse impact to innovation be minimized?[283]

MANAGING MARKET IMPERFECTIONS THROUGH MARKET-BASED INCENTIVES AND REGULATORY INTERVENTION

Elements within the private sector have begun to address the many challenges of integrating cybersecurity into their business policies. However, market imperfections exist and keep firms from sufficiently enhancing cybersecurity, partly because of the presence of negative externalities and imperfect information.[284] Moreover, given that cybersecurity is a public good – described in Chapter 1 as something that is underproduced by the private sector because it is both non-excludable and non-rivalrous – there is an argument that regulators have an important role to play in managing it.[285] As a CSIS Commission argued: "An appropriate level of cybersecurity

---

[281] *See, e.g.*, DATA BREACH, *supra* note 130, at 7.

[282] MURRAY, *supra* note 24, at 200.

[283] *See, e.g., The Administration Unveils its Cybersecurity Legislative Proposal*, WHITE HOUSE (May 12, 2011), http://www.whitehouse.gov/blog/2011/05/12/administration-unveils-its-cybersecurity-legislative-proposal (arguing for the need to strike a "critical balance between maintaining the government's role and providing industry with the capacity to innovatively tackle threats to national cybersecurity.").

[284] *See* Dan Assaf, *Government Intervention in Information Infrastructure Protection*, *in* CRITICAL INFRA-STRUCTURE PROTECTION 29, 33–36 (Eric Goetz & Sujeet Shenoi eds., 2007).

[285] Non-excludable signifies that it is impossible to prevent others from enjoying the benefit of the good, while non-rival means that one's use of the good does not detract from another's enjoyment. *Cf.* Paul Rosenzweig, *Cybersecurity and Public Goods: The Public/Private "Partnership"*, HOOVER INST., at 7–9 (2012), media.hoover.org/documents/EmergingThreats_Rosenzweig.pdf (arguing that "information

cannot be achieved without regulation, as market forces alone will never provide the level of security necessary to achieve national security objectives."[286] This sentiment has been echoed by the likes of General Hayden.[287] Debt, technical or otherwise, is rarely something that individuals, organizations, or institutions willingly address without necessity. The question becomes which inducements and regulations may be required to incentivize the private sector to enhance cybersecurity and secure CNI.[288] Just as regulation, lawsuits, and publicly disclosed ratings triggered better safety standards in the automobile industry, so may deterrents and incentives help to secure cyberspace.

This section considers the potential benefits and drawbacks of a few leading approaches to regulating cybersecurity. It begins by evaluating the current U.S. cybersecurity regulatory framework and the benefits and drawbacks of imposing liability for cyber attacks. Then, the potential of cyber-risk mitigation schemes focusing on insurance is analyzed.[289] Finally, oft-hyped public-private partnerships are considered, acknowledging both their limitations and importance. None of these approaches are magic bullets, but each has the potential to cajole, encourage, or even require the private sector to more proactively manage cybersecurity and foster cyber peace.

Regulatory Intervention to Manage Cyber Attacks

It took the automobile industry decades to be held liable for its "death seat," as the 1950 *Popular Science* article referred to it,[290] and as of yet, the makers of IT hardware and software are generally only liable to the extent that they offer customers purchase

about threat and vulnerability" is a public good, but that "the remaining elements are either private goods with recognized externalities and grave challenges for government regulation, or common pool resources with equally grave challenges for private sector coordination."). Professor Rosenzweig also considers whether, instead of a public good, cybersecurity may be considered a "club good," which he describes as resources "from which some users may be excluded but where access is controlled such that the resources are non-rivalrous." *Id.* at 11 n.46. As cyberspace becomes more enclosed through national regulation and the consolidation of the web, such a conceptualization may yield more robust cybersecurity policies.

[286] CSIS COMMISSION ON CYBERSECURITY, SECURING CYBERSPACE FOR THE 44TH PRESIDENCY 50 (Dec. 2008).

[287] *See* James Bamford, *The Secret War*, WIRED (June 12, 2013), http://www.wired.com/threatlevel/2013/06/general-keith-alexander-cyberwar/ (expressing concern "that this is going to break a threshold where the private sector can no longer handle it and the government is going to have to step in.").

[288] *See* Rosenzweig, *supra* note 285, at 9 (noting that if elements of cybersecurity are considered private goods, then externalities may arise. He identifies positive externalities in the form of securing systems and "raising the cost of attack" throughout cyberspace, as well as negative externalities, namely "diversion" – diverting attacks to other less protected systems – and "pricing," which refers to firms not internalizing the costs of cyber attacks, as will be discussed later in the chapter).

[289] *See, e.g.*, H. Republican Cybersecurity Task Force, 112th Cong., Recommendations of the House Republican Cybersecurity Task Force 5, 8, 14 (2011) [hereinafter House Cybersecurity Task Force].

[290] *See* Waltz, *supra* note 173.

warranties. To understand this issue, imagine that you bought a defunct toaster.[291] You do nothing wrong, but it catches fire and destroys your laptop in the process. The manufacturer would likely be liable for its defective product and any damage that it caused.[292] Alternatively, imagine that your laptop is running software that includes a known vulnerability for which a patch has not yet been released. A cyber attacker strikes, and your laptop crashes. Once again you would argue that you as the consumer did nothing wrong; there was no patch that you forgot to install. But in this context, unless it is covered by a warranty, the repair cost is on you.

Recall the box that you click at the end of a long scroll when installing a new piece of software, like the more than thirty pages of terms and conditions for iTunes.[293] Clicking on "accept" also typically means that you agree not to hold the software company liable across a range of situations.[294] In some ways, this makes sense. Toasters are not that complicated and have been around since at least 1919, so we know how to make them relatively well, and companies should be held responsible for not doing so. However, software is difficult to make vulnerability-free, and there are not yet agreed-upon ways to conduct the cyber equivalent of crash tests,[295] so arguably the market is not yet mature enough to permit regulators to hold firms responsible for their products. But on the other hand, this seems counterintuitive. Toasters are uncomplicated, and many consumers understand how they work better than how their laptops function. As a result, perhaps consumers should be more responsible for safely using simple machines like toasters, while companies should be responsible for ensuring the safety of sophisticated software, which is too complex for the typical consumer to be expected to understand. This line of reasoning has led to calls for software developers to be held liable for their code. In fact, the EU Commission has debated extending the EU Sales and Guarantees Directive to software.[296]

---

[291] Interview with Jim Dempsey, vice president for Public Policy, Center for Democracy and Technology, in San Francisco, Cal. (Feb. 22, 2011).

[292] *See* Restatement (Third) of Torts: Products Liability § 402(A) (1965).

[293] *See Apple Terms and Conditions*, Apple, http://www.apple.com/legal/internet-services/itunes/ww/# north-america (last visited Jan. 22, 2014).

[294] For the enforceability of these types of contracts, see, e.g., *Are "Click Through" Agreements Enforceable?*, Wilmer Hale (Mar. 22, 2000), http://www.wilmerhale.com/pages/publicationsandNewsDetail .aspx?NewsPubId=86850 (arguing that many courts have tended to enforce these types of contracts under certain circumstances).

[295] *Cf.* DARPA, National Cyber Range: A National Testbed for Critical Security Research 1, http://www.whitehouse.gov/files/documents/cyber/DARPA%20-%20NationalCyberRange_FactSheet .pdf (last visited Jan. 22, 2014) ("The National Cyber Range will allow classified and unclassified researchers to measure their progress in either a classified or unclassified environment, against appropriate threats, with sufficient timeliness and accuracy to allow for corrections and identify new capability needs.").

[296] *See* EU Consumer Aff., Eur. Union., http://ec.europa.eu/consumers/rights/gen_rights_en.htm#gar (last visited May 26, 2013); Tom Espiner, *EC Wants Software Makers Held Liable for Code*, ZDNet (May 8, 2009), http://www.zdnet.com/news/ec-wants-software-makers-held-liable-for-code/300769.

For now, whether it is reasonable or not, many software and hardware vendors continue to enjoy immunity from liability for three main reasons. First, few good options exist for how corporate liability should work in the cyber context, and those that have been proposed come with significant downsides.[297] Second, there are the technical reasons of contractual limitations in agreements, and inadequate information sharing.[298] Third, and perhaps most importantly, are indirect costs. For example, making companies liable will likely increase the price of software.[299] Neither firms nor consumers are yet being hurt by such negative externalities, but that cannot last, according to Palmer.[300] He calls this phenomenon "technical debt for consumers," noting that although we have enjoyed the plunging prices of hardware and software over the past decade, we can no longer ignore the accumulated debt.[301]

There is also the issue of what to do about free and open-source software. Cybersecurity specialist Bruce Schneier, for example, has argued that free and open-source software developers should not be held liable in the absence of a contractual relationship.[302] As long as humans write code, mistakes will happen. For its part, Microsoft considers the occurrence of vulnerabilities as a product quality issue that must be addressed by programmer training and supervision.[303] Holding software firms liable for problems raises a host of issues, which, although not insurmountable, make such regulation unlikely for the foreseeable future.

Beyond software liability, there is an array of domestic regulatory interventions and international laws in place to protect users from cyber threats, and still more are being debated. For example, the Fair Credit Reporting Act (FCRA) and the Gramm-Leach-Bliley Act (GLBA), which allow commercial banks, investment banks, and insurance companies to consolidate and regulate some aspects of corporate liability to safeguard private information, also have cybersecurity components.[304] The FCRA regulates cybersecurity mainly retrospectively, requiring that an agency issues an alert and tries to block further exploitation after it receives word of an identity theft.[305] There are no built-in checks on the employees who manage data or on hackers who would seek to gain access to such data through clandestine means. The GLBA

---

[297] See Tyler Moore, *Introducing the Economics of Cybersecurity: Principles and Policy Options*, Proc. Workshop Deterring Cyber Attacks: Informing Strategies & Developing Options for U.S. Policy (Nat'l Res. Council, 2010), at 10 (exploring the potential of imposing ex post liability on software developers, and discussing the downsides of doing so including negatively impact innovation).

[298] See Joseph R. Tiano, Jr., *The Liability of Computerized Information Providers: A Look Back and a Proposed Analysis for the Future*, 56 U. Pitt. L. Rev. 655, 656–57 (1995).

[299] Palmer, *supra* note 13.

[300] *Id.*

[301] *Id.*

[302] See Glyn Moody, *Should Software Developers Be Liable for Their Code?*, Linux J. (May 9, 2009), http://www.linuxjournal.com/content/should-software-developers-be-liable-their-code.

[303] See Lipner, *supra* note 156.

[304] See 15 U.S.C. § 1681 (2000); 15 U.S.C. §§ 6801–6827 (2000).

[305] See 15 U.S.C. § 1681(m).

was established to protect individuals' personal financial data preserved by financial institutions.[306] It requires covered firms to provide consumers privacy notices explaining the institutions' information-sharing practices and to ensure against unauthorized access of customer records.[307] So, too, does the Identity Theft and Assumption Deterrence Act, which enables the Federal Trade Commission (FTC) to investigate cases of identity theft and criminalizes the possession of any means of identification without lawful authority,[308] making it punishable by more than 20 years in federal prison plus fines under some circumstances.[309]

Still, although some businesses, like financial institutions under the GLBA, have a legal duty to safeguard customer data, as of October 2012 none has a duty to disclose a security breach to consumers unless the SEC or state law mandates it.[310] The Health Insurance Portability and Accountability Act (HIPAA) requires the disclosure of data breaches, but it applies only to private health information.[311] However, Sarbanes-Oxley has created an incentive for firms to enhance their cybersecurity because of its emphasis on internal control procedures including security.[312] Myriad other federal laws require cybersecurity compliance by covered firms and an entire industry has arisen to help them comply with statutory requirements,[313] which are oftentimes sector specific. Generally, though, the public sector has been more heavily regulated than the private sector in this domain as is exemplified by the Federal Information Security Management Act (FISMA), which, among other things, empowers the Office of Management and Budget to coordinate information security standards developed by federal agencies and their contractors.[314] The Identity Theft Penalty Enhancement Act of 2004, which establishes a new federal crime known as aggravated identity theft,[315] as well as the Electronic Communications Privacy Act

---

[306] *See, e.g.*, M. Maureen Murphy, *Privacy Protection for Customer Financial Data, Privacy Protection for Customer Financial Information*, CONG. RES. SERV., RS20185 at 2 (2012).

[307] *See id.* at 3; 15 U.S.C. § 6801(b)(1–3).

[308] *See Identity Theft and Assumption Deterrence Act*, Pub. L. No. 105–318, 112 Stat. 3007 (1998), http://www .ftc.gov/os/statutes/itada/itadact.pdf. Section 5 of the Federal Trade Commission Act, which regulates "unfair or deceptive acts and practicees that affect commerce," is also applicable to managing cyber attacks given that the FTC has charged firms at times for "failure to adopt reasonable information security practices." Moore, *supra* note 297, at 10 (citing 15 U.S.C. § 45).

[309] 18 U.S.C. § 1028(b)(3).

[310] *See* WSGR ALERT, *supra* note 37.

[311] *See* Murphy, *supra* note 306, at 6; 42 U.S.C. § 1320(d)(2) (1998).

[312] *See* Gordon, *supra* note 42, at 6.

[313] *See, e.g., Industry/Compliance*, SOURCEFIRE, http://www.sourcefire.com/industry-compliance (last visited Jan. 22, 2014).

[314] *See, e.g., FISMA*, SOURCEFIRE, http://www.sourcefire.com/industry-compliance/compliance-solutions/ fisma (last visited June 21, 2013).

[315] *See* 18 U.S.C. § 1028A (2008). ECPA specifies standards for government surveillance of Internet communications, but has not been updated since it was passed in 1986, despite efforts to enhance its privacy protections. *See* Press Release, U.S. Senator Patrick Leahy, Leahy Introduces Benchmark Bill To Update Key Digital Privacy Law (May 17, 2011), http://www.leahy.senate.gov/press/leahy-introduces-benchmark-bill-to-update-key-digital-privacy-law.

(ECPA) are also applicable,[316] but a comprehensive review of U.S. federal legislation is beyond the scope of this book. Suffice it to say, though, that U.S. federal law maintains a largely sector-specific and fragmented approach to enhancing cybersecurity, though it is far from alone in that regard.[317]

Aside from federal law, as of August 2012, forty-six states have passed some kind of data breach notification requirements, but variations create a complex and at times contradictory regulatory environment for firms operating across jurisdictions.[318] For example, a handful of states have a "no-harm threshold law," meaning that it does not matter whether lost information was used in a way that hurt consumers or not.[319] States also have more- or less-inclusive lists of personally identifiable information that must be lost for a breach to warrant disclosure. In states that do not have any data breach notification laws as of 2012, such as Alabama and South Dakota, a company could knowingly have its customers' social security numbers breached, not inform them, and may still be legally compliant under state law.[320] But these breach notification laws were designed to manage the problem of identity theft, not IP loss. The Obama administration's mid-2011 Cyberspace Policy Review discussed in Chapter 7 laid out some proposals to address this issue.[321]

Any legislation dealing with cybersecurity faces daunting prospects on Capitol Hill, given that, according to Senator John McCain, "at least seven committees claim some jurisdiction over the issue."[322] If attempts to pass anti-piracy legislation are any indication, comprehensive reform will likely face broader challenges from

---

[316] 18 U.S.C. §§ 2701-12 (2006).

[317] *See, e.g.*, Nicole Henderson, *Canadian Government Approach to Cybersecurity Fragmented: Auditor General Report*, WHIR (Oct. 24, 2012), http://www.thewhir.com/web-hosting-news/canadian-government-approach-to-cybersecurity-fragmented-auditor-general-report; Karine Silva, *Europe's Fragmented Approach Towards Cyber Security*, INTERNET POL'Y REV. (Oct. 10, 2013), http://policyreview.info/articles/analysis/europe%E2%80%99s-fragmented-approach-towards-cyber-security.

[318] *See State Security Breach Notification Laws*, NAT'L CONF. OF ST. LEGISLATURES (last updated Jan. 21, 2014), http://www.ncsl.org/research/telecommunications-and-information-technology/security-breach-notification-laws.aspx; *see also* Kevin J. O'Brien, *Europe Weighs Requiring Firms to Disclose Data Breaches*, N.Y. TIMES (Jan. 17, 2013), http://www.nytimes.com/2013/01/17/technology/17iht-data17.html (reporting that a proposed EU directive would require EU-wide data breach reporting for all firms that "run large databases, those used for Internet searches, social networks, e-commerce or cloud services.").

[319] Mike Tsikoudakis, *Patchwork of Data Breach Notification Laws Poses Challenge*, BUS. INS. (June 5, 2011), http://www.businessinsurance.com/apps/pbcs.dll/article?AID=/20110605/ISSUE03/306059998.

[320] *See* Jacqueline May Tom, *A Simple Compromise: The Need for a Federal Data Breach Notification Law*, 84 ST. JOHN'S L. REV. 1569, 1570 (2011).

[321] *See* WHITE HOUSE, CYBERSPACE POLICY REVIEW: ASSURING A TRUSTED AND RESILIENT INFORMATION AND COMMUNICATIONS INFRASTRUCTURE, at iv (2011), http://www.whitehouse.gov/assets/documents/Cyberspace_Policy_Review_final.pdf [hereinafter CYBERSPACE POLICY REVIEW].

[322] Press Release, U.S. Senator John McCain, Senator John McCain Calls for a Select Committee on Cyber Security and Electronic Intelligence Leaks (July 13, 2011), http://www.mccain.senate.gov/public/index.cfm/press-releases?ID=250e73df-04c9-0fe5-5417-7701b0ec3945 [hereinafter McCain Press Release]; *see also* Ben Pershing, *On Cybersecurity, Congress Can't Agree on Turf*, WASH. POST (July 18, 2011), http://www.washingtonpost.com/politics/on-cybersecurity-congress-cant-agree-on-turf/

the private sector and non-profit community. In January 2012, U.S. Senate and House attempts to pass the Protect IP Act and the Stop Online Piracy Act (SOPA) were halted after more than 100 companies (including Google and Facebook), public interest organizations, and cybersecurity specialists, among others, rallied against them.[323] A core concern was about the degree to which the bills would undermine the 1998 Digital Millennium Copyright Act (DMCA) "safe harbor" provision, which limits an ISP's liability for copyrighted content that users upload onto their sites.[324] Many organizations also expressed concern about the way in which the bills would impact free expression and innovation by allowing courts to take down websites that facilitate limited copyright infringement regardless of their intentions or more general purpose.[325] Still, these and other legislative initiatives may be pushing ISPs to implement more self-policing mechanisms, including efforts to notify and educate users about their illegal activities,[326] which may be considered a limited move toward polycentric governance.

Dozens of bills have been proposed to shore up U.S. cybersecurity. These include the Lieberman-Carper-Collins Bill, which would have required the DHS to develop a government-wide security strategy,[327] as well as the Rockefeller-Snowe Bill, which relied more on incentives to urge the private sector to collaborate with the government on developing standards to secure CNI.[328] Other provisions in these and other bills are designed to improve private-sector defenses, including mandatory audits and incentives for information sharing including legal immunity after certain kinds of cyber attacks.[329] However, other ideas, such as giving tax breaks for

2011/07/18/gIQACGCWMI_story.html (asking, "Congress already has more than 40 committees and well over 100 subcommittees. Does it really need one more?").

[323] *See List of Those Expressing Concern With SOPA and PIPA*, Ctr. Democracy & Tech. (Jan. 25, 2012), https://www.cdt.org/report/list-organizations-and-individuals-opposing-sopa; *see also* Hayley Tsukayama, *Web Activists Celebrate 'Internet Freedom Day*,' Wash. Post (Jan. 18, 2013), http://www .washingtonpost.com/business/technology/web-activists-celebrate-internet-freedom-day/2013/01/18/ 45655826-617d-11e2-9940-6fc488f3fecd_story.html?wpmk=MK0000200 (reporting on the first annual "Internet Freedom Day" on January 18, 2013, which in part commemorates the defeat of SOPA and calls on activists to demand updates to privacy regulations).

[324] 17 U.S.C. § 512(c) (2006).

[325] *See, e.g.*, David Sohn, *House Copyright Bill Casts Dangerously Broad Net*, Ctr. Democracy & Tech. (Oct. 27, 2011), https://www.cdt.org/blogs/david-sohn/2710house-copyright-bill-casts-dangerously-broad-net.

[326] *See* Doug Gross, *With SOPA Shelved, Anti-Piracy Advocates Take New Approaches*, CNN (Mar. 22, 2012), http://www.cnn.com/2012/03/22/tech/web/isps-sopa-piracy/index.html; Mathew Ingram, *Should You Fear the 'Six Strikes' Anti-Piracy Rule?*, Bloomberg Businessweek Tech. (Feb. 27, 2013), http:// www.businessweek.com/articles/2013-02-27/should-you-fear-the-six-strikes-anti-piracy-rule (reporting on "[a] new system designed to combat copyright infringement" launched by "content companies and internet service providers known as the Copyright Alert System.").

[327] *See* Protecting Cyberspace as a National Asset Act of 2010, S. 3480, 111th Cong. §§102(a), 246, 249(a) (2010), http://www.gpo.gov/fdsys/pkg/BILLS-111s3480is/pdf/BILLS-111s3480is.pdf.

[328] *See* Cybersecurity Act of 2009, S. 773, 111th Cong. (2009), http://www.gpo.gov/fdsys/pkg/BILLS-111s773is/pdf/BILLS-111s773is.pdf.

[329] *See* Rachel M. Zahorsky, *What Law Firms Should Know About Cyberattacks and the FBI*, ABA J. (May 23, 2013), http://www.abajournal.com/news/article/what_law_firms_should_know_about_cyber_

upgrading cybersecurity defenses, are noticably absent in many of these efforts, although the 2011 House Cybersecurity Recommendations do encourage Congress to consider expanding existing tax credits.[330]

To cut through the morass, Senator McCain proposed the creation of a Select Committee on Cybersecurity and Electronic Intelligence Leaks, which could produce comprehensive legislation on the subject.[331] As of June 2013, though, the proposal had not been enacted, leading other policymakers such as Senator Jay Rockerfeller to take additional steps including sending letters to the CEOs of every Fortune 500 company asking them to describe their cybersecurity practices.[332] The tenor of the debate changes, however, when considering how much power to give the government in a cyber emergency. The Rockefeller-Snowe bill would, for example, give the president the power to shut down sections of the private Internet in an emergency, a cyber "kill switch."[333] Debates remain fluid especially given continuing revelations from former NSA contractor Edward Snowden,[334] and although cybersecurity remains an area in which some bipartisan consensus is apparent, the ultimate form that legislation may take, including the controversial Cyber Intelligence Sharing and Protection Act (CISPA), remains to be seen.[335] However, the NIST cybersecurity framework introduced in Chapter 4 has the potential to shift the debate in the United States and perhaps around the world even without Congressional action, including potentially helping to define a cybersecurity duty of care, with which courts have been wrestling.[336]

attacks_and_the_fbi/ (reporting that requests for information from the FBI after cyber attacks are voluntary and do not come with legal immunity); Tony Romm, *NSA's Keith Alexander Seeks Cyber Shield for Companies*, POLITICO (June 16, 2013), http://www.politico.com/story/2013/06/ nsa-keith-alexander-cyber-shield-92880.html (discussing General Alexander's arguments in favor of granting legal immunity to companies "that help the feds fight cyberattackers.").

[330] *See* House Cybersecurity Task Force, *supra* note 289, at 8.

[331] *See* McCain Press Release, *supra* note 322.

[332] Siobhan Gorman, *Senator Presses on Cybersecurity*, WALL ST. J. (Sept. 19, 2012), http://online.wsj .com/news/articles/SB10000872396390044372020457800469000629961 4.

[333] *See, e.g.,* Declan McCullagh, *Bill Would Give President Emergency Control of Internet*, CNET (Aug. 28, 2009), http://news.cnet.com/8301-13578_3-10320096-38.html. Former Senators Joseph Lieberman and Susan Collins, however, refrained from including a "kill switch" in their draft cybersecuity legislation. *See* Chloe Albanesius, *Senators Introduce Cyber Bill with Ban on 'Internet Kill Switch,'* PC MAG. (Feb. 21, 2011), http://www.pcmag.com/article2/0,2817,2380680,00.asp.

[334] *See* Adam Mazmanian, *Lawmakers: Leaks Slowed Cybersecurity Legislation*, FCW (Sept. 12, 2013), http://fcw.com/articles/2013/09/12/snowden-cybersecurity-legislation.aspx.

[335] *See, e.g.,* Eric Engleman, *Reid to Move on Cybersecurity Measure in Early 2012*, BLOOMBERG (Nov. 17, 2011), http://www.bloomberg.com/news/2011-11-17/reid-to-move-on-senate-cybersecurity-legislation-in-early-2012.html; Julian Sanchez, *CISPA Is Dead. Now Let's Do a Cybersecurity Bill Right*, WIRED (Apr. 26, 2013), http://www.wired.com/opinion/2013/04/cispas-dead-now-lets-resurrect-it/.

[336] *See* Executive Order 13636: Improving Critical Infrastructure Cybersecurity, 78 Fed. Reg. 33, 11739 (Feb. 12, 2013); Gerald Ferguson, *NIST Cybersecurity Framework: Don't Underestimate It*, INFO. WK. (Dec. 9, 2013), http://www.informationweek.com/government/cybersecurity/ nist-cybersecurity-framework-dont-underestimate-it/d/d-id/1112978. President Obama has stated that his executive action was intended to, among other objectives, "strengthen our cyber defenses

Despite gaps in the legal framework, courts are increasingly willing to hold both organizations and firms liable for not protecting private information. For example, the Michigan Court of Appeals held a union responsible for failing to safeguard the private information of members who became victims of identity theft.[337] Another federal court judge in Michigan ruled that a local bank was at fault for not detecting earlier the losses its customers sustained through a phishing attack.[338] There have also been major class actions filed in invasion of privacy lawsuits. Two such cases filed in 2003 against several of the largest information brokers in the United States also implicated the state of Florida for not protecting the privacy of its residents.[339] Damages sought were more than $2,500 per violation, adding up to billions under the federal Driver Privacy Protection Act.[340] Ultimately, one of the defendant banks in the case was fined $50 million for purchasing data containing the personal information of hundreds of thousands of Florida residents for just $5,656.[341] In another case the FTC fined ChoicePoint, a large "data broker that maintains digital dossiers on nearly every adult in the United States," with a $10 million penalty – "the largest civil penalty in the agency's history" to that point.[342] In all, hundreds of millions of personal records have been exposed in thousands of incidents. A single breach in 2006 involving the theft of a laptop owned by the Veterans Administration that led to the loss of 26 million social security numbers of retired and active duty military personnel resulted in a class action lawsuit claiming some $26.5 billion in

---

by . . . developing standards to protect our national security, our jobs, and our privacy." Press Release, Office of the Press Sec'y, Remarks by the President in the State of the Union Address (Feb. 12, 2013), http://www.whitehouse.gov/the-press-office/2013/02/12/remarks-president-state-union-address. Among its many requirements, the Executive Order empowered the director of the National Institute of Standards and Technology to "lead the development of a framework to reduce cyber risks to critical infrastructure." 78 Fed. Reg. 33, 11740–41. This "Cybersecurity Framework" seeks to harmonize private sector best practices to "provide a prioritized, flexible, repeatable, performance-based, and cost-effective approach" to managing cyber risk. *Id.* at 11741.

[337] *See* Audrey Bell et al. v. Dentry Berry et al., Wayne Cir. Ct. LC No. 01–107819-NO, Mich. Ct. Appeals (Feb. 15, 2005).

[338] *See ACH Liability up for Grabs as Court Finds Against Bank in Second US Cyber-Heist Suit*, FINEXTRA (June 17, 2011), http://www.finextra.com/news/fullstory.aspx?newsitemid=22674.

[339] *See* Dan Christensen, *Major Information Brokers Face Class Action for Invasion of Privacy*, DAILY BUS. REV. (June 24, 2003), http://www.dailyreportonline.com/id=900005535773?slreturn=20140023140436.

[340] *See id.*; 18 U.S.C. § 2724(a) (2000).

[341] *See* K. C. Jones, *Bank to Pay $50 Million for Buying Personal Data*, INFO. WK. (Aug. 29, 2006), http://www.informationweek.com/bank-to-pay-50-million-for-buying-person/192500171.

[342] Gary Rivlin, *Keeping Your Enemies Close*, N.Y. TIMES (Nov. 12, 2006), http://www.nytimes.com/2006/11/12/business/yourmoney/12choice.html?_r=1; *see* AppleInsider Staff, *Google Agrees to Pay Largest Fine in FTC History for Bypassing Safari Privacy Settings*, APPLE INSIDER (Aug. 9, 2012), http://appleinsider.com/articles/12/08/09/google_agrees_to_pay_largest_fine_in_ftc_history_for_bypassing_safari_privacy_settings (reporting on a $22.5 million FTC fine levied against Google). In a similar instance the personal information of more than 540,000 New Yorkers was compromised when sensitive computer hardware went missing from a supposedly secure facility. CS Stars, a Chicago-based insurance broker, was responsible for the system, which was ultimately recovered by the FBI. *See, e.g., 540,000 New Yorkers at Risk of Identity Theft*, MSNBC (July 24, 2006), http://www.msnbc.msn.com/id/14015598/ns/technology_and_science-security/t/new-yorkers-risk-identity-theft/.

damages.[343] Yet litigation is by no means universally successful. In late 2012, for example, a federal judge dismissed a case against Sony resulting from its massive data breach on the grounds that its users signed a privacy policy that contained "clear admonitory language that Sony's security was not 'perfect,' [and therefore] no reasonable consumer could have been deceived."[344]

Other courts have considered whether victims of identity theft may bring a claim against financial institutions that have carelessly handled their personal information, sometimes arriving at contradictory rulings.[345] Still other decisions have recognized a broad tort duty of confidentiality, which suggests that banks and other protectors of private information have a duty to keep their customers' personal information secure and confidential.[346] Some scholars are getting creative, advocating for an independent tort of "negligent enablement of cybercrime" based on principles of premises liability (requiring that landowners who open their land to the public must use reasonable care in ensuring safety for their guests), product liability (holding producers liable for defective products), and warranty.[347] Such a tort is meant to get around mass-market license agreements (the "accept" checkbox) that typically include liability waivers for negligent software design, and could help protect consumers against breaches caused by foreseeable software flaws, shifting the burden to the party best able to evaluate cybersecurity.[348] Other lawsuits have been brought under the theory of "negligent enablement of imposer fraud."[349] However, many of these cases have so far been unsuccessful because of an absence of the duty element required in a negligence suit.[350] Absent cybersecurity reform legislation, attorneys will continue to advocate and courts will weigh the merits of novel legal arguments that could hold stakeholders more accountable. This could over time (depending on the uptake of the 2014 NIST Cybersecurity Framework) encourage industry to define a reasonable standard of cybersecurity care that would help internalize the

---

[343] *See* Joris Evers, *Veterans Affairs Faulted in Data Theft*, ZDNET (July 12, 2006), http://www .zdnet.com/news/veterans-affairs-faulted-in-data-theft/148782; Cindy Waxer, *The Hidden Cost of IT Security*, NETWORK SEC. J. (Apr. 16, 2006), http://www.networksecurityjournal.com/features/ hidden-cost-of-IT-security-041607/.

[344] In re: Sony Gaming Networks, 903 F. Supp. 2d 942, 968 (2012); *cf.* Schnall v. The Hertz Corp., 78 Cal.App.4th 1144, 1163–64, 93 Cal. Rptr. 2d 439 (2000) ("finding that disclaimers do not give notice to the reasonable consumer when they are incomprehensible and needlessly complex.").

[345] *See* Brandon McKelvey, *Financial Institutions' Duty of Confidentiality to Keep Customer's Personal Information Secure from the Threat of Identity Theft*, 34 U.C. DAVIS L. REV. 1077, 1077–78 (2001).

[346] *E.g.*, Peterson v. Idaho First Nat'l Bank, 367 P.2d 284, 290 (Idaho 1961).

[347] *See* Michael L. Rustad & Thomas H. Koenig, *The Tort of Negligent Enablement of Cybercrime*, 20 BERKELEY TECH. L.J. 1553, 1553, 1569, 1607 (2005).

[348] *Id.* at 1610–11.

[349] *See* Huggins v. Citibank, 585 S.E.2d 275, 333 (S.C. 2003).

[350] *Id.* at 334; Chris Jay Hoofnagle, *Putting Identity Theft on Ice: Freezing Credit Reports to Prevent Lending to Impostors*, in SECURING PRIVACY IN THE INTERNET AGE 207, 214 (Anupam Chander, Lauren Gelman, & Margaret Jane Radin eds., 2008). *See also* Willingham v. Global Payments, Inc., 2013 U.S. Dist. LEXIS 27764 (N.D. Ga., Feb. 5, 2013) ("Courts have found that no duty of care exists in the data breach context where, as here, there is no direct relationship between the plaintiff and the defendant.").

cost of cyber attacks and potentially increase market efficiency, but in the short term it also risks compounding uncertainty in the cyber regulatory environment. As Judge Learned Hand wrote in 1932 in a case requiring tugboat owners to have radios even though that was not yet statutorily required or an established industry custom, "Courts must in the end say what is required; there are precautions so imperative that even their universal disregard will not excuse their omission."[351]

The legal standards on which U.S. and other lawmakers settle will be important in shaping firms' cybersecurity investments. According to McAfee, "[f]or many companies, security and risk management decisions are based on strict adherence to compliance standards, not on protecting their intellectual capital."[352] Indeed, another McAfee survey found that compliance with regulation is the "key motivator" for security decisions "in Dubai, Germany, Japan, the U.K., and the U.S."; only in India and China did surveyed companies more often base security decisions on gaining or maintaining competitive advantages.[353] These surveys point to a trend showing that regulations are critical to firms' security investment decisions, even if businesses at times balk at additional regulatory compliance burdens. Consequently, regulatory intervention can play a vital role in enhancing the public good of cybersecurity. But how much is too much?

Survey data from PwC indicates that since 2008, many firms around the world are increasingly unhappy with cybersecurity regulations.[354] As many as 57 percent of Indian, 58 percent of U.S., and 72 percent of Chinese companies agreed that their regulatory environments were becoming "more complex and burdensome."[355] A Symantec report argued that "enterprises are buried with IT compliance efforts," ranging from HIPAA to Sarbanes-Oxley, which, among other things, impose severe fines on companies and even jail time for managers who are found to be noncompliant.[356] Some worry that well-meaning regulations may force companies to focus more on compliance than security (so-called "check-box compliance"), and others disagree about the effectiveness of existing regulations and argue that the onus should be on proponents of greater regulation to justify further interventions.[357] In the 2007 CSI survey, 25 percent of respondents "strongly disagreed" that Sarbanes-Oxley, for example, has improved its organizations' information security, and just

---

[351] Harold F. Tipton & Micki Krause, Information Security Management Handbook 2736 (6th ed. 2007) (citing In re Eastern Transportation Co. (The T.J. Hooper), 60 F.2d 737 (2d Cir. 1932)).

[352] Underground Economies, *supra* note 80, at 16.

[353] Unsecured Economies, *supra* note 132, at 6.

[354] *See Trial by Fire, supra* note 202, at 36.

[355] *Id.*

[356] State of Enterprise Security Study, *supra* note 27, at 12 (reporting that surveyed "enterprises are currently exploring a staggering 19 separate IT standards. . . . "). *See* Health Insurance Portability and Accountability Act (HIPAA) of 1996, Pub. L. No. 104–191, 110 Stat. 1998, §§ 669(a), 1347(2); HIPAA, Sourcefire, http://www.sourcefire.com/industry-compliance/compliance-solutions/HIPAA (last visited June 23, 2013) (reporting that HIPAA fines can range "up to $250K and/or imprisonment up to 10 years for knowing misuse of individually identifiable health information.").

[357] *See* Brito & Watkins, *supra* note 149, at 39–40, 82–83.

12 percent "strongly agreed" that the regulation had positive effects.[358] Similarly, only slightly more than one third of respondents to a 2011 McAfee survey said that they "feel that compliance regulations imposed by their home country are very useful and aim at the heart of the problem to protect their corporation's intellectual capital."[359] These findings point to the fact that more needs to be done to fashion effective cybersecurity interventions where needed, and to streamline compliance so that the focus is on enhancing cybersecurity and not checking boxes – not only in the United States, but also around the world.

Given the interconnected nature of the cyber regulatory environment, firms must consider applicable national and international laws beyond U.S. regulations. Analyzing the full breadth of the global cybersecurity regulatory landscape is beyond the scope of this book, but firms must be aware of the complexity in order to better understand their exposure. For example, for firms active in Canada, the Canadian Personal Information Protection and Electronic Documents Act requires that organizations secure private information.[360] In Europe, the German state of Hesse passed the first data protection law in 1970.[361] Many other European nations followed suit, eventually resulting in 1995 with the adoption of a EU directive harmonizing national data protection laws of the member states and preventing the transfer of data to third states with inadequate protections.[362] Moreover, in 2013 an EU cybersecurity directive was proposed requiring companies to harden their cybersecurity to meet EU-developed standards – a development that could cause any firm providing online services in Europe to "fundamentally have to change the way its business operates. . . ."[363] Among much else, as was described in Chapter 4, this regime would require many firms with some nexus to the Internet to invest in new technologies, develop procedures to prove compliance to national and EU regulators, and undertake enhanced cyber risk mitigation measures to better manage attacks.[364] Firms drawn into civil litigation over the protection of information assets under these or other laws may

---

[358] 2007 CSI Survey, *supra* note 49, at 24–25. *Cf.* Gordon, *supra* note 42, at 6 (making the empirical case that Sarbanes-Oxley has actually "created a strong incentive for organizations to increase their cybersecurity investments.").

[359] UNDERGROUND ECONOMIES, *supra* note 80, at 8.

[360] *See* Personal Information Protection and Electronic Documents Act, 23 C. Gaz. 1, ch. 5 (2000), http://laws.justice.gc.ca/en/P-8.6/.

[361] FRED H. CATE, PRIVACY IN THE INFORMATION AGE 32 (1997).

[362] *Id.* at 41–47; Patrick J. Murray, *The Adequacy Standard Under Directive 95/46/EC: Does U.S. Data Protection Meet This Standard?*, 21(3) FORDHAM INT'L L.J. 932, 932–37 (1997).

[363] Warwick Ashford, *How Will EU Cyber Security Directive Affect Business?*, COMPUTER WKLY (Feb. 19, 2013), http://www.computerweekly.com/news/2240178256/How-will-EU-cybersecurity-directive-affect-business (citing Stewart Room, a partner at Field Fisher Waterhouse, who argues that this directive will mean that other firms beyond telecom companies will face regulatory burdens related to cybersecurity. These will include "e-commerce platforms; [I]nternet payment gateways; social networks; search engines; cloud computing services; app stores.").

[364] *Id*; *see also Cybersecurity Strategy of the European Union: An Open, Safe and Secure Cyberspace*, EUR. COMM'N, at 2–6 (Feb. 7, 2013) (espousing an Internet freedom agenda including universal access, democratic and "efficient multi-stakeholder governance," and a focus on attaining "cyber

rely on insurance to help reduce costs, with varying degrees of success, as will be discussed. Some applicable international laws are considered in Chapter 6.

Even if certain sectors complain about burdensome compliance standards, regulations do play a vital role in firms' security investment decisions. Thus, although imposing direct liability on software developers for latent vulnerabilities remains controversial, an array of national and international regulations is shaping the cyber regulatory environment. How effective these regulations are at enhancing overall cybersecurity is an issue considered in Chapter 7. President Obama has said that his administration would not "dictate security standards for private companies."[365] Although the Obama administration's approach may have evolved over time, this sentiment is in keeping with the three regulatory stages identified by Professor Murray of first seeking to control or curtail a new disruptive technology (such as encryption), then working to protect the status quo, and finally adapting to it by incorporating it into business plans.[366] One way that firms are adapting to the cyber threat is by turning to the insurance market as a way to hedge losses, which is the subject we turn to next.

Cyber Risk Mitigation: Analyzing the Role of Cyber Risk Insurance in Enhancing Cybersecurity

In the wake of the cyber attacks on Sony, a legal battle has been brewing, pitting Zurich American Insurance Company against Sony over the question of responsibility for the more than 100 million data breaches that the company experienced in 2011.[367] Zurich claims that it should be absolved of any liability in the 58 punitive class-action lawsuits that have been filed against Sony because its policy did not include cyber attacks.[368] Sony expected to spend nearly $180 million on

---

resilience." To achieve this, the Directive sets out a number of goals, including setting national-level cybersecurity standards, creating national and regional CERTs, sharing private-sector best practices, and regularly assessing cyber risk – especially for firms operating critical infrastructure – so as to build a "cybersecurity culture."). *But see* Stephen Gardner, *Member States Reportedly Unconvinced on Need for EU Cybersecurity Directive*, BLOOMBERG BNA (June 3, 2013), http://www.bna .com/member-states-reportedly-n17179874317/ (reporting on questions from ministers arising from this mandate approach and noting that "other parts of the world, such as the USA, appear to opt for a more voluntary and flexible approach with regard to cybersecurity standards" such as the NIST Framework and worrying about creating "inconsistencies for companies whose operations span several jurisdictions. . . .").

[365] Press Release, Office of the Press Sec'y, Remarks by the President on Securing Our Nation's Cyber Infrastructure (May 29, 2009), http://www.whitehouse.gov/the_press_office/Remarks-by-the-President-on-Securing-Our-Nations-Cyber-Infrastructure.

[366] *See* MURRAY, *supra* note 24, at 201–02.

[367] *See* Zurich American Insurance Company v. Sony Corporation of America, No. 651982/2011 (N.Y. Sup., July 20, 2011).

[368] *See* Nicole Perlroth, *Insurance Against Cyber Attacks Expected to Boom*, N.Y. TIMES (Dec. 29, 2012), http://bits.blogs.nytimes.com/2011/12/23/insurance-against-cyber-attacks-expected-to-boom/.

breach-related costs, including litigation, in 2011 alone,[369] though it has had some success in getting claims dismissed in 2012.[370] Despite the substantial cost of cyber attacks, as the Sony episode demonstrates many boards have failed to manage their cyber risk exposure – indeed, many have failed to recognize that it exists in the first place. "I don't think it's a topic that occupies a significant place in board considerations," argues Charles M. Elson, director of the University of Delaware's Corporate Governance Center.[371] This conclusion is buttressed by the findings of a 2010 report from Carnegie Mellon's CyLab. The survey interviewed "board members at companies with between $1 billion and $10 billion in revenues" and "found that 56% considered improving risk management to be a top priority," but "0% considered improving computer and data security to be a priority."[372] Though there is evidence that attitudes are changing,[373] given this state of affairs, how useful is cyber risk insurance, and should nations view it as an important part of enhancing private-sector cybersecurity?[374] Does it really protect at-risk companies, or is it true that "[t]here aren't many success stories where cyber insurance [has played] a significant role in reducing the costs of incidents"?[375] Ultimately, does cyber risk insurance make firms less proactive in enhancing cybersecurity, damaging the prospects for cyber peace?

Commentators have been calling insurance a "key part of the [cybersecurity] solution" for years, and there is some evidence that it is catching on.[376] One reason for the delay goes back to the trouble of assessing risk and calculating costs. If firms cannot determine these values for themselves, then how can an insurance company that needs to establish reasonable premiums? Despite these concerns, cyber risk insurance policies are entering the mainstream. Even the U.S. government has considered encouraging firms to invest in them.[377] In the best case, this could help quantify risk and shield proactive firms from the fallout of cyber attacks. In the worst

---

[369] *See, e.g.*, Jaikumar Vijayan, *Zurich Lawsuit Against Sony Highlights Cyber Insurance Shortcomings*, COMPUTERWORLD (July 26, 2011), http://www.computerworld.com/s/article/9218639/Zurich_lawsuit_against_Sony_highlights_cyber_insurance_shortcomings.

[370] *See* Kerr, *supra* note 117.

[371] Chris Costanzo, *Is Your Company Prepared for Cyber Risk?*, BOARDMEMBER.COM (Feb. 24, 2011), https://www.boardmember.com/Print.aspx?id=5943.

[372] *Id.*; JODY R. WESTBY, GOVERNANCE OF ENTERPRISE SECURITY: CYLAB 2010 REPORT, at 11 (2010), http://www.fbiic.gov/public/2010/jul/cylab-governance-2010.pdf; *cf. Security 500*, SEC. MAG. (2010), http://www.securitymagazine.com/articles/2010-security-500-tables-1?v=preview (reporting that 82 percent of surveyed firms in 2010 either increased cybersecurity spending or held spending levels constant, though this figure includes spending on physical security, drug and alcohol testing, and a number of other responsibilities.).

[373] *See, e.g.*, Catherine Dunn, *Cybersecurity Becoming No. 1 Concern for GCs and Directors*, CORP. COUNSEL (Aug. 15, 2012), http://www.corpcounsel.com/id=1202567476954?slreturn=20140023145506.

[374] House Cybersecurity Task Force, *supra* note 289, at 14.

[375] *Lawsuit Against Sony Highlights Cyber Insurance Shortcomings*, SLASHDOT (July 27, 2011), http://it.slashdot.org/story/11/07/27/1720248/Lawsuit-Against-Sony-Highlights-Cyber-Insurance-Shortcomings.

[376] Palmer, *supra* note 13.

[377] *See* WHITE HOUSE, THE NATIONAL STRATEGY TO SECURE CYBERSPACE 24 (2003), http://www.giac.org/paper/gsec/2875/national-strategy-secure-cyberspace-in-depth-review/104847; Cybersecurity Act of

case, it could merely shift costs and contribute to a more reactive focus, reinforcing the unsustainable cybersecurity status quo. In order to assess which scenario is more likely and how to ensure that cyber risk insurance becomes an effective tool for firms seeking to cover costs and mitigate cyber risk, it is necessary to investigate how cyber risk insurance has evolved and what the major roadblocks are to its continued adoption and evolution.

Insurance companies have been dropping losses caused by cyber attacks from general insurance policies since at least 2003,[378] requiring firms to seek additional coverage beyond the typical Errors and Omissions, Directors and Officers, and Employment Practices Liability plans.[379] If, for example, an organization simply carries a Commercial General Liability policy, it is unlikely that it would provide sufficient protection against a cyber attack.[380] As such, many insurance companies are also now undertaking a proactive analysis of cyber risk as part of their overall insurance investigations, and have begun to offer specific cyber risk policies.[381]

The major players in the cyber risk insurance market include a list of usual suspects. "Hiscox, a Lloyd's of London syndicate," has begun offering "a policy for telecommunications, media, and technology companies that covers" losses caused by cyber attacks – for example, covering a company with 70 employees and approximately $8 million in revenue could cost roughly $420 per month for a $1.6 million indemnity.[382] A Chubb policy covers losses caused by a range of attacks and includes such services as privacy notifications and business interruption expenses.[383] Zurich North America even began offering "a reward for information leading to the conviction of" cyber terrorists in 2002.[384] Companies such as InsureTrust provide cyber risk insurance quotes.[385] Notably, geography plays an important role in what insurance options are available to companies. More policies have historically been available in

---

2009, *supra* note 328, at § 15(1) (providing for the creation of "a market for cybersecurity risk management, including the creation of a system of civil liability and insurance (including government reinsurance). . . .").

[378] *See* Jon Swartz, *Firms' Hacking-Related Insurance Costs Soar*, USA TODAY (Feb. 9, 2003), http://usatoday30.usatoday.com/tech/news/computersecurity/2003-02-09-hacker_x.htm; DHS, CYBERSECURITY INSURANCE WORKSHOP READOUT REPORT 5–6 (2012), http://www.dhs.gov/sites/default/files/publications/cybersecurity-insurance-read-out-report.pdf (making the case that cyber risk insurance has been available "since the late 1970s. . . .").

[379] *See* Anna Lee, Note, *Insuring Cyberspace: Why Traditional Insurance Policies Are Not Enough: The Nature of Potential E-Commerce Losses & Liabilities*, 3 VAND. J. ENT. L. & PRAC. 84, 84–86 (2001).

[380] *See* Denis Drouin, *Cyber Risk Insurance: A Discourse and Preparatory Guide*, SANS INST. INFOSEC READING ROOM (Feb. 9, 2004), at 4, http://www.sans.org/reading_room/whitepapers/legal/cyber-risk-insurance_1412.

[381] *See, e.g.*, Perlroth, *supra* note 368; *Rockwood Programs Adds Cyber Liability to Coverage Portfolio*, INS. J. (June 18, 2013), http://www.insurancejournal.com/news/national/2013/06/18/295976.htm.

[382] Swartz, *supra* note 378; *see* Press Release, Hiscox, Safeonline Launches Internet Security Insurance, http://www.hiscox.com/news/press-releases/archive/2000/18-10-00.aspx (last visited Oct. 9, 2012).

[383] *See Cyber Crime/Liability*, CHUBB GROUP OF INS. COS., http://www.chubb.com/businesses/csi/chubb912.html (last visited Oct. 9, 2012).

[384] Swartz, *supra* note 378.

[385] *See* Insuretrust, http://www.insuretrust.com/ (last visited Jan. 24, 2014).

the United States, for example, than other advanced markets like Canada because of smaller insurance premium bases.[386] Though this status quo is changing, it will impact the extent to which this form of cyber risk mitigation is available to at-risk firms around the world, including in emerging markets. In total, there are more than nineteen available sources for cyber risk insurance in the United States, according to Betterley,[387] although the actual figure is difficult to estimate.

Alongside an expanding industry is a growing insurance market, increasing from $100 million in 2003 to approximately $750 million as of 2011.[388] According to surveys, the customer base has expanded in step. From 2004 to 2008, CSI/FBI and CSI surveys show that 25 to 34 percent of companies had external insurance policies to help manage cyber risk.[389] However, according to a 2010 estimate by Betterley, another 25 percent of surveyed companies said they plan to purchase coverage in the next 18 months.[390] More firms may also choose to increase their insurance coverage in response to new regulations such as the SEC guidelines discussed earlier in the chapter.[391] However, an informal, non-randomized survey of IT security professionals predominantly working in higher education found that more than half of the organizations represented still lacked any form of cyber risk insurance coverage as of October 2012. These data are summarized in Figure 5.2.[392]

As the 2008 CSI Survey puts it, "cyber insurance is a concept that has a great deal of intellectual appeal, has seen a degree of implementation, but that isn't taking the enterprise world by storm."[393] The expense of first-party policies may partially explain the relatively slow growth of cyber risk insurance policies, which had ranged from roughly "$5,000 to $30,000 a year for $1 million in coverage,"[394] although they have become increasingly affordable for small to mid-sized businesses.[395] This has worked to the advantage of firms like Brookeland Fresh Water Supply in East Texas,

---

[386] Drouin, *supra* note 380, at 5.

[387] *See* BETTERLEY 2010, *supra* note 118, at 6.

[388] *See id.*; Perlroth, *supra* note 368; Robert Lemos, *Should SMBs Invest in Cyber Risk Insurance?*, DARK READING (Sept. 9, 2010), http://www.darkreading.com/smb-security/167901073/security/security-management/227400093/index.html.

[389] *See* 2004 CSI Survey, *supra* note 123, at 7; 2005 CSI Survey, *supra* note 123, at 9; 2006 CSI Survey, *supra* note 45; 2007 CSI Survey, *supra* note 49, at 10; 2008 CSI Survey, *supra* note 45.

[390] BETTERLEY 2010, *supra* note 118, at 6.

[391] *See* Perlroth, *supra* note 368.

[392] This survey was conducted with the help of EDUCASE, and was drawn from 37 distinct responses in October 2012. Results are on file with the author.

[393] 2008 CSI Survey, *supra* note 45, at 11.

[394] Swartz, *supra* note 378.

[395] *See* Lemos, *supra* note 388; *see also* *Travelers Adds Cyber Protection Tailored to Small Businesses*, INS. J. (Jan. 22, 2013), http://www.insurancejournal.com/news/national/2013/01/22/278157.htm#.UQa_cqq8nF8.email (reporting that Travelers is introducing cyber risk insurance for small businesses with fewer than 100 employees based in part on a survey finding that only 29 percent of smaller firms possessed such coverage). DHS summarized the current state of cyber risk insurance in 2012, noting that "[w]hile a sizable third-party market exists to cover losses suffered by a company's customers, first-party policies that address direct harms to companies themselves remain expensive, rare, and largely unattractive." DHS, *supra* note 378, at 1.

Suffered Cyber Attack in Past 12 Months?

Approach Favored in Managing Cyber Attacks?

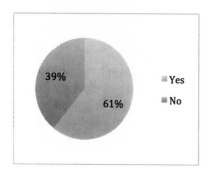

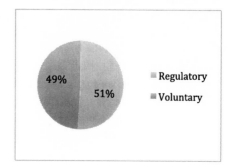

Possess Cyber Risk Insurance?

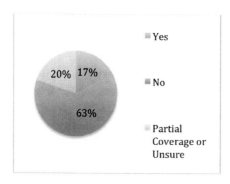

FIGURE 5.2. CYBER ATTACK SURVEY DATA

from which cybercriminals stole $35,000; because of its insurance policy, it only lost its $500 deductible.[396] Nevertheless, businesses must still pay upfront costs to have their network integrity assessed. Typically, firms also have to answer a series of questions regarding their prior incident history.[397] If businesses are not forthcoming, then the insurance company may decline coverage. And since many firms are only irregularly targeted by attackers, but must pay out in some cases significant annual premiums, some argue that the cost of protection may not always be in line with the magnitude of the problem.[398]

---

[396] *See The Case for Cybersecurity Insurance, Part II*, KREBS ON SEC., http://krebsonsecurity.com/2010/07/the-case-for-cybersecurity-insurance-part-ii/ (last visited Jan. 23, 2014).

[397] *See, e.g.*, Brooke Yates & Katie Varholak, *Cyber Risk Insurance – Navigating the Application Process*, SHERMAN & HOWARD (June 6, 2013), http://www.sah.com/NewsAndEvents/View/1AFCBA99-5056-9125-63918F3AD79A2940/.

[398] *See* Denise Dubie, *Corporate Security Spending Not in Line with Real-World Requirements*, NETWORK WORLD (May 2003), http://www.networkworld.com/news/2003/0505nemertes.html; Riva Richmond,

Calculating insurance premiums is, as was previously suggested, no simple matter. Still, many companies attempt to quantify the unquantifiable by requiring a long history of actuarial data. That is often difficult given the lack of incentives for effective information sharing, so calculations are oftentimes skewed.[399] Another issue is adverse selection, in which firms that have been hit by a cyber attack are more likely to purchase insurance. Insurance companies manage this uncertainty in their calculations by requiring information security audits – the virtual equivalent of the physical exam required for health insurance coverage.[400] Even after a successful audit, insurance companies may worry about companies' behavior when insulated from risk. This may be addressed through monetary incentives like deductions for firms that avoid bad behaviors,[401] analogous to a safe driving discount, or premium reductions for firms that enhance their cybersecurity. Already, Bryce and AIG have a history of offering discounts for firms using particular hardware and software packages.[402]

Policies differ with regard to what types of cyber incidents are covered. Plans can include post-breach response costs, including hiring computer forensic experts and arranging for credit monitoring services. There is also the possibility of purchasing different types of insurance for different types of cyber attacks. The market in cyber risk insurance is still developing with options of first-party risk, which applies to actions of the company, and third-party risk, which protects against the actions of another, as in the case of cyber attacks.[403] Some have even called for additional insurance options for at-risk firms, including a public option for insuring e-commerce.[404]

In short, although the market for cyber risk insurance must still surmount problems of accurately assessing and quantifying risk along with information sharing,[405] it is growing in importance and sophistication and is becoming better able to meet the needs of firms of all sizes, which could help to mitigate the threats of cybercrime and espionage.[406] Understanding what a firm's particular exposure is will be important to finding the right premium and engaging business executives in discussions about investing in it. This could provide management with a sense of the importance of insurance and infuse it with responsibility for protecting the organization and

---

How to Determine If Cyber Insurance Coverage Is Right for You, ENTREPENEUR (June 5, 2012), http://www.entrepreneur.com/article/223921.

[399] *See* DHS, *supra* note 378, at 1.

[400] *See* Lawrence A. Gordon et al., *A Framework for Using Insurance for Cyber-Risk Management*, 46 COMM. ACM 81, 82 (Mar. 2003).

[401] *Id.* at 83.

[402] *Id.*

[403] *Id.*; DHS, *supra* note 378, at 1.

[404] *See* Amy R. Willis, Note, *Business Insurance: First Party Commercial Property Insurance and the Physical Damage Requirement in a Computer Dominated World*, 37 FLA. ST. U.L. REV. 1003, 1021 (2010).

[405] *See* DHS, *supra* note 378, at 6.

[406] *Id.* at 6–7.

its intellectual property.[407] However, there is the danger of firms using cyber risk insurance to put off enhancing cybersecurity, which is why policies should be setup that would "reward" firms that make proactive cybersecurity investments.[408] Firms can and must do more to mitigate their enterprise risk.[409] Consider how a small dry cleaner business in a difficult Detroit neighborhood handles street crime. Insurance is likely part of its strategy, but so is investing in better locks and security cameras to catch intruders. Due to the limitations of cyber risk insurance, firms need to proactively enhance their cybersecurity and protect data through investing in the virtual equivalent of padlocks and security cameras discussed in Chapter 3. These policies should not be used as a substitute for proactively instilling best practices. Like the market-based solution of insurance, partnerships between the private and public sectors are also often touted as a critical component of enhancing cybersecurity. It is this final concept to which we turn to next.

Public-Private Partnerships for Cybersecurity

Along with regulatory intervention and risk mitigation mechanisms, public-private partnerships are another facet of enhancing private-sector cybersecurity and securing critical infrastructure. Like the building of the 46,876 mile-long U.S. national highway system,[410] managing the Internet requires that government and the private sector work together.[411] The question of how best to manage the private sector's role in cyberspace is one of the most challenging problems in the cybersecurity realm. A series of reports have argued that public-private partnerships (P3) introduced in Chapter 2 have the potential to enhance private-sector cybersecurity.[412] Lawmakers such as former Senator Joseph Lieberman, who chaired the Senate Homeland Security and Governmental Affairs Committee, asserted: "Right now, there is not enough joint private-public cyberdefense."[413] Some commentators, like Melissa Hathaway, former acting senior director for Cyberspace for the National Security and Homeland Security Councils, argue the reverse: that there are *too many* P3s already, and

---

[407] *See* Gordon, *supra* note 400, at 85.

[408] DHS, *supra* note 378, at 6.

[409] *Id.* at 1 ("Companies purchase cybersecurity insurance and other classes of coverage in order to transfer risk to other parties – namely, insurance carriers. Risk transfer is just one of four risk management strategies, however, that also include risk acceptance (i.e., bearing a risk and budgeting for potential losses accordingly); risk mitigation (i.e., taking steps to contain and minimize anticipated risk losses); and risk avoidance (i.e., eliminating a risk entirely by removing the conditions that create it).").

[410] *See Interstate FAQ*, U.S. DEP'T TRANSP., http://www.fhwa.dot.gov/interstate/faq.htm#question3 (last visited Jan. 23, 2014).

[411] *See Addressing Cyber Security Through Public-Private Partnership: An Analysis of Existing Models* 3 (Nov. 2009) [hereinafter *Addressing Cyber Security*].

[412] *See, e.g.*, CYBERSPACE POLICY REVIEW, *supra* note 321, at i.

[413] Tim Starks, *Cybersecurity: Learning to Share*, CQ POLITICS (Aug. 1, 2010), http://www.cqpolitics.com/wmspage.cfm?docID=weeklyreport-000003716158&cpage=1.

they have been ineffective at enhancing cybersecurity.[414] Hathaway believes that these programs should be deepened and consolidated.[415] How much public-private partnership then is warranted, and what form should it take?

Part of the problem in answering this question lies in determining which infrastructure is critical, as was explored in Chapter 4. The original President's Commission on Critical Infrastructure Protection (PCCIP) identified nine such institutions, which has later been revised to sixteen;[416] the European Commission classifies eleven.[417] Indeed, what counts as "critical" is often in the eye of the beholder. A common example is the U.S. power grid. The Federal Energy Regulatory Commission (FERC) has worked closely with groups including the nonprofit North American Electric Reliability Council (NERC) on rules that promote the reliability of electrical flow and impose tougher requirements on utilities.[418] However, the debate over protecting critical national infrastructure goes far beyond utilities, and includes telecommunications, the financial sector, and beyond. This debate has far-reaching implications for businesses operating in one of these sectors since designating an industry as critical could harken greater regulation.

Another divisive issue in fashioning P3s involves regulating disclosure requirements. It is difficult to know how secure CNI is if firms are not required to disclose when and what type of cyber attacks have occurred. Some programs are geared toward incentivizing companies to share information anonymously about the threats and attacks they encounter. But robust information sharing – by both the government and the private sector – still faces many hurdles. Some of these are legal and resource driven because security clearances and state secrets are at play.[419] Others are technical. After a cyber attack simulation exercise called Cyber ShockWave in 2010, former Homeland Security Secretary Michael Chertoff, who participated in the exercise,

---

[414] *See, e.g.,* Melissa Hathaway: *America Has Too Many Ineffective Private-Public Partnerships,* NEW INTERNET (Oct. 12, 2010), http://www.thenewnewinternet.com/2010/10/12/melissa-hathaway-america-has-too-many-ineffective-private-public-partnerships/.

[415] *Id.*

[416] *See* CRITICAL FOUNDATIONS, THE PRESIDENT'S COMMISSION ON CRITICAL INFRASTRUCTURE PROTECTION 3–4 (Oct. 1997), http://www.cyber.st.dhs.gov/docs/PCCIP%20Report%201997.pdf (including transportation, oil and gas, water, emergency, government, banking and finance, electrical, telecommunications, and communications services); *What is the ICS-CERT Mission?,* http://ics-cert.us-cert.gov/Frequently-Asked-Questions (last visited Jan. 17, 2014).

[417] *See* Bart Smedts, *Critical Infrastructure Protection at the European Level,* 64 STUDIA DIPLOMATICA 71, 73 (2011), http://www.nonproliferation.eu/documents/other/bartsmedts4ec14cddo11bd.pdf (citing Commission of the European Communities, Brussels. (COM) 576 (Nov. 17, 2005)) (noting that "[t]he proposal for the directive . . . retained 11 sectors and 29 sub-sectors . . . [but] [t]he directive itself only mentions 2 sectors (energy and transport). . . . ").

[418] *See* FERC Order N. 706, *Mandatory Reliability Standards for Critical Infrastructure Protection,* Docket No. RM06-22-000 (Jan. 18, 2008), http://www.ferc.gov/whats-new/comm-meet/2008/091808/E-26.pdf.

[419] *See* Rosenzweig, *supra* note 285, at 13 (arguing that the main barrier to public-private information sharing is simply a lack of resources to attain the necessary security clearances, though the overall lack of "individualized treatment" differentiating private-sector entities hamstrings the effectiveness of entities such as US-CERT).

said there was not a "user-friendly process" to allow government "defenders to effectively collaborate with the private sector" during the response to a cyber attack.[420] This stands in contrast to the situation in Estonia, as will be discussed.

Many ideas exist for incentivizing deeper public-private collaboration in the United States and beyond. These include additional funding for research and development programs, and even allowing the U.S. Department of Defense to have a role in building defenses into private-sector networks responsible for protecting CNI. So far, however, most of these ideas have not moved past the drawing board. If anything, there has been more progress through specific private-sector partnerships such as the ISACs. According to Microsoft's Paul Nicholas, forums like the IT-Sector Coordinating Council and the ISACs help provide a "fluid mechanism that allows subject matter experts to come in and work on solving particular problems with the government. These groups work best when they are focused on solving specific problems."[421] The danger of public-private partnerships or collaborative security efforts, though, as has been stated is that we may simply "wind up with checklists that don't translate into meaningful security."[422] Indeed, Professor Paul Rosenzweig has made the case that so far ISACs have been "[a]t best . . . a moderate success."[423]

A more comprehensive approach has been considered by the Intelligence and National Security Alliance (INSA), which published a report in 2009 arguing in part that effective P3s require: (1) "[a] representative group of members, large enough to be sufficiently inclusive, but small enough to retain the ability to act quickly"; and (2) "[a] circumscribed role for government with" the private sector "tak[ing] the lead."[424] The report also recommended establishing a cybersecurity panel composed of members from the public and private sectors to partner with a government agency to aid in detection, protection, and response.[425] These recommendations flow from an analysis of existing P3 models, such as NERC. This organization was originally created as a group of companies that came together voluntarily in an effort to protect against blackouts.[426] NERC standards, however, were eventually sanctioned by FERC in the aftermath of the northeast blackout of 2003,[427] an example of an organic code of conduct that was voluntarily adopted and subsequently reinforced by government consistent with Professor Ostrom's polycentric design principles

---

[420] Michael Chertoff, *Cyber ShockWave Exposed Missing Links in U.S. Security*, GCN (Mar. 10, 2010), http://gcn.com/articles/2010/03/15/commentary-chertoff-cyber-shockwave.aspx.

[421] Nicholas, *supra* note 164.

[422] *Id.*

[423] Rosenzweig, *supra* note 285, at 18.

[424] *Addressing Cyber Security, supra* note 411, at 3.

[425] *Id.* at 3, 8. An alternative proposal by Professor Rosenzweig is to create a "Cybersecurity Assurance Corporation" to gather and disseminate "information about cyber attacks." Rosenzweig, *supra* note 285, at 18–19.

[426] *Addressing Cyber Security, supra* note 411, at 7.

[427] *Id.*; Peter Behr, *A Decade After the Northeast Blackout, Reliability Increases but Human Issues Persist*, E&E (Aug. 12, 2013), http://www.eenews.net/stories/1059985876/print.

from Chapter 2.[428] In particular, recognizing the need for industry best practices to proactively adopt to the rapidly changing cyber threat matrix is central to the "collective-choice arrangements and minimal recognition of rights" criterion, while effective monitoring speaks to the importance of robust P3s.[429] Actions such as these could become a model for polycentric regulation in cyberspace. Expanding this FERC initiative to include other CNI sectors could promote effective outcome-based regulatory intervention without sacrificing innovation. U.S., EU, and NATO procurement could also be leveraged to spur on reluctant companies. On the world stage, however, the buying power of the U.S. government is no longer market driving, and is growing less so over time.[430] Indeed, in 2011, the U.S. DOD accounted for approximately .1 percent of all IT expenditures worldwide.[431]

Taking P3 to an extreme, some models for government and industry partnership include preemptive action. So far, no companies have gone on record as taking offensive action to safeguard their networks, though there have been calls for a more "active defense" model.[432] The underlying theory behind such proposals is that, due to being potentially better informed and more adaptable, private firms may be better positioned to protect their own systems from cyber attackers than is the government. Indeed, some companies are hiring consultant security firms, such as CrowdStrike, that provide a "menu of active responses" to targeted firms, including deception, that in some cases could risk running afoul of U.S. and foreign laws,[433] potentially opening multinational firms to litigation in foreign jurisdictions.[434] Such a

---

[428] *See* Elinor Ostrom, *Polycentric Systems: Multilevel Governance Involving a Diversity of Organizations, in* GLOBAL ENVIRONMENTAL COMMONS: ANALYTICAL AND POLITICAL CHALLENGES INVOLVING A DIVERSITY OF ORGANIZATIONS 105, 118 (Eric Brousseau et al., eds., 2012) (citing ELINOR OSTROM, GOVERNING THE COMMONS: THE EVOLUTION OF INSTITUTIONS FOR COLLECTIVE ACTION 90 (1990)).

[429] *Id.* at 120–21.

[430] Starks, *supra* note 413.

[431] Kristin M. Lord & Travis Sharp, *Executive Summary, in* AMERICA'S CYBER FUTURE: SECURITY AND PROSPERITY IN THE INFORMATION AGE 7, 33 (Kristin M. Lord & Travis Sharp eds., CNAS, 2011).

[432] Joseph Menn, *Hacked Companies Fight Back With A Controversial Move: Retaliation,* REUTERS (June 17, 2012), http://www.huffingtonpost.com/2012/06/17/hacked-companies-fight-ba_n_1603430.html.

[433] *Id.; see also* Rosenzweig, *supra* note 285, at 21–22 (discussing legal issues with the active defense model, including Fourth Amendment concerns). Among the legal barriers to active cyber defense under U.S. law is the Computer Fraud and Abuse Act (CFAA), which criminalizes accessing a computer "without authorization." 18 U.S.C. § 1030(a)(1)-(7). This prohibits firms from infiltrating or otherwise manipulating attacking networks, even if they are located in foreign jurisdictions, due to the extraterritorial reach of the CFAA, though strategies that do not infiltrate other networks such as using certain "honeypots" (traps) to fool cybercriminals may be permissible. *See* Charles Doyle, *Cybercrime: An Overview of the Federal Computer Fraud and Abuse Statute and Related Federal Criminal Laws,* CONG. RES. SERV., at 6–7 (2010); Ellen Messmer, *Hitting Back at Cyberattackers: Experts Discuss Pros and Cons,* NETWORKWORLD (Nov. 1, 2012), http://www.networkworld.com/news/2012/110112-cyberattackers-263885.html. The broad scope of the CFAA has also come under fire with the 2013 suicide of Aaron Swartz, who was an Internet freedom pioneer facing felony charges under the CFAA for downloading millions of academic articles from JSTOR, an online archive, leading to calls for reform. *See* Marcia Hofmann, *How to Honor Aaron Swartz,* SLATE (Jan. 14, 2013), http://www.slate.com/articles/technology/future_tense/2013/01/aaron_swartz_suicide_honor_his_memory_by_fixing_the_computer_fraud_and_abuse.html.

[434] NAT'L RES. COUNCIL, TECHNOLOGY, POLICY, LAW, AND ETHICS REGARDING U.S. ACQUISITION AND USE OF CYBERATTACK CAPABILITIES 211–12 (William A. Owens et al. eds., 2009).

self-help approach also risks escalation if private attacks are attributed back to the U.S. government under a theory of imputed responsibility,[435] even as it also promises some relief (however temporary) for affected firms. Still, some are calling for governments to work more closely with the private sector to better manage cyber attacks. In the United States, for example, DHS Secretary Janet Napolitano has commented that officials have even been considering whether to authorize "'proactive' private-entity attacks" in some situations.[436]

Going several steps further, Estonia is developing a state-sponsored cyber militia to defend its digital assets from future attacks and is partnering with the private sector to make it a reality.[437] Since being attacked in 2007, Estonia has been at the forefront of developing novel offensive and defensive solutions to cybersecurity challenges.[438] Among these is the Estonian "Cyber Defence League," an organization "aimed at protecting Estonian cyberspace" as part of the National Defense League.[439] The league was formed in the wake of a long history "of invasion and occupation[,]" including "by the Soviet Army in 1939, followed by the Germans in 1941[,] and" again by the Soviet Union from post-World War II until 1991.[440] This means that "[i]nsurgent activity against an occupying force sits deep in the Estonian under-standing of fighting back," according to Estonian Minister Jaak Aaviksoo.[441] Enter the cyber militia.

Rain Ottis, formerly of the NATO Cooperative Defense Center of Excellence, defines a cyber militia as "a group of volunteers who are willing and able to use cyber attacks in order to achieve a political goal."[442] Ottis notes that Estonia's cyber militia consists of volunteers only insomuch as they act of their own free volition, without contractual obligations or government payments.[443] The objectives of the league are quite broad, ranging from protecting Estonians' e-lifestyle to securing CNI. In an emergency, the league would work with Estonia's CERT to respond to attacks as provided for under the 2009 Emergency Preparedness Act.[444] Any Estonian with an

---

[435] *See* Jay P. Kesan & Carol M. Hayes, *Mitigative Counterstriking: Self-Defense and Deterrence in Cyberspace*, 25(2) HARV. J. L. & TECH. 415, 463–66 (2012).

[436] Joseph Menn, *Hacked Companies Take Controversial Steps*, STUFF.CO.NZ (June 18, 2012), http://www .stuff.co.nz/technology/digital-living/7122288/Hacked-companies-take-controversial-steps.

[437] *See* Rain Ottis, *Proactive Defense Tactics Against On-Line Cyber Militia*, in PROC. OF THE 9TH EUR. CONF. ON INFO. WARFARE & SEC. 233, 233 (Josef Demergis ed., 2010).

[438] *See* Kalev Aasmae, *The Poster Child for Cybersecurity Done Right: How Estonia Learnt from Being Under Attack*, ZDNET (Feb. 5, 2013), http://www.zdnet.com/the-poster-child-for-cybersecurity-done-right-how-estonia-learnt-from-being-under-attack-7000010628/.

[439] *What is the Cyber Defence League?*, FAQ, (copy on file with author); *Government Formed Cyber Defence Unit of the Defence League*, EST. MINISTRY DEF. (Jan. 20, 2011), http://www.kmin.ee/en/ government-formed-cyber-defence-unit-of-the-defence-league.

[440] Tom Gjelten, *Volunteer Cyber Army Emerges in Estonia*, NPR (Jan. 4, 2011), http://www.npr.org/2011/ 01/04/132634099/in-estonia-volunteer-cyber-army-defends-nation.

[441] *Id.*

[442] Ottis, *supra* note 437, at 233, 233.

[443] *Id.* at 233, 234.

[444] *See Estonia Defence League Cyber Unit FAQ*, KAITSELIIT, http://uusweb.kaitseliit.ee/en/ frequently-asked-questions (last visited Jan. 23, 2014).

information security background may apply to join.[445] As of 2011, it was unknown how many members of the Estonian National Defense League were also part of the cyber branch, though estimates range from 80 to 150 individuals.[446]

The private sector is at the forefront of the Estonian league because of a long history of effective public-private cooperation in Estonia. So far, reportedly "no other democratic country in the world has a comparable force."[447] Could something similar be attempted in the United States? Such efforts would inevitably be hampered by scale – Estonia has a population of only 1.3 million people, roughly the size of San Diego. Nevertheless, according to Stewart Baker, such a group could prove helpful during attacks: "It means people are keeping their skills up to date in the private sector, and those skills can be called on in an emergency. . . . "[448] Despite the benefits, though, Baker does not consider it very likely that the United States might establish a similar organization.[449] Businesses may also worry that such collaboration with national governments may damage their international reputations and access to certain emerging markets. In an age of globalization when companies are marketing themselves to cultures around the world, few firms would want to seem so beholden to their states of incorporation or principal places of business, especially if those differ.[450] The impact of Snowden's revelations regarding certain U.S. tech companies' ties with the U.S. government is a case in point.[451]

The future of P3, especially in the United States, may not lie with Estonia's League, but it is clear that steps can be taken to enhance public-private cybersecurity cooperation as the line between public and private blurs especially regarding CNI. The creation of a cybersecurity panel or other independent entity like that advocated for in the INSA report, more secure and anonymous information sharing mechanisms between public- and private-sector entities, spelling out what companies can and cannot do in terms of proactive defense, and drafting outcome-based regulations that reinforce corporate cybersecurity best practices could all go a long way toward building trust and promoting cyber peace.

SUMMARY

A great deal of confusion exists over assessing the cyber threat to the private sector and deciding what to do about it. Leaving cybersecurity to the market alone through

---

[445] Id.

[446] See id.; *Around 150 Experts Associated with Estonia's Cyber Defence League*, EST. REV. (Oct. 3, 2011), http://www.vm.ee/?q=en/node/12674.

[447] Gjelten, *supra* note 440.

[448] Id.

[449] Id.

[450] See, e.g., Tom Gjelten, *NSA Leak Could Be Bad Business for U.S. Tech Companies*, NPR (June 21, 2013), http://www.npr.org/blogs/alltechconsidered/2013/06/21/194330376/NSA-Leak-Could-Be-Bad-Business-For-U-S-Tech-Companies.

[451] *See* Li & McElveen, *supra* note 269.

self-governance is likely insufficient to enhance cybersecurity because of the presence of market imperfections and the problem of free riders representing a strategic disincentive for firms to invest the necessary capital.[452] However, the market has functioned to some extent in enhancing private-sector cybersecurity. Success stories such as Microsoft's SDL, Facebook's scalp wall, Google's Chrome and effective P3 partnerships, and survey results highlighting organizational, technological, and budgetary best practices all illustrate that some firms are taking this problem seriously, and are in the process of making cybersecurity into a competitive advantage. Yet many other firms lag behind in part because the cost of cyber attacks still are not always internalized, and as a result, they are putting consumers and CNI at risk. The market functions, but only so well.[453]

Consequently, the potential of market-based incentives and regulatory interventions were analyzed, combined with P3. Market-based incentives are being increasingly favored in Congress and can help to enhance private-sector cybersecurity, but voluntary measures only take us so far.[454] Regulators have a role to play in addressing negative externalities and correcting market imperfections where they exist as is explored further in Chapter 7.[455] Although public-private partnerships can be effective, they are often not the panacea that they are sometimes made out to be. Part of the problem lies in rapidly advancing disruptive technology, as discussed in Chapter 3. This can lead to firms undertaking a series of responses to perceived threats, including attempting to control or curtail a technology, and seeking legal mechanisms to protect the status quo.[456] A useful first step might be expanding joint DHS and FBI training sessions for managers to educate more corporate leaders about the nature and extent of the cyber threat as well as to instill best practices for mitigating it.[457] Regulatory intervention has inherent drawbacks and must be carefully calibrated to minimize distortions. As Professor Rosenzweig has succinctly

---

[452] *See* MURRAY, *supra* note 24, at 168, 176.

[453] *Id.* at 200.

[454] The survey results from Figure 5.2 help to illustrate the divide between individuals favoring a more voluntary or regulatory approach to enhancing cybersecurity. For example, on the one hand, respondents in favor of a more voluntary approach in this survey stated reasons that included perceived shortcomings in regulations such as an inability to quickly adapt, over-broadness, lack of cost effectiveness, and short lifespans before obsolescence. On the other hand, respondents in favor of more regulation cited concerns including potential market failure, the lack of effective information sharing, and the public interest worries surrounding CNI. The same debate playing out here among IT professionals is also evident at the national and even international levels, as may be seen in the debates surrounding the EU's 2013 cybersecurity directive. *See* Gardner, *supra* note 364.

[455] *See Examining the Homeland Security Impact of the Obama Administration's Cybersecurity Proposal: Hearing before the H. Comm. on Homeland Sec.*, 112th Cong. 8, 16 (2011) (statement of Melissa E. Hathaway, Hathaway Global Consulting), http://www.gpo.gov/fdsys/pkg/CHRG-112hhrg72253/pdf/CHRG-112hhrg72253.pdf (arguing that "[a]n overly restrictive approach should be avoided yet, we cannot afford to pass legislation that would prove to be feckless.") [hereinafter Hathaway Testimony].

[456] MURRAY, *supra* note 24, at 201.

[457] Hathaway Testimony, *supra* note 455, at 16.

argued in this context, "first, do no harm."[458] Firms would be well advised, though, to get in front of both investor expectations and the regulatory environment by proactively implementing private-sector cybersecurity best practices to better manage the cyber threat, using insurance to help mitigate any remaining risk, and in the process better secure corporate intellectual property, consumer records, and CNI. By doing so, firms could become norm entrepeneurs, as Microsoft, Facebook, and Google have done, establishing "new normative standards" for industry.[459] Eventually, after a tipping point is reached, such bottom-up efforts could catalyze positive network effects and even cause a "norm cascade" in which normative standards, in this context cybersecurity best practices, become internalized and perhaps eventually codified in national and international laws benefiting global cybersecurity through polycentric action.[460]

The market will punish firms that suffer data breaches, but only once the playing field is defined and level. Outstanding legal questions need to be addressed before best practices can be enforced. In order to understand not only the domestic but also international legal mechanisms at play in regulating cyberspace and enhancing cybersecurity, it is necessary then to analyze the applicable international law, which is the subject of the next chapter.

This chapter has analyzed private-sector cybersecurity, noting the main types of attacks that companies face, approximately how much they cost, which industries are being targeted, and how companies are responding technologically, organizationally, and with new investments. The uncertainty of existing survey data has also been explored, along with some of the benefits and drawbacks of regulatory intervention and cyber risk mitigation measures in the competitive marketplace. All of these tools are critical to help make business less risky, but by themselves they are insufficient to attain cyber peace. The market, laws, norms, and code all have roles to play within a polycentric framework. In order to complete our analysis of that framework, however, the international law and politics of Internet reform must be engaged as they are critical to enacting the technical, economic, legal, and policy lessons identified throughout this study. Gauging the promise of cyber peace, then, is the goal of Part III.

---

[458] Rosenzweig, *supra* note 285, at 26.

[459] ANNEGRET FLOHR ET AL., THE ROLE OF BUSINESS IN GLOBAL GOVERNANCE: CORPORATIONS AS NORM-ENTREPRENEURS 10 (2010).

[460] *See* Martha Finnemore & Kathryn Sikkink, *International Norm Dynamics and Political Change*, 52 INT'L ORG. 887, 895–98 (1998) (describing the three stages of "the norm 'life cycle,'" including "norm emergence," "norm cascade," and "norm internalization."); Neal K. Katyal, *The Dark Side of Private Ordering: The Network/Community Harm of Crime*, in THE LAW AND ECONOMICS OF CYBERSECURITY 193, 193–94 (Mark F. Grady & Francesco Parisi eds., 2006) (exploring network effects and network externalities in cyberspace).

PART III

The Law, Politics, and Promise of Cyber Peace

[P]owerful nations are going to try to wield ... [the Internet] and shape it to reflect their interests. The network will increasingly, I fear, look like what they want it to look like.

– Professor Jack Goldsmith[1]

---

[1] Tom Gjelten, *Seeing the Internet as an 'Information Weapon'*, NPR (Sept. 23, 2010), http://www.npr .org/templates/story/story.php?storyId=130052701.

6

An Introduction to the Law of Cyber War and Peace

We don't know when or if a cyberattack rises to the level of an 'armed attack.'

– Retired National Defense University Professor Dan Ryan[2]

If nations don't know what the rules are, all sorts of accidental problems might arise.... One nation might do something that another nation takes to be an act of war, even when the first nation did not intend it to be an act of war.

– Professor Jack Goldsmith[3]

At a time of great upheaval about a naval arms race and its costs, Russia proposed a series of measures aimed at disarmament and pacification. Putting aside their mutual suspicions, the great powers came together to open a dialogue about the future of armed conflict. The year was 1899, and the result of this initiative, the first Hague Peace Conference, was a new era in international relations that laid the foundations for the laws of war and served as a prototype for future United Nations gatherings.[4] Can we repeat the achievement of our ancestors who undertook this challenge at another time in which multipolar politics dominated international relations?[5] And how can this legacy of international law that was first framed in the late nineteenth century apply to new frontiers of international conflict in the twenty-first century, namely cyberspace?

Beginning with the Hague Conferences of 1899 and 1907, the international community has fashioned international laws to limit the number and type of offensive

---

[2] Tom Gjelten, *Extending the Law of War to Cyberspace*, NPR (Sept. 22, 2010), http://www.npr.org/templates/story/story.php?storyId=130023318. This chapter represents an updated version of *From Nuclear War to Net War: Analogizing Cyber Attacks in International Law*, as 27 BERKELEY J. INT'L. L. 192 (2009).

[3] Gjelten, *supra* note 2.

[4] Geoffrey Best, *Peace Conferences and the Century of Total War: The 1899 Hague Conference and What Came After*, 75 INT'L AFF. 619, 619–20, 631–33 (1999).

[5] *See* C. DALE WALTON, GEOPOLITICS AND THE GREAT POWERS IN THE 21ST CENTURY: MULTIPOLARITY AND THE REVOLUTION IN STRATEGIC PERSPECTIVE 3 (2007).

weapons through numerous treaties and accords, including the Hague and Geneva Conventions as well as the Rome Statute, which established the International Criminal Court.[6] The path has not been an easy one. Indeed, it is getting less so with the emergence of new power centers that have made reaching consensus on multilateral weapons regulation more problematic.[7] Cyber politics, however, is a subject for Chapter 7. The question for our present purposes is whether it is time for the international community to follow this long tradition of arms controls and adopt a new treaty to enhance global cybersecurity, and if so, what might such a treaty look like? Or, failing that, how can current law be clarified to enhance cybersecurity, both during times of war and peace? Put more simply, can international law help improve cybersecurity, and if so, how?

A great debate is currently raging in academic and policy circles about the applicability of international law generally, and the Law of Armed Conflict (LOAC) in particular, to cyberspace. The field may be broken down into at least four camps. First, some assert that there is no difficulty in applying certain established laws to cyberspace, such as the LOAC. This is the position taken by the U.S. government, as expressed by the Departments of Defense and State.[8] Second, others maintain that cyberspace is a unique environment necessitating a novel regulatory structure, such as a new comprehensive treaty for cyberspace.[9] A third camp holds out little hope for the usefulness of international law to enhance cybersecurity. Stewart Baker, former assistant secretary for policy at DHS, for example has said simply: "International law isn't going to save us."[10] Fourth, some commentators, including Richard Clarke, hold out hope for the ability of international law to promote some degree of cyber

---

[6] *See* David Caron, *War and International Adjudication: Reflections on the 1899 Peace Conference*, 94 AM. J. INT'L L. 4, 4, 7 (2000).

[7] Consider the context of the cluster munitions treaty negotiations. These talks have been ongoing for years, whereas the more focused Dublin-Oslo accord has had success in a relatively short time operating outside of the UN framework. *See, e.g.*, Jeff Abramson, *107 Countries Approve Cluster Munitions Treaty*, ARMS CONTROL ASSOC. (July 2008), http://www.armscontrol.org/print/3098.

[8] *See, e.g.*, U.S. DEP'T DEF., OFF. GEN. COUNS., AN ASSESSMENT OF INTERNATIONAL LEGAL ISSUES IN INFORMATION OPERATIONS 8–10 (2d ed. 1999) [hereinafter DOD ASSESSMENT]; U.S. DEP'T DEF., CYBERSPACE POLICY REPORT 9 (2011) ("International legal norms, such as those found in the UN Charter and the law of armed conflict, which apply to the physical domains (i.e., sea, air, land, and space), also apply to the cyberspace domain."); Aram Roston, *U.S.: Laws of War Apply to Cyber Attacks*, NAVY TIMES (Sept. 18, 2012), http://www.navytimes.com/news/2012/09/dn-laws-of-war-apply-cyber-attacks-091812/.

[9] *See, e.g.*, Rex Hughes, *A Treaty for Cyberspace*, 86(2) INT'L AFF. 523, 541 (2010); Henning Wegener, *Cyber Peace*, in THE QUEST FOR CYBER PEACE 77, 80 (Int'l Telecomm. Union & Permanent Monitoring Panel on Info. Sec. eds., 2011), http://www.itu.int/dms_pub/itu-s/opb/gen/S-GEN-WFS.01-1-2011-PDF-E.pdf (citing Toward a Universal Order of Cyberspace: Managing Threats from Cybercrime to Cyberwar, Report and Recommendations, World Federation of Scientists Permanent Monitoring Panel on Information Security, Nov. 19, 2003, Submission to the World Summit on the Information Society, http://www.itu.int/dms_pub/itu-s/md/03/wsis/c/S03-WSIS-C-0006!!PDF-E.pdf).

[10] Interview with Stewart Baker, former assistant secretary for Policy, Department of Homeland Security, in Wash., D.C. (Jan. 4, 2011); *see also* Stewart Baker, *Denial of Service*, FOREIGN POL'Y (Sept. 30, 2011), http://www.foreignpolicy.com/articles/2011/09/ 30/denial_of_service (expanding on this argument).

peace, but a peace based on state responsibility. "I think that there needs to be a well-articulated national obligation to police any activities coming out of your country,"[11] explains Clarke. "So if you find yourself suddenly under attack from a server in Uganda then you can – in real time – tell Uganda exactly what's going on . . . and then they must step up and do something about it."[12]

As these differing opinions about the utility of international law in this domain help illustrate, greater clarity is needed in the international legal system to help manage cyber attacks and define both what the law is, and "what it could and should be."[13] Defining the threshold at which a cyber attack becomes an armed attack, for example, is critical because that determines when the LOAC is triggered. For example, Harold Koh, formerly the State Department's chief legal adviser, has said that for a cyber attack to "constitute a 'use of force' under international law," it would have to "proximately result in death, injury or significant destruction."[14] Ultimately, however, the determination of whether a cyber "attack is an act of war is a political decision[,]" which in the United States rests with the President and Congress.[15] An "important consideration in that calculus is whether the attack is the work of a lone hacker, a criminal group," terrorist organization, or a foreign government.[16] Attribution, therefore, is a key component to building a robust legal regime,[17] but that is far from the only issue.

Cyber war raises a host of legal concerns, which may be broken down into at least three queries. First, does cyber conflict represent a qualitative change in the meaning and nature of warfare, and if so, which laws should apply to govern it?[18] Second, if

---

[11] Interview with Richard Clarke, chairman for Good Harbor Consulting, in Wash., D.C. (Jan. 4, 2011).

[12] *Id. But see* Michael N. Schmitt, *International Law in Cyberspace: The Koh Speech and Tallinn Manual Juxtaposed*, 54 HARV. INT'L L.J. ONLINE 13, 16 (2012), http://www.harvardilj.org/2012/12/online-articles-online-54-schmitt/ (noting that the International Group of Experts for the *Tallinn Manual* unanimously agreed that "international law applies to cyber activities").

[13] Duncan Blake & Joseph S. Imburgia, *"Bloodless Weapons"? The Need to Conduct Legal Reviews of Certain Capabilities and the Implications of Defining Them as "Weapons"*, 66 A.F. L. REV. 157, 161 (2010) (discussing the extent to which international law is lagging behind weapons technologies, including in the context of cyberspace); *see* Susan W. Brenner, *Toward a Criminal Law of Cyberspace: Distributed Security*, 10 B.U. J. SCI. & TECH. L. 1, 94 (2004) (arguing for the applicability of criminal law penalties, including sanctions, to cybersecurity lapses).

[14] Roston, *supra* note 8.

[15] Cheryl Pellerin, *Dempsey: Joint Force Must Be Versatile, Affordable*, AM. FORCES PRESS SERV. (July 26, 2011), http://www.defense.gov/news/newsarticle.aspx?id=64815. *See* BRIEN HALLETT, DECLARING WAR: CONGRESS, THE PRESIDENT, AND WHAT THE CONSTITUTION DOES NOT SAY 8 (2012) (discussing the framers' attempt "unsuccessfully to separate" the power to make war in the U.S. constitution); David I. Lewittes, *Constitutional Separation of War Powers: Protecting Public and Private Liberty*, 57 BROOKLYN L. REV. 1083, 1187 (1992) ("The Framers opted in favor of denying Congress the power to make war. Instead, the Constitution grants the legislative branch only the limited authority to declare war.").

[16] Gjelten, *supra* note 2.

[17] *See* Erik M. Mudrinich, *Cyber 3.0: The Department of Defense Strategy for Operating in Cyberspace and the Attribution Problem*, 68 A.F. L. REV. 167, 172–73 (2012) (discussing the attribution issue from a U.S. military perspective).

[18] *See, e.g.*, Roston, *supra* note 8.

the LOAC applies to cyber attacks, then which specific laws of war are relevant; for example, can a cyber attack be a "use of force" as defined by the UN Charter?[19] If so, then would such an attack activate the right of self-defense?[20] The concept of preemptive self-defense – that is, stopping cyber attacks before they are launched – is especially problematic. Taking this doctrine to an extreme would give State A the legal right to attack State B if, at some point in the undefined future, State A deems State B to be a threat to its national security. That is unlawful under international law,[21] and is a recipe for international instability. Yet former U.S. Defense Secretary Leon Panetta has indicated that U.S. forces may take certain preemptive actions if a sufficiently grave and imminent cyber threat is detected.[22] The doctrine of imminence, though, is stretched in the cyber context given the fast pace of attacks potentially requiring more lead-time for defenders to deter incoming assaults.[23] Clear rules of engagement need to be established to limit the danger of escalation,[24] both in peacetime and wartime. Lawyers and policymakers are working on such doctrines,[25] but thorough oversight will be critical domestically, in the U.S. Congress and in the courts, as well as globally to enhance accountability and build trust.[26]

Third, what role should other areas of international law, such as international human rights law (IHRL), play to manage cyber attacks, especially below the armed attack threshold?[27] For example, the LOAC assumes that harm will occur and seeks only to limit the extent of harm.[28] In contrast, human rights norms tradition-ally operate in peacetime during law enforcement investigations, but also have a

---

[19]　UN Charter, art. 2, para. 4.

[20]　UN Charter, art. 51.

[21]　*See, e.g.*, Mary Ellen O'Connell, Am. Soc'y Int'l L. Task Force Terrorism, The Myth of Pre-emptive Self-Defense 2 (2002), http://www.unza.zm/index2.php?option=com_docman&task=doc_view&gid=347&Itemid=43.

[22]　*See* Phil Stewart, *U.S. Defense Chief Says Pre-Emptive Action Possible Over Cyber Threat*, Reuters (Oct. 11, 2012), http://www.reuters.com/article/2012/10/12/net-us-usa-cyber-pentagon-idUSBRE89B04Q20121012.

[23]　*See* Ellen Nakashima, *As U.S. Builds a Cyberwarfare Force, Rules of Engagement Still Hard to Define*, Wash. Post (Mar. 10, 2013), http://www.washingtonpost.com/world/national-security/in-cyber warfare-rules-of-engagement-still-hard-to-define/2013/03/10/0442507c-88da-11e2-9d71-fofeafdd1394_story.html (noting that "the definition of 'imminent' is, like the definition of an 'act of war,' subjective and dependent upon circumstances.").

[24]　*See id.* One idea is to move from preemptive to preventive self-defense models, which the ITU argues is a key to cyber peace by calling for the recognition of "a shared responsibility of all digital stakeholders" to "secure networks and systems" through the use of best practices such as those summarized in Chapter 7. Wegener, *supra* note 9, at 77, 84–85.

[25]　*See* Roston, *supra* note 8.

[26]　*See* Tom Gjelten, *U.S. Seeks to Define Rules on Cyberwar*, NPR (June 3, 2010), http://www.npr.org/templates/story/story.php?storyId=127411091.

[27]　*See* Helen Stacy, professor, Stanford Univ., International Humanitarian Law Issues, Remarks at the Meeting of the Committee on Policy Consequences and Legal/Ethical Implications of Offensive Information Warfare (Apr. 11, 2007).

[28]　*See* Jefferson D. Reynolds, *Collateral Damage on the 21st Century Battlefield: Enemy Exploitation of the Law of Armed Conflict, and the Struggle for a Moral High Ground*, 56 A.F. L. Rev. 1, 1–2 (2005).

growing applicability to armed conflicts.[29] In a cyber conflict, under the Hague and Geneva Conventions "military targets would presumably have to be distinguished from civilian targets, with civilian computer networks off limits."[30] However, with most U.S. military communications traveling over private networks, distinguishing military from civilian targets is no easy matter.[31] These issues underscore the difficulty of relying exclusively on international law to manage cyber attacks.

As Chapter 4 showcased, cyber attacks are a grave threat to international peace and security, especially given the relative lack of international norms shaping how governments should respond to cyber attacks. This means that it is important to use all the tools at our disposal to enhance cybersecurity, including looking to analogies such as communications law, space law, and the law of the sea, among others.[32] These diverse regimes could function together to better manage the vast majority of cyber attacks that fall below the armed attack threshold,[33] but there is no perfect analogy for cyber war. Each regime of international law examined throughout the chapter is inadequate in one way or another to the task. By fitting together elements

---

[29] *See* Kenneth Watkin, *Controlling the Use of Force: A Role for Human Rights Norms in Contemporary Armed Conflict*, 98 AM. J. INT'L L. 1, 1–2 (2004).

[30] Gjelten, *supra* note 2; *see* Jeffrey T. G. Kelsey, Note, *Hacking into International Humanitarian Law: The Principles of Distinction and Neutrality in the Age of Cyber Warfare*, 106 MICH. L. REV. 1427, 1429–30 (2008).

[31] *See, e.g.*, Kevin Baron, *Cyber Strategy: Take a More Active Role in Preventing Attacks*, STARS & STRIPES (July 14, 2011), http://www.stripes.com/news/cyber-strategy-take-a-more-active-role-in-preventing-attacks-1.149204.

[32] Among the other potential analogous regimes is aviation law, given that aviation treaties would bar cyber attacks against the civil aviation sector, as well as public health. *See* Oona A. Hathaway et al., *The Law of Cyber-Attack*, 100 CAL. L. REV. 817, 868–70 (2012) (citing Protocol for the Suppression of Unlawful Acts of Violence at Airports Serving International Civil Aviation, Feb. 24, 1988, 1589 U.N.T.S. 474); SCOTT CHARNEY, MICROSOFT, COLLECTIVE DEFENSE: APPLYING PUBLIC HEALTH MODELS TO THE INTERNET 4–5 (2010) (applying lessons from the public health context to enhancing cybersecurity ranging from promoting hygiene to quarantining infected systems). Sustainable development is another rich area from which to analyze cybersecurity challenges, such as the concepts of polluter pays (which could be applied to require organizations responsible for launching spam or not taking basic security precautions to help pay mitigation costs), and common but differentiated responsibilities. *See The New Politics of the Internet*, ECONOMIST (Jan. 5, 2013), http://www.economist.com/news/briefing/21569041-can-internet-activism-turn-real-political-movement-everything-connected; THE PRINCIPLE OF COMMON BUT DIFFERENTIATED RESPONSIBILITIES: ORIGINS AND SCOPE, CISDL LEGAL BRIEF (2002), cisdl.org/public/docs/news/brief_common.pdf ("[T]he principle of common but differentiated responsibility evolved from the 'common heritage of mankind' and" recognizes the "historical differences" between "the contributions of developed and developing States" to global commons challenges and their capacities to help face these challenges). The latter notion, for example, could be applied to future agreements relating to cyber attacks and would put the onus on the cyber powers, especially the United States and China given their sophistication in this area and status as leading sources of cyber attacks, to take the lead in better managing the cyber threat. However, international political divisions would need to be overcome, though progress in the multilateral climate change negotiations context shows some promise. *See* Nitin Sethi, *World Agrees to Framework for New Global Climate Deal, US May Walk Out Later*, TIMES INDIA (Dec. 8, 2012), http://articles.timesofindia.indiatimes.com/2012-12-08/developmental-issues/35688596_1_climate-change-climate-convention-kyoto-protocol.

[33] *See* Hathaway et al., *supra* note 32, at 821; Matthew C. Waxman, *Cyber-Attacks and the Use of Force: Back to the Future of Article 2(4)*, 36 YALE J. INT'L L. 421, 425 (2011).

of these legal regimes, however, it is possible to craft two frameworks that help to address the recently posed questions and are analyzed in turn: one applicable in peacetime – a "Law of Cyber Peace" – and the other after an armed attack occurs – the "Law of Cyber War."

Cyber attacks have demonstrated both the need for a more regulated cyberspace and the difficulty of crafting and enforcing new regulations.[34] For example, the transnational reach of cyberspace suggests that although legal norms found in UN Charter law are helpful, existing legal frameworks are insufficient for managing the cyber threat because they take for granted sovereign control and established state responsibility.[35] The unsatisfactory status quo suggests two options: adapt current regimes, or create a new framework. The best way to ensure a positive cyber peace may well be through a new international accord dealing exclusively with cyberse-curity and its status in international law.[36] Determining the bounds of such a treaty and how it should function, however, is difficult. As Lewis points out, "[W]hat are you going to do – say 'you can't use laptops for bad purposes?'"[37] In addition, such a comprehensive treaty is likely politically unpalatable for the cyber powers given that it would involve core national security interests.[38] Clarifying existing national and international laws to cyber attacks is more politically feasible than negotiating a new treaty[39] – even though this may represent a second-best solution. Incremen-tal steps such as the creation of targeted protocols and norms should be taken to foster cybersecurity collaboration consistent with polycentric governance, discussed here as an approach in which many independent entities existing at multiple lev-els make "mutual adjustments . . . within a general system of rules" to address a common problem.[40] The goal of this chapter, then, is to analyze some of the inter-national legal aspects of cyber conflict and determine which laws and norms may help bring greater accountability and peace to cyberspace.

---

[34] *See* Andrew W. Murray, The Regulation of Cyberspace: Control in the Online Environment 53 (2006).

[35] Christopher C. Joyner & Catherine Lotrionte, *Information Warfare as International Coercion: Ele-ments of a Legal Framework*, 12 Eur. J. Int'l L. 825, 858 (2001).

[36] *See* Hathaway et al., *supra* note 32, at 822 (making a similar argument).

[37] Interview with James A. Lewis, director and senior fellow, Center for Strategic and International Studies, in Wash., D.C. (Jan. 5, 2011).

[38] *See* Joseph S. Nye, *Power and National Security in Cyberspace*, *in* America's Cyber Future: Security and Prosperity in the Information Age 5, 19–20 (Kristin M. Lord & Travis Sharp eds., CNAS, 2011) [hereinafter America's Cyber Future].

[39] *See* Deltev Wolter, *The UN Takes a Big Step Forward on Cybersecurity*, Arms Control Assoc. (Sept. 2013), http://www.armscontrol.org/act/2013_09/The-UN-Takes-a-Big-Step-Forward-on-Cyber security; UN General Assembly, Group of Governmental Experts on Developments in the Field of Information and Telecommunications in the Context of International Security, UN Doc. A/68/98 (June 24, 2013).

[40] Elinor Ostrom, *A Polycentric Approach for Coping with Climate Change* at 35 (World Bank Policy Research, Working Paper No. 5095, 2009) (citing Vincent Ostrom, *Polycentricity – Part 1*, *in* Poly-centricity and Local Public Economies 57 (Michael D. McGinnis ed., 1999)). Space constraints prohibit a full accounting of the applicable international law to cyber peace, but other areas ripe for investigation include non-intervention, sovereignty, and jurisdiction.

THE LAW OF CYBER PEACE

It is rarely disputed whether the use of chemical or biological weapons should be viewed as "force" within the classic meaning of armed attacks in international law.[41] More contentious to date has been the characterization of cyber war. For example, some scholars have argued that cyber attacks "that directly and intentionally result in non-combatant deaths and destruction . . . breach modern prohibitions on the use of force."[42] However, relatively little attention has been paid to critically assessing legal analogies to use as a baseline for regulatory responses to cyber attacks. Some have argued that the extraordinary nature of a worst-case cyber attack could be analogous to the electromagnetic pulse (EMP) of a nuclear weapon.[43] Elements within Russia and the United States have noted the similarity between cyber war and nuclear war, with a former Russian official stating: "An attack against the telecommunications and electronic power industries of the United States would, by virtue of its catastrophic consequences, completely overlap with the use of weapons of mass destruction."[44] Such hawkish statements point to the danger that great powers see in cyber war, as well as the harm that could result in not laying out an appropriate legal framework from the outset to limit the risk of escalation. Time is of the essence. Is there a possibility, for example, that cyber attacks could be outlawed as nuclear weapons nearly were by the International Court of Justice (ICJ)?[45] Answering such questions is critical to understanding the utility of international law in securing cyberspace.

As has been discussed, direct legal intervention has often proven ineffective at enhancing cybersecurity because of collective action problems and free riders, among other issues. Nations, and for that matter private firms remaining outside established legal frameworks, can create safe harbors that increase the risk to other stakeholders.[46] In response, states may invest resources and extradite cyber attackers where feasible under domestic laws,[47] and work with vulnerable states to enhance their cybersecurity and craft international norms. Given the difficulty of such interventions, however, along with the scale of the problem, it is necessary to consider law and norms alongside market-based incentives and code as part of a polycentric

---

[41] *See, e.g.,* HARV. UNIV., PROGRAM ON HUMANITARIAN POLICY & CONFLICT RESEARCH, HPCR MANUAL AND COMMENTARY ON INTERNATIONAL LAW APPLICABLE TO AIR AND MISSILE WARFARE § (C)(6) (2009), http://www.ihlresearch.org/amw/manual.

[42] Joyner & Lotrionte, *supra* note 35, at 850.

[43] *See* Natasha Solce, *The Battlefield of Cyberspace: The Inevitable New Military Branch – The Cyber Force,* 18 ALB. L.J. SCI. & TECH. 293, 306–07 (2008).

[44] Joyner & Lotrionte, *supra* note 35, at 831 (citation omitted).

[45] *See generally* Legality of the Threat or Use of Nuclear Weapons, Advisory Opinion, 1996 I.C.J. 226 (July 8) [hereinafter Legality of Nuclear Weapons].

[46] MURRAY, *supra* note 34, at 229; Tamisin Ford, *Ivory Coast Cracks Down on Cyber Crime,* BBC (Jan. 16, 2014), http://www.bbc.co.uk/news/business-25735305.

[47] *See* MURRAY, *supra* note 34, at 229.

system to further cyber peace.[48] In order to understand the role of law within that system, we must first examine analogies applicable below the armed attack threshold. At the outset, this requires a brief grounding in the primary sources and purpose of international law.

A Brief Introduction to International Law

International law may be defined as "the body of legal rules," norms, and standards that applies "between sovereign states"[49] and non-state actors, including international organizations and multinational companies, enjoying legal personality. The primary sources of international law are treaties, general principles of law,[50] and custom, the latter of which requires evidence of state practice that nations follow out of a sense of legal obligation.[51] The subsidiary sources of international law include judicial decisions and scholarly writing.[52] Provisions of international law "are [sometimes] enforceable by domestic institutions. . . . "[53] Unlike U.S. law, however, there is often no effective enforcer for international law, no coercive power such as an executive branch to penalize nations that do not live up to their obligations.[54] The International Court of Justice, for example, has from time to time found a state to be in breach of international law, but it lacks the ability to levy sanctions or other punishments without the support of the UN Security Council, which itself can be hobbled by political divisions.[55] Other institutions, such as the World Trade Organization, enjoy other enforcement mechanisms and may have some applicability to cyber attacks.[56] But this general drawback of international law limits its usefulness

---

[48] *See id.* at xi.

[49] *Definition of International Law*, Int'l Labor Org., http://www.actrav.itcilo.org/actrav-english/telearn/global/ilo/law/lablaw.htm (last visited June 25, 2013).

[50] *See* Linda A. Malone, International Law 27 (2008) ("General principles are losing importance in modern international law" because they have often been incorporated into custom or codified in treaties).

[51] *See* Statute of the International Court of Justice, art. 38, June 26, 1945, 59 Stat. 1055, http://www.icj-cij .org/documents/index.php?p1=4&p2=2&p3=0. Custom will be an increasingly important source of international cyber law going forward given the relative lack of binding law below the armed attack threshold and the political difficulties involved with negotiating new accords as discussed in Chapter 7.

[52] *See id.*; Malcolm N. Shaw, International Law 68–72 (4th ed. 1997).

[53] Nat'l Res. Council, Technology, Policy, Law, and Ethics Regarding U.S. Acquisition and Use of Cyberattack Capabilities 241 (William A. Owens, Kenneth W. Dam, & Herbert S. Lin eds., 2009) [hereinafter National Academies].

[54] *Id.*

[55] *See id.*; Mary Ellen O'Connell, *Prospects for Enforcing Monetary Judgments of the International Court of Justice: A Study of Nicaragua's Judgment against the United States*, 30 Va. J. Int'l L. 891, 891–92 (1990); Security Council – Veto List, http://www.un.org/depts/dhl/resguide/scact_veto_en.shtml (last visited Mar. 14, 2014).

[56] *See, e.g.*, Mark L. Movesian, Essay, *Enforcement of WTO Rulings: An Interest Group Analysis*, 32 Hofstra L. Rev. 1, 1–2 (2003) (describing the WTO Dispute Settlement Understanding and noting that trade disputes between nations "are to be resolved in adversarial proceedings before impartial panels of experts" under this system); James A. Lewis, *Conflict and Negotiation in Cyberspace*, Ctr.

in enhancing cybersecurity, though as we will see, certain approaches offer some promise.

Regulating Cyber Weapons through International Law

As difficult a challenge as banning chemical, biological, or nuclear weapons may present, it is even more complex to prohibit the use of cyber weapons under international law, due in no small part to technical challenges, verification issues, and the attribution problem.[57] This difficulty stems from the fact that the code comprising cyber weapons is similar to information requests, such as DDoS attacks. Nevertheless, some nations, such as Russia, potentially fearing Western digital dominance, are pushing for such an arms control-style cyber treaty, as discussed in Chapter 7. In an effort to determine the extent to which such a ban is even possible, this section considers lessons from other treaty systems that have sought to limit the use of weapons to help build out the law of cyber peace, including arms control treaties during the interwar period, nuclear weapons law, space law, and the Antarctic Treaty System (ATS).

Interwar Arms Control

The major arms-control treaties of the 1920s and 1930s determined national strength in terms of fleet size.[58] This changed in the post-WWII period, when "strategic nuclear capability . . . replaced fleets as the measure of global power status."[59] However, the interwar years do convey "an image of a policy environment not unlike our own today," replete with the military grappling with the consequences of a technological revolution along with the complexities of navigating multipolar politics.[60] The interwar arms control regime was based on the 1922 Washington Treaty that placed limits on naval fleet sizes and was followed by a slew of other treaties designed to ward off another arms race.[61] They failed. Among the lessons learned from this experience by scholars was that "by ignoring underlying sources of conflict, technical agreements may exacerbate insecurity."[62] An example is the 1930 London Naval Treaty, which "reaffirmed Japan's defensive superiority in the Pacific," but failed to address Western and Japanese policy differences toward a unified China.[63] Thus,

---

STRATEGIC & INT'L STUD. 48–51 (2013) (discussing the applicability of the WTO dispute resolution processes to help manage cyber espionage).

[57] *But see* Neil C. Rowe et al., *Challenges in Monitoring Cyberarms Compliance*, 1 INT'L J. CYBER WARFARE & TERRORISM 1, 1, 12 (2011) (discussing the challenges of and potential paths to cyber arms control, including making use of digital forensics and usage monitoring to verify compliance).

[58] *See* Caroline F. Ziemke, *Peace Without Strings? Interwar Naval Arms Control Revisited*, WASH. Q., Fall 1992, at 87.

[59] *Id.*

[60] Robin Ranger, *Learning from the Naval Arms Control Experience*, 10(3) WASH. Q., Summer 1987, at 47 (writing in the 1980s, but still with some application to the present).

[61] EMILY O. GOLDMAN, SUNKEN TREATIES: NAVAL ARMS CONTROL BETWEEN THE WARS 33–34 (1994).

[62] *Id.* at 30.

[63] *Id.*

whereas cyber arms control is not necessarily impossible, agreements must be as comprehensive as possible and take into account the likely reasons that a cyber war would start. A cyber weapons treaty would do little good, for example, if negotiators ignored its status during an armed conflict or the geopolitical context in which a conflict could arise, such as U.S.-China relations over Taiwan. Consequently, the interwar arms control treaties provide a fruitful cautionary tale for what can happen when good intentions race ahead of good policy that takes realpolitik into account.

The Analogy of Nuclear War

According to Lewis, we understand nearly as much about the relationship between cyber conflict and international security now as we did about strategic thinking related to nuclear weapons in the early 1950s.[64] If that is true, then it is important to consider the conventions and applicable case law on nuclear warfare to frame contemporary efforts aimed at controlling cyber weapons. During the 1950s and 1960s, nuclear policy was a tightly veiled secret with relatively little public discussion.[65] That was until Herman Kahn's books, including *On Thermonuclear War* and *Thinking About the Unthinkable*, began a renaissance in scholarly work on the topic that had a great impact on U.S. nuclear policy.[66]

The most significant legal decision on the use of nuclear weapons came in 1994, when the UN General Assembly voted to submit a request for an advisory opinion to the ICJ on the question of "whether the threat or use of nuclear weapons would be lawful. . . . "[67] The U.S. argued in the case that nuclear weapons cannot be banned in the abstract, but rather each case "must be examined individually."[68] Ultimately, the court stated that the threat or use of nuclear weapons "would generally be contrary to the rules of international law. . . . "[69] However, the court did not define whether "the threat or use of nuclear weapons would be lawful or unlawful in an extreme circumstance of self-defense, in which the very survival of a State would be at stake."[70] Even though the ICJ did not declare all nuclear weapons illegal, the logic of its holding that "methods and means of warfare . . . which would result in unnecessary suffering to combatants, are prohibited"[71] is applicable to cyber conflict given the interconnectivity of cyberspace and resulting potential for collateral damage as seen in attacks like Stuxnet.[72]

---

[64] James A. Lewis, *The "Korean" Cyber Attacks and Their Implications for Cyber Conflict*, CTR. STRATEGIC & INT'L STUD., Oct. 2009, at 2.

[65] *See* NATIONAL ACADEMIES, *supra* note 53, at xi.

[66] *Id.*; *see* HERMAN KAHN, ON THERMONUCLEAR WAR (1960); HERMAN KAHN, THINKING ABOUT THE UNTHINKABLE (1962).

[67] FOREIGN & INT'L LAW COMM., N.Y. COUNTY LAWYERS' ASS'N (NYCLA), ON THE UNLAWFULNESS OF THE USE AND THREAT OF NUCLEAR WEAPONS 5 (2000) [hereinafter NYCLA, UNLAWFULNESS OF NUCLEAR WEAPONS], http://www.nuclearweaponslaw.com/JournalsReport/NYCLA_Report.pdf.

[68] *Id.* at 4.

[69] Legality of Nuclear Weapons, 1996 I.C.J. at 266.

[70] *Id.*

[71] *Id.* at 262.

[72] Lewis, *supra* note 64, at 4.

There are several differences and similarities between nuclear weapons and cyber weapons. First, unlike nuclear testing, which remains rare,[73] cyber weapons are used frequently by state and non-state actors. Second, attributing a nuclear attack is possible through satellite tracking and radiological analysis,[74] but as we have seen, attributing cyber attacks is far more difficult. Third, the technology for cyber weapons has already diffused, making non-proliferation nearly impossible.[75] Nevertheless, similarities also persist, such as the superiority of offense over defense, ability to challenge power asymmetries, and potential for unintended consequences.[76]

Although the United States has not embraced a rule banning the use of nuclear weapons, it acknowledges that the LOAC governs such use, "including the rules of proportionality, necessity, moderation, discrimination, civilian immunity, [and] neutrality.... "[77] These concepts are explored in the next section on the law of cyber war. Similarly, the destructive potential for cyber weapons renders discussion on how these weapons may be limited, or banned outright, a worthwhile if problematic endeavor. The ICJ has not explicitly considered the legality of cyber weapons to this point.[78] In fact, there is little customary international law on the use of cyber attacks beyond the basic principle in the *Nicaragua Case* that "every sovereign State [has a right] to conduct its affairs without outside interference."[79] Custom, as was mentioned earlier in this chapter, requires widespread state practice that is undertaken out of a sense of legal obligation.[80] State practice in the aftermath of cyber attacks seems to suggest a lack of consensus on how best to respond. Consider the initial reaction, or lack thereof, from states including Iran following Stuxnet.[81] However, the fact that states often attempt to hide their cyber activities through intermediaries or other obscurations could be understood as implicitly acknowledging the unlawfulness of the actions and may suggest a growing recognition that certain

---

[73] *See, e.g.,* RICHARD L. MILLER, UNDER THE CLOUD: THE DECADES OF NUCLEAR TESTING 1–11 (1999) (describing the history of U.S. nuclear testing and development); Tia Ghose, *Nuclear Weapons Sensors Could Monitor Environment,* LIVESCIENCE (Feb. 14, 2013), http://www.livescience.com/27143-weapons-sensors-monitor-environment.html (reporting that "nuclear tests are rare.... ").

[74] *See* AM PHYS. SOC. & AM. ASSOC. ADVANCEMENT SCI., NUCLEAR FORENSICS: ROLE, STATE OF THE ART, AND PROGRAM NEEDS 3 (2008).

[75] *See* Joseph S. Nye, Jr., *Nuclear Lessons for Cyber Security?,* STRATEGIC STUD. Q., Winter 2011, at 18, 36 (discussing the extent to which cyber attack technologies have diffused to non-state actors, complicating efforts at international arms control as compared to the nuclear analogy).

[76] *See* NATIONAL ACADEMIES, *supra* note 53, at 295.

[77] NYCLA, UNLAWFULNESS OF NUCLEAR WEAPONS, *supra* note 67, at 9.

[78] *See* Legality of Nuclear Weapons, 1996 I.C.J. at 262.

[79] Military and Paramilitary Activities in and Against Nicaragua (Nicar. v. U.S.), 1986 I.C.J. 14, para. 106 (June 27) [hereinafter *Nicaragua*].

[80] *See* N. Sea Continental Shelf (F.R.G./Den. v. Neth.), 1969 I.C.J. 41, 72 (Feb. 20); *Assessment of Customary International Law,* ICRC, http://www.icrc.org/customary-ihl/eng/docs/v1_rul_in_asofcuin (last visited Jan. 29, 2014) ("To establish a rule of customary international law, State practice has to be virtually uniform, extensive and representative.").

[81] *But see* Ian Traynor, *Russia Accused of Unleashing Cyberwar to Disable Estonia,* GUARDIAN (May 16, 2007), http://www.guardian.co.uk/world/2007/may/17/topstories3.russia (discussing state responses to the cyber attacks on Estonia).

cyber attacks breach the customary international law norm of nonintervention.[82] Yet, even in the relative absence of custom, several treaty regimes may provide a basis for the regulation of some cyber attacks under international law that fall below the armed attack threshold at least until new regimes come online.

From the Digital Frontier to the Final Frontier: Arms Limitation in Space Law as an Analogy for Cyber War

Outer space is similar to cyberspace; both are vast areas encompassing both territorial and extraterritorial components. Like the weapons systems that have been developed to attack satellites, cyber attacks could have a large-scale strategic impact.[83] In short, the use of either anti-satellite or sophisticated cyber weapons can be game changers. More broadly, both outer space and cyberspace are domains in which intelligence gathering has been widely tolerated, even though the outcry has been greater in the case of cyber espionage than orbital reconnaissance.[84] The nature of cyberspace also makes comprehensive tracking difficult, because even though the physical Internet is routed in particular jurisdictions, controlling the packets of information that comprise cyberspace is another matter as was described in Chapters 2 and 3. Similarly, "[s]pacecraft and satellites in orbit pass above many different sovereign jurisdictions...."[85] Both the United States and the former Soviet Union began launching spy satellites that crossed over one another's territory in the late 1950s.[86] With few objections to these intrusions, this practice soon became part of customary international law and eventually was codified in the 1967 Outer Space Treaty (OST), which laid the foundations for space governance and may well have some application to cybersecurity.[87]

Space and telecommunications systems are intertwined, including in such areas as imagery collection, navigation, and signals intelligence.[88] However, space law's failure to address whether the legal regime applies during an armed conflict limits its utility as an analogy for cyber war. Moreover, the military use of space was not

---

[82] *See* Hathaway et al., *supra* note 32, at 843. *Cf.* James Blitz, *UK Becomes First State to Admit to Offensive Cyber Attack Capability*, Fin. Times (Sept. 29, 2013), http://www.ft.com/intl/cms/s/o/9ac6ede6-28fd-11e3-ab62-00144feab7de.html#axzz2rohGeqFy (illustrating the divergent state practice challenging norm development in cyberspace).

[83] National Academies, *supra* note 53, at 296–97.

[84] *See, e.g.*, James W. Gabberty, *Understanding Motives of Recent Cyber Attacks Against US*, Hill (Mar. 11, 2013), http://thehill.com/blogs/congress-blog/technology/287425-understanding-motives-of-recent-cyber-attacks-against-us.

[85] Julie J. C. H. Ryan, Daniel J. Ryan, & Eneken Tikk, *Cybersecurity Regulation: Using Analogies to Develop Frameworks for Regulation*, *in* International Cyber Security Legal & Policy Proceedings 76, 89 (Eneken Tikk & Anna-Maria Talihärm eds., 2010).

[86] *See* Thomas Graham, Jr. et al., Spy Satellites and Other Intelligence Technologies that Changed History 36–38 (2007).

[87] *See* Treaty on Principles Governing the Activities of States in the Exploration and Use of Outer Space, Including the Moon and Other Celestial Bodies, Jan. 27, 1967, 18 U.S.T. 2410, 610 U.N.T.S. 205 (entered into force Oct. 10, 1967) [hereinafter OST]; National Academies, *supra* note 53, at 296–97.

[88] DOD Assessment, *supra* note 8, at 26.

forbidden by the OST, as evidenced by the existence of earth-orbiting military reconnaissance satellites. Further, according to the DOD, "[t]here is no legal prohibition against developing and using space control weapons,"[89] for example, save for placing nuclear weapons or other WMDs into orbit.[90] A growing list of nations are developing space weapons.[91] Vision for 2020, a 1998 U.S. government report, explains that the United States should dominate space, a view shared by retired General Joseph W. Ashy, formerly of U.S. Space Command, who has said: "It's politically sensitive, but it's going to happen . . . we're going to fight *in* space."[92]

International efforts to form a legal regime for space weapons have been nearly as happenstance as those aimed at limiting cyber weapons.[93] Russia and China have advocated for an expanded regime to control both space and cyber weapons, as discussed in Chapter 7.[94] Yet unlike the sophisticated infrastructure and advanced technology needed to develop and deploy space weapons, nearly all nations participate in the Information Age to some degree, whereas only some eighty nations have engaged with space exploration, and fewer still could be considered actively spacefaring.[95] Barring a major conflict, most states do not expect or have the resources "to be either an attacker or a defender" in space in the near term.[96] In contrast, nearly "all states can reasonably expect to be both"[97] an attacker and defender in cyberspace to some degree, which can make reaching consensus difficult.

Space law illustrates that it is possible to regulate an area of the global commons to bar the most egregious military weapons systems. Space law, however, does not fit the mold of cyber peace given the many types of cyber attacks, none of which are equivalent to a WMD attack.[98] There is no cyber equivalent of a nuclear weapon – no

---

[89] *Id.* at 31 (The use of space control systems in peacetime would be subject to both the general principles of international law and to treaty obligations. . . . These obligations would probably be suspended during an international armed conflict. . . . ").

[90] OST, art. 4.

[91] *See* Jeremy Hsu, *Is a New Space Weapon Race Heating Up?*, SPACE.COM (May 5, 2010), http://www .space.com/businesstechnology/space-war-weapons-heats-up-100505.html (reporting that the United States, China, Russia, and India in January 2010, have all either begun or reinvigorated their anti-satellite weapons programs).

[92] Karl Grossman & Judith Long, *Waging War in Space*, NATION (Dec. 9, 1999) http://www.thenation .com/article/waging-war-space (emphasis in original).

[93] *See, e.g.*, Turner Brinton, *Obama's Proposed Space Weapon Ban Draws Mixed Response*, SPACE.COM (Feb. 4, 2009), http://www.space.com/news/090204-obama-space-weapons-response.html.

[94] *See* Press Release, General Assembly, Prevention of Outer Space Arms Race, Ratification of Nuclear Test-Ban Treaty Among Issues Addressed by Texts Introduced in First Committee, UN GA/DIS/3233 (Oct. 15, 2002), http://www.un.org/News/Press/docs/2002/gadis3233.doc.htm; Duncan Hollis, *Should There Be an International Treaty on Cyberwarfare?*, OPINIO JURIS (June 13, 2012), http://opiniojuris .org/2012/06/13/should-there-be-an-international-treaty-on-cyberwarfare/.

[95] *See* Scott Horowitz, *Nations in Space*, AMERICA.GOV (July 29, 2008), http://www.america.gov/st/space-english/2008/July/20080817210902SrenoD0.1624262.html.

[96] DOD ASSESSMENT, *supra* note 8, at 48.

[97] *Id.*

[98] Other space law treaties relating to liability claims resulting from space activities, registration of objects launched into space, the governance of the moon, or satellite regulations have little if any applicability

single attack now known that can, by itself, bring a country to its knees. Even Stuxnet may be thought of as more of a "smart bomb."[99] A more apt analogy may be the collective action problem of space junk. Some estimates place the total number of objects capable of damaging spacecraft at more than 35 million, making attribution difficult.[100] As with a stray bolt damaging a satellite, a piece of malware can wreak havoc with disparate websites and networks. As of 2013, however, there has been little multilateral agreement on how to better manage orbital debris, though limited polycentric initiatives have been undertaken that could be informative to cyber peacebuilding.[101]

Freeze the Code: The Antarctic Treaty System Approach to Cyber Weapons

Rather than banning only certain types of cyber weapons, it may be more useful to regulate all cyber attacks. The Antarctic Treaty, which besides managing a continent was the first arms control treaty of the Cold War, provides a fruitful analogue because it goes further than the OST and bans *all* military activities.[102] The main objective of the ATS is to ensure "in the interests of all mankind that Antarctica shall continue forever to be used exclusively for peaceful purposes. . . ."[103] Like Antarctica, the Internet is a rich resource, being a repository of knowledge and a vital channel for commerce and communications. However, imposing a freeze on developing new types of software that could be used to launch malicious attacks, even if it were possible, might not be preferable given that it could stifle innovation, among other concerns.[104] Nor would a traditional international accord likely be capable

to cyber attacks and so are beyond the bounds of this study. *See* Convention on International Liability for Damage Caused by Space Objects, arts. 14–20, Mar. 29, 1972, 24 U.S.T. 2389, 961 U.N.T.S. 187 (entered into force Sept. 1, 1972); Convention on Registration of Objects Launched Into Outer Space, Nov. 12 & 14, 1974, art. I, 28 U.S.T. 695, 1023 U.N.T.S. 15 (entered into force Sept. 15, 1976); Agreement Governing the Activities of States on the Moon and Other Celestial Bodies, Dec. 18, 1979, U.N. GAOR, 34th Sess., Supp. No. 46, at 77, U.N. Doc. A/34/46 (1980), 18 I.L.M. 1434; Agreement Relating to the International Telecommunications Satellite Organization, "INTELSAT," Aug. 20, 1971, 23 U.S.T. 3813.

[99] Steven Cherry, *Sons of Stuxnet*, IEEE Spectrum (Dec. 14, 2011), http://spectrum.ieee.org/podcast/ telecom/security/sons-of-stuxnet.

[100] *See* Ronald L. Spencer, Jr., *International Space Law: A Basis for National Regulation*, in National Regulation of Space Activities 1, 4 (Ram S. Jakhu ed., 2010).

[101] *See* Frank A. Rose, Remarks at the UN Institute for Disarmament Research, Space Security Conference, in Geneva, Switzerland: Laying the Groundwork for a Stable and Sustainable Space Environment (Mar. 29, 2012), http://www.state.gov/t/avc/rls/187090.htm (reporting that Japan, Australia, the EU, and the United States have agreed to develop a code of conduct for space debris mitigation); COPUOS *Space Debris Mitigation Guidelines* (2010), U.N. OOSA, http://www.oosa.unvienna.org/ pdf/publications/st_space_49E.pdf (last visited Nov. 11, 2013); Scott J. Shackelford, *Governing the Final Frontier: A Polycentric Approach to Managing Space Weaponization and Debris*, 51 Am. Bus. L.J. __ (2014).

[102] Antarctic Treaty, art. 1, para. 1, Dec. 1, 1959, 12 U.S.T. 794, 402 U.N.T.S. 72 (defining "peaceful purposes" in Antarctica as banning "any measures of a military nature. . . .").

[103] *Id.* at pmbl.

[104] *See, e.g.,* Jack Goldsmith, *Cybersecurity Treaties: A Skeptical View*, Hoover Inst., at 12 (2011), http://media.hoover.org/sites/default/files/documents/FutureChallenges_Goldsmith.pdf   (arguing

of keeping up with rapidly changing IT, necessitating a kind of standing public-private committee of cybersecurity experts that could analyze industry best practices and help identify new security threats as they arise. Subsequent enforcement and coordination would thereafter pose significant challenges. On the surface, then, it appears that neither barring certain malignant code nor all possible variations of cyber attacks under international law is an effective, efficient response to the cyber threat without substantial technological improvements.[105] What then about the potential of using either international communications or domestic law to prosecute attackers and their facilitators?

Determining Liability for Cyber Attacks through International Communications and U.S. Cyber Law

International communication law in many ways represents the most direct analogue to cybersecurity, but it, too, has its drawbacks. Given that so many international accords fail to offer a comprehensive legal system to manage cyber attacks, domestic mechanisms should also be considered. The United States is used as a case study in this regard, building from the analyses begun in Chapters 4 and 5.

International Communications Law and Cyber Attacks

In many ways, the development of international communications law was the direct precursor to cyber law, beginning with agreements dating from the 1800s designed to protect submarine cables.[106] Modern communications law is crafted by the International Telecommunication Union, the oldest still-active intergovernmental organization in the world.[107] For nearly 150 years, it has been the primary organization responsible for multilateral telecom governance,[108] and more recently it has also played a role in Internet governance as discussed in Chapters 1 and 7. The ITU Convention militates against "harmful interference," defined in Annex 3 of the document as that which "endangers . . . *safety services*, or seriously degrades, obstructs or repeatedly interrupts a radiocommunication service. . . . "[109] "Safety services" include technologies "used permanently or temporarily for the safeguarding

---

"that the fundamental clash of interests concerning the regulation of electronic communications, the deep constraints the United States would have to adopt to receive reciprocal benefits in a cybersecurity treaty, and the debilitating verification problems will combine to make it unfeasible to create a cybersecurity treaty that purports to constrain governments.").

[105] *But see* Rowe et al., *supra* note 57, at 12 (making the case that cyber arms control is possible using current technology).

[106] *See* DOD Assessment, *supra* note 8, at 4, 32–33.

[107] *See International Telecommunication Union*, UN, https://www.un.org/Pubs/ourlives/itu.htm (last visited June 25, 2013).

[108] *See* Hathaway et al., *supra* note 32, at 867 (citing Charles H. Kennedy & M. Veronica Pastor, An Introduction to International Telecommunications Law 30–33 (1996)).

[109] International Telecommunication Convention, Nairobi, annex 2, at para. 2003, Nov. 6, 1982, 32 U.S.T. 3821 (emphasis added).

of human life and property[,]" which could conceivably refer to public services such as health, police, and public transport, along with CNI more generally, all of which are vulnerable to cyber attacks.[110] However, the lack of mandatory enforcement mechanisms and its failure to apply during armed conflicts limits the efficacy of this regime, as does political resistance from some stakeholders to empower the ITU to have a larger role in enhancing global cybersecurity, as is explored in Chapter 7.

The ITU Convention also gives governments wide discretion in regulating private activity that "may appear dangerous to the security of the State[,]"[111] including acts "contrary to . . . public order, or to decency."[112] Unlike space law or the Antarctic Treaty System, this provision does have an exception for military activities, and state practice suggests that it does not apply during an armed conflict.[113] Ever since the British "cut the five submarine cables serving Germany" at the outbreak of WWI, "communications facilities" have been regarded as "priority military targets."[114] Critically, at least according to the U.S. DOD, international communications law currently "contains no direct and specific prohibition" against the use of cyber attacks "by military forces, even in peacetime."[115] As a result, whereas elements within the ITU Charter may help the international community manage cyber attacks, the Charter offers limited guidance in crafting a comprehensive legal framework to hold attackers more accountable.

U.S. Cyber Law Applied to Cyber Attacks

Cyber law is relatively new. It has to be – in 1988, there were only some 60,000 computers connected to the Internet, all at research institutions.[116] As the threats posed by cyber attacks have grown, so too has U.S. regulatory response to cyber attackers. U.S. laws have begun to divide the responsibilities of cybersecurity between various governmental agencies along with the private sector, as was introduced in Chapter 4, including defining the distinction between "covert" and "clandestine" action – in other words, cyber espionage. The former may be considered "activities that are intended to influence the conduct, behavior, or actions of an adversary without the involvement of the United States becoming known. . . . "[117] Simply put, covert actions occur "when you are changing something, and you're trying to maintain

---

[110] The Protection of Safety Services from Unwanted Emissions, ITU-R SM.1535 at (c) (2001).

[111] DOD Assessment, *supra* note 8, at 33–34.

[112] Constitution of the International Telecommunications Union, art. 34, Dec. 22, 1992, http://itu.int/net/about/basic-texts/index.aspx [hereinafter ITU Constitution].

[113] *Id.* at art. 48 ("Member States retain their entire freedom with regard to military radio installations.").

[114] DOD Assessment, *supra* note 8, at 33.

[115] *Id.* at 34.

[116] *See* Howard Rheingold, The Virtual Community: Homesteading on the Electronic Frontier 272 (1993); *Internet History: 1980s*, Computer Hist. Museum, http://www.computerhistory.org/internet_history/internet_history_80s.html (last visited Jan. 28, 2014).

[117] National Academies, *supra* note 53, at 285.

deniability when you do it," according to Clarke.[118] Covert action is highly regulated and requires a number of procedural steps, beginning with a written presidential finding and ending with a CIA operation, whereas clandestine action requires no special approval and is governed by an entirely separate part of the U.S. Code.[119] If cyber attacks were categorized as the former, bureaucratic delay may result. Any postponement in a setting where milliseconds count highlights one of the many ambiguities persistent in U.S. cyber law. Nevertheless, turf wars remain unresolved.

Aside from clandestine and covert actions, U.S. law does contain certain provisions that pertain to victims of cyber attacks.[120] For example, the Computer Fraud and Abuse Act was originally intended to protect against the unauthorized access of government computers and those of financial institutions.[121] However, the CFAA also may be interpreted to prohibit individuals and corporations from launching cyber attacks.[122] This, combined with prohibitions under international law, limits proactive defense strategies and domestic cyber militias discussed in Chapter 5 from being legally formed in the United States to protect CNI. A number of questions, however, remain unresolved. It is unclear, for example, whether the U.S. government can "use [the] private computers of Americans without owner permission" to conduct cyber attacks in an attempt to mask attribution.[123] Even fewer protections are sometimes afforded to persons and corporations outside the United States. As a result, there seems to be at present no bar in domestic law "for the U.S. government to commandeer the computers of private citizens abroad" to launch cyber attacks.[124] This risks alienating U.S. citizens, friends, and businesses, the consequences of which may be seen in the 2013–14 NSA revelations.[125] Proposals to request permission, or even pay users for allowing U.S. government botnets to operate on their machines, have so far gone nowhere.

The federal Wiretap Act of 1968, known as Title III, also shapes the U.S. cybersecurity landscape by limiting the use of real-time surveillance to situations in which the authorities have received a warrant from a judge.[126] Beginning "in 1978, the Foreign Intelligence Surveillance Act (FISA) established a framework for" collecting

---

[118] Clarke, *supra* note 11.

[119] *Id.*

[120] *See* Hathaway et al., *supra* note 32, at 874.

[121] 18 U.S.C. § 1030(a)(2)(C).

[122] Hathaway et al., *supra* note 32, at 874 (listing, at the U.S. federal level, provisions that address fraud; the "malicious interference in communications . . . systems; electronic communication interception; illicit access to electronic communications records; and recording of dialing, routing, addressing, and signaling information.") (footnotes omitted); 18 U.S.C. §§ 1029–30 (2012).

[123] National Academies, *supra* note 53, at 289.

[124] *Id.*

[125] *See NSA Spying Shows How to Lose Friends and Alienate Allies*, Wash. Post (Oct. 29, 2013), http://www.washingtonpost.com/opinions/nsa-spying-shows-how-to-lose-friends-and-alienate-allies/2013/10/29/0doc2928-40cf-11e3-a624-41d661b0bb78_story.html.

[126] *See* Wiretap Act of 1968, Pub. L. No. 90-351, 82 Stat. 197, 211–23 (1968) (passed as Title III of the Omnibus Crime Control and Safe Streets Act).

intelligence,[127] though the FISA court set up to adjudicate such matters has lost much of its substantive review and enforcement powers since amendments were passed in 2008.[128] Some types of cyber espionage fall under Title III regulation. In fact, on June 12, 2007, an FBI agent requested that a judge support an application for the FBI "to send a message to a computer used to administer a specific MySpace.com user account."[129] The message was "designed to cause this computer to transmit back to the FBI technical data identifying the computer and/or the users of the computer."[130] The judge's ruling is not publicly available.[131] However, in January 2014, President Obama announced reforms to the FISA court that include encouraging the U.S. Congress to install a public advocate to argue for civil liberties.[132]

Certain U.S. Executive Orders and other statutes also apply to cyber attacks. For example, "Executive Order 12333 regulates the conduct of U.S. intelligence activities," including cyber espionage.[133] However, it may also "restrict the ability of government agencies to collect information" on cyber attacks "within the United States.... "[134] Similarly, the Posse Comitatus Act, which was originally a Reconstruction-era law designed to limit the powers of the federal government to enforce state laws, may operate to forbid U.S. armed forces from launching cyber attacks in support of domestic law enforcement.[135] In addition, several U.S. criminal statutes could also build out the beginnings of a polycentric system for managing cyber attacks.[136] For example, U.S. felony statutes criminalize violations of international accords dealing with international radio or wire communications as well as malicious interference with satellites, similar to wire fraud.[137] These statutes could extend to cyber attacks that do not reach the level of an armed attack and be harnessed to prosecute cyber attackers and thus promote cyber peace.[138]

---

[127] NATIONAL ACADEMIES, *supra* note 53, at 286; 50 U.S.C. § 1806(f) (2012).

[128] *See* NATIONAL ACADEMIES, *supra* note 53, at 287; Nina Totenberg, *Why the FISA Court is Not What it Used To Be*, NPR (June 18, 2013), http://www.npr.org/2013/06/18/191715681/why-the-fisa-court-is-not-what-it-used-to-be.

[129] NATIONAL ACADEMIES, *supra* note 53, at 287.

[130] *Id.*

[131] *Id.* at 288.

[132] *See* Fred Kaplan, *Pretty Good Privacy*, SLATE (Jan. 17, 2014), http://www.slate.com/articles/news_and_politics/war_stories/2014/01/obama_s_nsa_reforms_the_president_s_proposals_for_metadata_and_the_fisa.html (noting that the Obama administration has not endorsed other proposed revisions to the FISA court including the way current FISA judges are named, or limiting the use of the FBI's National Security Letters).

[133] NATIONAL ACADEMIES, *supra* note 54, at 290; W. Hays Parks, *Memorandum of Law: Executive Order 12333 and Assassination* (Nov. 2, 1989), http://www.hks.harvard.edu/cchrp/Use%20of%20Force/October%202002/Parks_final.pdf.

[134] NATIONAL ACADEMIES, *supra* note 53, at 291.

[135] *Id.* at 288 (citing 18 U.S.C. § 1385 (2012)).

[136] *See* Wire and Electronic Communications Interception and Interception of Oral Communications, 18 U.S.C. § 2511 (2012); Malicious Mischief, 18 U.S.C. § 1362 (2012); Fraud and Related Activity Related in Connection with Access Devices, 18 U.S.C. § 1029 (2012).

[137] *See* 47 U.S.C. §502 (2006); 18 U.S.C. §§ 1343, 1367 (2006).

[138] *See, e.g.,* 18 U.S.C. § 2331 (2000).

Aside from executive orders and statutes, the fact that most CNI in the United States is in private hands signifies that the principles of tort law and other related common law doctrines could prove instrumental in developing a U.S. legal regime to better manage cyber attacks. For example, consider vicarious liability, a type of strict liability that arises under the common law doctrine of agency.[139] Under this theory, the principal is responsible for the acts of the subordinate, or as applied to cyberspace, the network administrator for network integrity. In a broader sense, a third party that has the right, ability, or duty to control the activities of a violator, but refuses or neglects to do so, may in some cases be liable for the violator's actions.[140] Applied to cybersecurity, this principle could provide an avenue for holding firms liable for knowingly or negligently failing to safeguard the persons or resources under their care during a cyber attack, a duty of care that could crystallize depending on the uptake of the National Institute of Standards and Technology Cybersecurity Framework mentioned in Chapter 5.[141]

Several U.S. Supreme Court precedents help lay the foundation for a regime of vicarious liability applied to cyber attacks. For example, if a technology company is aware of a nefarious act and the firm refuses to develop filtering tools to diminish the infringing activity, then, as an extension of existing precedent, the firm could be held liable for any resultant criminal or terrorist consequences.[142] The Court has also found defendants liable for having control over copyright infringers.[143] These cases could help place the onus of surveillance on the private sector were they to be applied beyond the copyright context. In doing so, however, companies (notably ISPs) cannot be overzealous and block innocent websites.[144] Nor do firms have secondary liability for providing Internet services if they have no knowledge of the violation or infringement.[145] This discussion, begun in Chapters 2 and 5, raises the specter of the role that the private sector should play in enhancing cybersecurity as part of a larger polycentric system to promote cyber peace.

The Role of the Private Sector in Managing Cyber Attacks under International Law

The private sector was marginalized when legal regimes were created to govern much of the global commons, including outer space and the deep seabed. Over time, though, a changing geopolitical landscape, technological advancement, and resource shortages have transformed the role of the private sector in these areas,

[139] RESTATEMENT OF AGENCY § 219 (1958).
[140] See Meyer v. Holley, 537 U.S. 280, 284 (2003).
[141] See Executive Order 13636: Improving Critical Infrastructure Cybersecurity, 78 Fed. Reg. 33, 11739 (Feb. 12, 2013).
[142] See Metro-Goldwyn-Mayer Studios, Inc. v. Grokster, Ltd., 545 U.S. 913 (2005).
[143] See Fonovisa v. Cherry Auction, Inc., 76 F.3d 259 (9th Cir. 1996).
[144] See Ctr. for Democracy & Tech. v. Pappert, 337 F. Supp. 2d 606 (E.D. Pa. 2004).
[145] See Hendrickson v. eBay, Inc., 165 F. Supp. 2d 1082 (C.D. Cal. 2001).

including the law of the sea (LOS). Some of the same lessons may be applied to cyberspace given the key role that private-sector actors play in Internet governance.

The LOS, like outer space, enjoys many parallels with cyberspace. The process that ultimately resulted in the first United Nations Convention on the Law of the Sea (UNCLOS) treaty began in 1945 and finally resulted in UNCLOS I in 1958.[46] However, UNCLOS I did not sufficiently address concerns about the legal status of the deep seabed lying underneath the high seas.[47] Little was accomplished at UNCLOS II, mostly owing to political opposition from "Arab States and the Communist bloc.... "[48] This served as an impetus for UNCLOS III, which was tasked with, among other things, regulating the use, exploration, and exploitation of all living and non-living resources of the high seas.[49] Still, the role of the private sector remained truncated. As the deep seabed mining provisions of UNCLOS proved unsatisfactory to the developed world, the treaty was amended in 1994 to better comport with economic development.[50] The story of the evolution of UNCLOS is in part the imperative that the private sector must be included if progress is to be made, which has ramifications for Internet governance and the role of the ITU.

Several provisions of UNCLOS III might be applied to cybersecurity. UNCLOS Article 19, for example, states that nations should not use another "nation's territorial sea to engage in activities prejudicial to the peace, good order, or security of the coastal State."[51] This includes the collection of information, distribution of propaganda, or interference with any systems of communications.[52] Article 113 requires domestic criminal legislation to punish willful damage to submarine cables.[53] As a result, UNCLOS is important for its prohibition on staging attacks that interfere with the security of coastal states.[54] An argument could be made that this Article 19 prohibition should also apply to Articles 21 and 113 claims involving submarine cables.[55] This would mean that cyber attackers who send code through submarine cables to a coastal state would be in breach of UNCLOS. However, this accord does

---

[46] Susan J. Buck, The Global Commons: An Introduction 85 (1998).

[47] *See* Christopher C. Joyner, *Antarctica and the Law of the Sea: An Introductory Overview*, 13 Ocean Dev. & Int'l L. 277, 281 (1983); Buck, *supra* note 146, at 86.

[48] Buck, *supra* note 146, at 86.

[49] *Id.* at 50, 87.

[50] *Id.* at 91; Agreement Relating to the Implementation of Part XI of the United Nations Convention on the Law of the Sea of 10 December 1982, § 5, July 28, 1994, S. Treaty Doc. No. 103-39, 1836 U.N.T.S. 41; *see* David Shukman, *Deep Sea Mining 'Gold Rush' Moves Closer*, BBC (May 17, 2013), http://www .bbc.co.uk/news/science-environment-22546875.

[51] United Nations Convention on the Law of the Sea, art. 19, para. 1, Dec. 10, 1982, 1833 U.N.T.S. 397 [hereinafter UNCLOS]; DOD Assessment, *supra* note 8, at 34.

[52] UNCLOS at art. 19(1)(c-d, k).

[53] *Id.* art. 113. *See also* art. 21(1)(c) (granting coastal states the option of passing laws to protect cables and pipelines); DOD Assessment, *supra* note 8, at 37 (expanding on these arguments).

[54] UNCLOS, art. 19(1).

[55] *See* DOD Assessment, *supra* note 8, at 37.

not specify its status during wartime, nor does it include enforcement mechanisms beyond calls for domestic criminal legislation.

UNCLOS is an important example of a regime that was unsuccessful until it better recognized the needs of the private sector. If an international legal regime is to be created with the purpose of enhancing cybersecurity, it must similarly ensure sufficient protections for private enterprise to promote engagement and spur innovation, providing a cautionary tale to certain nations and stakeholders seeking to sideline private entities as Internet governance evolves.[156] Relatedly, the history of UNCLOS also underscores the importance of including non-state actors and effective public-private partnerships in polycentric efforts aimed at managing global common pool resources,[157] including arguably the Internet.

Analogizing Other Applicable Accords to Cyber Attacks

Numerous bilateral and multilateral treaties dealing with everything from legal assistance, extradition, diplomatic relations, and friendship, to status of forces agreements include provisions that impact cybersecurity. The United States, for example, is a party to dozens of Mutual Legal Assistance Treaties (MLAT) that could be used to seek criminal prosecution of cyber attackers, especially those MLATs that either explicitly mention IT or are termed broadly enough to cover *all* law enforcement investigations.[158] However, there are often no enforceable obligations under these treaties, limiting their utility, as seen in the Estonia-Russia saga from Chapter 4, and the 2013 episode regarding Russian President Vladimir Putin's refusal to extradite accused NSA leaker Edward Snowden to U.S. authorities despite the presence of a U.S.-Russia MLAT.[159] The United States is also "a party to more than a hundred bilateral extradition treaties. . . ."[160] Without such accords, national governments would "have neither an international obligation nor the domestic authority to deliver custody of an individual" for prosecution in a foreign jurisdiction.[161] These treaties could be amended to more effectively bring the perpetrators of cyber attacks to justice, such as by including incentives for information sharing and sanctions for

---

[156] John D. Negroponte et al., Defending an Open, Global, Secure, and Resilient Internet 14 (Council on Foreign Rel. Independent Task Force Rep. No. 70, 2013) ("Various nations – China, Russia, Iran, Pakistan, and Saudi Arabia among them – want to extend national sovereignty into cyberspace and are pushing for a more state-centric system to manage the Internet.").

[157] *See* Buck, *supra* note 146, at 91.

[158] *See, e.g.,* US-Canada MLAT, S. Treaty Doc. No. 100–14; 100th Cong., 2nd Sess. Exec. Rept. 100–28; 100th Cong, 2nd Sess. Exec. Rept 101–10; 101st Cong., 1st Sess. XXIV ILM No. 4, 7/85, 1092–99.

[159] *See* Tom Balmforth, Tom Philips, & Alex Spillius, *Vladimir Putin Bluntly Rejects US Appeals to Hand Over Edward Snowden*, Telegraph (June 25, 2013), http://www.telegraph.co.uk/news/worldnews/northamerica/usa/10142233/Vladimir-Putin-bluntly-rejects-US-appeals-to-hand-over-Edward-Snowden.html; US-Russia MLAT, S. Treaty Doc. No. 106-22 (1999).

[160] DOD Assessment, *supra* note 8, at 33; *see* U.S. Treaties of Extradition, Cornell Univ. L. Sch., at 6–9, http://www.state.gov/documents/organization/71600.pdf.

[161] DOD Assessment, *supra* note 8, at 35.

noncompliance. However, harmonizing disparate national criminal laws remains problematic even though progress is being made, as discussed later in this chapter.

Another avenue would be to safeguard certain tempting targets such as embassies. The 1961 Vienna Convention on Diplomatic Relations enshrines the right of "inviolability of the premises" of a diplomatic mission, its archives, private residences and property of its agents, and its communications.[162] Applied to the law of cyber peace, then, this regime could protect all transmissions made to and from government embassies and missions against cyber attacks or espionage. This regime would be applicable in attacks that have already been waged against Russian and Japanese embassies, among others.[163] The reverse has also occurred, such as when the United States declared Venezuela's consul general a persona non grata after she allegedly planned cyber attacks against U.S. networks.[164]

The vast majority of treaties of friendship, commerce, and navigation are archetypical examples of agreements that will likely be suspended during an international armed conflict, but may have some applicability to managing cybercrime, espionage, and terrorism.[165] Tourism is antithetical to a war zone, but many NATO Status of Forces Agreements (SOFA) would remain in place even during an armed conflict.[166] Typically, the stationed forces must "notify the host nation" of any change in operations,[167] including, arguably, cyber warfare. This would help decrease the possibility of foreign soldiers launching cyber attacks on other nations without the host government's tacit consent. Bilateral investment treaties and trade agreements also offer an invaluable, if underappreciated, path to enhance global cybersecurity such as by protecting trade secrets, though they are imperfect as well because of controversies of enforcement through investor-state arbitration and the limiting factor of national security clauses.[168] Other applicable frameworks to a law of cyber peace

---

[162] *Id.* at 38; *see* Vienna Convention on Diplomatic Relations, arts. 2, 24, 27, 30, Apr. 18, 1961, 23 U.S.T. 3227, http://untreaty.un.org/ilc/texts/instruments/english/conventions/9_1_1961.pdf; DOD Assessment, *supra* note 8, at 38 (expanding on this argument).

[163] *See, e.g.,* Eduard Kovacs, *DDoS Attack Targets Russian Embassy Website,* SOFTPEDIA (Sept. 12, 2011), http://news.softpedia.com/news/DDoS-Attack-Targets-Russian-Embassy-Website-221257.shtml; *Cyber War on Japanese Embassies,* EXPATICA (Oct. 26, 2011), http://www.expatica.com/nl/news/dutch-news/cyber-war-on-japanese-embassies_184525.html.

[164] *See US Expels Venezuela's Miami Consul Livia Acosta Noguera,* BBC (Jan. 8, 2012), http://www.bbc.co.uk/news/world-us-canada-16461697.

[165] *See* DOD Assessment, *supra* note 8, at 39.

[166] *Id.* at 39–40.

[167] *Id.* at 40.

[168] Bilateral investment treaties (BITs) are an increasingly important component of international investment law. There are currently more than 3,000 BITs involving the vast majority of countries around the world. These agreements cover a huge range of industry sectors and business activities, including intellectual property. *See* GUS VAN HARTEN, INVESTMENT TREATY ARBITRATION AND PUBLIC LAW 171 (2007). The United States and China are negotiating an expansive BIT that may include the difficult issue of securing trade secrets and thereby enhancing cybersecurity. *See* Annie Lowrey, *U.S. and China to Discuss Investment Treaty, but Cybersecurity Is a Concern,* N.Y. TIMES (July 11, 2013), http://www.nytimes.com/2013/07/12/world/asia/us-and-china-to-discuss-investment-treaty-but-cybersecurity-is-a-concern.html?_r=0. However, nations often reserve

include countermeasures allowing states to respond to violations below the armed attack threshold (discussed later in this chapter),[169] several UN General Assembly resolutions relating to cybersecurity,[170] limited regional initiatives such as NATO's cybersecurity efforts analyzed in Chapter 4, along with the Council of Europe, Organization of American States, and Shanghai Cooperation Organization's cyber-security initiatives returned to later in this chapter.[171]

Summary

Taken together, these diverse bodies of law provide the beginnings of an (admittedly unsettled) legal framework to manage cyber attacks during peacetime. If a host nation's domestic laws criminalize cyber attacks, then applicable MLATs and extradition treaties would apply to make perpetrators accountable in various jurisdictions. If the attack were directed against a foreign mission or embassy, then the Vienna Convention on Diplomatic Immunity would provide certain remedies and potentially reparations to the victim nation. Moreover, provisions under UNCLOS III regulating submarine cables, the ability to prosecute private parties in breach of the ITU treaty in telecommunications law, and interference with satellite transmissions in space law, all place restrictions on cyber attackers. This regime has been criticized as "patchwork[,]"[172] partly because few if any of these treaties, with the exception of SOFAs, would remain in force during a true cyber war. But it is a foundation, however limited, from which to build the edifice of cyber peace. The next task is defining the legal framework applicable to those relatively few cyber attacks that rise to the level of an armed attack activating the LOAC, which we turn to next.

THE LAW OF CYBER WAR

At what point is a cyber attack an act of war? According to Leon Panetta, "[I]f a cyber attack . . . crippled our power grid . . . took down our financial systems, took down

---

the right to deny protection to foreign investments in the name of national security and/or the health and safety of the people, calling into question the utility of this regime in furthering the law of cyber peace. *See* KENNETH J. VANDEVELDE, U.S. INTERNATIONAL INVESTMENT AGREEMENTS 196–99 (2009); Scott J. Shackelford et al., *Using BITs To Protect Bytes: Promoting Cyber Peace and Safeguarding Trade Secrets through Bilateral Investment Treaties*, 52 AM. BUS. L.J. __ (forthcoming 2014), *available at* http://ssrn.com/abstract=2324619.

[169] *See* Hathaway et al., *supra* note 32, at 856.

[170] *Id.* at 860 (citing G.A. Res. 58/32, U.N. Doc. A/RES/58/32 (Dec. 8, 2003); G.A. Res. 59/61, U.N. Doc. A/RES/59/61 (Dec. 3, 2004); G.A. Res. 60/45, U.N. Doc. A/RES/60/45 (Jan. 6, 2006); G.A. Res. 61/54, U.N. Doc. A/RES/61/54 (Dec. 19, 2006); G.A. Res. 62/17, U.N. Doc. A/RES/62/17 (Jan. 8, 2008); G.A. Res. 63/37, U.N. Doc. A/RES/63/37 (Jan. 9, 2009); G.A. Res. 64/25, U.N. Doc. A/RES/64/25 (Jan. 14, 2010)).

[171] *Id.* at 860–66.

[172] *Id.* at 859.

our government systems, that that [sic] would constitute an act of war."[173] Defining this threshold is controversial but critical to developing a functional legal regime to enhance cybersecurity.[174] To better understand the legal context surrounding the Law of Cyber War, it is first necessary to have an understanding of the Law of Armed Conflict itself. This field may be broken down into two parts. The first body of law describes "when . . . [it is] legal for a nation to use force against another nation[.]"[175] This is called *jus ad bellum*, Latin for the "right to declare and wage war."[176] The second body of law addresses what rules "govern the behavior of combatants" during war.[177] This is known as *jus in bello*, or justice in wartime.[178] *Jus ad bellum* has its roots in just war theory dating back to Cicero.[179] The central idea is that conflict can and ought to meet certain philosophical or political criteria.[180] Today, *jus ad bellum* is governed by customary international law and the UN Charter, particularly Articles 2(4), 39, 42, and 51.[181] *Jus in bello* is regulated by the Hague Conferences of 1899 and 1907 mentioned in the introduction to this chapter, as well as "the Geneva Conventions, and customary international law."[182] These will be discussed after an investigation into the utility of *jus ad bellum* as applied to cyber war.

The UN Charter generally divides conflict into three zones. The first threshold is defined by Article 2(4), which makes the threat or use of force illegal without UN Security Council (UNSC) authorization.[183] There are many examples of acts that states have not treated as breaching Article 2(4)'s prohibition on the use of force, including trade disputes, space-based surveillance, espionage, and economic sanctions.[184] But even though state practice has shown that such acts do not activate Article 2(4) protections, it is an open question how threats of force may be regulated in cyberspace; for example, "[d]oes introducing vulnerabilities into an adversary's

---

[173] Jake Tapper, *Leon Panetta: A Crippling Cyber Attack Would Be 'Act of War'*, ABC NEWS (May 27, 2012), http://abcnews.go.com/blogs/politics/2012/05/leon-panetta-a-crippling-cyber-attack-would-be-act-of-war/; *see also* TALLINN MANUAL ON THE INTERNATIONAL LAW APPLICATION TO CYBER WARFARE 17 (Michael N. Schmitt ed., 2013) (discussing when a cyber attack could trigger the right of self-defense) [hereinafter TALLINN MANUAL].

[174] *See* Roston, *supra* note 8.

[175] NATIONAL ACADEMIES, *supra* note 53, at 242.

[176] EDMUND JAN OZMANCZKY, ENCYCLOPEDIA OF THE UNITED NATIONS AND INTERNATIONAL AGREEMENT, VOL. II 1209 (Anthony Mango ed., 2003).

[177] NATIONAL ACADEMIES, *supra* note 53, at 242.

[178] *Id.*; OZMANCZKY, *supra* note 176, at 1209; Robert Kolb, *Origin of the Twin Terms* Jus Ad Bellum/Jus In Bello, 320 INT'L REV. RED CROSS (1997), http://www.icrc.org/eng/resources/documents/misc/57jnuu .htm.

[179] *See* Mark Edward DeForrest, Note, *Just War Theory and the Recent U.S. Strikes Against Iraq*, 1 GONZAGA J. INT'L L. 11, 14 (1997) (citing St. Augustine of Flippo, *Against Faustus the Manichaean* XXII 73–79, *in* AUGUSTINE: POLITICAL WRITINGS 222 (Michael W. Tkacz & Donald Kries, trans., Ernest L. Fortin & Donald Kries, eds., 1994)).

[180] *See* Kolb, *supra* note 178.

[181] *See* NATIONAL ACADEMIES, *supra* note 53, at 242.

[182] *Id.* at 246.

[183] *See* Bruno Simma, *NATO, the UN, and the Use of Force*, 10 EUR. J. INT'L L. 1, 2–3 (1999).

[184] NATIONAL ACADEMIES, *supra* note 53, at 242.

system . . . constitute a threat of force . . . ?"[185] The second zone includes the thresh-olds encompassed in Articles 39 and 42, at which point the UNSC may designate a breach to international peace and security and take action to restore order.[186] Examples of times in which the UNSC has used this authority include cases of ethnic cleansing, apartheid, and genocide.[187] The final threshold is Article 51, which allows for the "right of individual or collective self-defense" in response to an armed attack.[188] Such acts of self-defense are warranted until the UNSC takes action "to maintain international peace and security."[189] International law requires that for self-defense to be permissible, there must be an attack "so egregious that the victim would be justified" in responding in kind.[190] Many contend that an armed attack is more serious than a use of force, and constitutes the equivalent of an invasion by military forces.[191] The natural question, then, is can a cyber attack meet that threshold, activating the laws of war?

There are at least three tests to help determine whether a cyber attack is an armed attack.[192] The first is the equivalent effects test mentioned earlier, which requires that for a cyber attack to be an armed attack, it must have the same results as a physical invasion by traditional military forces.[193] This approach has been supported by the U.S. DOD General Counsel's office, among other entities.[194] It was also reaffirmed by James A. Baker, former U.S. associate deputy attorney general, when he testified to Congress that "'acts [in cyberspace] that would be equivalent . . . to kinetic attacks on the United States' would constitute an 'act of war.'"[195] The second test is based on the "scope, duration, and intensity" of a cyber attack and was propounded by Walter Gary Sharp of the U.S. DOD.[196] Finally, the third test is the Schmitt analysis,

---

[185] *Id.* at 242, 257 (noting that prohibited threats under Article 2(4) might include "verbal threats, initial troop movements, initial movement of ballistic missiles, [or the] massing of troops on a border. . . . ").

[186] *Id.* at 242 (discussing Articles 39 and 42 as the "two exceptions to this prohibition on the use of force.").

[187] *See* John Quigley, *Repairing the Consequences of Ethnic Cleansing*, 29 PEPP. L. REV. 33, 34, 37 (2001).

[188] UN Charter, art. 51; NATIONAL ACADEMIES, *supra* note 53, at 243.

[189] UN Charter, art. 51.

[190] DOD ASSESSMENT, *supra* note 8, at 12; *see also* G.A. Res. 2625 (XXV) (Oct. 24, 1970) (declaring a war of aggression "a crime against the peace" and exhorting states to refrain from "acts of reprisal involving the use of force . . . [and] from organizing, instigating, assisting, participating in acts of civil strife or terrorist attacks in another State."); Definition of Aggression, G.A. Res. 3314 (XXIX), art. 1, U.N. GAOR, 29th Sess., Supp. No. 31, at 142, U.N. Doc. A/9631 (1975), 13 I.L.M. 710 (Dec. 14, 1974).

[191] *See* JEFFERY CARR, INSIDE CYBER WARFARE: MAPPING THE CYBER UNDERWORLD 49–51 (2009).

[192] *Cf.* Hathaway et al., *supra* note 32, at 846–47 (arguing that there are three approaches, including: the so-called "instrument-based" approach, which maintains that a cyber attack can only be an armed attack if "military weapons" are used; the "target-based" approach, which classifies an armed attack based upon the importance of the targeted computer system; and the "effects-based" approach explained in the text).

[193] *See* NATIONAL ACADEMIES, *supra* note 53, at 34, 67.

[194] *See* Roston, *supra* note 8; DOD ASSESSMENT, *supra* note 8, at 18.

[195] Aliya Sternstein, *Threat of Destructive Coding on Foreign-Manufactured Technology is Real*, NEXTGOV (July 7, 2011), http://www.nextgov.com/nextgov/ng_20110707_5612.php.

[196] *See, e.g.*, Graham H. Todd, *Armed Attack in Cyberspace: Deterring Asymmetric Warfare with an Asymmetric Definition*, 64 A.F. L. REV. 65, 69 n.9 (2009); NATIONAL ACADEMIES, *supra* note 53, at 53, 170.

named for Professor Michael Schmitt of the U.S. Naval War College and the University of Exeter. The Schmitt analysis examines a number of factors on a case-by-case basis to determine whether or not a cyber attack constitutes a use of force.[197] These simplified factors include:

- *Severity* – how many people were killed, and how much damage was sustained?
- *Immediacy* – how fast and unexpected was the military action?
- *Directness* – is there a clear cause and effect relationship?
- *Invasiveness* – have the nation's borders been violated?
- *Measurability* – how accurately do we know the effects?
- *Presumptive legitimacy* – is this an action that presumably takes a country to accomplish, indicating a high level of coordination?
- *Responsibility* – which nation's military forces were responsible?[198]

On one end of the spectrum, therefore, Professor Schmitt "argues that a cyber attack on an air traffic control system" causing crashes and numerous casualties would be a use of force, whereas an attack on a "university computer system designed to" delay a government research program would not be.[199] However, even this analysis leaves pertinent questions unanswered. What, for example, is the minimum amount of time that CNI must be disrupted, and to what effect, before such action may be considered an armed attack?

All three approaches to analyzing armed attacks have the drawback of being cumbersome to a greater or lesser degree. Waiting to see what an attack does may help uncover intent, but it has the rather significant drawback of standing by while damage occurs. In an environment where nanoseconds matter, neither soldiers nor politicians may have the luxury to undertake such detailed analyses. In the search for clarity, Harold Koh, for example, has taken a somewhat different approach and stated that the right of self-defense potentially includes proportionate responses to illegal uses of force that result in "death, injury, or significant destruction" and that may fall short of what other nations classify as an armed attack.[200] Ultimately, though, in the United States at least the political threshold for determining that a serious cyber attack is an act of war is likely high with few, if any, unambiguous bright lines.[201] However, given the vital importance of information technology to modern society, Leon Panetta's comment that a serious cyber attack on the nation's CNI could be an armed attack is indicative of the current tenor of the debate.[202] As shown in the

---

[197] Michael N. Schmitt, *Computer Network Attack and the Use of Force in International Law: Thoughts on a Normative Framework*, 37 COLUM. J. TRANSNAT'L L. 885, 900 (1999).

[198] *Id.*; NATIONAL ACADEMIES, *supra* note 53, at 357.

[199] NATIONAL ACADEMIES, *supra* note 53, at 254.

[200] Ellen Nakashima, *U.S. Official Says Cyberattacks Can Trigger Self-Defense Rule*, WASH. POST (Sept. 18, 2012), http://www.washingtonpost.com/world/national-security/us-official-says-cyberattacks-can-trigger-self-defense-rule/2012/09/18/c2246c1a-0202-11e2-b260-32f4a8db9b7e_story.html.

[201] *See* Lewis, *supra* note 64, at 7.

[202] *See* Tapper, *supra* note 173.

Estonia case study from Chapter 4, the main legal hurdles in pursuing a self-defense rationale are: (1) proving that the cyber attack rose to the level of a traditional armed attack by military forces, or at least was an illegal use of force; and (2) that this attack can be attributed to a particular state. The former may well be an easier question to answer than the latter.

First, although controversial, it is likely possible for a cyber attack to rise to the level of an armed attack as traditionally recognized under the LOAC.[203] Cyber war is an expansive category of military activities. It includes blended physical attacks on networks by kinetic means, as well as "psychological operations, military deception, and 'electronic warfare' operations such as jamming. . . . "[204] Cyber war is not the first arena of high technology to fall under the LOAC framework. EMP weapons and certain lasers, among other devices, operate similarly enough to traditional weapons that they trigger LOAC protections.[205] The difficult issue arises in the context of a pure cyber attack. Using "electronic means to gain access" or to "change information in a targeted information system" does not damage any physical components in the traditional sense.[206] The real question thus turns on a definition of "force," which could be interpreted strictly in accordance with the text, or consistent with the broad object and purpose of the UN Charter.[207] Although it is a contentious issue, the boundaries of "force" may not correspond to those of armed force only, even though efforts to expand its scope "to include violations of sovereign domain" have not met with much success.[208] As was stated, however, it is theoretically possible for a cyber attack to rise to the level of an armed attack, especially as technology advances, as Koh among others has maintained.[209] A cyber weapon itself is only an instrument to carry out an attack in the same way as any other twenty-first century weapon.

Second, states that unwittingly or permissively allow their territory to be used to carry out attacks may be committing an act of aggression.[210] The problem becomes one of attribution, and defining the rights and responsibilities of neutrals, as discussed later in this chapter. To take one example, many of the zombie computers used to carry out the botnet attacks against Estonia turned out to be located in

[203] *See, e.g.*, Hathaway et al., *supra* note 32, at 817, 821; Roston, *supra* note 8.
[204] DOD Assessment, *supra* note 8, at 5.
[205] *Id.*
[206] *Id.*
[207] *See* United Nations Conference on International Organization, Doc. 784, I/1/27, 6 U.N.C.I.O. Docs. 331, 334, 609 (April 25, 1945).
[208] Waxman, *supra* note 33, at 430.
[209] *See* Harold Hongju Koh, Legal Advisor, U.S. Dep't of St., Remarks at USCYBERCOM Inter-Agency Legal Conference: International Law in Cyberspace (Sept. 18, 2012), http://www.state.gov/s/l/releases/remarks/197924.htm ("A State's national right of self-defense, recognized in Article 51 of the UN Charter, may be triggered by computer network activities that amount to an armed attack or imminent threat thereof.").
[210] *See* G.A. Res. 41/38 (Nov. 20, 1986).

the United States.[211] Should Estonia then have a right of self-defense against the United States? The difficulties in defining the boundaries of this legal regime test fundamental assumptions in international law regarding self-defense and the use of force. After all, the UN Charter anticipates situations such as "the presence of troops and the use of traditional military weapons" on another nation's territory,[212] not simultaneous multimodal network attacks on a state. In the case of cyber war, "fundamental questions arise" over what types and degrees of cyber attacks may fall within the scope of the LOAC.[213] Only through an analysis of the available legal frameworks may a compromise position be synthesized that responds to the unique challenges posed by cyber attacks, while also preserving the integrity of the UN Charter system that provides the primary bulwark against the proliferation of violence in international relations. The doctrine of state responsibility for cyber attacks is critical for such a legal regime to be functional in this new era of cyber conflict.

State Responsibility for Cyber Attacks

At a time in which the sovereign authority of states is breaking down in many areas, state responsibility remains a key component of international security.[214] However, "[t]he speed and anonymity of cyber attacks makes distinguishing among the actions of terrorists, criminals, and nation states difficult, a task which often occurs only after the fact, if at all."[215] As has been alleged in the cyber attacks on Estonia, "a sponsoring state may not cooperate in the investigation, apprehension, and extradition of those who" committed criminal or terrorist acts on its behalf.[216] Defining thresholds is also a difficult, if necessary, starting point. Should the cyber attack on Estonia, for example, be characterized as: cybercrimes backed by Russian Nashi su hackers, cyber terrorism by a group pursuing particular political goals, cyberwarfare by Russian intelligence operatives, or merely a cyber riot? Delineating these classifications shapes responses, including the proper involvement of civilian law enforcement or, if necessary, the military.

---

[211] *See* Mark Landler & John Markoff, *Digital Fears Emerge after Data Siege in Estonia*, N.Y. TIMES (May 29, 2007), http://www.nytimes.com/2007/05/29/technology/29estonia.html?pagewanted=all&_r=0.

[212] DOD ASSESSMENT, *supra* note 8, at 15.

[213] Joyner & Lotrionte, *supra* note 35, at 845.

[214] *See* Mudrinich, *supra* note 17, at 193 (discussing, among other strategies, imputed responsibility as one potential solution to the attribution issue); David E. Graham, *Cyber Threats and the Law of War*, 4 J. NAT'L SEC. L. & POL'Y 87, 93–95 (2010) (expanding on the imputed responsibility option to prevent host states from forming safe havens for cyber attackers).

[215] WHITE HOUSE, NATIONAL STRATEGY TO SECURE CYBERSPACE viii (2003), http://energy.gov/sites/prod/files/National%20Strategy%20to%20Secure%20Cyberspace.pdf.

[216] Susan Brenner, *At Light Speed: Attribution and Response to Cybercrime/Terrorism/Warfare*, 97 J. CRIM. L. & CRIMINOLOGY 379, 422 (2007); *see, e.g.*, Agreement on Legal Assistance and Legal Relations in Civil, Family and Criminal Matters, Est.-Russ., Jan. 26, 1993, Riigi Teataja II 1993, at 16, 27.

Classic conceptions of terrorism are distinct from warfare, the latter of which should not target civilians.[217] Yet history is replete with examples from WWII to the genocide at Srebrenica of those bright lines between terrorism and warfare blurring, creating ambiguity.[218] Boundaries are continuing to break down in the twenty-first century. In the words of Professor Susan Brenner, "[S]tates generate crime and terrorism as well as war, and individuals wage war in addition to committing crimes and carrying out acts of terrorism."[219] Given the clandestine nature of cyberspace, states may incite civilian groups within their own borders to commit cyber attacks and then hide behind a (however sheer) veil of plausible deniability to escape accountability. The alleged use of hackers by several governments, including China and Russia,[220] speaks to the urgent necessity of addressing the critical question of state responsibility. For example, a cyber attack uncovered in May 2012 codenamed Flame reportedly targeted more than 600 entities in the Middle East and North Africa and was likely state sponsored,[221] but proving attribution is technically and legally difficult.[222] Despite the evolution of sovereignty in some areas as discussed in Chapter 2, state responsibility and attribution remain at the core of the international security system.

Determining an appropriate standard for attribution is a critical element in building the law of cyber war. The U.S. National Research Council succinctly summarizes the problem, arguing "it may be difficult to identify even the nature of the involved party (e.g., a government, a terrorist group, an individual), let alone the name of the country or the terrorist group or the individual."[223] A critical part of this analysis lies in defining the "degree of certainty" needed "about the identity of an attacker . . . before a cyberattack may be launched to neutralize it[.]"[224] The laws of war require that a state must identify itself when it attacks another state under *jus in bello*, although this convention is sometimes honored more in the breach than

---

[217] *See* UN Off. High Comm'r Hum. Rights, Geneva Convention Relative to the Protection of Civilian Persons in Time of War, Aug. 12, 1949, http://www.unhchr.ch/ html/menu3/b/92.htm.

[218] The Srebrenica Massacre was the July 1995 killing of an estimated 8,000 people in the region of Srebrenica in Bosnia and Herzegovina by units of the Serbian Army during the Bosnian War. *See* Steven L. Burg & Paul S. Shoup, The War in Bosnia-Herzegovina: Ethnic Conflict and International Intervention 140–42 (2000).

[219] Brenner, *supra* note 216, at 404–05.

[220] *See, e.g.*, Lolita C. Baldor, *U.S. Report Blasts China, Russia for Cybercrime*, USA Today (Nov. 3, 2011), http://usatoday30.usatoday.com/money/industries/technology/story/2011-11-03/Cyber-attacks/51058852/1; Oliver Joy, *Mandiant: China is Sponsoring Cyber-Espionage*, CNN (Feb. 20, 2013), http://edition.cnn.com/2013/02/19/business/china-cyber-attack-mandiant.

[221] *See* Dave Lee, *Flame: Massive Cyber-Attack Discovered, Researchers Say*, BBC (May 28, 2012), http://www.bbc.co.uk/news/technology-18238326.

[222] *See, e.g.*, Mandiant, APT1: Exposing One of China's Cyber Espionage Units 58 (2013) (noting some of the difficulties involved with attributing a cyber attack back to a particular individual).

[223] National Academies, *supra* note 53, at 252.

[224] *Id.*

the observance.[225] When there is a question about state sponsorship of aggression opening the door to countermeasures or even a claim of self-defense, Article 8 of the International Law Commission's Draft Articles on the Responsibility of States for International Wrongful Acts comes into play. Article 8 implicates state control when state actors or official organs are "acting on the instructions of, or under the direction or control of, that State in carrying out the conduct."[226] An exact definition of "control," however, has been left up to the courts to interpret, which has resulted in two main approaches: the effective and overall control standards.[227]

The effective control doctrine recognizes a country's control over paramilitaries or other non-state actors only if the actors in question act in "complete dependence" on the state.[228] In contrast, the overall control doctrine requires that where a state has a role in organizing and coordinating a group's acts during an international armed conflict, then the group's acts may be attributable back to the state.[229] Thus, the two standards differ over whether or not the state must be in direct control of operational planning. The ICJ has consistently used the more restrictive effective control standard in its jurisprudence regarding state responsibility, including in the *Bosnian Genocide* case,[230] all of which falls outside the cybersecurity context. In essence, the Court has required smoking-gun evidence or its equivalent.[231] The standard laid down was "beyond *any* doubt," not beyond a *reasonable* doubt.[232] Such a high burden of proof was difficult to satisfy in the kinetic attacks at issue in *Bosnian Genocide*. Proving specific intent behind state-sponsored cyber attacks would be harder still, though the standard of proof varies with context. In a sophisticated global cyber attack, missing or corrupted data commands could be sufficient to disprove state control and defeat accountability even with other evidence of state sponsorship. If state responsibility is to have sufficient applicability to the cyber realm, a more flexible approach similar to the overall control standard should be adopted as part of an international regime to enhance cybersecurity.[233]

---

[225] *See* Hague Convention No. III, Relative to the Opening of Hostilities art. I, Oct. 18, 1907, 36 Stat. 2259, 2271, T.S. 598 (1907), *entered into force* 26 Jan. 1910, art. 1.

[226] *State Responsibility*, UN Y.B. Int'l. L., Vol. II 47 (2001).

[227] *See* Tallinn Manual, *supra* note 173, at 31–33 (noting that state responsibility arises when the non-state actor is "exercising elements of governmental authority.").

[228] Nicaragua, 1986 I.C.J. at para. 110.

[229] *See* Prosecutor v. Tadic, Case No. IT-94-1-I ICTY (Oct. 2, 1995), at 1541 [hereinafter Tadic]; Ademola Abass, Complete International Law 258–61 (2011) (discussing the competing standards of state responsibility).

[230] Application of the Convention on the Prevention and Punishment of the Crime of Genocide (Bosn. & Herz. v. Serb. & Mont.), 2007 I.C.J. 1, 140 para. 391 (Feb. 26) [hereinafter *Bosnian Genocide*].

[231] *See* David Luban, *Timid Justice: The ICJ Should Have Been Harder on Serbia*, Slate (Feb. 15, 2007), http://www.slate.com/articles/news_and_politics/jurisprudence/2007/02/timid_justice.html.

[232] *See* Bosnian Genocide, 2007 I.C.J. at 422 (emphasis added).

[233] *But see* Tallinn Manual, *supra* note 173, at 33 (arguing that state responsibility requires that a state "issued specific instructions or directed or controlled a particular operation," and noting that even the overall control standard still requires that control "go beyond 'the mere financing and equipping of such forces and involv[e] also participation in the planning and supervision of military operations.'")

Attribution is a fundamental problem in cybersecurity, and as a result, a burden of proof analysis is essential to satisfying state responsibility for cyber attacks. This could include relying more on digital clues left behind by attackers – as Stewart Baker puts it, "The bad news is that our security sucks. The good news is that their security sucks too."[234] Because of the ongoing technical difficulties of proving attribution for cyber attacks discussed in Chapter 3, though, along with the high standards of proof that have been imposed by the ICJ, this subsection has argued for the adoption of a flexible approach like the overall control standard. But there is little agreement on the issue among jurists or policymakers, and the law remains unsettled. More broadly, according to Michael DuBose, "If we began to look at Internet access as a right with attendant responsibilities, as opposed to just a right, society might be willing to require greater authentication measures for certain Internet uses and transactions," thus helping attribution.[235] Yet this can also be a slippery slope, as seen in China where authorities began requiring Internet users to register their names in December 2012.[236] Ultimately, though, determining a standard for state responsibility is but one element of enhancing cybersecurity. Another critical challenge is defining self-defense.

Cyber Attacks and Self-Defense

As was discussed earlier in this chapter, there is a zone of ambiguity beneath the armed attack threshold in which it is difficult to determine which laws to apply. Defining that threshold is challenging, but even if it were successfully drawn, how

---

(citing Tadic, at 145). At least two other more flexible approaches are also evident. The first is the government awareness standard, stating that if a government was aware of its obligations under international law and failed to comply with these responsibilities then it could be held in breach of international law. *See* United States Diplomatic and Consular Staff in Tehran (U.S. v. Iran), 1980 I.C.J. 3, 29 (May 24). However, this approach assumes that the applicable international law is clear. Moreover, many nations around the world would likely be in breach of this approach without major improvements in their own domestic cybersecurity, including the United States. The second is the sliding scale approach, which simply requires that "the graver the charge the more confidence there must be in the evidence relied on." Oil Platforms (Iran v. U.S.), 2003 I.C.J. 161, 234 (Nov. 6) (separate opinion of Judge Higgins). One potential problem with this approach is that some states could have a perverse incentive to sponsor more devastating attacks so as to raise the necessary burden of proof and potentially defeat accountability, illustrating the necessity of further research on this topic including an analysis of what constitutes good faith and reasonability in this context.

[234] Stewart Baker, *Cybersecurity and Attribution – Good News At Last?*, VOLOKH CONSPIRACY (Oct. 7, 2012), http://www.volokh.com/2012/10/07/cybersecurity-and-attribution-good-news-at-last/ (making the case that attribution may in fact be getting easier with the help of new investigative techniques).

[235] Electronic Interview with Michael DuBose, head of cyber investigations at Kroll Advisory Solutions and former chief of the Computer Crime & Intellectual Property Section, Criminal Division, Department of Justice, in Wash., D.C. (Apr. 18, 2011).

[236] *See* Keith Bradsher, *China Toughens Its Restrictions on Use of the Internet*, N.Y. TIMES (Dec. 28, 2012), http://www.nytimes.com/2012/12/29/world/asia/china-toughens-restrictions-on-internet-use.html ?_r=1&.

would the doctrine of self-defense work in practice to manage cyber attacks? If the attack is real or the threat imminent, the victim state of a cyber attack may invoke self-defense "to justify reasonable, necessary, and proportional measures to safeguard its security" under Article 51 of the UN Charter.[237] This section of the UN Charter seeks to maintain international peace and security. Armed attacks that destabilize the peace fall within Article 51's scope.[238]

A valid exercise of self-defense in cyberspace would require proof of aggression to satisfy state responsibility.[239] International law forbids forcible retaliation.[240] Rather, self-defense permits a state to defend itself against armed attacks, or imminent danger of an armed attack.[241] But not just any imminent danger will suffice for Article 51 purposes.[242] The threat must be "real and credible and create an imminent need to act" in accordance with the so-called "*Caroline* criteria."[243] These criteria arose from the *Caroline* incident involving a Canadian insurrection in 1837. After suffering defeat, according to Professor Schmitt, "Canadian insurgents retreated into the United States where they recruited and planned further operations."[244] In doing so, they used the vessel *Caroline*. Next, "British troops crossed the border and destroyed the vessel. Britain justified the action on the grounds that the United States was not enforcing its laws along the frontier and that the action was a legitimate exercise of self-defense."[245] What does a nineteenth century Canadian insurrection have to do with cybersecurity? From this episode came the criteria of necessity, immediacy, and proportionality being required as part of a valid exercise of self-defense under international law.[246] Military necessity, for example, limits targets to "those that make a direct contribution to the enemy's war effort. . . ."[247] Proportionality requires the weighing of the amount of collateral damage against the military advantage of an attack.[248] Immediacy means that the threat of an attack must be imminent.[249] Therefore, preemptive Israeli airstrikes on invasion forces about to attack in the 1967 Six-Day War were largely held to be consistent with international law,[250]

---

[237] Joyner & Lotrionte, *supra* note 35, at 851; UN Charter, art. 2, para 4.

[238] *See* NATIONAL ACADEMIES, *supra* note 53, at 34.

[239] *See* Joyner & Lotrionte, *supra* note 35, at 846, 853.

[240] *Id.* at 852.

[241] *Id.* at 854.

[242] *See* TALLINN MANUAL, *supra* note 173, at 63.

[243] Joyner & Lotrionte, *supra* note 35, at 854.

[244] Schmitt, *supra* note 197, at 930 n.124.

[245] *Id.*; Joyner & Lotrionte, *supra* note 35, at 857 n.112; TALLINN MANUAL, *supra* note 173, at 63–64; Letter from Daniel Webster to Lord Ashburton (Aug. 6, 1842), *in* 2 JOHN MOORE DIG. INT'L L. 411–12 (1906), http://avalon.law.yale.edu/19th_ century/br-1842d.asp#web2.

[246] *See* Joyner & Lotrionte, *supra* note 35, at 860.

[247] NATIONAL ACADEMIES, *supra* note 53, at 246.

[248] *See id.*; TALLINN MANUAL, *supra* note 173, at 62–63.

[249] NATIONAL ACADEMIES, *supra* note 53, at 243.

[250] *See* Anthony Clark Arend, *International Law and the Preemptive Use of Military Force*, 26 WASH. Q., Spring 2003, at 89, 94–95 (discussing the political responses to Israel's strikes ahead of the six-day war).

whereas the Bush administration's interpretation of this doctrine to justify the invasion of Iraq was questionable, to say the least.[251] These cases help guide a nation's response to an impending cyber attack crossing the armed attack threshold.[252] There is no strict prohibition on the preemptive use of cyber attacks so "long as the perceived threat is demonstrated to be real and immediate," and the state adheres to "the criteria of proportionality and necessity" in applying coercion.[253] Whether the international community would accept such a use of force depends entirely on context.[254]

In addition to Article 51 protections, the UN Security Council can also legally determine whether an attack would constitute a threat to international peace and security.[255] It has the power to call on member states to apply "measures not involving the use of armed force" including the "complete or partial interruption of . . . telegraphic, radio, and other means of communications. . . . "[256] Similarly, the U.S. DOD has stated, "a computer network attack that caused widespread damage, economic disruption, and loss of life could well precipitate action by the Security Council."[257] Consequently, there is the potential for UNSC action in response to a cyber attack such as by using the framework from UNSC Resolution 1373, which requires states to rein in terrorist financing.[258] This resolution, passed in the wake of 9/11, gave the UN Security Council greater influence over the domestic law of member states.[259] But such a departure from the original intent of Resolution 1373 would likely require an additional UNSC Resolution, and there is little likelihood that such an approach would be supported by all of the permanent UNSC members, including Russia and China, given the sensitive national security issues in play.

The DOD has argued that attacks "that cannot be shown to be state-sponsored generally do not justify acts of self-defense in another nation's territory."[260] Rather, a nation harmed "by the private conduct of an individual" acting "within the territory of another nation" should request the latter's government to stop such conduct.[261] However, the appropriate response when a state, and not a private individual, stands behind such an act remains unclear, although efforts have been made to clarify the

---

[251] *See* Ivo H. Daalder, *Policy Implications of the Bush Doctrine on Preemption*, COUNCIL FOREIGN REL. (Nov. 16, 2001), http://www.cfr.org/international-law/policy-implications-bush-doctrine-preemption/p5251.

[252] *See* Koh, *supra* note 209; Schmitt, *supra* note 12, 14–15 (noting the substantial similarities and limited differences between the *Tallinn Manual* and Legal Adviser Koh's speech).

[253] Joyner & Lotrionte, *supra* note 35, at 858–59.

[254] *See* Schmitt, *supra* note 197, at 903.

[255] UN Charter, art. 1, para. 2.

[256] UN Charter, art. 41.

[257] DOD ASSESSMENT, *supra* note 8, at 15.

[258] *See* Toby L. Friesen, *Resolving Tomorrow's Conflicts Today: How New Developments Within the U.N. Security Council Can Be Used to Combat Cyberwarfare*, 58 NAVAL L. REV. 89, 107–08 (2009).

[259] *Id.* at 108.

[260] DOD ASSESSMENT, *supra* note 8, at 22.

[261] *Id.*

1. **Is the technique employed in the cyber attack a use of armed force?**
   a. It is if the attack is intended to directly cause physical damage to tangible objects or injury to human beings.
2. **If it is not armed force, is the cyber attack nevertheless a use of force as contemplated in the U.N. Charter?**
   a. It is if the nature of its consequences track those consequence commonalities which characterize armed force.
3. **If the cyber attack is a use of force (armed or otherwise), is that force applied consistent with Chapter VII, the principle of self-defense, or operational code norms permitting its use in the attendant circumstances?**
   a. If so, the operation is likely to be judged legitimate.
   b. If not and the operation constitutes a use of armed force, the cyber attack will violate Article 2(4).
   c. If not and the operation constitutes a use of force, but not armed force, the cyber attack will violate Article 2(4).
4. **If the cyber attack does not rise to the level of the use of force, is there another prohibition in international law that would preclude its use?**
   a. The most likely candidate would be the prohibition on intervening in the affairs of other States.

FIGURE 6.1. PROFESSOR MICHAEL SCHMITT'S CHECKLIST FOR CYBER ATTACKS UNDER INTERNATIONAL LAW. Figure redrawn from Michael N. Schmitt, *Computer Network Attack and the Use of Force in International Law: Thoughts on a Normative Framework*, 37 COLUM. J. TRANSNAT'L L. 885, 934–35 (1999).

situation, as is exemplified in Figure 6.1. In practice, these two scenarios may be hard to tell apart because of the problem of attribution.[262]

One option to resolve the problem of self-defense involving cyber attacks is through a graduated scheme that would shift the emphasis away from "customary law enforcement and counterintelligence" to a "national defense mode."[263] Such a strategy would need to be tempered by procedural and institutional safeguards, including: establishing criteria for national security responses to be followed for different levels of cyber attacks, as well as identifying policymakers who would take part in the decision to use force.[264] These procedures would help institute a test for the reasonableness of self-defense in response to cyber attacks given the greater stakes of a national security response making use of armed forces.

Still, it is unclear to what extent the international community will regard cyber attacks as unlawful acts or uses of force, which in turn clouds how doctrines of self-defense and countermeasures apply to such situations.[265] For countermeasures

---

[262] *Cf.* Baker, *supra* note 234 (making the case that the attribution problem is not as insurmountable as it may seem).

[263] DOD ASSESSMENT, *supra* note 8, at 22.

[264] *Id.* at 24.

[265] *See* UN Int'l Law Comm'n Draft Articles on Responsibility of States for Internationally Wrongful Acts, Rep. of the Int'l Law Comm'n, U.N. GAOR, 53d Sess., Supp. No. 10, U.N. Doc. A/56/10 (2001), at 128 (defining countermeasures as "measures that would otherwise be contrary to the international

to be permissible, after all, the identity of the attacker must be known, and the countermeasure must be sufficiently onerous and targeted to disincentivize the unlawful conduct and must cease when the responsible state is once again compliant with its legal obligations.[266] Interpretations are likely to turn on the consequences of such an attack. In the case of the cyber attacks on Estonia, the international community likely would not have condoned an Estonian armed response, however infeasible, against Russia. What is unclear is how that collective perspective would have changed if the cyber attacks on Estonia had resulted in numerous deaths or significant destruction. Would lawful countermeasures have been warranted? If so, given the attribution problem, against whom do you levy countermeasures?[267] Few answers seem immediately forthcoming, though the independent experts who authored the *Tallinn Manual on the International Law Applicable to Cyber Warfare* argued that cyber countermeasures "should, to the extent feasible, [be proportionate and] consist of measures that have temporary or reversible effects."[268] The issue is made murkier still when contemplating how international human rights law may be applied to cyber attacks.

The Intersections of International Humanitarian and Human Rights Law as Applied to Cybersecurity

In order to determine what combination of LOAC and international human rights law should apply to cyber attacks that rise to the level of an armed attack, it is necessary to investigate the intersections between these systems. International human rights law and the LOAC differ in formulation, structure, application, and enforcement.[269] Although the distinctions between the two regimes are far from merely "semantic and contextual[,]"[270] there are areas of overlap. Since WWII, a growing international consensus has led to the establishment of numerous norms and standards in both human rights and humanitarian law aimed at better protecting human integrity.[271] Faced with the threat of cyber attacks, can these norms and standards meet distinctive societal needs during times of cyber war and peace?

---

obligations of an injured State vis-à-vis the responsible State, if they were not taken by the former in response to an internationally wrongful act by the latter in order to procure cessation and reparation.").

[266] Hathaway et al., *supra* note 32, at 859.

[267] *See* TALLINN MANUAL, *supra* note 173, at 37 (noting that "the law on countermeasures [is] ambiguous" in the cyber context).

[268] *Id.* at 38; Wegener, *supra* note 9, at 77, 83 ("Under the concept of cyber peace, priority must be given to the maintenance or early restoration of a peaceful and stable environment.").

[269] *See, e.g.*, RENE PROVOST, AID AND INTERVENTION: INTERNATIONAL HUMAN RIGHTS AND HUMANITARIAN LAW 345 (2002); INT'L COMM. RED CROSS, INTERNATIONAL HUMANITARIAN LAW AND INTERNATIONAL HUMAN RIGHTS LAW: SIMILARITIES AND DIFFERENCES (2003), http://www.ehl.icrc.org/images/resources/pdf/ihl_and_ihrl.pdf [hereinafter Red Cross Report]. However, it should be noted that some scholars consider IHRL to be part of the LOAC. *See, e.g.*, NATIONAL ACADEMIES, *supra* note 53, at 242 n.4.

[270] PROVOST, *supra* note 269, at 343.

[271] *See* JACK DONNELLY, INTERNATIONAL HUMAN RIGHTS 4 (1998).

Human rights law along with criminal law enforcement and the LOAC can all overlap when a conflict involves non-state actors.[272] Human rights conventions generally impose obligations on states, including during armed conflicts. In contrast, the LOAC was created to protect members of specific groups during armed conflicts exclusively.[273] The provisions of the 1907 Hague Convention, the 1949 Geneva Conventions, and the 1977 Additional Protocols protect the rights of identified subgroups such as combatants, POWs, and unarmed civilians.[274] Although international human rights law and the LOAC were originally designed to apply in different circumstances, the two bodies of law may cross-fertilize. Both IHRL and the LOAC are rooted in "respect for human values and the dignity of the human person[;]"[275] first principles from which little if any derogation is permitted.[276] The point of departure for LOAC is the need to balance humanity with military necessity during an armed conflict.

The "nature and scale of violence in interstate conflicts" have a distinct impact on the control of force in the LOAC.[277] A human-rights paradigm normally would address the "internal use of force...."[278] LOAC, on the other hand, applies to both international and certain domestic armed conflicts.[279] But, as has been noted by former Judge Advocate General Kenneth Watkin, "[T]he relationship between the two is much more complex than this division of responsibilities implies."[280] For example, IHRL applies during armed conflicts, as the ICJ "decided in the *Nuclear Weapons* Advisory Opinion,"[281] whereas the LOAC determines whether there has been "an arbitrary deprivation of the right to life...."[282] An elaborate system of treaties on the law of war governs many aspects of the conduct of modern warfare, from permissible weapons to the treatment of POWs and non-combatants. However, some questions remain with regard to how these treaties apply to cyber war.

Applying the LOAC to Cyber Attacks

A host of issues arise when applying the laws of war, developed to govern traditional armed attacks decades ago, to a twenty-first century digital battleground. The United States, for example, is "party to eighteen law-of-war treaties," all of which were

---

[272] *See* Watkin, *supra* note 29, at 2.

[273] *See* Red Cross Report, *supra* note 269, at 1.

[274] *See* BRENT G. FILBERT & ALAN G. KAUFMAN, NAVAL LAW: JUSTICE AND PROCEDURE IN THE SEA SERVICES 208 (1998).

[275] Watkin, *supra* note 29, at 9.

[276] *See* Red Cross Report, *supra* note 269, at 1 (noting that "IHRL treaties permit governments to derogate from certain rights in situations of public emergency threatening the life of the nation.").

[277] Watkin, *supra* note 29, at 2.

[278] *Id.*

[279] *See id.*

[280] *Id.*

[281] *Id.*; Legality of Nuclear Weapons, 1996 I.C.J. at para. 240.

[282] Watkin, *supra* note 29, at 2.

negotiated before cyberspace in its current form existed.[283] Issues range from the legal options of victim nations in responding to a cyber attack to the offensive use of cyber weapons by state and non-state actors.

For the LOAC to effectively regulate contemporary armed conflict, rules on "the use of deadly force ... [should] reflect the levels of violence and the nature of the threat posed to society."[284] As has been shown, however, applying *jus ad bellum* and *jus in bello* to cyber conflicts is difficult. For example, clarity about what constitutes an armed attack and a use of force is lacking. Few doubt that the LOAC should apply during a cyber conflict, but how? What constitutes a military target given the interconnectedness of civilian and military information infrastructures? And might cyber attacks be ethically preferred to traditional kinetic attacks under some circumstances? A few dozen crashed websites might be more desirable, for example, than bombs landing on your capital city.[285] In all, though, applying LOAC rules to cyber attacks is possible and was even required by the U.S. Congress in their 2011 authorization for the Defense Department to conduct offensive cyber attacks upon direction by the president.[286] The question is how this should be done in practice. To help address this issue, some of the primary LOAC norms are addressed in turn, including: (1) the distinction between combatants and non-combatants, (2) between civilian and military infrastructure, (3) the prohibition against disproportionate attacks, and (4) protecting the rights of neutrals.

First, distinction requires armed forces "to distinguish between civilian and military assets ... and to refrain from deliberately attacking civilians. . . . "[287] The principle applies to cyber attacks, though there are some lawful exceptions such as the use of psychological operations against civilian populations.[288] According to the distinction between combatants and non-combatants, civilians "forfeit their protection from attacks" if they participate in cyber operations, and cyber attackers forfeit the combatant privilege if they do not identify themselves as combatants.[289] The combatant privilege under the Hague Conventions holds that "only members of a nation's

---

[283] DOD ASSESSMENT, *supra* note 8, at 6. For a survey, see U.S. DEPT. ST., TREATIES IN FORCE (2007), http://www.state.gov/s/l/treaty/treaties/2007/index.htm.

[284] Watkin, *supra* note 29, at 34.

[285] *See* THOMAS RID, CYBER WAR WILL NOT TAKE PLACE 37–38, 172 (2013). *But see Iran Sees Cyber Attacks as Greater Threat than Actual War*, REUTERS (Sept. 25, 2012), http://www.reuters.com/article/2012/09/25/net-us-iran-military-idUSBRE88O0MY20120925 (reporting that elements within Iran's Revolutionary Guard would prefer a traditional kinetic war to a cyber war as they consider the former to be potentially less damaging).

[286] *See* H.R. Rep. No. 112–329, at § 954 (Conf. Rep.), http://www.gpo.gov/fdsys/pkg/CRPT-112hrpt329/pdf/CRPT-112hrpt329-pt1.pdf.

[287] NATIONAL ACADEMIES, *supra* note 53, at 247.

[288] *See* TALLINN MANUAL, *supra* note 173, at 110–11 (noting that the principle of distinction is one of the two core LOAC principles recognized by the ICJ, which has called the rule "intransgressible") (citing Legality of Nuclear Weapons, para. 79).

[289] *Id.* at 104.

regular armed forces are entitled to use force against the enemy."[290] Given the lack of markers indicating combatants such as insignia, would the Hague Conventions apply to captured cyber attackers?[291] What about patriot hackers, or members of a nation's cyber militia – digital weekend warriors? If private hacktivists based in the United States did launch crippling attacks against a foreign government, then could that government respond against the United States under the LOAC as if the U.S. government itself had committed an act of aggression, assuming attribution existed?[292] Would a failure to suppress the activities of such groups constitute de facto support? Questions abound and few answers are forthcoming, though it seems unlikely that state responsibility would be fulfilled unless the private group received detailed instructions, was directed, or was otherwise clothed in governmental authority.[293]

Second, the scope of cyber attacks tests the LOAC limitation on permissible objectives. The LOAC distinguishes between military and civilian personnel, objects and installations, and requires limiting attacks to military objectives.[294] Infrastructure that makes "no direct contribution to the war effort" and whose destruction would not offer a military advantage, then, is legally "immune from deliberate attack."[295] Civilians that are "engaged in self-help" are subject to domestic criminal laws such as the U.S. Computer Fraud and Abuse Act.[296] Given the comingling of civilian and military networks, during a cyber conflict, distinction is difficult, thereby necessitating an analysis of dual-use targets. These targets are typically "defined as those used for both military and civilian purposes, such as power plants that provide electricity" to the civilian and military grids.[297] Accounts differ as to whether and how such dual-use targets may be properly targeted.[298] The attacking state could argue, akin to

---

[290] DOD Assessment, *supra* note 8, at 6; *see* Additional Protocol to the Geneva Conventions of Aug. 12, 1949, and Relating to the Protection of Victims of Non-International Armed Conflicts (Protocol I) art. 43(2), June 8, 1977, 1125 U.N.T.S. 609 [hereinafter Protocol I].

[291] *See* Tallinn Manual, *supra* note 173, at 96–97.

[292] *See* G.A. Res. 41/38 (Nov. 20, 1986).

[293] *See* Tallinn Manual, *supra* note 173, at 31–33.

[294] *See id.* at 100; Protocol I art. 48.

[295] DOD Assessment, *supra* note 8, at 6; *see* Koh, *supra* note 209; Heather Harrison Dinniss, Cyber Warfare and the Laws of War 185 (2012) ("Article 52(2) requires that any military objective must by its nature, location, purpose or use make an effective contribution to military action.").

[296] *See* National Academies, *supra* note 53, at 267.

[297] Arie J. Schaap, *The Development of Cyber Warfare Operations and Analyzing Its Use Under International Law*, 64 Air Force L. Rev. 121, 156 (2009).

[298] *See* Françoise Bouchet-Saulnier et al., The Practical Guide to Humanitarian Law 270 (2007) (noting that in situations of dual-use targets "[t]he nature, the place, the purpose or the use of the object must effectively contribute to military action . . . [and] [t]he destruction of the object – in whole or in part – capturing it or neutralizing it must show a specific military advantage" for the attack to be lawful, along with ensuring that civilians are evacuated and that disproportionate harm does not come to noncombatants); National Academies, *supra* note 53, at 266 ("Traditional LOAC allows attacks on dual-use targets if the conditions of military necessity, proportionality, distinction, and discrimination are met.").

the role that Radio Milles Collines played in inciting the Rwandan genocide,[299] that these facilities were used for command and control and thus were, in fact, military objectives.[300] This is a fine line, requiring the evacuation of civilians before an attack, if possible, while avoiding the disproportionate use of force against noncombatants so as to mitigate the risk of collateral damage and civilian casualties.[301] Recognizing this facet of cyber attacks, the U.S. DOD has required that targeting analysis be conducted for cyber attacks as it would for attacks using more traditional weapons systems.[302]

Third, and relatedly, the LOAC places much of the responsibility for collateral damage resulting from disproportionate attacks on defending forces that have "failed to properly separate military targets from noncombatants and civilian property."[303] This principle entails a balancing act between military advantage and the harm to civilians.[304] Once again, however, drawing the line is difficult and depends on context.[305] Koh has offered a three-part assessment that nations should undertake to determine whether a cyber attack during a conflict is in fact proportionate:

> [consider] (1) the effects of cyber weapons on both military and civilian infrastructure and users, including shared physical infrastructure (such as a dam or a power grid) that would affect civilians; (2) the potential physical damage that a cyber attack may cause, such as death or injury that may result from effects on critical infrastructure; and (3) the potential effects of a cyber attack on civilian objects that are *not* military objectives, such as private, civilian computers that hold no military significance, but may be networked to computers that are military objectives.[306]

However, predicting the collateral damage of cyber attacks is difficult (case in point: Stuxnet),[307] and such an attack could open Pandora's box by leaving a state's

---

[299] *See* David Yanagizawa-Drott, *Propaganda and Conflict: Theory and Evidence From the Rwandan Genocide*, HARV. UNIV. 1, 1 (2010), http://www.hks.harvard.edu/fs/dyanagi/Research/RwandaDYD.pdf (arguing that roughly "9 percent of the genocide ... can be explained by the radio station.").

[300] *See* Final Report to the Prosecutor by the Committee Established to Review the NATO Bombing Campaign against the Federal Republic of Yugoslavia, paras. 71–79, 39 I.L.M. 1257, 1277 (June 13, 2000), http://www.icty.org/x/file/Press/nato061300.pdf (noting that NATO's targeting of Serbian TV and radio stations during the Kosovo conflict could also have been lawful if it had been justified on grounds of mitigating incitement to genocide and not as being an incidental "aim of its primary goal of disabling the Serbian military command and control system[s]. . . . ").

[301] BOUCHET-SAULNIER ET AL., *supra* note 298, at 270.

[302] *See* DOD ASSESSMENT, *supra* note 8, at 8; TALLINN MANUAL, *supra* note 173, at 110.

[303] DOD ASSESSMENT, *supra* note 8, at 9.

[304] *See id.*

[305] *See* DINNISS, *supra* note 295, at 103–04 (noting that "[t]he principle of proportionality requires the weighing of the response against its permitted purpose of halting and repelling the attack. . . . ").

[306] Koh, *supra* note 209 (emphasis in original).

[307] *See, e.g.*, Matthew J. Schwartz, *Cyber Weapon Friendly Fire: Chevron Stuxnet Fallout*, INFO. WK. SEC. (Nov. 12, 2012), https://www.informationweek.com/security/attacks/cyber-weapon-friendly-fire-chevron-stuxn/240115344 (reporting on Chevron's infection by Stuxnet).

own population vulnerable to reprisals potentially developed from the same cyber weapon.[308]

Fourth, the neutrality problem mentioned earlier similarly complicates the legal situation because cyber attacks are often routed through neutral countries because of the Internet's distributed architecture discussed in Chapters 1 and 3.[309] The doctrine of neutrality allows a state to retain immunity from attack so long as it does not "assist either side" or allow its territory to be used by a belligerent state.[310] In a cyber context, the question is how aggressive must neutral states be in securing their networks from attackers? A number of proposals have been made to answer this query regarding how to treat neutral parties in a cyber conflict, drawing from naval, air, and space warfare analogies. Some go so far as to argue that a victim nation should have the right to stop cyber attackers from making use of a neutral state's networks by any means necessary.[311] However, there is support for the opposite conclusion as well. For example, the 1907 Hague Convention states in pertinent part, "A neutral power is not called upon to forbid or restrict the use on behalf of the belligerents of telegraph or telephone cables or of wireless telegraphy apparatus belonging to it or to companies or private individuals."[312] Some commentators rely on this "telecommunication exception" to suggest that the only behavior that is required in order to "remain neutral in a cyber conflict" is that the neutral state "not originate" the attack,[313] whereas others argue that the state must take some "action to prevent . . . [the] attack from transiting" through its nodes and routers.[314] Placing the onus on states assumes relatively equal capacity, whereas in actuality, as was previously mentioned, states possess a wide range of cybersecurity capabilities. Yet this risks giving the cyber powers too free a hand at infiltrating, or even controlling, neutral networks to thwart attackers if the neutral state did not use the "means at its disposal" to repel attackers.[315] The authors of the *Tallinn Manual* have argued that there is a standard requiring either actual or constructive knowledge on the part of the neutral state that its infrastructure is being used in a cyber conflict.[316] However,

---

[308] *Cf.* DINNISS, *supra* note 295, at 104 (arguing that a kinetic attack may be used in response to a cyber attack under certain circumstances, but that these circumstances had not yet arisen, at least from attacks discussed in the public domain).

[309] *See* Joshua E. Kastenberg, *Non-Intervention and Neutrality in Cyberspace: An Emerging Principle in the National Practice of International Law*, 64 A.F. L. REV. 43, 53 (2009).

[310] DOD ASSESSMENT, *supra* note 8, at 7.

[311] *See* George K. Walter, *Information Warfare and Neutrality*, 33 VAND. J. TRANSNAT'L L. 1079, 1199–1200 (2000) (drawing from the law of naval warfare).

[312] Hague Convention v. Respecting the Rights and Duties of Neutral Powers and Persons in Case of War on Land, Oct. 18, 1907, art. 8, 36 Stat. 2310, T.S. 540, 1 Bevans 654, http://www.unhcr.org/refworld/pdfid/3ddca4e14.pdf.

[313] Kastenberg, *supra* note 309, at 57; *see* Stephen W. Korns & Joshua E. Kastenberg, *Georgia's Cyber Left Hook*, 38 PARAMETERS – U.S. ARMY WAR C. Q. 60, 62 (2008).

[314] Schaap, *supra* note 297, at 153.

[315] Kelsey, *supra* note 30, at 1445.

[316] *See* TALLINN MANUAL, *supra* note 173, at 252–53.

they were split on whether this implies that neutral states have an affirmative duty to actively monitor their networks for cyber attacks.[317]

What can be done about these LOAC ambiguities? Two options are often discussed. First, for the purpose of clarifying distinction, some have argued for the principle's expansion, allowing "greater flexibility" for states to launch and respond to cyber attacks that have a low potential for the loss of human life.[318] Unfortunately, this would likely do relatively little to stem the flood of cyber attacks. A second – and potentially more politically palatable clarification – lies in applying the telecommunication exception, which could alleviate many of the concerns that neutral states have about policing their networks.[319] However, such a legal regime may encourage non-neutral powers to feign neutrality and still collaborate with belligerent powers. Taken to an extreme, and depending on the interpretation adopted, it could also provide incentives for a race to the bottom, allowing states the benefits of launching cyber attacks while relieving them of the responsibility to police their networks and augment security.

Together, the aforementioned LOAC provisions point to a basis in the law of war for the use of limited, targeted, and proportionate cyber attacks in wartime.[320] In fact, according to the DOD, "[t]he law of war is probably the single area of international law in which current legal obligations can be applied with the greatest confidence to information operations."[321] This fact is especially important given how many treaties lose effect during armed conflicts. Collectively, these principles form the foundation for a law of cyber war, but determining exactly how to apply these laws in such a novel context will occupy military commanders, policymakers, and attorneys for the foreseeable future.

Cyber Warfare, International Criminal Law, and Human Rights Law

According to Kenneth Watkin, "[e]fforts to control the power of the state and its impact on individual citizens spawned human rights norms" that were "'concerned with the organization of State power vis-à-vis the individual'...."[322] Increasingly, and especially in the aftermath of the 9/11 attacks, "the use of force during armed conflict is being assessed through the perspective of human rights law...."[323] These principles are important in the cyber context for attacks then that fall both above and

---

[317] *See id.* at 253.

[318] Kelsey, *supra* note 30, at 1445, 1448.

[319] *See* Koms & Kastenberg, *supra* note 313, at 69, 72.

[320] For a more comprehensive treatment of these and other related issues in the law of cyber warfare, see generally TALLINN MANUAL, *supra* note 173; DINNISS, *supra* note 295.

[321] DOD ASSESSMENT, *supra* note 8, at 11.

[322] Watkin, *supra* note 29, at 13 (quoting Robert Kolb, *The Relationship Between International Humanitarian Law and Human Rights Law: A Brief History of the 1948 Universal Declaration of Human Rights and the 1949 Geneva Conventions*, 38 INT'L REV. RED CROSS 409, 410 (1998)).

[323] *Id.* at 1.

below the armed attack threshold, though especially the latter because, according to Anthony Cordesman of CSIS, "some 95 percent of all the problems and challenges posed by criminals...and hackers will have to be...treated as normal actuarial losses and the 'cost of doing business.'"[324] As discussed in Chapter 5, this means that a significant part of the burden of managing cyber attacks and promoting cyber peace lies with the private sector, requiring coordination by multiple stakeholders within an emerging polycentric system.[325]

The first multilateral efforts to prevent cybercrime and terrorism stretch back nearly three decades, with the goal being to ensure that no criminal receives a "safe haven" anywhere in the world.[326] For example, in a Justice and Home Affairs Communiqué on May 11, 2004, the G-8 argued that "all countries must continue to improve laws that criminalize misuses of computer networks and that allow for faster cooperation on Internet-related investigations."[327] Various other regional bodies and the UN have since enacted initiatives to manage cyber attacks such as through harmonizing divergent national laws.[328] The previously mentioned Budapest Convention remains the best known, but it is by no means alone.[329] Myriad criminal offenses are defined under the Budapest Convention, including: illegal access, illegal interception, data interference, system interference, and misuse of devices.[330] The Convention calls on signatories to adopt domestic laws to criminalize these offenses, and to establish a regime to enhance international cooperation. As of January 2014, forty-one nations had ratified the accord,[331] although enforcement mechanisms for noncompliance remain absent. Asian-Pacific Economic Cooperation leaders have also agreed to "strengthen their respective economies' ability to combat cybercrime by enacting domestic legislation consistent with the provisions of international legal instruments, including the Convention on Cybercrime...."[332] Similarly, the Organization of American States has also encouraged member states to join the Budapest

---

[324] ANTHONY H. CORDESMAN & JUSTIN G. CORDESMAN, CYBER-THREATS, INFORMATION WARFARE, AND CRITICAL INFRASTRUCTURE PROTECTION 9 (2002).

[325] *See* Susan W. Brenner & Marc D. Goodman, *In Defense of Cyberterrorism: An Argument for Anticipating Cyber-Attacks*, 2002 U. ILL. J.L. TECH. & POL'Y 1, 27 (2002).

[326] GRAHAM, *supra* note 214, at 94 (discussing the issue of safe havens).

[327] Communiqué, Meeting of G-8 Justice and Home Affairs Ministers para. 10, (May 11, 2004), http://www.justice.gov/ag/events/g82004/Communique_2004_G8_JHA_Ministerial_051204.pdf.

[328] *See* Henning Wegener, *Cyber Peace*, *in* THE QUEST FOR CYBER PEACE, supra note 9, at 77, 79.

[329] Convention on Cybercrime, Nov. 23, 2001, 2296 U.N.T.S. 167, http://conventions.coe.int/Treaty/en/Treaties/Html/185.htm; *see also* INT'L TELECOMM. UNION, UNDERSTANDING CYBERCRIME: PHENOMENA, CHALLENGES AND LEGAL OPTIONS 11, 127–28 (2012), http://www.itu.int/ITU-D/cyb/cybersecurity/docs/Cybercrime%20legislation%20EV6.pdf (listing other relevant model laws, including the Commonwealth Model Law on Computer and Computer-related Crime).

[330] Budapest Convention, arts. 2–6.

[331] *See Convention on Cybercrime*, COUNCIL OF EUR. TREATY OFF., http://www.conventions.coe.int/Treaty/Commun/ChercheSig.asp?NT=185&CM=8&DF=28/06/2013&CL=ENG (last updated Feb. 3, 2014).

[332] APEC, SIXTEENTH APEC MINISTERIAL MEETING: JOINT STATEMENT 14 (2004), http://aimp.apec.org/Documents/2004/MM/AMM/04_amm_jms.doc.

Convention and to ratchet up regional cooperation to mitigate cybercrime,[333] whereas a nonbinding UN General Assembly Resolution calls on states to "eliminate safe havens" for cybercriminals.[334] Together, these and other accords and regional initiatives have made some progress in the fight to unify diverse national cybercrime laws into a polycentric framework potentially applicable during both cyber war and peace.[335]

It may also be possible to integrate cyber attacks into other leading international criminal treaties such as the International Criminal Court (ICC). The jurisdiction of the ICC is limited to "the most serious crimes of international concern."[336] These include instances of genocide, crimes against humanity, war crimes, and aggression.[337] A decade of debate ensued about how to define "aggression," ultimately concluding in 2010 with a perhaps still somewhat ambiguous common view that aggression included "manifest violation of the Charter of the United Nations."[338] The difficulties of classifying cyber attacks as uses of force in violation of the UN Charter have already been discussed, but this definition could potentially provide a forum for holding certain state sponsors of cyber attacks more accountable.[339]

Aside from international criminal law, as has been mentioned, there is confusion over the role that human rights law should play in armed conflicts. It is unclear, for example, whether human rights treaties such as the International Covenant on Civil and Political Rights (ICCPR) should apply extraterritorially, including to U.S. actions abroad.[340] Without clarification, the utility of the ICCPR and human rights law generally will be undermined as part of the law of cyber peace. If the international community takes a broad view, then several ICCPR provisions – including Article 19 (protecting the right to seek information) and Article 17 (protecting the right to privacy) – would have new life as applied to cybersecurity.[341] The UN General Assembly took action on this topic in late 2013, passing a consensus resolution

---

[333] *See* OAS AG/RES. 2040 (XXXIV-O/04), § IV(8) (June 8, 2004), http://www.oas.org/juridico/english/cyber.htm.

[334] G.A. Res. 55/63, U.N. Doc. A/RES/55/63 (Jan. 22, 2001), http://www.itu.int/ITU-D/cyb/cybersecurity/docs/UN_resolution_55_63.pdf.

[335] *See* Marco Gercke, Regional and International Approaches to Cybercrime, Asia Pacific Regional Mock Court Exercise on Fighting Cybercrime, Sept. 18–19, 2012, in Jakarta, Indon., at 7, http://www.itu.int/ITU-D/asp/CMS/Events/2012/mockcourt/S3.3_Mr_Marco_Gerke.pdf.

[336] Rome Statute of the International Criminal Court, United Nations Diplomatic Conference of Plenipotentiaries on the Establishment of an International Criminal Court, art. 1, July 17, 1998, U.N. Doc. A/CONF. 183/9 (1998), 2187 U.N.T.S. 90 (1998).

[337] *Id.* art. 5.

[338] INT'L CRIM. CT., Special Working Group's Proposal on the Crime of Aggression, http://www.iccnow.org/?mod=swgca-proposal.

[339] *See* Jonathan A. Ophardt, *Cyber Warfare and the Crime of Aggression: The Need for Individual Accountability on Tomorrow's Battlefield*, 2010 DUKE L. & TECH. REV. 3 (2010). Other potential forums could include investor-state arbitration, or a dedicated international tribunal for cyberspace. *See supra* note 168; *infra* note 367 and accompanying text.

[340] *See* Michael J. Dennis, *Application of Human Rights Treaties Extraterritorially in Times of Armed Conflict and Military Occupation*, 99 AM. J. INT'L L. 119, 119 (2005); NATIONAL ACADEMIES, *supra* note 53, at 281.

[341] NATIONAL ACADEMIES, *supra* note 53, at 281–82.

in the wake of NSA revelations sponsored by Germany and Brazil on "[t]he right to privacy in the digital age" affirming that human rights including privacy and freedom of expression apply online in a move that could contribute to a positive cyber peace.[342]

State-sponsored cyber attacks straddle the worlds of IHRL and the LOAC. Non-state actors that engage in international violence at the behest of states, regardless of whether such violence rises to the level of an armed attack, do not fit easily within either paradigm. Aggressive acts in cyberspace are not only assessed by their consequences, but also by their intentions. The difficulty lies in proving those intentions, and applying these diverse accords to foster cyber peace by holding attackers accountable for their actions.

SUMMARY

Neither the LOAC nor any of the other treaty systems or legal principles discussed in this chapter serves as a panacea for cybersecurity. Yet the issue is becoming ever more pressing and complex, especially as the international community is confronted with the growing specter of state-sponsored cyber attacks. Even though these attacks have not risen to the level of an armed attack required to activate the LOAC, sponsor states should not be able to avoid accountability. The digital fog of cyber war necessitates the creation of legal regimes that take into account an inherent level of uncertainty – cyber law must scale and evolve alongside governance and security. Specifically, this requires a two-tiered system for responding to cyber attacks – a default state for peacetime, and another triggered by an armed attack. Thus far, the latter has received more attention from scholars and policymakers and is now better defined than the former, despite the fact that the former includes the vast majority of cyber attacks.

Consider the case of Estonia. There, the 2007 cyber attacks disrupted the functioning of the Estonian government and thus arguably endangered the "safety services" referred to in the ITU Charter.[343] Therefore, if Russia were attributed blame for this incident, it may well have been in breach of the ITU Charter and Estonia could potentially institute countermeasures and bring international pressure to bear for reparations, although there is no enforcement mechanism available under this treaty. The Estonian government could also have held those companies most affected by cyber attacks liable if they were aware of the nefarious activity and did not adequately prepare for or respond to the threat, as some U.S. courts have done in the

---

[342] The Right to Privacy in the Digital Age, Nov. 1, 2013, UN Doc. A/C.3/68/L.45 (2013), http://daccess-dds-ny.un.org/doc/UNDOC/GEN/N13/544/07/PDF/N1354407.pdf?OpenElement; *see* Violet Blue, *Despite US Opposition, UN Approves Rights to Privacy in the Digital Age*, ZDNET (Nov. 27, 2013), http://www.zdnet.com/despite-us-opposition-un-approves-rights-to-privacy-in-the-digital-age-7000023708/ ("It is the first such document to establish privacy rights and human rights in the digital sphere.").

[343] International Telecommunication Convention, annex 2.

context of copyright infringement and as part of an emerging cybersecurity duty of care, as discussed in Chapter 5. Similarly, Estonia could possibly have invoked UNCLOS, which prohibits the staging of any attacks that interfere with the security of a coastal state. Arguably, this prohibition could also apply to claims involving submarine cables.[344] This would mean that states could prosecute cyber attackers who send subversive code through fiber-optic submarine cables to a coastal state, potentially opening up another route to reparations and possible sanctions from the UNSC.[345] Targeted economic sanctions are permissible under international law, whereas blockades are illegal absent a UNSC Resolution, although drawing the line between the two in cyberspace may be difficult.[346] Together, these and other bodies of law, along with the emerging norms discussed in Chapter 7, form the beginnings of a law of cyber peace that both defines inappropriate conduct and provides for reparations or other compensation to affected nations.[347]

After a cyber attack rises to the level of an armed attack, an international security system may be activated combining elements from the LOAC with human rights law to ensure that civil rights are respected. Both regimes have much to offer in forming a polycentric system to promote positive cyber peace. A framework that considers human rights alone is insufficient because it would not address the relative importance of CNI nor provide a proportionate assessment regarding non-combatant casualties, whereas a pure LOAC regime could violate base human rights protections.[348] Moreover, command responsibility is well established under the laws of war, and commanders should apply these same principles to cyber attacks as "they do to the use of bombs and missiles."[349] To enable the LOAC to regulate contemporary armed conflict effectively, this area of law "must set forth realistic rules governing the use of deadly force that reflect the levels of violence and the nature of the threat posed to society."[350] Armed conflict does not occur in isolation.

---

[344] *See* UNCLOS, arts. 19, 113.

[345] *See* UN Charter, chap. VII, art. 52.

[346] *See* NATIONAL ACADEMIES, *supra* note 53, at 260; Lewis, *supra* note 56, at 48–51 (noting the array of actions that may be taken by states "to indicate displeasure," including "canceling official visits, freezing visa issuance, ending scientific cooperation, and, in extreme cases, imposing sanctions").

[347] *See* ABRAHAM D. SOFAER, DAVID CLARK & WHITFIELD DIFFIE, NAT'L ACAD. SCI., *Cyber Security and International Agreements*, 2010 PROC. ON DETERRING CYBERATTACKS: INFORMING STRATEGIES & DEVELOPING OPTIONS FOR U.S. POL'Y 179, 205 (discussing the potential for bottom-up mechanisms to build toward an international regime to improve cybersecurity).

[348] One proposal for addressing cyber attacks on CNI is amending the Convention on Certain Conventional Weapons to include this category alongside blinding laser weapons and certain incendiary weapons. *See* Jody R. Westby, *A Call for Geo-Cyber Stability*, *in* THE QUEST FOR CYBER PEACE, *supra* note 9, at 66, 74.

[349] Reynolds, *supra* note 28, at 62.

[350] Watkin, *supra* note 29, at 34. For example, the law of neutrality should be clarified in the context of cyberspace, defining whether or not victim nations could hold neutral nations through which cyber attacks transited accountable for not being diligent in repelling attackers. *See* Kelsey, *supra* note 30, at 1445; TALLINN MANUAL, *supra* note 173, at 252–53.

Incorporation of IHRL principles such as accountability, for example, "can have a positive impact on the regulation of the use of force during armed conflict."[351]

However, this framework remains imperfect because few of these laws specify how armed conflict should change their applicability. Critically, many treaties also lack enforcement mechanisms. The limitations of such regimes, created by analogy and the extension of principles developed to suit different challenges, demonstrate the limits of existing international laws to enhance cybersecurity. Internet freedom arguments about the "unregulatability of bits" and the ability of attackers to circumvent national borders remain powerful especially given rapid technological advancements, but have been partly undermined by scholars such as Professor Joel Reidenberg who have advocated for the potential of private regulatory regimes to serve as proxies for laws.[352] However, the fundamental difficulty of enforcing regulations in cyberspace remains apparent given problems of attribution, environmental plasticity, and the inter-networked nature of cyberspace, among other challenges.[353] This means that although regulation is possible in cyberspace, it is fraught with difficulties, as has been shown throughout this book. It is best, then, to consider law and norms alongside market-based incentives and code as part of a polycentric system for fostering cyber peace given the absence of a comprehensive legal regime.

If political impasses explored in Chapter 7 are overcome, negotiators could craft a new cybersecurity treaty to improve upon the suboptimal status quo that: (1) defines appropriate graduated sanctions against nations harboring or sponsoring cybercriminals and terrorists, and sets out when a cyber attack rises to the level of an armed conflict; (2) clarifies which international legal provisions apply above and below the armed attack threshold; (3) establishes a regime for attribution that includes robust information sharing; (4) provides for enforcement mechanisms; and (5) a system of dispute resolution.[354] Several proposals have been made along these lines. One early scheme is the International Convention on Cyber Crime and Terrorism drafted at Stanford University, otherwise known as the "Stanford Proposal."[355] The findings section of the Stanford Proposal include several arguments for greater international cooperation in managing cyber attacks based on shared

---

[351] Watkin, *supra* note 29, at 34.

[352] MURRAY, *supra* note 34, at 203–04.

[353] *Id.* at 205.

[354] *See* Hathaway et al., *supra* note 32, at 880 (arguing in particular for "a shared definition of cyber-crime, cyber-attack, and cyber-warfare" and establishing "a framework for more robust international cooperation in information sharing, evidence collection, and criminal prosecution of those participating in cross-national cyber-attacks"). *Cf.* Deltev Wolter, *The UN Takes a Big Step Forward on Cybersecurity*, ARMS CONTROL ASSOC. (Sept. 2013), http://www.armscontrol.org/act/2013 09/The-UN-Takes-a-Big-Step-Forward-on-Cybersecurity (reporting on an agreement that included several leading cyber powers on "the full applicability of international law to state behavior in cyberspace.").

[355] ABRAHAM D. SOFAER ET AL., STAN. UNIV., A PROPOSAL FOR AN INTERNATIONAL CONVENTION ON CYBER CRIME AND TERRORISM (2000), http://www.iwar.org.uk/law/resources/cybercrime/stanford/cisac-draft .htm.

danger.[356] Article 12 of the Stanford Proposal, for example, argues for the creation of an International Agency for Information Infrastructure Protection (IAIIP), the goal of which is "to serve as a formal structure in which interested groups cooperate with experts in countries around the world in developing standards and best practices concerning cyber security."[357] However, national security concerns at present limit the likelihood of the creation of such a World CERT, though we have seen progress in the realm of global cybersecurity P3s such as IMPACT, discussed in Chapters 1 and 7. Additionally, the Stanford Proposal, like the Budapest Convention, has other drawbacks; for example, it excludes state conduct, focusing instead on private individuals and groups.[358] This underscores the fact that insufficient effort has been made to frame an appropriate legal framework for state-sponsored cyber attacks, though the IAIIP's inclusion of the private sector at least avoids some of the problems that plagued UNCLOS III.

An international treaty on cyber attacks should make use of the effects doctrine discussed in Chapter 2 as a mechanism for taking into account concerns over regulating cyberspace.[359] Each area of the global commons has lessons on how, and how not, to regulate cyberspace to better manage attacks. The goal of commons regulation is typically to preserve the commons; that is, in this case, the cyber pseudo commons generally, and arguably the generative Internet in particular, for future generations. However, unlike barring a military presence in Antarctica through the ATS, cyber weapons cannot be easily outlawed for political, technical, and legal reasons. What might be better suited instead is a polycentric approach to Internet governance and cybersecurity drawing from Professor Ostrom's design principles, as is laid out in Chapter 7. For example, the proportionality criterion speaks to the importance of creating a level, equitable playing field in which legal ambiguities are addressed both above and below the armed attack threshold.[360] Relatedly, monitoring states for compliance with international legal regimes along with developing robust enforcement and dispute settlement mechanisms including sanctions and forums where victims of cyber attacks can air their grievances would do much to build out the law of cyber war and peace.[361]

What other options exist in enhancing cybersecurity beyond adapting existing treaties? Some argue for the widespread use of preventative self-defense with its attendant dangers of international instability and escalation.[362] Others would prefer a regime of universal jurisdiction, whereby any state would be able to prosecute cyber

---

[356] *Id.*

[357] *Id.* at iv.

[358] *Id.* at 21.

[359] *See* TALLINN MANUAL, *supra* note 173, at 19–20.

[360] Elinor Ostrom, *Polycentric Systems: Multilevel Governance Involving a Diversity of Organizations, in* GLOBAL ENVIRONMENTAL COMMONS: ANALYTICAL AND POLITICAL CHALLENGES INVOLVING A DIVERSITY OF ORGANIZATIONS 105, 120 (Eric Brousseau et al. eds., 2012).

[361] *See id.*

[362] *See* Joyner & Lotrionte, *supra* note 35, at 858–59.

attackers.[363] An extreme option is a movement toward a surveillance society such that every state would have greater information awareness, raising obvious privacy implications but also not necessarily contributing to overall cybersecurity.[364] Among other issues, each of these approaches raises the thorny problem of harmonization as well as reciprocity. Given that the United States remains a leading cyber power, U.S. cybersecurity policy may well be mirrored back; we have to be comfortable with the reflection. Still others call for a multilateral counterterrorism approach through the UNSC. This would involve the Security Council using its authority to issue binding rules on all UN member states to enhance global cybersecurity through better prevention and monitoring.[365] The current international political situation, however, makes the likelihood of such an approach questionable, meaning that in the near term at least "the United States will have to pursue its . . . [cybersecurity] strategies on an uncertain and unstable international legal terrain."[366] And issues of accountability remain. The LOAC has been violated with relative impunity in many armed conflicts. How can the international community ensure that similar transgressions would not happen during a cyber war? Defining attribution is a prerequisite to accountability – as is greater clarity about when the laws of war should apply to cyber conflicts, and which forums should have jurisdiction over attackers. In 2010, for example, Norway's Judge Stein Schjolberg advocated for the creation of an International Criminal Tribunal for Cyberspace to hear the most serious cybercrime cases.[367] Though such an approach is fraught with political difficulties, it does demonstrate the innovative thinking required to better manage the cyber threat.[368]

International law changes with events: as Justice Oliver Wendell Holmes wrote, "The life of the law has not been logic; it has been experience."[369] It is essential for policymakers to consider cyber attacks as the revolutionary threat that they are to the security and welfare of citizens around the world for real and lasting progress to be made. But it is equally necessary for scholars, jurists, and negotiators to place a greater emphasis on developing and clarifying the law of cyber peace given that

---

[363] *See* Kelly A. Gable, *Cyber-Apocalypse Now: Securing the Internet Against Cyberterrorism and Using Universal Jurisdiction as a Deterrent*, 43 VAND. J. TRANSNAT'L L. 57, 57 (2010).

[364] *See* Clyde Wayne Crews, Jr., *'Partial' Information Awareness*, CATO INST. (Jan. 9, 2003), http://www.cato.org/publications/commentary/partial-information-awareness; Denver Nicks, *Report: Usefulness of NSA Mass Surveillance 'Overblown*,' TIME (Jan. 13, 2014), http://swampland.time.com/2014/01/13/report-usefulness-of-nsa-mass-surveillance-overblown/.

[365] *See* Friesen, *supra* note 258, at 107–08.

[366] Waxman, *supra* note 33, at 459.

[367] *See* STEIN SCHJOLBERG & SOLANGE GHERNAOUTI-HÉLIE, A GLOBAL TREATY ON CYBERSECURITY AND CYBERCRIME 67 (2d ed. 2011).

[368] Equally imperative is jumpstarting a conversation on the ethics of cyber conflict, especially for cyber attacks falling below the armed attack threshold. *See* NAT'L RES. COUNCIL, EMERGING AND READILY AVAILABLE TECHNOLOGIES AND NATIONAL SECURITY – A FRAMEWORK FOR ADDRESSING ETHICAL, LEGAL, AND SOCIETAL ISSUES (Jean-Lou Chameau et al. eds., 2014).

[369] DOD ASSESSMENT, *supra* note 8, at 1–2.

this legal regime will be responsible for managing responses to most cyber attacks.[370] This chapter has taken a non-comprehensive look at how some existing legal regimes may be applied in cyberspace. As has been shown, there is not an absence of law in cyberspace. It is far from the untamed digital Wild West that it is at times made out to be. The issue is one of reconceptualizing cyber attacks and determining appropriate responses within an evolving polycentric system. As with many breakthroughs in weapons technology, cyber weapons are racing ahead of the law. Nevertheless, that does not mean that the laws discussed here have no application to enhancing cybersecurity. Existing regimes should not be abandoned in favor of a new cyber weapons treaty because little clarity exists as to what such a treaty would look like even if it were politically feasible to negotiate and ratify it. Better, one might think, to begin the process of legal clarification and norm building now, and not let the great be the enemy of the good.

The existing legal regime to manage cyber attacks is useful, but is oftentimes ineffective and underdeveloped. International law then must be one tool, alongside diplomatic, political, economic, and military mechanisms, to foster cyber peace. Enhancing cybersecurity, however, ultimately depends on politics. It is to that final subject, along with assessing the promise and peril of polycentric regulation in cyberspace, which we turn to next.

---

[370] *See* Mary Ellen O'Connell, *Cyber Security without Cyber War*, 17 J. CONFLICT & SEC. L. 187, 187 (2012) (arguing for the application of the international law governing "economic activity and communications" instead of the LOAC to better manage cyber attacks).

7

Cyber Peace

'Cyber peace' to me would be an entire weekend without my Blackberry going off.

– Managing Director at Kroll Advisory Solutions Michael DuBose[1]

In July 2004, the world's first dedicated international treaty to mitigate cybercrime came online.[2] Although an important achievement that (as of January 2014) has been ratified by nations that are home to more than one-third of Internet users,[3] the hard-fought Budapest Convention has experienced limited success. Many nations, including cyber powers like China, Russia, and Israel, have yet to ratify the accord. A common criticism is that, unlike UN treaties, the negotiation process was not open to all nations.[4] It is a product of the Council of Europe, although both member and non-member states have joined it including the United States and Japan.[5] Moreover, the treaty is now "somewhat outdated" given the rapid pace of technological advancements,[6] and as discussed in Chapter 6 it does not address issues of cyber terrorism, war, or state-sponsored cyber attacks generally.[7] Consequently, many governments and organizations are pushing for a new cybersecurity accord

---

[1] Electronic Interview with Michael DuBose, head of cyber investigations at Kroll Advisory Solutions and former chief of the Computer Crime & Intellectual Property Section, Criminal Division, Department of Justice, in Wash., D.C. (Apr. 18, 2011).

[2] See Council of Europe, *Convention on Cybercrime*, Mar. 2002, 41 I.L.M. 282 (2001), http://conventions .coe.int/Treaty/EN/Treaties/Html/185.htm [hereinafter Convention on Cybercrime].

[3] See, e.g., Brian Harley, *A Global Convention on Cybercrime?*, COLUMBIA SCI. & TECH. L. REV. (Mar. 23, 2010), http://www.stlr.org/2010/03/a-global-convention-on-cybercrime/; *Convention on Cybercrime*, COUNCIL OF EUR. TREATY OFF., http://www.conventions.coe.int/Treaty/Commun/ChercheSig .asp?NT=185&CM=8&DF=28/06/2013&CL=ENG (last updated Feb. 3, 2014).

[4] See Harley, *supra* note 3.

[5] See COUNCIL OF EUR. TREATY OFF., *supra* note 3.

[6] Harley, *supra* note 3.

[7] Cf. Emilio Godoy, *Cybercrime Treaty Could Be Used to Go After Cyberespionage*, INTER PRESS SERV. (Oct. 3, 2013), http://www.ipsnews.net/2013/10/cybercrime-treaty-could-be-used-to-go-after-cyberespionage/ (reporting on efforts by some scholars to argue for including cyber espionage under the Budapest Convention).

in tandem with revisions to Internet governance.[8] The ITU, with the support of many developing countries, has been identified as a potential focal point to lead such efforts.[9] In early 2011, the ITU and UN Office on Drugs and Crime (UNODC) signed a Memorandum of Understanding to work together to help member states fight cybercrime.[10] This represents the first time that two UN organizations have cooperated on cybersecurity.[11] However, the divergent views about the best ways to enhance cybersecurity within a system often requiring consensus engender questions about the potential for it to lead the push for a new convention,[12] though the ITU has had some success in helping to establish national cyber emergency response teams among other cybersecurity accomplishments.[13]

The saga of the Budapest Convention reveals much about the state of global cyber politics. Given that all nations have a vested interest in managing cybercrime, the lack of consensus on this topic bodes ill for more divisive issues such as holding state sponsors of cyber attacks accountable under international law or reshaping Internet governance. There remains a great deal of uncertainty over best practices even as governance becomes more fragmented.[14] This is partly caused by differing national interests shaping the Internet, as was analyzed in Chapter 4, as well as an array of other factors, including threats to the Domain Name System, the ongoing transition to IPv6, the rise of Internet censorship, and stresses on the Internet standards process, to name a few.[15] The influence of non-state actors, especially the private sector, further complicates the question in part because of pushback among business leaders who are weary of mounting regulations, as discussed in Chapter 5.[16] This lack of coordination is weakening the resolve of the international community to manage cyber threats – criminals are cooperating with one another even if states, for the most part, are not. Many nations are not on the same page in terms of enhancing cybersecurity – in fact, they are not even reading the same book.

Opportunities are present, however, in such times of flux, as emerging polycentric systems flex and shape the cyber regulatory environment. This final chapter

---

[8] *See* Harley, *supra* note 3.

[9] *See, e.g., IMPACT: Mission & Vision,* IMPACT, http://www.impact-alliance.org/aboutus/mission-&-vision.html (last visited June 30, 2013).

[10] *UN Agencies Team Up to Make the Online World Safer: MoU Signed Between ITU and UNODC at WSIS Forum 2011,* ITU NEWSLOG: CYBERSECURITY SPAM AND CYBERCRIME (May 19, 2011), http://www.itu.int/osg/blog/CategoryView,category,Cybersecurity%2BSpam%2Band%2BCybercrime .aspx.

[11] *Id.*

[12] Harley, *supra* note 3.

[13] *See, e.g., Kenya, ITU Sign Agreement on Cyber Security,* BIZTECH AFRICA (Feb. 21, 2012), http://www .biztechafrica.com/article/kenya-itu-sign-agreement-cyber-security/2049/.

[14] JONAH FORCE HILL, INTERNET FRAGMENTATION: HIGHLIGHTING THE MAJOR TECHNICAL, GOVERNANCE AND DIPLOMATIC CHALLENGES FOR U.S. POLICY MAKERS 5–6 (2012), http://belfercenter.hks .harvard.edu/files/internet_fragmentation_jonah_hill.pdf.

[15] *Id.*

[16] *See Zuckerberg and Schmidt Warn on Over-Regulation of Web,* BBC TECH. (May 25, 2011), http://www.bbc.co.uk/news/technology-13553943 [hereinafter Zuckerberg & Schmidt].

explores the confused world of cyber politics, both within the United States and around the world, which is giving form to these emerging regimes. In particular, the future of Internet governance is analyzed, along with the promise and peril of using polycentric governance to enhance cybersecurity. Best practices of key stakeholders identified throughout this book are also summarized. The book concludes by investigating what cyber peace might mean in this new era of cyber conflict.

CYBER POWER AND POLITICS IN THE INFORMATION AGE

Beginning in May 2011, Syrian activists used social media sites like Facebook and Twitter to help catalyze anti-government demonstrations.[17] The Syrian government and its allies responded, using bits along with bullets to attempt to quell the uprisings in what came to be known as "Repression 2.0."[18] Such tactics only continue a trend begun in nations like China and Iran, which, according to former U.S. Secretary of State Clinton, has resulted in "democracy and human rights activists . . . [having] their emails hacked . . . [and being] tortured so they would have to reveal their passwords and implicate their colleagues."[19] In several Arab nations including Bahrain, activists have reported receiving "anonymous death threats via e-mail, Facebook and Twitter."[20] For example, a 24-year-old Bahraini human rights campaigner named Mohammed al-Maskati had his name, picture, and home address posted by government supporters along with urgings that he be killed.[21] In a similar vein, the Iranian Cyber Army has targeted opposition news sites,[22] along with reportedly lashing out at U.S. banks and the Saudi Arabian state oil firm Aramco.[23]

These events point to the flip side of the Internet freedom agenda, what Evgeny Morozov calls "The Net Delusion," which is the notion that social media and the Internet can be a boon to authoritarian governments and activists alike.[24] To help tip the scale toward the activists, the U.S. State Department has funded training

---

[17] *See* Mary Beth Sheridan, *Autocratic Regimes Fight Web-Savvy Opponents with their Own Tools*, WASH. POST (May 22, 2011), http://www.washingtonpost.com/world/autocratic-regimes-fight-web-savvy-opponents-with-their-own-tools/2011/04/19/AFTfEN9G_story.html?hpid=z4.

[18] *Id.*; *see also* Mark Clayton, *Syria's Cyberwars: Using Social Media Against Dissent*, CSM (July 25, 2012), http://www.csmonitor.com/USA/2012/0725/Syria-s-cyberwars-using-social-media-against-dissent (reporting on how the Syrian government used social media to its own advantage).

[19] Hillary Rodham Clinton, U.S. Sec'y of State, Remarks on Internet Freedom (Jan. 21, 2010), http://www.state.gov/secretary/rm/2010/01/135519.htm.

[20] Sheridan, *supra* note 17.

[21] *See id.*; *Bahrain: Death Threats Against Messrs. Mohammed Al-Maskati, Nabeel Rajab and Yousef Al-Mahafdha*, WORLD ORG. AGAINST TORTURE (Dec. 2011), http://www.omct.org/human-rights-defenders/urgent-interventions/bahrain/2011/12/d21549/.

[22] *See* Sheridan, *supra* note 17; FREEDOM HOUSE, FREEDOM ON THE NET: A GLOBAL ASSESSMENT OF INTERNET AND DIGITAL MEDIA 88, 187 (2011), http://www.freedomhouse.org/sites/default/files/FOTN%202012%20summary%20of%20findings.pdf.

[23] *See, e.g.*, Mike Mount, *U.S. Officials Believe Iran Behind Recent Cyber Attacks*, CNN (Oct. 16, 2012), http://www.cnn.com/2012/10/15/world/iran-cyber/index.html.

[24] EVGENY MOROZOV, THE NET DELUSION: THE DARK SIDE OF INTERNET FREEDOM xvii, 100 (2011).

programs to educate opposition members about best practices to elude detection and, in some cases, equipping them with "Internet in a Suitcase" technology to bypass government censorship.[25] Google has also gotten into the game of eluding censors, as discussed in Chapter 2.[26] Some groups have even planned to launch private communications satellites into orbit to undermine government censorship.[27] Such initiatives demonstrate the extent to which cyber power is diffusing as Internet governance fragments. Understanding the political forces shaping Internet governance and cybersecurity trends is therefore critical. This section briefly reviews recent U.S. efforts at reform before moving on to discuss the political opposition both at home and abroad to a global agreement on cybersecurity.

Tweet Softly, but Carry a Big Stick: U.S. Cybersecurity Reform Efforts

Within the United States, a morass of partisan politics and sometimes-conflicting regulations complicates cybersecurity reform efforts, as discussed in Chapters 4 and 5. Some vested interests disregard reforms as either being too costly for businesses,[28] or not going far enough to protect CNI.[29] To help break the logjam, the Obama administration released a Cyberspace Policy Review in early May 2009.[30] The review recognized the unacceptable status quo and the fact that U.S. responses have not kept pace with the evolving cyber threat.[31] In response, the administration offered a series of policy recommendations laid out in Table 7.1. Some of these sought to clarify the bureaucracy, such as by appointing a cybersecurity policy official with real authority over disparate cybersecurity efforts within the federal government,[32] whereas other measures were aimed at enhancing security by establishing standardized "performance metrics."[33] The Obama administration then worked to push cybersecurity reform through Congress. Domestically, among much else, the administration

---

[25] James Glanz & John Markoff, *U.S. Underwrites Internet Detour Around Censors*, N.Y. TIMES (June 12, 2011), http://www.nytimes.com/2011/06/12/world/12internet.html?pagewanted=all&_r=0.

[26] *Google Unveils Service to Bypass Government Censorship, Surveillance*, AL JAZEERA (Oct. 21, 2013), http://america.aljazeera.com/articles/2013/10/21/google-inc-unveilsservicetobypassgovernmentcensor shipsurveillanc.html.

[27] *See* David Meyer, *Hackers Plan Space Satellites to Combat Censorship*, BBC (Dec. 30, 2011), http://www.bbc.co.uk/news/technology-16367042.

[28] *See* Ken Dilanian, *U.S. Chamber of Commerce Leads Defeat of Cyber-Security Bill*, L.A. TIMES (Aug. 3, 2012), http://articles.latimes.com/2012/aug/03/nation/la-na-cyber-security-20120803.

[29] *See* David Brancaccio, *Why the U.S. Should Worry about Cyber Security*, PBS MARKETPLACE (Apr. 25, 2012), http://www.marketplace.org/topics/tech/why-us-should-worry-about-cyber-security; Judy Woodruff, *Critical U.S. Infrastructure Vulnerable to Cyber Attack, Congress Fails to Act*, PBS NEWS HOUR (Aug. 8, 2012), http://www.pbs.org/newshour/bb/science/july-dec12/cybersecurity_08-08.html.

[30] CYBERSPACE POLICY REVIEW: ASSURING A TRUSTED AND RESILIENT INFORMATION AND COMMUNICATIONS INFRASTRUCTURE (2009), http://www.whitehouse.gov/assets/documents/Cyberspace_Policy_Review_final.pdf [hereinafter CYBERSPACE POLICY REVIEW].

[31] *Id.* at iii–v, 4.

[32] *Id.* at 7.

[33] *Id.* at vi, 11.

TABLE 7.1. *Obama administration cyberspace policy review near-term action plan*[34]

1. Appoint a cybersecurity policy official responsible for coordinating the nation's cybersecurity policies and activities.
2. Prepare for the president's approval of an updated national strategy to secure the information and communications infrastructure.
3. Designate cybersecurity as one of the president's key management priorities and establish performance metrics.
4. Designate a civil liberties official to the National Security Council cybersecurity directorate.
5. Convene appropriate interagency mechanisms to formulate a coherent cybersecurity policy across the federal government.
6. Initiate a national public awareness and education campaign to promote cybersecurity.
7. Develop U.S. Government positions for an international cybersecurity policy framework and strengthen our international partnerships to create cybersecurity initiatives.
8. Prepare a cybersecurity incident response plan and initiate a dialog to enhance public-private partnerships.
9. Develop a research and development framework focusing on game-changing technologies that have the potential to enhance the security of digital infrastructure and provide the research community access to relevant data.
10. Build a cybersecurity-based identity management vision and strategy that addresses privacy and civil liberties' interests.

called for increasing penalties for cybercrimes, giving the DHS more authority to protect the dot-gov domain, creating a national cybersecurity education campaign, and establishing reporting requirements for data breaches in order to standardize divergent state laws.[35] Globally, the administration has explicitly affirmed what has been apparent for some time – international cooperation is vital to enhancing cybersecurity.[36]

The reception that these cybersecurity proposals received in Congress was initially welcoming, with former Senator Joe Lieberman saying that without such action the Internet would become a "digital Dodge City."[37] Senators Susan Collins and Tom Carper also praised the review's call for enhanced public-private partnerships, which mirrored provisions from the Lieberman-Carper-Collins bill discussed in Chapter 5.[38] Criticisms focused on the need "to spell out presidential authority" over

---

[34] CYBERSPACE POLICY REVIEW, *supra* note 30, at iii.

[35] *See id.* at iv–vi; Siobhan Gorman, *White House Cybersecurity Plan Boosts Chances of Bipartisan Bill*, WALL ST. J. (May 12, 2011), http://online.wsj.com/article/SB10001424052748704681904576319 613484927634.html?mod=googlenews_wsj.

[36] *See* CYBERSPACE POLICY REVIEW, *supra* note 30, at i; INTERNATIONAL STRATEGY FOR CYBERSPACE: PROSPERITY, SECURITY, AND OPENNESS IN A NETWORKED WORLD, WHITE HOUSE 20–21 (2011) [hereinafter INTERNATIONAL STRATEGY FOR CYBERSPACE].

[37] Josh Smith, *Lawmakers Express Optimism, Concerns Over White House Cybersecurity Plan*, NAT'L J. (May 24, 2011), http://www.nationaljournal.com/tech/lawmakers-express-optimism-concerns-over-white-house-cybersecurity-plan-20110523.

[38] *Id.*

the Internet during "a national emergency[,]"[39] and the lack of binding requirements for CNI operators.[40] With continuing White House support, as well as encouragement from the U.S. Chamber of Commerce among other groups, cybersecurity may be an area where bipartisan compromise is possible if ideological divides may be overcome.[41] As of this publication, though, cooperation has proven elusive,[42] though there has been progress made especially regarding the 2014 NIST Cybersecurity Framework.[43] Outstanding questions remain as to whether galvanized action will only occur in the event of a major cyber attack, and to what part U.S. reform efforts will play in shaping global cyber politics.

The Global Politics of Internet Reform

What more should the international community do to regulate cyberspace? Some nations including Russia have publicly sought a cyber weapons treaty to enhance cybersecurity, which could morph into a Treaty for Cyberspace in the mold of the Outer Space Treaty or the UN Convention on the Law of the Sea.[44] In the best case, such a treaty could help mitigate a cyber arms race and clarify the principles

---

[39] Eric Chabrow, *Obama Cybersecurity Package Praised, Criticized*, GovInfoSecurity.com (May 23, 2011), http://www.govinfosecurity.com/articles.php?art_id=3669.

[40] *See* Gorman, *supra* note 35.

[41] *See* Grant Goss, *Cybersecurity Bill Fails in U.S. Senate*, Computer World (Nov. 14, 2012), http://www.computerworld.com/s/article/9233656/Cybersecurity_bill_fails_in_U.S._Senate; Brancaccio, *supra* note 29.

[42] See Alexei Alexis, *House Homeland Security Leaders Said Close to Unveiling Cybersecurity Bill*, Bloomberg BNA (June 10, 2013), http://www.bna.com/house-homeland-security-n17179874424/ (reporting on cybersecurity reform efforts in the House and Senate as of June 2013); Carl Franzen, *Outcry Over PRISM Spying Delays CISPA and Other Cyber Bills from Moving Forward*, Verge (June 28, 2013), http://www.theverge.com/2013/6/28/4474438/prism-fallout-delays-advance-of-other-cyber-bills (suggesting that cybersecurity bills would not be introduced until the fall of 2013 because of blowback from revelations regarding the NSA's PRISM program).

[43] *See* Executive Order 13636: Improving Critical Infrastructure Cybersecurity, 78 Fed. Reg. 33, 11739 (Feb. 12, 2013); Gerald Ferguson, *NIST Cybersecurity Framework: Don't Underestimate It*, Info. Wk. (Dec. 9, 2013), http://www.informationweek.com/government/cybersecurity/nist-cybersecurity-framework-dont-underestimate-it/d/d-id/1112978. *See also* Nelson Peacock, *Cybersecurity Could Be the Next Bipartisan Breakthrough*, Hill (Jan. 30, 2014), http://mobile.thehill.com/blogs/congress-blog/technology/196026-cybersecurity-could-be-the-next-bipartisan-breakthrough (discussing the potential of a cybersecurity bill passing Congress in 2014, and reporting that a January 2014 "bill in its present form would codify and strengthen civilian cybersecurity authorities within DHS consistent with policy doctrine under both President Bush and Obama, help DHS expand its work with the private sector, and amend the Safety Act to establish a threshold for qualifying cyber incidents to help address liability issues related to cybersecurity."). *But see* Tony Romm, *Cybersecurity in Slow Lane One Year After Obama Order*, Politico (Feb. 9, 2014), http://www.politico.com/story/2014/02/cybersecurity-in-slow-lane-one-year-after-obama-order-103307.html?hp=f1 ("Nearly a year after President Barack Obama issued an executive order to improve the cybersecurity of the nation's vital assets, the administration doesn't have much to show: The government is about to produce only some basic standards, with little incentive for the private sector to participate.").

[44] *See* Duncan Hollis, *Should There Be an International Treaty on Cyberwarfare?*, Opinio Juris (June 13, 2012), http://opiniojuris.org/2012/06/13/should-there-be-an-international-treaty-on-cyberwarfare/ (responding to a *US News*-sponsored debate on the desirability of an international cyber weapons treaty).

of the law of cyber war and peace explored in Chapter 6, such as by better defining which targets are legal in a cyber conflict as well as formally establishing the rights and responsibilities of neutral states.[45] Putting aside for the moment whether or not such rules would be well-designed, useful, or followed, at least the players would finally know the rules of the game. This could by itself prove helpful, as cybersecurity policymaking has been likened to a "five-year old soccer game, with everyone chasing the ball in a cluster and without a clear game plan."[46] Because of deep geopolitical and sociocultural divisions between the cyber powers, however, a grand bargain is unlikely for the foreseeable future.[47] A targeted cybercrime treaty, or one that focuses on common "environmental" effects and protects "the core working of the Internet" including CNI holds more promise.[48] However, because of differing priorities and national strategies discussed in Chapter 4, even there the international political situation may not be aligned for significant progress.

Because cyber technology is so new and promising as a tool for achieving geopolitical goals, some find benefit in the *"status quo* of strategic ambiguity,"[49] including the United States.[50] For example, whereas the U.S. government ostensibly pushes an Internet freedom agenda built on a vision of the Internet as a "global networked commons,"[51] China, in a 2010 Internet White Paper, highlighted the importance of Internet sovereignty and governments' rights to control content within their sovereign networks.[52] These differences, which were explored in Chapter 2, are undermining efforts to collaborate, even in the face of common interests, such as working to prevent a third-party organization from launching a cyber attack designed to instigate a U.S.-China conflict.[53]

Otto von Bismarck famously said, "Politics is the art of the possible, the attainable, the art of the next best."[54] This begs the question: what can stakeholders do

---

[45] *See id.* (reporting that a treaty could accomplish an array of other functions beyond arms control from establishing norms to regulating third-party attacks on CNI).

[46] Doug DePeppe, *A Taxonomy for the National Cybersecurity Doctrine,* CSO (Jan. 21, 2013), http://www.csoonline.com/article/727099/a-taxonomy-for-the-national-cybersecurity-doctrine?page=1.

[47] *See* Joseph S. Nye, Jr., *Power and National Security in Cyberspace, in* AMERICA'S CYBER FUTURE: SECURITY AND PROSPERITY IN THE INFORMATION AGE 5, 19–20 (Kristin M. Lord & Travis Sharp eds., CNAS, 2011) [hereinafter AMERICA'S CYBER FUTURE].

[48] *Id.*

[49] Rex B. Hughes, *NATO and Cyber Defence: Mission Accomplished?,* ATLANTISCH PERSPECTIEF 3 (Apr. 2009), http://www.carlisle.army.mil/DIME/documents/NATO%20and%20Cyber%20Defence.pdf.

[50] *See, e.g.,* David E. Sanger, *Obama Order Sped Up Wave of Cyberattacks Against Iran,* N.Y. TIMES (June 1, 2012), http://www.nytimes.com/2012/06/01/world/middleeast/obama-ordered-wave-of-cyberattacks-against-iran.html?pagewanted=all.

[51] Hillary Rodham Clinton, U.S. Sec'y State, Remarks on Internet Freedom (Jan. 21, 2010), http://www.state.gov/secretary/rm/2010/01/135519.htm.

[52] Evan Osnos, *Can China Maintain "Sovereignty" Over the Internet?,* NEW YORKER (June 11, 2010), http://www.newyorker.com/online/blogs/evanosnos/2010/06/what-is-internet-sovereignty-in-china.html.

[53] *See* Nye, Jr., *in* AMERICA'S CYBER FUTURE, *supra* note 47, at 5, 20.

[54] PATRICK DUNLEAVY, DEMOCRATIC POLITICS AND THE STATE 23 (2011).

now, while a grand cyber treaty is beyond reach, to improve global cybersecurity? Many nations, including China, Russia, and the United States, have established formal command authorities in cyberspace, as discussed in Chapter 4, and more still have organized CERTs.[55] However, the United States has also envisioned something grander than a state-centric approach to cybersecurity, having put forth one of the more comprehensive global visions for cyberspace to date – the "International Strategy for Cyberspace," which the Obama administration unveiled, somewhat belatedly, in May 2011.[56] In it, the White House set forth goals for "defense, diplomacy, and international development" in cyberspace.[57] Analyzing this document holds clues for the promise and perils of polycentric mechanisms to improve global cybersecurity.

The name "International Strategy for Cyberspace" itself marks a departure from earlier U.S. positions on cybersecurity, suggesting that cyberspace is not viewed as a realm that the United States should unilaterally dominate.[58] Instead, the strategy promotes multilateral cooperation to reduce cyber threats and to ensure that the Internet remains "free, secure, and reliable."[59] It does this by advocating key policy priorities, including enhancing cybersecurity; strengthening "national and international" regulations to combat cybercrime; promoting multi-stakeholder governance; building "secure networks[,]" especially in developing nations; and promoting Internet freedom, including guaranteeing privacy and freedom of expression and association online.[60] Embedded in this list are some bedrock principles of U.S. ideology at which some nations might balk, although somewhat surprisingly, Russia signed off on many of these principles in a 2011 G-8 communiqué.[61] Yet the geopolitical ground shifted in 2013 because of NSA revelations resulting in a UN General Assembly resolution on the right to privacy in the digital age mentioned in Chapter 6, which voices support for extending human rights protections into cyberspace and received

---

[55] *Oman's CERT Designated as Regional Cyber Security Centre in the Arab World*, ITA (Dec. 15, 2012), http://www.ita.gov.om/ITAPortal/MediaCenter/NewsDetail.aspx?NID=476 [hereinafter Regional Cybersecurity Center].

[56] *See* David Gerwitz, *The Obama Cyberdoctrine: Tweet Softly, but Carry a Big Stick*, ZDNET (May 17, 2011), http://www.zdnet.com/blog/government/the-obama-cyberdoctrine-tweet-softly-but-carry-a-big-stick/10400.

[57] Ellen Nakashima, *Obama Administration Outlines International Strategy for Cyberspace*, WASH. POST (May 16, 2011), http://www.washingtonpost.com/world/obama-administration-outlines-international-strategy-for-cyberspace/2011/05/16/AFokL54G_story.html?hpid=z3.

[58] *But see* Sanger, *supra* note 50 (reporting how the Obama administration continued, and in fact accelerated, the Bush administration's policy of launching cyber attacks on Iranian uranium enrichment facilities).

[59] Clinton, *supra* note 51.

[60] INTERNATIONAL STRATEGY FOR CYBERSPACE, *supra* note 36, at 10, 12, 23–24.

[61] *See* G8 DECLARATION: RENEWED COMMITMENT FOR FREEDOM AND DEMOCRACY, May 26–27, 2011, para. 5, http://ec.europa.eu/commission_2010-2014/president/news/speeches-statements/pdf/deauville-g8-declaration_en.pdf (reporting that "for the first time . . . we agreed . . . on a number of key principles, including freedom, respect for privacy and intellectual property, multi-stakeholder governance, cyber-security, and protection from crime, that underpin a strong and flourishing Internet.").

widespread support in late 2013.[62] In China, state-run media has been increasingly critical of the U.S. position on Internet governance, suggesting that the United States is pushing cooperation and "the Internet freedom agenda" as a farce to maintain its "technological lead" in cyberspace.[63] Multi-stakeholder governance that includes the private sector is par for the course in the United States – not necessarily so in Russia or China, nor in many other emerging markets.[64] Yet the strategy itself fails to provide examples for how to make successful multi-stakeholder governance work.[65] Instead of acting solely as a call for international collaboration, then, the strategy may also be read as an opening salvo to move toward a cyber Pax Americana before other nations solidify opposing ideologies built on a more robust role for the state in governance and security.[66] Even if that was the intention, though, Snowden's leaks caused an "unintended Internet revolution" in 2013-14 in which core Internet institutions including ICANN and IETF allied themselves with nations such as Brazil in an attempt to globalize Internet governance, as discussed later in the chapter.[67]

The strategy is just a beginning with prescriptions omitted because, as former Secretary of State Clinton remarked, "There is no one-size-fits-all, straightforward route" to a cyberspace that is, in the words of President Obama, "open, interoperable, secure, and reliable. . . ."[68] Important questions remain to be answered about

---

[62] The Right to Privacy in the Digital Age, Nov. 1, 2013, UN Doc. A/C.3/68/L.45 (2013), http://daccess-dds-ny.un.org/doc/UNDOC/GEN/N13/544/07/PDF/N1354407.pdf?OpenElement ("A total of 55 drafts were passed without a vote, including a text on the emerging question of cyberspace privacy. By the terms of that text, titled 'Right to privacy in the digital age', the Assembly established, for the first time, that human rights should prevail irrespective of the medium, and therefore the need for protection both offline and online.").

[63] Adam Segal, *Chinese Responses to the International Strategy for Cyberspace*, COUNCIL FOREIGN REL. (May 23, 2011), http://blogs.cfr.org/asia/2011/05/23/chinese-responses-to-the-international-strategy-for-cyberspace/.

[64] *See* Robert M. McDowell, *The U.N. Threat to Internet Freedom*, WALL ST. J. (Feb. 21, 2012), http://online.wsj.com/article/SB10001424052970204792404577229074023195322.html.

[65] Different camps in the Internet governance debate use the term "multi-stakeholder" to describe their position, which can be confusing. The crux of the difference, as explained by Brendan Kuerbis, though is "between state-centric multilateral and non-state multistakeholder governance." Brendan Kuerbis, *The 'Iron Cage' of Multistakeholder Governance*, INTERNET GOVERNANCE FORUM (Jan. 28, 2014), http://www.internetgovernance.org/.

[66] For a more comprehensive discussion of the strategy and its geopolitical implications, see David P. Fidler, *International Law and the Future of Cyberspace: The Obama Administration's International Strategy for Cyberspace*, 15 ASIL INSIGHTS (June 8, 2011), http://www.asil.org/pdfs/insights/insight110608.pdf.

[67] *See* Andrew Leonard, *Edward Snowden's Unintended Internet Revolution*, SALON (Oct. 15, 2013), http://www.salon.com/2013/10/15/edward_snowdens_unintended_internet_revolution/; *Montevideo Statement on the Future of Internet Cooperation*, ICANN (Oct. 7, 2013), http://www.icann.org/en/news/announcements/announcement-07oct13-en.htm.

[68] Chris Lefkow, *White House Unveils Global Cyberspace Strategy*, AFP (May 16, 2011), http://www.google.com/hostednews/afp/article/ALeqM5j0YrkwYuuRQt8WzDHiF-VOJ3OfKw; *see also* INTERNATIONAL STRATEGY FOR CYBERSPACE, *supra* note 36, at 3, 8 (stating the overriding U.S. goal in cyberspace is to "work internationally to promote an open, interoperable, secure, and reliable" cyberspace).

how to achieve these lofty principles.[69] However, the fact that these goals have been enumerated is significant, as is the extent to which they highlight several themes explored throughout this book, including the need to clarify national and international laws to help hold cyber attackers more accountable, the necessity of increasing information sharing between stakeholders, the importance of norms, and, implicitly, the rise of polycentric governance in cyberspace.[70]

One specific component of the International Strategy for Cyberspace is a proposal to create "international standards with penalties for countries and organizations that f[a]ll short."[71] This initiative requires DHS, Pentagon, Justice, Commerce, and State Department officials "to work with their counterparts around the world" to negotiate and adopt best practices.[72] Such an approach may reinforce an evolving polycentric cybersecurity regime, bringing "like-minded nations together on a host of issues, such as technical standards and acceptable legal norms regarding territorial jurisdiction, sovereign responsibility, and use of force."[73] Professor Nye has argued that such a bilateral approach catalyzed nuclear disarmament talks once they focused on common environmental issues, such as atmospheric testing.[74] Similarly, focusing on common irritants, such as spam, could help lay a foundation on which to build a more comprehensive agreement. By 1985, Professor Nye points out, Presidents Ronald Reagan and Mikhail Gorbachev were able to agree: "Nuclear war cannot be won and must never be fought."[75] Although it is unlikely that Presidents Obama and Putin will pronounce that "Cyber war cannot be won and must never be fought" in 2014, bilateral talks between the key established and emerging cyber powers might lay the groundwork of both the technical expertise and goodwill necessary for such a day to come.[76] For example, although the U.S. and Russian governments have long held

---

[69] *See* Helene Cooper, *U.S. Calls for Global Cybersecurity Strategy*, N.Y. TIMES (May 17, 2011), http://www.nytimes.com/2011/05/17/us/politics/17cyber.html.

[70] *See* INTERNATIONAL STRATEGY FOR CYBERSPACE, *supra* note 36, at 3, 9–11.

[71] Cooper, *supra* note 69.

[72] *Id.; see* INTERNATIONAL STRATEGY FOR CYBERSPACE, *supra* note 36, at 21.

[73] CYBERSPACE POLICY REVIEW, *supra* note 30, at iv.

[74] *See* Nye, Jr., *in* AMERICA'S CYBER FUTURE, *supra* note 47, at 5, 20; Abraham D. Sofaer, David Clark, & Whitfield Diffie, *Cyber Security and International Agreements, in* PROCEEDINGS OF A WORKSHOP ON DETERRING CYBERATTACKS: INFORMING STRATEGIES AND DEVELOPING OPTIONS FOR U.S. POLICY 179, 205 (2010) (arguing that "[b]ilateral and information arrangements could be used to build toward a broader set of understandings sufficient to justify attempting to create a more conventional, multilateral [cybersecurity] agreement.").

[75] Nye, Jr., *in* AMERICA'S CYBER FUTURE, *supra* note 47, at 5, 20 (citing Joseph S. Nye, Jr., *Nuclear Learning and U.S.-Soviet Security Regimes*, STRAT. STUD. Q. 18, 29 (Winter 2011)).

[76] *See* US and Russia Sign Cyber Security Pact, ATLANTIC COUNCIL (June 18, 2013), http://www .atlanticcouncil.org/blogs/natosource/us-and-russia-sign-cyber-security-pact (reporting on the creation of a joint U.S.-Russian cybersecurity working group that includes information sharing about cyber attacks); *cf.* Hamadoun I. Touré, *The International Response to Cyberwar, in* THE QUEST FOR CYBER PEACE 86, 91 (Int'l Telecomm. Union & Permanent Monitoring Panel on Info. Sec. eds., 2011), http://www.itu.int/dms_pub/itu-s/opb/gen/S-GEN-WFS.01-1-2011-PDF-E.pdf ("Bilateral approaches have also been ventured, but they fall far short of a comprehensive strategy to improve cybersecurity and ensure cyber peace since they only involve a very small fraction of the relevant players in the

high-level bilateral discussions on cybersecurity,[77] U.S.-Chinese discussions were mostly relegated to informal meetings. These talks in recent years have yielded progress on certain topics such as Internet fraud, but mostly continue to expose the "wide gap" between Washington and Beijing on cybersecurity and Internet governance.[78] Nevertheless, in 2011, for the first time, "[t]he annual cabinet-level U.S.-China Strategic and Economic Dialogue included cybersecurity," although the session was reportedly "just 90 minutes long, cut in half by translation and produced no breakthroughs."[79] Still, it is a beginning, and as of March 2013 China expressed willingness to engage in dialogue with the United States to help foster cyber peace.[80] These talks began in June 2013 at a "40,000 foot level," according to President Obama.[81] Focusing on bilateral and regional[82] efforts is also a reflection of the fact that multilateral diplomacy has, so far, borne few fruits.

United Nations-sponsored cyber disarmament discussions have been ongoing since the late 1990s.[83] More recently, ITU Secretary-General Touré has suggested that the ITU "could 'broker' a cyber disarmament accord."[84] Many emerging markets and developing countries support the idea of such an accord, but it makes the United States and certain other developed nations wary, as discussed later in the chapter.[85] This push follows several moves by the ITU to take on a larger role for enhancing global cybersecurity in support of its Member States. For example, in 2007, the

---

cyber peace equation."). Another analogy to consider is the investment context and the rise of bilateral investment treaties. *See* GUS VAN HARTEN, INVESTMENT TREATY ARBITRATION IN PUBLIC LAW 3–5 (2007). These treaties symbolize a bottom-up regulatory response to a multilateral problem – in this case, guaranteeing investor property rights to spur development and potentially protect trade secrets. For further information on this topic, see Scott J. Shackelford et al., *Using BITs To Protect Bytes: Promoting Cyber Peace and Safeguarding Trade Secrets through Bilateral Investment Treaties*, 52 AM. BUS. L.J. __ (forthcoming 2014).

[77] *See* Nye, Jr., *in* AMERICA'S CYBER FUTURE, *supra* note 47, at 5, 20.

[78] Diane Bartz & Paul Eckert, *Great Wall: U.S. and China Face Vast Divide on Cyber Issues*, REUTERS (July 14, 2011), http://www.reuters.com/article/2011/07/14/us-usa-china-cyber-idUSTRE 76D3K020110714.

[79] *Id.*

[80] *See* Terril Yue Jones, *China Says Willing to Discuss Cyber Security with the U.S.*, REUTERS (Mar. 12, 2013), http://www.reuters.com/article/2013/03/12/us-usa-china-cybersecurity-idUSBRE92A0 XO20130312.

[81] *See* Amanda Sakuma, *US, China Enter 'Uncharted Waters' in Cybersecurity Talks*, MSNBC (June 8, 2013), http://tv.msnbc.com/2013/06/08/a-enter-uncharted-waters-in-cybersecurity-talks/; *cf. Spying Revelations Affect US-China Cyber Security Talks*, VOICE OF AM. (June 25, 2013), http://www.voanews .com/content/spying-revelations-affect-us-china-cyber-security-talks/1688596.html (reporting on the impact of U.S. government cyber espionage programs on U.S.-China cybersecurity talks) [hereinafter *Spying Revelations*].

[82] *See, e.g.*, Regional Cybersecurity Center, *supra* note 55 (discussing regional cybersecurity collaboration in the Arab world).

[83] *See* Tom Gjelten, *Seeing the Internet as an 'Information Weapon,'* NPR (Sept. 23, 2010), http://www .npr.org/templates/story/story.php?storyId=130052701.

[84] *Id.*

[85] *Id.*

ITU launched the Global Cybersecurity Agenda (GCA) to serve as a "framework for international cooperation aimed at enhancing confidence and security in the information society."[86] The GCA was operationalized through the International Multilateral Partnership Against Cyber Threats (IMPACT), which has been billed as the "world's first comprehensive alliance against cyber threats" and is tasked with "providing cybersecurity assistance and support to ITU's 193 Member States and also to other organisations within the UN system."[87] IMPACT has helped strengthen cybersecurity defenses in a number of nations and regions,[88] though some argue that the fact that the ITU has historically been a somewhat state-centric organization with a relatively circumscribed role for the private sector militates against expanding its scope to include cybersecurity.[89]

The global politics of Internet reform have long been inconsistent with a multi-lateral cyber arms control treaty, in part because of varying interpretations for what the end goal should be. According to Jim Dempsey, a global treaty could "prohibit stuff that we like and authorize stuff that we don't like all in the name of cyber peace. I mean, the harmonious Internet, that's the Chinese concept – they want a peaceful Internet too, just on their terms."[90] Until 2009, the United States had worked to thwart attempts at international cyber arms-control "for fear that this could lead to rigid global regulation of the internet" that would undermine U.S. technological dominance, stymie innovation, and restrict openness.[91] But this stance has begun to change under the Obama administration,[92] potentially because of a growing recognition that the United States, as a country increasingly reliant on cyberspace,

---

[86] *Global Cybersecurity Agenda*, ITU, http://www.itu.int/osg/csd/cybersecurity/gca/ (last visited June 30, 2013). In the aftermath of the 2010 WSIS and 2010 ITU Plenipotentiary Conference, the ITU similarly acknowledged that "a fundamental role of the ITU . . . is to build confidence and security in the use of information and communication technologies." *ITU Activities Related to Cybersecurity*, ITU, http://www.itu.int/cybersecurity/ (last visited Jan. 30, 2014) (listing the GCA and IMPACT, as well as other initiatives designed to protect children online and aid in secure standards development).

[87] *About Us*, IMPACT, http://www.impact-alliance.org/aboutus/ITU-IMPACT.html (last visited Feb. 9, 2014); *see Strategy*, ITU, http://www.itu.int/en/ITU-D/Cybersecurity/Pages/Strategy.aspx (last visited Jan. 24, 2014); IMPACT, http://www.impact-alliance.org/aboutus/mission-&-vision.html (last visited Jan. 24, 2014).

[88] *See, e.g.*, Regional Cybersecurity Center, *supra* note 55.

[89] *See* ROBERT K. KNAKE, COUNCIL ON FOREIGN RELATIONS, INTERNET GOVERNANCE IN AN AGE OF CYBER INSECURITY 8 (2010), http://i.cfr.org/content/publications/attachments/Cybersecurity_CSR56.pdf; Andrea Renda, *Cybersecurity and Internet Governance*, COUNCIL FOREIGN REL. (May 3, 2013), http://www.cfr.org/cybersecurity/cybersecurity-internet-governance/p30621.

[90] Interview with Jim Dempsey, vice president for public policy, Center for Democracy & Technology, in San Francisco, Cal. (Feb. 22, 2011).

[91] *Cyberwar: The Threat from the Internet*, ECONOMIST (July 1, 2010), http://www.economist.com/node/16481504 [hereinafter *Cyberwar*]; *see also US Joins UN Cyber Arms Control Collaboration*, COMPUTER WKLY. (July 20, 2010), http://www.computerweekly.com/news/1280093311/US-joins-UN-cyber-arms-control-collaboration (reporting on growing U.S. support for a cyber arms control treaty).

[92] *See* TIM MAURER, CYBER NORM EMERGENCE AT THE UNITED NATIONS: AN ANALYSIS OF THE ACTIVITIES AT THE UN REGARDING CYBER-SECURITY 3 (2011).

is also among the most vulnerable to cyber attacks.[93] The development of U.S. and other nations' cyber weapons increases the urgency of negotiations.[94]

As the cyber threat mounts, some nations are now joining a chorus of others "calling for a cyber arms-control treaty," with the loudest voice singing in Russian.[95] Since 1998, Russia has regularly introduced a UN resolution to combat "information terrorism."[96] In 2009, it went even further, successfully sponsoring a "cyber disarmament proposal" at the Shanghai Cooperation Organization that in part defined "information war" as an effort by a state to undermine another's "political, economic, and social systems."[97] Russia, however, is far from being alone in its views.[98] As was explored in Chapter 2, governments around the world are seeking to both manage cyber weapons and to exert greater influence in Internet governance. Engagement is critical, which is why General Alexander, formerly of CYBERCOM, has welcomed "Russia's longstanding calls for a treaty as a 'starting point for international debate.'"[99] If attacks like Stuxnet do "cross the Rubicon," steps must be taken to control these weapons before we move further into "uncharted territory."[100]

One of the main advances toward addressing cybersecurity multilaterally thus far occurred on July 16, 2010 when fifteen nations – including the United States, Russia, and China – presented a report to the UN Secretary General that included a framework for cooperative measures to address cyber threats.[101] The report was the culmination of a diplomatic process begun by the United States, China, and Russia in 2005 when then-UN Secretary-General Kofi Annan appointed the Group of Governmental Experts on Developments in the Field of Information and Telecommunications in the Context of International Security[102] – a complex name for an equally complex undertaking. The group was tasked with identifying cyber threats and reporting back to the United Nations. Although important issues were sidestepped,[103] there was agreement to continue multilateral efforts "to reduce collective risk and

---

[93] *See Cyberwar, supra* note 91.

[94] *See, e.g.,* Sanger, *supra* note 50; James Blitz, *UK Becomes First State to Admit to Offensive Cyber Attack Capability,* FIN. TIMES (Sept. 29, 2013), http://www.ft.com/intl/cms/s/0/9ac6ede6-28fd-11e3-ab62-00144feab7de.html#axzz2rohGeqFy.

[95] MAURER, *supra* note 92, at 20.

[96] Gjelten, *supra* note 83.

[97] *Id.*; Richard Fontaine & Will Rogers, *Internet Freedom and its Discontents: Navigating the Tensions with Cyber Security, in* AMERICA'S CYBER FUTURE, *supra* note 47, at 145, 152.

[98] *See, e.g.,* Letter, International Code of Conduct for Information Security, Sept. 12, 2011, from the Permanent Representatives of China, the Russian Federation, Tajikistan and Uzbekistan to the United Nations addressed to the Secretary-General, http://www.rusemb.org.uk/policycontact/49.

[99] *Cyberwar, supra* note 91.

[100] Misha Glenny, *A Weapon We Can't Control,* N.Y. TIMES (June 25, 2012), http://www.nytimes.com/2012/06/25/opinion/stuxnet-will-come-back-to-haunt-us.html.

[101] *See* John Markoff, *Step Taken to End Impasse Over Cybersecurity Talks,* N.Y. TIMES (July 16, 2010), http://www.nytimes.com/2010/07/17/world/17cyber.html.

[102] Report of the Secretary-General, UN General Assembly, A/60/150 (Aug. 5, 2005).

[103] *See US Joins UN Cyber Arms Control Collaboration, supra* note 91.

protect critical national and international infrastructures."[104] Indeed, in late 2013 the group agreed on a "substantial and forward-looking" follow-up report that, among much else, recognized "the full applicability of international law to state behavior in cyberspace."[105] These reports could serve as a stepping-stone to build consensus on more substantive agreements that engage core issues and provide a firmer foundation for effective Internet governance and enhancing global cybersecurity.[106]

THE FUTURE OF INTERNET GOVERNANCE

Two meetings, one a G-8 conference in May 2011 and the other in December 2012, demonstrate divergent views on the future of Internet governance. First, in May 2011 the G-8 group of developed countries met to discuss – among much else – Internet governance, ultimately agreeing "on a number of key principles, including freedom, respect for privacy and intellectual property, multi-stakeholder governance, cyber-security, and protection from crime, that underpin a strong and flourishing Internet."[107] Another shadow G-8 meeting was occurring at the same time – a meeting of the virtual masters of the universe called the "e-G8," including Eric Schmidt of Google and Mark Zuckerberg of Facebook.[108] In the face of mounting government regulation, these business leaders called for the private sector to remain the driving force behind the Internet, echoing themes from the International Strategy for Cyberspace including openness and transparency.[109] Schmidt and Zuckerberg warned of legislating before understanding the consequences and cherry-picking aspects of the web to control.[110] Others in attendance included Professor Lessig, who reportedly insisted that government should exercise a "light touch" online.[111] Whether such a light touch is possible in nations that have already proven their

[104] UN Secretary-General, Report of the Group of Governmental Experts on Developments in the Field of Information and Telecommunications in the Context of International Security, 8, UN Doc. A/65/201, art. 18(i) (July 30, 2010).

[105] Deltev Wolter, *The UN Takes a Big Step Forward on Cybersecurity*, ARMS CONTROL ASSOC. (Sept. 2013), http://www.armscontrol.org/act/2013_09/The-UN-Takes-a-Big-Step-Forward-on-Cybersecurity; UN General Assembly, Group of Governmental Experts on Developments in the Field of Information and Telecommunications in the Context of International Security, UN Doc. A/68/98 (June 24, 2013). *See also* Timothy Farnsworth, *UN Creates New Group on Cyberspace Issues*, ARMS CONTROL ASSOC. (Dec. 2013), http://www.armscontrol.org/act/2013_12/UN-Creates-New-Group-on-Cyberspace-Issues (reporting the formation of a new group of experts comprised of twenty nations with "a mandate to examine 'developments in the field of information and telecommunications in the context of international security.'").

[106] *See* MAURER, *supra* note 92, at 47 (noting that there are "clear signs of nascent cyber norms slowly emerging.").

[107] Deauville G-8 Declaration, Renewed Commitment for Freedom and Democracy (May 27, 2011), http://ec.europa.eu/commission_2010-2014/president/news/speeches-statements/pdf/deauville-g8-declaration_en.pdf [hereinafter 2011 G-8 Declaration].

[108] *See* Zuckerberg & Schmidt, *supra* note 16.

[109] *See* INTERNATIONAL STRATEGY FOR CYBERSPACE, *supra* note 36, at 3, 9.

[110] Zuckerberg & Schmidt, *supra* note 16.

[111] *Id.*

propensity for heavy-handed regulation, or desirable in terms of enhancing cybersecurity, is another question.

Jump ahead to December 2012, when the World Conference on International Telecommunications (WCIT) was held by the ITU. During the WCIT, the 193 ITU member states reviewed and considered revising the International Telecommunication Regulations (ITRs), which were last negotiated in 1988 and "facilitate international interconnection and [the] interoperability of information and communication services. . . ."[112] Concerns abounded regarding WCIT more so than is typical of many ITU proceedings. Vint Cerf told the U.S. Congress that new ITRs could undermine the Internet's openness and "lead to 'top-down control dictated by governments. . . .'"[113] Numerous U.S. congressional representatives expressed similar sentiments.[114] Concerns centered on the prospect of the summit being "hijacked" by nations including China and Russia seeking to codify greater state control of Internet governance and security.[115] These worries seemed to have been legitimated in June 2012 when preparatory documents were leaked purportedly "show[ing] that many ITU member states want to use international agreements to regulate the Internet by crowding out bottom-up institutions, imposing charges for international communication, and controlling the content that consumers can access online."[116] Critics worried that such proposals would give the UN too much power over the Internet,[117] though Internet governance likely falls outside of the ITU's mandate. The U.S. government has opposed a larger Internet governance role for foreign nations or the ITU,[118] but authoritarian regimes lobbied UN member states to vote their way.[119] Eighty-nine countries signed the WCIT final resolution that on the one

---

[112] World Conference on International Telecommunications (WCIT-12), http://www.itu.int/en/wcit-12/Pages/default.aspx (last visited Jan. 30, 2014); *see* INT'L TELECOMM. UNION, FINAL ACTS OF THE WORLD CONFERENCE ON INTERNATIONAL TELECOMMUNICATIONS (2012) [hereinafter ITU RESOLUTIONS], http://www.itu.int/en/wcit-12/Documents/final-acts-wcit-12.pdf.

[113] Declan McCullagh, *U.N. Takeover of the Internet Must be Stopped, U.S. Warns*, CNET (May 31, 2012), http://news.cnet.com/8301-1009_3-57444629-83/u.n-takeover-of-the-internet-must-be-stopped-u.s-warns (quoting Cerf, who opined that "the open Internet has never been at a higher risk than it is now.").

[114] *See id.* (quoting Rep. Fred Upton and Rep. Anna Eshoo, who both expressed their disapproval over the prospect of greater ITU involvement in Internet governance).

[115] Carl Franzen, *U.N. Telecom Agency Releases Secret Treaty, Critics Unswayed*, TPM (July 13, 2012), http://idealab.talkingpointsmemo.com/2012/07/un-telecom-agency-releases-secret-treaty-critics-unswayed.php; *see also* Int'l Telecomm. Union, Proposals Received from ITU Member States for the Work of the Conference, Doc. WCIT12/DT/1-E (2012), at 99, http://www.soumu.go.jp/main_content/000188223.pdf (listing a Russian proposal for Article 3A: "Member States shall have equal rights to manage the Internet, including in regard to the allotment, assignment and reclamation of Internet numbering, naming, addressing and identification resources and to support for the operation and development of the basic Internet infrastructure.").

[116] L. Gordon Crovitz, *The U.N.'s Internet Power Grab*, WALL STREET J. (June 17, 2012), http://online.wsj.com/article/SB10001424052702303822204577470532859210296.html.

[117] *Id.*

[118] *See, e.g.*, Leo Kelion, *US Resists Control of Internet Passing to UN Agency*, BBC (Aug. 3, 2012), http://www.bbc.co.uk/news/technology-19106420.

[119] *See id.* (voicing the ITU's opposition to voting and affirming that any changes to the ITRs must have unanimous support).

hand embraces multi-stakeholder governance, but on the other determines that "all governments should have an equal role and responsibility for international Internet governance and for ensuring the stability, security and continuity of the existing Internet. . . ."[120] This language only appears in a non-binding resolution entitled "Fostering an Enabling Environment for the Internet," but it has been seized on by some as heralding a growing state-centric view of cyberspace held in many nations, especially in Asia (with the notable exceptions of India, Japan, and Australia) and Africa.[121] Such a view could lead to more regulations on content – what we generally think of as censorship – among other restrictions, though at least some of the opposition stemmed from a change in voting practices from consensus to a one-nation, one-vote basis.[122]

These meetings seem to demonstrate two very different visions of Internet governance – one a top-down approach with national governments at the center, the other bottom-up governance favoring the private sector amidst multiple stakeholders. But, as discussed in Chapter 2, this debate between Internet freedom and sovereignty is an oversimplification and ultimately a false choice. Instead of a black and white comparison, what may be more accurate is investigating the myriad shades of gray that comprise the complexion of global Internet regulations to find common ground. After all, even the G-8 countries that espouse Internet freedom and a decentralized approach to Internet governance still envision a role for national governments,[123] while the WCIT declaration discusses the importance of multi-stakeholder governance and was negotiated at a meeting with hundreds of private firms present.[124] Yet even if we are not heading for an age of outright Internet balkanization, we may be in for a period of greater state involvement in Internet governance. Whether through the ITU or on their own initiative, states will likely continue to assert greater power online in the name of controlling restive populations, fighting cybercrime, or securing CNI. The open questions are: what costs will this impose in terms of innovation

---

[120] *Resolution Plen/3 (Dubai 2012): To Foster an Enabling Environment for the Greater Growth of the Internet*, in FINAL ACTS OF THE WORLD CONFERENCE ON INTERNATIONAL TELECOMMUNICATIONS 20 (2012), http://www.itu.int/en/wcit-12/Pages/default.aspx [hereinafter ITU Resolution].

[121] *See WCIT-12 Final Acts Signatories*, INT'L TELECOMM. UNION (Dec. 14, 2012), http://www.itu.int/osg/wcit-12/highlights/signatories.html [hereinafter ITU Signatories].

[122] *See ITU Phobia: Why WCIT Was Derailed*, INTERNET GOVERNANCE PROJ. (Dec. 18, 2012), http://www.internetgovernance.org/2012/12/18/itu-phobia-why-wcit-was-derailed; Ambassador Terry Kramer, *Remarks*, U.S. DEP'T ST. (Dec. 13, 2012), http://www.state.gov/e/eb/rls/rm/2012/202040.htm (explaining U.S. opposition to changing the multi-stakeholder model of Internet governance including the extension of national or intergovernmental control online). Though subsequent ITU meetings have met with more success, such as the World Summit on the Information Society 2013, paranoia about the ITU's role in Internet governance continues in many countries, including the United States. *See* WSIS Forum 2013, http://www.itu.int/wsis/implementation/2013/forum/ (last visited Jan. 30, 2014); Steven Cherry, *Paranoia Update: U.N. to Take Over the Internet*, IEEE SPECTRUM (Dec. 3, 2012), http://spectrum.ieee.org/podcast/telecom/internet/paranoia-update-un-to-take-over-the-internet.

[123] 2011 G-8 Declaration, *supra* note 107 ("Governments have a role to play . . . in helping to develop norms of behaviour and common approaches in the use of cyberspace.").

[124] *See* ITU Resolution, *supra* note 120, at 20; *see* WTPF 2013, INT'L TELECOMM. UNION, http://www.itu.int/en/wtpf-13/Pages/overview.aspx (last visited Feb. 28 2012) (noting that additional conferences are also set to deal more directly with issues surrounding multi-stakeholder Internet governance).

and interconnectedness, and how can we manage the growing reach of the leviathan to minimize distortions and enhance cybersecurity while protecting civil liberties? An opportunity to instill the Internet freedom agenda may have been missed at the WCIT-2012, but that does not mean that the Internet as we know it is over. Instead, it should be taken as a call to action for professed Internet freedom proponents, including the United States, to practice what it preaches, and to work with partners around the world to build consensus on the future of Internet governance in an increasingly multipolar world. The April 2014 Global Multistakeholder Conference on the Future of Internet Governance may well be just the first in a series of opportunities to reach such a consensus since,[125] even though the U.S. is negotiating from a weakened position in the wake of NSA revelations, the multi-stakeholder status quo has weathered similar storms in the past.[126]

Beginning with a few researchers' informal ideas, today thousands of entities – including private firms, international organizations, and governments – have a stake in regulating cyberspace, together forming a regime complex.[127] On the one hand, this fracturing makes solving continued questions over Internet governance such as cybersecurity difficult. But on the other hand, it is an opportunity for innovation if political deadlock and turf battles can be overcome, and if the dangers of a "new 'digital divide'" can be mitigated.[128] The two creators of TCP/IP themselves, Vinton Cerf and Robert Kahn, maintain differing views about the desirability and feasibility of various Internet governance reform initiatives, with Cerf reportedly preferring the status quo and Kahn being more open to working with institutions such as the ITU.[129] As arguably both the most important and difficult issue in Internet governance, the promotion of cybersecurity is a crucial test for both the Internet and

---

[125] *See* Milton Mueller, *Booting Up Brazil*, INTERNET GOVERNANCE PROJECT (Nov. 19, 2013), http://www .internetgovernance.org/2013/11/19/booting-up-brazil/ (reporting on a Brazilian news release stating, "The meeting will aim to produce universal internet principles and an institutional framework for multistakeholder internet governance. The framework will include a roadmap to evolve and globalize current institutions, and new mechanisms to address the emerging internet governance topics.").

[126] Milton Mueller & Ben Wagner, *Finding a Formula for Brazil: Representation and Legitimacy in Internet Governance*, INTERNET GOVERNANCE FORUM 26–27 (2014), http://www.internetgovernance .org/wordpress/wp-content/uploads/MiltonBenWPdraft_Final.pdf (discussing, among much else, the desire by private Internet governance organizations such as ICANN "to legitimize their own governance institutions."). *But see* Craig Timberg, *U.S. to Relinquish Remaining Control Over the Internet*, WASH. POST (Mar. 14, 2014), http://www.washingtonpost.com/business/technology/us-to-relinquish-remaining-control-over-the-internet/2014/03/14/0c7472d0-abb5-11e3-adbc-888c8010c799_ story.html?wpmk=MK0000200 (reporting on a March 2014 decision not to renew the contract between ICANN and the U.S. Department of Commerce paving the way for the U.S. government "to relinquish federal government control over the administration of the Internet. . . . ").

[127] *See* Kal Raustiala & David G. Victor, *The Regime Complex for Plant Genetic Resources*, 58(2) INT'L. ORG. 277, 277 (2004).

[128] Larry Downes, *Requiem for Failed UN Telecom Treaty: No One Mourns the WCIT*, FORBES (Dec. 17, 2012), http://www.forbes.com/sites/larrydownes/2012/12/17/no-one-mourns-the-wcit/.

[129] *See* John Markoff, *Viewing Where the Internet Goes*, N.Y. TIMES (Dec. 30, 2013), http://www.nytimes .com/2013/12/31/science/viewing-where-the-internet-goes.html?pagewanted=1&_r=0.

polycentric governance that will help determine whether either a modified system or new regimes are required to help secure cyberspace.

The Rise of Polycentric Governance in Cyberspace

An early international Internet regime came into being during the 1990s with the common acceptance of the TCP/IP protocol.[130] In the years since, however, the notion of minimal national government involvement in Internet governance has been challenged, as has been discussed. State involvement in cyberspace is "the major issue for the next decade," according to Greg Rattray, senior vice president for security at the Financial Services Roundtable and Founding Partner at Delta Risk.[131] And it is also an opportunity with some states being norm entrepreneurs identifying and hastening the uptake of cybersecurity best practices such as with regards to CNI protection.[132] However, aside from national regulations, a mixture of soft law, bilateral and regional accords, customary international law, and multilateral treaties now govern the Internet, though none has the power or mandate to manage the entirety of cyberspace, and gaps persist. For example, according to Rattray, the whole Internet governance debate misses routing: "[t]he major mountain on the landscape is ungoverned."[133] From ICANN to the IETF, national governments to the ITU, differing governance strategies illustrate both the benefits and drawbacks of polycentric governance, as discussed in Chapter 1. The IETF, for one, may be considered a model polycentric system, publishing standards for Internet governance through a time of explosive growth. It represents an organic, bottom-up response to a common problem, as opposed to an externally imposed system such as ICANN.[134] Yet as the "center of gravity" for global telecom competition has shifted eastward,[135] and Chinese companies like Huawei have until recently had relatively little influence on

---

[130] *See* MARKUS FRANDA, GOVERNING THE INTERNET: THE EMERGENCE OF AN INTERNATIONAL REGIME 203 (2001).

[131] Telephone Interview with Greg Rattray, senior vice president for security, BITS Financial Services Roundtable (Feb. 23, 2011). Even a degree of Internet balkanization is a possibility. *See* Marietje Schaake, *Stop Balkanizing the Internet*, HUFF. POST (July 17, 2012), http://www.huffingtonpost.com/marietje-schaake/stop-balkanizing-the-internet_b_1661164.html. Consider China's National Network Information Center's policy of gaining "a worldwide monopoly over the key governing mechanisms of all Internet service in the Chinese language." FRANDA, *supra* note 130, at 209–10. This led the PRC to adopt its own DNS system in 2006, before ICANN accepted internationalized domain names, as discussed in Chapter 1. *See China Adds Top-Level Domain Names*, PEOPLE'S DAILY ONLINE (Feb. 28, 2006), http://english.people.com.cn/200602/28/eng20060228_246712.html. Such policies could eventually result in the fracturing of DNS itself if left unchecked, leading to the formation of distinct national Internets, or intranets. *But see* Markoff, *supra* note 129 (quoting Cerf as saying, "Balkanization is too simple of a concept. . . . [However,] [e]nd-to-end connectivity will vary depending on location.").

[132] *See* MAURER, *supra* note 92, at 47.

[133] Rattray, *supra* note 131.

[134] *See* ANDREW W. MURRAY, THE REGULATION OF CYBERSPACE: CONTROL IN THE ONLINE ENVIRONMENT 233 (2006).

[135] JACK GOLDSMITH & TIM WU, WHO CONTROLS THE INTERNET?: ILLUSIONS OF A BORDERLESS WORLD 101 (2006).

the IETF,[136] the ITU has reemerged as a viable alternative standards body.[137] What potential does polycentric governance have for conceptualizing these governance trends and enhancing global cybersecurity, and can Internet governance organizations conceived in a different era of Internet governance adapt to a multipolar, or even nonpolar, twenty-first century cyberspace?[138] This section analyzes emerging polycentric regimes in cyberspace. The following discussion addresses issues of regime effectiveness and best practices.

As was analyzed in Chapter 2, a basic notion of polycentric governance applied to cyberspace is that diverse organizations and governments working at multiple levels can create policies "that increase levels of voluntary cooperation or increase compliance with rules established by governmental authorities."[139] Among other lessons, this approach suggests that "a single governmental unit" is often incapable of managing global collective action problems, in part because of free riders,[140] such as nations that either lack the resources or refuse to prosecute domestic cybercriminals. Instead, the importance of "smaller-scale effects" and local actors – be they technical communities, individual firms, or even nations – should be recognized within a polycentric framework.[141]

The range of entities now active in cyberspace demonstrates the extent to which governance is fragmenting. Polycentric governance can help conceptualize such a dynamic system, given its embrace of multiple stakeholders, norms, bottom-up

---

[136] U.S. and other Western firms such as Cisco, IBM, and Microsoft are among the most active in drafting and publishing RFCs. *See* Document Statistics, IETF, http://www.arkko.com/tools/docstats (last visited Jan. 31, 2014). *Cf. Huawei Hosts 88th Internet Engineering Task Force Meeting*, IETF (Oct. 29, 2013), www.ietf.org/media/2013-10-29-huawei-hosts-ietf88.html.

[137] *See ITU-T Recommendations*, INT'L TELECOMM. UNION, http://www.itu.int/en/ITU-T/publications/Pages/recs.aspx (last visited Jan. 31, 2014) (noting that ITU standards are often employed in voice over IP (VoIP), videoconferencing, and video compression, which are useful for YouTube, the iTunes store, and Adobe flash player); *Huawei Joins Hands with ITU to Promote ICT Development*, HUAWEI (Oct. 31, 2007), http://www.huawei.com/en/about-huawei/newsroom/press-release/hw-089415-news.htm; Carolyn Duffy Marsan, *IETF vs. ITU: Internet Standards Face-Off*, NETWORKWORLD (Dec. 3, 2012), http://www.networkworld.com/news/2012/120312-argument-ietf-itu-264594.html; Nerea Rial, *ITU, Huawei to Bridge Standards Gap in India*, NEW EUR. (Nov. 26, 2012), http://www.neurope.eu/article/itu-huawei-bridge-standards-gap-india-0.

[138] *See* Richard N. Haass, *The Age of Nonpolarity: What Will Follow U.S. Dominance*, 87(3) FOREIGN AFF., May/June 2008, at 44, 44.

[139] Elinor Ostrom, *A Polycentric Approach for Coping with Climate Change* 12 (World Bank Policy Research Working Paper No. 5095, Oct. 2009).

[140] *Id.* at 35; *see also* Robert O. Keohane & David G. Victor, *The Regime Complex for Climate Change*, at 2 (Harv. Proj. on Int'l Climate Agreements Discussion Paper No. 10-33, 2010) (published as 9 PERSP. ON POL. 7 (2011)), http://belfercenter.ksg.harvard.edu/files/Keohane_Victor_Final_2.pdf (arguing that "regime complexes are not just politically more realistic but they also offer some significant advantages [over comprehensive systems] such as flexibility in substantive content and scope.").

[141] Ostrom, *supra* note 139, at 35, 53; Elinor Ostrom, *Polycentric Systems: Multilevel Governance Involving a Diversity of Organizations, in* GLOBAL ENVIRONMENTAL COMMONS: ANALYTICAL AND POLITICAL CHALLENGES INVOLVING A DIVERSITY OF ORGANIZATIONS 105, 117 (Eric Brousseau et al. eds., 2012) (noting that polycentric systems frequently enjoyed better outcomes than those of central governments).

regulation, and targeted measures to enhance cybersecurity in the face of multipolar politics.[142] As has been shown, regulation is happening at various levels and through various modalities, including laws, norms, markets, code,[143] self-regulation, and multilateral collaboration, all of which can contribute to enhancing global cybersecurity. Each of these regulatory approaches has unique benefits and drawbacks, but together they contribute to a governance regime that is multi-level, multi-purpose, multi-type, and multi-sectoral in scope[144] and that could complement the top-down governance model increasingly favored by certain nations.[145]

Direct regulatory intervention is possible despite the arguments of cyber libertarians – if not through traditional means, then by private regulatory systems that are either contractual or built into network architecture and promulgated by standards bodies such as IETF.[146] These bodies may serve as "proxies for courts," a notion that has become "the dominant school of cyber-regulatory theory," according to Professor Andrew Murray.[147] Yet the fundamental difficulty of enforcing regulations in cyberspace remains apparent given problems of attribution, "environmental plasticity," and the inter-networked nature of cyberspace.[148] Consequently, norms of behavior should also be created to supplement legal regimes.

According to Professor Ron Diebert and Masachi Crete-Nishihata, "states learn from and imitate" one another, and "[t]he most intense forms of imitation and learning occur around national security issues because of the high stakes and urgency involved."[149] In part because of many states' perception that cyber risk is "escalating out of control," there exists an opportunity to engage in constructive international dialogue on norm building.[150] Potential cyber norms could include a duty to cooperate

---

[142] *See* Michael D. McGinnis, *An Introduction to IAD and the Language of the Ostrom Workshop: A Simple Guide to a Complex Framework*, 39(1) POL'Y STUD. J. 163, 171–72 (Feb. 2011) (defining "polycentricity" as "a system of governance in which authorities from overlapping jurisdictions (or centers of authority) interact to determine the conditions under which these authorities, as well as the citizens subject to these jurisdictional units, are authorized to act as well as the constraints put upon their activities for public purposes.").

[143] *See* LAWRENCE LESSIG, CODE: VERSION 2.0 125 (2006).

[144] McGinnis, *supra* note 142, at 170–72.

[145] *See* ITU Signatories, *supra* note 121.

[146] MURRAY, *supra* note 134, at 204.

[147] *Id.*

[148] *Id.* at 57, 205.

[149] Ronald J. Deibert & Masachi Crete-Nishihata, *Global Governance and the Spread of Cyberspace Controls*, 18 GLOBAL GOVERNANCE 339, 350 (2012).

[150] James A. Lewis, *Confidence-Building and International Agreement in Cybersecurity*, DISARMAMENT FORUM: CONFRONTING CYBERCONFLICT 51, 52 (2011). Though norms do not bind states like a treaty, Lewis notes that "[n]on-proliferation provides many examples of non-binding norms that exercise a powerful influence on state behavior." *Id.* at 53. This position has also been supported by other scholars. *See, e.g.*, Roger Hurwitz, *An Augmented Summary of The Harvard, MIT and U. of Toronto Cyber Norms Workshop* 5 (2012), http://citizenlab.org/cybernorms/augmented-summary.pdf (noting "[a]t the very least, acceptance of a norm by a state puts the state's reputation at risk. If it fails to follow the norm, other states which accept that norm, will typically demand an explanation or account, rather than ignoring the violation or dismissing it as self-interested behavior.").

with victim nations if an attack occurred through information systems in a state's territory, and a duty of care to secure systems and warn potential victims.[151] The Obama administration has also encouraged the development of norms for respecting intellectual property, mitigating cybercrime, valuing privacy, and working toward global interoperability, reliable access, multi-stakeholder governance, and cybersecurity due diligence.[152] Yet despite the "general agreement on a norms-based approach" to enhancing cybersecurity,[153] "even simple norms face serious opposition. Conflicting political agendas, covert military actions, espionage[,] and competition for global influence" have created a difficult context for cyber norm development and diffusion,[154] a situation that WCIT-12 and NSA revelations arguably exacerbated.[155] As a result, to be successful in such a difficult climate, norms must be "clear, useful, and do-able,"[156] such as beginning with areas of common concern like protecting CNI.[157] These norms and other confidence-building measures could eventually lead to a cyber code of conduct that meets the needs of key stakeholders.[158] In addition to the U.S. government's work, NATO has also begun efforts aimed at constructing

---

[151] Eneken Tikk, *Ten Rules of Behavior for Cyber Security*, NATO CCDCOE at 5–6, 8–9 (2011). Other proposed norms such as creating a rebuttable presumption to attribute a cyber attack back to a given state because it was launched from its networks beg questions of legitimacy given the technical and legal issues with attribution discussed in Chapters 3 and 6. *Id.* at 5.

[152] INTERNATIONAL STRATEGY FOR CYBERSPACE, *supra* note 36, at 10.

[153] Lewis, *supra* note 150, at 55.

[154] *Id.* at 58.

[155] Hurwitz, *supra* note 150, at 7 ("States today differ in their visions of cyberspace, especially with regard to issues of information access, sovereign authority and sovereign responsibilities. Also, they do not similarly rank the threats or even have the same sets for ranking. China and Russia construe the flows of dissident political information – Internet Freedom, by another name – as a threat and are less concerned than the U.S. about industrial espionage. Consequently, there might be little agreement on where to begin and the specification of norms might be slow and piecemeal."); David P. Fidler, *Becoming Binary Amidst Multipolarity: Internet Governance, Cybersecurity, and the Controversial Conclusion of the World Conference on International Telecommunications in December 2012*, ARMS CONTROL L. (Feb. 8, 2013), http://armscontrollaw.com/2013/02/08/becoming-binary-amidst-multipolarity-internet-governance-cybersecurity-and-the-controversial-conclusion-of-the-world-conference-on-international-telecommunications-in-december-2012/.

[156] Martha Finnemore, *Cultivating International Cyber Norms*, in AMERICA'S CYBER FUTURE, *supra* note 47, at 90, 90.

[157] *See* Richard A. Clarke, *A Global Cyber-Crisis in Waiting*, WASH. POST (Feb. 7, 2013), http://www.washingtonpost.com/opinions/a-global-cyber-crisis-in-waiting/2013/02/07/812e024c-6fd6-11e2-ac36-3d8d9dcaa2e2_story.html?tid=wp_ipad; Hurwitz, *supra* note 150, at 8. Over time, a hierarchy of cyber norms may also be established and married with escalating sanctions as is common across a range of international legal instruments. *Cf.* Jure Vidmar, *Norm Conflicts and Hierarchy in International Law: Towards a Vertical International Legal System?*, in HIERARCHY IN INTERNATIONAL LAW: THE PLACE OF HUMAN RIGHTS 13, 14 (Erika De Wet & Jure Vidmar eds., 2012) (questioning "whether the jus cogens-based substantive norm hierarchy is more than theoretical.").

[158] *See* Timothy Farnsworth, *China and Russia Submit Cyber Proposal*, ARMS CONTROL ASSOC. (Nov. 1, 2012), http://www.armscontrol.org/act/2011_11/China_and_Russia_Submit_Cyber_Proposal ("outlining a proposal for an International Code of Conduct for Information Security."). A nonbinding cyber weapon anti-proliferation pledge embodying emerging codes of conduct could also be negotiated, potentially modeled after the nuclear non-proliferation pledge codified in the Nuclear Non-Proliferation Treaty. *See, e.g., The Nuclear Non-Proliferation Treaty*, U.S. DEP'T ST. (1968), http://history.state.gov/milestones/1961-1968/NPT.

cyber norms through identifying best practices.[159] Firms, states, and regional bodies such as NATO and the EU can, and in some instances already are, acting as norm entrepeneurs that could eventually cause a "norm cascade" in which cybersecurity best practices become internalized and eventually codified in national and international laws benefiting global cybersecurity through polycentric action.[160]

Aside from the role of laws and norms in enhancing cybersecurity, the competitive market is also critical to polycentric governance. As was analyzed in Chapter 5, norm entrepreneurs such as Microsoft, Google, and Facebook have built proactive methods for threat management, but voluntary mechanisms have inherent limitations. Other companies with more lax security become free riders that increase the risk of attacks on other stakeholders, including suppliers.[161] Cyber risk-mitigation strategies favored by factions within the U.S. Congress, such as cyber risk insurance, can help firms limit their exposure in the event of a data breach,[162] but they may do little to enhance overall cybersecurity absent a proactive strategy that infuses best practices from the beginning.[163] SEC cybersecurity guidelines should be further refined to help ensure that all major cyber attacks on publicly traded firms are disclosed (including arguably the techniques used so that other firms do not fall pray to similar tactics), which would have the dual benefit of improving information sharing to the benefit of consumers, investors, and policymakers, as well as internalizing the cost of attacks to allow the competitive market to function more efficiently.[164] Strengthening the DHS Homeland Security Enterprise with deeper public-private partnerships[165] and expanding DHS and FBI training sessions for managers may also help by better educating corporate leadership and policymakers about the nature

[159] *See* Blake Williams, *Developing Norms, Deterring Terrorism Expected Topics of NATO's Difficult Cybersecurity Discussion*, MEDILL NAT'L SEC. ZONE (May 9, 2012), http://nationalsecurityzone .org/natog8/developing-norms-deterring-terrorism-expected-topics-of-natos-difficult-cybersecurity- discussion/. *See also* MONROE E. PRICE & STEFAN G. VERHULST, SELF-REGULATION AND THE INTERNET 22 (2005) (arguing in the domestic U.S. context for codes of conduct to be adopted "to ensure that Internet content and service providers act in accordance with principles of social responsibility.").

[160] *See* Martha Finnemore & Kathryn Sikkink, *International Norm Dynamics and Political Change*, 52 INT'L ORG. 887, 895–98 (1998).

[161] *See* Trial by Fire: *What Global Executives Expect of Information Security*, PwC at 14, 32–33 (2010), http://www.pwc.com/en_GX/gx/information-security-survey/pdf/pwcsurvey2010_report.pdf [hereinafter *Trial by Fire*].

[162] *See, e.g.*, House Republican Cybersecurity Task Force, 112th Cong., Recommendations of the House Republican Cybersecurity Task Force 5, 8, 14 (2011) [hereinafter House Cybersecurity Task Force].

[163] *See* Trial by Fire, *supra* note 161, at 6 (reporting that just 43 percent of surveyed organizations with cybersecurity strategies called those strategies "effective" and themselves "proactive" at implementing their plans).

[164] *See* Eamon Javers, *Cyberattacks: Why Companies Keep Quiet*, CNBC (Feb. 25, 2013), http://www .cnbc.com/id/100491610 ("Only a limited number of companies disclosed cyberattacks occurring in 2012, CNBC found after a review of 2012 SEC filings. That's even though the SEC specifically asked companies to reveal significantly damaging attacks in guidance the commission issued to companies in the fall of 2011. The volume of disclosures to the SEC doesn't bear out the picture painted by the U.S. intelligence community of massive, economy-draining cyberthreat.").

[165] *See* DEP'T HOMELAND SEC., BLUEPRINT FOR A SECURE CYBER FUTURE: THE CYBERSECURITY STRATEGY FOR THE HOMELAND SECURITY ENTERPRISE 36 (Nov. 2011).

and extent of the cyber threat,[166] initiatives that could be informed by the DOD's Enduring Security Framework program.[167] Effective public-private partnerships and market-based incentives such as tax credits for enhancing security is also important elements of reform efforts,[168] along with addressing technical vulnerabilities given the rapid advance of disruptive technologies.

As Chapter 3 demonstrated, technical vulnerabilities comprise a key component of the cyber threat. Best practices must be implemented at each layer of the Internet's architecture to address vulnerabilities from the bottom-up starting with hardware because each layer only uses functions from the layer below, exporting "functionality to the layer above."[169] Better quality control and supply chain management is critical for the physical layer. One step in this regard would be requiring U.S. government contracts for sensitive computer hardware to be domestically sourced to the extent feasible, such as by amending the COTS program.[170] Because the industry does not yet exist to support U.S. government needs, long-term commitments should be made to U.S. firms, which could both enhance cybersecurity and catalyze economic growth so long as such protection was targeted, transparent, and justifiable on national security grounds.[171] Further research must be undertaken to understand the benefits and drawbacks of both end-to-end application-level security measures like HTTPS and protocol-level security measures like DNSSEC and IPsec to secure the logical infrastructure. If protocol-level security measures are deemed effective, then the extension of DNSSEC to the root and TLDs as an example of polycentric governance should be followed. Vulnerabilities in underlying code also require more

---

[166] *See Examining the Homeland Security Impact of the Obama Administration's Cybersecurity Proposal: Hearing before the H. Comm. on Homeland Sec.,* 112th Cong. 8, 16 (2011) (statement of Melissa E. Hathaway, Hathaway Global Consulting), http://www.gpo.gov/fdsys/pkg/CHRG-112hhrg72253/pdf/CHRG-112hhrg72253.pdf.

[167] *See* William J. Lynn, *Cyber Security: Defending a New Domain,* Dep't Def., http://www.defense .gov/home/features/2010/0410_cybersec/lynn-article1.aspx (last visited Jan. 31, 2014) (stating that corporate executives "meet regularly" with Defense Department officials through the Enduring Security Framework to exchange information and discuss how to better meet the cyber threat). Participating in simulated cyber attacks is also a useful way to test readiness. *See* Andrew Tangel, *Wall Street Gears Up To Battle Cyber Attacks with 'War Game,'* L.A. Times (July 1, 2013), http://www.latimes.com/business/money/la-fi-mo-wall-street-plans-cyber-war-game-20130628,0,7197348.story (reporting that the Securities Industry and Financial Market Association coordinated "a simulated cyber attack with about 50 firms [along with the U.S. Treasury and DHS participation] in an exercise called Quantum Dawn 2" in 2013).

[168] *See* House Cybersecurity Task Force, *supra* note 162, at 8.

[169] Murray, *supra* note 134, at 43; Yochai Benkler, *From Consumers to Users: Shifting the Deeper Structure of Regulation Toward Sustainable Commons and User Access,* 52 Fed. Comm. L.J. 561, 562 (2000).

[170] *See* Richard A. Clarke & Robert K. Knake, Cyber War: The Next Threat to National Security and What to Do About It 86 (2010).

[171] *See* Allan A. Friedman, *Cybersecurity and Trade: National Policies, Global and Local Consequences,* Brookings Inst. 4–5 (2013), http://www.brookings.edu/~/media/research/files/papers/2013/09/19%20 cybersecurity%20and%20trade%20global%20local%20friedman/brookingscybersecuritynew.pdf; Raphael Satter, *Report: NSA Intercepts Computer Deliveries,* AP (Dec. 29, 2013), http://hosted.ap.org/dynamic/stories/E/EU_NSA_SURVEILLANCE?SITE=AP&SECTION=HOME&TEMPLATE=DEFAULT.

comprehensive attention, such as through mandatory automatic updating and providing incentives to phase out old software and hardware, whereas better education of users is vital to limiting the effectiveness of social engineering attacks, as will be explored later in this chapter. However, focusing solely on technical vulnerabilities and code could further "regulatory competition"[172] absent a wider discussion about the role of self-organization that is so critical to the polycentric thesis.

Online communities have an important role to play in securing the pseudo, or "imperfect," commons of cyberspace.[173] There are many types of such communities, ranging from commercial organizations such as eBay to gaming communities like World of Warcraft, knowledge communities like TripAdvisor, and creative communities such as Wikipedia.[174] In some of these communities, such as eBay – which Professor Murray describes as "Lockean" because users have given over some power to a central administrator – democratic governance can coexist with an established authority such as by empowering users to police and report errant behavior.[175] This state of affairs may be compared to so-called Rousseauen communities in which power remains decentralized.[176] However, such groupings are often ineffective, according to Professor Murray, because they are "simply too large and too diverse. . . ."[177] If, however, such communities could increase collaboration in the vein of IETF working groups, then power may not have to be centralized to the degree that it is in Lockean communities such as Facebook. This may be accomplished through forming even smaller communities potentially by making use of social networking, as well as the so-called "cognitive surplus" of populations.[178]

Polycentric theorists, including Professor Ostrom, have extolled the benefits of self-organized communities in the context of managing common resources,[179] and anthropological evidence confirms that groups of humans function more efficiently

---

[172] MURRAY, *supra* note 134, at 46.

[173] Joseph S. Nye, Jr., *Cyber Power*, HARV. KENNEDY SCH. 15 (May 2010).

[174] MURRAY, *supra* note 134, at 148.

[175] *Id.* at 163. John Locke was a seventeenth-century philosopher who is popularly known as the Father of Liberalism. *See* Michael Welbourne, *The Community of Knowledge*, 31(125) PHIL. *Q.* 302, 302–04 (1981).

[176] MURRAY, *supra* note 134, at 163. Jean-Jacques Rousseau was an eighteenth-century Genevan philosopher who argued that individuals are best protected from one another by forming a moral community of equals. *See* Katrin Froese, *Beyond Liberalism: The Moral Community of Rousseau's Social Contract*, 34 CAN. J. POL. SCI. 579, 581–82 (2001).

[177] MURRAY, *supra* note 134, at 163.

[178] *See The New Politics of the Internet: Everything Is Connected*, ECONOMIST (Jan. 5, 2013), http://www.economist.com/news/briefing/21569041-can-internet-activism-turn-real-political-movement-everything-connected [hereinafter *New Politics*] (discussing the ideas of Professor Kevin Werbach who has suggested that the Internet "lowers the barriers to organisation," potentially to the point that mailing lists could replace painstaking institution building); *Digital Do-Gooders: Why Do We Help Strangers Online?*, BBC (Sept. 25, 2013), http://www.bbc.co.uk/news/magazine-24207047 (reporting that "educated people around the world have about a trillion hours of free time each year that could be contributed to collaborative projects, a phenomenon . . . [Clay Shirky] calls 'cognitive surplus.'").

[179] *See, e.g.*, Elinor Ostrom et al., *Revisiting the Commons: Local Lessons, Global Challenges*, 284 SCI. 278, 278 (1999) (questioning policymakers' use of Garrett Hardin's theory of the "tragedy of the commons,"

along certain metrics when they are kept relatively small in scale.[180] However, micro-communities – like those focused on a single issue such as P2P file sharing – can ignore the wider impact of their actions.[181] To overcome such apathy, as discussed in Chapter 2, such communities must have a defined stake in the outcome to effectuate good governance. The Internet is comprised of both types of communities, but a Lockean hybrid model favoring organic, bottom-up governance composed of small cybersecurity cohorts with a role for centralized coordination that can codify and enforce best practices as well as protect against free riders may be most appropriate to enhance security.[182] Such self-regulation has the flexibility "to adapt to rapid technological progress"[183] better than black letter law, which often changes incrementally. It also has the potential to be more efficient and cost-effective than command and control-style regulation while instilling civic virtue,[184] though it is not a panacea, which is why communal self-governance is but one component of polycentric governance.[185] Yet as Professor Murray argues: "[I]n cyberspace the power to decide is, it seems, vested ultimately in the community. We have the power to control our destiny."[186]

in light of the empirical data showing self-organizing groups can communally manage common-pool resources).

[180] *See, e.g.,* Gregory A. Johnson, *Organizational Structure and Scalar Stress, in* THEORY AND EXPLANATION IN ARCHEOLOGY 389, 392–94 (Colin Renfrew et al. eds., 1982).

[181] *See* MURRAY, *supra* note 134, at 164 (explaining how members of micro-communities tend to focus only on what directly impacts their own activities); *cf. New Politics, supra* note 178 (discussing "the virtues of 'commons-based peer production' like that seen in open-source software communities, where volunteers write and debug code as a gift to the community at large.").

[182] *See* MURRAY, *supra* note 134, at 164. The DHS's Cybersecurity Awareness Month every October helps to highlight the important role played by bottom-up efforts to enhance cybersecurity, noting, "Every Internet user has a role to play in securing cyberspace and ensuring the safety of ourselves, our families, and our communities online." *National Cyber Security Awareness Month,* DEP'T HOMELAND SEC., http://www.dhs.gov/national-cyber-security-awareness-month (last visited Jan. 24, 2013). Competitions rewarding communities that distinguish themselves in enhancing their cybersecurity along defined metrics such as through grants could also help build awareness and increase the potential for successful polycentric governance, especially when coupled with other hallmarks such as effective dispute resolution.

[183] PRICE & VERHULST, *supra* note 159, at 21. According to Notre Dame Professor Don Howard, different online communities "have a complicated topology and geography, with overlap, hierarchy, varying degrees of mutual isolation and mutual interaction. There are also communities of corporations or corporate persons, gangs of thieves, and . . . on scales small and large." Don Howard, *Civic Virtue and Cybersecurity* 15 (Working Paper, 2014). What is more, Professor Howard argues that these communities will each construct norms in their own ways, and at their own rates, but that this process has the potential to make positive progress toward addressing multifaceted issues such as enhancing cybersecurity. *Id.* at 22.

[184] *See* PRICE & VERHULST, *supra* note 159, at 21–22; Gary M. Shiffman & Ravi Gupta, *Crowdsourcing Cyber Security: A Property Rights View of Exclusion and Theft on the Information Commons* 7 INT'L J. COMMONS 92 (2013).

[185] Elinor Ostrom, *Polycentric Systems as One Approach for Solving Collective-Action Problems* 2–3 (Ind. Univ. Workshop in Political Theory and Policy Analysis, Working Paper Series No. 08-6, 2008).

[186] MURRAY, *supra* note 134, at 125.

Polycentric analysis provides an avenue to conceptualize the regulatory complexity of the Internet and how to model efforts aimed at enhancing cybersecurity.[187] But determining the shape of a polycentric governance model is difficult because it necessitates a dynamic view of Internet governance before effective interventions may be undertaken to enhance cybersecurity.[188] Such a complex model requires recognition of the large number of regulators online, including the public and private sectors, the plasticity of the environment, and the "high degree of regulatory competition."[189] Predicting the outcome of interventions in such a regime complex is difficult to say the least, as seen in the parallel criticisms surrounding ICANN.[190] Instead of external bodies such as ICANN being imposed on online communities, bottom-up regulation in the vein of the IETF should be prioritized and best practices reinforced. Examples of this approach include the NERC standards discussed in Chapter 5 that were eventually sanctioned by the U.S. government,[191] as well as the NIST Cybersecurity Framework.[192] Disruptive regulation should be minimized, according to Professor Murray, in favor of complimentary or "symbiotic" interventions that take into account existing relationships between different stakeholders.[193]

While patterns of communications may be easily mapped in an analog world, in a digital environment like cyberspace the patterns are constantly changing. The discipline of system dynamics helps model complexity,[194] such as by fashioning mechanisms that help regulations adapt to feedback coming from affected stakeholders.[195] The benefits of such an approach to help manage the rapidly evolving cyber threat are many, and could help to minimize market distortions resulting from regulatory interventions. Modeling tools such as iThink are available to help regulators track millions of variables and predict the outcome of interventions before they are made,[196] and could be put to use in crafting cybersecurity regulations along with emerging techniques in the field of data analytics.[197] However, the political cost

---

[187] *See* Ostrom, *supra* note 185, at 2–3 (discussing some of the benefits and drawbacks of polycentric governance).

[188] *See* MURRAY, *supra* note 134, at 250 (explaining the dynamic nature of the regulatory environment, where all parties can act as both "regulator and regulatee").

[189] *Id.* at 234.

[190] *Id.* at 234–37.

[191] *See* INTELLIGENCE & NAT'L SEC. ALLIANCE, ADDRESSING CYBER SECURITY THROUGH PUBLIC-PRIVATE PARTNERSHIP: AN ANALYSIS OF EXISTING MODELS 7 (Nov. 2009), www.insaonline.org/i/d/a/Resources/Addressing_Cyber_Security.aspx.

[192] *See* Executive Order 13636, *supra* note 43.

[193] *See* MURRAY, *supra* note 134, at 243–44.

[194] *Id.* at 247 (citing Jay Forrester, *Industrial Dynamics – A Major Breakthrough for Decision Makers*, 36(4) HARV. BUS. REV. 37 (1958)).

[195] *Id.* at 249.

[196] *See id.*; *iThink*, ISEESYSTEMS, http://www.iseesystems.com/softwares/Business/ithinkSoftware.aspx (last visited Jan. 31, 2014).

[197] *See, e.g.*, Ramon Barquin & Silka Gonzalez, *Cybersecurity: The Role for Data Analytics*, BEYENETWORK (July 17, 2012), http://www.b-eye-network.com/view/16206.

of such an approach could be high given that such a regime would require constant attention, and it would increase uncertainty for firms if regulations constantly changed. Such concerns may be partially assuaged, though, if mechanisms were put into place allowing regulations to reinforce evolving industry best practices such as those emerging from the NIST Cybersecurity Framework process along with affected industries enjoying regular consultation with regulators. Ultimately, system dynamics teaches us that successful interventions in cyberspace require: dynamic mapping; analysis of all affected stakeholders; and a willingness to experiment, identify, and reinforce best practices.

Applying the conceptual framework of polycentric management to cybersecurity underscores the importance of strengthening mutual reinforcement "to form an interlocking suite of governance systems. . . . "[198] As with the Montreal Protocol, which in 2009 became the first treaty in the history of the UN "to achieve universal ratification[,]"[199] this study has shown that there is some utility in negotiators focusing on facets of common problems, such as spam and cybercrime, through targeted forums with limited membership.[200] The idea, to oversimplify the points raised by Professors Ostrom and Victor among others, is for policymakers to start small and local, but to start somewhere. This is the opposite of the classic approach to global commons governance, which focuses on consensual multilateral UN treaties, and is a more apt reflection of the current multipolar state of international relations.[201] Yet even the UN Convention on the Law of the Sea already calls for cooperation at multiple scales, including regional and global, to support its provisions.[202] This example should be followed as policymakers seek to use polycentric instruments

---

[198] ARCTIC GOVERNANCE PROJECT, ARCTIC GOVERNANCE IN AN ERA OF TRANSFORMATIVE CHANGE: CRITICAL QUESTIONS, GOVERNANCE PRINCIPLES, WAYS FORWARD 13 (2010), http://arcticgovernance .custompublish.com/arctic-governance-in-an-era-of-transformative-change-critical-questions-govern ance-principles-ways-forward.4774756-156783.html (discussing the regime complex comprising Arctic governance). The Arctic Council may be considered as another example of a successful regional intergovernmental forum that is is increasingly important in Arctic governance and has helped to promote security and sustainable development in the area by focusing on areas of common concern, such as search and rescue. *About Arctic Council*, ARCTIC COUNCIL, http://arctic-council.org/article/ about (last visited Jan. 31, 2014); Scott J. Shackelford, *Time for a South China Sea Council*, HUFF. POST (June 18, 2013), http://www.huffingtonpost.com/scott-j-shackelford/time-for-a-south-china-se_b_ 3442529.html (comparing the geopolitical situation in the Arctic with the South China Sea).

[199] UN Envt. Prog., *The Evolution of the Montreal Protocol*, http://ozone.unep.org/new_site/en/montreal_ protocol.php (last visited Feb. 3, 2014).

[200] *See* Daniel H. Cole, *From Global to Polycentric Climate Governance*, 2 CLIMATE L. 395, 395 (2011) (taking a similar approach in the climate change context in discussing the potential of polycentric governance to better address that global collective action problem given the slow pace of multilateral efforts).

[201] *Cf.* Oona A. Hathaway et al., *The Law of Cyber-Attack*, 100 CAL. L. REV. 817, 877 (2012) (calling for an international treaty to better manage cyber attacks).

[202] United Nations Convention on the Law of the Sea, art. 197, Dec. 10, 1982, 1833 U.N.T.S. 397 [hereinafter UNCLOS].

as a means of strengthening existing and creating new regulatory regimes at multiple levels, such as IMPACT's efforts aimed at fostering regional cybersecurity cooperation in the Arab world.[203] Such a proposal is in keeping with the findings of scholars such as Professor Christopher Joyner who has implicitly argued for the importance of polycentric partnerships to help galvanize the political will of states to adhere to the principles laid out in legal regimes.[204] There is also evidence that the Obama administration has recognized the importance of coupling national and international action to enhance cybersecurity,[205] but a successful polycentric framework ultimately must address Professor Ostrom's design principles discussed in Chapter 2, including effective monitoring, graduated sanctions, and efficient dispute resolution.[206] The International Strategy for Cyberspace represents some progress along these lines, such as promoting due diligence and sanctions for violators,[207] but further research and negotiations remain to be done.

To summarize and modestly update the design principles from Chapter 2 for the cybersecurity context, five design principles are suggested for further study. First, local, national, regional, and global authorities should work to define group boundaries by laying out the scope and powers of communities comprising the cyber regime complex. This may be done organically through codes of conduct developed by communities such as Microsoft, NERC, and NIST, which may then be subsequently reinforced by national and international regulation.[208] Second, building off of corporate social responsibility at the firm level and the

---

[203] *See, e.g.,* Regional Cybersecurity Center, *supra* note 55; *see also* Cole, *supra* note 200, at 396 (arguing that "*effective* global governance institutions inevitably are 'polycentric' in nature[,]" and that "polycentric governance requires a certain level of independence, as well as interdependence, between governance institutions and organizations at various levels. The key issue – applicable to climate policy as much as to other areas of global or international concern – is to determine the appropriate division of responsibility and authority between governance institutions and organizations at global, national, state, and local levels.").

[204] *See* Christopher C. Joyner, *Rethinking International Environmental Regimes: What Role for Partnership Coalitions?*, 1(1–2) J. INT'L L. & INT'L REL. 89, 118–19 (2005) (making the case that "[t]he creation of multinational, multi-group partnerships can contribute to" the effective management of the global commons, but that such action is insufficient without "financial support by governments. . . . ").

[205] *See, e.g.,* Williams, *supra* note 159.

[206] *See* SUSAN J. BUCK, THE GLOBAL COMMONS: AN INTRODUCTION 31 (1998). *See also* Henning Wegener, *Cyber Peace, in* THE QUEST FOR CYBER PEACE, *supra* note 76, at 77, 78 (arguing that cyber "[p]eace implies the prevalence of legal and general moral principles, possibilities and procedures for settlement of conflicts, durability and stability.").

[207] *See* INTERNATIONAL STRATEGY FOR CYBERSPACE, *supra* note 36, at 10.

[208] *See* WHITE HOUSE PRESS SEC'Y, EXECUTIVE ORDER ON IMPROVING CRITICAL INFRASTRUCTURE CYBERSECURITY (Feb. 12, 2013), http://www.whitehouse.gov/the-press-office/2013/02/12/executive-order-improving-critical-infrastructure-cybersecurity-o (discussing Obama administration efforts aimed at identifying and instilling cybersecurity industry best practices to help secure vulnerable CNI); *cf.* David Lacey, *Whither Cyber Security*, COMPUTER WKLY. (June 29, 2013), http://www.computerweekly.com/blogs/david_lacey/2013/06/whither_cyber_security.html (arguing that "[t]o stop advanced threats we need advanced countermeasures, not corporate governance systems.").

common heritage of mankind concept globally, the equitable and human rights aspects of cyber peace must be addressed by managers and policymakers to avoid free riders and help ensure that some "users [do not] get all the benefits and pay few of the costs."[209] As was shown in Chapter 5, for example, the absence of a level playing field provides misaligned incentives for the uptake of cybersecurity best practices.[210] Third, robust monitoring of and information sharing between cybersecurity communities is necessary at multiple scales.[211] Chapters 1 and 5 demonstrated that while there is growing agreement on the severity of the cyber threat and that more organizations are participating in bodies such as the Information Sharing and Analysis Centers,[212] overall public-private information sharing remains insufficient to monitor and assist affected entities.[213] Fourth, addressing legal ambiguities and establishing norms of behavior are critical to defining graduated sanctions for rule violators and fostering effective dispute resolution, as was discussed earlier in this chapter as well as in Chapter 6.[214] Fifth, promoting nested enterprises as part of a multilevel system of Internet governance is central to building trust and securing cyberspace. According to Professor Ostrom, this principle posits that larger institutions are important for "govern[ing] the interdependencies among smaller [governance] units,"[215] highlighting the need for effective multi-stakeholder governance with some degree of higher-order coordination. The ITU or another body could act as such a coordinating "umbrella" organization "under which many different efforts proceed,"[216] but it will be critical to avoid the crowding out of smaller-scale

---

[209] Ostrom, *supra* note 141, at 105, 120.

[210] *See, e.g.,* Nicole Perlroth, *Lax Security at LinkedIn Is Laid Bare,* N.Y. TIMES, (June 10, 2012), http://www.nytimes.com/2012/06/11/technology/linkedin-breach-exposes-light-security-even-at-data-companies.html. The same lessons may be applied globally in the context of an international agreement on cybersecurity. *See Spying Revelations, supra* note 81 (reporting on the cyber arms race underway between the United States and China, and quoting Benjamin Koo, a professor at China's Tsinghua University, that "[w]hoever is holding the lower end in this game is not going to feel comfortable."). The level playing field criterion is also applicable to the IPv6 allocation debate. *See ITU and IPv6,* http://www.itu.int/net/ITU-T/ipv6/ (last visited Jan. 26, 2014).

[211] *See, e.g.,* Alexis, *supra* note 42 (reporting on industry councils being proposed in the United States "to develop and coordinate the enforcement of cybersecurity guidelines for key U.S. sectors."); Regional Cybersecurity Center, *supra* note 55.

[212] *See, e.g., Survey: SMBs are Getting Serious about Information Protection,* SYMANTEC (2010), http://www.symantec.com/about/news/resources/press_kits/detail.jsp?pkid=smbsurvey2010; Joe Waldron, *Comments of VeriSign, Inc, VeriSign Response to NOI* 100721305–0305-01, DEP'T COMM. INTERNET POL'Y TASK FORCE (Sept. 13, 2010), at 2–3, http://www.nist.gov/itl/upload/VeriSign_Cybersecurity-NOI-Comments-9-13-10.pdf.

[213] *See, e.g.,* VERIZON, DATA BREACH INVESTIGATIONS REPORT 44 (2012), http://www.verizonbusiness.com/resources/reports/rp_data-breach-investigations-report-2012_en_xg.pdf (discussing the difficulty of quantifying the amount and type of records lost to cyber attackers due in part to insufficient information).

[214] Ostrom, *supra* note 141, at 105, 122.

[215] *Id.* at 121.

[216] Keohane & Victor (2010), *supra* note 140, at 23.

innovative efforts aimed at enhancing global cybersecurity.[217] These principles are necessarily abstract, but with further refinement they could help inform debates in boardrooms, national legislatures, and in the international community about how best to catalyze a positive cyber peace through polycentric action.

Defining cyber peace is only a starting point for thinking about meta goals for enhancing global cybersecurity, with polycentric governance being but one conceptual framework to help get us there. At best, the analytical framework of polycentrism as applied to cybersecurity is a tool to help understand the dynamic nature of cyberspace and how diverse organizations that are multi-level, multi-purpose, multi-type, and multi-sector in scope can work together to help manage cyber attacks.[218] Scholars have identified many preconditions for success in polycentric endeavors, such as the following traits summarized by Professor Michael McGinnis: "[p]olycentricity in the organization of (1) market arrangements; (2) the legal community; (3) constitutional rule; and (4) political conditions. . . . "[219] As has been shown, market conditions in cyberspace, as well as aspects of the applicable law and politics, demonstrate some features of polycentricity. But there is not a cohesive system of constitutional law in cyberspace, though there are the beginnings of a law of cyber war and peace from which to build, as discussed in Chapter 6. Professor Ostrom, among others, have also identified four overarching stipulations for collective action, including: (1) affected organizations recognizing their responsibility for the problem and agreeing on the need for change, (2) robust information existing regarding the issue of concern, (3) monitoring being available as a means of ensuring compliance, and (4) communication occurring among at least some participants.[220] Yet even if all the necessary preconditions were met, polycentricity says relatively little about the processes for how to bring about needed reforms. Informed

---

[217] *See, e.g.,* Elinor Ostrom, *Beyond Markets and States: Polycentric Governance of Complex Economic Systems,* 100 AM. ECON. REV. 641, 656 (2010) (citing Andrew F. Reeson & John G. Tisdell, *Institutions, Motivations and Public Goods: An Experimental Test of Motivational Crowding,* 68 J. ECON. BEHAVIOR & ORG. 273 (2008) (finding "externally imposed regulation that would theoretically lead to higher joint returns 'crowded out' voluntary behavior to cooperate.")).

[218] *See* Michael D. McGinnis, *Updated Guide to IAD and the Language of the Ostrom Workshop: A Simplified Overview of a Complex Framework for the Analysis of Institutions and their Development,* at 7 (Working Paper Ver. 2c, 2013), http://php.indiana.edu/~mcginnis/iad_guide.pdf.

[219] *Id.* at 7.

[220] Ostrom, *supra* note 139, at 12–13. Still other preconditions of polycentric governance that have been mentioned by scholars include greater autonomy given to lower-level political units (such as, in this context, states) relative to supranational governance. *See id.* at 15 (discussing the importance of local initiatives to help mitigate global climate change). This has been demonstrated to an extent in the cyber context such as by the increase in national regulations analyzed in Chapter 2. Critically though, "cooperative arrangements among government units to undertake joint activities of mutual benefit" must be better defined, and "the correspondence of different units of government [should be matched] to the scales of effect for diverse public goods." McGinnis, *supra* note 218, at 7. In the cyber context, this could involve clarifying governance responsibilities, establishing a more formalized dispute resolution system, and identifying opportunities for collaboration between key stakeholders taking into account the global, interconnected nature of cyberspace.

experimentation, then, should be encouraged that takes into account the cyber-security best practices summarized below and makes use of all the modalities of regulation at multiple scales[221] – such experimentation, after all, is at the heart of both the Internet's history and polycentric governance, and is vital to enhancing cybersecurity.

Regime Effectiveness in Cyberspace

An effective system of polycentric governance for cyberspace would use a mixture of laws and norms; market-based incentives; code; self-regulation; public-private partnerships; and bilateral, regional, and multilateral collaboration to enhance cyber-security. Yet even if such a system could be put into practice, polycentric networks are susceptible to institutional fragmentation and gridlock caused by overlapping authority.[222] Thus, before summarizing best practices, it is useful to assess the desirability of such an approach by analyzing the current state of affairs. But measuring the effectiveness of current regimes is problematic and is posed here merely to couch the debate in greater context, and to help illustrate the difficulties involved with realizing the promise of polycentric governance in promoting cyber peace.

Regime effectiveness has become a "driving force . . . in the analysis of international relations."[223] Empirical studies have concluded that there is modest support for the proposition that international agreements improve on the status quo.[224] However, the array of literature on regime effectiveness that has arisen in fields such as international environmental and human rights law has not been applied to Internet governance partly because of the difficulty of making causal inferences under a variety of conditions given the lack of robust data.[225] Moreover, measuring the effectiveness of regime complexes is a challenging proposition since the governance structures at work are diverse and not easily amenable to quantifiable comparison.[226] At best, correlations may be highlighted. A comprehensive analysis of the effectiveness of cyber laws is thus beyond the scope of this book. Nevertheless, some

---

[221] See MURRAY, *supra* note 134, at 249 (arguing that regulators need not rely on "'trial and error' regulatory models" if they make use of dynamic modeling tools).

[222] See Keohane & Victor (2010), *supra* note 140, at 14, 17 (explaining that different components within a partially fragmented regime complex may compete with each other, resulting in a gridlock of innovation).

[223] Michael Zürn, *The Rise of International Environmental Politics: A Review of Current Research*, 50(4) WORLD POLITICS 617, 649 (1998).

[224] See Scott Barrett, *Self-Enforcing International Environmental Agreements*, 46 OXFORD ECON. PAPERS 878, 892 (1994); Carsten Helm & Detlef Sprinz, *Measuring the Effectiveness of International Environmental Regimes*, 44 J. CONFLICT RES. 630, 639 (2000).

[225] See, e.g., Oona A. Hathaway, *Do Human Rights Treaties Make a Difference?*, 111 YALE L.J. 1935, 1938 (2002) (declaring that a quantitative approach to tracing the effectiveness of relationships within human rights law is typically difficult, if not impossible).

[226] See Helm & Sprinz, *supra* note 224, at 632 (suggesting that scholars "focus on observable political effects of institutions rather than directly on environmental impact" because of the difficulty of measuring the actual impacts resulting from a given regulatory action).

qualitative and quantitative analysis of the performance of legal regimes governing cyberspace is possible by comparing the performance of those regimes to an ideal type in which a positive vision of cyber space is attained, as well as to a no-regime counterfactual. The literature on international environmental regime effectiveness is helpful toward this end. Professor Oran Young has been among the most prolific scholars in this area, positing five main approaches for measuring effectiveness: the problem-solving, legal, economic, normative, and political approaches.[227] A combination legal-political approach is used here to analyze some aspects of the cyber law underpinning Internet governance.

Ascertaining the effectiveness of cyber law is difficult, particularly because of the relative lack of binding international law below the armed attack threshold, as was explored in Chapter 6. Diverse bodies of law and custom are applicable in the cybersecurity arena to help fill in the law of cyber peace. For example, a cyber attack that is not an armed attack could potentially activate the following legal provisions: (1) Article 35 of the ITU dealing with the suspension of communications services,[228] (2) domestic cyber law, (3) Articles 19 and 113 of the UN Convention on the Law of the Sea,[229] (4) applicable mutual legal assistance treaties and status of forces agreements, and (5) pertinent bilateral investment treaties or even UN Security Council Resolutions. Yet, it is possible to investigate the status of these and other treaties active in somewhat analogous arenas, such as those governing the global commons, a sampling of which are summarized in Table 7.2.

These data allude to at least three important trends.[230] First, reservations may be found in 44 percent of the surveyed accords included in Table 7.2; including the Budapest Convention, which permits states to opt out of specific provisions, thus potentially weakening the regime even as it functions to expand membership and speeds entry into force.[231] Second, more than half of the total agreements are regional or subregional in scope,[232] underscoring the move toward a regime complex.[233] And third, enforcement provisions are often lacking,[234] as are information sharing and

---

[227] Oran R. Young & Marc A. Levy, *The Effectiveness of International Environmental, in* THE EFFECTIVENESS OF INTERNATIONAL ENVIRONMENTAL REGIMES: CAUSAL CONNECTIONS AND BEHAVIORAL MECHANISMS 1, 4–6 (Oran R. Young ed., 1999).

[228] INT'L. TELECOMM. UNION, CONSTITUTION OF THE INTERNATIONAL TELECOMMUNICATIONS UNION art. 35 (2010), http://www.itu.int/dms_pub/itu-s/oth/02/09/s02090000115201pdfe.pdf.

[229] UNCLOS, arts. 19, 113.

[230] There are more than 124 multilateral agreements regulating areas of the global commons ranging in scope and purpose that were included in these estimates drawn from the work of Professor John Vogler and updated using publicly available information from the listed sources in Table 7.2. For more information, see JOHN VOGLER, THE GLOBAL COMMONS: A REGIME ANALYSIS 156 (1995); *see also* JOHN VOGLER, THE GLOBAL COMMONS: ENVIRONMENTAL AND TECHNOLOGICAL GOVERNANCE 152–81 (2000) (representing an updated treatment of regime effectiveness in the global commons).

[231] *See* Convention on Cybercrime, arts. 42–43; VOGLER (2000), *supra* note 230, at 159.

[232] VOGLER (1995), *supra* note 230, at 156 (noting that participation of states in various regimes is a key issue in mitigating global governance challenges).

[233] *See* VOGLER (2000), *supra* note 230, at 179.

[234] *Id.* at 172.

TABLE 7.2. *Selection of international agreements governing the global commons*[235]

Name	Subject	Year	Full members	Ratifications for Entry Into Force (EIF)	Signature to EIF (months)	Amendment requirements	Reservations allowed?
ICRW	Whaling	1946	88	6	23	Three-quarters	Yes
Antarctic Treaty	Antarctica	1959	49	All	19	All	Yes
London Convention	Marine pollution	1972	87	15	21	Two-thirds	Yes
MARPOL Convention	Marine pollution	1973 & 1978	152	15	119	Two-thirds	Yes
UNCLOS III	Oceans	1982	166	60	143	Two-thirds or 60; three-quarters for seabed	No
Vienna Convention	Atmospheric ozone	1985	197	20	44	Three-quarters	No
Montreal Protocol	Ozone	1987	197	11	15	20	No
UNFCCC	Climate	1992	195	50	21	Three-quarters	No
Kyoto Protocol	Climate	1995	192	*Marrakesh Accords	99	Three-quarters	No
Outer Space Treaty	Outer space	1967	102	5	8	Simple majority	Yes
Rescue Agreement	Outer space	1968	92	3	7	All	No
Liability Convention	Outer space	1972	89	5	6	Simple majority	No
Registration Convention	Outer space	1976	60	5	20	Simple majority	No
Moon Treaty	Outer space	1984	15	5	55	None	No
Convention on Cybercrime	Cybercrime	2001	41	5	31	All	Yes
ITU Constitution & Convention	Telecom	1992	193	July 1, 1994	19	Two-thirds	Yes

* The rules setting out the implementation of the Kyoto Protocol were adopted at COP 7 in Marrakesh in 2001, and are called the "Marrakesh Accords." UNFCCC: Kyoto Protocol, http://unfccc.int/kyoto_protocol/items/2830.php (last visited Feb. 3, 2014).

[235] Table adapted from JOHN VOGLER, THE GLOBAL COMMONS: ENVIRONMENTAL AND TECHNOLOGICAL GOVERNANCE 157–59 (2000), and updated from data available at: the International Maritime Organization, the United Nations, International Whaling Commission, the Secretariat of the Antarctic Treaty, and the London Convention and Protocol. *E.g.*, U.N. Treaties and Principles on Outer Space, U.N. Sales No. E.08.I. 10 (2008); International Maritime Organization, International Convention for the Prevention of Pollution from Ships (MARPOL) (adopted 1973), http://www.imo .org/About/Conventions/ListOfConventions/Pages/International-Convention-for-the-Prevention-of-Pollution-from-Ships-%28MARPOL%29.aspx; Int'l Whaling Comm'n, *Membership and Contracting Governments*, http://iwc.int/members.htm (last visited Feb. 3, 2014); Secretariat of the Antarctic Treaty, *Parties*, http://www.ats.aq/devAS/ats_parties.aspx?lang=e (last visited Feb. 3, 2014) (including both consultative and non-consultative parties); London Convention and Protocol, *Convention on the Prevention of Marine Pollution by Dumping of Wastes and Other Matter*, http://www.imo.org/ OurWork/Environment/SpecialProgrammesAndInitiatives/Pages/London-Convention-and-Protocol .aspx (last visited Feb. 4, 2014); UN Envt. Prog., *Ozone Secretariat*, http://ozone.unep.org/new_site/en/ treaty_ratification_status.php?treaty_id=&country_id=&srchcrit=1&input=Display (last visited Feb. 4, 2014).

verification mechanisms.[236] The overall effectiveness of these regimes has been varied.[237]

Focusing on cyberspace, some scholars such as Professor Ostrom have argued that, in fact, cyberspace is being successfully governed relative to other parts of the global commons.[238] The growing membership of the Budapest Convention, relative rarity of cyber terrorist incidents, absence of genuine cyber war, increasing rates of e-commerce, and the TCP/IP's successful accommodation of rapid growth all support this view. However, the growth of cybercrime and espionage,[239] as well as the apparent proliferation of sophisticated cyber weapons and state-sponsored attacks, calls it into question.[240] Moreover, the rate of multilateral regulation governing the global commons peaked from 1972 to the late 1980s and now seems to be decreasing, showing the difficulty of crafting new consensual treaties in a multipolar world – even the Budapest Convention was, after all, a Council of Europe initiative. From a political perspective, which is concerned with the extent to which regimes transfer authority from a national to an international level, most of these regimes are relatively weak.[241] Cyberspace is no exception. As we have seen, nations are exerting increasing control over Internet governance, and the outcome of ongoing multilateral negotiations could well reinforce this state of affairs.[242]

The experience of one large U.S. organization of more than 500 employees provides a telling example of the challenges associated with gauging the regime effectiveness of cyber law. This organization, which wishes to remain anonymous, shared its data on cyber attacks targeting its systems from May 2006 to June 2011.

---

[236] *See id.* at 167–69. Other trends are also prevalent in Table 7.2, such as regarding the space law treaties. For example, while the amount of time it has taken for space law treaties to enter into force has gradually increased, there was a concurrent decrease in both the number of ratifying and signatory states to the principal space law treaties from 1967 to 1984.

[237] *Id.* at 18, 161, 170–71 (providing that effectiveness in some of the more recently established regimes proves difficult to ascertain beyond a level of informed speculation).

[238] *See* Interview with Elinor Ostrom, distinguished professor, Indiana University-Bloomington, in Bloomington, Ind. (Oct. 13, 2010).

[239] *See, e.g.,* DETICA, THE COST OF CYBERCRIME 2–3 (2011), http://www.iwar.org.uk/ecoespionage/resources/cost-of-cybercrime/full-report.pdf (estimating that cybercrime costs the British economy approximately $43 billion annually).

[240] To take one other example of the continued difficulty of enhancing cybersecurity, consider the case of online voting. This is becoming more popular in parts of the world, but a pilot program in Washington, DC, in late 2012 resulted in security specialists finding a number of lapses – a team from the University of Michigan was even able to hack the website so that the University's fight song would play after a vote was cast. *See* Timothy B. Lee, *The Michigan Fight Song and Four Other Reasons to Avoid Internet Voting*, ARS TECHNICA (Oct. 24, 2012), http://arstechnica.com/tech-policy/2012/10/the-michigan-fight-song-and-four-other-reasons-to-avoid-internet-voting/.

[241] *See* VOGLER (2000), *supra* note 230, at 162.

[242] As an analogy to cyberspace, space law, despite having more directly applicable international treaties than cyber law, has also experienced a multilateral weakening along with a concurrent move toward polycentric governance notably in the arena of orbital debris mitigation. *See* Scott J. Shackelford, *Governing the Final Frontier: A Polycentric Approach to Managing Space Weaponization and Debris*, 51 AM. BUS. L.J. 429 (2014).

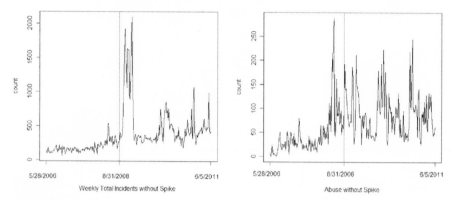

FIGURE 7.1. TOTAL NUMBER OF CYBER ATTACKS AFFLICTING ONE LARGE ORGANIZATION, 2006 TO 2011. Note that for "Weekly Total Incidents" and "Abuse", there was a spike at 1/25/2009, which was artificial due to spam abuse service issue. Data from this week was excluded from the analysis.

Over this five-year period, there was an upward trend in the total number of incidents, though perhaps not as dramatic as one might expect after reviewing the, at times, alarmist surveys summarized in Chapter 5. Overlaid on Figure 7.1 is the date of August 2008 when the U.S. Computer Fraud and Abuse Act was amended,[243] representing a targeted national measure designed to better manage cybercrime. Although DOJ cybercrime prosecutions have quadrupled from 2005 to 2009,[244] the experience of this organization illustrates that the problem of cyber attacks is far from solved. Indeed, a University of Cambridge study estimated that despite the United States accounting for half of the law enforcement effort against cybercrime worldwide – not counting the billions invested by private industry – losses continue to mount, with eighteen people per second falling victim to cybercrime in 2013.[245] Analyzing any causation between the CFAA and trends in cyber attacks, however, is nearly impossible given the presence of confounding variables, so at best Figure 7.1 offers a correlation of data.

This brief study of regime effectiveness in cyberspace is necessarily limited and littered with caveats because of the lack of hard, verifiable data and binding law – though it does perhaps help illustrate why existing governance structures are in some cases inadequately managing the cyber threat. While these data may form part of an assessment of the impact of cyber law on cybersecurity, broader conclusions about regime effectiveness require additional research, data, and innovative methodologies. Yet it does seem evident that, while current laws fall short of an ideal

---

[243] *See* 18 U.S.C. § 1030(a)(4) (2008) (strengthening the CFAA through, among other revisions, making it a felony to damage ten or more computers).

[244] Electronic Interview with Michael DuBose, head of cyber investigations at Kroll Advisory Solutions and former chief of the Computer Crime & Intellectual Property Section, Criminal Division, Department of Justice (July 27, 2011).

[245] *See* Wieland Alge, *Cyber Security and the Scramble to Invest*, PS PUBLIC SERV. (Jan. 18, 2013), http://www.publicservice.co.uk/feature_story.asp?id=21942.

type fostering a positive cyber peace (unpacked later in this chapter), these legal systems are preferable to a no-regime counterfactual. That is, given the anarchy possible in the absence of any regulation, it is clear that current laws are preferable to none at all. Although ambiguities and gaps persist, the progress we have seen in enhancing cybersecurity would likely not have been possible without these and other legal systems.[246] That does not mean, though, that identifying and instilling cybersecurity best practices at multiple scales could not help improve these regimes.

CYBERSECURITY BEST PRACTICES

Crafting an effective and secure regulatory regime for cyberspace is no small feat given the malleability and complexity inherent in the environment. Each of the stakeholders identified must utilize best practices, including users, companies, countries, and the international community. This book has undertaken an inter-disciplinary analysis of some of those practices, which are summarized here. The first step is education – after all, "The weakest link in any system of information assurance is the human user."[247] Many cyber attacks, from DDoS to spear phishing, can be better managed by having an understanding of secure computing, as was recognized in the Obama administration's Cyberspace Policy Review.[248] Therefore, what follows is an analysis of personal security best practices as well as some concise lessons from the technical community, companies, and countries studied.

Personal Cybersecurity

Much can be done to make it less likely that you will be one of the approximately 12.6 million annual U.S. victims of fraud or identity theft.[249] For example, as of 2010 according to one study the most common password remained "123456," whereas the tenth most common was "abc123."[250] Putting in the effort that it takes to create strong passwords can not only save you time and money (the average victim of identity theft in 2011 reportedly spent 12 hours and $365 to fix the problem),[251] but also enhances

---

[246] *See, e.g.,* VOGLER (1995), *supra* note 230, at 181; *Europeans Charged in US Over Destructive Computer Virus,* BBC (Jan. 23, 2013), http://www.bbc.co.uk/news/world-us-canada-21174685 (reporting that Russian, Latvian, and Romanian defendants were in the process of being extradited to the United States to stand trial for launching a virus named Gozi that was responsible for the theft of millions of dollars) [hereinafter *Europeans Charged*].

[247] Fred Cate, *Comments to the White House 60-Day Cybersecurity Review,* WHITE HOUSE, Mar. 27, 2009, at 3, http://www.whitehouse.gov/files/documents/cyber/Center%20for%20Applied%20Cyber security%20Research%20-%20Cybersecurity%20Comments.Cate.pdf.

[248] *See* CYBERSPACE POLICY REVIEW, *supra* note 30, at iv.

[249] *See Identity Theft First Aid,* CAL. OFF. PRIVACY PROTECTION, http://oag.ca.gov/idtheft (last visited Jan. 31, 2014); *Protect Yourself from Identity Theft,* IRS (Jan. 2012), http://www.irs.gov/uac/Protect-Yourself-from-Identity-Theft-1.

[250] David Coursey, *Study: Hacking Passwords Easy As 123456,* PC WORLD (Jan. 21, 2010), http://www.pcworld.com/businesscenter/article/187354/study_hacking_passwords_easy_as_123456.html (this survey relied on data from Rockyou.com account users).

[251] *Identity Theft First Aid, supra* note 249.

the overall level of cybersecurity by, for example, making it less likely that your computer will become part of a botnet. To illustrate the latter, consider Burma.

Burma, at one time one of the most censored nations on Earth, was knocked off the Internet entirely in October 2010. Cyber attacks beginning in late October overwhelmed Burma's Internet connection just days ahead of elections scheduled for November 7.[252] Some reports speculate that the Burmese military was behind the attacks,[253] but they may have had unlikely accomplices – you and me. The cyber attacks that crippled Burmese networks were DDoS and phishing attacks making use of botnets.[254] Even though there is not any direct evidence that the attacks originated from U.S. systems, there are a few simple steps that can help keep your computer from turning into a zombie of a foreign military. According to Microsoft and ZDNet, these include: keeping antivirus, antispyware, firewalls, and other software up to date on all your devices; creating passwords of at least fourteen characters that consist of numbers, punctuation, or symbols for added complexity; using flash drives cautiously; being weary of the information you share on social media; encrypting sensitive information with programs like Identify Finder; avoiding "pirated or cracked software"; treating unsolicited emails prudently, especially those including attachments or links; avoiding public Wi-Fi hotspots whenever possible without using a VPN; and checking your credit report regularly for fraudulent activity.[255] Nor are Mac users immune, as discussed in Chapter 3. By taking these simple steps, we can all help make it harder to launch the kinds of attacks that crippled Burmese systems. This is a critical, but difficult, part of the polycentric partnerships necessary to enhance global cybersecurity.

According to a 2011 survey conducted by the University of Cambridge branch of YouGov, a market research agency, many users are still not taking basic precautions.[256] Some results of the study were promising. For example, 85 percent of respondents reported that their anti-virus and anti-spyware software was up to date. And fully 80 percent of respondents stated that cybersecurity was either "very important" or "important." But dig a little deeper and the situation is not so encouraging. Only 34 percent of respondents said that they "always" installed updates at the system's first request. Age plays a significant role in the outcome, with only 18 percent of 18–24-year-olds updating software at the first prompting, compared to

---

[252] See *Burma Hit by Massive Net Attack Ahead of Election*, BBC (Nov. 4, 2010), http://www.bbc.co.uk/news/technology-11693214 [hereinafter *Burma Hit*].

[253] See *Cyber Attack Cripples Myanmar Days Before Vote*, MSNBC (Nov. 4, 2010), http://www.msnbc.msn.com/id/40006682/ns/world_news-south_and_central_asia.

[254] See *Burma Hit*, *supra* note 252.

[255] *Microsoft Protect*, MICROSOFT, http://www.microsoft.com/protect/fraud/phishing/feefraud.aspx (last visited Feb. 1, 2014); Kenn Hess, *10 Security Best Practice Guidelines for Consumers*, ZDNET (Mar. 5, 2013), http://www.zdnet.com/10-security-best-practice-guidelines-for-consumers-7000012171/.

[256] This survey was conducted using an online interview administered by YouGov. For further information about the results or methodology of this survey, please contact YouGov@Cambridge, (+44)(0)20-7-012-6000.

44 percent of those older than 60. Similarly, whereas 32 percent of 18–24-year-old respondents admit to "sometimes" turning off their firewall or disregarding security warnings, only 7 percent of those respondents 60 or older reported doing so. In fact, putting social networking aside, people age 60 or older were actually more cautious when it comes to cybersecurity than the average twenty-something. Also troubling is the propensity of users to use the same password for email, online banking, and social networking sites. Only 35 percent of respondents reported that they "never" do this, with 11 percent saying that they "always" do so. Encrypting data was also uncommon, with only 6 percent reporting the use of programs to protect sensitive data, as was the case with Do Not Track programs like TorButton. Nor did many respondents seem to be paying close attention to the litany of press reports on cyber attacks, with only 25 percent stating that they had heard of either the Aurora attacks on Google or the Night Dragon attacks on Exxon, Shell, and BP.

Personal cybersecurity is the foundation on which cyber peace is built.[257] Without an informed and engaged online community, malicious actors will continue to take advantage of unknowing or apathetic users to perpetuate crimes and launch cyber attacks. Internet use comes with both rights and responsibilities. More public- and private-sector campaigns are needed to educate users about best practices starting at an early age, potentially equating good cybersecurity citizenship with good hygiene such as the importance of washing your hands.[258] The goal is to create a culture of responsibility, such as that for which Microsoft strives, as discussed in Chapter 5.[259] Toward that end, some such as Professor Susan Brenner have called for "distributed security," which may be considered a facet of polycentric governance and requires pushing down responsibility to lower levels of a multi-tiered system coupled with fining noncompliant entities.[260] Through proactive engagement, users can decrease their likelihood of becoming a victim, reduce the millions of insecure devices online,[261] and in so doing, help do their parts to crowdsource cybersecurity. However, administrators also have a vital role to play because a single breach can compromise

---

[257] Wegener, *supra* note 206, at 77, 84.

[258] *See* Lisa Daniel, *Cyber Command Synchronizes Services' Efforts*, U.S. DEP'T DEF. (July 9, 2010), http://www.defense.gov/news/newsarticle.aspx?id=59965 (quoting Navy Vice Admiral Carl V. Mauney); SCOTT CHARNEY, MICROSOFT, COLLECTIVE DEFENSE: APPLYING PUBLIC HEALTH MODELS TO THE INTERNET 4–5 (2010) (discussing the application of the public health model to cybersecurity).

[259] *See New Politics*, *supra* note 178, at 17 (discussing Manuel Castells's concept of the "culture of the Internet" as including the beliefs in "technological progress, the free flow of information, virtual communities and entrepreneurialism."). The growing strength of such cultural movements could be leveraged to help enhance both self-governance and cybersecurity if members came to see core principles such as the free flow of information being threatened.

[260] Susan W. Brenner & Leo L. Clarke, *Distributed Security: Preventing Cybercrime*, 23(4) J. MARSHALL J. COMPUTER & INFO. L. 659, 660–61 (2005).

[261] *See Whole Internet Probed for Insecure Devices*, BBC (Mar. 21, 2013), http://www.bbc.co.uk/news/technology-21875127 (reporting on a study that found millions of insecure devices online ranging from printers to webcams).

even the most protected systems.[262] As part of this multifaceted effort, more needs to be done to address underlying technical vulnerabilities, as was analyzed in Chapter 3 and is reviewed next.

Technical Cybersecurity

For much of its early history, a cadre of dedicated professionals and volunteers managed the Internet's communications and address system. As governance became more formalized, security has received greater attention, but vulnerabilities persist in the physical and logical infrastructures. Cyber attacks are the result of a complex threat ecosystem to which these vulnerabilities contribute. Their effective management requires taking targeted measures at every level as was recently discussed,[263] but noting that mitigation strategies are most efficiently introduced from the bottom-up, leading to both opportunities and challenges for regulators and illustrating the potential for polycentric governance in this context.[264] Owing to the continuing lack of scientific and political consensus over how best to meet the cyber threat, for example in the case of Border Gateway Protocol vulnerabilities, private-sector competitions such as a Cybersecurity X Prize should be organized and federal grants offered to researchers to help establish best practices.[265] Once this is accomplished, refined solutions to TCP, IP, DNS, and BGP vulnerabilities should be widely implemented; hardware and software must be improved, such as through securing supply chains and clarifying liability structures; and users must be incentivized to become better educated and responsible. In addition, after greater consensus is achieved, regulatory interventions may be undertaken to help codify industry codes of conduct, protect against free riders, and ensure a level playing field. This effort may be conceptualized as polycentric given that it encourages experimentation at multiple levels,[266] including self-regulation to manage vulnerabilities and foster cyber peace.

Corporate Cybersecurity

The private sector is at the front line of enhancing cybersecurity.[267] As with individuals, it is in firms' best interests to take cybersecurity seriously to protect their intellectual property and safeguard their customers' personally identifiable data and

---

[262] *See* Dep't Energy, 21 Steps to Improve Cyber Security of SCADA Networks 5–6 (emphasizing the importance of network administrators for cybersecurity).

[263] *See, e.g.,* D. Thaler & B. Aboba, What Makes for a Successful Protocol? 11, IETF RFC 5218, (2008), http://tools.ietf.org/html/rfc5218#page-11.

[264] Murray, *supra* note 134, at 44–45.

[265] *See* Knake, *supra* note 89, at 26–27.

[266] *See* Ostrom, *supra* note 139, at 31.

[267] *See, e.g.,* Tom Gjelten, *Bill Would Have Businesses Foot Cost of Cyberwar*, NPR (May 8, 2012), http://www.npr.org/2012/05/08/152219617/bill-would-have-businesses-foot-cost-of-cyber-war.

their own reputations. The strategic management literature has shown that cyber-security should be viewed as a "value creator" supporting e-business.[268] To reduce their risk exposure, firms should adopt a proactive, systemic approach to cyber-security through three steps.[269] First, companies should regularly conduct cyber risk assessments and invest in enhancing security consistent with their risk exposure. This first step could include requiring data encryption, air gapping vital systems, and conducting regular penetration testing with third party audits.[270] Second, managers should assess their insurance coverage as part of a comprehensive risk mitigation effort making use of cost-benefit analysis to determine whether additional protec-tion is warranted.[271] Third, firms should analyze their cybersecurity organization to ensure that it is optimized for coordination and information sharing, both within the company and with relevant industry groups and public-private partnerships. This third step serves both to help better inform policymakers and to protect their own company against known threats. Some degree of centralization is important, whether through a Chief Information Security Office or an analogous position.[272] As losses mount, investors will likely stop treating cyber attacks as a corporate nuisance, and start treating them as the serious threat that they are to the survival of firms, and at a macro level, the long-term competitiveness of knowledge economies built on innovation.[273]

National Cybersecurity

As was demonstrated by the WCIT-2012 Conference and reinforced by NSA reve-lations in 2013–14, the U.S. government can no longer dictate Internet governance. Nor is the United States alone in pursuing offensive cyber weaponry. In fact, it has been reported that "[t]he vast majority of the industrialized countries in the world today have cyber-attack capabilities."[274] As governance fragments and the playing field becomes more dangerous and crowded with public- and private-sector actors, which, if any, of the nations surveyed are getting cybersecurity right?

---

[268] Huseyin Cavusoglu, *Economics of IT Security Management, in* ECONOMICS OF INFORMATION SECURITY 71, 73 (L. Jean Camp & Stephen Lewis eds., 2004).

[269] *Cf. Incentives for Improving Cybersecurity in the Private Sector: A Cost-Benefit Perspective*, H. Comm. Homeland Security, 110th Cong. 8 (2007) (statement of Lawrence. A. Gordon, professor, University of Maryland) (discussing the business case for cybersecurity investments through five steps).

[270] *See Trial by Fire, supra* note 161, at 32–33 (noting that only 30 percent of surveyed North American firms conducted "enterprise risk assessment[s] at least twice a year."); Lacey, *supra* note 208.

[271] Gordon, *supra* note 269, at 1–2.

[272] PONEMON INST., ANNUAL STUDY: U.S. COST OF A DATA BREACH 32 (2010), http://www.fbiic.gov/public/ 2011/mar/2010_Annual_Study_Data_Breach.pdf [hereinafter DATA BREACH].

[273] *Cf.* Lacey, *supra* note 208 (arguing that firms have four options: (1) "ignore the danger," (2) implement a basic security management system that "won't stop any sophisticated attacks but it's cheap to put in place and it will satisfy the auditors and lawyers," (3) air gap vital networks, and (4) "invest in a small army of monitoring staff, equipped with an arsenal of state-of-the-art security technology.").

[274] CLARKE & KNAKE, *supra* note 170, at 64.

No country has perfected cybersecurity. Indeed, many policymakers cannot even agree on a common definition of the problem, or for that matter a single conception of CNI.[275] Still, at least five important elements of more successful national cybersecurity strategies are worth noting. First, national cybersecurity strategies that specify cybercrime laws and establish cyber emergency response teams and national authorities with clear responsibility in the vein of Israel's eGovernment initiative are needed to help protect CNI and intellectual property.[276] Second, better cybersecurity education is critical to help establish "shared situation awareness"[277] because citizens around the world are both willing and unwilling participants in cyber attacks. Estonia, to take one example, has become a leader in this regard.[278] Third, more robust public-private and cross-border information sharing is required to improve investigations and better manage cyber attacks, such as the exchanges envisioned under the Cybersecurity Act of 2012.[279] Fourth, greater emphasis should be placed on how to make multi-stakeholder Internet governance work both within and between nations. Deeper cooperation globally is unlikely without agreement on this topic, specifically how to balance the important roles played by nations and non-state actors, including international organizations and the private sector. And fifth, nations should incentivize regular cyber risk assessment and mitigation programs for government contractors and firms operating CNI, including the development of sensible cybersecurity performance standards and user-friendly cybersecurity rating systems that are as consistent as possible between nations to avoid creating an overly complex regulatory environment.[280] The NIST Cybersecurity Framework is an important

---

[275] *See, e.g., Cybersecurity Update: Key US and EU Regulatory Developments*, SKADDEN, ARPS, SLATE, MEAGHER & FLOM LLP (June 25, 2013), https://www.skadden.com/insights/cybersecurity-update.

[276] *See* JOHN HALLER, BEST PRACTICES FOR NATIONAL CYBER SECURITY: BUILDING A NATIONAL COMPUTER SECURITY INCIDENT MANAGEMENT CAPABILITY, VER. 2.0, at v (Software Engineering Inst., 2011), https://www.cert.org/archive/pdf/11tr015.pdf; CYBERSECURITY POLICY MAKING AT A TURNING POINT: ANALYZING A NEW GENERATION OF NATIONAL CYBERSECURITY STRATEGIES, OECD (2012) (summarizing the national cybersecurity strategies of ten nations).

[277] HALLER, *supra* note 276, at v.

[278] *See Cyber Security*, E-STONIA, http://e-estonia.com/e-estonia/digital-society/cyber-security (last visited Jan. 24, 2013); *cf.* Ben Weitzenkorn, *New FBI Program Teaches Kids How to Stay Safe Online*, LIVESCI. (Oct. 17, 2012), http://www.livescience.com/24063-fbi-teach-cybersecurity-kids.html (reporting on an FBI program to teach elementary and middle school students about safe mobile, social networking, and chat room use).

[279] *See* HALLER, *supra* note 276, at v; Cybersecurity Act of 2012, S. 2105, 112th Cong. § 703 (2012).

[280] *Cf.* Steven P. Bucci, Paul Rosenzweig, & David Inserra, *A Congressional Guide: Seven Steps to U.S. Security, Prosperity, and Freedom in Cyberspace*, HERITAGE FOUND. (Apr. 1, 2013), http://www.heritage.org/research/reports/2013/04/a-congressional-guide-seven-steps-to-us-security-prosperity-and-freedom-in-cyberspace (summarizing "seven key components that need to be included in truly effective cyber legislation[,]" including:

1. "Enabling information sharing instead of mandating it;
2. Encouraging the development of a viable cybersecurity liability and insurance system;
3. Creating a private-sector structure that fosters cyber-supply-chain security ratings;
4. Defining limited cyber self-defense standards for industry;

step forward in this direction, and, depending on its uptake, may well help shape an international cybersecurity duty of care especially in other jurisdictions such as the UK and India that are experimenting with similar voluntary models.[281]

The U.S. government remains at the forefront of the cybersecurity arena in part because of its historic role in the creation of the Internet and its robust IT sector. As such, the U.S. approach to regulation will likely have a significant impact on other nations' efforts. Getting it right is thus critical not only for U.S. interests, but for global cybersecurity. One important step in U.S. efforts would be a requirement that all firms operating CNI to report the types of attacks that they are detecting through a standardized methodology similar to the EU's proposed cybersecurity strategy,[282] creating a resource to better understand the composition and scale of the cyber threat. More U.S. firms are already starting to meet cybersecurity performance requirements codified from industry best practices such as through the NIST process.[283] Augmented SEC guidelines could also require the disclosure of all major cyber attacks,[284] helping to internalize costs and increase market efficiency again similar to the EU draft strategy illustrating an area of policy convergence that could foster norm building.[285] In addition, Congress should act to revise the extraterritorial reach of U.S. cybercrime laws to assist with prosecutorial efforts, clarify the use of countermeasures against aggressors,[286] work with industry to develop supply chain rating systems for sensitive hardware, and consider implementing deep-packet inspection and other intrusion detection techniques to help guard against

---

5. Advocating for more private-sector efforts to promote general awareness, education, and training across America;
6. Reforming science, technology, engineering, and mathematics (STEM) education to create a strong cyber workforce within industry and government; and
7. Leading responsible international cyber engagement.").

[281] *See* UK CYBER SECURITY STRATEGY: PROTECTING AND PROMOTING THE UK IN A DIGITAL WORLD 28 (2011), http://www.carlisle.army.mil/dime/documents/UK%20Cyber%20Security%20Strategy.pdf; *Official: EU Eying NIST Framework With 'Great interest,'* INSIDE CYBERSECURITY (Feb. 5, 2014), http://insidecybersecurity.com/index.php?option=com_user&view=login&return=aHRocDovL2luc 2lkZWN5YmVyc2VjdXJpdHkuY29tL0N5YmVyLURhaWx5LLU5ld3MvRGFpbHktTmV3cy9vZm ZpY2lhbC1ldS1leWluZy1uaXNoLWZyYW1ld29yay13aXRoLWdyZWF0LWludGVyZXNoL211bnUta WQtMTA3NS5odG1sP3VobV9jb250ZW50PGxicic5pdCZidWVkaXVtPXR3aXR0ZXI=.

[282] *See Joint Communication to the European Parliament, the Council, the European Economic and Social Committee and the Committee of the Regions: Cybersecurity Strategy of the European Union: An Open, Safe and Secure Cyberspace* 4–5, 17–19 (Feb. 7, 2013) [hereinafter *EU Cybersecurity Strategy*].

[283] *See* NAT'L INST. OF STANDARDS & TECH., CYBERSECURITY FRAMEWORK DEVELOPMENT OVERVIEW (2013), http://www.nist.gov/itl/upload/cybersecurity_framework_presentation_05292013.pdf.

[284] *See* Chris Strohm, *SEC Chairman Reviewing Company Cybersecurity Disclosures,* BLOOMBERG (May 13, 2013), http://www.bloomberg.com/news/2013-05-13/sec-chairman-reviewing-company-cybersecurity-disclosures.html (reporting that the SEC is exploring strengthening cyber attack disclosure requirements).

[285] *EU Cybersecurity Strategy*, *supra* note 282, at 5 (noting requirements to report "significant security breaches.").

[286] Hathaway et al., *supra* note 201, at 880; Bucci, Rosenzweig, & Inserra, *supra* note 280.

sophisticated encroachments.[287] Other measures should include clarifying under what circumstances the private sector may undertake active defense strategies,[288] creating micro grids to decrease the potential of widespread blackouts during a cyber attack on CNI,[289] refining cybersecurity insurance and liability schemes, supporting the implementation of trusted mail systems with sender verification, expanding public-private cybersecurity training programs along with prioritizing STEM education and R&D for secure protocols, and providing incentives such as tax credits for firms that implement cybersecurity best practices.[290] Elements within the private sector could also begin developing the digital equivalent of LEED standards,[291] identifying firms with best-in-class cybersecurity. Cybersecurity responsibilities should also be streamlined, such as by clarifying the Federal Trade Commission's power to enhance consumer cybersecurity.[292]

The list goes on, but the salient point is that much more could be done to enhance U.S. cybersecurity. To the extent possible, though, new regulations should use outcome-based rather than prescriptive criteria so that the government is not in the business of picking winners and losers in the rapidly changing cyber-threat matrix, but instead reinforcing best practices such as regular penetration testing with timelines for remediation.[293] Moreover, a targeted approach in which smaller pieces of legislation are prioritized could pay dividends, and help dispel the myth of the "comprehensive solution" to the nation's cybersecurity challenges. Partisan gridlock should not scuttle reform – cybersecurity is not a liberal or conservative issue. The time for action is now.

As the groundwork for new international agreements is being laid, countries should continue work on polycentric norms and accords "that would raise the political [and economic] cost of cyber-attacks."[294] These initiatives could include measures to fight spam and some of the more common varieties of malware as discussed earlier in this chapter, and requirements that stakeholders make anti-malware and

---

[287] *See, e.g., Detecting Cyber Threats*, BOOZ ALLEN, http://www.boozallen.com/insights/ideas/booz-allen-ideas-festival/winning-ideas/detecting-cyber-threats (last visited July 1, 2013) (advocating for the use of multivariate statistics to help identify cyber attackers); Bucci, Rosenzweig, & Inserra, *supra* note 280.

[288] *See* Paul Rosenzweig, *Cybersecurity and Public Goods: The Public/Private "Partnership"*, HOOVER INST. (2012), at 21–22, media.hoover.org/documents/EmergingThreats_Rosenzweig.pdf.

[289] *See* Melissa C. Lott, *Are Microgrids the Key to Energy Security?*, SCI. AM. (Dec. 18, 2012), http://blogs.scientificamerican.com/plugged-in/2012/12/18/guest-post-are-microgrids-the-key-to-energy-security/.

[290] *See* Bucci, Rosenzweig, & Inserra, *supra* note 280; House Cybersecurity Task Force, *supra* note 162, at 8.

[291] *See* LEED, US GREEN BUILDING COUNCIL, http://new.usgbc.org/leed (last visited Jan. 24, 2013) (defining "LEED (Leadership in Energy and Environmental Design)" as "a voluntary, consensus-based, market-driven program that provides third-party verification of green buildings.").

[292] *See, e.g.,* Brent Kendall, *FTC Fires Back in Cybersecurity Case*, WALL ST. J. (May 24, 2013), http://blogs.wsj.com/law/2013/05/24/ftc-fires-back-in-cybersecurity-case/.

[293] *See, e.g.,* Nat'l INST. OF STANDARDS & TECHNOLOGY, SPECIAL PUBLICATION 800-53A, E1, http://csrc.nist.gov/publications/nistpubs/800-53A-rev1/sp800-53A-rev1-final.pdf (representing one iteration of penetration testing best practices).

[294] *Cyberwar, supra* note 91.

anti-spyware tools available to their citizens for free along with open source encryption technologies to better safeguard private data, which in the U.S. context would have the added value of helping to rebuild the reputation of technology firms that have been tarnished in the wake of Snowden's disclosures. Legal assistance treaties could be strengthened and forums created to help prosecute attackers when national courts are unable or unwilling to exercise jurisdiction, such as through investor-state arbitration for trade secrets violations.[295] NATO could make it clear that certain types of cyber attacks will provoke a given response by issuing and practicing norms of conduct. Similarly, countries should spell out their military responses to cyber attacks, as is beginning to happen with the U.S. DOD.[296] Sanctions and countermeasures could be used against nations that launch or sponsor cyber attacks.[297] Eventually, an independent, multilateral CERT could be created as a resource to help monitor and investigate cyber attacks, similar to the original International Agency for Information Infrastructure Protection called for as part of the Stanford Proposal from Chapter 6, but with an expanded scope to include state action.[298] Through mission creep and trust building initiatives particularly in North America and Western Europe, IMPACT could become such an organization given its mandate to act as a "global multi-stakeholder and public-private alliance against cyber threats."[299]

None of these suggestions are a magic bullet, but together they can begin the process of building a global culture of cyber peace. Low-hanging fruit should also not be missed, though, given that some of these suggested reforms are difficult to implement. The Australian government, for example, has reportedly been succcessful in preventing 85 percent of cyber attacks through following three common sense techniques: application whitelisting (only permitting pre-approved programs to operate on networks), regularly patching applications and operating systems, and "minimizing the number of people on a network who have 'administrator' privileges."[300]

[295] *See* STEIN SCHJOLBERT & SOLANGE GHERNAOUTI-HELIE, A GLOBAL TREATY ON CYBERSECURITY AND CYBERCRIME 67 (2d ed. 2011).

[296] *See* DEP'T OF DEF., DEPARTMENT OF DEFENSE CYBERSPACE POLICY REPORT, at 2 (2011), http://www.defense.gov/home/features/2011/0411_cyberstrategy/docs/NDAA%20Section%20934%20Report_For%20webpage.pdf.

[297] *See* Mary Ellen O'Connell, *Cyber Security without Cyber War*, 17(2) J. CONFLICT & SEC. L. 187, 204–05 (2012) (noting that, under the international law on countermeasures, "[i]f a State is the victim of a cyber-attack or cyber espionage, and it has clear and convincing evidence that the wrong is attributable to a foreign sovereign State, the victim State may itself commit a wrong against the attacking state, so long as the wrong is commensurate with the initial wrong (proportionality) and so long as the response is aimed at inducing an end to the initial wrong (necessity) or the provision of damages.").

[298] *See* ABRAHAM D. SOFAER ET AL., STAN. UNIV., A PROPOSAL FOR AN INTERNATIONAL CONVENTION ON CYBER CRIME AND TERRORISM, art. 12 (2000), http://www.iwar.org.uk/law/resources/cybercrime/stanford/cisac-draft.htm.

[299] ITU-IMPACT, http://www.itu.int/en/ITU-D/Cybersecurity/Pages/ITU-IMPACT.aspx (last visited July 1, 2013).

[300] James A. Lewis, *Raising the Bar for Cybersecurity*, CSIS, at 1, 7–8 (Feb. 12, 2013), http://csis.org/files/publication/130212_Lewis_RaisingBarCybersecurity.pdf.

Nations will exert increasing power over the Internet going forward. Engaging in a constructive dialogue is critical to harmonizing divergent approaches and reaching a workable middle ground between Internet sovereignty and freedom that both respects civil rights and secures vital systems. Mixtures of regulatory modalities across multiple levels and sectors are required to enhance cybersecurity throughout the system. In this vein, self-regulatory agencies such as industry councils should be encouraged to create and enforce self-generated codes of conduct organically.[301] Nations should commence similar negotiations,[302] incentivize two-way information sharing, regulate to avoid market failures while minimizing distortions through dynamic modeling and outcome-based frameworks, and form deeper partnerships to share intelligence and better manage the multifaceted cyber threat.[303] But as President Obama wrote in the *Wall Street Journal*, "[S]imply sharing more information is not enough. Ultimately, this is about security gaps that have to be filled . . . We have the opportunity – and the responsibility – to take action now and stay a step ahead of our adversaries."[304] An all-of-the-above approach is needed to accomplish this feat, and to move us toward some measure of cyber peace.

TOWARD CYBER PEACE

The World Federation of Scientists first put forward "the concept of cyber peace" during a program "at the Vatican's Pontifical Academy of Sciences in December 2008."[305] After this conference, the Erice Declaration on Principles for Cyber Stability and Cyber Peace (Erice Declaration) was published.[306] The Erice Declaration called for enhanced cooperation and stability in cyberspace through instilling six lofty principles ranging from guaranteeing the "free flow of information" to forbidding exploitation and avoiding cyber conflict.[307] Each principle is controversial to

---

[301] *See* PRICE & VERHULST, *supra* note 159, at 22; Alexis, *supra* note 42.

[302] *See* Jeremy Kirk, *Russia Pushes for Online Code of Conduct at United Nations General Assembly*, COMPUTER WORLD UK (Oct. 3, 2011), http://www.computerworlduk.com/news/public-sector/3307976/russia-pushes-for-online-code-of-conduct-at-united-nations-general-assembly/.

[303] *See, e.g.*, Anthony Reuben, *Davos 2013: UK Signs Up to Online Safety Plan*, BBC (Jan. 25, 2013), http://www.bbc.co.uk/news/business-21197171 (reporting that the UK has signed up to an initiative sponsored by the World Economic Forum's Partnering for Cyber Resilience to help nations and the private sector better manage the cyber threat).

[304] Barack Obama, *Taking the Cyberattack Threat Seriously*, WALL ST. J. (July 20, 2012), http://online.wsj.com/article/SB10000872396390444433090457753549269304465o.html.

[305] Jody R. Westby, *Conclusion, in* THE QUEST FOR CYBER PEACE, *supra* note 76, at 112, 112.

[306] *Id.; see* WORLD FED'N OF SCI., ERICE DECLARATION ON PRINCIPLES FOR CYBER STABILITY AND CYBER PEACE (2009), www.ewi.info/system/files/Erice.pdf.

[307] The six principles of the Erice Declaration are as follows:

   1. All governments should recognize that international law guarantees individuals the free flow of information and ideas; these guarantees also apply to cyberspace. Restrictions should only be as necessary and accompanied by a process for legal review.
   2. All countries should work together to develop a common code of cyber conduct and harmonized global legal framework, including procedural provisions regarding investigative assistance and

one group or another. Many governments are reticent to guarantee the free flow of information, as discussed in Chapter 2, while as Chapter 6 demonstrated developing a harmonized global legal framework to manage cyber attacks is difficult, either above or below the armed attack threshold. However, less aspirational ideas are also embedded in the Erice Declaration, such as creating incentives for nations to create cyber non-aggression pacts.[308]

Cyber peace is more than simply the inverse of cyber war; what might a more nuanced view of cyber peace resemble? First, stakeholders must recognize that a positive cyber peace requires not only addressing the causes and conduct of cyber war, but also cybercrime, terrorism, espionage, and the increasing number of incidents that overlap these categories.[309] Taking each in turn, it is unlikely that a multilateral accord will be negotiated to deal explicitly with cyber war doctrines or cyber weapons for the foreseeable future as has been explained.[310] States may, however, begin the process of limiting the escalation of a cyber arms race through norm building. Like-minded groups of nations and key industry players could come together to form a "Cybersecurity Forum" in the vein of the Major Emitters Forum discussed in Chapter 2 and the Arctic Council to negotiate targeted measures that address common problems as has been called for by the Obama administration.[311] Membership in such a forum could begin with the United States and its close NATO and non-NATO allies that share a common vision for Internet governance and cybersecurity, and expand to include emerging markets and perhaps eventually

cooperation that respects privacy and human rights. All governments, service providers, and users should support international law enforcement efforts against cyber criminals.

3. All users, service providers, and governments should work to ensure that cyberspace is not used in any way that would result in the exploitation of users, particularly the young and defenseless, through violence or degradation.

4. Governments, organizations, and the private sector, including individuals, should implement and maintain comprehensive security programs based upon internationally accepted best practices and standards and utilizing privacy and security technologies.

5. Software and hardware developers should strive to develop secure technologies that promote resiliency and resist vulnerabilities.

6. Governments should actively participate in United Nations' efforts to promote global cyber security and cyber peace and to avoid the use of cyberspace for conflict.

Wegener, *supra* note 206, at 77, 79–80.

[308] *Id.* at 81. Other suggestions in the Erice Declaration such as a cyber code of conduct, a non-first use norm, prohibition on harboring cybercriminals or terrorists, and more support for law enforcement are also echoed in this study. *Id.* However, vague calls for implementing "comprehensive security programs based upon internationally accepted best practices . . ." require further refinements, as has been explored. *Id.* at 79–81.

[309] This is consistent with building out the notion of "geo-cyber stability," which may be defined as "the ability of all countries to utilize the Internet for economic, political, and demographic benefit while refraining from activities that could cause unnecessary suffering and destruction." Jody R. Westby, *Introduction, in* The Quest for Cyber Peace, *supra* note 76, at 1, 4–5.

[310] *See* Nye, Jr., *in* America's Cyber Future, *supra* note 47, at 5, 19.

[311] *See* Cyberspace Policy Review, *supra* note 30, at iv.

even antagonistic cyber powers.[312] Such limited groupings could help bypass some of the issues with consensus-based rulemaking shown in the climate change context, although political divides would likely remain prevalent.[313]

Managing cybercrime requires deeper cooperation between Member States of the Budapest Convention, as was recognized by the United Kingdom in its 2011 Cyber Security Strategy,[314] along with budgeting more resources for prosecutions and forming bilateral relationships with cybercrime havens to limit free riders.[315] Cyber terrorism remains a nascent threat,[316] but ensuring that it stays that way necessitates many of the same responses previously discussed, including close collaboration between law enforcement as well as the infiltration of non-state networks.[317] Tackling the interrelated problem of cyber espionage internationally is even more delicate, but the tipping point might be reached when nations begin to cooperate – in fact, there is some evidence that this may already be happening.[318] Until more progress is made on this facet of the cyber threat, though, defense through the instillation of cybersecurity best practices should be prioritized to protect valuable IP and state secrets.[319]

Ultimately, as discussed in Chapter 1, parsing cyber attacks by category is an insufficient means of achieving cyber peace because of problems of overlap, among other

---

[312] Participating nations in WCIT-2012 that did not sign on to the accord, thus implicitly expressing reservations about a state-centric vision for cyberspace, may also be natural allies in this initiative. *See* ITU Signatories, *supra* note 121. However, NSA revelations have likely changed the geopolitical situation with nations such as Brazil altering their views on Internet governance. *See* Max Fisher, *How Anti-NSA Backlash Could Fracture the Internet Along National Borders*, WASH. POST (Nov. 1, 2013), http://www.washingtonpost.com/blogs/worldviews/wp/2013/11/01/how-anti-nsa-backlash-could-fracture-the-internet-along-national-borders/.

[313] As was discussed in Chapter 2, there are both moral and political problems with this approach, including an application of Garrett Hardin's "lifeboat ethics," and an unwillingness of some states to be politically pressured in smaller forums. *See* Garrett Hardin, *Lifeboat Ethics: The Case Against Helping the Poor*, PSYCHOL. TODAY (Sept. 1974), at 38–40, 123–124, 126 (examining, from an ethical viewpoint, when swimmers surrounding a lifeboat should be taken aboard).

[314] *See* CABINET OFF., THE UK CYBER SECURITY STRATEGY: PROTECTING AND PROMOTING THE UK IN A DIGITAL WORLD 7 (2011), http://www.carlisle.army.mil/dime/documents/UK%20Cyber%20Security %20Strategy.pdf.

[315] *See* INTERNATIONAL STRATEGY FOR CYBERSPACE, *supra* note 36, at 7.

[316] *See, e.g., Assessing The Threat of Cyberterrorism*, NPR (Feb. 10, 2010), http://www.npr.org/templates/ story/story.php?storyId=123531188.

[317] NAT'L RES. COUNCIL, TECHNOLOGY, POLICY, LAW, AND ETHICS REGARDING U.S. ACQUISITION AND USE OF CYBERATTACK CAPABILITIES 313–15 (William A. Owens, Kenneth W. Dam, & Herbert S. Lin eds., 2009) [hereinafter NATIONAL ACADEMIES].

[318] *See, e.g., US Accuses China Government and Military of Cyber-Spying*, BBC (May 7, 2013), http:// www.bbc.co.uk/news/world-asia-china-22430224; Richard Esposito, *'Astonishing' Cyber Espionage Threat from Foreign Governments: British Spy Chief*, ABC NEWS (June 25, 2012), http://abcnews .go.com/Blotter/astonishing-cyberespionage-threat-foreign-governments-british-spy-chief/story?id=166 45690#.T-vyFXBvDL2 (noting that the United States, the United Kingdom, and other European allies have begun to coordinate in an effort to combat cyber espionage by China).

[319] Wegener, *supra* note 206, at 77, 84–85 (noting that cyber peace requires "the principle of prioritizing comprehensive self-defence over offence.").

concerns. Moreover, a top-down, monocentric approach focused on a single treaty regime or institution could crowd out innovative bottom-up best practices developed organically from diverse ethical and legal cultures. Instead, a polycentric approach is required that recognizes the dynamic, interconnected nature of cyberspace, the degree of national and private-sector control of this plastic environment, and a recognition of the benefits of multi-level action. Local self-organization, however – even by groups that enjoy legitimacy – can be insufficient to ensure the implementation of best practices.[320] There is thus also an important role for regulators,[321] who should use a mixture of laws, norms, markets, and code[322] bound together within a polycentric framework operating at multiple levels to enhance cybersecurity. Modeling such a dynamic environment is beyond the scope of this book, but requires an understanding of all the stakeholders, the linkages between them, and ultimately embracing some amount of uncertainty.[323] As with quantum physicists who found value in the Heisenberg Uncertainty Principle that helped give birth to quantum mechanics,[324] cyber regulators also face an increasingly complex task. Dynamic regulation in which all stakeholders are also regulators both increases the type and number of choices for possible interventions, and complicates the task of enhancing cybersecurity. Nevertheless, harmony may be found even within chaotic systems,[325] such as through developing new tools to model the multi-dimensional effects of regulations and fine-tuning them as necessary. Ultimately, however, if we are to further our understanding of how such a polycentric system may operate, we must accept that there are currently limits to our knowledge and thus rely on informed experimentation, much like the early twentieth-century physicists and, for

---

[320] *See* Nye, Jr., *supra* note 173, at 15 (arguing that the conditions that Professor Ostrom associates with self-governance "are weak in the cyber domain because of the large size of the resource, the large number of users, and the poor predictability of system dynamics (among others)."). But the growing enclosure of cyberspace that Professor Nye highlights, along with the movement towards more robust virtual communities, could make cyberspace more amenable to self-governance, especially if more communities adopted a Lockean hybrid model.

[321] It is important to note that polycentric governance is distinct from notions of network governance, which can "attribute too little importance to central coordination. . . ." McGinnis, *supra* note 218, at 8. The trick in the Internet governance context is balancing multilevel regulations with existing laws and treaties to create an adaptable and efficient system of governance. Further research is required to better understand the contours of such a regime.

[322] *See* LESSIG, *supra* note 143, at 125.

[323] *See* MURRAY, *supra* note 134, at 252; *cf.* Zuckerberg & Schmidt, *supra* note 16 (quoting Eric Schmidt as saying, "Technology will move faster than governments, so don't legislate before you understand the consequences.").

[324] MURRAY, *supra* note 134, at 254. This principle states that an observer may know the path that an electron takes through space or its location at a given moment but not both. *Cf.* Geoff Brumfiel, *Common Interpretation of Heisenberg's Uncertainty Principle Is Proved False*, SCI. AM. (Sept. 11, 2012), http://www.scientificamerican.com/article.cfm?id=common-interpretation-of-heisenbergs-uncertainty-principle-is-proven-false (reporting on an experiment that challenges the assumption of quantum uncertainty).

[325] MURRAY, *supra* note 134, at 250.

that matter, Internet pioneers.[326] Where, though, does that leave our discussion of cyber peace?

What is the best that we can reasonably hope for in terms of "peace" on the Internet? States, organizations, and individuals will continue to engage in cyber espionage so long as it functions as such an effective tool for intelligence gathering.[327] In response, globally the "five eyes" should be expanded and negotiations begun to curtail state-sponsored industrial espionage,[328] and domestically the U.S. DOD program called "Defense Industrial" designed to help protect at-risk firms should be enlarged.[329] A tiered approach to cybercrime should also be implemented. Step one would enable enhanced public-private and private-private information sharing to identify cybercrime trends and spread best practices to promote positive network effects.[330] Step two would seek to stabilize and then gradually reduce cybercrime levels through budgeting more resources to law enforcement, stepping-up prosecutions along with harmonizing cybercrime laws, and incentivizing cyber risk mitigation strategies to limit exposure and protect consumers through norm building. Targeted forums should be created to manage the risk of escalation of cyber conflicts, with states recognizing "that cyber attacks will be a significant component of any future conflict, whether it involves major nations, rogue states, or terrorist groups."[331] Military doctrines should be updated accordingly. Ultimately, nations – including the United States – must secure not only government networks, but also private CNI, which requires using laws, norms, markets, and code[332] to enhance cybersecurity

---

[326] *Id.* at 257.

[327] The political cost of espionage may, though, at times outweigh the advantages gained, as may be seen in the aftermath of the 2013–14 NSA revelations necessitating a rebalancing to appease allies and protect civil liberties. *See, e.g., Transcript of President Obama's Jan. 17 Speech on NSA Reforms,* WASH. POST (Jan. 17, 2014), http://www.washingtonpost.com/politics/full-text-of-president-obamas-jan-17-speech-on-nsa-reforms/2014/01/17/fa33590a-7f8c-11e3-9556-4a4bf7bcbd84_story.html ("[J]ust as [we] balance security and privacy at home, our global leadership demands that we balance our security requirements against our need to maintain the trust and cooperation among people and leaders around the world. For that reason, the new presidential directive that I've issued today will clearly prescribe what we do and do not do when it comes to our overseas surveillance."); Siobhan Gorman, *White House Added Last-Minute Curbs on NSA Before Obama Speech,* WALL ST. J. (Jan. 31, 2014), http://online.wsj.com/news/articles/SB10001424052702303743604579355221879331080?mg=reno64-wsj&url=http%3A%2F%2Fonline.wsj.com%2Farticle%2FSB10001424052702303743604579355221879331080.html.

[328] *See, e.g., Germany Seeks Admission to Spooks' Club,* DW.DE (Nov. 4, 2013), http://www.dw.de/germany-seeks-admission-to-spooks-club/a-17203578 (proposing an expanded system of "no-spy agreement[s] . . . [as a way] to set common standards for Western intelligence services and declare[] the NSA spying affair case over."); *State-Backed Data Spies Hunt Industrial Secrets,* BBC (Apr. 22, 2013), http://www.bbc.co.uk/news/technology-22248700.

[329] William J. Lynn, *Remarks on the Department of Defense Cyber Strategy,* U.S. DEP'T DEF. (July 14, 2011), http://www.defense.gov/speeches/speech.aspx?speechid=1593.

[330] Neal K. Katyal, *The Dark Side of Private Ordering: The Network/Community Harm of Crime, in* THE LAW AND ECONOMICS OF CYBERSECURITY 193, 193–94 (Mark F. Grady & Francesco Parisi eds., 2006).

[331] *Id.*

[332] *See* LESSIG, *supra* note 143, at 125.

and build effective multi-type, multi-sector, and multi-level partnerships to promote Internet access, human rights, and the uptake of best practices.[333]

Cyber peace, then, will likely not mean the absence of cyber attacks or a "wholesome state of tranquility. . . ."[334] Rather, cyber peace is the construction of a network of multilevel regimes promoting global, just, and sustainable cybersecurity. Various frameworks have been proposed to attain this positive vision of cyber peace in addition to the Erice Declaration, including from the ITU[335] and the UK government.[336] Regional attempts have also been made at defining the principles of cyber peace, such as a Council of Europe initiative that, among other things, has sought "to protect human rights in cyberspace, and a responsibility to prevent and minimize transboundary harm or interference to the cross-border flow of the Internet."[337] Though differences exist between these approaches, such as with respect to protecting intellectual property, a prohibition on launching first strikes, and the role of the

---

[333] *See* McGinnis, *supra* note 218, at 6–7.

[334] Henning Wegener, *A Concept of Cyber Peace*, in THE QUEST FOR CYBER PEACE 77, 78 (Hamadoun I. Touré & Permanent Monitoring Panel on Information Security, 2011). Wegener, *supra* note 206, at 79.

[335] *See* Touré, *supra* note 76, at 103 (listing five principles of cyber peace):

1. Every government should commit itself to giving its people access to communications;
2. Every government will commit itself to protecting its people in cyberspace;
3. Every country will commit itself not to harbor terrorists/criminals in its own territories;
4. Every country should commit itself not to be the first to launch a cyber attack on other countries; and
5. Every country must commit itself to collaborate with each other within an international framework of co-operation to ensure that there is peace in cyberspace.

[336] *See* Daniel J. Ryan, Maeve Dion, Eneken Tikk, & Julie J. C. H. Ryan, *International Cyberlaw: A Normative Approach*, 42 GEO. J. INT'L L. 1161, 1172 (2011) (citing William Hague, U.K. Foreign Sec'y, Speech at the Munich Security Conference: Security and Freedom in the Cyber Age – Seeking the Rules of the Road (Feb. 11, 2011), http://www.fco.gov.uk/en/news/latest-news/?view=Speech&id=545383882) (laying out a list of seven cyber peace principles):

1. The need for governments to act proportionately in cyberspace and in accordance with national and international law.
2. The need for everyone to have the ability – in terms of skills, technology, confidence and opportunity – to access cyberspace.
3. The need for users of cyberspace to show tolerance and respect for diversity of language, culture, and ideas.
4. Ensuring that cyberspace remains open to innovation and the free flow of ideas, information, and expression.
5. The need to respect individual rights of privacy and to provide proper protection to intellectual property.
6. The need for us all to work collectively to tackle the threat from criminals acting online.
7. The promotion of a competitive environment which ensures a fair return on investment in network, services, and content.

[337] *Id.* at 1172 (citing Council of Eur. Steering Comm. on the Media & New Commc'ns Servs., Terms of Reference of the Ad Hoc Advisory Group on Cross-border Internet (2010), http://www.coe.int/t/dghl/standardsetting/media/MC-S-CI/MC-S-CI(2009)Rev_mandat_en.asp).

United Nations in fostering cyber peace, significant similarities also exist including a common desire to support international legal mechanisms to enhance cybersecurity, along with promoting tolerance and taking steps to protect citizens in cyberspace.

In an attempt to build on common ground in conceptualizing cyber peace, a modification of the Erice Declaration is proposed comprised of five main recommendations that builds from these earlier definitions and is consistent with the findings in this book. First, nations "should work together to develop a common code of conduct" that incorporates baseline norms, including a prohibition on harboring cybercriminals or terrorists and not unduly limiting certain Internet freedoms such as the free flow of information, while supporting existing international law and continuing negotiations on a harmonized global cybersecurity legal framework that addresses difficult subjects like attribution.[338] Second, governments and CNI operators should establish proactive, comprehensive cybersecurity policies and frameworks that meet global best practices and require hardware and software developers to promote resiliency in their products.[339] Third, consensual recommendations of stakeholders such as technical organizations including IETF should be made enforceable by nations when taken up as industry best practices to help guard against free riders in the vein of NERC and NIST. Fourth, governments and NGOs should not only continue to participate in UN efforts to mitigate the risk of cyber conflict [340] and refine multi-stakeholder Internet governance, but also create formal and informal cybersecurity forums to enable faster progress on core issues of common concern such as protecting critical international infrastructure like the global financial system, fighting spam, safeguarding trade secrets, and protecting human rights, including the establishment of baseline privacy rights and stopping the exploitation of vulnerable populations online.[341] Fifth and finally, training campaigns and more robust public-private partnerships should be undertaken to share information and educate stakeholders at all levels about the nature and extent of the cyber threat.[342] Together, these polycentric initiatives could help to foster cyber peace in an age of cyber conflict.

---

[338] Wegener, *supra* note 206, at 77, 79.

[339] *Id.* at 79–80.

[340] *Id.* at 80.

[341] These groups need not be formalized; informal efforts should also be encouraged. For example, the successful Conficker Working Group was made up of "the cybersecurity community, including Microsoft, ICANN, domain registry operators, anti-virus vendors, and academic researchers organized to block the infected computers from reaching the domains...." CONFICKER WORKING GROUP: LESSONS LEARNED ii (2011), http://www.confickerworkinggroup.org/wiki/uploads/Conficker_Working_Group_Lessons_Learned_17_June_2010_final.pdf.

[342] *See* Touré, *supra* note 76, at 86, 90, 99–100 (arguing that "an effective strategy for cyber peace must be flexible and adaptable enough to manage and respond to the fast-pace of technological advancement, ICT growth and their attendant security challenges. Countries must also agree on procedures and approaches for tracing points of origin and identities in order to address anonymous cyber attacks and the international entanglements they threaten to create.").

From Aurora and Stuxnet to Flame and the Great Firewall of China, the power of cyberspace both as a tool for social and political development and as a weapon should not be underestimated. Cyber criminals launch attacks against individuals, firms, and even states often without fear of prosecution given problems of attribution and jurisdiction.[343] States are using cyberspace as an unprecedented tool for espionage, stealing a treasure trove of intellectual property and state secrets from the NSA allegedly spying on German Chancellor Angela Merkel and foreign companies to seemingly endless waves of Chinese state-sponsored cyber attacks.[344] But instead of cyber peace appearing on bumper stickers, so far the public is not engaged.[345] So, gazing into the crystal ball, what hope is there for cyber peace? Myriad views pervade discussions about a cyber end game.

Professor Ryan simply defines cyber peace as "when bad stuff isn't happening, you're at peace. We're never going to see that again in cyberspace."[346] However, just because negative cyber peace is likely impossible does not mean that we are in a constant state of war. "War is characterized by widespread, harmful effects, like WWII when 80 million people died . . . in this case, absent such serious effects, the reality is that we're going to continue to be in a state of low-level hostilities that won't rise to the level of war, but will never be what I like to think of as peace . . . we're going to have to be on guard all the time."[347] In this way, a component of positive cyber peace may be thought of as being akin to law enforcement and counterinsurgency operations, recognizing that the threat of cyber attacks is real, but not all encompassing. If and when a true "attack" occurs, then all elements of national power would be needed to restore the relative calm.[348]

According to Chris Palmer, "[c]yber peace can't mean mutually assured destruction . . . That's one view of cyber peace that I really don't want."[349] Instead, Palmer

---

[343] *But see Europeans Charged, supra* note 246 (showing that law enforcement agencies are having some success at apprehending cybercriminals, though it remains unclear to what extent such arrests are impacting overall cybercrime rates).

[344] *See* Stephen Brown, *Berlin and Washington Still 'Far Apart' on NSA, Merkel Says,* REUTERS (Jan. 29, 2014), http://uk.reuters.com/article/2014/01/29/uk-germany-usa-merkel-idUKBREA0S0ZW20140129; Steven Musil, *Snowden Accuses NSA of Conducting Industrial Espionage,* CNET (Jan. 26, 2014), http://news.cnet.com/8301-13578-3-57617823-38/snowden-accuses-nsa-of-conducting-industrial-espionage/; *China's 'State Sponsored Hackers Renew Attacks on US,'* BBC (May 20, 2013), http://www.bbc.co.uk/news/technology-22594140.

[345] *Cf. National Cyber Security Awareness Month, supra* note 182.

[346] Interview with Dan Ryan, professor, National Defense University, in Wash., D.C. (Jan. 5, 2011).

[347] *Id.* This comment brings up the notion of international "cyber peacekeepers" to help police the Internet for criminal activity. This idea, though, has been criticized as redundant given ongoing national and inter-governmental efforts aimed at enhancing global cybersecurity. *See, e.g.,* Ellyne Phneah, *Idea of Cyber Peacekeepers Premature, 'Redundant,'* ZDNET (Feb. 6, 2012), http://www.zdnet.com/idea-of-cyber-peacekeepers-premature-redundant-2062303742/.

[348] *Id.*

[349] Interview with Chris Palmer, Google engineer and former technology director, Electronic Frontier Foundation, in San Francisco, Cal. (Feb. 25, 2011).

envisions economic interdependence gradually making cyber war unthinkable, the same philosophy behind the European Union, born out of two world wars, that was central to its winning the 2012 Nobel Peace Prize.[350] Under this view, therefore, trade and investment would become the main vehicle for cyber peace, which is encouraging considering the deepening U.S.-China economic relations.[351] However, so long as nations think they enjoy plausible deniability, even economic integration may be insufficient to ward off escalation.

For Jim Dempsey, one aspect of cyber peace is the protection of personal privacy: "Cyber peace would be the ability to control information about yourself and use it only for purposes for which it was collected."[352] NSA revelations driving the evolution of Internet governance underscore the importance of multilateral and multi-stakeholder discussions on privacy.[353] From a military perspective, Dempsey thinks there is little hope of banning cyber weapons: "Look at the success of Stuxnet; if I'm a warrior there's no way that I want to give this up, its served our foreign policy goals and avoided some of the worst forms of retaliation."[354] In the end, then, Dempsey believes that cyber peace will look a lot like regular peace: "It's going to be incomplete and messy," and each country is going to want to do it on its own terms.[355]

Richard Clarke argues that a first step toward cyber peace requires creating the right community of people who are well informed and know one another: "We haven't done this yet for cyber. Real progress can be made only after that foundation is laid."[356] Creating these communities requires that first, "[y]ou've got to introduce the diplomats in every country to their own technical people, you've got to educate them about what the technical issues are, frequently they're scared because after all, if they could do math, they wouldn't be diplomats."[357] Such a feat is easier in a small nation like Estonia than a large one like the United States, but highlights the importance of multi-stakeholder dialogue both within and between nations along with active engagement from technical communities.

---

[350] *See, e.g., Nobel Peace Prize Awarded to European Union,* BBC News (Oct. 12, 2012), http://www.bbc .co.uk/news/world-europe-19921072.

[351] *See Trade in Goods with China,* U.S. Census Bureau, http://www.census.gov/foreign-trade/balance/ c5700.html (last visited July 1, 2013). The opportunity for a U.S.-China bilateral investment treaty that includes trade secrets protections could also deepen this component of bilateral cyber peace between the G2, which could then extend to other trading partners and beyond. *See US, China Move Forward on Bilateral Investment Treaty,* Voice of Am. (July 11, 2013), http://www.voanews.com/ content/us-china-to-focus-on-economy-on-final-day-of-talks/1699526.html.

[352] Dempsey, *supra* note 90.

[353] *See, e.g.,* Ewan MacAskill, *Independent Commission to Investigate Future of Internet After NSA Revelations,* Guardian (Jan. 22, 2014), http://www.theguardian.com/world/2014/jan/22/independent-commission-future-internet-nsa-revelations-davos.

[354] Dempsey, *supra* note 90.

[355] *Id.*

[356] Interview with Richard Clarke, chairman for Good Harbor Consulting, in Wash., D.C. (Jan. 4, 2011).

[357] *Id.*

Professor Fred Cate equates cyber attacks with bad weather: "We want to predict, identify, and survive these attacks."[358] The best way to assure this, according to Professor Cate, is to require that security be built into the system. For example, he explains that Congress required all television manufacturers to include UHF tuners in 1961 so that local television stations could be viewed.[359] For some reason, however, the thought of doing something similar for cybersecurity remains a non-starter. As he puts it, "[i]f I had my way, every router and cable box would have to be secured."[360] For the time being, though, he argues "the best thing that I can hope for from a smart phone is that it doesn't ruin my life when a breach happens."[361]

Cyber attacks will continue to happen, even with enhanced security features. That is why this book takes the approach of managing cyber attacks, not stopping them. Using a biological analogy, cybersecurity is like the human body, in that viruses will inevitably infiltrate critical systems – the trick is to build in resilience and triage to fight off the most virulent strands quickly.[362] Moreover, even if it were possible to stop cyber attacks, scholars such as Professor Goldsmith have argued that we would not want to: "On the private side, hacktivism can be a tool of liberation. On the public side, the best defense of critical computer systems is sometimes a good offense."[363]

Although views diverge, what is clear is that cyber peace is not the absence of attacks or exploitations, that is, negative cyber peace, which has been shown to be technically and politically unattainable in the near term, as well as being insufficient to build a robust global culture of cybersecurity. Rather, it is the construction of a network of multilevel regimes that share the common end of promoting cybersecurity by clarifying the rules of the road for companies and countries alike so as to gradually reduce the risk of cyber conflict, along with the cost of cybercrime and espionage, to levels comparable to other business and national security risks. Achieving this goal requires using the technical, legal, political, and economic tools discussed throughout this book couched within a polycentric framework. That is not easy; in fact, "achieving and maintaining cyber-peace can be as demanding as starting

---

[358] Telephone Interview with Fred Cate, distinguished professor and C. Ben Dutton Professor of Law and director, Center for Applied Cybersecurity Research, Indiana University Maurer School of Law (June 10, 2011).

[359] *See* All-Channel Receiver Act, Pub. L. No. 87-529, 76 Stat. 150 (1962) (codified at 47 U.S.C. §§ 303(s), 330 (1976)).

[360] Cate, *supra* note 358.

[361] *Id.*

[362] *See* Marlene Cimons, *The Science of Cyber Security*, U.S. NEWS & WORLD REP. (Aug. 4, 2011), http://www.usnews.com/science/articles/2011/08/04/the-science-of-cyber-security. *See also* Alex Stark, Book Review, E-INT'L REL. (Jan. 6, 2014), http://www.e-ir.info/2014/01/06/review-cybersecurity-and-cyberwar/ (reviewing PETER W. SINGER & ALLAN FRIEDMAN, CYBERSECURITY AND CYBERWAR: WHAT EVERYONE NEEDS TO KNOW 170–72 (2014)) (discussing the concept of resilience in cybersecurity policymaking).

[363] Jack Goldsmith, *Can We Stop the Global Cyber Arms Race?*, WASH. POST (Feb. 1, 2010), http://articles.washingtonpost.com/2010-02-01/opinions/36895669_1_botnets-cyber-attacks-computer-attacks.

a Cyberwar."[364] Working through polycentric partnerships, however, and with the leadership of engaged individuals and institutions, we can stop cyber war before it starts by moving toward a positive vision of cyber peace that respects human rights, spreads Internet access along with the cybersecurity best practices outlined in this chapter, and strengthens Internet governance mechanisms by eschewing false choices and fostering global multi-stakeholder collaboration.[365]

[364] *Talk: On Cyber-Peace – Towards an International Cyber Defense Strategy*, DEEPSEC (Nov. 4, 2011), http://blog.deepsec.net/?p=702.

[365] *See, e.g.,* Touré, *supra* note 76, at 86, 100 (arguing that, among other considerations, Article 19 of the Universal Declaration of Human Rights is fundamental to promoting cyber peace, as is deeper international engagement analogous to the Outer Space Treaty's guiding principles stating that "all states should pursue cooperation and mutual assistance in the exploration and use of outer space.").

Conclusion

This book has examined the issue of cyber peace and argued for the "movement towards a global culture of cybersecurity" in which individuals, organizations, and nations enjoy the rights and responsibilities of an open and secure Internet.[1] Achieving this goal, needless to say, is easier said than done. Governance in cyberspace remains relatively fragmented. The international community must come together to craft a common vision for cyberspace and cybersecurity. But given the difficulties of accomplishing this feat in the near term, alternative paths forward should be considered, including polycentric governance.

Particular attention has been paid to some of the consequences of the current state of Internet governance – notably, the potential for a new digital divide to emerge and the impact of an increasingly state-centric cyberspace on enhancing global cybersecurity. Economically, insufficient progress has been made toward addressing this issue with losses to cybercrime showing little sign of abating, although information here is imperfect, and collective action problems remaining prevalent. Politically, the growth of regime complexes is evident, with an increasing array of actors competing for influence at multiple levels. Legally, applicable national and international law is largely insufficient to adequately enhance cybersecurity, requiring clarification domestically as well as globally both above and below the armed attack threshold.[2] Thorny issues of attribution must be addressed, even if some ambiguity remains.[3]

---

[1] Henning Wegener, *A Concept of Cyber Peace*, *in* THE QUEST FOR CYBER PEACE 77, 77 (Int'l Telecomm. Union & Permanent Monitoring Panel on Info. Sec. eds., 2011).

[2] *See* Harold Hongju Koh, Legal Advisor, U.S. Dep't of State, Remarks at USCYBERCOM Inter-Agency Legal Conference: International Law in Cyberspace (Sept. 18, 2012), http://www.state.gov/s/l/releases/remarks/197924.htm; James B. Michael et al., *Measured Responses to Cyber Attacks Using Schmitt Analysis: A Case Study of Attack Scenarios for a Software-Intensive System*, IEEE PROC. TWENTY-SEVENTH ANNUAL INT. COMPUTER SOFTWARE & APPLICATIONS CONF. 621 (Dallas, Tex., Nov. 2003), http://www.au.af.mil/au/awc/awcgate/nps/ws09-with-pub-info.pdf.

[3] *See* Stewart Baker, *Cybersecurity and Attribution – Good News At Last?*, VOLOKH CONSPIRACY (Oct. 7, 2012). http://www.volokh.com/2012/10/07/cybersecurity-and-attribution-good-news-at-last/. Some

Overall, the international legal system is unlikely to soon operate a coherent law of cyber war and peace. Many of the relevant international treaties do not specify whether or how they apply after an armed attack. Nor do many of these treaties include adequate enforcement provisions including countermeasures. Still, there are the beginnings of a law of cyber peace present, which could be built upon by the international community using all of the tools available to tackle the global collective action problem of cyber attacks. Nations, criminals, spies, and terrorists are increasingly using cyber attacks to further their own ends, sometimes in conjunction with one another. International law needs to better reflect this reality. A multilateral cybersecurity accord should be negotiated in this vein that: (1) defines graduated sanctions against nations harboring or sponsoring cybercriminals and terrorists where possible, and sets out when a cyber attack rises to the level of an armed conflict; (2) clarifies which international legal provisions apply above and below the armed attack threshold; (3) establishes a regime for attribution that includes robust information sharing; (4) provides for enforcement mechanisms; and (5) implements a system of dispute resolution.[4] All interested stakeholders should push for a constructive dialogue through such tactics as creating targeted forums with limited membership, making every effort to proactively assess and mitigate cyber risk, and building consensus on crafting regulations to help make cyberspace as secure and open as possible while avoiding the creation of safe harbors. There is no perfect forum in a multipolar world; both top-down and bottom-up approaches have benefits and drawbacks. Even though the Internet has vastly changed since IETF's creation, for example, there is still room for bottom-up governance in the form of industries creating norms of conduct that encompass best practices. There is also space for governments to regulate at-risk CNI for the public good. However, without concerted action, the international community will lurch from crisis to crisis that could mount in severity to a point that not only cripples societies and challenges the very existence of the cyber pseudo commons, but could also shake the Information Age to its foundations.

Direct regulatory interventions are only one element of promoting cybersecurity. There are myriad other modalities identified by Professor Lessig and others that deserve further research and attention by scholars and policymakers.[5] These include developing norms, relying on norm entrepeneurs and the competitive market whenever possible to self-regulate and thus minimize market distortions, providing incentives for the uptake of cybersecurity best practices, and addressing technical vulnerabilities. If nations undertake these efforts alongside the private sector and

---

scholars, for example, have introduced a spectrum featuring both active and passive responsibility for cyber attacks depending on whether the accused aggressor state ignored, abetted, or conducted the attacks. *See* Jason Healey, *Beyond Attribution: A Vocabulary for National Responsibility for Cyber Attacks*, CYBER CONFLICT STUD. ASSOC., May 21, 2010, at 15.

[4] *See* Oona A. Hathaway et al., *The Law of Cyber-Attack*, 100 CAL. L. REV. 817, 880 (2012).

[5] LAWRENCE LESSIG, CODE: AND OTHER LAWS OF CYBERSPACE 71 (1999).

other key stakeholders, we may enter a more global and collaborative Phase Four of Internet governance, making it possible to craft a common twenty-first century vision for cyberspace. An amount of uncertainty must be embraced in this process, along with the necessity for dynamic regulatory models such as polycentric governance that recognize the diversity of public and private stakeholders operating at multiple scales and take technological change as a given.[6] No nation is an island in cyberspace. Enhanced multilateral cooperation is essential to promoting cybersecurity, as is education. Ignorance and apathy are the enemies of cybersecurity and the allies of attackers. There likely will not be a technological magic bullet that solves the problem, although plenty of fixes may help (such as DNSSEC and IPsec), as well as federated identity schemes to create a system for authenticating secure digital identities.[7] But as Paul Saffo, director of the Institute of the Future, has stated, "We tend to invest our fondest hopes and our deepest fears in new technology, and in fact it turns out that neither our hopes nor our fears are realized."[8] We should look to the tools of social science, then, as well as computer science and information systems management, to enhance global cybersecurity.

It is common to think that one is living through a pivotal moment in human history. Often that is incorrect, but here it may be right. We are seeing a fundamental change in the methods of communication and the nature of cyberspace that will only continue with the rapid introduction of new technologies comprising the "Internet of things," such as self-driving cars, that promise to enhance efficiency as well as multiply vulnerabilities.[9] It is time to get off the surfboard and examine the wave. The domestic and global implications of human society's increasing dependence on the Internet makes our ability to deter, detect, and minimize the effects of cyber attacks ever more necessary,[10] even as fracturing governance has made the task more challenging. Today, the international community is at the point of determining how governance of cyberspace should develop in the twenty-first century. The strategies and practices assumed in the short-term will impact how this fast-evolving body of law and policy is shaped and systems are secured. Policymakers and managers

---

[6] *See* ANDREW W. MURRAY, THE REGULATION OF CYBERSPACE: CONTROL IN THE ONLINE ENVIRONMENT 25–52 (2006).

[7] Kristin M. Lord & Travis Sharp, *Executive Summary*, *in* AMERICA'S CYBER FUTURE: SECURITY AND PROSPERITY IN THE INFORMATION AGE 7, 31 (Kristin M. Lord & Travis Sharp eds., CNAS, 2011) (noting the major cybersecurity successes of the Obama administration as of 2011, including "a 60-day Cyberspace Policy Review, creating U.S. Cyber Command, elevating the role of DHS, increasing funding for key programs, and unveiling the National Strategy for Trusted Identities in Cyberspace and an international cyberspace strategy.").

[8] SALLY RICHARDS, FUTURENET: THE PAST, PRESENT, AND FUTURE OF THE INTERNET AS TOLD BY ITS CREATORS AND VISIONARIES 200 (2002).

[9] *See* Aliya Sternstein, *Do We Need Cyber Cops for Cars?*, NEXTGOV (Nov. 13, 2012), http://www.nextgov .com/cybersecurity/2012/11/do-we-need-cyber-cops-cars/59477/; *The Internet of Things*, IBM, http:// www.ibm.com/smarterplanet/us/en/overview/article/iot_video.html (last visited Feb. 3, 2014).

[10] HOWARD F. LIPSON, CERT COORDINATION CTR., TRACKING AND TRACING CYBER-ATTACKS: TECHNICAL CHALLENGES AND GLOBAL POLICY ISSUES 3 (2002), http://www.dtic.mil/cgi-bin/GetTRDoc? AD=ADA408853&Location=U2&doc=GetTRDoc.pdf.

should consider not only what serves short-term military and commercial interests, but also the shared long-term interest of building a secure, interconnected, and robust cyberspace for the world's existing 2.5 billion Internet users, and the billions more to come.

In 3001: *The Final Odyssey*, Arthur C. Clarke envisions a future where humanity had the foresight to rid itself of the worst weapons of mass destruction that it had created and place them in a vault on the moon.[11] A special place in this vault was reserved for the most malignant computer viruses that, in his speculative fiction, had caused untold damage to humanity over the centuries.[12] Before the great-grandchild of Stuxnet does untold damage to our Information Society, it is in our own best interest to educate and regulate our way to a steady state of cybersecurity where we can all enjoy the benefits of an open and secure cyberspace. Remember, the Internet is written in ink. The best and worst of our collective history, including our creations, will be preserved for posterity, and maybe that is as it should be. After all, in 3001, the cyber weapons that humanity had created to destroy one another eventually were called on to save us from an alien invasion. However unlikely that scenario might be, if there is one thing that science fiction has taught us, it is the wonder of the future, both good and bad. As Alfred Tennyson wrote, "When I dipt into the future far as human eye could see; [s]aw the Vision of the world, and all the wonder that would be."[13] Whether or not that future includes the security and prosperity of cyber peace is up to us.

---

[11] ARTHUR C. CLARKE, 3001: THE FINAL ODYSSEY 219–23 (1997).

[12] *Id.*

[13] ALFRED TENNYSON, THE POETICAL WORKS OF ALFRED LORD TENNYSON 160 (2004).

Appendix

Illustrative Timeline of Significant Cyber Attacks as Catalogued by the Center for Strategic and International Studies[1]

Date of Attack	Popular Name of Attack or Target	Alleged Source Country	Target Country/Firm	Description of Event
February 1998	Solar Sunrise	Attacks were widespread and included: Israel, the United Arab Emirates, France, Taiwan, and Germany	United States	Computers based in the United Arab Emirates managed to breach U.S. government networks including the DOD.
March 1999	Kosovo Campaign	Multiple sources including, allegedly, Serbia and the United States	Former Yugoslavia, NATO nations	NATO web servers came under sustained attacks, while NATO forces similarly targeted Milosevic's command and control capabilities online.
May 1999	Chinese Embassy Bombing	China	China, United States	In the wake of the U.S. bombing of the Chinese embassy in Belgrade, there were multiple reports of cyber attacks directed at U.S. government networks.

(continued)

[1] *Significant Cyber Incidents Since 2006*, CSIS, http://csis.org/files/publication/131010_Significant_Cyber_Incidents_Since_2006_0.pdf (last visited Feb. 3, 2014). The CSIS defines "significant" cyber attacks as those "that were successful, targeted government agencies, defense and high tech companies, or economic crimes with losses of more than a million dollars." *Id.* Information about pre-2006 cyber attacks was compiled from the following sources: Global Security: Solar Sunrise, http://www.globalsecurity.org/military/ops/solar-sunrise.htm (last visited Feb. 4, 2014); The Israeli-Palestinian Cyber Conflict, RUSI (Feb. 2001), http://www.mafhoum.com/press2/74T42.htm; Technology, Policy, Law, and Ethics Regarding US Acquisition and Use of Cyberattack Capabilities 278–79 (William A. Owens, Kenneth W. Dam, & Herbert S. Lin eds., 2009).

Appendix (continued)

Date of Attack	Popular Name of Attack or Target	Alleged Source Country	Target Country/Firm	Description of Event
October 2000	Israeli-Palestinian Cyber Conflict	Israel, Palestine	Israel, Palestine	As part of the so-called 'Al-Aqsa Intifada' in the Israeli-occupied Palestinian territories, the Israelis and the Palestinians attacked one another's national web presences.
January 2001	U.S./Chinese Aerial Confrontation	United States, China	United States, China	After a U.S. reconnaissance aircraft collided with a Chinese figure, hackers from both sides defaced one another's websites.
April 2001	Moonlight Maze	Former Soviet Union	United States	Allegedly state-sponsored hackers from the former Soviet Union penetrated DOD computers for more than a year to secure technology from U.S. agencies such as the DOE and NASA, as well as from military contractors and universities.
December 2002	Apolo Ohno	South Korea	United States	DDoS attacks hit several U.S.-based servers from machines that appeared to be based in South Korea in the context of the 2002 Olympic Games.
2003–2006	Titan Rain	China	United States	Designated by the U.S. government as a series of cyber attacks on U.S. systems, including those of Lockheed-Martin and NASA, these attacks began in 2003 and were ongoing for at least three years. Although the true source and rationale behind the attacks has not been publicly revealed, the SANS Institute has attributed them most likely to Chinese military hackers.
May 2006	U.S. State Department		United States	The Department of State's networks were hacked, and unknown foreign intruders downloaded terabytes worth of information.
November 2006	U.S. Military War College		United States	Hackers attempted to penetrate U.S. military War College networks, resulting in a two-week shutdown at one institution while infected machines were restored.
December 2006	NASA		United States	NASA was forced to block emails with attachments before the shuttle launched out of fear that the agency would be hacked. *Business Week* reported that unknown foreign intruders obtained the plans for the latest U.S. space launch vehicles.
April-May 2007	Web War 1 – Cyber Riot in Estonia	Russia	Estonia	Russian hackers are widely believed to have attacked Estonia's digital infrastructure.

Date of Attack	Popular Name of Attack or Target	Alleged Source Country	Target Country/Firm	Description of Event
June 2007			United States	The U.S. Secretary of Defense's unclassified email account was hacked by unknown foreign intruders as part of a larger series of attacks designed to access and exploit DOD networks.
August 2007		China	United Kingdom, France, Germany	The British Security Service, the French Prime Minister's Office, and the Office of German Chancellor Angela Merkel all complained to China about intrusions on their government networks.
September 2007	Israeli Raid on Syria	Israel	Syria	Israel disrupted Syrian air defense networks (with some collateral damage to its own domestic networks) during the bombing of an alleged Syrian nuclear facility.
September 2007	France and UK Defense Sectors	China	France, United Kingdom	Francis Delon, Secretary-General of National Defense in France, stated that groups from China had infiltrated information systems in France. British authorities also reported that hackers, believed to have come from China's People's Liberation Army, penetrated the network of the Foreign Office and other key departments.
October 2007		Taiwan, United States	China	China's Ministry of State Security reported that foreign hackers, allegedly 42 percent from Taiwan and 25 percent from United Sates, had been stealing information from Chinese systems.
October 2007	Oak Ridge National Labs		United States	More than one thousand staffers at Oak Ridge National Labs received an email with an attachment that, when opened, provided unknown outsiders with access to the Lab's databases.
March 2008		China	South Korea	South Korean officials claimed that China had attempted to hack into Korean Embassy and Korea military networks.
May 2008		India	China	The *Times of India* reported that an Indian official accused China of hacking into government computers. The official stated that the core of the Chinese assault is the scanning and mapping of India's official systems to gain access to content in order to plan how to disable or disrupt networks during a conflict.

(continued)

Appendix (continued)

Date of Attack	Popular Name of Attack or Target	Alleged Source Country	Target Country/Firm	Description of Event
June 2008	U.S. Congressional Offices	China	United States	The networks of several Congressional offices were hacked by unknown foreign intruders. Some infiltrations involved offices with an interest in human rights in Tibet.
Summer 2008	Republican and Democratic Presidential Campaigns		United States	The databases of both Republican and Democratic presidential campaigns were hacked and downloaded by unknown foreign intruders.
Summer 2008			Marathon Oil, ExxonMobil, Conoco Phillips	Marathon Oil, ExxonMobil, and ConocoPhillips were hacked and lost data detailing the quantity, value, and location of oil discoveries around the world.
August 2008	Invasion of Georgia	Russia	Georgia	Computer networks in Georgia were hacked by unknown foreign intruders, most likely at the behest of the Russian government. Much press attention was given to annoying graffiti on Georgian government websites. There was little disruption of services but the hacks did put political pressure on the Georgian government and were coordinated with Russian military actions.
October 2008			United Kingdom	Police discovered a highly sophisticated supply chain attack where credit card readers made in China and used in UK supermarkets had a wireless device inserted in them. The device copies a credit card when it is inserted, stores the data, and transfers the data it has collected once a day via Wi-Fi connection to Lahore, Pakistan. Estimated losses were $50 million or more.
November 2008	Royal Bank of Scotland		United Kingdom, United States	Hackers breached networks at Royal Bank of Scotland's WorldPay, allowing them to clone 100 ATM cards and withdraw over $9 million dollars from machines in 49 cities.
December 2008	TJX		TJX	Retail giant TJX was hacked. The one hacker captured and convicted (Maksym Yastremskiy) is said to have made $11 million from the hack. Total losses were estimated at over $250 million.

Date of Attack	Popular Name of Attack or Target	Alleged Source Country	Target Country/Firm	Description of Event
January 2009		Israel	Criminal Organizations in the former Soviet Union, but paid for by Hamas or Hezbollah	Hackers attacked Israel's Internet infrastructure during the January 2009 military offensive in the Gaza Strip. The attack, which focused on government websites, was executed by at least 5,000,000 computers.
January 2009	Indian Music Download Sites	India	Pakistan	Indian Home Ministry officials warned that Pakistani hackers had placed malware on popular music download sites used by Indians in preparation for cyber attacks.
February 2009	FAA		United States	FAA computer systems were hacked. Increased use by FAA of IP-bases' networks also increases the risk of the intentional disruption of commercial air traffic.
February 2009	Conficker		France	French naval aircraft planes were grounded after military databases were infected with the "conficker" worm. Naval officials suspected someone at the Navy had used an infected USB key. In all, the worm has been detected in over 200 nations, making it among the most prolific in history.
March 2009	GhostNet	China	103 countries	Canadian researchers found a computer espionage system that they believe China implanted on the government networks of 103 countries.
March 2009			United States	Reports in the press say that the plans for a new Marine one, the presidential helicopter, were found on a file-sharing network in Iran. The program was cancelled in April 2009 due to cost overruns.
May 2009			Merrick Bank	In May 2009, Merrick Bank, a leading issuer of credit cards, claimed it lost $16 million after hackers compromised as many as 40 million credit card accounts.
July 2009			United States, South Korea	Cyber attacks against websites in the United States and South Korea, including a number of government websites, were launched by unknown hackers. South Korea accused North Korea of being behind the attacks.

(*continued*)

Appendix (continued)

Date of Attack	Popular Name of Attack or Target	Alleged Source Country	Target Country/Firm	Description of Event
August 2009				Albert Gonzalez was indicted on charges that between 2006 and 2008, he and unidentified Russian or Ukrainian colleagues allegedly stole more than 130 million credit and debit cards by hacking into the computer systems of five major companies. This was the largest hacking and identity theft crime in U.S. history to that point.
November 2009	Climategate	Russia		Jean-Pascal van Ypersele, the vice-chairman of the United Nations' Intergovernmental Panel on Climate Change, ascribed the hacking and release of thousands of emails from the University of East Anglia's Climatic Research Unit to Russia as part of a plot to undermine the Copenhagen climate talks.
December 2009		Iraq	United States	Downlinks from U.S. military UAVs were hacked by Iraqi insurgents using laptops and $24.99 file-sharing software, allowing them to see what the UAV has viewed.
January 2010		China	United Kingdom	The UK's MI5 Security Service warns that undercover intelligence officers from the People's Liberation Army and the Ministry of Public Security have approached UK businessmen at trade fairs and exhibitions with the offer of "gifts" – cameras and memory sticks – containing malware that provides the Chinese with remote access to users' computers.
January 2010	Aurora	China	More than 30 multinational firms	Corporations targeted in Aurora included, most prominently, Google, Adobe Systems, Intel, Yahoo, Symantec, and Dow Chemical. The goal of the penetrations, which Google ascribed to China, was to collect IP and gain access to Google's Gaea password management system.
January 2010		Iran	China	A group named the "Iranian Cyber Army" disrupted service of the popular Chinese search engine Baidu. Users were redirected to a page showing an Iranian political message. Previously, the "Iranian Cyber Army" had hacked into Twitter in December with a similar message.

Date of Attack	Popular Name of Attack or Target	Alleged Source Country	Target Country/Firm	Description of Event
March 2010		China	NATO and EU States	NATO EU leaders warned that the number of cyber attacks against their networks have increased significantly over the past 12 months, with China being among the most active players.
March 2010			Vietnam	Google announced that it had found malware targeted at Vietnamese computer users. Google said that the malware was not especially sophisticated and was used to spy on "potentially tens of thousands of users who downloaded Vietnamese keyboard language software." The malware also launched distributed denial of service attacks against blogs containing political dissent, specifically, opposition to bauxite mining efforts in Vietnam.
April 2010		China	India	Chinese hackers reportedly broke into classified files at the Indian Defense Ministry and Indian embassies around the world, gaining access to Indian missile and armament systems.
April 2010		China		A Chinese telecommunications firm transmitted erroneous routing information for roughly 37,000 networks, causing Internet traffic to be misrouted through China. The incident lasted 20 minutes and exposed traffic from more than 8,000 U.S. networks, 8,500 Chinese networks, 1,100 Australian networks, and 230 French networks.
July 2010		Russia	United States	A Russian agent (allegedly named Alexey Karetnikov) was arrested and deported after working for nine months as a software tester at Microsoft.
October 2010	Zeus		Banks in U.S. and UK	The *Wall Street Journal* reported that hackers using "Zeus" malware, available in cybercrime black markets for about $1,200, were able to steal over $12 million from five banks in the U.S. and UK.
October 2010	Stuxnet	Unknown (potentially U.S. and/or Israel)	Iran	Stuxnet, a complex piece of malware designed to interfere with Siemens Industrial Control Systems, was discovered in Iran, Indonesia, and elsewhere, eventually disrupting the Iranian nuclear program as well as causing collateral damage in thousands of systems around the world.

(*continued*)

Appendix (continued)

Date of Attack	Popular Name of Attack or Target	Alleged Source Country	Target Country/Firm	Description of Event
December 2010		Pakistan	India	India's Central Bureau of Investigation (CBI) website (cbi.nic.in) was hacked and data erased. India blames Pakistani hackers.
January 2011			EU	Hackers penetrated the European Union's carbon trading market, which allows organizations to buy and sell their carbon emissions quotas, and steal more than $7 million in credits, forcing the market to shut down temporarily.
January 2011		China	Canada	The Canadian government reported a major cyber attack against its agencies, including Defense Research and Development Canada, a research agency for Canada's Department of National Defense. The attack forced the Finance Department and Treasury Board, Canada's main economic agencies, to disconnect from the Internet. Canadian sources attribute the attack to China.
March-April 2011		Chinese firms	U.S. firms	Between March 2010 and April 2011, the FBI identified twenty incidents in which the online banking credentials of small-to-medium sized U.S. businesses were compromised and used to initiate wire transfers to Chinese economic and trade companies. As of April 2011, the total attempted fraud amounted to approximately $20 million; the actual victim losses were $11 million.
March-April 2011	RSA	China	RSA	Hackers used phishing techniques in an attempt to obtain data that would compromise RSA's SecureID authentication technology.
May 2011	PlayStation Network		Sony	Cybercriminals masquerading as members of the hacktivist group "Anonymous" penetrated the PlayStation network. Sony estimated that personal information for more than 80 million users was compromised and that the cost of the breach was over $170 million.
July 2011		China	South Korea	South Korea said hackers from China had penetrated an Internet portal and accessed phone numbers, email addresses, names, and other data for 35 million Koreans.

Date of Attack	Popular Name of Attack or Target	Alleged Source Country	Target Country/Firm	Description of Event
August 2011			Japanese firms	According to sources in the Japanese government, Mitsubishi Heavy Industries and twenty other Japanese defense and high tech firms were the target of an effort to extract classified defense information. Japanese officials believed the exploits all originated from the same source. The intruder used email with a malicious attachment whose contents were the same as a legitimate message sent 10 hours earlier.
September 2011			Dutch firm	Unknown attackers hacked a Dutch certificate authority, allowing them to issue more than 500 fraudulent certificates for major companies and government agencies. The certificates are used to verify that a website is genuine. By issuing a false certificate, an attacker can pretend to be a secure website, intercept email, or install malicious software. This was the second hack of a certificate authority in 2011.
September 2011			Australia	Australia's Defense Signals Directorate stated that defense networks are attacked more than 30 times a day, with the number of attacks increasing by more than 350 percent by 2009.
October 2011		China	U.S. firms	Networks of 48 companies in the chemical, defense, and other industries were penetrated for at least six months by a hacker looking for intellectual property. Symantec attributes some of the attacks to computers in Hebei, China.
November 2011			Norway	Norway's National Security Agency (NSM) reported that at least 10 major Norwegian defense and energy companies were hacked. The attacks were specifically "tailored" for each company, using an email phishing scheme. NSM said that the attacks came when the companies, mainly in the oil and gas sectors, have been involved in large-scale contract negotiations. The hacking occurred over the course of 2011, with hackers gaining access to confidential documents, industrial data, usernames, and passwords.

(continued)

Appendix (continued)

Date of Attack	Popular Name of Attack or Target	Alleged Source Country	Target Country/Firm	Description of Event
December 2011		China	U.S. Chamber of Commerce	U.S. Chamber of Commerce computer networks were penetrated for more than a year by hackers who, according to press reports, had ties to the People's Liberation Army. The Hackers had access to everything in Chamber computers, including member company communications and industry positions on U.S. trade policy.
March 2012			United States	NASA's Inspector General reported that 13 APT attacks successfully compromised NASA computers in 2011. In one attack, intruders stole 150 user credentials that could be used to gain unauthorized access to NASA systems. Another attack at the Joint Propulsion Laboratory involving China-based IP let the intruders gain full access to key JPL systems and sensitive user accounts.
March 2012			United States	The U.S. Department of Homeland Security issued amber alerts warning of a cyber intrusion campaign on U.S. gas pipelines, dating back to December 2011. Press reports indicated that Industrial Control Systems Cyber Emergency Response Team (ICS-CERT) described the attack as a sophisticated spear phishing campaign emanating from a single source.
May 2012			United Kingdom	UK officials told the press that there had been a small number of successful perpetrations of classified MOD networks.
May 2012	Flame	United States	Israel, Syria, Sudan, and other Middle Eastern nations	An espionage toolkit named "Flame" was discovered in computers in the Iranian Oil Ministry, as well as in other Middle Eastern countries, including Israel, Syria, and Sudan.
June 2012				A global fraud campaign using automated versions of SpyEye and Zeus Trojans targeted high-value personal and corporate accounts, bypassing two-factor authentication.
June 2012			UK firm	The head of the UK Security Service stated that a London-listed company lost an estimated $1.2 billion as a result of state-sponsored cyber attacks.

Date of Attack	Popular Name of Attack or Target	Alleged Source Country	Target Country/Firm	Description of Event
July 2012	Madhi		Israel and Iran	A Trojan nicknamed "Mahdi" found gathering data from approximately 800 critical infrastructure engineering firms, government agencies, financial houses, and academia throughout the Middle East and beyond, predominantly in Israel and Iran. The virus contains Persian language strings.
July 2012		China	India	Indian naval officials confirmed that a virus had collected data from sensitive computer systems at the country's Eastern Naval Command headquarters and sent the data to Chinese IP addresses. The virus allegedly entered the Navy's network via infected USB drives, which were used to transfer data from standalone computers holding sensitive files to networked systems.
July 2012			United States	The Director of the National Security Agency said that there had been a 17-fold increase in cyber incidents at U.S. infrastructure companies between 2009 and 2011.
July 2012		"State Actors"	India	Regarded as the largest attack on Indian government networks, over 10,000 email addresses of top Indian government officials were hacked, including officials in the Prime Minister's Office, Defense, External Affairs, Home, and Finance ministries, as well as intelligence agencies. India blames the attack on state actors.
August 2012	Gauss		Lebanese banks	Malware nicknamed "Gauss" infected 2,500 systems worldwide. Gauss appears to have been aimed at Lebanese banks, and contains code whose encryption has not yet been broken.
August 2012	Aramco	Iran	Aramco, RasGas	A group called "Cutting Sword of Justice" linked to Iran claimed it has used the "Shamoon" virus to attack Aramco, a major Saudi oil supplier, deleting data on 30,000 computers and infecting (without causing damage) control systems. The attack also affected the Qatar company RasGas, a major LNG supplier. Other oil companies may have also been infected.

(continued)

Appendix (continued)

Date of Attack	Popular Name of Attack or Target	Alleged Source Country	Target Country/Firm	Description of Event
September 2012	Operation Ababil		Bank websites and NY Stock Exchange	Izz ad-Din al-Qassam, a hacker group linked to Iran, launched "Operation Ababil" targeting bank websites for sustained denial-of-service attacks. Targets include Bank of America, New York Stock Exchange, Chase Bank, Capital One, SunTrust, and Regions Bank.
October 2012	Red October		Nations in Eastern Europe, the former USSR, and Central Asia	The Russian firm Kaspersky discovered a worldwide cyber-attack dubbed "Red October," that had been operating since at least 2007. Hackers gathered information through vulnerabilities in Microsoft's Word and Excel programs. The primary targets of the attack appear to be countries in Eastern Europe, the former USSR and Central Asia, although Western Europe and North America reported victims as well. The virus collected information from government embassies, research firms, military installations, energy providers, nuclear and other critical infrastructures, although the full extent of the damage is unknown.
December 2012			U.S. electric utilities	The U.S. Industrial Control Systems Cyber Emergency Response Team (ICS-CERT) reported that two power plants in the U.S. suffered sophisticated malware infections using unprotected USB drives as an attack vector. In both cases, a lack of basic security controls made it easier for the malicious code to reach critical networks.
December 2012				Al-Qaida websites were taken off line for two weeks. This followed a 2008 website disruption aimed at damaging recruiting and propaganda efforts by the group.
December 2012			Council on Foreign Relations, Turbine Corp.	The Council on Foreign Relations and Capstone Turbine Corporation were targeted by hackers who used a zero-day vulnerability in Microsoft's Internet Explorer web browser to compromise the computers of those who visited the websites. Both CFR and Capstone Turbine are believed to have been used as a 'watering hole' – a target of opportunity that is used access the real targets, presumably individuals known to frequent the sites. Capstone Turbine fits the profile of companies that are believed to be high-value targets for industrial espionage from firms based in China.

Date of Attack	Popular Name of Attack or Target	Alleged Source Country	Target Country/Firm	Description of Event
January 2013	Operation Ababil, phase two	Iran	U.S. banks	Izz ad-Din al-Qassam claimed responsibility for another series of distributed denial-of-service attacks against U.S. Bank websites, as part of "Operation Ababil," phase two. Targets included: Ally Financial, BB&T, Capital One, Fifth Third Bank, HSBC, PNC, Wells Fargo, SunTrust, and Zions Bank. U.S. officials speculate that the group is a front for a state-sponsored campaign attributed to Iran.
January 2013			Japanese Ministry of Foreign Affairs	The Japanese Ministry of Foreign Affairs (MOFA), after being notified by the National Information Security Center, discovered it had been hacked and had lost "at least" twenty files, including highly classified documents.
January 2013		China	U.S. media outlets	The *New York Times*, *Wall Street Journal*, *Washington Post*, and *Bloomberg News* came forward and revealed that they had been the victims of persistent cyber attacks, presumably originating from China.
February 2013		China	U.S. Department of Energy	The U.S. Energy Department was confirmed to have been hit by a major, sophisticated cyber attack. Fourteen computer servers and 20 workstations were reportedly penetrated during the attack, compromising the personal information of several hundred employees. The sophistication of the attack suggests foreign government involvement and could have been aimed at obtaining other sensitive information, such as information held by the National Nuclear Security Administration. China is the primary suspect behind the attack.
February 2013		China	EADS and ThyssenKrupp	*Der Spiegel* revealed that EADS (European Aeronautic Defence and Space Company) and German steelmaker ThyssenKrupp recorded major attacks by Chinese hackers in 2012.
February 2013		China	U.S. gas pipeline firms	The U.S. Department of Homeland Security issued a restricted report, revealing that from December 2011 through June 2012, cyber criminals targeted 23 gas pipeline companies and stole information that could be used for sabotage purposes. The report does not mention China, but experts traced the digital signatures of the attacks to a Chinese cyber espionage group.

(continued)

Appendix (continued)

Date of Attack	Popular Name of Attack or Target	Alleged Source Country	Target Country/Firm	Description of Event
March 2013		North Korea	South Korea	South Korean television stations and financial institutions were hit with a cyber attack thought to have originated in North Korea. The attack involved a piece of malware called DarkSeoul that was designed to evade popular South Korean anti-virus software. The U.S.-based Committee for Human Rights in North Korea was also attacked in the same time frame.
March 2013		South Korea, United States	North Korea	North Korea blames the United States and South Korea for a series of attacks that severely restricted Internet access in the country.
March 2013		China	Indian Defence Research and Development Organisation	The Indian Defence Research and Development Organisation was hacked by an unknown source, believed to be Chinese. The organization is responsible for developing intelligence for the Indian military. Thousands of documents were uploaded to a server with an IP address in Guangdong, China.
March-June 2013			U.S. financial institutions	The Jihadi group Izz ad-din al-Qassam cyber fighters continued to target U.S. financial institutions throughout these months. Known as Operation Ababil, several major U.S. banks were subjected to DDoS attack.
March-June 2013		Syrian Electronic Army	Western media	The Syrian Electronic Army, a pro-Assad hacktivist group, hacked into major Western media organizations as part of a propaganda campaign.
April 2013			Android mobile devices	On April 19, an Internet security firm announced that they discovered malware on millions of Android mobile devices. The incident primarily affected Russia and Russian-speaking countries.
May 2013		China	U.S. Department of Labor	Chinese hackers are believed to have compromised the U.S. Department of Labor. A similar attack targeted at least 9 other agencies, including the Agency for International Development.
May 2013		China	U.S. Army Corps of Engineers	Chinese Hackers are believed to have infiltrated the Army Corps of Engineers' National Inventory of Dams.

Date of Attack	Popular Name of Attack or Target	Alleged Source Country	Target Country/Firm	Description of Event
May 2013			Iran	And unknown attacker utilized a DDoS attack to bring down the website of the Iranian Basij military branch (basij.ir).
May 2013			Middle Eastern banks	U.S. authorities accuse a gang of eight hackers of committing a massive $45 million heist against several Middle Eastern banks. The targeted attacks eliminated the withdrawal limits on prepaid debit cards, permitting the hackers to withdraw massive amounts of funds. The hackers targeted banks in the UAE and Oman.
May 2013	OpSaudi	Anonymous	Saudi Arabia	Anonymous' Saudi branch launched OpSaudi and took down several government websites such as the Ministry of Foreign Affairs, Ministry of Finance, and the General Intelligence Presidency via DDos attack.
May 2013		Western hackers	Al-Qaeda	It is believed that Western actors scrambled the contents of Al-Qaeda's English language web forum referencing the Boston bombings.
May 2013			Western automotive parts suppliers	Over the course of this month, unknown hackers breached several major automotive parts suppliers in North America and Europe.
May 2013		Syrian Electronic Army	Saudi Arabia	The Syrian Electronic Army claims to have breached the Saudi Arabian Ministry of Defense email system, and leaked several confidential emails.
May 2013	Operation Hangover	India	Pakistan	"Operation Hangover" is disclosed as a massive espionage effort conducted by India. Telenor is the highest profile target, but many Pakistani mining, automotive, legal, engineering, food service, military, and financial entities were also affected.
May 2013		Iran	U.S. electrical grid	The United States reported that its electrical grid is under near constant attack on a daily basis from multiple unattributed actors. On May 23, the *Wall Street Journal* reported that Iranian actors have increased efforts to compromise U.S. corporations and utility providers.
May 2013		Syrian Electronic Army	Israel	Israeli officials reported on a failed attempt by the Syrian Electronic Army to compromise water supply to the city of Haifa.

(*continued*)

Appendix (continued)

Date of Attack	Popular Name of Attack or Target	Alleged Source Country	Target Country/Firm	Description of Event
May 2013		China	Australia	An alleged Chinese hacker stole the blueprints for the Australian Security Intelligence Organization's new $631 million building.
June 2013				President Obama signed a directive instructing the U.S. to aid its allies increasingly coming under Iranian and North Korean cyber attacks.
June 2013	Edward Snowden	United States	China	Edward Snowden, a former systems administrator at the NSA, revealed documents showing among other things that the U.S. conducted cyber espionage against Chinese targets.
June 2013				The U.S. and Russia signed a 'cyber pact,' which establishes hotlines of communications between the two countries in the event of a crisis in cyberspace.
June 2013			South Korea, North Korea, United States	On the 60th Anniversary of the Korean War, a wave of cyber-incidents in Korea began involving South Korea, North Korea, and the United States. The incidents began with DDoS attacks on major South Korean websites. North Korean websites also went down including those of the communist party and the national airlines. The U.S. was drawn into the ongoing cyber dispute by the hacking of tens of thousands of soldiers' personal information.
July 2013		Ukrainian and Russian hackers		Five Ukrainian and Russian hackers were charged by the FBI with stealing over 160 million credit card numbers, and causing hundreds of millions in losses.
August 2013			China	A massive DDOS took down China's dot-cn country code top level domain for several hours
August 2013		Syrian Electronic Army	Western media sites	The Syrian Electronic Army hijacked and rerouted major Western social media and media sites to a malicious hosting site in Russia.
September 2013		North Korea	South Korea	North Korea again hacked South Korean targets, including think tanks, the South Korean Ministry of Defense, and Korean defense industry firms.
September 2013		Iran	U.S. Navy	The U.S. Navy stated that Iran hacked into unclassified computers as part of an escalating cyber conflict.

Index

cyber warfare
  definition of, 152
  example of, xvi
  The New Cyber Warfare, 151
cyber weapon
  example of, xv
CYBERCOM, xvi, xxxvii, 177, 192, 195, 324
  purpose of, 177
cybercrime, 11
  computer crime, 12
  cyber criminals, xvi, xxiii, 13, 14, 15, 17, 18, 57,
    64, 187, 208, 210, 211, 215, 231, 250, 255, 305,
    308, 330, 363, 368
  Piracy of software, 12
  quickswapping, xxxv
  statistics on, xxi, 12
Cybersecurity Act of 2012, xviii, 156, 178, 179, 204,
    352
cyberspace, 55
  and the global commons, 57
  as an anti-commons, 64
  cyber pseudo commons, 61, 84, 88, 368
  definition of, xxxi, 55
  global networked commons, 75, 77, 318
  tragedy of the cyber commons, xviii, 6, 55
Cyberspace Policy Review, xi, 117, 176, 239, 252,
    315, 316, 321, 347, 357, 369
cybersquatting, 28, 29, 33

Deibert, Robert, 6, 53, 54, 57, 58, 62, 63, 66, 67,
    68, 72, 73, 74, 76, 78, 95, 195
Denial of Service (DoS) attacks, 140
Department of Defense (DOD), xxii, xxxvii, 21,
    54, 72, 116, 154, 265, 355, 360
  breaches, 160
  information operations, 7
  IT expenditures, 255
  purchasing, 116, 117, 179
  targeting analysis, 301
Department of Homeland Security (DHS), xxxvii,
    16, 36, 106, 147, 264, 380
  training for managers, 258, 333
Department of Justice (DOJ), xxxvii, 12, 16,
    346
  Computer Crime and Intellectual Property
    Section (CCIPS), 16
Digital Millenium Copyright Act (DMCA),
    240
Distributed Denial of Service (DDoS) attacks,
    xxxvii, 59, 62, 136, 139, 140, 141, 142, 147, 160,
    161, 164, 170, 171, 172, 202, 207, 208, 210, 214,
    271, 284, 347, 348, 372
Domain Name Security Extensions (DNSSEC),
    xxxvii, 125, 127, 128, 129, 130, 136, 149, 150, 334,
    369

Domain Name System (DNS), xxxvii, 19, 26, 27,
    28, 29, 36, 118, 125
  DNS Wars, 29, 31
  Susie's Wonderful Bank (SWB), 120
Driver Privacy Protection Act, 242
DuBose, Michael, xxxv, 12, 15, 16, 293, 312, 346
Dynes, Scott, 222, 223, 226, 228, 230, 231, 233

eBay, 14, 49, 50, 98, 205, 281, 335
  AuctionWeb, 49, 205
e-commerce, 33, 45, 56, 64, 193, 205, 224, 239, 245,
    251
Edelman, Benjamin, 67, 71
Electronic Frontier Foundation (EFF), xxxvii, 3,
    5, 225
end-to-end design, 23, 24, 132, 334
Enlai, Zhou, xxx
equivalent effects test, 287
Erice Declaration on Principles for Cyber
    Stability and Cyber Peace (Erice
    Declaration), 356, 357, 361
Estonia
  "eStonia", 162
  Cyber Defence League, 256, 257
  Cyber Emergency Response Team
    (CERT-EE), 165
EU Directive on Privacy and Electronic
    Communications, 91
Executive Order, 179, 280
  by President Obama, 179
  by President Reagan, 280

Facebook, 16, 50, 67, 69, 75, 82, 83, 126, 133, 134,
    179, 187, 200, 217, 224, 228, 234, 240, 258, 259,
    314, 325, 333, 335
  Facebook Immune System (FIS), 228
Fair Credit Reporting Act (FCRA), xxxvii, 237
Federal Bureau of Investigation (FBI)
  Cyber Division, 15
  Office of Infrastructure Protection and
    Computer Intrusion Squad, 16
Federal Energy Regulatory Commission (FERC),
    xxxvii, 253, 254, 255
Federal Trade Commission (FTC), 12, 143, 238,
    242, 354
Federal Wiretap Act of 1968, 279
Filter King, 74
Financial Services Technology Consortium, 232
Foreign Intelligence Surveillance Act (FISA),
    279, 280
four main approaches to secure cyberspace, 65
  common property solutions, 65
  nationalization, 55, 62, 84
  polycentric regulation, 65, 88
  privatization, 55, 65, 79, 81, 84

CPSIA information can be obtained at www.ICGtesting.com
Printed in the USA
LVOW07*0403221114

414608LV00003B/34/P